BUSINESS ECONOMICS
PRINCIPLES AND CASES

BUSINESS ECONOMICS
PRINCIPLES AND CASES

Seventh Edition

Marshall R. Colberg
The Florida State University

Dascomb R. Forbush
Clarkson University

Assisted by the Contribution to
Previous editions of
Gilbert R. Whitaker, Jr.

1986

Homewood, Illinois 60430

ISBN 0-256-03341-2

Library of Congress Catalog Card No. 85–82617

Printed in the United States of America

1 2 3 4 5 6 7 8 9 0 K 3 2 1 0 9 8 7 6

Preface

This book combines text and cases for use in courses where economic analysis is applied to the solution of business problems. These courses, which may have such titles as Business Economics, Managerial Economics, or Economics of the Firm, are offered both by schools of business administration and departments of economics. They may serve either as alternatives for, or complements to, traditional courses in microeconomics. The cases involve the student more fully in the application of such basic economic concepts as opportunity cost, marginality, discounting, and profit maximization, as well as providing factual information about many firms and types of business activity.

The authors have attempted to write the book for undergraduates who have had a course in principles of economics. With appropriate supplementation, this book is suitable for first-year graduate students in business administration. Some prior training in accounting, finance, and statistics is desirable, but not essential, to an understanding of this volume. Mathematical formulations, apart from geometrical figures, are not emphasized except where necessary for precision, as in the case of capitalization formulas.

Comments from users and reviewers of the 6th edition have been useful in pointing out places where improvement was needed, and the authors have attempted to respond to many comments. An additional chapter has made it possible to expand the theoretical treatment of competition and monopoly. More data for statistical estimation of demand are included in view of the increasing availability of computers. Intracompany transfer pricing, a matter of concern to many firms, has now been included as a topic in the text. The veritable explosion of new financial markets and the great takeover movement have led to complete change of the associated chapters. New trends in antitrust policy and the AT&T breakup are covered.

This edition contains 79 cases compared with 62 in the 6th edition. Almost half are either new or substantially updated. Both short and long cases are included, permitting the instructor much latitude in assignments and in length of course, even up to a full academic year.

Thanks for suggestions are due especially to John H. Lauck, Joseph W. Meador, Nicola Vulkovic, George Macesich, Herbert W. Uppitt, Carl Housley, James I. Stewart, Larry A. Webb, and Arnt Spandau.

At Florida State University, thanks go to Grace Colberg for her manuscript and indexing work, and to Esther Glenn and Chrys Ivey Biederman.

From Clarkson University, thanks are due to Janet M. C. Forbush for her help in manuscript and computer work; to Jeff Hermann, Catherine Barton, Paul Oates, and Professor Donald Dutkowsky for computer work on demand models; and to Faroukh Gandhi, Daniel H. Forbush, and John A. Larson for supplying case materials.

Marshall R. Colberg
Dascomb R. Forbush

Contents

1 The Nature of Business Economics 1

The Perspective and Decisions of Business Economics. The Challenge of Consumerism. The Challenge of the Environmental Movement. The Provision of Equal and Challenging Employment Opportunities. The Organization of Business Economics.
  Case 1-1, Leeway in Accounting, 9

2 Speculation, Hedging, and Profit 12

Accounting and Economic Profit. Balance Sheet View. The Problem of Uncertainty. Decision Making under Certainty. Decision Making under Risk and the Concept of Expected Profits. Decision Making under Uncertainty. The Use of Criteria Other than Maximization of Profits. The Transforming of Uncertainties. Long and Short Positions. Future Markets. Hedging by Selling Futures. Hedging by Buying Futures. Interest Rate Futures. Foreign Exchange Futures. Options. Options on Stock Indexes. Commodity Futures Options.
  Case 2-1, Cow Pastures or Condominiums, 32
  Case 2-2, Haloid to Xerox, 35
  Case 2-3, On Broadway, 39
  Case 2-4, Puts, Calls, and Straddles, 40
  Case 2-5, Options on Stock Indexes, 43
  Case 2-6, Arbitrage in Stocks, 44

3 Forecasting Methods 45

Projection and Extrapolation Methods. Complex "Naive" Methods. Leading Indicators. Leading Indicators in Detail. Coincident Indicators. Lagging Indicators. Rational Expectations. Econometric Methods. Survey Methods. Consumer Attitudes. Requirements

Forecasting. Loaded Dice Techniques.

   Case 3-1, Bad Times for the Forecasters, 59
   Case 3-2, Problems in Forecasting, 60
   Case 3-3, Leading Indicators and Cyclical Turning
         Points, 61
   Case 3-4, Ratio of Coincident to Lagging
         Indicators, 63

4 Demand Analysis for Industry 66

Demand, the Relationship between Quantity and Price. Slope and Elasticity. Elasticity and Revenue. Computation of Price Elasticity. Quantity and Income. Income Elasticity of Demand. Substitutes and Complements. Cross Elasticity of Demand. Quantity and Population. Quantity and Advertising. Quantity and Stock. Empirical Demand Functions.

   Case 4-1, Demand for Frozen Orange
         Concentrate, 83
   Case 4-2, The Demand for Refrigerators, 89
   Case 4-3, Problems in Demand Analysis for
         Industry, 96
   Case 4-4, The Demand for California and Arizona
         Lemons, 97
   Case 4-5, Demand for California and Florida
         Avocados, 99

5 Demand Analysis for the Firm 102

Demand Facing a Monopolist. Some Qualifications. Demand Facing Pure Competitor. Pure Competition is Uncommon. Demand Under Oligopoly. Monopoly as Limiting Case of Oligopoly. Market Share. Duopoly. Game Theory Approach. Business Situation with a Saddle Point. Business Situation without a Saddle Point. Some Other Possible Applications. General Observations on Game Theory and Business.

   Case 5-1, Market Shares in Soft Drinks, 118
   Case 5-2, Women in Business, 120
   Case 5-3, Chicago-Vancouver Route Controversy, 121
   Case 5-4, Hul Gul—An Application of Game Theory, 123
   Case 5-5, Problems in Demand Analysis for the
         Firm, 124

6 Production Functions and Short-Run Costs of Production 126

The Short Run and the Long Run. Opportunity Cost. Production Functions. The Two-Input, One-Good Production Function. Fixed and Variable Costs. Relationship of Costs to Production Function.

Hypothetical Cost Data. Average and Marginal Cost Curves. Output under Competitive Conditions. All-or-None Decision. Adaptability and Divisibility of Plant. Standard Costs and Volume Variances. Break-Even Charts. Statistical Cost Analysis. Optimum Inventory Policy Models and Linear Programming Methods.

Case 6-1, Sunland Tailoring Company, 143

Case 6-2, Badger and Siegel, 145

Case 6-3, Nordon Manufacturing Company, 146

Case 6-4, L. E. Mason Company and Optimal Inventory Policy, 148

Case 6-5, Linear Programming Methods—A Graphic Example, 154

7 Investment Decisions and Long-Run Cost 163

Flexibility of Plant. Replication and the L-Shaped LRAC Function. Size of Firm and Cost. Limited Production Run. Value of Equipment. Value of a Machine. Decision to Purchase a Machine. Should a New Model be Purchased? Alternative Formulation of Replacement Criterion. Revenue Considerations. Determination of Long-Run Cost (Planning) Curves.

Case 7-1, The Use of Interest Rate Formulas by Managers and Engineers, 182

Case 7-2, Problems in Capital Investment, 184

Case 7-3, Robbins Manufacturing Company, 187

Case 7-4, Productivity in Air-Conditioning and Related Industries, 188

Case 7-5, The Trend toward Smaller Plants, 189

Case 7-6, The Learning Curve and Military Aircraft, 191

8 Capital Budgeting and Financing 192

Aftertax Cash Flows. The Demand for Capital Funds by a Firm. Supply of Capital Funds. Sources of Funds. Cost of Capital from Specific Sources. Cost of Debt. Cost of Preferred Stock. Cost of Common Stock. Cost of Internally Generated Funds. Overall Cost of Capital. Capital Structure. Supply Schedule for Capital Funds. Dealing with Inflation. New Era of Corporate Takeovers.

Case 8-1, Problems in Capital Budgeting, 206

Case 8-2A, The Paragon Parking Lot, 207

Case 8-2B, How Much Insulation? 208

Case 8-3, The Component Manufacturing Company, 209

Case 8-4, That First House: Inflation, Interest, and Taxes, 212

9 Employment of Human Resources 214

Marginal Productivity of Labor. Fixed Proportions. Monopolist's Demand for Labor. Monopsony. Bilateral Monopoly. Right-to-Work Laws. Minimum Wage Rates. Davis-Bacon Act. Training of Workers. Worker Alientation. Executive Incentives.

Case 9-1, Union and Nonunion Rubber Plants (March, 1979), 229
Case 9-2, Combating Worker Alienation, 230
Case 9-3, Discrimination and Employment, 232
Case 9-4, Collective Bargaining in the Basic Steel Industry, 234
Case 9-5, How the Government Measures Unemployment, 236
Case 9-6, How High a Minimum Wage? 239

10 Plant Location—Domestic and Multinational 242

Nonpecuniary Factors in Location. Cost. Market Orientation. Location at Both Ends. Milling-in-Transit Privilege. Multiple Sources of Materials. Processing Costs. Land Rent. Demand as a Locational Factor. Demand Interdependence. Competition in Location. Location along a Highway. Agglomeration of Sellers. Multinational Business.

Case 10-1, Nissan in Tennessee, 256
Case 10-2, Reed, Waite, and Gentzler, 257
Case 10-3, Dow Chemical in Europe, 263
Case 10-4, Pepsi-Cola for Vodka, 264

11 Price Determination under Competition 266

Very Short-Run Price Determination. Fixed Supply without Reservation Prices. Fixed Supply with Reservation prices. Rationing of Seasonal Output. Short Run and Long Run under Competition. Rent and Other Price Controls. Price Supports. Summary of Implications of the Competitive Model. Government Interference with Prices.

Case 11-1, Prices in Philately, 277
Case 11-2, Moscow's Taxi Business, 282
Case 11-3, Even the Cows are Laughing, 283

12 Monopolistic Pricing 286

Other Sources of Monopoly Power. Monopoly Demand. Marginal Revenue. Monopoly Price for Existing Supply. Short-Run Output and Prices. Long-Run Adjustments. Cartels. Government Regulation. Airline Deregulation. Geometric Analysis of Regulation.

Case 12-1, Nixon Price Controls, 298
Case 12-2, Hundreds of Ways to Chisel on Price, 301
Case 12-3, Medical Advertising, 307
Case 12-4, De Beers and the CSO, 308
Case 12-5, Selected Problems in Monopoly Pricing, 311

13 Price Discrimination and Price Differentials 313

Price Differentials and Discrimination. Elements of Monopoly and
Market Imperfection as Requisites for Discrimination. Separation of
Markets as a Requisite for Price Discrimination. Perfect Price
Discrimination. Fixed Supply Case. Continuous Production.
International Dumping. Discrimination and Differentials when
Products are Differentiated. Geographic Price Discrimination.
Basing-Point Pricing in Steel. Market Penetration. Price Differentials
and Discrimination when Marginal Costs Differ. The Legality of
Price Discrimination. Price Dispersion.
Case 13-1, *The Country Doctor, 328*
Case 13-2, The Urban Electric Company, 330
Case 13-3, Frito-Lay, Inc., 345
Case 13-4, Generic Drugs, 346
Case 13-5, Price Dispersion in Optical Products in Califonia, 348
Case 13-6, Price Discrimination at Harvard, 349

14 Price Strategies when Sellers are Few 351

Reactions to Price Changes under Oligopoly. Concentration of
American Industry and Oligopoly. Pure and Differentiated
Oligopoly. The Variety of Oligopolistic Situations as an Influence on
Business Decisions. Cartelization or Formal Agreements. Price
Leadership and other Conventions. Emphasis on Policies that are
Difficult to Retaliate Against. Independent Action with Little
Concern for Reactions.
Case 14-1, The Riverside Metal Company, 365
Case 14-2, Price Publicity in the Aluminum
            Industry, 376
Case 14-3, Price-Level Determination by General
            Motors, 377
Case 14-4, Traditional Department Stores, Inc., 383

15 Nonprice Competition 392

Competition in Services and Other Terms of Trade. Types of
Product Competition. Varieties of Sales Promotion. The Magnitude
of Product and Selling Competition. An Economic Model of
Product Differentiation. A Marginal Approach. Consumerism,
Product, and Promotion Policies.

Case 15-1, Refrigerators and Kilowatt-Hours, 403
Case 15-2, Upheaval in the Cigarette Industry, 408
Case 15-3, The Big Advertisers, 424

16 Product Line Policy 426

Growth through Diversification. Joint Costs. Joint Costs and
Monopoly. Multiple Products to Utilize Capacity. Industry
Development and Integration. Integration in Food Distribution.
Pitfalls in Integration. Intracompany Transfer Pricing. Demand-
Related Goods. Seasonal Demand. Brand-Name Carryover. Internal
Brand Competition. Commodities Related in Advertising and
Distribution. Commodities Related in Research. The Free-Form
Product Line. Takeovers and Mergers in the Mid-1980s. Typical
Takeover Scenario.

Case 16-1, The Redeployment of LTV, 448
Case 16-2, General Electric and the $10 Light Bulb, 459
Case 16-3, American Natural Resources Takeover in 1985, 460

17 Production and Social Costs 463

Private Bargaining. Pollution and Common Property. Solution by
Merger. Regulation by Authorities. Taxes on Pollutants. Summary of
Some Important Principles. A More Political View.

Case 17-1, Pollution Problems in the Diary Industry, 471
Case 17-2, Noise in Moscow, 473
Case 17-3, The Bees and the Flowers in Florida, 475
Case 17-4, Atomic Waste Management, 476

18 Antitrust Limitations on Business Decisions 480

The Prohibition of Price Fixing and Related Agreements.
Exceptions from the Prohibition on Price Fixing. Monopolization.
The Demise of Mother Bell. Price Discrimination. Exclusion of
Competitors. The Decision to Merge. Setting a Plane for
Competition.

Appendix—The Antitrust Laws, 497
Case 18-1, The Electrical Price Conspiracy Cases and General
         Electric Directive 20.5, 504
Case 18-2, Telex versus IBM: The Problem of Plug Compatible
         Peripherals, 512
Case 18-3, Xerox before and after the 1975 Consent Order, 518
Case 18-4, Kellogg Company versus the FTC, 522

Index 527

1

The Nature of Business Economics

The chief business of the American people is business.
—*Calvin Coolidge*

Economics is the study of the optimal use of scarce resources to satisfy human needs and wants. It consequently deals with both the extent to which labor and capital are employed and the way in which these factors are allocated among alternative goods and services. Economics is primarily a social science rather than one that has as its purpose the analysis of efficient behavior on the part of the individual business firm. Nevertheless, social economy requires that business enterprises be well located, be alert to the demands of consumers, be of efficient size, be operated efficiently, and be compelled by competition to pass on to buyers the advantages of their efficiency. Consequently, a good deal of economic analysis is concerned with principles of efficient action applicable to the firm. This book will discuss some of these principles and will present business cases the solution of which should be facilitated by the application of the associated analysis. Good business people need not be economists, but a knowledge of economics is likely to sharpen their thinking about their own firm's problems and sometimes will aid them in making wise decisions that would not otherwise be obvious. Certain types of business decisions are sufficiently difficult and important to justify use not only of all relevant theoretical analysis but also of expensive empirical investigation.

THE PERSPECTIVE AND DECISIONS
OF BUSINESS ECONOMICS

Business economics is primarily concerned with the applicability of economic concepts and analysis to five types of decisions made by businesses: the selection of the product (or service), the choice of production methods, the determination of prices and quantities, the promotional strategy, and the place (or location) decision. In brief, how can businesses mind their p's and q's.

The perspective of business or managerial economics is quite different from that of conventional microeconomics in studying these decisions. The major interest of the latter is to predict equilibrium prices and quantities in demonstrating how resources are allocated to the production of goods and services throughout the economy. The firm is recognized as a leading actor on the economic stage but is typically a rather bloodless abstraction. It is usually convenient to assume that the firm seeks to maximize profit. Somewhat sophisticated revenue and cost functions lead to price and quantity predictions using this criterion. Whether a particular firm is successful or not is not usually a central issue in the analysis that is primarily concerned with industry or market performance.

The emphasis of business economics is on managerial decisions rather than on predicting the equilibrium position of an industry. Forecasting the probable outcomes of alternative actions is seen as part of this decision-making process. It is not necessary to assume the goal of profit maximization; part of the decision-making process is to determine the firm's objectives (and profit is likely to be important among them). The success of the particular firm is of considerable consequence to its managers and owners, though it may be of minor importance to the economy.

While the viewpoint of the participating manager is far different from that of the observing economist, the participant can make use of much of what the economist has noted. Concepts such as marginal revenue and opportunity cost that have been developed by economists making deductions about rational behavior, forecasting techniques such as leading indicators and regression analysis, analytical frameworks such as the classification of market structures, and institutional observations on the impact of antitrust policy or a minimum wage law can all prove useful to managers.

Each type of decision of primary concern to business economics has many manifestations:

1. Selection of products. The product decision may range from the launching of a major innovation following a long period of research, such as Du Pont's introduction of nylon, to a minor alteration in form, like producing saltines as single crackers instead of blocks of four. It may be a routine annual decision such as whether to plant the "back forty" in soybeans or corn, or it may be a decision that is rarely made, such as the changing of the formula of an established soft drink. It may be made by a new firm or an established firm, through a merger, or by building a new plant.

2. The choice of production methods. When highly generalized, this choice is the selection of the cost-minimizing combination of labor and capital necessary to produce a particular output and is dependent on the state of technology and the relative prices of the factors. In specific business cases it may involve changes as small as a switch to longer runs and larger inventory holdings of replacement parts for equipment. On the other hand, it could involve a multibillion dollar switch to a newer technology such as the substitution of oxygen converters for open-hearth furnaces in the steel industry, which was substantially accomplished in the 1960s. Instead of the two factors of production (labor and capital) in generalized economic analysis, the detailed decisions of firms will involve choices among the numerous types of labor, capital, land, raw materials, and intermediate goods. Nevertheless, the principles guiding factor substitution that will minimize cost are the same for two or for 100 factors.

3. The determination of prices and quantities. Price and quantity can be viewed as two aspects of the same decision. For the price taker in a competitive market (for example, a cattle rancher), the decisions are entirely quantity decisions: the size of herd and the number of young steers sold to feeding lots at a particular time. Current and anticipated price information guides the quantity decisions. For firms with sufficient market power to have some discretion over price, the quantity that can be sold will be determined by the price charged. When firms do formulate price policies, a close relationship is likely to exist with product and promotional decisions. A list price of $22,000 for a car is determined after a sequence of decisions regarding particular product specifications and the image of the car that has been projected partly as a result of promotional strategy.

4. Promotional strategy. As long as the assumption of given tastes and preferences of consumers is made, economic analysis has no place for a consideration of promotional expenditures. With the relaxation of this assumption, promotion, defined as expenditures made by the firms to shift demand curves, becomes important. Advertising expenditures involving such media as television, radio, magazines, newspapers, direct mail, and outdoor signs have run in the range of 3 percent to 4 percent of total consumption expenditures. Sales promotion also includes the personal selling efforts by the Avon salesperson, the telephone solicitor, the drug company representative visiting doctors, and the system analysis experts representing computer companies.

5. The place (or location) decision. Most traditional economic analysis makes the simplifying assumption that the production and distribution of goods occurs at one point in space and thus does not bear on locational decisions. For most businesses, major locational decisions are relatively infrequent. New distribution outlets may be set up or a warehouse system reorganized, but shifts in the location of major plants with long depreciation periods and established labor forces are infrequent. The importance of the decisions and the applicability of economic analysis with the spatial dimension added, as it has been in location, transportation, regional and international economics, justify treating the place decision as the fifth type of decision with which business economics is primarily concerned.

It has already been suggested that price, product, and promotional decisions may be closely interrelated. Other types of decisions are also interrelated; for example, a decision to substitute plastic for wood as a raw material for clothespins involves both product and production methods. The introduction of large-scale, high-density chicken production concentrated the location of chicken production geographically, notably in Georgia and the Delmarva area.

THE CHALLENGE OF CONSUMERISM

The old slogan, "let the buyer beware" can sometimes be reversed, as shown by the greatly increased number of malpractice suits against doctors and lawyers and by the volume of automobile recalls where sellers pay for needed repairs. The major business decisions often under attack by consumer groups and others are those concerned with product quality, safety, and promotion. The Motor Vehicle Safety Act has led to increasing controls such as seat belt regulations and may eventually lead to compulsory air bags. Producers must attempt to balance safety against cost, keeping an eye on the possibility of mandatory laws if their compromise becomes legally unacceptable. A perfectly safe passenger car might resemble an army tank but would not promote the social welfare.

Both product and promotional issues have been raised in the drug industry but have ramifications for other businesses as well. New drug legislation requiring stricter testing procedures followed the tragedy in which thousands of deformed babies were born in Europe (notably Germany and England) as the result of the use of thalidomide, a new analgesic. The United States was spared not so much because of strong laws but because of the administrative firmness of one medical official, Dr. Frances Kelsey. She was awarded a medal by President Kennedy for her important work with thalidomide.[1] Laws requiring more extensive testing of drugs before public sale have contributed to a reduction in the rate of new drugs being introduced. Under certain circumstances, such strict testing requirements might prove harmful to the public. For example, it may be that drugs that can mean the difference between life and death cannot be purchased in the United States even after they have been tested abroad.

What is being asked of the drug industry and of American business in general is "fuller disclosure" of the relevant facts about products. For drugs, food additives, some cosmetic preparations, and so forth, full disclosure requires more knowledge about long-range side effects of mate-

---

[1]Arthur Hailey in his latest well-researched novel *Strong Medicine* (Garden City, N.Y.: Doubleday Publishing, 1984) gives much credit to Dr. Helen Taussig who testified before Congress on the European disaster of thalidomide and to Morton Mintz, a *Washington Post* reporter who broke the story.

rials ingested into the complex human body. For American industry as a whole, greater candor has been called for under such legislation as Truth in Lending and the Fair Packaging Act, under administrative decrees such as the warning requirement on cigarette packages and advertising, under the threat of private damage suits using the common-law concept of warranty, and under voluntary programs such as unit pricing and listing nutritional content of foods. The increasing complexity of products and the variety of product choices suggest further moves away from "caveat emptor" or "let the buyer beware" doctrines, moves that on the whole should prove a welcome although sometimes inconvenient challenge for business. A fuller discussion of the economic aspects of, and implications for, product and promotional strategies of fuller disclosure developments is contained in later chapters.

THE CHALLENGE OF THE ENVIRONMENTAL MOVEMENT

A broad range of business decisions are being conditioned by the several aspects of environmentalism. Decisions based on production methods must meet the clean air and pure water standards of state and federal acts. The economic case for charges per unit of pollutant that would confront the firm with increased costs in proportion to the effluent discharged has been largely rejected in favor of maximum discharge limits. The degree to which these maxima can be reduced over time will largely be a function of the success some business firms have in developing technology that will reduce pollution at costs that the public is willing to bear. It is easy to put the finger on corporations as polluters, but the ultimate cost of abatement must largely be carried by the consumers whose demands are being presently met by lower cost production methods that involve effluent discharges.

That product decisions of firms are and will be affected is most conspicuously illustrated in the challenge to auto manufacturers to meet the engine emission standards set by the Environmental Protection Agency under the Clean Air Act of 1970. Some observers were highly critical of the technological solution proposed by the auto companies of the catalytic converters. Critics claimed the converters were expensive to the consumer ($300 to $400 a car were estimates), unreliable, and costly in terms of fuel. Unfavorable comparisons were made with the progress made by the Japanese particularly in the Honda's stratified charge technology. Other types of product decision involve packaging. The growing dominance of the nonreturnable container for beer and soft drink was being questioned to the point where stringent legal restrictions were passed in such states as Oregon and Vermont. The environmental issues raised by the nonreturnables include the contribution of such containers to the solid waste disposal problem; the visual desecration of roadways, beaches, and parks by discarded containers; and the extra energy requirements of producing containers that were eventually thrown away. Recycling of aluminum cans has made a contribution both to the economy in the use of resources and to the environment as an example of good use of the price system.

The electric utilities are prime examples of new constraints on place decisions. The strictures extend, however, to heavy industry in general and in some locations such as Greenwich, Connecticut, to light, smokeless industrial or commercial establishments whose presence would tend to increase population or automotive densities. The growth in zoning and land use restrictions, in requirements for environmental impact studies, and in legal and political activities by environmentally concerned citizens adds new complexities to location decisions. It has become difficult to find locations for nuclear-powered utility plants and for oil refineries that will not stir public protest. And almost all communities say they want "clean" industry, although the cleanest may often be capital intensive rather than semi-skilled labor intensive.

THE PROVISION OF EQUAL AND CHALLENGING EMPLOYMENT OPPORTUNITIES

The provision of equal and challenging employment opportunities has two distinct strands that challenge management's decision making. The first is that of fairness in hiring and promotion so that equal opportunities are provided in all categories of employment to men and women regardless of race and ethnic background. The second is that of reducing what some observers have noted as increasing job alienation.

Both strands could be classified as influences on decisions involving production methods. Efforts to make jobs more meaningful could involve restructuring manufacturing processes to reduce the input of labor in purely repetitive, quasi-mechanical tasks epitomized by assembly-line operation. Some means toward this end could be substituting automatic equipment, increasing job content to cover a broad range of operations, and encouraging greater worker participation in restructuring operating procedures.

It could be argued that pressures for equal opportunities in employment do not result in changes in production methods, since the same labor skills in a black or female form are being substituted for those of white males. In fact, however, the occupations in which female and black participation rates are the lowest are business-related professions such as accounting, engineering, and management. Readjustments are likely to be called for by white males toward taking the technical advice of women or black professionals and taking orders from women or black managers. That the ability, training, and experience of those from economically underprivileged groups will be precisely the same is also in doubt. The long history of exclusion from these occupations is likely to mean continued shortages of those educated for and experienced in these fields.

Location decisions of firms must also be influenced if equality of opportunity in a wide range of occupations is to be increased for black minorities (and to a lesser extent, for Spanish-speaking minorities). Most new manufacturing and retailing locations are being selected at the periphery of metropolitan areas despite the fact that black population growth is almost entirely occurring in the central cities. It is doubtful that free market decisions of firms will be effective in equalizing employment opportunities to inner city residents without various subsidies that would influence locational decisions.

THE ORGANIZATION OF BUSINESS ECONOMICS

Basic economic decisions that firms make have been outlined, and several challenges to how such decisions are made have been considered. It is now appropriate to look at the structure of an economic approach to the problems involved.

The success of a business enterprise depends on its ability to cover at least the cost of its operations with revenues. In recent years, success or failure in many fields of activity has begun to depend also on operations in organized markets in stocks, stock options, bonds, commodities, and international currencies. Takeover attempts and voluntary mergers of large corporations make use of many types of devices that were not common even a decade ago. Consequently, Chapter 2, "Speculation, Hedging, and Profit," devotes a good deal of attention to these new markets and procedures as well as to profit and goals, both pecuniary and nonpecuniary.

Chapter 3 examines some popular methods of forecasting for firms and the economy. Forecasts for the economy as a whole are shown as the most important but the least reliable forecasts.

Economic analysis is firmly based on the concepts of demand and supply. Either could be taken up first. We chose to start with demand because economic forecasting has paid particular attention to the forecasting of demand functions in which the quantity demanded of a product is determined by the key decision variables of price and promotion as well as by externally determined variables such as population and income. The sequence chosen of first looking at the demand for industries (Chapter 4) and then the demand facing firms (Chapter 5) reflects a frequent practice of businesses in which a forecast for the economy as a whole precedes the forecast for the industry. The industry forecast then serves as a framework for forecasting the firm's share of the market.

Chapters 6 through 10 are concerned mainly with the costs that determine the ability of a firm to be an effective supplier of various quantities of a good. The student should recognize the use of *ceteris paribus*, keeping many variables constant while the effects of other key variables are examined. Much of the quality of an economist depends on his or her judgment in treating *ceteris paribus*. Milton Friedman, especially, has warned against assuming constant, important variables that cannot possibly remain unchanged when those we are examining are assumed to change (e.g., the price of butter when the price of oleomargarine changes sharply).

Chapter 6 deals with short-run costs—the variable costs of producing at different rates when plant capacity is assumed to remain fixed. A broader choice of production methods becomes available when capital inputs are also allowed to vary as in Chapter 7.

Chapter 8, "Capital Budgeting and Financing," stresses the key time dimension of business decision making in which capital resources are invested in time periods prior to the realization of benefits in the form of revenues or cost savings. Together with Chapter 7, it presents key concepts included in such courses as engineering economics and managerial finance. Chapter 9, "Employment of Human Resources," is a logical successor, since production requires the combining of capital and human resources. Employment and unemployment are, of course, basic concerns all over the world. Some U.S. legislation affecting employment opportunities is examined. Chapter 10 is devoted to the theory and practice of plant location, both domestic and multinational.

Chapters 11 through 16 bring together supply and demand to show determination of prices and outputs. Chapter 11 summarizes the competitive model that plays a basic role in business economics since predictions can often best be made by proceding "as if" an industry is fully competitive even when this is not strictly true. Chapter 12 deals with monopolistic pricing, since together the moves toward and away from competitive behavior tell much about the real business world.

Chapter 13 deals with price discrimination and price differentials. Price discrimination is a common device for increasing profits and the utilization of capacity (as seen in first-class, tourist, standby, and other air fares.) In Chapters 14, 15, and 16, oligopolistic pricing and promotion policies are considered as these loom very large in business activity. Conglomerate mergers, concentration, and corporate takeovers are also involved, along with recognition that most firms handle many products in spite of the popularity of the single-product firm for simplicity of analysis.

Chapter 17 is devoted to the vexing problem of pollution and congestion and with some possible devices for their amelioration. Such pollution as acid rain and runoff from toxic dumps correctly claims much public attention.

The final chapter, Chapter 18, summarizes the present status of antitrust activity, with special reference to important considerations of the 1980s. Throughout the text, government regulation has been recognized as an important constraint on business decision making. The final chapter on government parameters to business decisions acts both as a reference back to some previous parts of the course and as a concluding note on public policies designed to influence present and future decision making.

The chapters are followed by cases that give practice to students in applying material within (and sometimes outside of) the corresponding chapter to real-world problems. Chapter 1 has only one case, "Leeway in Accounting." The purpose is to show the student at the outset a need to go behind statements promulgated by accountants, executives, lawyers, politicians, bureaucrats, and even professors, and to try to separate analysis from propaganda.

CASE 1–1
Leeway in Accounting*

Sometimes flexibility in calculating earnings comes from having several strikingly different ways to account for a single set of facts. Managers sometimes have leeway because situations call for highly subjective estimates. While there is a lot less room to manipulate earnings today than a decade ago, the rules still are mighty spacious.

The bailout of the Continental Illinois National Bank has focused new attention on the extraordinary discretion that banks have in establishing loss reserves and accruing interest on shaky loans. The present system allows banks to report rising earnings even as loans sour. The Securities and Exchange Commission has made inadequate bank loss reserves a top enforcement priority.

Most well-known instances of managed earnings involve companies trying to make profits look robust. But the process often is considerably subtler. Most executives prefer to report earnings that follow a smooth, regular, upward path. They hate to report declines, but they also want to avoid increases that vary wildly from year to year: it's better to have two years of 15 percent earnings increases than a 30 percent gain one year and none the next. As a result, some companies "bank" earnings by understating them in particularly good years and use the banked profits to polish results in bad years.

A recent study by accounting professor Paul Healy of the Massachusetts Institute of Technology bolsters Briloff's assertions. Healy documents a connection between bonus schemes and the accounting choices executives make. Executives whose bonus plans rewarded them up to a ceiling tended to choose accounting options that minimized reported profits, while executives on bonus plans without upper limits chose profit-boosting options. In other words, if no additional bonus is paid once profits hit a certain level, it's not in the executive's interest for reported earnings to exceed that amount. The executive is better off deferring any

---

*SOURCE: Selected portions of an article by Ford S. Worthy, "Manipulating Profits: How It's Done," *Fortune*, June 25, 1984. © 1984 Time Inc. All rights reserved.

profits above the maximum bonus level until the profits are needed to sustain personal income.

The oil industry offers one of the best examples of how different accounting options can drastically alter reported income. In mid-1978, Occidental Petroleum changed the way it accounted for the costs of finding oil and gas. The change, which was merely a different way to record the same economic events, slashed reported profits by a third. Under the old method, Oxy's earnings per share were $2.92 in 1977. Restated, 1977 earnings dropped to $1.93 a share.

Companies can't switch back and forth between accounting methods. But the fact that they can change to "preferable" methods stirs up critics who argue that if there is a preferable way, there ought not to be another way. Says John C. Burton, a former chief accountant for the SEC and now dean of Columbia University's Graduate School of Business, "I feel very strongly that there should be fewer areas where alternative accounting principles are permitted."

But the opportunity for judgment in accounting matters to affect earnings is most potent in two industries: (1) banking and (2) property and casualty insurance. Banks must make a provision to cover loans that will ultimately go bad. Property and casualty companies establish reserves to cover claims they ultimately will pay out on current insurance policies. These amounts are deducted from profits in the year they are added to reserves, not in the year a claim is paid or a loan becomes worthless. When a loan is written off, for example, the bank removes it from assets and deducts an equal amount from the pool of loss reserves, which is a bookkeeping entry that doesn't affect the income statement.

Ideally, the total amount held in reserve should be just enough to cover all loans on the books that the bank has reason to believe will eventually go bad. The addition to reserves that is charged against income each year should be just enough to keep total reserves at the appropriate level.

A company's management and its auditors sometimes have different opinions about what level of reserves is appropriate. But they can generally agree on the range of acceptable estimates. Within this range, earnings can be managed. Since total reserves can exceed a bank's annual earnings, "a small percentage variation in the loan loss estimate can have a huge effect on the bottom line," says Roger Cason, a partner at Main Hurdman/KMG, a New York accounting firm.

Executives usually are most eager to boost earnings in hard times, just when they also are especially anxious to reduce inventories. As a result, it is difficult for auditors and SEC investigators to know whether a company is liquidating inventory for sound business reasons or to manipulate earnings. L. Glenn Perry, the chief accountant for the enforcement division of the SEC, wants the LIFO rules tightened.

U.S. Steel has reported $1.7 billion in LIFO profits since 1976, while the company's steel business has been shrinking. "The magnitude of their liquidations is so large that you wonder if they're not doing it purposely," says Ted. O'glove. "I don't think it's an indication of real profit." U.S. Steel has broken out the accounting profits each year and says they resulted from a long-term program to reduce inventories permanently.

Questions

1. To the extent there is leeway in accounting, name some considerations that can cause executives to attempt to:
   a. Overstate profits
   b. Understate profits
2. Should corporations make charitable contributions on a substantial scale?
3. Large loans to South America and to the U.S. oil industry may well affect some accounting decisions of banks in the United States. Comment.

2

Speculation, Hedging, and Profit

He who sells what isn't his'n
Must buy it back or go to pris'n
—*Daniel Drew*

It is often said that nothing is certain except death and taxes. In an important sense, not even these qualifications need be made. The entire institution of life insurance (a euphemism for death insurance) is based on the uncertain duration of the life of an individual in comparison with the calculability of mortality rates for large numbers of persons. Also, the amount and nature of taxes are important uncertainties to the family and the firm.

If the future could be known with certainty, correct economic decisions could be made by everyone. The worker could know precisely where and how to earn the largest income, the business executive would know in advance the outcome of alternative ventures that might be undertaken, and the investor would be fully cognizant of the relative desirability of various investment opportunities. Decision making would not be difficult, and professional decision makers (business executives) would not be highly paid. Investment in a newly formed uranium mining company would be as safe as investment in a well-established utility company.

In the actual world the existence of uncertainty causes future incomes to be imperfectly predictable. Often it is possible for the individual to choose between receiving income that is definite in amount according to terms either of a contract or an unwritten agreement, or receiving income that depends, instead, on the outcome of the economic activity in which the individual participates. In the first case, the individual can be fairly sure what his or her income will be in the near future, while in the second case the degree of predictability is lower. A fisherman, for example, may work for a regular daily wage or, alternatively, may share in the proceeds of the sale of the catch. The latter arrangement is very common because of the unusually high degree of uncertainty regarding the production function (relation of output to input) in the fishing industry. Similarly, a manager may be employed at a specific salary rate by a chain grocery store or, alternatively, may operate his or her own store where the return for labor and capital investment depends on the success of the operation. Similarly, a person wanting to invest funds in a particular corporation may become a bondholder, a preferred stockholder, or a common stockholder. In the first case, the person would be a creditor of the firm, receiving interest in a fixed annual amount. His or her income would not depend on the success of the firm except that a sufficiently unprofitable situation might endanger both receipt of interest and safety of principal. As a preferred stockholder the degree of uncertainty of return would be somewhat lower, while as a common stockholder the investor would face the greatest degree of uncertainty, both in terms of return and safety of principal.[1]

ACCOUNTING AND ECONOMIC PROFIT

The accountant designates as *profit* or *net income* (before taxes) the amount left over after deducting from gross income all payments to hired factors and an allowance for depreciation of capital equipment. The economist also thinks in terms of deducting cost from revenue but has a different concept of costs. The economist considers alternative present opportunities, while the accountant must adhere to historical costs. (This is not to say that good accountants neglect the economic way of thinking when they are making recommendations and that they are not bound by tax law or similar restrictions.)

Economic profit can be defined as *income minus opportunity costs*. Opportunity cost is the value of the best alternative that is sacrificed in order to engage in an activity. The alternative may be inferior, equal, or superior to the present activity. Suppose a skilled surgeon became a commercial fisherman for a year. Even if the surgeon happened also to be skilled in fishing, the opportunity cost of each catch would be high because a surgeon's time should be considered to be worth what could have been earned as a surgeon. The economic profit of the surgeon would be negative, and this would be a signal to abandon commercial fishing. Of course, any intelligent surgeon would have already known this and probably had some important objective such as improving his or her own health. In less obvious situations of resource misallocation, however, close measurement of opportunity costs may give useful information. For example, the owner of a filling station who shows an accounting profit of $21,000 in a given year is probably making a negative economic profit. If the owner could now sell out for $50,000 and invest the money elsewhere at 10 percent, and if the owner could earn $20,000 per year by working

---

[1]Over a long period of time, however, common stock may offer the investor more nearly a guarantee of stability or gain in *real* income and real value of principal. This is traceable primarily to the propensity of governments to follow inflationary monetary and fiscal policies.

for another firm, economic profit by choosing not to sell would clearly be negative. The opportunity costs would be $25,000 per year so far as labor and capital were concerned. (This calculation neglects possible depreciation or appreciation in selling value if the business were kept.)

The habit of thinking in terms of opportunity cost is a most valuable one for personal, business, and even governmental decision making. Any expenditure of time or money forecloses many other possibilities: the value of the most attractive one is the opportunity cost.

Some of the explicit costs deducted by the accountant, such as wage payments, maintenance expenditures, and utility bills, are also costs from the economist's point of view since payments to outsiders clearly foreclose opportunities for using the funds elsewhere. The most important difference in viewpoint relates to capital. Interest actually paid (e.g., on mortgages and bonds) is an accounting cost, whereas interest on the present value of the plant (which could be obtained in an alternative investment of similar riskiness if the plant were sold) is the corresponding cost from an economic point of view. Similarly, "depreciation" entered in a company's income statement is typically based on original cost and is calculated as a published uniform amount over the estimated life of the asset. For tax purposes much more rapid write-offs are permitted. Except at the time of purchase, original cost is irrelevant to the economist. Depreciation in the economic view is the expected loss in selling value over an interval relevant to the problem at hand. Negative depreciation (appreciation) is also possible. This opportunity cost approach is brought out in Case 2–1, "Cow Pastures or Condominiums."

The distinction can perhaps be most easily made by reference to a simple type of firm—the household. Interest paid on the mortgage is an allowable deduction for family income tax purposes. However, even if the house is fully owned by the family, there is an opportunity interest cost equal to the amount that could be earned if the house were sold and the proceeds invested elsewhere. This selling value may have little relation to original cost of the house. Expected changes in selling value (negative or positive) are depreciation or appreciation that should also be considered in the family's decision whether to retain the house. For example, if the house originally cost $40,000 and could now be sold for $70,000 the implicit interest cost of living there is $7,000 per year (at 10 percent). If the selling value is expected to decline by $1,000 in the next year, the annual interest and depreciation from an economic point of view would be $8,000, and this figure should enter into decision making. The original cost is irrelevant unless it affects the capital gain on which an income tax will be paid if the house is sold. Of course, many additional factors should enter into an actual selling decision including the price of alternative housing and nonpecuniary factors.

The most important consequence of the distinction between economic and accounting profit derives from the corporation income tax. Theoretically, the tax should be levied on economic profit. In actuality, it is based on accounting profit. This base gives the corporation an incentive to make more of its costs explicit, and the most important way in which this can be done is to raise part of its capital by selling bonds rather than relying entirely on the sale of stock and the retention of earnings. Corporate financial structures are undoubtedly weighted more heavily with "bonds payable" than would be the case if there were no corporation income taxes. This can cause special stress when business conditions are poor because bond interest payments must be met, whereas dividends could be skipped.

In theory, an interest cost is involved in using equity capital, whether it is derived from the sale of stocks or from retained earnings. In practice it would be a difficult change to put into effect, although some moves in that direction have been made by authorities such as the Financial Accounting Standards Board (FASB) and the Cost Accounting Standards Board (CASB). Unless the very disruptive change of eliminating interest as a deduction for income tax purposes were made by the U.S. Congress, it would be necessary to apply an interest rate to equity capital. Two practical choices are to use: (1) the company's own pretax rate for borrowed funds or (2) some standard rate published by appropriate authorities.[2] The FASB approach is to use the company's own pretax interest rate for borrowed funds. Like other suggestions this has its problems. For example, a corporation might deliberately pay an unnecessarily high interest rate on a bond sale if this would give a more-than-compensating deduction for interest on equity capital. The concept of marginal cost comes into play. Like other decisions, it should not be made on too narrow a view.

Reform to make accounting cost more nearly approach economic cost would do much to improve the image of large corporations. All or most of the sometimes "obscene" profits now reported are actually a "normal" or market rate of return on equity capital. Some profits, of course, are actually far above any level that seems reasonable, especially if monopolistic practices have contributed strongly.

From the point of view of a potential *buyer* of a firm, it may be important to view opportunity cost in terms of his or her own alternatives rather than those of the seller. This is especially likely to be significant with respect to labor earnings. The decision regarding purchase of a business involves *anticipated* rather than past incomes, and these anticipations are fraught with uncertainty. In the absence of better information, anticipations may have to be based on past performance.

BALANCE SHEET VIEW

In order to decide whether a somewhat marginal enterprise is worth continuing, the business executive may do well to think in terms of an "economist's balance sheet." Such a balance sheet would value individual

---

[2]Robert N. Anthony, "Recognizing the Cost of Interest on Equity," *Harvard Business Review*, January–February 1982, pp. 91–96.

assets according to their income-earning potential in their best use, that is, according to their present market prices. Historical costs, which provide the basis for the accountant's balance sheet, would not enter into consideration. If the total market value of such individually evaluated assets exceeded their value as a whole to the enterprise, as calculated from future earnings prospects, the indicated decision would be to liquidate the business by selling assets separately. The process of discounting anticipated future earnings of the business as a whole in order to find the present value of its net assets (assets minus liabilities) will be discussed in some detail in a later chapter.

Even if the decision is to remain in business, this way of thinking about the opportunity cost of retaining assets may lead to useful decisions. For example, the present market value of an asset may be so high that the firm in question should sell the asset. This is especially likely to happen with land that is vacant or that supports a well-depreciated building. A periodic check of its value to other possible users might lead a firm to a more rational decision on whether this particular parcel of land should remain in the business.

One of the pressures that has resulted in the movement of firms to the rural fringes of metropolitan areas is that of rising land values in more central locations making the land asset too valuable for continuation of its present use. Higher property taxes that usually accompany such increases in land value add to the pressure to act. One recreational industry that has been particularly affected is that of the private golf course. In the face of a rapid growth in the number of golfers, the number of golf courses has remained relatively constant, essentially because well-located suburban courses are sold off for residential and commercial development as the land becomes literally too valuable for the land-extensive game of the Scots. The results are escalating green fees and increased congestion with line-ups at 5:00 AM on weekends for an early tee off at public urban courses.

The value of alternative uses of a scarce resource may prove to be a financial solace to firms faced with unfavorable shifts in demand. For example, the scarce waterfront property that was an indispensable part of the northern New England boys' or girls' camp may now be valued at $150 a foot for second-home use. For a camp owner struggling against competition from European tours and specialized sports camps for a youth market impatient with reveille and woodcraft, $150,000 for lake frontage could be substantial inducement for early exit.

THE PROBLEM OF UNCERTAINTY

The process of decision making is one of making a choice among alternatives. Were there no uncertainty in predicting the outcome of a decision, no ambiguity in measuring the desirability of the results, and no difficulty in listing all the possible courses of action, it would be a very simple process. A payoff table of the following sort could be constructed. The alternative actions could be listed vertically, and the results of each action could be listed next to the alternative:

Choice	Payoff
1	a
2	b
3	c

If b were larger than a or c, choice 2 would be made.

Classical economic analysis of the static equilibrium type takes this relatively simple form. The firm is assumed to maximize measurable profits. Many alternative courses of action in the form of different price and output combinations are shown quite succinctly with demand and cost curves from which profit consequences are easily derived. No specific provision, however, is made for uncertainty. The economist recognizes, of course, that the firm's forecasts of demand and cost functions may be faulty, especially under changing circumstances. Economic theories of profit rest heavily on the entrepreneurial role in operating under uncertainty. The standard equilibrium analysis, however, is designed to show the eventual price-output adjustment to given demand and supply conditions. It assumes that knowledge of these given conditions would, over time, perhaps with some trial and error, be sufficient to establish specific demand and cost functions and prices.

For business managers in a dynamic economy, demand and cost functions will never be known with certainty. The very conditions underlying a particular equilibrium are continually being transformed. A range of outcomes to a particular business decision is a possibility. Estimates of the demand for the product are at best central points of a comparatively narrow range of possibilities.

Assume a very simple case of a firm that is considering three strategies: expand, maintain, or reduce output. The firm conceives of three discrete states of nature that would affect the outcome of its decision: an upturn in business conditions, a downturn in business conditions, or stability. It then calculates the profit possibilities of each strategy under each state of nature as shown in Figure 2–1.

FIGURE 2–1

Strategy	State of Nature		
	Upturn	Stability	Downturn
1. Expand output	$20,000	$5,000	$ – 10,000
2. Maintain output . . .	12,000	6,000	–0–
3. Contract output . . .	4,000	3,000	2,000

DECISION MAKING UNDER CERTAINTY

Suppose it is assumed that stability conditions are certain and that the profit consequences of the strategies are correctly specified. The indicated decision would be to maintain output and obtain a profit of $6,000. Two reservations must be made. The first question—whether expected profits would necessarily be the measure in which the payoff matrix was expressed—will be discussed later. The second is whether unlisted strategies are available that would be more profitable than those specified. The cost and revenue curves used by the economist cover a multitude of possible variations in product specifications, promotion, and production methods. A real problem for management is the range and number of alternatives it can afford to evaluate.

DECISION MAKING UNDER RISK AND THE CONCEPT OF EXPECTED PROFITS

If the outcome is unknown and the firm does not choose to act as though it were certain, two different cases can be assumed: decision making under risk and decision making under uncertainty. The distinction is this. Risk is used to designate a situation where the particular outcome is unknown but there is a substantial basis for estimating the probabilities (p) for a number of possible outcomes. Uncertainty is used to designate a situation where there is no basis for expecting one rather than another of the universe of possible outcomes.

Under conditions of risk, it is possible to compute the expected profits from a particular strategy by the following formula:

$$E = p_1 G_1 + p_2 G_2 + \cdots + p_n G_n$$

where E is expected profit, and G_1, G_2, $\cdots$, G_n represent the payoffs (gains) resulting from the various possible outcomes (or "states of nature"). The series $p_1 + p_2 \cdots + p_n$ equals 1, since it is assumed that one of the possible outcomes will occur even though the specific outcome is uncertain.

If the probabilities of various states of nature were estimated at 0.6 for an upturn, 0.3 for stability, and only 0.1 for a downturn, the expected profits could be evaluated as follows:

$$E(1) = 0.6(20,000) + 0.3(5,000) + 0.1(-10,000) = \$12,500$$
$$E(2) = 0.6(12,000) + 0.3(6,000) + 0.1(0) \qquad\quad = \$\ 9,000$$
$$E(3) = 0.6(4,000)\ + 0.3(3,000) + 0.1(2,000) \quad\ = \$\ 3,500$$

The strategy that maximizes expected profits is that of expanding output. Case 2–3, "On Broadway," involves this sort of calculation.

DECISION MAKING UNDER UNCERTAINTY

Suppose now that the decision maker is completely uncertain about the state of nature, that is, which outcome is the most likely. What criteria might she use? A number of decision criteria that might be chosen have been suggested, but we deal with just two.[3]

One approach is to make the assumption associated with LaPlace and Bayes that in the absence of other information, all of the possible states of nature are equally likely. Under this assumption, expected profits can be computed as suggested above. They are at a maximum of $6,000 for maintaining output. Two difficulties should be noted in the application of this approach to business decisions.

First, the listing of the possible states of nature may be incomplete. In this illustrative example, there is an element of arbitrariness in selecting only three business conditions. Depending upon what additional possibilities were included, the expected profits would be estimated differently. In typical examples from another book, "war," "peace," and "depression" or "perfect weather," "variable weather," and "bad weather" have been included as the three possible states of nature, and yet the gradations in each of these sets are many.[4] For example, depression could include the almost imperceptible break in growth which occurred in early 1967 (called a minirecession) and the Great Depression of the 1930s with many other possibilities such as more recent recessions which have been accompanied by continued inflation.

Second, even if all possibilities were listed, information is likely to be available that would suggest greater probabilities for one outcome than for another. This point is important to keep in mind in reading this chapter where the distinction between uncertainty and risk is made. Many, if not most, business problems fall between the two, a grey area where probabilities are not known but the outcome is not completely uncertain either. Much business information gathering and forecasting is designed to reduce the uncertainty and make the decision one that deals with manageable risks.

THE USE OF CRITERIA OTHER THAN MAXIMIZATION OF PROFITS

One of the criteria most frequently suggested for decision making under uncertainty is the maximin, that is, the maximization of the minimum level of profits, or more generally, of utility expected. If this were applied to the payoff matrix of Figure 2–1, it would be noted that the poorest result from each strategy would result from a downturn. The best payoff for this would be $2,000 for the strategy of contraction; and if it used the maximin criterion, the firm would elect this course. Every other strategy could, under some outcome, result in greater losses. This could be termed

---

[3]The student who is interested in a further discussion of decision theory will find both a summary discussion and further references in chaps. 4 and 5 of the D. W. Miller, S. Martin, K. Starr, *Executive Decisions and Operations Research* (Englewood Cliffs, N.J.: Prentice-Hall, 1969;) and in chap. 24 of W. Baumol, *Economic Analysis and Operations Research*, 3d ed. (Englewood Cliffs, N.J.: Prentice-Hall, 1972).

[4]Miller et al., *Executive Decisions, chap. 5.*

FIGURE 2–2

Strategy	State of Nature or Outcome		
	Upturn	Stability	Downturn
1. Expand output	16,000	6,000	− 14,000
2. Maintain output . . .	11,500	6,500	500
3. Contract output . . .	2,000	1,000	–0–

---

the criterion of pessimism. Its counterpart, the criterion of optimism, would be the maximax, that is, the maximization of maximum profits. Expansion would be the maximax decision.

An absolute measure of profits does not necessarily convey the total of utility that is involved to the decision maker. The application of the maximin criterion to a payoff matrix implies that the certainty of some minimum level of profits could take precedence over the assumption of the maximization of profits. Another more relevant payoff matrix could be expressed in terms of utility which could embrace more than the magnitude of profits.

Assume that the owner of this hypothetical firm had the following concept of measuring his or her preferences:

1. A dollar of profits in the range of $0–$10,000 represented one unit of utility.
2. Profits above $10,000 added 0.5 units of utility per dollar of profits; each dollar of loss was equivalent to − 1.5 units of utility.
3. The act of expansion itself was worth 1,000 units of utility; a decision to contract represented a negative 2,000 units of utility; maintaining output represented 500 units of utility.

The payoff matrix in utility units would now look like that shown in Figure 2–2.

The student should confirm these choices: under equally likely probabilities, or under maximin criterion, "maintain output" would be chosen; with very small probabilities of a downturn and significant possibilities of an upturn, "expansion" would be chosen; and "contracting output" would never be chosen.

THE TRANSFORMING OF UNCERTAINTIES

It is useful to distinguish between transformable and nontransformable uncertainties. The latter provide the basic explanation for the existence of profits in an economy of private, competitive industry. Nevertheless, a good deal of knowledge and judgment are required by business executives in order to transform successfully and economically the types of uncertainties that are avoidable at a certain cost. The time and effort that must be spent in this type of activity vary a great deal from business to business.

One process of transforming uncertainties into definite costs is called *hedging*.

Hedging, in essence, involves the purposive holding of two opposite positions at the same time. Roughly, it can be described as betting in two opposite ways at the same time. The purchase of insurance is of this nature and can be thought of as hedging. When business people buy fire insurance, they are essentially betting that a fire will occur on their premises; the insurance company is betting that this will not happen. Even if the fire does occur, the directors of the insurance company are unlikely to be dismayed because the company will undoubtedly win its bets with numerous other persons who bought fire insurance, and the successful wagers will likely at least offset the unsuccessful ones. As the owner of a building and its contents, business people are, of course, hoping that no fire will occur, since this would bring financial loss. For protection, the owner must take an opposite stand—that is, bet that a fire will occur. Whatever the actual outcome, disaster will be averted since an important risk has been converted into a definite cost—the cost of the insurance premiums.[5]

LONG AND SHORT POSITIONS

Hedging in the business world often consists of taking offsetting "long" and "short" positions. This strategy is appropriate when the firm is forced into one position as an incident of doing business. If the position is a dangerously speculative one, it is conservative to hedge against it, thereby incurring a small, certain cost rather than risking a large loss.

An individual is in a "long" position whenever he or she owns any commodity, security, or other valuable asset. The hope is then that the asset will increase in money value as a result of the operation of supply-demand forces.[6] The fear is that market forces will reduce the value of the asset. On the other hand, a person in a "short" position hopes that the market price will decline rather than rise, since a contract has been made to deliver a commodity, security, or other asset at a future date for a specific price. The more cheaply the asset can be purchased when the delivery date rolls around, or the more cheaply it can be produced in time to meet the delivery requirement, the larger the gain will be. A contractor who has agreed, for example, to construct a building, road, or other proj-

---

[5]Even apart from the consequences of the disruption of business, the insured person is apt not to recover the entire loss, since insurance companies normally do not sell policies to cover the whole value of inflammable property. To do so might overtly tempt some policyholders to win their bets with the company. Even beneficiaries of life insurance policies have been known to take steps to secure the proceeds prematurely!

[6]It is also possible to be long on money itself. This occurs whenever a cash balance is held. The hope of the individual is then that the purchasing power of the cash will increase—that is, that prices will fall. Conversely, someone is "short" on money when in debt, since it is necessary to make future delivery of principal and interest to a creditor. The latter condition tends to be chronic among college students.

ect for a specified sum is considered to be in a "short" position with respect to that asset. One of the problems, once that contract has been signed, is that the cost of materials, labor, and other inputs may increase during the construction period, so as to make the job an unprofitable one. In order to hedge against this contingency, the contractor must take a long position with respect to the needed inputs.

The contractor may, for example, sign a lease to rent the needed equipment at a specified price for the period of construction; or she or he may buy the equipment. Alternatively, the contractor may attempt to secure a contract with the labor unions involved, which will make labor costs more predictable. With respect to materials, there are two alternatives: (1) buying all of the necessary materials ahead of time and storing them until needed; or (2) contracting to have them delivered at specified prices at specified future dates. Either alternative is a hedge against a price increase. Once the contractor has protected "long" positions on most of the inputs required for construction of the project, the uncertainty of unfavorable price changes is transformed into predictable costs.

FUTURE MARKETS

Hedging operations in many lines of activity are made possible by the existence of organized markets in which commodities are traded both at *spot* or *cash* prices for immediate delivery and at *future* prices for deferred delivery. Futures contracts are regularly bought and sold for dozens of relatively homogeneous commodities including wheat, corn, oats, soybeans, soybean meal, soybean oil, copper, gold, silver, platinum, mercury, cocoa, coffee, orange juice, sugar, and pork bellies. (The last-mentioned commodity has been made rather famous in several moving pictures.)

A *futures contract* is a firm, legal agreement between a buyer or seller and an established commodity exchange. A seller agrees to deliver a specified amount of the commodity during a designated period. Quality and delivery conditions are specified, but there are usually some alternatives available with respect to the grade or place of delivery, with a set of premiums or discounts applying to deviations from the basic contract. Delivery must be made during the month specified in the futures contract, but the actual day of the month is selected by the seller and notice is given in the form of a warehouse receipt, shipping certificate, or bill of lading.[7]

A buyer also deals directly with the commodity exchange, agreeing to accept delivery at a specified price and according to other stated conditions. However, most buyers do not actually take possession of the commodity (nor do most sellers actually deliver) since more than 98 percent

---

[7]This and some other information in this section is from an excellent book by R. J. Teweles, C. V. Harlow, and H. L. Stone, *The Commodity Futures Game* (New York: McGraw-Hill, 1974). Detailed information is given for a large number of commodities.

of all futures contracts are settled by offset transactions.[8] That is, a buyer of a futures contract can sell a similar contract, and a seller can buy a similar contract, to cancel the obligation. Consequently, most transactions are bookkeeping entries with the actual act of buying or selling occurring only after an intent to deliver is shown. At that time, a specific buyer and seller are paired. More than 20 times the actual crop may be traded before expiration of the crop year.[9]

The futures market is a great convenience to both speculators and hedgers, since the actual commodity need not be handled, and since buyers and sellers normally do not have to be concerned about selection of the specific grade, place of delivery, and other details. A speculator who believes that a presently quoted futures price is too low—that is, that demand will be stronger in relation to supply than present quotations indicate—is able to *buy* a futures contract. If the speculator's expectation is correct, this purchase can later be offset with a similar sale at a higher price. On the other hand, a speculator who believes that a presently quoted futures price is too high can *sell* futures, profiting by a later offsetting purchase if this "bearish" expectation turns out to be correct.

Instead of attempting to take advantage of a change in a single price over time, a speculator may, instead, attempt to turn to his or her advantage a difference between two prices when that difference appears to be out of line. Suppose that a study of market conditions suggests strongly that July oats futures are underpriced relative to September oats. This would suggest an arbitrage transaction in which July oats would be bought and September oats would be simultaneously sold. It would then not matter whether the more normal differential were established by a rise in the price of July oats, by a fall in September oats, or any other combination of change, so long as a smaller difference in price came to be established. Similarly, an improper price differential between two markets can be the source of arbitrage profits. Some years ago a law student on the west coast noticed that rare coins were more expensive in the East. He made a large profit by buying them in the West and shipping them eastward.

The arbitrager can be considered to be "betting two ways at once." This action differs, however, from that of the hedger in that the latter is forced to assume one position (make one of the available bets) as an incident to carrying on a regular line of business activity. The arbitrager takes both positions as a speculative matter. In practice, it is often impossible to characterize an individual as purely a hedger or purely a arbitrager on a particular transaction, since a hedger is not averse, of course,

---

[8]John Maynard Keynes, a noted speculator as well as economist, once greatly pleased the chaplain of his college by borrowing the chapel for three days, as Keynes was known to be nonreligious. It turned out, however, that he wanted to use the chapel for the worldly purpose of storing grain that was unexpectedly being delivered to him on a futures purchase! (Story told by Harry G. Johnson to writer.)

[9]Teweles et al., *Commodity Futures Game*, p. 25.

FIGURE 2–3

Date	Events	Receipts and Payments
July 20	Farmer has growing wheat with estimated yield of 10,000 bushels in September. Wishing to assure himself the September futures price of $3 (spot price is also $3), he sells futures contract for 10,000 bushels. He puts up margin of $3,000 and pays commission of $200.	September futures receipts . . . .$30,000 Commission payment 200
Sept. 20	Spot and futures prices have declined to $2.50. Farmer sells wheat in spot market (10,000 bushels). He buys September futures for $2.50. He pays off margin loan with 10 percent annual interest.	Cash receipts . . . . 25,000 September futures payments . . 25,000 Interest payment 50
	Result: Farmer nets $25,000 for wheat plus $4,750 on futures contract.	Net 29,750
	Note: Had cash and futures prices increased to $3.25 he still would have netted $29,750 rather than the $32,500 with no hedge.	

---

to making an arbitrage profit, whenever possible, in the process of protecting himself or herself from an adverse price change.

HEDGING BY SELLING FUTURES

A wheat farmer, contemplating his growing crop in July, realizes that he is an involuntary speculator in wheat on the "long" side. He may decide to hedge by selling September wheat, perhaps in about the quantity he expects to harvest in that month. By taking this action, he has, roughly speaking, already sold his growing crop at a specific price for delivery at harvest time, and he is in no danger of suffering a speculative loss between July and September. Actually, he is unlikely to deliver his own wheat on the futures contract; he will probably offset his short position in late August or September by buying September futures in the same amount he had previously sold. Then he will sell his own wheat in the cash market.

If we assume that the quantity of wheat involved was 10,000 bushels and make certain price assumptions, the transactions can be summarized as shown in Figure 2–3.

In the situation pictured, the farmer would be glad that he hedged, since he has a net gain of $29,750, whereas his crop would have brought him $25,000 if he had not hedged. The cash price of wheat declined 50 cents a bushel between July 20 and September 20, but this was offset by the 50-cent decline in September futures over the same period. The protection received from this sort of hedging is based on the fact that cash and futures prices generally move in the same direction. However, these two prices may not move by the same amount; consequently, the hedger is apt to either make a speculative gain or suffer a loss of moderate proportions.[10] If the price of cash wheat had increased from, say, $3 per bushel on July 20 to $3.25, the farmer would have had a larger net income by not hedging. The existence of government price supports at some designated percentage of "parity" may make hedging by farmers less necessary. (However, both spot and futures prices can fall below support levels.) The price-support program thus places part of the speculative risk of a price decline on the shoulders of the taxpayers. Nevertheless, U.S. farmers have been reported to engage extensively in this sort of hedging.

Hedging is practiced extensively by certain types of processors. The practice has expanded in recent years, for example, in the case of southern textile mills. These mills buy spot cotton early in the season and sell cotton futures as a hedge. Offsetting futures purchases are made as orders are received for textiles. This gives them substantial protection against losses on their long position in cotton. If cotton has declined in price between the time it is purchased and a textile order is received, the mill may have to quote a price on textiles which reflects the lower price of cotton. In this case, however, a profit will be made on the futures transactions, and this may equal or even exceed the reduction in revenue occasioned by the need to cut the price of textiles.

A soybean processing mill converts soybeans into oil and meal. An unusual assortment of hedging possibilities is available here since there are separate futures markets for soybean meal, soybean oil, and soybeans. To protect a long position in beans (because of having an inventory on hand), the mill managers can sell beans, meal, or oil futures or some combinations of these, later offsetting such contracts by futures purchases as the inventory is reduced. The choice of which futures to deal in will depend in part on judgment as to which commodity seems to have a relatively favorable price when the futures sales take place. In practice, hedging usually involves elements of speculation and arbitrage; it is not just neat insurance against loss.

HEDGING BY BUYING FUTURES

If the business in which a business executive participates requires taking a short position, the executive may be able to hedge by taking an opposite position in a relevant futures market. Suppose that during the summer months orders are taken by a candy manufacturer for candy to be deliv-

---

[10]Actually, the farmer did not engage in a pure hedging transaction, since he was short on mature wheat but long on immature wheat prior to harvest time. If he had held wheat in storage and had sold wheat futures in the same amount, the long and short positions would have been more definitely offsetting. With a growing crop, an unfortunate hailstorm could have left him short.

ered at specified prices before Christmas. The candy should not be produced until November. The firm is then short on candy and can protect itself from a price increase in sugar and chocolate by buying November futures in sugar and cocoa during the summer. This can be very important protection since both of these commodities tend to fluctuate rather violently in price. When the time arrives to produce the candy, the business executive will probably not take delivery on the sugar and cocoa contracts that were bought but instead will buy in a spot market the exact kind of sugar and chocolate required. If the executive has to pay more than was anticipated at the time a definite price was given for the candy, a profit on the futures contract will be helpful and perhaps even vital to the company's financial solvency.

INTEREST RATE FUTURES

Since late 1975 there has been an important futures market based on interest rates. The market deals in U.S. Treasury bonds and notes.[11] Since bond prices and interest rates vary inversely in a precise way, these markets can be called bond futures, debt futures, or interest rate futures.

Banks, savings and loan associations, insurance companies, pension funds, mutual funds, and other large-scale owners of private or government bonds can suffer severe capital losses if market interest rates rise. Existing bonds compete with new bond issues; if the latter pay a higher interest rate, old bonds must fall in price to match this yield. The institutions mentioned are long on bonds, just as a cotton mill is long on cotton in storage. To hedge, the financial institution has to go short—that is, sell bonds for future delivery.

Suppose an institution owns $100 million worth of 20-year U.S. government bonds currently yielding 11 percent in interest. If market interest rates should rise to 12 percent (due, perhaps, to an unexpected increase in the rate of inflation), the value of the institution's bond portfolio would decline by a few million dollars. If the institution has hedged against this contingency, it will have sold bond futures earlier and can now buy back a similar contract for a few million dollars less than the amount for which it was sold. This multimillion-dollar gain in interest rate futures should rather closely offset the decline in the value of the bond portfolio, except for commissions and related costs. If, instead, market interest rates had declined, the institution's managers would be sorry they had hedged since there will not be the capital gain that could otherwise have been enjoyed.

Speculation as well as hedging occurs in interest rate futures. An

---

[11]Treasury bonds and notes pay a fixed rate of interest semiannually. Bonds are issued for maturities of more than 10 years. Notes mature in 1 to 10 years. Treasury bills are issued in maturities of 13, 26, or 52 weeks, with interest paid in the form of a discount from their principal amount.

FIGURE 2–4   Treasury Bond Futures as of October 22, 1985 (settle prices)

December 1985	$77.28
March 1986	76.00
June	74.87
September	73.84
December	72.91
March 1987	72.03
June	71.25
September	70.53

SOURCE: *The Wall Street Journal,* October 23, 1985, p. 50.

individual or fund manager who has reason to expect a decline in interest rates can buy bonds for future delivery at a price now quoted. If this expectation is correct, the bonds at delivery time will be worth more than was paid. Before the delivery date the speculator may sell the contract at a profit instead of actually acquiring the bonds.

Hedging in bond futures can have personal as well as social value. A few years ago when interest rates rose sharply, some persons in charge of bond portfolios lost their jobs because they had failed to hedge. Of course it is also possible to lose a good position by selling bond futures when interest rates are about to decline substantially. Figure 2–4 illustrates Treasury bond futures.

FOREIGN EXCHANGE FUTURES

Futures markets also exist for trading major foreign currencies, such as the British pound, Canadian dollar, French franc, Swiss franc, West German mark, and Japanese yen. These futures (or forward) markets are especially valuable to business managers by making it possible to have a guaranteed price on a foreign currency in which they will be paid, or will have to pay, at a future date within the time span of the quotations.

A foreign exchange rate is the price of one currency relative to another. The market consists primarily of trading by the world's international banks. Supply and demand, affected by a multiplicity of forces, largely determine exchange rates. Many international firms have found their profits in particular periods to be sharply affected by exchange rate fluctuations. Wise use of the futures market in foreign currency can avoid many unpleasant surprises.

OPTIONS

Although options are an old financial device, *puts* and *calls* applicable to common stocks have attained much greater importance in recent years with the establishment of the Chicago Board Options Exchange and initi-

FIGURE 2–5 Example of Option Pricing on the CBOE

Option and N.Y. Close	Strike Price	Calls—Last			Puts—Last		
		Dec.	Mar.	June.	Dec.	Mar.	June.
Sears 33½. .							
	30	3¾	4¼	4½	⅛	—	—
	35	⁷⁄₁₆	1⅛	1⁹⁄₁₆	2¹⁄₁₆	—	—
	40	¹⁄₁₆	³⁄₁₆	⁷⁄₁₆	—	—	—

SOURCE: *The Wall Street Journal*, October 21, 1985, p. 56.

ation of options trading on the American Stock Exchange, the Philadelphia Stock Exchange, the New York Stock Exchange, the Pacific Stock Exchange, the Chicago Board of Trade, and the Chicago Mercantile Exchange.

A *call* is an option to buy a particular stock, usually in the amount of 100 shares, at a specified ("striking") price within a stated period. The buyer is "bullish," expecting that the price of the stock will rise above the striking price. Alternatively, the option can be sold at a gain if the underlying stock has appreciated in price.

The advantage in buying a call instead of buying the stock outright is the much lower cost. To buy 100 shares of a stock selling at $40 per share requires capital of $2,000 even if it is bought on a 50 percent margin, the remainder being borrowed from the broker. A call option on the same stock might cost $250, the exact price depending on the expiration date, the volatility of the stock, the relation between the striking price and the present market price, and the demand/supply situation for the option. (When the stock market is going up, buyers are more interested in options.) The call buyer can lose only the amount he or she spends on the option but can make a large profit if the price of the stock rises well above the striking price and the call is exercised or sold.

The seller of a call is seeking additional income. If the stock on which he or she *wrote* the call rises above the striking price and is exercised, the stock will be *called away* at the specified price, and the option seller will be deprived of a capital gain that could have been realized. (The seller may have some capital gain, however, as the option may have been sold with a striking price above the market price of the stock at the time of writing the option.)

The form in which prices of calls and puts are reported is shown in Figure 2–5 for a popular stock. Similar data can readily be found for several hundred of the relatively active common stocks on the New York Stock Exchange, the American Stock Exchange, the Philadelphia Stock Exchange, and the Pacific Stock Exchange.

The first column shows the name and the closing price of the stock for the same day. The "strike price" (also called "striking price") pertains to both calls and puts. For example, if one were bullish on Sears, a call option to buy 100 shares of the stock at a price of $35 per share would have cost $156 for the option expiring in June 1986.[12] Earlier expirations are less costly because the stock has less time in which to go up in price. High strike prices are less costly because of the low probability that they will be reached. If, instead, one anticipated disappointing Christmas sales volume at Sears, one could buy a December put option for $206.25, giving the right to sell the stock at a price of $35 before the option expires. If the call buyer is correct in his or her anticipation, Sears can either be bought for $35 when it is worth more than that amount or the option can be sold for more than it cost. If the put buyer is correct, the stock can be sold for $35 when it is worth less than that price, or the option, which will have gained in value, can be sold. Of course, brokers' fees and taxes must be considered in either case.

Buying a put resembles short selling but is less dangerous in that the buyer's loss is limited to the cost of the option. In short selling, the speculator borrows the stock from the broker and sells it, waits for a period of time, then buys the stock in order to repay the shares to the broker. If the bearish expectations prove correct, the price decline brings profits, but a large price increase produces heavy losses. Short selling is said to have originated with Daniel Drew in the 19th century, and its nature is suggested by the quotation in the heading of this chapter.[13]

OPTIONS ON STOCK INDEXES

In recent years a veritable explosion of new futures and options contracts has become available to speculators and hedgers. They are apt to be bewildering to the nonprofessional. Fortunately, the underlying principles and terminology are much the same in all the variations.

Among the popular, relatively new, variations are put and call options on stock indexes. These permit speculation and hedging on general market movements rather than on individual stocks. A well-utilized variety is based on the Standard & Poor's index of 100 common stocks. Figure 2–6 shows quotes on these options (they must be multiplied by $100 to obtain their cost). The S&P 100 index closed at 181.96 on the same day.

Suppose one felt strongly that the stock market would rise substantially by late January 1986. A January call on the index at a striking price of 180 could have been purchased for $475 (plus commissions and taxes). This option would already be "in the money" since the striking price is below the current level of the index.

If the bullish forecast turned out to be a good one and the index rose to 200 by late January, a cash settlement could be secured by the option

---

[12]Usually expiring the Saturday immediately following the third Friday of the expiration month.

[13]Bouck White, *The Book of Daniel Drew* (Larchmont, N.Y.: American Research Council, 1965) is recommended reading, especially for those interested in financial skulduggery.

FIGURE 2–6 Options on the S&P 100 Index as of October 24, 1985

Strike Price	Calls—Last			Puts—Last		
	Nov.	Dec.	Jan.	Nov.	Dec.	Jan.
170	12	12¼	13	1/16	5/16	⅝
175	7	7¼	9	⅜	1 1/16	1½
180	2 11/16	3¾	4¾	1⅝	2⅝	3⅛
185	11/16	1⅝	2 7/16	4¾	5½	6
190	⅛	7/16	1	8½	9¾	—

SOURCE: *The Wall Street Journal,* October 25, 1985, p. 56.

buyer based on the difference between 200 and 180. Net gain would be $2,000 minus $475 and commissions and taxes. Possible loss, if the market went down, would be the outlay for the option. As in the case of options on individual stocks, a bearish expectation can be effected by purchasing a put.

COMMODITY FUTURES OPTIONS

To further complicate the student's life, not only do commodity futures markets exist, but *options* on such futures have recently been introduced in the United States for certain agricultural products and metals. At the time of this writing, the former includes corn, soybeans, cotton, sugar, cattle, and hogs; the latter are gold and silver. Their nature can be seen in Figure 2–7, which pertains to corn on the Chicago Board of Trade.

Option prices on these futures resemble those on other "financial products" in that various strike prices are listed and separate prices for calls and puts at these strike prices are quoted. This provides an alternative way to speculate in commodities or to hedge.

Referring to Figure 2–7, suppose a speculator expects a sharp rise in the price of May corn. (The May futures price was about $2.41 per bushel on October 3, 1985.) A May call could be purchased at a strike price of

FIGURE 2–7 Options on Corn Futures as of October 3, 1985 (cents per bushel)

Strike Price	Calls			Puts		
	Dec.	Mar.	May	Dec.	Mar.	May
$2.00	24½	—	—	¼	⅜	—
2.10	14¾	25½	—	⅝	⅞	1¾
2.20	7	18	—	2½	2½	3¼
2.30	2⅛	11½	15¾	7¾	5½	6
2.40	½	6½	10¾	15½	10	9
2.50	¼	3⅜	7½	25¼	16½	15½

SOURCE: *The Wall Street Journal,* October 4, 1985, p. 33.

$2.30, $2.40, or $2.50, the last being the least expensive. Since the options are traded in units of 5,000 bushels, the cost of a May call at $2.50 would be $375 (5,000 × .075) plus commissions. If May corn rose in price to more than $2.50 per bushel, the option owner could still buy it at $2.50. More likely, the typical speculator would sell the option at a price above $.075.

A hedger, such as a corn farmer, fearing a disastrous drop in the price of corn, could buy a put option; for example, a May put at a striking price of $2.40 for $450 (5,000 × .09). More than one put might have to be bought to provide sufficient protection. The advantage to the farmer of dealing in options rather than directly in futures (as described earlier in the chapter) may be the lower cash outlay and limitation of possible loss to the amount paid for the option.

SUMMARY

1. A "bullish" speculator may buy stocks, bonds, real estate, or other assets that he or she believes will increase in price. Alternatively, on many stocks, a call option may be purchased, guaranteeing a "striking price" at which 100 shares of the security can be bought until a specified expiration date. Most options are resold rather than exercised, so the bull may think primarily in terms of speculating in options.

2. A "bearish" speculator in stocks can sell short by borrowing the security, selling it, waiting, and then buying the stock, hopefully at a lower price.

3. A less dangerous bear strategy involves buying a put option which gives the holder the right to sell the underlying stock at a specific price before the expiration date. If the market price of the stock declines below the strike price, it can be profitably "put to" the option maker.

4. In recent years it has become possible to deal in calls and puts on stock indexes such as the popular one maintained by Standard & Poor's on 100 common stocks. This makes it feasible to speculate on the general movement of stock prices. Settlement is in cash. Those who originate options are seeking additional income and on the whole are probably successful in securing good rates of return.

5. Options can be used in hedging as well as for speculating, and this tends to be emphasized by those in the business because of the wide social acceptability of insurance. (See Case 2–4, Puts, Calls, and Straddles.)

6. Arbitrage transactions have long been popular in all sorts of markets. They are meant to take advantage of price differentials between markets. The arbitrageur buys in the relatively underpriced market and sells in the dearer one, often simultaneously. (See Case 2–6, Arbitrage in Stocks.) The widespread use of computers has multiplied arbitrage possibilities—for example, between stocks and stock index futures.

7. Speculation in agricultural and other commodities is facilitated by futures markets and even by options on selected futures.

8. The same is true for foreign exchange for major currencies and for interest rates futures. That is, both futures and options on futures are available. Some of these markets are suitable mainly for institutions rather than for even moderately affluent individuals.

9. Hedging commodity positions is a very important business practice. It may even be essential, as in the case of egg cold storage where banks will not lend money to carry an unhedged inventory. A firm or grower that is long on a commodity hedges by going short (selling futures). A firm in a short position goes long by buying futures in the commodity or in related commodities. A successful hedge shifts much of the price risk onto speculators, more nearly permitting profits to depend on the principal business operation.

10. Miscellaneous futures and options markets, current and pending, are almost too numerous to mention. Options may cover just a small number of stocks, such as those of electronics companies. The innovative Montreal Exchange has a plan to introduce options on gold with settlement in cash rather than in the metal. Inflation futures based on the U.S. consumer price index for urban wage earners are currently sold on a small scale. Potentially, they may be used to provide predictable real value annuities and pensions. The quoted inflation futures also provide a market appraisal of expected inflation (or possibly deflation) rates.

11. The proliferation of futures and options markets, together with the new generation of computers, makes sophisticated strategies an interesting (and sometimes profitable) pursuit for many groups that handle financial matters. For example, it is usually safe to originate and sell options that are about to expire, even at a low price. But for a situation in which the strategy can backfire, see Case 2–5, Options on Stock Indexes.[14]

CASE 2–1
Cow Pastures or Condominiums*

Until 1960, there were more cows than people in Vermont. As a matter of fact, after 1830, Vermont's population never changed by as much as 5 percent in a decade—the major demographic development was the heading south or west of most of the natural increase in population. Between 1960 and 1970, a population explosion by Vermont's very modest stan-

---

[14]A great deal of detailed information on futures and options is now available in booklets, from employees of the exchanges, and from brokers. An early article, which includes analysis of options arbitrage and functions of the conversion house, is C. B. Franklin and M. R. Colberg, "Puts and Calls: A Factual Survey," *Journal of Finance*, March 1958.

*SOURCE: This case is designed to be representative of frequent choices made in northern New England. The characters are fictional, and the facts rest on some familiarity with the region. Part of the idea for the case came from "Cows and Cambodia" published in Edward Hoagland's *Walking the Dead Diamond River* (New York: Random House, 1973).

dards, occurred. The number of Vermonters increased by 14 + percent, slightly more than the national average, and accompanying this population surge was a great increase in land valuations.

As for the cow pastures of northern Vermont it was the increase in land values that counted. It was not necessary for people to commit themselves to vigorous winters and limited full-time employment opportunities of the Green Mountain state for its land to become more valuable. The potential of nearby ski slopes in the winter, air-conditionless summers, woodland trails, and mountain vistas when contrasted with the congestion and pollution of Megalopolis increased the demand for second homes and land on which something eventually might be built. Many are capable of being moved by a view of Mt. Mansfield to the southwest and Jay Peak to the north such as found around Morrisville, Vermont. The inflation of the late 1960s and early 1970s enhanced the values of the tangibles such as land; and the four-lane ribbons of concrete and asphalt named Interstate 89 and Interstate 91 promised seven-hour access from New York and five hours from Boston.

The production function of a northern Vermont farm can be largely described in terms of this same land. Given 1 acre of land for hay and another acre of land for grazing plus 3,000 pounds of purchased grain, a Holstein can give close to 15,000 pounds of milk a year. After allowing for all out-of-pocket expenses plus depreciation, the yearly monetary yield per acre averaged $100 at prices prevailing in the late 1960s and early 1970s.

To be more specific, take the Vermont farm of Mr. Aiken, which encompasses 225 acres of Lamoille County in northern Vermont. Aiken maintained 75 dairy cows on the 150 acres suitable for hay and pasture.

Since Vermont is the least horizontal of the 50 states, 75 acres of Aiken's hilly land yielded only $5 an acre for maple sugar and pulpwood. In order to maintain a herd of 75 cows with family labor, Mr. Aiken had to invest considerable capital in hay loaders, milking machines, sterilizers, buildings, and fences as well as dairy cows, amounting to $75,000 in depreciated value. The market value of the portable, salable assets approximated $55,000 should the land be taken out of dairy farming. Aiken's labor skills were specialized toward dairying; and with the limited industrial labor market in Vermont (what he considers the fleshpots and beehives a few hundred miles to the south and east have no attraction for him), the market value of his alternative employment was only $5,000 annually. Aiken recognized that his dairy business was a bit risky. The per capita consumption of milk had not been moving favorably; despite reasonable contributions to the campaigns of Nixon and his opponents, the milk price support program had not always compensated for unfavorable changes in milk-grain price ratio; hay crops varied with precipitation; and mastitis and Bang's disease remained around as possible cattle afflictions. No less than 10 percent would seem to be the risk-equivalent return to be used in looking at alternative investments.

In 1971, Ecological Condominiums & Open Spaces, Inc., made an offer for the Aiken farm of $90,000 exclusive of salable equipment. The $400 an acre was in line with the bids it was making elsewhere in the area. EC & OS was a relatively ethical and responsible operator in a field not noted for burning-bush honesty and extraordinary environmental concern. Standards were called for since Vermont, concerned with the land speculation and population increases, had strict land use controls by comparison with the nation's standards. The developer's general plan was to buy 4,000 reasonably contiguous areas at $400 an acre and establish a recreational-retirement community with an eventual 1,600 residential units, about half of them in clustered condominiums. This arrangement made the provision of central facilities such as sewage disposal economical and was to be balanced by leaving a quarter of the area completely undeveloped except for riding and walking trails. If all went reasonably well, the corporation could expect to net about $1,250 an acre on the sales of the land, the yield running anywhere from a significant minus amount for such necessary amenities as a golf course, $500 an acre for a steep 20-acre plot (which might be just enough to find a level area for a house and septic system), to $15,000 an acre for prime locations in a shopping center. The $5 million prospective net for land costing $1.6 million would seem to be a handsome return, but the corporation recognized it would have another $1.5 million in capital tied up before the dollar inflow from land and condominium sales could be expected to offset the continuing development expenses needed. Thus, it would be unreasonable to expect to complete the sale of land in less than 10 years.

When Mr. Aiken was approached, the corporation had already secured the key parcels it needed to start and it was operating openly, since preliminary plans had already been submitted to town and state governments. The plans were flexible enough so that no particular farm was necessary (some operating farms in the area would be an advantage to the corporation, providing local color and added green space). Thus, Aiken had no particular bargaining power on price. He knew there were opportunities for selling a few of his most desirable acres for more than $400, but his acreage that was redundant to farming was far from the road. He saw no desecration to the land in development per se and was confident that the ecological people were probably better than most. He did think it would be a bit strange to operate a farm in an area with a peak population of 5,000 rather than 300.

In brief, Aiken felt he could approach the decision on the basis of economic profitability without emotional involvement. He started out by including tax consequences, but after getting into a muddle on capital gains, which would depend on the cost of a new house and income averaging, and so forth, he decided to look at the problem before taxes. This made some economic sense because the income tax advantages of keeping the farm were approximately offset by the fact that there was an excellent chance that the new assessor would increase his land taxes and that substantial barn and fence repair would reduce his future operating net below the present. As he was completing his calculations, Mrs. Aiken called down to remind him that a roof over their heads should be considered part of the farm income. Mr. Aiken put down $1,500 (heating and maintenance costs were very high for the old house) and concluded that while this made the calculation close, economic profitability favored selling.

The next morning his neighbor stated he wasn't selling. His calculations were pretty much the same, except that he left out the opportunity cost for receipts received from the land sale on the grounds that in view of inflation and the pressure from city folk for country homes, prices for land would rise 10 percent a year in the future. Mr. Aiken was only partly convinced—he knew of cases where the appreciation had been even greater, but most of these had been for scarce property; lakefront, hilltop with spectacular mountain view and proven water, or a quiet street in a desirable community near Burlington and Essex Junction where IBM had located. When the ecological man called later in the day he indicated his indecision and was told that while the base price would not be increased, the corporation would be glad to buy an option to purchase the farm in five years for the $90,000. Five thousand dollars would be paid now and for each of the next four years, and then the corporation would pay the full $90,000 or drop the commitment leaving Mr. Aiken the land to use or sell as he saw fit. The $5,000 a year and the right to farm would be guaranteed for five years.

Questions

1. Show why it is economically unprofitable to continue to farm the land under the initial assumptions.
2. Was the neighbor's decision correct on the basis of his assumption of a 10 percent annual rise in land valuation?
3. Was the option deal probably a better one for both Aiken and the company than the original offer?

CASE 2–2
Haloid to Xerox*

In 1972, Xerox, Inc., had sales of $2,419,103,000 and its net income of close to a quarter of a billion dollars amounted to $3.16 and permitted a dividend payment of $0.84 for each of 78.5 million shares of stock. During the first half of 1973, the price per share of Xerox stock sold in a range of $140 to $170 as sales rose 22 percent and profits 21 percent over the year before.

---

*Case 18–3 also deals with Xerox, Inc., especially with recent antitrust problems in the copier industry.

In 1935, the Haloid Company had sales of $1,232,596 and its net income of $145,530 amounted to $4.85 a share. This permitted a dividend payment of $2 for each of 30,000 shares of stock. Each of these shares, if held from 1935 to 1973, would have become 540 shares of Xerox stock. In 1936, after a three-to-one stock split, a public offering of 55,000 new shares brought $20 a share which helped to finance the purchase of the Rectigraph Company, the producer of a photocopy machine, to add to Haloid's capacity to produce 10 miles of 41-inch photographic paper a day.

Chester F. Carlson, a physicist and patent attorney, produced his first xerographic image in 1938 and received a patent on his process in 1940. He was unable to interest any business firm (IBM was one he visited) in his electrostatic, dry writing process (in Greek, xeros means "dry" and graph is the Greek stem of "write"). In 1944, Battelle Memorial Institute in Columbus did undertake the expensive job of perfecting the process in return for 60 percent of any proceeds that developed.

A Haloid vice president read about xerography in a technical magazine; and in 1947 the company president, John C. Wilson, arranged a patent license with Battelle and shortly afterward negotiated exclusive commercial rights to xerography in return for financing research at Battelle.

The first Xerox copy machine, designed to make masters for offset printing, was introduced in 1949. All but a handful of Americans turned down the chance to become millionaires (not until 1954 were there more than 1,500 Haloid stockholders). Haloid's stock sold in the range of $14–$22 despite the increase of sales to $7,723,651 and modest national coverage (for example, in *Time* of November 1, 1948) of its rights in xerography. Haloid badly needed funds to finance research and market development and was successful in selling 47,183 shares of common stock (at $28.50 to its shareholders and $29.50 to outsiders), and over two million dollars' worth of convertible stock in 1950 (almost all of this preferred issue was converted to 68,000-odd common shares in 1954).

The year 1954 was also the year in which Haloid arranged to buy outright all of some 100 Battelle patents on xerography for what amounted by 1965 to 5,400,000 shares (1973 basis) of Xerox. Mr. Carlson, who received 40 percent of the proceeds, was finally able to resign from his position in a patent law office. In 1956, Rank-Xerox was formed with a 50 percent Haloid interest to handle the world market. In 1957, the 914 copier, which could copy individual documents up to 9 × 14 inches (hence the name), was developed. This was the machine Haloid had been seeking for decisive penetration into the photocopy market. The marketing job seemed too formidable for a small company so Haloid sought IBM as a distributor. But IBM rejected this second chance after receiving a research report that "prospects for such a big expensive unit were dim."[15]

---

[15]William Hammer, "There Isn't Any Profit Squeeze at Xerox," *Fortune*, July 1962, pp. 151 ff.

Haloid split its stock four for one, changed its name first to Haloid-Xerox in 1957 and then to Xerox Corporation in 1961, and prepared a merchandising plan for the 914. It decided to lease the copier for $95 a month plus 3½ cents for each copy above 2,000 a month. To meet capital requirements it borrowed heavily, including debentures convertible to stock. It marketed its last issue of common stock by granting rights to its current stockholders to buy additional shares of the split stock at $24.

By 1961 it was clear that the 914 was a mint. The average user made 10,000 copies a month and paid annual rentals of $4,000 on a machine costing $2,500 to manufacture with a conservative depreciation period of five years. Plans were made to launch a smaller copier, the 813, and a copy duplicator, the Xerox 2400, numbered after its hourly production rate. The ability to reproduce nonchemically and on ordinary paper vastly expanded the market for copying, an expansion underestimated by the company president when he looked forward to only a 15 percent to 20 percent annual increase in xerography products after 1962 and an eventual goal of $1 billion sales in a broader communications market. To reach that goal the company acquired companies with publishing and reproduction interests. Xerox moved into the computer field with the acquisition of Scientific Data Systems in 1969, a product addition that has not yet led to profits in 1973. (IBM almost concurrently inaugurated the production of copiers.) The original Carlson patents had run out by 1962, but by then Xerox had built a structure of 250 improvement patents to protect its position.

In January 1973, the FTC filed a complaint against Xerox alleging the monopolization of the copier market. The complaint sought unrestricted licensing of all Xerox patents and know-how, divesture of the Rank-Xerox in which Xerox now held 51 percent control, and permission for other companies to maintain and service copiers leased to Xerox customers. In its 1973 report the company stated, "We consider the Commission's case without merit," in explaining its refusal to negotiate a consent settlement. "What is really at issue here is the right of any organization to earn success through the creativity, imagination, and dedication of its people. . . . It is in effect an attack on the very foundation of the patent system. . . . Moreover, given the fact that there are already 50 competitors in the U.S. market alone . . . the Commission's charges are in our view without foundation."

The 1973 report also stressed the following recent or new products: the Xerox 7000 reduction duplicator, the color copier, Cyclex 400 (a copier-duplicator paper from 100 percent recycled materials), the Xerox 400 telecopier-transceiver for facsimiles, Xeroradiography (a dry process for X-ray pictures), and the Xerox 530 (a general-purpose computer).

Very large rewards have been paid to Xerox stockholders—to some extent in dividends and to a greater extent in capital appreciation. Exhibit 2–2A is designed to show the origins of the roughly 78.5 million shares of Xerox stock outstanding in 1972. The first category, 1935 initial holders, owned shares that have since been split into 540 shares: 1936, three for

EXHIBIT 2–2A

	No. of 1972 Shares	Multiplier (1972 shares ÷ initial issue)	Price per 1972 Share
Initial holders (1935 or before)	16.2	540	0.09(†)
Purchases or conversions to stock:	(38.8)	—	—
1936 stock sale @ $20	9.3	180	0.11
1950 stock sale @ $29.50	8.5	180	0.15
1954 conv. 1950 pref. @ $35.80	12.3	180	0.20
1960 stock sale @ $24	5.0	15	1.60
1963 conv. 1960 deb. @ 100	2.2	15	6.66
1966–67 conv. 1964 deb. @ 92	1.5	3	30.67
Stock for patent rights to Battelle and Carlson (1955–65)	5.4	3–60	*
Stock options to executives 1960 to date	3.3	15	0.85(‡)
Stock for acquisitions:	(14.8)	—	—
Scientific data systems, 1969	10.0	1	100.00(†)
All others, 1962–72	4.8	1–15	*

*Various
†Based on average market value for year.
‡Various. The figures given represent an option to purchase a share in 1960 for $12.75.

one; 1955, three for one; 1959, four for one; 1963, five for one; 1969, three for one. The $20 a share average price in 1935 can be divided by 540 to get approximately $0.09 as the price of a 1972 share in 1935. To put it the opposite way, the holder of one share in 1935 could have sold 540 shares in 1972 for $81,000. In addition, such a holder of one share in 1935 would have received $123 in dividends from 1936 to 1962 and $2,370 from 1963 to 1972 (after the 914 copier had become an established success).

The second category represents the sale of additional shares of stock either directly or indirectly through the issuance of convertible preferred stock and debentures. This financing was used for expansion into the photocopy machine business (1936), the Xerox duplicating business and xerography research (1950), and xerox copiers and continuing research (1960–64). All such purchases were rewarding to the investors with prices for a 1972 share ranging from 11 cents in 1936, 20 cents in 1954, and $30.67 in 1966–67.

The other categories are the shares exchanged in compensation for the patent rights of Battelle and inventor Carlson (5.4 million shares); the stock options used to reward executives (3.3 million shares); and the 14.8 million shares exchanged in the acquisition of companies, which includes the 10 million shares for Scientific Data Systems, the yet-to-be-profitable foothold in the computer industry.

Many current stockholders acquired these shares by simple purchases of already issued stock. As late as 1953 this could be done for $0.19 a 1973 share or less; in the later 1950s the range was $0.36 to $2.50; from 1960 to 1967 the range was $1.50 to $33. Only in 1968 was the price over $50 ranging upward to the 1973 price of $150.

EXHIBIT 2–2B Xerox: Ten Years in Review (columns 1–4 in $ millions)

	(1)	(2)	(3)	(4)	(5)	(6)	(7)
					Income ÷		
	Operating	Net			Average	Income	Dividends
	Revenues	Income	Equity	R&D	Equity	per Share	per Share
1963	$176	$23	$85	$15	34.4	$0.39	$0.08
1964	318	44	155	24	36.4	0.68	0.14
1965	549	66	229	38	34.2	0.92	0.20
1966	752	87	326	53	31.2	1.20	0.31
1967	983	106	474	51	26.6	1.42	0.40
1968	1,224	129	601	60	24.0	1.88	0.50
1969	1,483	161	738	84	24.1	2.08	0.58
1970	1,719	188	893	98	23.0	2.40	0.65
1971	1,961	213	1,052	104	21.9	2.71	0.80
1972	2,419	250	1,253	132	21.7	3.16	0.84

Exhibit 2–2B shows that the company's rapid growth continued from 1963 to 1972.

Questions

1. Suppose you had purchased 100 shares of Xerox stock in 1935, or in 1950, or in 1960, and held for sale in 1972, what would your rewards have been? Would you have performed any service to justify these returns? Why would the rewards be so much less if you bought in the 1970s?

2. Consider the services performed by other groups who received or bought Xerox stock: the 1935 holders of Haloid stock, the executives who received stock options, the stockholders of acquired firms, persons who bought Haloid or Xerox stock over the counter or on the N. Y. Stock Exchange (starting in 1961). For what, if anything, were they rewarded?

3. Did Xerox make economic profits in the 1963–72 period (assume a rate of return on capital of 6 percent)? Is there any evidence these were diminishing?

CASE 2–3
On Broadway

In the postwar period, the theatrical production on Broadway was a risky and uncertain business. The profits on a few hits each year sometimes exceeded and sometimes fell below that of the losses of the many failures, depending upon whether the successful plays were so outstanding that the realization from such ancillary enterprises as national tours and recording, movie, and television rights was great. Exhibit 2–3A sum-

EXHIBIT 2–3A

	Number of Productions	Average Profit of Loss	Total Profit or Loss
Total losses	42	$ – 150,000	$ – 6,300,000
Partial losses	6	– 50,000	– 300,000
Moderate hits	9	180,000	1,620,000
Smash hits	3	1,700,000	5,100,000

marizes outcomes for a representative season. Simplifications such as having an average cost of $150,000, even though musicals would generally cost more and straight plays less, have been used. The outcomes for investors are approximations for the 60-production year.

Investor George Tompkins considered whether to invest $15,000 for a 10 percent share in a new production. Assume his alternative was to keep the $15,000 in short-term government bonds at 8 percent annual interest. Since it would take a prolonged run and subsequent sale of other rights to realize the profits on a smash hit, interest should be calculated for a three-year period.

Questions

1. Suppose the probabilities of the four summarized outcomes were computed on the basis of past experience. What decision would have maximized expected profits?

2. How might theatrical productions continue to command new capital even though economic losses exceeded economic profits?

3. The 1973–74 theatrical season was particularly bad. Out of 46 productions, only 10 had prospects of financial success, and there were no smash hits. An alternative riskless investment in treasury notes yielded 8 percent. Assume the unsuccessful plays averaged a loss of $200,000 and that the successes eventually would average profits of $500,000. Was it surprising that producers found it increasingly difficult to raise money for new shows? Explain.

CASE 2–4
Puts, Calls, and Straddles

Puts and calls on stocks have become much more popular in recent years since the development of organized markets for these options. Their nature has been described in Chapter 2. By far, the most popular reason to buy calls (and to a lesser extent puts) is the hope of speculative gain. Sellers (makers) of options are seeking additional income. It is also pos-

EXHIBIT 2–4A   Mr. Anderson's Decision

		Profit Outcome If Price of Stock in Six Months Is:					
	$30	$40	$50	$60	$70	$80	$90
Buy X stock	$ – 3,000	$ – 2,000	$ – 1,000	$ 0	$1,000	$2,000	$3,000
Buy X stock and put	– 525	– 525	– 525	– 525	475	1,475	2,475

EXHIBIT 2–4B   Mr. Bunderson's Decision

		Profit Outcome If Price of Stock in Six Months Is:					
	$30	$40	$50	$60	$70	$80	$90
Buy X stock	$ – 3,000	$ – 2,000	$ – 1,000	$ 0	$1,000	$2,000	$ 3,000
Buy a call on X stock . .	– 600	– 600	– 600	– 600	400	1,400	2,400
Buy 10 calls on X stock	– 6,000	– 6,000	– 6,000	– 6,000	4,000	14,000	24,000

sible to use options as a hedging device, which involves taking simultaneous long and short positions.

To show how puts may be used to reduce risk, let's look at the situation of Mr. Anderson. He is attracted by the prospects of a rise in the price of stock X and purchases 100 shares for $60 a share. He is quite uncertain that the rise will be immediate and without substantial downward fluctuations. He therefore buys the put option to sell the 100 shares for $60 during the next six months. In the matrix of Exhibit 2–4A we have shown his prospective gain or loss for prices from $30 to $90. The first line shows the results from buying the stock only, and the second line gives the results of the stock purchase plus $525 paid for the put. Actually, there are many intermediate prices for which the stock might sell in six months; nevertheless, a very good approximation of his gains and losses is possible by lumping all of the intermediate possibilities into these seven outcomes. If his expected gains or losses considering each of the seven outcomes are assumed to be equally likely, the second course of action involving the put has the higher expected profits. If you give very large probability to the prices from $60 to $90, Mr. Anderson as a profit maximizer would not purchase the put, although if his goal was to maximize the minimum profit to be expected, he would still wish to use the option.

Mr. Bunderson considered different alternatives in making a similar decision (see Exhibit 2–4B). As an alternative to buying 100 shares of stock X for $6,000, he considered the possibility of purchasing an option to buy, that is a call, that would run for just over six months, with a striking price of $60. Such an option would limit his losses to $600 and reduce prospective gains by the same amount. It then occurred to him

EXHIBIT 2–4C Mr. Callison as the Investor Who Sells Options

| | Profit Outcome If Price of Stock in Six Months Is: | | | | | | |
	$30	$40	$50	$60	$70	$80	$90
(A) Sell call ... .$	600	$ 600	$ 600	$ 600	$ – 400	$ – 1,400	$ – 2,400
(B) Sell put	– 2,475	– 1,475	– 475	525	525	525	525
(C) Sell straddle	– 1,875	– 875	125	1,125	125	– 875	– 1,875

that by using the whole $6,000 for 10 calls he could open up possibilities of very large gains if the stock rose to $80–$90.

Clearly, options are being used speculatively with the potential long position being extended rather than offset with the call option if this third course is followed.

The selling of options represents a way of increasing returns on a stock portfolio with the acceptance of some risk from price fluctuations. The payoff matrix for Mr. Callison shown in Exhibit 2–4C illustrates the general prospects from options sold in a particular period. For simplicity in the decision matrix, no dividends have been put in and the assumption has been made that the investor in effect maintains his portfolio holdings in face of declines and rises in the stock prices. The possibilities of increased return in the stock can readily be seen, since dividends are retained by the stock owner and two six-month options might be sold in a year. The table assumes one transaction in the six-month period, a striking price of $60, sale of a call for $600, or sale of a put for $525, or of a straddle for $1,125, and disregards brokers' commissions and transfer taxes.

Questions

1. Evaluate each of the decision matrices on the basis:
    a. Equal probabilities for each of the seven prices;
    b. Probabilities of 0.05, 0.10, 0.20, 0.30, 0.20, 0.10, and 0.05 for the outcomes from $30 to $90;
    c. Probabilities of 0.01, 0.04, 0.15, 0.25, 0.25, 0.20, and 0.10 for the outcomes from $30 to $90;
    d. Probabilities of 0.10, 0.20, 0.25, 0.25, 0.15, 0.04, and 0.01 for the outcomes from $30 to $90.

2. Compare the profit-maximizing decision with the maximin decision for the three men under the probability assumptions of (a), (b), (c), and (d) above.

3. Which decisions would represent a shifting of uncertainty; which represent a speculative willingness to undertake greater uncertainties?

CASE 2–5
Options on Stock Indexes*

"It was late afternoon on April 19th, a sleepy Thursday for the security markets—the last trading day before the Easter holiday weekend. A professional trading concern called Chicago Research and Trading Group was, as usual, trading various stock index options. . . .

"As part of its sophisticated strategy, the firm, a day or so earlier, had sold on the Chicago Board Options Exchange call options on the Standard & Poor's 100-stock index. The calls, which give the holders the right to buy from the sellers the cash value of the index at a set price for a set time, by the afternoon of the 19th were rapidly losing value because they were due to expire that day.

"Suddenly, the price of the S&P call options began surging. The 11th hour rally continued to the closing bell when those particular options ceased to exist. Chicago Research and Trading lost $200,000. Total losses by CBOE floor traders have been estimated at $1 million to $2 million."

Investigation by exchange officials disclosed that at least one element in the sudden increase in price of these call options was that a large security trading firm was about to buy some $100 million of at least half the stocks in the S&P index.

Traders who learned of the purchase flooded the CBOE with purchase orders for calls on the S&P index, driving their prices up sharply. Chicago Research and Trading and others had to pay out much more than the modest premium they collected when they sold the index options they had expected to expire without value to the buyers.

Questions

1. Explain the essential similarity between:
    a. Buying a call on a specific stock and buying a call on a stock index.
    b. Selling a call on a specific stock and selling a call on a stock index.
    c. Buying a put on a specific stock and buying a put on a stock index.
    d. Selling a put on a particular stock and selling a put on a stock index.
2. Different stock indexes that are traded on options markets are based on unlike numbers of stocks. Also, the number and activity of shares outstanding can vary greatly. Would a sudden, unpleasant surprise such as that of April 19 be more likely to occur on a narrow index than on a broad one? Why?

---

*SOURCE: Extracted from Richard E. Ruston and Pamela Sebastian, "Some Option Trading Raises New Questions on Market's Fairness," *The Wall Street Journal*, July 11, 1984, p. 1, with permission.

3. In a sense, options on specific stocks are options on an index containing just that one stock. Is "front running" (trading in options with inside knowledge of coming large deals in associated stocks) more probable on specific stocks than on broad indexes? Why?

CASE 2–6
Arbitrage in Stocks

An interesting and unusual opportunity for arbitrage occurred when the American Writing Paper Company was reorganized after experiencing severe financial losses. As part of the reorganization plan, the judge decreed that two shares of preferred stock would exchange for one share of common stock in 30 days.

At the time of this judicial action the common and preferred stocks were each selling at $6 per share.

Questions

1. What arbitrage transactions would ensure that a profit could be made in this situation?
2. Would the amount of profit be the same regardless of how the prices of the common and preferred stock moved?
3. If put and call options had been available on both common and preferred shares of American Writing Paper, how could the arbitrage transaction have been carried out with options alone?

3

Forecasting Methods

Never prophesy, especially about the Future.
—*Samuel Goldwyn*

In the previous chapter it was pointed out that many businesses protect against unfavorable price changes by hedging. If hedging is "pure"—that is, if it does not include an element of speculation—a forecast is not necessary, because the business is protected regardless of which way the relevant price moves. For most business decisions, however, no perfect hedge is available, and reasonably accurate forecasting is necessary for profitable operations.

Forecasting is not always carried out as an explicit function, but it is necessarily implicit in numerous decisions that must be made within the firm. If forecasting is not a centralized, explicit activity, there is danger that, in effect, important forecasts will be made by persons who are not in the best position to engage in this activity. For example, the sales forecast may be implicit in decisions made by an order clerk using rule-of-thumb methods, rather than taking advantage of all available information which could be brought to bear on the problem.

While business economists and management consultants engage in many kinds of analysis, such as plant location, pricing, financing, and relations with government, most of them are active to some degree in economic and business forecasting. Economic forecasting applies to *general* business activity such as movements of national income, aggregate industrial production or employment, total exports or imports, or fluctuations in the international value of the dollar. Business forecasting pertains more directly to the activity of a particular industry or firm, consisting of short- and long-term forecasts of sales, prices of important raw materials and equipment, availability of resources at plant sites under investigation, and a host of other matters of specific interest. The separation between economic and business forecasting is not always sharp, however, and the two are frequently intertwined in the same forecasting process. For example, a forecast of industry sales is dependent on an economic forecast of general business conditions. In turn, a firm's forecast of its sales uses the industry projection as well as such specific factors as its own promotional campaigns or new products. The firm's sales may be highly correlated with the sales of the industry of which it is a member, but this relation does not necessarily hold, especially over the longer run (during which new firms may enter or leave the field). In view of this difficulty of classification, no sharp division will be drawn in this chapter between economic and business forecasting. Instead, several popular methods of forecasting, which are applicable to both general and specific prediction, will be discussed.

Forecasting the broad economic measures such as Gross National Product is more interesting than making specific or microeconomic forecasts, but there has been considerable disillusionment about the ability of economists to do a worthwhile job on the former. Case 3–1 deals with the consequent shift of forecasting emphasis to the less aggregate measures.

It has been said by an expert that the personal computer in the second half of the 1980s probably will be as indispensable for economists as the electronic calculator was in the 1970s and the slide rule was in the 1950s.[1] The personal computer is a great help in personal forecasting and in reducing the cost of such work; it also makes experimentation with models much easier. It is often possible to transfer information from the large mainframe computers to the personal computers, securing a flexibility that would be absent with reliance only on the big computers.

PROJECTION AND EXTRAPOLATION METHODS

Probably the most common way of forecasting the future is simply to construct a chart depicting the actual movement of a series and then to project (extrapolate) the apparent trend of the data as far into the future as is desired for the purpose at hand. The projection is usually a straight line, but it may be curvilinear. This is sometimes classified as a "naive" method of forecasting since it is based on no particular theory as to what causes the variable to change, but merely assumes that forces that have contributed to change in the recent past will continue to have the same effect. Trend projectors are often able to show a high percentage of forecasts that are correct (in direction, at least), but the method has the serious defect of missing sudden downturns or upturns—just the changes that it is most important to predict correctly.

On the other hand, trend projection may be the only available method when the variable under consideration is affected by a *large number of factors*, the separate influence of which cannot readily be measured because of lack of data, lack of time, or other reasons. For example, an analyst may have a feeling that a series is affected by the general growth of the economy as population increases, capital accumulates, and tech-

---

[1] Ray C. Fair, "How Personal Computers Are Changing the Forecaster's Job," *Business Week*, October 1, 1984, pp. 123–24.

FIGURE 3–1   Trend Projection

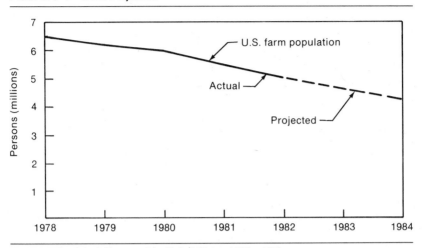

SOURCE: *Statistical Abstract of the United States,* 1984, p. 794.

nology improves. With confidence in this general underlying growth, the analyst may feel, quite rationally, that the observed upward trend in the series will continue. Simple extrapolation is then not entirely naive. However, provided the necessary data were available—on time—a more reliable forecast might be made by using more complicated methods.

In using any forecasting method it is important that the analyst be familiar with the product being forecast. It would be ridiculous to predict January retail sales of toys by measuring the increase of sales in December over November and projecting the result.

Trend projections may be made graphically, using only a pencil and ruler, or mathematically, by methods of curve fitting. In Figure 3–1, a simple example of graphic "eyeball" trending is illustrated. Total farm population in the United States seems to be declining in a roughly linear way, falling from 6,501,000 in 1978 to 5,620,000 in 1982. In the absence of important contrary information, the analyst might project a further decline similar to that indicated by the dashed line. Series that show an uptrend, such as sales of home security devices, could readily be found and perhaps be reasonably projected in the same manner.

It should be noted that different analysts can draw quite different trend projections from the same body of data. Some comparability can be achieved through the use of mathematical methods of curve fitting. A simple illustration of the "least squares" technique appears in Chapter 4. More on the subject can be found in many basic statistics texts.[2] It must

---

[2]For example, see William A. Spurr and Charles P. Bonini, *Statistical Analysis for Business Decisions,* rev. ed. (Homewood, Ill.: Richard D. Irwin, 1973). See also Roger Chisholm and Gilbert R. Whitaker, Jr., *Forecasting Methods* (Homewood, Ill.: Richard D. Irwin, 1971).

be noted that the particular mathematical function selected and the time span of past data will alter in significant ways the prediction obtained from trend projections.

Another extrapolation method used frequently is exponential smoothing.[3] This method uses the entire past data series available, but assigns weights to past observations, the most weight being given to the most recent observation. This method is based upon the familiar notion of a geometric series. Thus, if we let S_t represent actual sales in period t and $\hat{S}_t$ represent the exponentially smoothed value of sales for period t, and α equal a smoothing weight, we can write the following expression:

$$\hat{S}_t = \frac{S_t + (1 - \alpha) S_{t-1} + (1 - \alpha)^2 S_{t-2} + \cdots}{1 + (1 - \alpha) + (1 - \alpha)^2 + \cdots}$$

This says that one can obtain an estimate of the average value of sales by weighting all past observations with the set of weights:

$$1, (1 - \alpha), (1 - \alpha)^2, (1 - \alpha)^3, \ldots.$$

These weights are a geometric series whose sum can be shown to be $1/\alpha$. It can be demonstrated that the equation above can be written equivalently as:

$$\hat{S}_t = \alpha S_t + (1 - \alpha) \hat{S}_{t-1}$$

Thus, the new average value is determined by α times the new observation plus $1 - \alpha$ times the last estimate of the average value.

This particular formulation of exponential smoothing does not allow for either trend or seasonal variation. However, relatively simple modifications are possible that can take care of this deficiency. Determination of α is usually done on a trial and error basis using alternative values of α until a value is chosen which minimizes the sum of the squared errors between past observations and forecasts made. Use of exponential smoothing virtually requires that a computer be available to do all of the necessary calculations. Once the method is set up, it requires relatively little computer storage space and is very useful when large numbers of items are involved and rapid forecasts are needed.

COMPLEX "NAIVE" METHODS

All of the naive methods discussed so far have assumed that past data can be used in some specified fashion to predict future data. A specific set of weights is determined in advance and is then used to forecast future values.

In recent years, forecasting methods have been developed under the names of "Generalized Adaptive Filtering" and "Box-Jenkins." These are both methods that develop forecasts on the basis of past data and at the

---

[3]See R. G. Brown, *Statistical Forecasting for Inventory Control* (New York: McGraw-Hill, 1959).

same time assume no fixed weighting scheme. Each method attempts under different procedures to select the most appropriate forecasting model and to choose optimum parameters. Both methods are based upon the concept of autocorrelation. That is, they look to correlations over time in the variables in the data series that is to be forecast. These can be highly effective forecasting methods but are too complex to be dealt with in this text. The interested reader is referred to the footnote references.[4]

LEADING INDICATORS

As has been suggested, a shortcoming of linear projection methods as forecasting techniques is that they necessarily fail to foresee the vital turns, downward and upward, in the series under consideration. It is these turns that call for the most important changes in inventory policy, hiring policy, capital budgeting, debtor-creditor position adjustment, and other matters. A great deal of statistical research has been devoted to the problem of finding "leading indicators," that is, sensitive series that tend to turn up or down in advance of other series. The value of such indicators (if reliable) is obvious. If one could discover a series that would reliably lead stock or commodity price indexes, it would not be difficult to become rich (provided this method of prediction did not come into general use; in that event, it would cease to lead these speculative prices). Actually, stock prices themselves have been found to be significant leading series for industrial production and for other important indicators of business health. For example, the stock market crash of 1929 preceded the calamitous depression of the 1930s. However, stock market price movements reflect the opinions and actions of speculators and investors, and the more basic question still remains as to what information affects, or should affect, the opinions of the most alert and best-informed speculators.

In 1950, Dr. Geoffrey Moore of the National Bureau of Economic Research tested the cyclical behavior of over 800 statistical series. He selected 18 monthly and 3 quarterly series that appeared to be outstanding business indicators. These are not all leading indexes, however; some are coincident with business fluctuations, and others lag behind general business activity. Composition of the indexes varies over time as statisticians attempt to improve their usefulness.[5]

---

[4]G. E. P. Box and G. M. Jenkins, *Time Series Analysis, Forecasting and Control* (San Francisco: Holden Day, 1976); and Spyros Makridakis and Steven C. Wheelwright, *Interactive Forecasting*, 2d ed. (San Francisco: Holden Day, 1978).

[5]A revised list of indicators was published in 1967 by the National Bureau of Economic Research. See Geoffrey H. Moore and Julius Shiskin, *Indicators of Business Expansions and Contractions*, Occasional Paper 103 (New York: National Bureau of Economic Research, 1967). The name of the publication of indicators has been changed to *Business Conditions Digest*. During the period 1972–75, a new and comprehensive review resulted in a revised set of leading indicators. See U.S. Department of Commerce, *Handbook of Cyclical Indicators* (Washington, D.C.: U.S. Government Printing Office, May, 1977).

FIGURE 3–2   Economic Indicators Illustrated

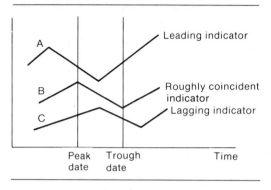

In Figure 3–2, the concept underlying the indicators is illustrated. The vertical lines represent the peak and trough of a general business cycle that has been identified. Line *A* represents an indicator that leads the general cycle by peaking in advance of the general peak and by also reaching its trough in advance of the general trough. Line *B* represents a roughly coincident indicator that peaks and troughs simultaneously with the general cycle. Line *C* represents a lagging indicator that peaks and troughs after the general cycle.

Data for representative leading indicators are available in the *Business Conditions Digest*. Also, an index of 12 leading indicators is given wide publicity, even on TV news broadcasts. This index is shown for 1979–84 in Case 3–3. One difficulty is immediately apparent: the indicators often point in different directions from month to month, so that until their movements become substantial in magnitude and similar in direction, it is hard to know where they are leading. Nevertheless, a downturn of some of these indicators after a consistent rise might at least warn the business executive that a general downturn is more likely than before. A downturn of a substantial number of leading indicators might well be a signal for action in anticipation of reduced business activity. The indicators of the index of leading indicators should not be utilized in a mechanical way but rather as one basis for judging coming business conditions. Their use requires alertness in watching for first publication of an index and for anticipating movements before they are published. For example, industrial stock averages are published daily as well as monthly.[6] It is also necessary to watch for revisions of indexes that have been published. Statisticians responsible for the indexes may have even *guessed* at some components in order to meet deadlines.

---

[6]See Arthur M. Okun, "On the Appraisal of Cyclical Turning-Point Predictors," *Journal of Business*, April 1960. For a corporation's use of indicators, see Robert L. McLaughlin, "Leading Indicators: A New Approach for Corporate Planning," *Business Economics*, May 1971.

LEADING INDICATORS IN DETAIL

The current selection of leading indicators is shown below. Each series has, or should have, a theoretical reason to lead general business activity.

Series 1: Average workweek in manufacturing reflects the tendency of plants to employ some of the existing work force overtime rather than hiring new workers when orders pile up. Similarly, it reflects the tendency to reduce hours of work rather than to lay off workers in the opposite situation.

Series 5: Average initial claims for state unemployment benefits (inverted) quite obviously should reflect layoffs of workers. (It is inverted because the indexes all need to show a rise as favorable.)

Series 8: New orders for consumer goods and materials are expressed in 1972 dollars in order to reflect "real" orders.

Series 32: Vendor performance, or the percentage of companies receiving slower deliveries, reflects the reduced ability of suppliers to deliver quickly when they are already at or near capacity. A downturn suggests that suppliers are more able to make quick deliveries.

Series 12: Net business formation is based on the increasing optimism or pessimism of entrepreneurs according to their outlook on the economy.

Series 20: Contracts and orders for plant and equipment are leading indicators since new orders and contracts clearly should precede actual production.

Series 29: New building permits for private housing should be a guide as to fairly near-term sales of building materials, appliances, furniture, and many other items needed in new homes although not all permits are followed by actual building.

Series 36: Net change in inventories on hand an on order is theoretically questionable as a series since an increase in inventories may be a sign of slowing economic activity due to difficulty in selling.

Series 96: When marked by an increase in selected prices, change in sensitive material prices should show that a stronger demand-supply situation is building up. However, if there is general fear of inflation, a rise is not obviously desirable. Also, the higher prices can raise production costs.

Series 19: Common stock prices should be a good leading indicator since speculators and investors are very sensitive to changes in the economic outlook and since they utilize all evidence that they believe to be important. It seems quite likely that an index of 100 rather than the 500 stock prices that are actually used would be better. Participants in stock index options have shown much more interest in the S&P 100 stock index than in the S&P 500 stock index.

Series 106: Money supply, M_2, reflects some faith in "monetarism" as developed and promulgated by Milton Friedman, Anna Schwartz, and others. Unfortunately, it has become more difficult to know which of the measures of the money supply is most relevant.

Series 111: Change in business and consumer credit outstanding is based on the theory that new borrowing will soon be translated into purchases.

COINCIDENT INDICATORS

The four coincident indicators currently in use are: (1) nonagricultural employment, (2) personal income less transfer payments, (3) industrial production, and (4) manufacturing and trade sales. These are good measures of the actual status of the economy so an index of coincident indicators can be considered to be what we are trying to forecast. Of course, there are other possible coincident indicators such as gross national product.

LAGGING INDICATORS

Six series are currently designated as lagging behind business activity: average duration of unemployment (inverted); ratio of constant dollar inventories to sales in manufacturing and trade; labor cost per unit of output, manufacturing, as percent of trend; average prime interest rate; commercial and industrial loans outstanding; and the ratio of consumer installment credit to personal income. Although the lagging indexes should not have direct forecasting value, see Case 3–4 for their use in connection with a possible forecasting method.

RATIONAL EXPECTATIONS

Increasing attention is being paid to the importance of expectations as an influence on the economy. The main idea is that there will be speedy adjustment to observed or even anticipated changes in such matters as federal monetary or fiscal policy, rather than gradual adjustment to the new situation. In the case of stock price movements, the "efficient-markets" theory refers to the same phenomenon. For example, an increase of say $4 billion in the money supply in a particular week would have no effect on stock prices if it were widely anticipated. But if a $4 billion increase were expected and a $6 billion increase occurred, the stock market would react to the news. Research results at the National Bureau of Economic Research indicate that the impact of a sharp, unanticipated increase in M_1 on stock prices would be negative.[7]

---

[7] *The NBER Digest*, National Bureau of Economic Research, Inc., October/November 1984.

Two reasons can be adduced for this reaction: (1) the Federal Reserve System may quickly move to a more restrictive monetary policy as an offset, and (2) a higher rate of inflation will be widely anticipated, causing lenders to raise interest rates. Both hypotheses suggest a decline in bond and stock prices, and the decline should occur very rapidly according to the efficient markets idea.

The rational expectations view is rather disturbing to one's faith in forecasting by such means as leading indicators. It suggests that a change in an indicator may not be significant unless it is unanticipated, and anticipations are hard to measure. One possibility is to assume that a trend line fitted to a series will govern general expectations for the near future. If so, the *deviation* of a new observation from the trend may be more relevant than the absolute change itself. For example, if real expenditures on plant and equipment have been rising at an 8 percent rate for two years, an estimate of a 6 percent rise for the next year might not be impressive.

ECONOMETRIC METHODS

The most elegant (and sometimes the best) method of forecasting is by the use of econometrics. This term covers a variety of analytical techniques, most of them blends of economics, statistics, and mathematics. Econometric models of the entire economy are constantly being worked upon and improved. These models contain among their variables such factors as net investment, consumption, government expenditures, taxes, and net export or import balance, since these are key determinants of national income. To the extent that some of the determining variables can be predicted, an econometric model may be useful in forecasting such overall measures of economic activity as gross national product and national income. If, for example, it could be shown by statistical study of the past that investment in one year is largely determined by profits of the previous year and that consumption is heavily influenced by the amount of liquid savings accumulated before January 1 of the year in question, the econometrician could use these relationships in a forecasting model. If past relationships continued to hold true (which may be a big "if"), the analyst could make a useful and accurate prediction.

In recent years, progress has been made in the development of econometric model building for the U.S. economy. Models have been developed that capture more of the detail of the complex economy and utilize monthly or quarterly data for more timely reporting of results.[8] Less accuracy for forecasts in the early 1980s could be partly attributed to sharp

---

[8]See D. B. Suits, "Forecasting and Analysis with an Econometric Model," *American Economic Review*, March 1962, pp. 104–32; J. S. Duesenberry, G. Fromm, L. R. Klein, and E. Kuh, eds. *The Brookings Quarterly Econometric Model of the United States* (Chicago: Rand McNally, 1965); and Michael K. Evans, *Macroeconomic Activity: Theory, Forecasting, and Control* (New York: Harper & Row, 1969).

FIGURE 3–3   Expenditures for New Plant and Equipment
($ billions)

	1982 (actual)	1983 (actual)	1984 (actual)	1985 (estimated)
All industries	282.71	269.22	353.54	386.10
Manufacturing	119.68	111.53	138.38	155.98
Mining	15.45	11.83	16.88	16.06
Railroad	4.38	3.92	6.77	7.35
Air transportation	3.93	3.77	3.55	4.09
Other transportation	3.64	3.50	6.17	6.21
Public utilities	41.95	42.00	47.39	47.74
Commercial and other . . .	93.68	92.67	134.40	148.67

SOURCE: U.S. Department of Commerce, *Survey of Current Business,* June 1985.

breaks with the past such as record trade and peacetime budget deficits. Econometric models necessarily depend on continuities with the past. Further, these new models are constructed so that various policy alternatives can be tried out in a model environment to reveal possible results of such policies if they were actually employed. While computer models are likely to have an interesting future, there is currently considerable skepticism about the usefulness of the forecasts being made by their users. Case 3–1 deals with recent appraisals of their forecasting accuracy.

SURVEY METHODS

The forecaster who wishes to make optimum use of econometric methods must constantly recompute the forecasting equations as more current data becomes available. Also, a forecaster should be willing to incorporate the work of others into the system if there is reason to believe that better estimates are available or if this procedure is worthwhile as a timesaver. Similarly, the results of intentions surveys on such matters as planned investment and consumption should be substituted if such data are more accurate than that computed from past relationships. On the other hand, the analyst is free to use computed relationships if the predictive value of a survey is in doubt.

The U.S. Department of Commerce conducts a well-known quarterly survey in order to ascertain recent expenditures for plant and equipment and investment plans for the near future. Figure 3–3 shows actual 1982, 1983, and 1984 expenditures for new plant and equipment and estimated 1985 expeditures based on reports by business in late April and May 1985. The analyst depending on this survey would probably be quite optimistic about business in 1985.

CONSUMER ATTITUDES

The University of Michigan's Institute for Social Research regularly publishes information on consumer attitudes based on a survey of about 700 families. An "index of consumer sentiment" stood at 91.6 in the third quarter of 1983 versus 91.5 a quarter earlier and a 1972 peak of 94.4.

More interesting are the consumer evaluations pertaining to individual "large-ticket items." For May 1984, these evaluations are:

	Large Household Goods	Houses	Cars
Good time to buy . . .	77%	58%	63%
Uncertain.	10	5	9
Bad time to buy	13	37	28

SOURCE: University of Michigan, Institute for Social Research, *Survey of Consumer Attitudes,* May 1984.

It is apparent that reluctance to purchase houses was relatively great, due probably to high mortgage interest rates. Comparison over time of such percentages can provide an indication of changes in consumer buying attitudes. The great importance of consumer spending in determining national income makes obvious the desirability of trying to anticipate changes in such expenditures. Also, sales forecasts by some individual industries may benefit from consumer intention surveys.[9] The small size of the sample of families and the lack of advance planning by many families probably makes this survey less dependable than the Commerce Department's survey of investment plans of business enterprises which are likely to include some firm commitments.

REQUIREMENTS FORECASTING

An important and very common type of sales forecasting is quite obviously open to all firms selling materials or components to other firms that set up production schedules for end items. Firms that regularly supply General Motors with components can clearly gauge their future sales prospects by securing the General Motors output schedules—assuming, of course, that these schedules are sufficiently "firm," that General Motors will not decide to make its own components, and that the company in question will continue to get the General Motors business.

In recent years an allied form of forecasting has become possible to the extent that the federal government establishes production programs

[9]The Conference Board, a business information service, also publishes surveys of consumer attitudes. Albert T. Sommers, of the Conference Board, in a recent book, *The U.S. Economy Demystified* (Lexington, Mass.: D. C. Heath, 1985), p. 54, says there is no close short-term correspondence between revealed consumer attitudes and current retail volume but that a prolonged rise or decline in sentiment, sustained over several months, has large and obvious significance. This book is an excellent source of information regarding American business statistics.

and schedules. During World War II, for example, President Roosevelt called for the production of 60,000 military airplanes in 1942 and 125,000 in 1943. These goals were followed by detailed production schedules that were supposed to add up to these totals. (Actually, they did not, especially for 1942.) From the detailed schedules of airplane production the federal statisticians were able to compute requirements for aluminum, engines, propellers, radio equipment, and thousands of other components. To the extent that end-product schedules were realistic for airplanes and other munitions, the detailed requirement schedules gave firms producing materials and components an excellent forecast of their own sales possibilities.

When the federal government formulated its huge interstate highway program, it became possible for the portland cement industry, asphalt industry, aggregates producers, pipe producers, steel industry, and others to make approximate calculations of their probable sales in support of this tremendous program. An advantage of this sort of program from the view of materials suppliers is its recessionproof nature. In fact, a business recession would probably increase their sales on this account, since the highway program would very likely be speeded up as an emergency public work.

A firm in one of these categories faces a number of problems in forecasting its sales as related to a government production program:

1. The end-item schedules usually reflect a combination of political, administrative, and economic considerations. They are likely to be placed deliberately too high in order to stimulate private firms to set their sights high. Often, the end-item schedules reflect more what government officials believe is required than what can actually be produced within the specified time period.
2. The firm may not get its share of the industry sales in support of a government program (or it may be able to get more than its share).
3. There are usually some opportunities for substitution of one material for another. Computation of requirements is complicated by this possibility, since there is usually no set "bill of materials" that can be depended upon. Portland cement and asphalt are important examples of substitute materials.
4. "Pipeline" requirements create difficulties. It is necessary for producers not only to turn out the materials and components needed for incorporation in end items but also to build up inventories at various stages in the transportation-production process. In part, these inventories are needed to "fill the pipeline" so that a steady input into end items can be secured. These inventory needs are often especially difficult to predict.

In general, as government activities have come to loom larger in our economy, it has become more and more important for firms in many lines to gear their activities to government procurement programs or to government scheduling of some private activities. This requires a sort of forecasting and suggests the importance of following not only federal government activities but also those of state and local governments.

LOADED DICE TECHNIQUES

Numerous other ways of looking into the future—some of which are more ethical than others—are based on getting information that is not generally available or on securing information sooner than other people get it. Simply knowing the status of the present and of the immediate past can be of great help in planning operations instead of, as in many situations, having to depend on facts that are weeks or even months old. For example, one use of computers by automobile and appliance manufacturers is keeping continual track of dealers' inventories so that the current rate of retail sales is known. A naive short-run forecast that next week's sales are going to be the same as this week's when current sales are known is probably superior to the most elaborate method of projection that depends on data that are several weeks old. An interesting historical example of the value of being alert occurred in 1815. By using their own news service, the Rothschilds received advance news of the outcome of the Battle of Waterloo, which gave them their chance to make a fortune on the London Stock Exchange.[10]

A similar situation in which advance news has value to speculators occurs when the U.S. Department of Agriculture compiles its crop estimates in Washington, D.C. If the estimates are larger than had been expected, futures prices will fall, and the speculator with advance news can profit by selling grain futures before the new estimates are publicly released. The opposite is true if the estimates are lower than had been expected. This situation has led some persons to attempt to communicate with cohorts outside the building as soon as the estimates have been assembled. It is said that a man was once caught passing a signal from a washroom by means of adjusting the height of the window shade. Strict security measures are employed by the Department of Agriculture to prevent the premature export of crop estimates from the building.

"Forecasting the forecast" obviously presents another possibility along these lines. If, for example, individuals were able to come up with a close approximation of their own to the federal crop estimate and were able to make the estimate soon enough, they might be in a position to make speculative profits. (Actually, the cost of gathering and analyzing the necessary data would, in this particular case, probably bring a net loss rather than a profit.) Airline pilots who were in an excellent position to view the freeze damage to Florida oranges in 1977 profited from their

---

[10]Cecil Roth, *The Magnificent Rothschilds* (London: Robert Hale, Ltd., 1939), p. 23, says that contrary to popular legend, Nathan Mayer Rothschild's news service was not based on pigeon post.

knowledge by buying frozen orange concentrate futures. A similar opportunity may have existed in the 1983 and 1985 freezes in Florida.

Methods of securing advance information vary from those that merely require alertness to those that are downright dishonest. Alertness was displayed by Andrew Carnegie, who secured advance information on industrial production by counting the number of smoking chimneys. A less clearly ethical way of forecasting land values is used in the oil industry, where workers are regularly employed to watch the drill rigs of other companies through field glasses and to rush to the nearest phone to take up all available options on adjacent land if they see oil struck.

Fortune magazine has recently updated the list of practices in common use for finding out what competitors are doing.[11] One drug company found that its sales declined in some territories due to competitors' gifts of cars, boats, and expensive junkets to physicians. When promotions were in part matched, company sales soared.

Especially in industries where growth has slowed, firms realize that sales gains must come mainly from reduced sales by their rivals. This fosters all sorts of industrial espionage. Consultants have even developed courses and seminars to train business executives in methods of finding out what competitors are doing. Even newspaper studies of employment opportunities for professional persons can yield important information about particular firms.

Taking a cue from Andrew Carnegie, some firms are measuring the amount of rust on the rails of sidings used by rivals. Trailers leaving loading platforms and the dimensions of cartons going out are observed. There is even a "science" of "crateology," developed especially by military intelligence, to predict the contents of sealed crates.

Reverse engineering is increasingly common. Competitors' products are purchased and taken apart to examine their components. Manufacturing methods can be ascertained, and even the cost of production can be estimated from such analyses.

Important information is often secured in job interviews with former employees of rival firms, especially if the individual left on bad terms or is anxious to impress the potential new employer. Similarly, hiring away important executives or other professional persons is almost certain to result in new information of importance. Consultants on design or other matters may be willing to divulge secrets or may do so inadvertently. Even the imprints on cartons used by competitors may disclose useful information, especially if followed up by some means of estimating sales of such cartons.

In "high-tech" fields, it may be highly profitable to lend engineers to important customers in the hope of influencing their subsequent requirements and purchases. The same sort of influence is commonly exerted on government agencies. An example was the lending of insurance company actuaries to the Veterans Administration when "G.I. insurance" was for-

---

[11]"Snooping on Your Competitors," Fortune, May 14, 1984.

mulated for soldiers in World War II. The $10,000 limitation on purchase may have been one important result.

At the bottom of the list ethically are a variety of sharp and often illegal practices that may be ways either of ascertaining what exists or of forecasting what is coming. It is illegal to make tours of plants or to attend certain types of seminars under false identity. A competitor's garbage may, however, be legally collected and inspected after it leave the premises. While many companies, following the lead of the armed services, systematically shred their important surplus papers, the ease of modern copying increases the likelihood of placing important information in the wastebasket in usable form for interested parties.

At the bottom of the list are such practices as breaking into offices and stealing industrial secrets, tapping telephone lines, and placing tiny transmitters under appropriate desks. It is strongly recommended that only the legitimate methods of forecasting be studied. Pinstripes are much more becoming than "penstripes."

CASE 3–1
Bad Times for the Forecasters*

The American economy is proving far stronger than most economists anticipated—and far peppier than the economic consulting business itself.

*   *   *   *   *

Perhaps the principal reason for their problems is an epidemic of wide-of-the-mark forecasts—forecasts that, moreover, looked particularly bad because many economists probably oversold their forecasting abilities in the first place. Other reasons for the slump range from corporate and governmental cost cutting to the spread of do-it-yourself analysis by means of personal computers.

*   *   *   *   *

A particularly glum assessment is offered by Michael K. Evans, a Washington-based consultant, who says, "We're a declining industry." Many analysts share the view of Donald H. Straszheim, the chief domestic economist at Wharton Econometric Forecasting Associates in Philadelphia. "As a profession," he says, "we couldn't deliver what we promised."

A similar appraisal comes from William Wilcox, the vice-president for planning at A. O. Smith Corp., a Milwaukee-based manufacturer of diversified industrial products: "Consulting on the overall economy isn't the

---

*SOURCE: Extracted from Lindley H. Clark, Jr. and Alfred L. Malabre, Jr., "Business Forecasters Find Demand Is Weak in Their Own Business," *The Wall Street Journal,* September 7, 1984, p. 1, with permission.

growth industry it once was," he says. "Getting the operating people in a company to take forecasts seriously has become difficult because of many economists' poor track records."

*   *   *   *   *

"We're trying harder to tailor our reports to a client's special needs," Mr. Malanga says, "and worrying less about predicting precisely what's ahead for the big macrosectors of the economy, like the gross national product."

Data Resources has launched a similar strategy, says Joseph Kasputys, the president of the McGraw-Hill Corp. subsidiary. "We've diversified into such areas as analyzing patient-discharge data, to help hospitals figure out what their market share is," he explains. "We're also collecting more of the primary data ourselves."

*   *   *   *   *

Despite the rough sledding, economic consulting continues to attract more and more practitioners. "With the advent of the personal computer, almost anyone with a few thousand dollars to invest in hardware and software can play the game," says Mr. Nakagama, whose firm is only a year and a half old; previously, he worked as an economist for Kidder, Peabody & Co., a large securities firm based in New York.

David Williams, executive vice president of the Cleveland-based National Association of Business Economists, also believes that forecasters' ranks are continuing to swell. His organization has a record 3,798 members up from 2,575 as recently as 1978. And apparently still more economists are in the pipeline. Allan H. Meltzer, an economics professor at Carnegie-Mellon University in Pittsburgh, says the number of students pursuing advanced degrees in economics there is rising sharply.

Questions

1. Why have many consultants moved toward forecasting that is specific to firms rather than to the economy?
2. What does the case suggest regarding the relative dependability of microeconomic and macroeconomic forecasts?
3. Why has the spreading use of personal computers tended to foster a "do-it-yourself" trend in forecasting? Will it necessarily reduce the business of consulting companies?

CASE 3–2
Problems in Forecasting

1. A possible use of commodity futures prices might be forecasting the actual tend of prices during the next 12 or more months. This is

because futures quotations represent the present opinions of experts regarding future demand/supply conditions—opinions on which they have risked their money.

Although there are several difficulties, including differences in the exact definition of the commodity specified in spot and futures quotations and the divergence of retail and wholesale prices, inspect futures prices in a recent edition of *The Wall Street Journal* in order to form an opinion regarding the trend of the following retail prices during the coming 12 months: *(a)* hamburger, *(b)* coffee, *(c)* cocoa, *(d)* orange juice, *(e)* sugar, *(f)* oleomargarine, and *(g)* gasoline.

2. Futures quotations for U.S. Treasury bonds may offer a clue as to the trend of long-term interest rates for the coming 12 months. On the basis of present quotations, what is your forecast of such interest rates? Explain.

3. There is also a futures market for Treasury bills. On the basis of present quotations, what is the outlook for short-term interest rates?

4. From the *Federal Reserve Bulletin* or other source, name the several definitions of the money supply. Which measure would you expect to have the greatest value in forecasting price movements? Why?

CASE 3–3
Leading Indicators and Cyclical Turning Points

There has been such interest in the use of leading indicators to predict upturns and downturns in general business conditions that the U.S. Department of Commerce through its Bureau of the Census has published for several decades *Business Conditions Digest,* a monthly available during the last week of the month following that of the data. Among other data it includes about 120 principal indicators—leading, coincident, and lagging—and draws heavily upon the pioneering work of the National Bureau of Economic Research in its selection of the indicators and in its presentation of analytical measures utilizing the indicators. Any business economist engaged in forecasting where general business conditions are important would find this publication a valuable source.

Exhibit 3–3A shows the Commerce Department's index of leading indicators by months for the period 1979–85. Unfortunately, the index is revised frequently as some of the underlying series may even be missing when the statisticians reach their deadlines. The *Business Conditions Digest* is also a source for individual economic series that may be of more immediate interest to a business enterprise.

U.S. Business Slumps
According to *The Wall Street Journal,* October 12, 1984, p. 1, the following tabulation shows 11 business slumps that have occurred in the United

EXHIBIT 3–3A   Index of 12 Leading Indicators (1967 = 100)

Month	1979	1980	1981	1982	1983	1984	1985
January	142.6	134.8	135.2	135.1*	145.2	164.5	166.3
February . . .	142.3	134.1	134.2	135.7	147.4	166.5	167.7
March	143.2	131.1	135.8	134.7	150.2	167.2	167.9
April	140.3	125.6	137.3	136.0	152.5	168.0	166.9
May	141.4	122.2	136.0	136.2	154.4	168.5	167.4
June	141.6	123.7	135.2	135.5	157.3	167.0	167.8
July	141.2	128.0	134.8	136.2	158.2	164.0	169.0
August	140.1	130.6	134.1	136.1	158.9	164.4	170.1
September . .	140.1	135.0	130.7	137.5	160.2	165.6	
October	137.2	136.0	128.3	138.6	162.5	164.0	
November . . .	135.6	137.6	128.2	139.4	162.6	164.8	
December . .	135.2	136.4	127.1	140.9	163.5	163.9	

*Not comparable to previous month due to change in composition of index.

SOURCE: U.S. Department of Commerce, *Business Conditions Digest,* September 1985 and earlier issues.

States from 1929 to 1982. The length of the slump, percentage drop that occurred in industrial output, and the peak rates of unemployment are summarized. Other data could have been shown in such a summary, such as GNP, national income, construction activity, etc., but the summary as given presents a useful view of the unfavorable periods of our economic history for over 50 years. It may be somewhat misleading for the 1930s which really constituted an entire decade of depression. The indicated slump in 1945 was of a different kind, since the sharp drop in output reflected a reconversion from munitions production to civilian goods. Unemployment was low, as is shown.

	Length in Months	Percent Drop in Industrial Output	Peak Jobless Rate
August 1929–March 1933	43	53.4	24.9
May 1937–July 1938	13	32.4	20.0
February 1945–October 1945	8	38.3	4.3
November 1948–October 1949	11	9.9	7.9
July 1953–May 1954	10	10.0	6.1
August 1957–April 1958	8	14.3	7.5
April 1960–February 1961	10	7.2	7.1
December 1969–November 1970 . . .	11	8.1	6.1
November 1973–March 1975	16	14.7	9.0
January 1980–July 1980	6	8.7	7.8
July 1981–November 1982	16	12.3	10.7

Questions

1. Draw a chart (graph) showing the index of leading indicators by month for the period of January 1979 through December 1982. On the same chart, indicate the two business slumps that occurred during that period by means

of light shading. As a business economist, would you have been aided substantially by the index of leading indicators in forecasting these slumps?

2. At the time you are preparing this case, would you, on the basis of recent leading indicators, forecast a turn in business activity?

3. Can you suggest a statistical procedure that might show when the index changes (in either direction) more than was generally anticipated?

CASE 3–4
Ratio of Coincident to Lagging Indicators

In recent years there has been considerable interest in an index derived by dividing a composite index of four roughly coincident indicators by an index of six lagging indicators. Improving business activity tends, of course, to raise the ratio by increasing the numerator. However, even if the numerator has been increasing, the ratio will decline if the composite of lagging indicators is rising faster. The underlying theory is that the lagging indicators—labor cost per unit in manufacturing, average prime interest rate charged by banks, ratio of consumer installment debt to personal income, and the others described in the text—represent inhibiting forces. Consequently, a substantial period in which the ratio of coincident to lagging indicators has been declining is an unfavorable portent for the future. Relevant data are shown in Exhibit 3–4A. This forecasting device has received a good deal of publicity in The Wall Street Journal.

EXHIBIT 3–4A Composite Economic Indicators, 1979–1985
(1967 = 100)

Year and Month	(1) Index of Four Roughly Coincident Indicators	(2) Index of Six Lagging Indicators	(3) (col. 1 ÷ col. 2) Ratio Coincident Index to Lagging Index
1979:			
January . . .	144.8	157.4	92.0
February . . .	144.9	158.5	91.4
March	146.8	158.5	92.6
April	144.2	161.9	89.1
May	145.6	162.5	89.6
June	145.0	163.6	88.6
July	145.3	164.8	88.2
August	143.7	166.4	87.2
September .	144.7	170.5	84.9
October . . .	144.8	175.9	82.3
November . .	144.9	179.0	80.9
December . .	145.1	177.9	81.6

EXHIBIT 3–4A (Continued)

Year and Month	(1) Index of Four Roughly Coincident Indicators	(2) Index of Six Lagging Indicators	(3) (col. 1 ÷ col. 2) Ratio Coincident Index to Lagging Index
1980:			
January ...	146.1	178.4	81.9
February ...	145.2	180.8	80.3
March	143.5	190.0	75.5
April	140.5	196.2	71.6
May	138.0	183.5	75.2
June	136.7	168.5	81.1
July	136.5	163.6	83.4
August	136.7	161.7	84.5
September .	138.1	164.2	84.1
October ...	139.7	168.5	82.9
November ..	140.8	175.6	80.2
December ..	141.3	191.0	74.0
1981:			
January ...	142.0	189.1	75.1
February ...	142.5	186.5	76.4
March	142.4	181.2	78.6
April	142.2	179.4	79.3
May	142.2	189.6	75.0
June	142.5	191.4	74.6
July	142.6	192.6	74.1
August	142.6	193.5	73.6
September .	142.0	194.1	73.1
October ...	140.0	189.5	73.8
November ..	138.4	184.9	74.9
December ..	136.5	181.7	75.1
1982:			
January ...	138.4	126.1*	109.8*
February ...	139.9	125.3	111.1
March	139.2	125.1	111.3
April	138.0	125.9	109.6
May	138.8	125.1	111.0
June	137.3	124.8	110.0
July	136.4	124.3	109.7
August	135.2	122.2	110.5
September .	134.5	121.4	110.8
October ...	132.9	120.2	110.6
November ..	132.7	118.2	112.3
December ..	132.6	116.7	113.6
1983:			
January ...	134.3	115.7	116.1
February ...	133.5	115.8	115.3
March	134.6	114.4	117.7
April	135.6	113.5	119.5
May	137.9	111.1	124.2
June	139.8	109.8	127.3
July	140.7	109.7	128.3
August	140.8	110.3	127.7
September .	143.3	109.7	130.6
October ...	145.0	109.6	132.3
November ..	145.9	110.0	132.6
December ..	147.5	110.9	133.0

EXHIBIT 3–4A (*Concluded*)

Year and Month	(1) Index of Four Roughly Coincident Indicators	(2) Index of Six Lagging Indicators	(3) (col. 1 ÷ col. 2) Ratio Coincident Index to Lagging Index
1984:			
January . . .	149.5	109.4	136.2
February . . .	150.6	111.3	135.3
March	151.0	112.9	133.7
April	152.6	114.5	133.3
May	153.9	116.3	132.3
June	155.5	117.6	132.2
July	155.7	118.9	131.0
August	155.7	119.9	129.9
September .	156.0	121.1	128.8
October . . .	156.2	122.3	127.7
November . .	157.3	122.1	128.8
December . .	158.4	122.2	129.6
1985:			
January . . .	158.2	124.2	127.4
February . . .	158.5	124.9	126.9
March	158.9	125.9	126.2
April	160.1	126.0	127.1
May	159.6	128.3	124.4
June	158.9	128.1 ·	124.0
July	159.3	128.3	124.2
August	160.7	128.3	124.7

*Not comparable to December 1981 due to changes by Department of Commerce.

SOURCE: U.S. Department of Commerce, *Business Conditions Digest,* September 1985 and earlier issues.

Questions

1. As shown in Case 3–3, the U.S. economy suffered a brief slump from January 1980 through July 1980 and a more serious slump from July 1981 through November 1982. Consider the index of four roughly coincident indicators to reflect the actual state of business activity and show (by a chart or other means) whether the ratio of coincident to lagging indicators was helpful in forecasting these slumps.

2. Using the *Business Conditions Digest,* or other sources, bring the ratio of coincident to lagging indicators up to date. What does this index now appear to forecast for future business activity?

3. The ratio under consideration has been said to have a long lead time. Is this an advantage or a disadvantage to a forecaster?

4

Demand Analysis for Industry

The cheaper an article is, the greater ordinarily is the demand for it.
—*Augustin Cournot**

Manufacturers, farmers, wholesalers, retailers, and others have demands for all sorts of things, but consumer demand is the ultimate regulator of these "derived demands." Main emphasis is consequently placed by economists on final demand as viewed by consumers. In this chapter, an industry may be thought of as a group of firms that produces the same or similar products or services. This rather vague definition suffices for most purposes. However, rigorous definition of an industry is difficult; the more substitutes a product has, the less clear-cut the industry description can be. This causes more difficulty in empirical work than in basic theory.

The quantity of a product that will be demanded by consumers can be viewed as being related to (or as being a function of) such factors as the product's consumers' disposable income, population and other demographic factors, prices of substitutes and complements, existing stock in consumers' hands, cash balances, consumer credit, and expectations regarding prices. Armed with such a function, the analyst has an opportunity to forecast sales by "plugging in" the best estimates of the independent variables. Some estimates (such as population and its composition) may be quite easy to make accurately; others will be difficult. Modern computers may be very useful in connection with forecasting a range within which sales will probably fall, since many alternatives can be tested quickly.

---

*Augustin Cournot, *Researches into the Mathematical Principles of the Theory of Wealth*, (New York: Macmillan, 1929), p. 46. Cournot, whose analysis was written in 1838, appears to have been the first writer to utilize demand curves. Modern textbooks usually substitute "amount demanded" for "demand" in Cournot's statement in order to distinguish between movement along a curve and a shift in the curve.

FIGURE 4–1   Hypothetical Demand Curve for Wheat

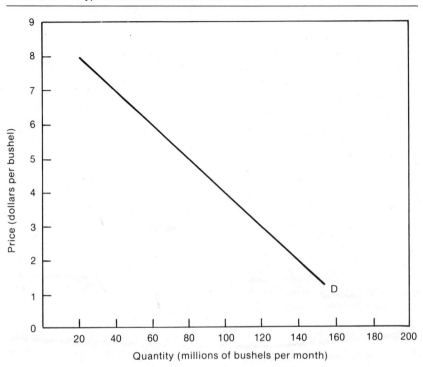

Quantity (millions of bushels per month)

DEMAND, THE RELATIONSHIP BETWEEN QUANTITY AND PRICE

For a great many analytical purposes, the price of a commodity may be considered the independent variable upon which the physical volume of sales depends. Other pertinent variables are then held constant for purposes of defining the demand function. (The student who has studied calculus may recognize that this is the process of finding the partial derivative of sales with respect to price of the same good, other variables being held constant.) The usual demand curve of economic analysis is a special case in which all variables except price of the commodity under consideration are placed in *ceteris paribus*—that is, in which other factors having an effect on sales are unchanged.[1]

---

[1]Some variables can logically be placed only provisionally in *ceteris paribus*. The price of butter is such a variable when demand for oleomargarine is being analyzed. See Milton Friedman, *Price Theory* (Chicago: Aldine Publishing, 1976), p. 23. Also there is a logical problem in assuming "all other" prices constant when one price is allowed to change (since prices are exchange rates between goods), but this question is unlikely to affect analysis of managerial problems.

Demand is based on human wants but should not be confused with wants, which are often said to be infinite. We may all want a new car every year, but our demand is effective only occasionally when we believe the necessary resources are available to cover the original price and the cost of upkeep.

A hypothetical demand curve is shown in Figure 4–1. (Although the commodity is specified as wheat, no attempt has been made to approximate the actual price-quantity relationship for the good—this is the task of empirical analysis as described later in the chapter.)

SLOPE AND ELASTICITY

As the demand curve is drawn in Figure 4–1, a $1 decrease in price per bushel brings about a 20 million bushel increase in quantity demanded per month. This relationship is unchanging along the straight line, giving a slope of $-\frac{1}{20}$, derived from the formula $S = \Delta P / \Delta Q$. Slope depends greatly on the units of measure used. For example, if price were measured in cents rather than dollars, the slope would be -5. ($-100 \div 20$). It is for this reason that Alfred Marshall devised the concept of elasticity of demand which is independent of the units of measure and also permits some comparison of completely different goods, for example, apples measured in bushels and natural gas measured in cubic feet.

Price elasticity of demand is defined as the ratio of the percentage change in quantity demanded to the corresponding percentage change in price. It is mathematically necessary to take the ratios of very small (strictly, infinitesimally small) percentage changes in order to measure elasticity at a particular price.[2] As Alfred Marshall suggested, a useful approximation is to consider price to change by 1 percent (up or down) and to observe the percentage change in quantity. If quantity also changes by exactly 1 percent, demand has an elasticity of 1. If the percentage change in quantity is greater than 1, demand is elastic, while if the percentage change in quantity is less than one, demand is inelastic.

Precise computation of price elasticity of demand by the formula shown in footnote 2 requires some knowledge of calculus. Fortunately, the exact elasticity at any point on the demand curve can easily be figured as illustrated in Figure 4–2. The demand curve D is extended until it touches the vertical axis at point T. A line is drawn horizontally from the point at which elasticity is to be measured, and the intersection with the vertical axis is labeled P. Then point elasticity is $OP \div PT$. Since the distances OP and PT are equal, elasticity is 1. (It is really -1, but it is

---

[2] If $\dfrac{dq}{q}$ denotes an infinitesimal percentage change in quantity demanded and $\dfrac{dp}{p}$ is an infinitesimal percentage change in price, elasticity of demand $(E) = \dfrac{dq}{q} \div \dfrac{dp}{p}$. This is often written as $E = \dfrac{dq}{dp} \cdot \dfrac{p}{q}$.

FIGURE 4–2   Geometric Calculation of Elasticity

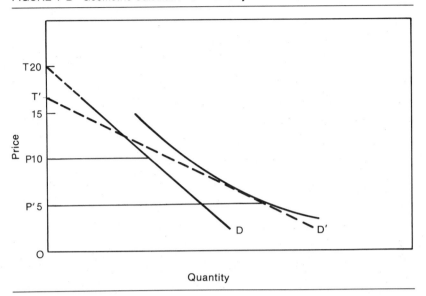

convenient geometrically to neglect the sign.) Above P, the elasticity is greater than 1; below P it is less than 1. It is vital in predictions to keep in mind the minus sign.

If the demand curve actually curves (D' in the figure) a tangent is drawn at the desired point and is treated in the same way. As drawn, elasticity at priceP' is well below 1 since OP' is less than P'T'. The test is a reminder that elasticity usually varies at every point along the demand curve.[3] When we speak of the demand for a commodity as being "elastic" or "inelastic," we probably refer to a typical or recent price. Referring back to Figure 4–1, the extended demand curve intersects the ordinate at a price of $9. From the geometric test, the elasticity at a price of $4 is ⅘ or 0.8. At this price its demand would be called "inelastic."

ELASTICITY AND REVENUE

The negative relationship between price and quantity demanded is known as the *law of demand* because it is so dependable. Economists sometimes enjoy, and even contribute usefully to, the investigation of other types of activity using the general idea behind the law of demand. For example, the quantity of excess speed is a function of the probability

---

[3]In the special case $Q = ap^b$, the elasticity is constant and many empirical studies make this assumption of constant elasticity when using functions that are linear in logarithmic form.

FIGURE 4–3 Relationships among Total Revenue, Average
Revenue, and Elasticity (not to scale)

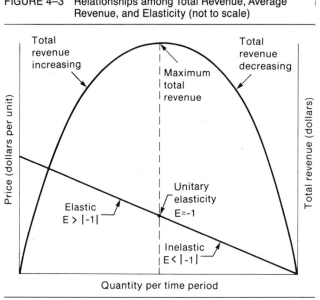

---

of being caught and the likely fine for the moving violation; the demand for shirking on a job is a function of the possible penalty; visits to a neighbor are inversely related to his unpleasantness or that of his dog, etc.

The relationship between total revenue and price (average revenue) is shown in Figure 4–3 for a linear demand curve. In this case since total revenue is equal to price times quantity ($TR = pq$), total revenue will be a parabola. At sales of zero due to a high price, there will be no revenue; and if price is zero, there will again be no revenue. In the diagram, the maximum value is reached where total revenue stops increasing as price decreases and begins to decrease for further reductions in price. Each of these regions of increasing, constant (maximum), and decreasing total revenue are related to the price elasticity of demand.

The ranges of elastic and inelastic demand and the point of unitary elastic demand are shown on Figure 4–3. Since where demand is elastic, a price decrease results in a more than proportionate increase in quantity, total revenue must be increasing. Also, where a decrease in price results in a less than proportionate increase in quantity, total revenue must be declining. Where there is a proportionate change in quantity as a result of a change in price, total revenue remains constant and the resulting elasticity measure is unitary.

It is often the case in attempting to learn something about the elasticity of demand that the analyst does not have enough information to derive the whole demand curve and must rely on inferences about elasticity from observed changes in total revenues. The relationships discussed above provide the necessary clues to make such inferences.

COMPUTATION OF PRICE ELASTICITY

Numerical computations of elasticity follow directly from the definition:

$$\text{Elasticity} = \frac{\text{Percentage change in quantity}}{\text{Percentage change in price}}$$

Strictly speaking, since elasticity is measured at a point, the changes should be very small to make the computation accurate. However, since the data is usually rough and prime interest is in knowing within limits how responsive quantity is to price changes, this approach provides a useful measure of elasticity. For example, suppose that as a result of a price decrease of 5 percent, quantity increases 10 percent, then

$$E = \frac{+10\%}{-5\%} = -2$$

The concept of arc elasticity allows one to compute an approximate measure of elasticity when only two observations on price and quantity are available. If p_1 and q_1 represent one observation and p_2 and q_2 the other, arc elasticity is calculated by

$$\textbf{ARC } \text{Elasticity} = \frac{\dfrac{q_1 - q_2}{q_1 + q_2}}{\dfrac{p_1 - p_2}{p_1 + p_2}}$$

This computes the elasticity midway between the two points on a straight-line demand curve; thus the approximation is better the closer the two points are to each other.

QUANTITY AND INCOME

When longer time periods are considered in discussing the demand for a product, price becomes only one of many factors that influence the quantities that consumers desire to purchase.[4] Income is a factor of considerable importance in explaining the demand for many products over the longer run. It is conventional to treat income as a factor that shifts the demand curve. For most products, it is expected that increases in con-

---

[4]An unusual factor affecting demand was the 1966 apostolic decree that permitted the Catholic Bishops of the United States to terminate obligatory meatless Fridays, except during Lent. Frederick W. Bell, "The Pope and the Price of Fish," *American Economic Review*, December 1968. Bell found a 12.5 percent decline in price of seven species of fish in the Northeast.

sumer income will result in a shift of the price-quantity relationship up and to the right. Figure 4–4 gives data on quantity, price, and income for a hypothetical product over five years. In this exhibit price remains constant yet quantity continues to increase over time, apparently due to the changes in per capita income.

If price and income both may vary, the chart shown in Figure 4–5 illustrates a price-quantity schedule that shifts as income changes. In order to *predict* the quantity for any point in time, it is necessary to know both the price and level of income. In this chart, price and quantity are shown on the axes, and each schedule represents a specified level of income.

In this discussion, the term income has been used rather vaguely. However, for particular products it may be quite important that great care be used in selecting the appropriate measure of income to relate to quantity. For example, if the concern is with the demand for tractors, then farm

FIGURE 4–4   Price, Income, Quantity Schedule

Year	Price ($)	Income ($ per capita)	Quantity (000 units)
1	$1	$2,000	2,000
2	1	2,500	2,500
3	1	3,000	3,000
4	1	3,500	3,500
5	1	4,000	4,000

FIGURE 4–5   Increase in Income—Shifts Demand Upward If Good Is Normal

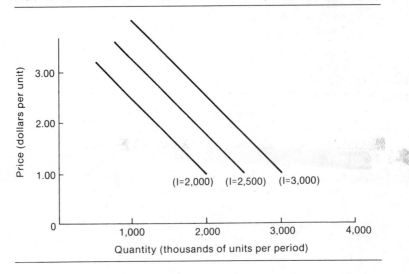

income may be the appropriate income measure, while disposable consumer income may be the appropriate measure when studying automobile demand.

INCOME ELASTICITY OF DEMAND

A popular measure of the responsiveness of quantity demanded to income (with price being held constant at a specified level) is known as *income elasticity of demand*. Again as in price elasticity, the percentage change in quantity is the numerator, and the formula *can* be written as:

$$\text{Income elasticity} = \frac{\text{Percent change in quantity}}{\text{Percent change in income}}$$

When changes are very small, the formula becomes $E = \dfrac{dq}{dy} \cdot \dfrac{y}{q}$, where y denotes income. Like price elasticity, income elasticity can be greater than, equal to, or less than unity. In Figure 4–4, income elasticity is clearly equal to unity. For "normal goods" income elasticity is positive in sign (as in Figure 4–4). For "inferior goods", the sign is negative, denoting a decline in sales (leftward shift of demand) as income increases. Secondhand clothing is a good example of an inferior good.

It is very helpful to a business if income elasticity of demand is positive and high, as this will bring greater industry sales with economic growth, and even if the number of rival firms increases, an existing firm may well find its own sales increasing. To enter into production of an inferior good while national income is rising is apt to be hazardous, as total demand will weaken. There are exceptions to all rules, however, and filling a need for an inferior good before others crowd the field can be profitable. In part the "garage" or "yard" sale is a response to the general lack of good secondhand markets for furniture, clothing, utensils, and other household items.

SUBSTITUTES AND COMPLEMENTS

All products compete for consumers' dollars and are consequently substitutes in a broad sense. The businessperson is likely to be much more aware, however, of close substitutes such as Tylenol for aspirin, letters for long-distance telephone calls, or rented for purchased automobiles. Other goods are complementary such as gasoline and oil, golf clubs and golf balls, and dress shirts and ties. Complements are very likely to be stocked by the same retailer since the customer who buys one product is a good prospect for a related item. Substitutes may also be carried by the same retailer in order to attract customers by the variety of choices provided. Close comparison may then be discouraged by such devices as keeping expensive dresses on the upper floors of a department store, far from the bargain basement.

When the price of a good changes (or if we merely contemplate different prices along a given demand curve), two separate effects on the buyer can be distinguished: (1) the substitution effect and (2) the income effect. The substitution effect derives from the tendency to shift to another good as the price of the good under consideration rises in relative price. The income effect derives from the effect of a change in the price of a good on the real income of a buyer. Usually the substitution effect is much more important. In recent years, however, the sharp increases in gasoline prices and utility bills have had a pronounced income effect on all of us, draining away purchasing power from other commodities.

CROSS ELASTICITY OF DEMAND

The above concepts are related to another popular elasticity measurement—*cross elasticity of demand*. Here, changes in the sales of one product are associated with changes in the price of a closely related product, other things, including price of the commodity in question, being held constant. If finite changes are examined the formula is:

$$\text{Cross elasticity of demand} = \frac{\text{Percent change in } Q_x}{\text{Percent change in } P_y}$$

where Q_x is sales of product X and P_y is the price of a substitute, complement, or independent (unrelated) good. If cross elasticity is positive, the goods are substitutes, for example, a rise in the price of oleomargarine raises the sales of butter, *ceteris paribus*. A decline in the price of coffee reduces the sales of tea. (Two minuses make a plus when divided.) If cross elasticity is negative, the goods are complements, for example, higher gasoline prices reduce the sale of oil (but not by very much). If cross elasticity is zero, the goods are independent (e.g., the sales of butter in the United States and the price of goats' milk in Iraq).[5]

When a demand curve is drawn for an industry, it is usually assumed for the sake of simplicity that the good is homogeneous, for example, sulphur, crude oil of a certain grade, wheat of a given variety, etc. Often the good is, instead, heterogeneous such as with automobiles, different species of fish, mountain and ocean vacations, etc. If goods are very similar, there may be little problem in treating them as exactly the same; if they are quite different but meet the same general category of service, they may be treated as one good only with great caution. For example, the substantial product and price variation in automobiles makes it difficult to estimate a demand curve for cars.

---

[5]The student should not regard measures such as cross elasticity to be of merely academic interest. For example, in a famous case, economists for Du Pont were able to show high positive cross elasticities between cellophane and such products as glassine, waxpaper, and other wrapping materials, helping Du Pont prove that monopoly power in cellophane was not a serious social problem as the "commodity," broadly defined, had many producers. Meetings of both private and public officials on business and legal matters are apt to involve many of the economist's concepts.

QUANTITY AND POPULATION

Another variable of considerable importance for demand studies when longer time periods are considered is population. Again, population may be considered as a variable that shifts the basic price-quantity relationships. In general, it is expected that the greater the population, the greater the demand for a product at a given price. That is, there is usually a positive relationship between population and quantity, all other variables held constant.

There are many aspects of the population—that is, demographic characteristics—that may be of critical importance in long-run demand studies. The age distribution of the population is one such aspect. Thus, if half the population is under 25, a producer of geriatric supplies may want to plan diversification, and a builder may want to give more attention to apartments than to single-family homes. Actually, the analysts would want to look at more than just the median age in their analysis. Marriage rates, family formation, urban concentration, and many other demographic factors are relevant in long-run demand studies, and the economist who ignores these factors is courting disaster.[6] For medium range (5 to 10 years) demand forecasts, population is a very useful variable as all the potential heads of households are already born, making forecasts much easier. Some of these persons will now be residing in other countries so that probable in-migration can be important also. A depressing factor for beer sales in the late 1980s and 1990s is the drop in births in the 1960s and 1970s.

QUANTITY AND ADVERTISING

An industry through its trade association may attempt to shift the demand curve through advertising expenditures. If successful, the result will be a change in consumers' tastes and in their willingness to purchase additional units at the same prices. The shift obtained should give the same kind of pattern as that observed for a normal good when income increases in Figure 4–5. (Demand for an inferior good such as used suits declines with an increase in income.)

An individual firm in a highly competitive industry (poultry and egg production, agricultural products, commercial fishing, etc.) usually has no need to advertise. Most company advertising is done where the number of firms producing a consumer good (cigarettes, beer, pantyhose, etc.) is limited. However, competitive industries may advertise with such slogans as "Eat More Oysters—Live Longer, Love Longer." The gas industry has recently been active in pushing its product in view of government-mandated conversions of many factories from gas to coal. This sort of

---

[6]See Haskel Benishay and Gilbert R. Whitaker, Jr., "Demand and Supply in Freight Transportation," *Journal of Industrial Economics*, July 1966, for a study using demographic variables.

advertising is designed to influence the opinions of legislators and voters as well as consumers.

QUANTITY AND STOCK

The effect of the existing stock of a good on current demand is most pronounced when the good being studied is a durable. However, some interesting studies have been done that use the notion of a stock as a proxy for tastes or habits.[7] For durable goods such as automobiles, not only is the existing stock important but knowledge of the stock is helpful in predicting replacement demand and also in a real sense the existing stock is a substitute for new goods. Both of these aspects of stock should be taken into account in analyzing the demand for a durable.

EMPIRICAL DEMAND FUNCTIONS

All of the variables discussed above and many more can affect the demand for a good or service. Recognition of the important factors can aid managers in making better informed judgments about the responsiveness of their products' demand to changes in these factors. Some of the variables such as price and promotion policy are to some extent controllable by a business. As to others, they can only react or plan their reactions if they are forewarned about changes to come. More precise quantitative estimates of demand may be possible through empirical or statistical demand functions.

The most common method of deriving statistical demand curves involves the use of time-series data on prices, sales, and other relevant variables.[8] The first step is usually to plot all of the price-sales data on a chart where price is measured vertically and quantity sold is measured horizontally. (This has become conventional, although theoretically it would be preferable to plot price, the independent variable, against the horizontal scale [X axis] and sales against the vertical scale [Y axis].) If the investigator is unusually fortunate, he or she can immediately draw the statistical demand curve merely by fitting a "regression" line to the price-sales data.[9] Even if the fit is very close and the regression line slopes nicely downward, it may not be a demand curve, as will become apparent in the subsequent discussion.

---

[7]See H. S. Houthakker and Lester D. Taylor, *Consumer Demand in the United States, 1929–1970* (Cambridge, Mass.: Harvard University Press, 1966).

[8]Family budget data have been used by statisticians to derive demand curves for some consumer goods. This method will not be considered in the present chapter.

[9]Such a line of "best" fit may simply be drawn freehand in such a way as to minimize approximately the sum of the deviations of the plotted points from the regression line. Or mathematical methods such as the "least squares" method may be employed. The least squares method may minimize the sum of the squared vertical distances, squared horizontal distances, or squared perpendicular distances from the regression line.

FIGURE 4–6   Shifting Supply and Demand May Trace No Pattern

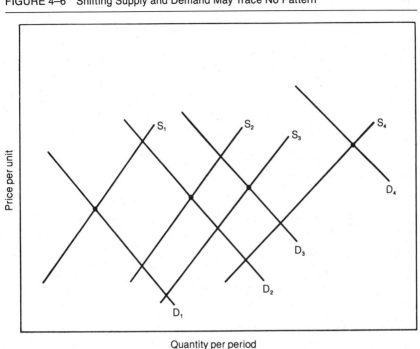

Quantity per period

In the case of a competitively produced commodity, each historically recorded price-sales point can be considered to have been determined by the intersection of a supply and a demand curve. This is illustrated in Figure 4–6 for a hypothetical situation in which both the demand and the supply curves have shifted over a period of time. Each of the intersections (D_1 and S_1, D_2 and S_2, etc.) indicates a price that existed at one time during the period studied. It is clear that if the demand and supply curves have both shifted to the right, as suggested by Figure 4–6, the price-quantity data plotted by the statistician would not trace out a demand curve, a supply curve, or any of the other curves of economic theory.

On the other hand, if the situation has been that of Figure 4–7 in which the demand curve was stable over the period while the supply curve shifted to several different positions (due, for example, to different crop yields in successive years), the price-sales data would trace out the demand curve which the statistician is seeking.[10] If the demand curve shifted only slightly while the supply curve shifted substantially, the

---

[10]The various possibilities are shown is a classic article by E. J. Working, "What Do Statistical Demand Curves Show?" *Quarterly Journal of Economics*, February 1927, pp. 212–35.

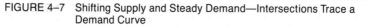

FIGURE 4–7   Shifting Supply and Steady Demand—Intersections Trace a
             Demand Curve

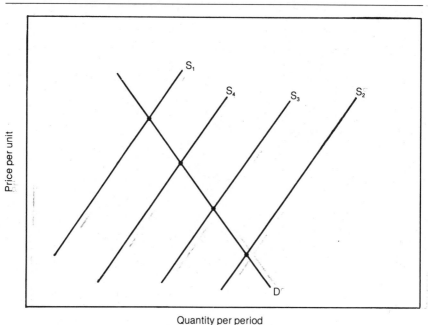

Quantity per period

intersections would appear to follow a single demand curve but would
not actually do so. If the supply curve were unchanged while the demand
curve shifted, the price-sales data would trace out a supply curve.

In practice, the demand curve usually shifts a good deal over the
period for which the statistician has price-sales data. Numerous statistical
devices are available for removing the shift and coming out with an approximation to the static demand curve of economic theory. A simple
graphical method for accomplishing this end may be illustrated by its
application to the hypothetical price-sales data of Figure 4–8. The "period" referred to is usually a year, but may be a shorter span of time. Price
must refer to a weighted average for the period unless, of course, a single
price persisted throughout the time interval.

As a first step in finding the influence of price on quantity sold, the
analyst would probably plot these data as in Figure 4–9. At this point, he
or she might be discouraged, because the plotted points do not even come
close to falling along a negatively declining demand curve such as would
be expected from a knowledge of the economist's "law of demand." Inspection of the original data reveals clearly, however, that there has been

FIGURE 4–8 Hypothetical
Price-Sales Data

Period	Quantity Sold	Price per Unit
1	50	$ 9
2	75	8
3	65	15
4	110	10
5	150	7
6	150	14
7	200	9

FIGURE 4–9   Price-Sales Data—May Show No Pattern

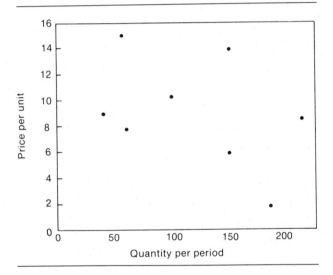

an upward trend in sales over the seven periods.[11] This is easily seen by reference to the fact that in period 1 a price of $9 was associated with sales of 50 units, while in period 7 the same price was coupled with sales of 200 units. One way of eliminating the trend in order to isolate the influence of price is to fit a trend line to the time series of sales. Such a line can be fitted freehand or, if more accuracy is desired, by the method of least squares.

---

[11]Trend is a "proxy" for all the factors other than price which may have caused the demand curve to shift over time. The assumed relationship is $q = f(p,t)$, where q = quantity, p = price, and t is the trend variable. This "shortcut" method is a two-step approach with trend removed in order to isolate the effect of price.

If time is designated by X and quantity by Y, a straight-line fit that minimizes the sum of the squared vertical deviations can be obtained by solving the equations:

$$\Sigma y = na + b\Sigma x$$
$$\Sigma xy = a\Sigma x + b\Sigma x^2$$

Where n is the number of observations, a is the Y-axis intercept, and b is the slope of the regression line. The following table gives necessary data related to Figure 4–8:

X	Y	X²	XY
1	50	1	50
2	75	4	150
3	65	9	195
4	110	16	440
5	150	25	750
6	150	36	900
7	200	49	1,400
28	800	140	3,885

Placing these values in the equations we have:

$$800 = 7a + 28b$$
$$3,885 = 28a + 140b$$

Multiplying each term in the first equation by 4 we get:

$$3,200 = 28a + 112b$$
$$3,885 = 28a + 140b$$

Subtracting the first equation from the second:

$$685 = 28b$$
$$b = 24.46$$

Substituting this value for b in either equation:

$$a = 16.45$$

Consequently the line of the best fit has the equation:

$$Y = 16.45 + 24.46X$$

This line can be readily plotted in Figure 4–10. It will hit the vertical axis at 16.45 (since $X = 0$). Suppose $X = 5$, then

$$Y = 138.75$$

Through these two points (or any other calculated two points) the regression line can be drawn.

FIGURE 4–10 Sharp Upward Trend in Sales—Has Obscured
Effect of Price

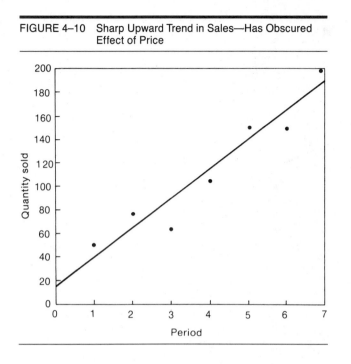

The next step in a shortcut method of deriving a demand curve is to measure the vertical deviations of observations from the regression line. If the line in Figure 4–10 had been fitted by freehand means, the deviations could be measured with a ruler. Since the line was fitted by least squares, the deviations can be found more accurately by comparing actual and calculated values of Y, as shown below:

X	Actual Y	Calculated Y	Deviation
1	50	40.91	+ 9.09
2	75	65.37	+ 9.63
3	65	89.83	− 24.83
4	110	114.29	− 4.29
5	150	138.75	+ 11.25
6	150	163.21	− 13.21
7	200	187.67	+ 12.33

The next step is to plot deviations against price. The underlying assumption is that the upward trend in quantity over time is due to such factors as growth of population and income. Consequently, periods in which price was relatively high should exhibit sales below "normal," that is, below the fitted trend line, while low prices should have stimulated

FIGURE 4–11 Effect of Price Appears—Because Trend Has Been Removed

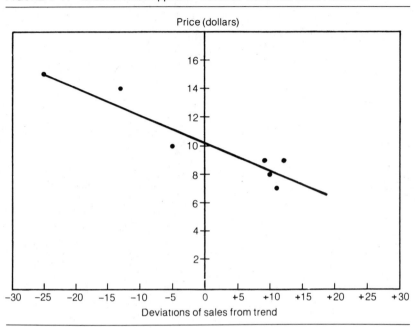

above-normal sales. (This relationship between price and deviations of sales works out nicely in Figure 4–11 because the data have been contrived to do so.) If a negative relationship does not appear at this point, the shortcut approach will not work for the commodity being investigated. It is possible that the difficulty is due to such factors as existence of a close substitute that has not been brought into the analysis, irregularity of factors such as disposable income, or even poor data.

Although the line that has been fitted freehand in Figure 4–11 indicates the effect that price had on sales, it is not a demand curve because the full quantity demanded is not shown. It is necessary to add back the trend value of quantity for whatever time period a demand curve is to be estimated. The following calculation would be made to show demand curves for periods 1, 4, and 7. Any two price-deviation combinations on the regression line of Figure 4–11 will be satisfactory. Arbitrary prices of 14 and 8 are used below:

	Trend Value	Deviation		Quantity	
		P = 14	P = 8	P = 14	P = 8
Period 1	40.91	− 20	+ 12	20.91	52.91
Period 4	114.29	− 20	+ 12	94.29	126.29
Period 7	187.67	− 20	+ 12	167.67	199.67

FIGURE 4–12   Upward Shifting Demand Curve—the Final Product of Analysis

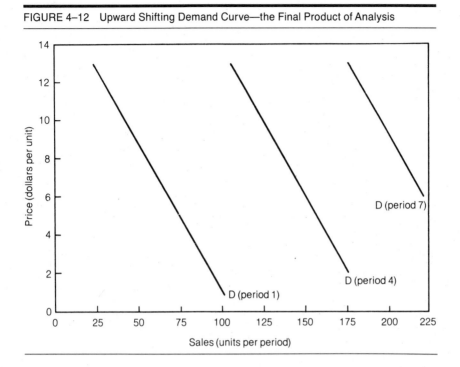

The end result is the shifting demand curve shown in Figure 4–12 plotted from the data in the right-hand columns. The upward shift of demand (which characterizes a great many actual commodities) should be taken into account in any attempt to judge current demand. A weakness of the shortcut method employed is that all of the demand curves have the same slope.

CASE 4–1
Demand for Frozen Orange Concentrate

The problem of deriving a statistical demand curve for an actual commodity, frozen orange concentrate, is illustrated in this case. A relatively new good, it was first produced and retailed during the 1945–46 orange crop season. Demand increased rapidly as consumers became acquainted with the product and as retail stores installed the necessary refrigerated cabinets.

Frozen orange concentrate is unusual in that monthly retail sales and price data are available. Most commodities are reported only on a yearly

EXHIBIT 4–1A   Frozen Orange Concentrate and Related Data

Month	Consumer Purchases* (000 gallons)	Retail Price* (cents per 6-ounce can)	Disposable Personal Income† (annual rate, $ billion)	Consumer Price Index‡ (1957–59 = 100)	U.S. Population§ (millions)
1963:					
September . . .	3,222	28.0	408.3	107.1	189.8
October	3,238	27.7	411.6	107.2	190.0
November . . .	3,263	27.4	413.1	107.4	190.4
December . . .	3,240	27.8	417.3	107.6	190.6
1964:					
January	3,398	27.3	420.8	107.7	190.8
February	3,283	27.4	422.8	107.6	191.0
March	3,494	27.4	424.1	107.7	191.2
April	3,649	27.0	430.8	107.8	191.4
May	3,527	25.7	434.3	107.8	191.6
June	3,551	25.7	435.9	108.0	191.9
July	3,349	25.6	437.3	108.3	192.1
August	3,290	25.6	440.7	108.2	192.3
September . . .	3,728	25.4	442.9	108.4	192.6
October	4,369	25.0	442.1	108.5	192.8
November . . .	4,090	25.2	445.9	108.7	193.1
December . . .	4,163	24.9	451.3	108.8	193.3
1965:					
January	5,076	22.8	450.6	108.9	193.5
February	5,046	21.3	450.4	108.9	193.7
March	4,931	21.1	453.0	109.0	193.8
April	5,353	19.7	454.3	109.3	194.0
May	5,105	18.1	458.8	109.6	194.2
June	5,044	18.0	462.3	110.1	194.4
July	4,801	17.8	469.7	110.2	194.6
August	4,936	17.7	472.1	110.1	194.8
September . . .	5,596	17.4	476.1	110.2	195.0
October	5,675	17.3	480.5	110.4	195.2
November . . .	5,519	17.3	486.5	110.6	195.5
December . . .	5,507	17.5	491.5	110.0	195.6
1966:					
January	6,401	16.7	490.7	110.0	195.8
February	5,744	17.1	495.2	111.6	196.0
March	5,709	17.8	499.5	112.0	196.2

SOURCE: * U.S. Department of Agriculture.
†Calculated from data in *Survey of Current Business,* U.S. Department of Commerce.
‡Bureau of Labor Statistics, as reported in *Survey of Current Business.*
§Bureau of the Census, as reported in *Survey of Current Business.*

basis. Ordinarily, the use of monthly figures requires that adjustment be made for a regular seasonal fluctuation in sales; however, no substantial seasonal pattern exists for frozen orange concentrate.

Some Problems in Statistical Measurement of Demand

Exhibit 4–1A shows the variables that were selected some years ago for close statistical examination in the measurement of demand for frozen orange concentrate. It should be recognized that all of these data are subject to problems of measurement, that problems of "multicollinearity" and "autocorrelation" exist, and that many other series have some relevance. For example, the price of substitutes such as grapefruit, fresh oranges, orange drinks, frozen lemonade, and frozen limeade could be included. The data are based on a survey of 6,500 demographically balanced families.

Sales and price data are affected by the reliability of the small sample of families, by lack of complete homogeneity of orange concentrate both over a period of time and at any point in time, and by weighting problems involved in getting an average retail price. Disposable personal income, like other aggregate measures of income, fails to pick up transactions that do not go through the market (e.g., housewives' services) and some that do go through the market (e.g., babysitting services). Personal taxes can be estimated only approximately on a monthly basis. The Consumer Price Index is especially vulnerable to quality changes in the commodities on which it is based, probably overstating the rise in the cost of living. Even population is measured only approximately, especially because census enumerators are unable to find many persons in the cities (particularly when welfare recipients fear that reporting their presence may be harmful to continued receipt of benefits). It is probable that the actual population to the United States is several million greater than official figures show. From the viewpoint of the present study there are problems also of relevance of total population to demand because age and geographical distribution also affect consumption. At the same time it should be realized that an excessively critical attitude toward available data will result in the loss of statistical studies that may be useful in prediction and interpretation of the real world.

The common statistical problem of multicollinearity refers to intercorrelation among independent variables. Such correlation makes it difficult to measure their separate influences on the dependent variables. Minimization of its influence requires careful selection of dependent variables. The problem of autocorrelation refers to the correlation of each item in a series with its succeeding item. Statistical methods used to reduce autocorrelation include the use of first differences (each item subtracted from the previous one) and removal of linear trends.

A useful way of reducing the number of independent variables in a demand study is sometimes found in the division of one series by another. For present purposes it was found desirable to divide both retail price and disposable personal income by the Consumer Price Index. (It was not found to be useful, however, to place sales on a per capita basis by dividing by population). "Deflated" retail price data and "real" disposable personal income are shown in Exhibit 4–1B. These two series, along with consumer purchases, are the ones entering the regression equation as independent variables. (The equation has been fitted by means of least squares analysis, minimizing the sums of squared vertical deviations.)

$$Q = 2{,}779 - 172P + 12.6Y$$

EXHIBIT 4–1B   Deflated Prices and Real
Disposable Income

Month	Deflated Price*	Real Disposable Income†
1963:		
September	26.1	381.2
October	25.8	384.0
November	25.5	384.6
December	25.8	387.8
1964:		
January	25.3	390.7
February	25.5	392.9
March	25.4	393.8
April	25.0	399.6
May	23.8	402.9
June	23.8	403.6
July	23.6	403.8
August	23.7	407.3
September	23.4	408.6
October	23.0	407.5
November	23.2	410.2
December	22.9	414.8
1965:		
January	30.9	413.8
February	19.6	413.6
March	19.4	415.6
April	18.0	415.6
May	16.5	418.6
June	16.3	419.9
July	16.2	426.2
August	16.1	429.2
September	15.8	432.0
October	15.7	435.2
November	15.6	439.9
December	15.8	442.8
1966:		
January	15.0	442.1
February	15.3	443.7
March	15.9	446.0

*Retail price divided by Consumer Price Index.
†Disposable personal income divided by Consumer Price Index.

where Q is consumer purchases in thousands of gallons per month, P is the deflated price in cents per 6-ounce can, and Y is real disposable income.[12]

Equation (1) shows that a 1-cent change in price brings about an opposite change in sales of 172.0 thousand gallons per month. A change of one billion in real disposable income brings about a change of 12.6 thousand gallons per month in the same direction.[13]

---

[12]The method of fitting such an equation is described in many statistics books.

[13]Both regression coefficients are significant at the 5 percent level. The coefficient of determination is 0.91, significant at the 5 percent level.

Since real disposable income shows mainly an upward trend during the period covered, the demand curve relating sales to price tends to move upward and to the right over time. If one wishes to measure elasticity of demand for frozen orange concentrate, it is necessary to specify which demand curve is to be used and also the price at which elasticity is to be calculated. If real income of 446.0 is substituted for Y in equation (1), we have:

$$Q = 8,399 - 172P \tag{2}$$

Substituting 15.9 for P, we have:

$$Q = 5,664 \tag{3}$$

4-1A

(This estimated value of Q compares with an actual quantity of 5,709.)

To find elasticity of demand at a price of 15.9 the following formula can be employed:

$$E = \frac{dQ}{dP} \cdot \frac{P}{Q} \quad \textit{point elasticity} \tag{4}$$

or

$$E = -172\left(\frac{15.9}{5,664}\right) \tag{5}$$

solving

$$E = -0.48 \tag{6}$$

Since this computed price elasticity of demand is less than unity, it is an example of "inelastic demand" at the prevailing price. From the point of view of the industry, a higher price would be more profitable. From the social point of view the situation appears to be favorable since quite a highly competitive situation appears to prevail.

Income elasticity of demand can also be computed from the formula

$$E = \frac{dQ}{dY} \cdot \frac{Y}{Q} \tag{7}$$

substituting:

$$E = 12.6\left(\frac{446}{5,664}\right) = \frac{5,620}{5,664} = +0.99$$

The positive sign indicates that during the period covered, frozen orange concentrate was a "superior" good. A 1 percent increase in real income brought about approximately a 1 percent increase in sales of frozen orange concentrate.

Questions

1. Before beginning a complicated demand study, it is desirable to make a simple check to see whether there is, in fact, a negative relationship between

EXHIBIT 4–1C   Frozen Orange Concentrate and Related Data

Month	Consumer Purchases* (000 gallons)	Retail Price* (cents per 12-ounce can)	Personal Income† ($ billions per year in 1972 $)	Consumer Price Index‡ (1967 = 100)
1981:				
January	68,700	69.8	1,227	260.5
February . . .	44,200	76.6	1,232	263.2
March	38,500	85.5	1,235	265.1
April	39,800	88.8	1,235	266.8
May	38,600	90.4	1,234	269.0
June	38,400	90.5	1,240	271.3
July	38,300	89.3	1,248	274.4
August	38,400	89.6	1,254	276.5
September . .	43,600	87.7	1,253	279.3
October	43,800	87.8	1,251	279.9
November . .	35,800	89.3	1,250	280.7
December . .	44,300	87.4	1,245	285.5
1982:				
January	56,600	86.0	1,246	282.5
February . . .	37,400	88.9	1,256	283.4
March	36,900	90.8	1,255	283.1
April	44,500	88.8	1,260	284.3
May	38,700	88.0	1,259	287.1
June	39,700	86.9	1,248	290.6
July	40,200	86.3	1,252	292.2
August	37,700	87.9	1,249	292.8
September . .	44,000	82.9	1,249	293.3
October	41,900	84.8	1,249	294.1
November . .	38,200	85.3	1,262	293.6
December . .	40,500	87.4	1,267	292.4
1983:				
January	43,000	84.9	1,264	293.1
February . . .	41,200	84.6	1,261	293.2
March	40,100	84.0	1,266	293.4
April	41,600	84.2	1,268	295.5
May	34,500	83.6	1,276	297.1
June	39,000	82.9	1,283	298.1
July	38,400	83.1	1,283	299.3
August	37,300	83.0	1,285	300.3
September . .	38,200	81.2	1,291	301.8
October	41,900	84.8	1,306	302.6
November . .	36,300	82.3	1,312	303.1
December . .	45,400	82.5	1,321	303.5
1984:				
January	49,600	81.5	1,333	305.2
February . . .	35,000	88.7	1,342	306.6
March	40,500	93.8	1,344	307.3
April	33,200	100.7	1,354	308.8
May	33,900	101.4	1,359	309.7
June	34,500	101.0	1,372	310.7

SOURCES: *Citrus Digest, Florida Department of Citrus, Market Research Department, June 1984. †Business Conditions Digest, U.S. Department of Commerce. ‡Bureau of Labor Statistics, as reported in Survey of Current Business, U.S. Department of Commerce (all items, wage earners and clerical workers).

changes in price and changes in sales. One useful check is to compare "first differences" in each series—that is, the absolute change from period to period in sales and prices. For example, in Exhibit 4–1A for the 1963 data, first differences in sales from September to October are +16 while price was −0.03; from October to November, first differences were +25 and −0.3; from November to December, −23 and +0.4.

Using the new data in Exhibit 4–1C, calculate enough first differences to assure yourself that price and quantity usually, but not always, move in opposite directions.

2. Using the new data and any available computer program for regression analysis, recompute the demand equation for frozen orange concentrate with Q denoting consumer purchases in thousands of gallons per month, P the deflated price in cents per 12-ounce can (instead of previous reporting per 6-ounce can), and Y the real personal income at an annual rate. (See Note at end of case.)

3. Does this now appear to be a "mature industry" in comparison with its situation in the 1960s?

4. Are the price elasticity and income elasticity estimates derived from your recomputed equations reasonably consistent with those reported for the earlier study?

5. Does your regression equation help you measure the effect of consumers' reactions to the freezing Florida weather of January 1981, January 1982, and December 1983? Explain. Do their reactions appear to be due to "rational expectations"?

Note

If you did not work out the model, use the following in which P represents the price deflated by the consumer price index; for example, P for January 1981 is 26.8 (69.8/2.605). The least squares equation is

$$Q = 155{,}550 - 1{,}195P - 62Y$$

CASE 4–2
The Demand for Refrigerators*

Refrigerators are a long-lived consumer durable good. Existing homes are saturated with refrigerators, but failures can be expected to result in replacement purchases. New homes and apartments usually require additions to the total stock of refrigerators. Therefore, total demand can be considered to consist of two basic components—replacement demand and new owner demand. However, sales data do not indicate the reason why a particular customer is buying a refrigerator. Also, there are no

---

*SOURCE: This case is based upon a study made in 1966 by the economic and market research department of the Whirlpool Corporation. It is used with their permission.

EXHIBIT 4–2A   Refrigerators: Replacement Schedule—16-year average life

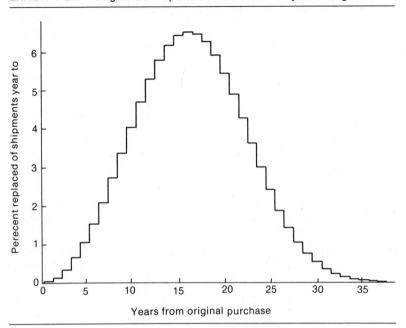

EXHIBIT 4–2B   Refrigerators: New-owner demand
+ replacement demand = shipments

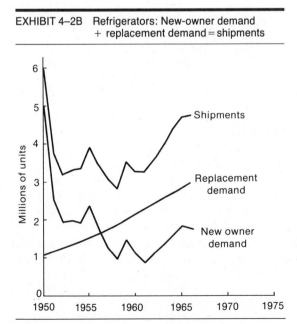

registration data available such as there are for automobiles to provide a basis for estimating scrappage. An approximate method was required to separate sales data into these two components.

Annual shipments for replacement were estimated under the assumption that replacement demand (scrappage and replacement of existing refrigerators) was a probabilistic function of prior refrigerator purchases. In order to make estimates of replacements for recent periods, it was necessary to utilize annual refrigerator sales data from the year 1920. The assumption of probabilistic replacement implies that some small fraction of the refrigerators sold in 1920 will be scrapped in 1921, a somewhat larger percentage in 1922, and so forth. A probability distribution, the Wiebull distribution illustrated in Exhibit 4–2A, was assumed. By applying the theoretical replacement percentages to annual sales, the scrappage through time of a particular year's sales may be estimated. Repeating the process for each year's sales since 1920 and summing the annual scrappage figures obtained, an estimate was made of replacement demand for each year. This process was repeated with different probability distributions until results were obtained which provided a reasonable check with available census data. The distribution that worked best was one with an average life of 16 years as shown in Exhibit 4–2A. This 16-year average life also checked well against life estimates made by other researchers using other methods.[14]

Exhibit 4–2B shows total refrigerator shipments for the period 1950–65; replacement demand is estimated using the procedure outlined above and the resulting "apparent" new-owner demand that was obtained by subtracting replacement demand from total shipments.

Replacement demand was readily extended for forecasting purposes once the basic series had been developed in the manner described above. However, this left unresolved the problem of forecasting new-owner demand.

Forecasting new-owner demand was explained in the following manner:

The next step is the construction of an econometric model capable of explaining the observed variation in the new owner demand curve. At this point, the statistical technique of multiple regression analysis is employed.

A number of sets of independent variables were used to explain the fluctuations in new owner demand. The group finally selected consisted of (1) the total U.S. population age 20–34, (2) housing starts, (3) change in current dollar disposable personal income, and (4) the consumer price index for refrigerators.

The number of people between 20 and 34 represents the primary market of "first appliance" buyers since most people have established by

---

[14]Jean L. Pennock and Carol M. Jaeger, "Household Service Life of Durable Goods," *Journal of Home Economics*, January 1964.

EXHIBIT 4–2C   Independent Variables for New-Owner Demand

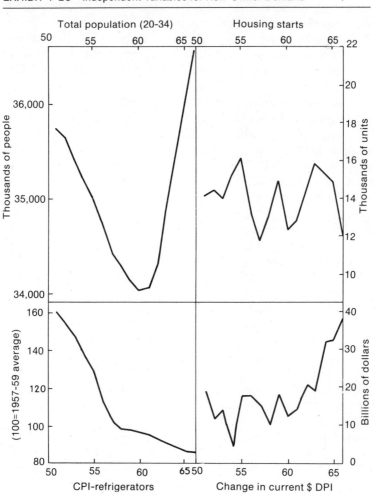

age 34 an independent household that has already triggered the purchase of a *new* refrigerator somewhere in the economy. Since the new owner segment excludes replacement purchases by definition, this demographic variable is most important in explaining the historic new owner series. The general weakness in appliance sales in the late 1950s can be traced directly to the depression-caused falloff in young adults entering this critical consumer segment at that time. On the other hand, the continued expansion of this age group in the next decade creates a strong basis for "bullish" forecasts of new owner purchases for appliances, particularly refrigerators.

Change in disposable personal income was used to pick up the short-term swings in the economy that caused deviations around the underlying demographic trend in new owners. People's immediate economic expectations are an important determinant of whether they decide to purchase a durable good now or to wait. The change in disposable personal income is a gross measure of people's personal buoyancy in that their current expectations are based on their most recent experiences. The use of this economic variable helps to explain the 1959 resurgence of refrigerator shipments in the face of continued decline in the number of younger adults.

The correspondence between the "apparent" new owner series and a curve computed from the multiple regression analysis was improved through the addition of two supplementary variables. Housing starts insofar as they contain multifamily units with their near-saturation installation rates of 95 percent are directly related to new owner purchases. The refrigerator consumer price index, which exhibits the continued increase in refrigerator values for the consumer, although modest in its effect, applies the finishing touches to this explanation of the historic new owner's demand series.

The variation which was inherent in the independent variables is shown in Exhibit 4–2C.

Multiple regression analysis was performed using "apparent" new-owner demand as the dependent variable and the four independent variables discussed above. This resulted in the following multiple regression equation for predicted new-owner demand:

Apparent new owners (000 units) =
  0.022 population + 0.7761 housing starts
  + 17,594 Consumer Price Index for refrigerators
  + 33,286 disposable personal income − 2,812

New owner demand explained as a function of:

(1) Population, age 20–34   (POP)   (000)
(2) Housing starts   (HS)   (000)
(3) Refrigerators CPI   (CPI)   (percent)
(4) Change in our $ DPI   (DPI)   ($ billions)

Apparent new owners = 0.0220 POP + 0.7761 HS + 17.594 CPI
  + 33,286 DPI − 2,812

The numbers were the regression coefficients estimated for the independent variables, and − 2,812 was the regression constant. Thus, given predictions of the independent variables, predictions could be made for the dependent variable. Using the actual values of the independent variables and substituting them into the equation above gave the dashed line "fit" as shown in Exhibit 4–2D. This equation explained 92.5 percent of the variation in new-owner demand. The graph indicated a close fit of the "predicted" values to the actual values especially with respect to the major turning points in the series.

EXHIBIT 4–2D   Refrigerators

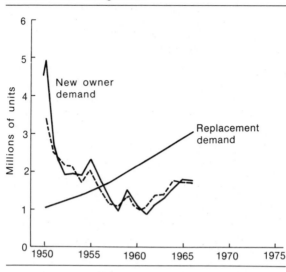

EXHIBIT 4–2E   Refrigerators: Ten-Year Projection of
Domestic Factory Shipments

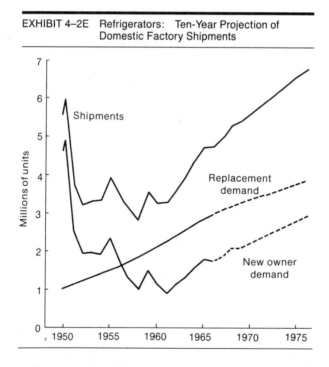

A 10-year forecast of refrigerator shipments was computed by recur-
sively adding the annual projections of replacement and new-owner demand. Using refrigerator shipments from 1930 to 1967, replacement
demand was projected for 1968. New-owner demand for 1968 was projected based upon substitution of forecasts of the independent variables

EXHIBIT 4–2F   Independent Variable Data, 1965–1972

Year	Population Age 20–34 (000s)	Total Private Housing Starts (000s)	Annual Average Consumer Price Index Refrig- erators (1957– 59 = 100)	Disposable Personal Income (annual rate, $ billions)	Change in Disposable Personal Income
1965	34,750	1,472	80.4	473.2	
1966	34,900	1,165	80.0	511.9	38.7
1967	35,953	1,292	79.4	546.3	34.4
1968	37,612	1,508	80.1	591.0	44.7
1969	38,906	1,467	81.5	634.4	43.4
1970	41,278	1,434	83.1	691.7	57.3
1971	44,012	2,052	85.1	746.0	44.3
1972	45,572	2,357	85.1	797.0	51.0

EXHIBIT 4–2G   Estimated Replacement Demand and Actual Sales, 1965–1971 (000 units)

Year	Estimated Replacement Demand*	Refrigerator Sales
1965	2,879	4,678
1966	2,984	4,685
1967	3,097	4,576
1968	3,198	5,023
1969	3,287	5,246
1970	3,366	5,099
1971	3,438	5,551

*From extrapolation Weibull distribution.

in the estimating equation reported above. Refrigerator shipments for 1968 were projected as the sum of these two components. This 1968 shipment estimate became an input in estimating the 1969 replacement demand. Exhibit 4–2E shows these projected demands for the 10-year period through 1979.

Questions

1. Exhibit 4–2F gives some additional values of the independent variables used in the new-owner demand equation. Substitute these into the equation and make forecasts of new-owner demand for these years.

2. Critically appraise the economic significance of the statistical results reported herein.

3. Exhibit 4–2G indicates a graphic extrapolation of the replacement demand and the actual data for refrigerator sales for the years indicated. Compare

the forecasts you obtained in Question 1 with actual demand and appraise the results. How would you attempt to do better if the results were not "good"?

CASE 4–3
Problems in Demand Analysis for Industry

1. When the Hudson and Manhattan Railroad company (which operates under the Hudson from New Jersey to Manhattan) raised its fare from 10 cents to 15 cents, passengers carried dropped off 15 percent in the first two days. The Lackawanna and Erie ferries, which offered free transportation to their commuting passengers (who constitute a large percentage of normal H–M traffic), had standing room only during rush hours.

   a. Was the demand indicated to be elastic or inelastic?

   b. Would you expect the elasticity to prove less or greater after a few days or weeks? After a year or two?

2. Beginning in 1973, the Organization of Petroleum Exporting Countries (OPEC) raised oil prices drastically. Consumption fell off in Western Europe, Japan, and the United States even though it had previously been in a sharp upward trend.

   What do you believe was the general relationship between "long-run elasticity of demand" and "short-run elasticity"? In the United States what were some long-run reactions to the OPEC price increases?

3. As a result of an increase in the price of coffee from $1.80 to $2.20 per pound, the sales of tea increased from 500,000 pounds per week to 600,000 pounds. What is the cross elasticity of demand? What important variable is assumed not to change, although in fact it would probably not remain constant?

4. If two linear demand curves intersect on a chart, with scales being the same for both, can they have the same price elasticity at the point of intersection? Explain.

5. Sales and prices of butter and oleomargarine in 1950 and 1960 were as follows:

	Butter		Margarine	
	Price per Pound (cents)	Per Capita Consumption (pounds)	Price per Pound (cents)	Per Capita Consumption (pounds)
1950	72.9	10.7	30.8	6.1
1960	83.0	5.5	28.4	10.8

What caution is suggested by the data if one wishes to derive a demand curve for a good with a very close substitute?

6. "An increase in demand means a higher price. A higher price leads to a decreased demand. An increased demand, therefore, is equivalent to a decreased demand." Comment.

7. If the quantity demanded of a product rose from 80,000 to 100,000 when the price of the product fell from $50 to $40, what was the arc elasticity of demand?

8. If a demand curve shifts to the right so that the measurement along the abscissa is twice as large as it formerly was at a price of $10, and this is due to a 50 percent increase in income, what is the income elasticity of demand?

9. From 1946 to 1977, total sales of chickens fell from 2,317,984,000 pounds to 1,099,561,000 pounds per year while price per pound fell from 27.6 cents to 12.1 cents. Broilers (young chickens of heavy breeds) increased in annual sales from 883,855,000 pounds to 12,992,359,000 pounds in the same period and price per pound fell from 32.7 cents to 23.6 cents. Since prices of chickens fell relative to those of broilers was this a contradiction of the "law of demand"? Why or why not?

CASE 4–4
The Demand for California and Arizona Lemons

California and Arizona produce virtually all of the lemons that are sold in the United States by American growers. Roughly half are sold fresh, and half are further processed. Arizona lemons are processed to a somewhat greater extent than are California lemons.

Exhibit 4–4A shows lemon production for the two states combined for 13 seasons from 1969–70 to 1981–2 (column 1). It also includes the average price per box (column 2), and the adjusted price per box (column 3) which was obtained by deflating with the implicit price deflator for GNP (1972 = 100) in column 4.

The production data clearly suggested that the supply shifted with weather conditions from year to year and had tended to expand over the long run, probably through more extensive plantings.

The identification problem here was to determine whether demand could best be approximated by a single price-quantity relationship, or whether a clear pattern of shifting demand over the period occurred. Drawing a scatter diagram of actual prices and quantity produced suggests that significant shifting has taken place (see Question 1). Economic demand analysis, however, stresses the importance of *relative* prices. In the period 1969–80, the price level more than doubled. To adjust for this the prices were expressed in 1972 constant dollars by dividing by an index of

EXHIBIT 4–4A   Production and Prices of Lemons 1969–1970 to 1981–1982.

	(1) Production (000s boxes)	(2) Price per Box	(3) P* (2)/0.01(4)	(4) GNP Deflator (1972 = 100)
1969–70	15,210	$4.85	$5.306	91.45
1970–71	16,450	4.98	5.188	96.0
1971–72	16,680	4.81	4.810	100.0
1972–73	22,200	4.38	4.140	105.75
1973–74	17,800	6.17	5.365	115.1
1974–75	29,400	3.85	3.060	125.8
1975–76	17,600	5.80	4.384	132.3
1976–77	25,600	( )	2.455	140.05
1977–78	26,100	( )	2.860	150.4
1978–79	19,600	( )	4.218	163.4
1979–80	20,800	8.09	4.530	178.6
1980–81	31,300	4.82	2.464	195.6
1981–82	24,800	5.29	2.546	207.4

Note: The values of the price index in column 4 are for the second of the two-crop years, for example, 1970 for 1969–70. Slight discrepancies among (2), (3), and (4) are due to rounding or index revisions.
   SOURCE: U.S. Department of Agriculture, *Citrus Fruits*, various dates, and U.S. Department of Commerce.

the price level. The index used was the implicit price deflator for the GNP. It is the broadest index and moves very closely with its personal consumption component. (It was preferred to the consumer price index [CPI] for this period because of the CPI's possible upward bias during this period reflecting its heavy weight on financing housing.)

Questions

1. Estimate the current dollar prices left blank in column 2 by taking the deflated 1972 prices (P^*) and using the price index to reverse the adjustment that has been made.

2. Draw a scatter diagram of the production and price data in columns 1 and 2. Use dated dots for your observations. Also plot the quantities and adjusted P^* on the diagram. Designate these dated observations with xs to distinguish them. Which set of data suggests a significant shifting of demand to the right over time, and which approximates a single demand curve, albeit with some shifting in either direction?

3. Fit a straight demand curve to the quantity and P^* data. It should go through the mean values ($Q = 21,800$ and $P^* = 3.95$). You should end up with a demand curve that approximates the equation ($Q = 38,525 - 4,235P^*$). If calculating capacity is available, you can confirm this by working out a simple regression model. You would also find out that the percent of variance explained by the model, R^2, is equal to 0.825, and that the standard errors of the intercept and slope are very small ($-2,404$ and -588, respectively) so that the model has high significance.

4. Estimate the elasticity of demand at the mean values using the information

in Question 3. How do increases and decreases in production affect the elasticity of demand under the straight-line assumption?

5. (Optional) Even after the addition of real incomes and population data, the demand curve in Question 3 is the best that can be obtained (subject to the assumption of a linear relationship and recognizing that the apparent rightward shift in demand reflects a change in absolute prices due to inflation). The values of other economic variables—real personal income, population (in 000s), per capita quantity (QPC), and real disposable income per capita (PCY)—are given below. Students with the computer capacity to do multi-regression analysis may wish to confirm that models that include additional variables add negligibly to explanatory power of the equation in Question 3. Suggested models are Q as a function of P*, population and real income, and QPC as a function of P* and PCY.

The student could attempt to get better results by altering the price index to reflect the average of two years for each crop season. For example, the implicit price deflator for 1969 was 86.8 and that for 1970 is given as 91.45; their mean is 89.1 and the calculated p^* would be $5.44 for 1969–70.

The student might also check to see whether the assumption of constant elasticities implied in $Q = aP^bY^c$ fit the data better. The linear regression would then be made on $\log Q = \log a + b \log P + c \log Y$, and b and c would be the constant elasticities of price and income respectively.

	(1) Population (000s)	(2) Income	(3) Quantity per Capita	(4) Income per Capita
1969	202,736	853.7		3,564
1970	205,089	876.9	0.07372	3,665
1971	207,692	900.2	0.07920	3,752
1972	209,924	951.4	0.07946	3,860
1973	211,939	1,007.2	0.10475	4,080
1974	213,898	1,003.7	0.08322	4,009
1975	215,981	1,009.7	0.13612	4,051
1976	218,086	1,056.2	0.08070	4,158
1977	220,289	1,105.2	0.11621	4,280
1978	222,629	1,162.2	0.11724	4,441
1979	225,106	1,201.0	0.08707	4,512
1980	227,654	1,209.6	0.09137	4,472
1981	229,872	1,248.6	0.13616	4,538
1982	232,050	1,254.6	0.10687	4,544

Notes: Income (2) is personal income in billions deflated by an implicit price deflator for personal consumption to get real income in 1972 dollars. Income per capita (4) is disposable income per capita in 1972 dollars as published in *Economic Report of the President*.

CASE 4–5
Demand for California and Florida Avocados

Virtually all domestic commercial production of avocados occurs in California and Florida, with California accounting for about 85 percent of the total.

EXHIBIT 4–5A

(1) Period	(2) Years	(3) Quantity	(4) Price	(5) P*
1 1964–65		36,740	402	529.64
2 1965–66		60,800	271	351.04
3 1966–67		80,300	204	256.93
4 1967–68		52,100	383	470.52
5 1968–69		73,700	289	341.61
6 1969–70		45,700	561	634.62
7 1970–71		85,800	357	385.95
8 1971–72		45,400	691	716.06
9 1972–73		89,300	499	499.00
10 1973–74		73,700	672	635.76
11 1974–75		127,400	450	386.93
12 1975–76		87,400	827	659.74
13 1976–77		141,100	567	430.85
14 1977–78		117,700	733	526.88
15 1978–79		152,400	488	327.33

Note: Column 5, *P**, represents prices in constant 1972 dollars. The deflation of column 4 was done with the implicit price deflator for personal consumption using the index value for the initial year of a growing season (1964 for 1964–65). Approximately identical results in the price-quantity relationships could have been achieved with either the consumer price index (with 1972 set as 100) or the implicit price deflator for the GNP.

SOURCE: U.S. Department of Agriculture, *Agricultural Statistics, 1979.*

Tons of avocados sold or utilized for the two states combined (column 3) and average price per ton (column 4) are shown for the seasons 1964–5 to 1978–9 in Exhibit 4–5A. You will note that with the exception of period 1, 1964–65, all of the odd periods have large crops and the even years small crops. This is a botanical quirk; no matter where or when the tree is planted, the tree yields abundantly only in odd seasons. The trend of supply to increase over time is thus interrupted with leftward shifts.

A plausible and simple hypothesis is that quantity demanded is a function of real price (column 5) and time (column 1). Time is a surrogate for regular changes in consumer tastes (such as more salads), population, and income. When Q is regressed on P^* and the period number (T), the following function is arrived at:

$$Q = 96360 - 147P^* + 7{,}284T$$

The R^2 is 0.97 (i.e., 97 percent of the variance from the mean is explained), and all of the parameters are highly significant. The student should be able to approximate these results without running a multiregression on the computer using methods suggested by the questions.

Questions

1. Compute the first differences in quantity (column 3) and real price (column 5). Plot them on a graph and fit a straight line. The slope should approximate

that of the equation (actually a simple regression gives a slope of −150). Hints: Put ΔQ on vertical and the ΔP on the horizontal axis to get the slope in equation form; graph your line of relationship through the mean point; to get means, divide the differences between year 15 and year 1 by 14.

2. Plot quantity against time. The shortcut method of simple regression is a bit cumbersome with 15 observations (it would yield an intercept of 32,725 and a slope of 6,485). Again a graphic fit would yield a tolerable approximation (perhaps closer to 7,224 of the demand function). Hint: As a guide to your graphing, have your trend line go through the mean point, quantity 84,600 at period (8).

3. Work out the price elasticity at the means for price (477) and period (8). Is this consistent with ability of the industry to usually at least maintain revenues in poor crop years?

4. (Optional) Economists often like to include real income in their models. The probability here is that it is so closely correlated with time that one cannot get a meaningful parameter if the period is included. One way to avoid this is to relate quantity per capita to real price and to real disposable income per capita (in 1972 dollars). The data is listed below:

Period	PCI	POP(000s)	Period	PCI	POP(000s)
1	$3,026	191,889	9	$3,860	208,846
2	3,171	194,303	10	4,083	210,410
3	3,290	196,560	11	4,013	211,901
4	3,389	198,712	12	4,055	213,559
5	3,493	200,706	13	4,161	215,152
6	3,564	202,677	14	4,266	216,880
7	3,665	204,878	15	4,409	218,717
8	3,752	207,053			

Your model will end up with a very high income elasticity (about 3). Why? Will it necessarily be correct?

5

Demand Analysis for the Firm

> Within the firm, individual bargains between the various cooperating
> factors of production are eliminated and for a market transaction is
> substituted an administrative decision.
> —*Ronald Coase*

As indicated above by a famous contemporary economist, Ronald Coase,
the firm is usually an efficient device for obtaining necessary cooperation
between factors of production. A family hiring the services of a baby sitter,
for example, can readily strike an individual bargain, but in more complicated situations, arriving at separate bargains involving a multitude of
owners of factors of production is usually not practicable.

The nature of the markets in which firms operate provides a primary
means of classifying them and analyzing the demand they face. Main
markets distinguished in economics are: competitive, monopolistic, and
oligopolistic, according to whether there are many, one, or a few sellers.
"Monopolistic competition" is often added as a category, but the analysis
draws mainly on the same principles that govern competitive and monopolistic behavior. The analysis of monopolistic competition, originated by
Edward H. Chamberlin in the 1930s does, however, provide insights into
business behavior that have enriched the field of business economics.[1]

DEMAND FACING A MONOPOLIST

Where the entire output of a commodity is accounted for by a single firm,
the demand curve facing the firm is identical to the market demand.
Monopoly demand curves consequently follow the "law of demand,"
sloping downward to the right.

In analyzing a monopolist's behavior, it is useful to employ the concept of "marginal revenue," which is the *additional* revenue secured by a
seller from the sale of an additional unit of product. (Strictly, the unit

---

[1]See Edward H. Chamberlin, *The Theory of Monopolistic Competition* (Cambridge,
Mass.: Harvard University Press, 1948).

FIGURE 5-1   Computation of Marginal Revenue

(1) Price of Product (per bushel)	(2) Quantity Demanded (millions of bushels per month)	(3) Value ($ millions)	(4) Change in Quantity (millions of bushels)	(5) Change in Total Revenue ($ millions)	(6) (col. 5 ÷ col. 4) Marginal Revenue (per bushel)
$4.00	50	200	10	$20	$2
3.50	60	210	10	10	1
3.00	70	210	10	0	0
2.50	80	200	10	−10	−1
2.00	90	180	10	−20	−2
1.50	100	150	10	−30	−3
1.00	110	110	10	−40	−4

should again be infinitesimally small.[2]) If there were only one producer of a hypothetical agricultural product—an unrealistic assumption but one that is no longer fanciful since farmers may act somewhat in concert through federal farm programs and by means of private marketing agreements—the demand schedule for the producer might resemble that of Figure 5–1, columns 1 and 2.[3]

Marginal revenue is shown in column 6; it is found by taking the difference between successive total revenues and dividing these by the differences between successive quantities demanded. Some economists prefer to show marginal revenue data *between* rows.

In order to get the change in quantity and in total revenue shown for the top row, it is necessary to assume that a quantity of 40 million bushels would have been demanded at a price of $4.50. This would have yielded a total revenue of $180 million; the difference between this amount and $200 million is the $20 million that is shown. Division of $20 million by the quantity increases of 10 million bushels sold added $2 per bushel to the seller's total revenue. In rows 4 through 7 marginal revenue is negative, showing that additional sales actually reduce total income because of the lower prices necessary to induce these sales.

It is clear that a profit-seeking monopolist would not sell any units which, through their depressing influences on price, would reduce total revenue. That is, monopolists will not knowingly sell in the region of negative marginal revenue. They set their price at $3.25 or higher. (The

[2]For those who like to think in terms of calculus, marginal revenue is the first derivative of total revenue with respect to quantity, that is, the rate of change of total revenue as quantity sold changes.

[3]On the basis of federal and some state laws, growers of certain agricultural products may draw up an agreement to limit supply and assign marketing quotas. Jack Hirshleifer, *Price Theory and Applications*, 2nd ed. (Englewood Cliffs, N.J.: Prentice-Hall, 1980), p. 358 shows the effects of such orders on some fruits and nuts produced in California and Oregon.

FIGURE 5–2   Price Exceeds Marginal Revenue under Monopoly

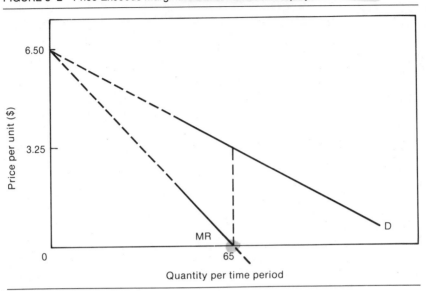

exact optimum cannot be defined until cost is brought into the picture, as will be done in a later chapter.) Monopolists should sell in the region where demand is of unitary elasticity or higher, rather than where demand is inelastic. Although total revenue would be the same at quantities of 50 million and 80 million bushels, for example, the cost of producing the smaller amount would obviously be less.

A tabular representation such as that in Figure 5–1 is easy to understand. However, it leaves questions such as "what are sales at prices other than those shown at 50-cent intervals?" The beauty of the demand curve in Figure 5–2 is that it shows prices and quantities that vary continuously, hitting all values rather than a finite few. This also permits an accurate showing of marginal revenue in relation to demand. If the linear demand curve is extended to reach the vertical axis, marginal revenue starts at the same point, then slopes downward at twice the rate of the demand curve. Where MR = 0, demand for that quantity is of unitary elasticity. Note that MR = 0 at the midpoint of the interval, 60–70 on Figure 5–1. For smaller quantities, demand is elastic; for larger quantities, it is inelastic. (These elasticities may be checked by using the geometric test of Figure 4–2.)

SOME QUALIFICATIONS

The demand curves that have been used so far show simplified "static" relationships that are especially useful in the theory of price determination. While they are useful tools for the business executive, it is important to keep in mind some complicating qualifications.

First, a reduction in price may temporarily reduce sales rather than increase them, since buyers may be led to expect further price cuts. This is a "dynamic" consideration that is neglected in the static theory of demand. Similarly, a price cut may "spoil the market" so that return to a higher price previously charged may not be feasible. Buyers are frequently more sensitive to changes in price than to the absolute level of price.

Second, even when some buyers immediately begin to buy more in response to a price cut, other buyers may be slower in changing their buying habits so that a considerable period of time may elapse before the full effect of the price change works itself out.[4]

Third, the demand and marginal revenue curves that have been drawn assume that all buyers are charged the same price. Actually, it may be possible to sell additional units by reducing price only to a new group of buyers, or only on additional sales to existing customers. The practice of price discrimination will be examined in some detail in a separate chapter.

Fourth, although it is theoretically irrational for a monopolist to sell in the region of inelastic demand—since he can gain revenue by raising price—he may still find it expedient to do so. By charging a less-than-optimum price, he may be able to discourage would-be competitors, build up consumer goodwill for the long run, and perhaps reduce the likelihood of prosecution under the federal antitrust laws if he is selling in interstate commerce.

DEMAND FACING PURE COMPETITOR

Economists define "perfect" or "pure" competition as a situation in which there are so many sellers of a particular commodity that none can individually affect the price. In the absence of governmental interference, many agricultural commodities are produced under such conditions. Even today, truck-garden vegetables, poultry, eggs, and fish, for example, are often turned out by perfectly competitive firms.

Under pure competition the demand curve for the produce of the individual firm is simply a horizontal line drawn at the price determined in the market. That is to say, market price is determined by overall supply and demand, and the individual firm can sell as much as it wishes at this price. It cannot charge more than the market price without losing all of its customers (who are assumed to be both rational and mobile) and need not, of course, accept less than the prevailing price.

The demand for the product of a purely competitive firm is represented in Figure 5–3. Such a horizontal line is infinitely elastic along its

---

[4]If consumers respond slowly to a cut in price, it is possible that revenue will drop for a time even if demand is elastic over a longer time span. See John M. Scheidell, *Advertising, Prices, and Consumer Demand* (Washington, D.C.: American Enterprise Institute for Public Policy Research, 1978), p.10.

FIGURE 5–3 Infinitely Elastic Demand Faces Perfectly Competitive Firm

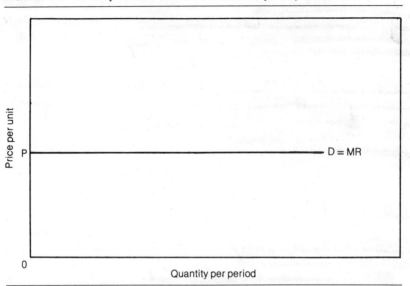

entire range. The firm has no control over price and can be designated as a "price taker" rather than as a "price maker." (The latter term is appropriate for a monopolistic firm.) Marginal revenue is equal to price for the perfectly competitive firm, since it is not necessary to lower price in order to sell additional units.

PURE COMPETITION IS UNCOMMON

The case of pure competition is, in practice, much less common than that of monopoly, when the latter term is used to cover all situations in which the demand facing the individual firm is downsloping rather than horizontal. Most firms have some power to fix prices, within limits, and hence are not fully competitive with others. The amount of this price-making power may be great—for example, in the case of a city-owned electric utility system where the rates set by the municipal authorities may be subject to no check by a regulatory commission. Or the amount of price–making power may be severely limited by the existence of close substitutes, as in the case of a seller of a particular brand of bath towel or tuna fish.

The "unrealism" of assuming pure competition for purposes of analysis should not lead one to believe that the economist's model of competition is unimportant. Many firms with a small degree of monopoly power can best be analyzed "as if" they are perfectly competitive. This is because the pure competition model incorporates and emphasizes important forces that will influence their business. Such quasi-purely competitive firms will act as "price takers," that is, as if their demand curves were horizontal.

In order to operate under conditions of perfect competition, a firm must sell an unbranded commodity (such as sweet corn) and must not be significantly separated spatially from other sellers of the same good. Many firms have a degree of locational monopoly due to their greater convenience to buyers. Vendors of refreshments at a football game, for example, have a separateness from other sellers which permits them to charge higher prices than those on the outside. Much advertising is designed simply to imprint brand names on the public mind, in order to lessen the severity of competition from similar or even identical goods.

DEMAND UNDER OLIGOPOLY

The demand curves that have been drawn so far were necessarily based on the assumption of *ceteris paribus*—that is, all other factors that would affect the quantity demanded were held constant. These include prices of competing products, incomes and their distribution, and consumers' tastes. Where there are only a few sellers of a particular commodity, however, this assumption is not useful. Instead, it must be recognized that each seller will carefully watch the action of close competitors and frequently will react to any change that they make in price, quality, or selling effort. This is called an "oligopolistic" situation—the case of a few sellers. It is an extremely common real-world situation. Oligopolistic firms may turn out identical homogenous products (e.g., brass tubing, aluminum sheet, or copper wire); or they may sell closely related but somewhat dissimilar goods (e.g., trucks, airplanes, typewriters, or soap powder). They may sell in national or international markets or only in local markets (e.g., if two or three brickyards serve an area).

A single demand curve cannot depict the price-quantity relationship faced by a firm for a commodity sold oligopolistically. If price is changed, the response of sales depends heavily on the actions that close rivals are induced to take. If, for example, price is lowered by one firm but rivals choose to maintain their prices and quality unchanged, the amount that buyers will purchase from the price cutter is likely to expand quite sharply. If rivals match a price cut, sales of the first price cutter are likely to increase only moderately, since others will share in the larger total sales volume. If rivals more than meet a price cut, the physical volume sold by the first price cutter may even fall off.

A general picture of the demand situation under differentiated oligopoly can be shown graphically.[5] Such a chart is suggestive only, since it cannot show the results of all of the possible combinations of action

---

[5]If a good is homogeneous and buyers are fully informed, sales would theoretically drop to zero if price were increased and rivals did not follow. Also, for a price cut that was not followed the demand curve for the price cutter would become perfectly elastic.

FIGURE 5–4   Oligopoly Demand Curves—Sales Depend on Rivals' Reactions

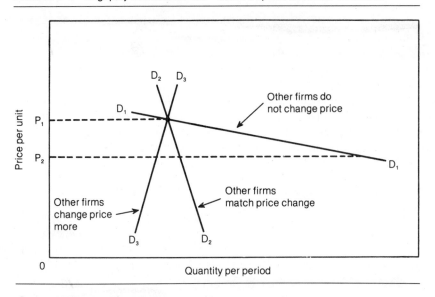

and reaction on the part of oligopolistic rivals. Figure 5–4 pertains to an individual firm that is assumed, first, to be charging price OP_1. If the firm then lowers its price to OP_2 and its rivals do not change their prices, the physical sales of the price cutter may expand sharply, as indicated by curve D_1. (Since this curve is elastic between prices OP_1 and OP_2, total revenue received by the firm will rise.) If, instead, rival firms match the price cut, the volume of sales may expand only moderately, as indicated by D_2. (Since this curve, as drawn, is inelastic between prices OP_1 and OP_2, the dollar volume of sales would be down, despite the rise in physical volume.) It is even possible that the firm under consideration will encounter a positively sloping demand curve such as D_3. This is only likely if rivals more than match the first firm's price cut.

Above the original price OP_1 the demand curves can be interpreted in a similar way. If our firm raises its price and its close rivals do not do so, sales may fall off sharply, as suggested by curve D_1. If the other sellers match the price increase, sales may fall off only moderately, as along D_2. If rivals should decide to raise their prices more than the first firm, that firm may enjoy higher physical and dollar sales, as indicated by D_3. A well–known construction, the "kinked oligopoly demand curve" is based on the assumption that rivals will match a price cut in order to protect their shares of the market but will not match a price increase. This means that D_2 becomes the demand curve below price P_1, while D_1 becomes the demand curve above that price. Like other models of oligopolistic behavior, this reaction cannot be depended upon by the analyst.

It is clear that there are so many possible combinations of oligopolistic price behavior (to say nothing of changes in such variables as quality, amount of advertising, premiums, credit terms, etc.) that demand curves for the individual firm are of limited usefulness. The same is not true of *market* demand curves for oligopolistic industries, however, and considerable effort has been expended in deriving statistical demand curves for such commodities as steel, automobiles, and cigarettes, where the number of producers is relatively small.

The consequences of the complex nature of demand under oligopoly will be examined in some detail in subsequent chapters. It is readily apparent, though, that a great many different results may ensue from a price change. The uncertainties inherent in the situation are conducive to the maintenance of stable prices through overt or tacit agreements between sellers. When such agreements break down, however, price wars may follow, especially when excess capacity exists.

MONOPOLY AS LIMITING CASE OF OLIGOPOLY

An insight to the relationship between oligopoly and monopoly can be gained by considering curves D_1 and D_2 of Figures 5–4. As drawn, it matters a great deal whether rivals match or do not match a price change by the firm in question, that is, D_1 and D_2 diverge sharply. To the oligopolist with a very strong market position, the reactions of rivals will be a much less significant matter, that is, D_1 and D_2 will not diverge greatly. Monopoly can usefully be considered to be a limiting case of oligopoly where D_1 and D_2 become coincident. That is, monopolists can determine their price without regard to rivals' reactions because they have no rivals in the market. In a near-monopoly situation, rivals' reactions may be disregarded because they have only a small effect on sales of the strong firm because its D_1 and D_2 curves are nearly coincident.

MARKET SHARE

Many business firms are not only concerned with the total demand for their product but are also concerned with their relative position. In fact, some are said to be more concerned with market share than with profits.[6] Market share is simply the percentage one firm's sales are of the total market.

Market share elasticity may be defined as the responsiveness of the market share of a firm to changes in price.

$$\text{Elasticity of market share} = \frac{\text{Percent change in market share of A}}{\text{Percent change in price of A}}$$

[6]William J. Baumol, *Business Behavior, Value and Growth* (New York: Macmillan, 1948).

FIGURE 5–5 Price Differentials versus Market Share
Changes

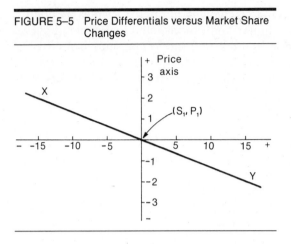

This concept can also be related to economists' measure of cross elasticity by placing the percent change of a close rival's price in the denominator.

A useful graphic device to illustrate market share response to price changes is given in Figure 5–5. In this diagram, P_1 represents either a price differential of zero, or some customary differential such as the usual 2-cent differential between major and independent brands of gasoline which results in no change in market share. S_1 represents the firm's usual market share if prices and other factors remain the same. The vertical axis, therefore, shows deviations from zero or from the customary differential, while the horizontal axis shows the resulting changes in market share. Data for such curves may be available from historical records of a firm and if used with care may provide some very useful insights into pricing problems. Similar concepts of market share elasticity can also be extended to such demand-influencing variables as promotion, with the percent change in advertising appearing in the denominator.

DUOPOLY

The indeterminate nature of demand facing the individual seller under oligopoly was first shown for the case of duopoly (two sellers) by the brilliant French mathematician and economist Augustin Cournot in 1838.[7] He analyzed the behavior of two neighbors each of whom owned an identical spring with uniquely beneficial mineral water. Marginal cost of providing the water was assumed to be zero, or at least negligible.

Cournot saw that it was impossible to specify the demand curve facing either seller without making some uniform assumption regarding the reaction of each to the actions of the other. He made the simple (though

---

[7] Augustin Cournot, *Researches into the Mathematical Principles of Wealth* (New York: Macmillan, 1929), chap 7.

FIGURE 5–6   Cournot's Duopoly Solution

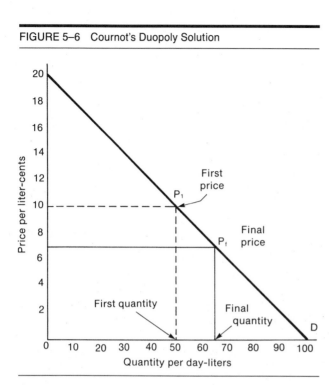

Quantity per day-liters

improbable) assumption that each owner would believe that the sales of the other would remain at the latest level observed.

Total demand for the water was represented by a curve such as D in Figure 5–6. (Cournot used a nonlinear demand curve; it is drawn as a straight line and given numbers along the scales for the sake of simplicity.)

If seller A was ready for business one day sooner than B, A would set price at 10 cents per liter and sell 50 liters the first day. This would be a revenue-maximizing monopolistic action. Elasticity of demand would be unitary at this initial price. Seller B would enter the market the next day and would believe (following Cournot's basic assumption) that A would continue to sell 50 liters per day. In effect, B would consider the vertical axis relevant to his own action to be the dashed vertical line above the 50-liter quantity. Regarding only the portion of the demand curve to the right of the dashed vertical line as available to him, B would set price at 5 cents per liter and sell 25 liters, Seller A would have to meet this price.

Next, seller A would be aware of the competitor and would expect B to continue to sell 25 liters per day. In effect this moves the hypothetical vertical axis to a quantity of 25 from A's viewpoint, and A will seek a new revenue-maximizing action. This will be to sell half the amount between 25 and 100, namely, 37½ units. Seeing this cutback in sales by A, seller B would find it desirable to increase his sales to 31¼ units. This will cause a slight diminution in A's sales, and B will increase sales a bit more.

Finally they will reach an equilibrium with each producing 33⅓ units, a total of 66⅔ liters sold at a price of 6⅔ cents per liter.[8]

Cournot observed that if the two owners came to an understanding, they would both be better off by moving to the monopoly price of 10 cents per liter and sharing the sales equally. He saw the possibility that the monopoly solution might be difficult to maintain stating: "In other words, this condition is not one of stable equilibrium; and, although the most favorable for both producers, it can only be maintained by means of a formal engagement; for in the moral sphere men cannot be supposed to be free from error and lack of forethought any more than in the physical world bodies can be considered perfectly rigid, or supports perfectly solid, etc."[9]

Although other duopoly models have been developed since the time of Cournot, all encounter the same types of problems. None can be considered to be *the* theory of duopoly. When sellers are more numerous than two, it is even more difficult to predict how price and output will be determined.

GAME THEORY APPROACH

An interesting mathematical development in relatively recent years by John von Neumann, known as the theory of games, is helpful in determining the outcome in certain conflict situations, including some that are found in oligopoly.[10]

The essential elements are two parties in conflict who can exert some control over the situation, each by devising a strategy of behavior. A game is called *zero-sum* when the gain by one party is wholly at the expense of the other, i.e., together their gain is zero. Zero-sum games are much simpler than the nonzero-sum variety, and the mathematics have been developed much more fully. Fortunately, it is possible to gain some knowledge of zero-sum games without making calculations more difficult than adding and subtracting.

The first step is to prepare a payoff matrix that shows the gain or loss of each player under various combinations of moves. Calling one player "North" and the other "West," suppose they decide to toss quarters, with West being required to match in order to win. The matrix, with positive numbers indicating payment by North to West and negative numbers payment by West to North, is shown in Figure 5–7.

---

[8]The equation of the market demand curve in Figure 5–6 is $Q = 100 - 5P$. From this equation the market price at which any total quantity will sell, or the total quantity that can be sold at any price, is readily obtained. At the final position, 66⅔ $= 100 - 5P$, and $P = 6⅔$.

[9]Cournot, *Researches into the Mathematical Principles of Wealth*, p. 83.

[10]The theory is set forth in most complete form in John von Neumann and Oskar Morgenstern, *Theory of Games and Economic Behavior* (Princeton: Princeton University Press, 1944). An application of game theory to competition and oligopoly is in Martin Shubik, *Strategy and Market Structure* (New York: John Wiley & Sons, 1959).

FIGURE 5-7

	North tosses	
	Head	Tail
West tosses · Head	+25¢	−25¢
West tosses · Tail	−25¢	+25¢

FIGURE 5–8

	North		
	A	B	Row minimum
West · A	+1	+2	+1
West · B	+4	+3	+3
Column maximum	+4	+3	

This is not a game of strategy because the players cannot exert control on the situation (especially if both toss simultaneously). If, instead, the players could exert control by playing either A or B and the payoff matrix (not related to any particular game) were as shown in Figure 5–8, the game would have a "saddle point."

The game of Figure 5–8 is very unfair to North since he must pay West no matter what combinations of plays are made. It is assumed that both players know the nature of the matrix so West will always play B where the gain is bound to be greater than in the first row. North will never play · A since he would lose 4. Both will always play B, and the *value of the game* is +3, which is called the *saddle value*. To discover whether a game has a saddle point it is only necessary to list the maximum figures in each column (these are +4 and +3) and the minimum figures in each row (these are +1 and +3). The game has a saddle point if the smaller of the column maxima equals the larger of the row minima. There is a saddle point since +3 fills this condition.

BUSINESS SITUATION WITH A SADDLE POINT

The theory of games seems to hold more promise of being useful in guiding executive decisions in repetitive situations such as pricing and advertising that in one-time decisions. It may, however, logically be applied to the latter type of decision also. Suppose that there are two large—but not

FIGURE 5–9 The Motel Game

		North installs				
		TV	Pool	Both	Neither	Row minima
West installs	TV	+2	−10	−20	+10	−20
	Pool	+10	+4	−10	+15	−10
	Both	+15	+5	+6	+20	+5
	Neither	−5	−10	−15	0	−15
Column maxima		+15	+5	+6	+20	

entirely modern—motels so located between a mountain range on one side and a national park on the other that while they are in vigorous competition with one another, they are well isolated from other accommodations for motorists. (This assumption makes a zero-sum game solution quite plausible, since the gains made by each will be mainly at the expense of the other.) The motels will again be named North and West.

Aware of the luxury demanded by American motorists, both motel owners begin to ponder the desirability of installing free television in all rooms and/or building a swimming pool on the premises in order to take business away from the rival firm. By chance, both hire the same management consultant, who, after considerable study, furnishes each manager with estimated payoffs from various combinations of actions. Payoffs are estimated increases and decreases of weekly net profits, positive figures being profit gains by West and negative figures being profit gains by North. Each entrepreneur learns that the other has access to the same payoff information, and each regards the other as an astute businessperson.

It will be noted in Figure 5–9 that the installation of TV, a swimming pool, or both is somewhat more favorable to West than to North. This may be because North's location is somewhat lower and shadier than West's location, which will force North to erect higher antennas and which will make swimming somewhat less attractive to guests. Nevertheless, it will not pay North to abstain entirely from these improvements. The matrix has a saddle point at "install both" for West and "install pool" for North.[11] North's weekly loss of net profits (after costs, including the new maintenance, repair, and depreciation) will be $5, because of the new investment by the two motels. However, if West installed both TV and a pool while his rival did nothing, he could deprive North of an estimated $20 a week in net profits.

---

[11]The saddle value is $5 because this figure is both the maximum of the row minima and the minimum of the column maxima.

FIGURE 5–10   A Loss-Leader Game

North uses as loss leader

		Butter	Coffee	Row minima
West uses as loss leader	Butter	0	+100	0
	Coffee	+150	−50	−50
	Column maxima	+150	+100	

BUSINESS SITUATION WITHOUT A SADDLE POINT

In the motel game just described the situation called for a one time investment by each firm. More interesting applications of game theory involve repetitive moves carried out according to a computed mixed strategy.

Suppose that two firms, which we shall again call North and West, are grocery stores located in the same area but are well isolated from other sellers. This makes them close rivals who watch each other's prices and selling activities warily. Every Thursday evening, each entrepreneur turns over his advertising copy to the local newspaper; included in the advertised items is a loss leader designed to attract customers to his store and away from the rival store. Experience has shown, we shall assume, that coffee and butter are the most satisfactory loss leaders; each Thursday, each manager chooses one of these to be the special bargain during the Friday-Saturday period. Suppose further that historical experience has taught each seller that the gains and losses from various possible actions are as shown in Figure 5–10, positive payoffs being gains in total dollar sales by West and losses of sales by North, and negative payoffs being gains in dollar sales by North at the expense of his rival, West.[12]

It is apparent that the whole practice of using loss leaders is more favorable to West than to North. However, experience has shown North that it is not wise to run no loss leader at all, in view of West's consistent policy of using leaders.[13] A glance at the row minima and column maxima shows that there is no saddle point. It is clear that it would not be desirable for West to use butter each week as the loss leader because North

---

[12]This assumption makes it a zero-sum game. Actually, it is quite possible that total sales will be somewhat increased by the loss leaders for the two stores taken together and that the gain of one will not be entirely at the expense of the other. If the assumption is close to the truth, however, the game theory solution may be of practical utility.

[13]The strategy on North's part of using either butter or coffee as a leader may be said to be "dominant" over a strategy on his part of using no leader at all. If a third column labeled "No Leader" were added to the matrix, the payoffs might be, for example, +80 and +200 in rows 1 and 2, respectively. This strategy is clearly so inferior from North's viewpoint that it should never be followed. Therefore, it can be eliminated from the matrix.

would do the same and no sales advantage would accrue to West. It would be undesirable for West to use coffee as the leader each week because North would also do so and would take $50 in sales away from West. Similarly, it would be foolish for North to settle on a policy of using butter each week as the leader because West would use coffee as the leader and gain $150 in sales at North's expense. It can similarly be seen that a constant strategy of using coffee as the leader would be unwise for North. Clearly, a mixture of strategies by each grocer is called for, with the loss-leader special for each week being kept a secret until it is too late for the rival firm to change its advertising copy in the newspaper.

The optimal mixture of the two alternative actions can be found by a simple process. To obtain North's best mixture, subtract each figure in row 2 from the figure just above it. This gives -150 and $+150$. Since these are equal in absolute value, this means that North should use each loss leader half the time. In order not to "tip his hand" by falling into some sort of routine, North could toss a coin once a week, perhaps using butter as the leader whenever heads turns up and coffee when tails turns up.

To obtain West's optimal mixture, subtract each figure in column 2 from the figure just to the left. This gives -100 and $+200$. Disregarding signs, these numbers apply to the *opposite row*. That is, 200 pertains to the use of butter and 100 to coffee. This means that West should use butter as a loss leader twice as often as he uses coffee, again using a chance device each week. (For example, two yellow marbles and one brown marble of equal size and texture can be kept in a jar that is shaken vigorously and one marble withdrawn. A yellow marble would call for the use of butter and the brown one for the use of coffee as the loss leader.) Why the use of a chance device? In the words of von Neumann and Morgenstern: "Ignorance is obviously a very good safeguard against disclosing information directly or indirectly."

The value of the loss-leader "game" can be calculated by using the best mixture of either seller against the results of either alternative strategy of the other. The average payoff according to the four methods of calculation is as follows:

$$1. \quad \frac{1(0) + 1(+100)}{2} = +50$$

$$2. \quad \frac{1(+150) + 1(-50)}{2} = +50$$

$$3. \quad \frac{2(0) + 1(+150)}{3} = +50$$

$$4. \quad \frac{2(+100) + 1(-50)}{3} = +50$$

Since the value of the game is positive, it is "unfair" to North and favorable to West. West should continue to use loss leaders, and this forces

North to do so also. North should try to convince West that it would be better to discontinue these special bargains and even offer West some valuable consideration if he will discontinue using loss leaders (so long as this consideration is not more damaging to his net profits than the loss of $50 a week in sales.) Another possibility is that North will hire a group of people to buy only the loss leader from West for a period of time, hoping to discourage the loss-leader practice. (This strategy would change the payoff matrix, and North would hope to make West believe the change to be permanent.)

SOME OTHER POSSIBLE APPLICATIONS

It has been suggested by other writers that two firms that share a market where the demand is more or less fixed might use game theory in deciding whether to use radio, television, or printed advertising. Depending on the calculated gains and losses, they may arrive at a saddle-point solution where they stick to one medium each (not necessarily the same one) or follow a mixed strategy.[14] The latter bears a resemblance to the loss-leader game which has been described. The saddle-point situation is similar to the motel game of this chapter.

The U.S. Army has made use of game theory in the assignment of personnel. The payoff matrix is derived from evaluation of the suitability of various persons in various jobs. Presumably an amateur radio operator will not end up as an army cook if the evaluations make sense.

Nonzero-sum games, where the gains of one player are not wholly at the expense of the other player, are potentially more useful. Unfortunately, the theory has not been fully worked out. It is, however, possible to set up some simplified models that can be useful in solving business problems. For example, a firm bidding on government contracts and possessing some knowledge of its competitors may be able to randomize its bids in such a way as to maximize its probability of winning only as many contracts as it has capacity to fulfill. Price wars, where survival depends heavily on the asset position of participants, expected demand, and other economic data have been analyzed as nonzero-sum games.

Checkerboard land buying, which may be just within the financial capability of a firm wishing to acquire a large tract of land, has also been the subject of analysis. The danger is that competitors may buy up strategic strips for later sale at high prices. The company must design its checkerboard buying pattern in such a way as to make competitor's holdings as costly as possible. The game is likely to be more successful when competitive buyers are financially weak and are consequently unable to hold out for long.

---

[14]Martin Shubik, "The Uses of Game Theory in Management Science," *Management Science*, October 1955, p. 339. Some of the other examples of possible uses of game theory are taken from this article.

GENERAL OBSERVATIONS ON GAME THEORY AND BUSINESS

A main difficulty in applying game theory to business decisions is getting reasonably accurate estimates of payoffs under various conditions. These estimates need not be perfectly accurate, but if they err too greatly they may lead to incorrect actions. In these respects the estimates do not differ from calculations made to guide executives in nongame situations, for example, whether to build a new plant when it is not clear whether rivals will react. Any decision based on inadequate work by statisticians, accountants, engineers, and other experts is apt to be nonoptimal. Acquiring information is itself costly, however, so an excessive research effort is also nonoptimal. It is easy to say that research should be carried to the point where marginal gains equal marginal costs, but application of the principle is usually difficult.

Another problem is choosing the best payoff criterion. In business this is usually assumed to be net profits to the firm. Sometimes, however, maximization of short-term profits is incompatible with maximizing long-term profits. In the case of the loss-leader problem, payoffs were in terms of gains and losses of sales by the two stores. This tacitly assumes that profits are positively correlated with storewide sales. Otherwise sales do not constitute a rational payoff criterion—unless short-run sales are considered to be positively correlated with long-run profits through their power to mold consumers' buying habits.

According to J. C. C. McKinsey, "the most crying need" in game theory is the development of a more satisfactory theory of nonzero-sum games and games where the number of players exceeds two. Nevertheless, game theory in its present state has been characterized by McKinsey as an important "intellectual breakthrough."[15] As a minimum, game theory teaches the importance of specifying alternatives systematically along with possible reactions of adversary.

CASE 5–1
Market Shares in Soft Drinks*

Back in the 1940s when Crawford Johnson Jr. was a Coca-Cola bottler in Birmingham, Alabama, one of his biggest worries was watermellon. "At a

---

[15]J. C. C. McKinsey, *Introduction to the Theory of Games* (New York: McGraw-Hill, 1952), p. 358.

*SOURCE: Information from Bill Abrams and John Koten, "Soft Drink Companies Prime Their Weapons in Market Share Battle," *The Wall Street Journal,* April 26, 1979, with permission.

dime each watermelon cost the same as a Coke," recalls his son Crawford III, president of Coca-Cola Bottling Co., United. "My father hated watermelon."

Soda pop makers like Mr. Johnson don't fret much anymore about the price of watermelon. Soft drinks have long since passed the fruit in popularity, just as they edged past coffee in 1975 and milk in 1976.

Today the soft drink companies are primarily concerned about each other and in maintaining their shares of the large market. Heavy advertising, including singing commercials on TV, is a prime device.

Coca-Cola is expected in 1979 to resume heavy price cutting and force the soft drink industry into more intense price competition than it would like. "We've got to see what Coke and Seven-Up will do," says John Scully, president of Pepsico's domestic soft drink unit. "We'll react to protect our share."

Seven-Up—the third-ranking soft drink, with 7 percent of the market compared with Coca-Cola's 25 percent and Pepsi-Cola's 18 percent—is expected to double its ad spending to about $40 million. Philip Morris, Inc., which acquired the beverage maker in a takeover battle last year, has its first chance to see whether its $545 million investment will pay off.

Soft drink companies, including fourth-ranked Dr Pepper, have to be concerned not only about rivalry among themselves but also about competitive products being introduced by other large companies. General Foods produces Country Time canned lemonade and has the funds and marketing experience to become an important factor in the soft drink industry.

Another entry, introduced in East Coast markets last year and going national this year, is Sunkist Orange Soda, marketed by a joint venture between Sunkist Growers, the fruit-raising cooperative, and General Cinema Corp., soft drink bottler and movie theater operator. Sales of Sunkist Orange, according to a Sunkist spokesman, "are exceeding even our wildest expectations." It has already picked up more than 2 percent of the New York market.

Questions

1. On the basis of information given, describe how cross elasticity of demand between commodities can change over time.

2. What cross elasticities of demand between soft drinks and other goods probably have a negative sign?

3. Devise a measure of elasticity of market share that uses a close rival's advertising outlay rather than price change as a key variable. Be careful to indicate which variables are assumed to be constant.

4. From information in the case and from personal experience, describe how soft drink companies experiment in price changes and other devices before instituting more general actions that could prove to be costly if incorrect.

CASE 5–2
Women in Business*

Under the leadership of Dr. Juanita Kreps, former Secretary of Commerce of the United States, special attention is being directed toward the problems of women as entrepreneurs. Referring to available data she said, "They showed that in 1972 only 4.6 percent of all American businesses—approximately 400,000—were owned by women. Furthermore, these businesses generated less than one half of 1 percent of all revenues received by American businesses. The survey also revealed that most female-owned businesses were sole proprietorships, that they were highly concentrated, 71 percent in the retail and nonprofessional services trades, and that only 13 percent of them had paid employees. The typical female business entrepreneur according to the survey had fewer than five employees and grossed less than $54,000—this at a time when the average American firm had annual gross receipts of more than three quarters of a million dollars."

The House report made numerous recommendations related to women-owned business, including the following:

1. That the president issue a directive to all federal procuring departments and agencies that purchases from women-owned businesses are to be encouraged. The directive should require such procurement activities to maintain statistics on the award of contracts by the sex of the person owning the business.
2. Impose a uniform definition of "woman-owned business" that would take into account both legal control and responsibility for day-to-day business management.
3. That the Department of Commerce continue and expand its present commendable activities to assist women in business by attempting to locate more domestic and international markets for their products and services.
4. Conduct and publish a statistical study covering the year 1977 similar to "Women-owned Businesses, 1972."
5. That the Small Business Administration consult with the U.S. Civil Service Commission and mutually agree upon a specific plan of action with clearly identifiable goals for employing more women in high level management positions within the agency.
6. Increase its efforts to make more loans to women-owned businesses and to explore all possibilities for attracting investors to establish small business investment companies which will

---

*SOURCE: A Report of the Committee on Small Business, House of Representatives, 95th Congress, House Report No. 95–1830, chap. 16 (Washington, D.C.: U.S. Government Printing Office, January 2, 1979).

have as a predominant investment policy assisting the female entrepreneur.

7. That the Department of Commerce and the Small Business Administration enter into an interagency agreement that will result in coordinated activities to (a) obtain an adequate data base on women in business, (b) isolate and define specific problems besetting female and minority female business persons, and (c) enumerate and evaluate both short-term and long-term strategies needed to correct or lessen the effect of such problems.

8. Jointly promote, in cooperation with appropriate federal agencies and departments, local boards of education and business people, an educational program designed to expose women to business opportunities and to inform them of the requisite skills for the business world. This program should be made available to women in their early high school years in order that they may begin proper preparation for careers as business owners.

Questions

1. There is a great difference between ownership and control of American corporations. In general (or with the aid of statistical information), how do women fare in the ownership of American corporations? What are the primary reasons for this situation?

2. Has control of large corporations been closely correlated with stock ownership? Why or why not?

3. Obtain some recent data on enrollment of women in professional education and give your opinion on whether sufficiently rapid progress has been made by females.

4. What are the dangers of making business-oriented courses available to women "in their early high school years" as recommended in the House Report?

5. Consider the problem of compiling a directory of women-owned businesses in the United States and discuss briefly some of the definitional problems that are certain to be involved.

6. What are likely to be some problems in giving women-owned firms special consideration in securing federal loans and contracts?

CASE 5–3 _____
Chicago–Vancouver Route Controversy*

Before the Airline Deregulation Act of 1978, the Civil Aeronautics Board (CAB) was especially active in making decisions on an accumulation of

---

*SOURCE: *Civil Aeronautics Board Reports,* October 1977–January 1978, CAB Docket 29597, adopted August 8, 1977.

cases pertaining to rates and routes. One of the controversies related to the granting of first nonstop authority in the Vancouver–Chicago market. Both United and Northwest airlines had requested the right to fly nonstop between these cities.

United had the advantage of an already-established service between Chicago and Vancouver with a stop in Seattle. Northwest argued that the public would be better served if it were awarded the nonstop route between Vancouver and Chicago while United maintained only its one-stop service.

The CAB ruled in favor of permitting United to initiate nonstop service. It pointed out that the general policy was to lift restrictions on incumbent carriers in preference to adding new carriers to the market when traffic justifies additional service.

United would not be in a monopoly position in this market, according to the CAB, because vigorous competition from Air Canada, already flying the Chicago–Vancouver route, could be expected. Northwest argued that it would have a greater incentive to provide good nonstop service since any such patronage it could develop would be new business rather than a diversion from its own one-stop service (since it had none). The CAB admitted that Northwest might have the greater incentive to cultivate the nonstop market but that this might be at the expense of the Vancouver–Chicago market as a whole.

Northwest claimed that it had a more efficient operation in general and should be awarded the nonstop route in part because of this efficiency. The problem that the CAB faced in this regard is shown in their statement:

> We continue to agree that it is important to encourage and reward efficiency and that one promising way of doing so would be to use relative efficiency as one of the bases for deciding which carriers should be given particular route awards. Our staff is therefore systematically exploring possible ways of doing this. Meanwhile, however, we must reject Northwest's proposed application of this principle in this case. The most important reason is— we do not have at our disposal analytical tools refined enough to enable us to measure to our satisfaction the relative efficiency of the several carriers absent the effect of the varying governmentally imposed restrictions to which they are subject. Until exogenous factors of the latter kind can be reliably separated out, interfirm comparisons of costs will not provide a reliable measure of managerial efficiency or of how effectively a carrier would perform in a particular market for which it is competing.

The CAB order was approved by President Jimmy Carter on January 13, 1978.

Questions

1. What definite cost savings in Vancouver would United have that would not be available to Northwest?

2. Explain how the then-existing state of regulation would affect cost comparisons in such a way as to greatly diminish their usefulness to the CAB, as the agency claimed.

3. Since the Airline Deregulation Act of 1978 how does route selection occur? What are some advantages and disadvantages of the new situation?

4. Consult an airline, a travel agency, or other source to find whether United has "walked away" from the one-stop Chicago–Vancouver route, as Northwest predicted would happen after deregulation.

CASE 5–4
Hul Gul—An Application of Game Theory

A simple game—Hul Gul—reputedly played by children, affords practice in the application of the theory of games and may suggest business (or gambling) applications of game theory beyond those mentioned in the text.

The game of Hul Gul is played with beans or other small objects. In the simplest version, only two beans are used. One player holds his hands behind his back, then brings forth one fist in which he holds either one or two beans. The other player must attempt to guess the number of beans. If he does so correctly, he gets the beans (or a more valuable remuneration); otherwise, he pays an amount to the other player equal to the difference between what he guessed and the actual number held.

It is quite obvious that the bean holder (call him North) will wish to hold one bean more often than two beans, since if he holds only one, that is all he can lose; if he holds two, he may lose two. He cannot hold one bean each time, however, for his strategy would soon be figured out and he would lose one every time.

To find what proportion of the plays he should hold one bean, and what proportion two beans, in order to lose the smallest amount is a suitable task for the theory of games as suggested by the loss leader example in the text. Also the optimal strategy for the guesser (West) can be calculated.

Questions

1. Arrange gains and losses in matrix form, showing who pays how much to whom under the four possible circumstances. Denote payments by North to West with positive numbers and payments by West to North with negative numbers.

2. Show the row minima and column maxima of the matrix. Is there a saddle point?

3. Compute the optimum strategy for the holder and for the guesser.
4. If each player had a tiny model of the Pentagon building in his possession, how could he use the model and why would it be sensible action?
5. Find the value of the game.

CASE 5–5
Problems in Demand Analysis for the Firm

A. The western Range Company manufactures a microwave oven that has a large share of total sales of this appliance. The principal rival is AMA Range, Inc., although several smaller firms also sell in this oligopolistic market.

On April 1, 1985, AMA cut its wholesale price from $600 to $500 while Western Range and the smaller companies maintained their prices at $600 per oven. Monthly sales before and after the AMA price cut were as shown below.

Month and Year	Western Range 24M Sales	Price	AMA Corporation Sales	Price	Other Companies Sales	Price 3 mil
March 1985 ..	40,000	$600	20,000	$600	5,000	$600
April 1985 ...	35,000	600	28,000	500	4,000	600 2.4mil

21M   14   480x500 = 2.4mil

Questions   42,000 x 500 = 21,000

1. What was the elasticity of market share for the Western Range Company for the period covered by the data?
2. What factors should management of Western Range take into account in deciding whether to match AMA's price cut? Total Rev.
3. What actions appear to be useful for the small companies in the industry?

B. You are trying to measure the price elasticity of demand for Qwerts, a portable manual typewriter produced by a small independent, Qwerts, Inc. You find that in 1984, at a price of $85, 50,000 units were sold, and that in 1985, at a price of $80, 60,000 were sold. From these data you compute price elasticity. ⌐3⌐

However, you are certain that "other things" did not remain constant during the years in question, and you want to make some allowance for them in your analysis of elasticity. So you make a list of them:

a. Consumer income rose 15 percent.
b. Your competitors increased their prices 10 percent.

c. You received news from your sales force that for some reason, apparently independent of price or income, they were finding increased sales resistance to Qwerts. They felt that perhaps the company was not improving Qwerts as rapidly as was the competition.

d. The proportion of their incomes spent by consumers for products of the typewriter industry dropped rather sharply—30 percent.

Questions

1. Indicate with a *diagram* (do not try to quantify) how much of the change in quantity that you measured was due to the change in price, and how much was due to the "*other factor.*" (Treat each event separately; do not try to sum them.)

2. In each case, was the measure you calculated greater than, equal to, or less than what was probably the "true" elasticity, that is, elasticity adjusted for the "other" factor? (Be sure to treat each of the four cases *independently.*)

C. Mr. Peck, president of Imperial Zinc Corporation, is approached by his sales manager who suggests that if prices are lowered on Item 345, sales and profits can be increased. At present, when sales are 100,000 units, variable costs are 40 percent of total revenue, the allocated fixed costs are 50 percent of total revenue, and profits are 10 percent. The product at present is selling for $2. The sales manager asserts that if prices are cut by 10 percent, total profits will be one and a half times what they are now. The president is told that the company has plenty of capacity and that there will be no increase in overhead if sales are as great as predicted.

Questions

1. How many units must be sold at the new price if the sales manager's prediction is to be correct?

2. What price elasticity is necessry if the sales manager's predictions are to be realized?   4.75

D. The Widget Manufacturing Company experienced the following weekly sales.

Week	Price	Sales
1	.$1.00	$1,200,000
2	1.10	1,100,000

Questions

1. What is the price elasticity of demand?

2. What factors could make this estimate incorrect?

6

Production Functions and Short-Run Costs of Production

> Relatively short and long period problems go generally on similar lines. In both use is made of that paramount device, the partial or total isolation for special study of some set of relations.
> —*Alfred Marshall*

The next five chapters are concerned with various aspects of costs of production. Preliminaries in this chapter deal with the distinction between the short and the long run that is often blurred in practice and a reemphasis on opportunity costs as those relevant for business decision making. The idea of the production function is developed in a simple two-factor model to emphasize the role of factor prices in the decision for the minimum cost method of production.

THE SHORT RUN AND THE LONG RUN

It is useful in economics to distinguish between short-run and long-run production possibilities and costs.[1] These periods are defined in terms of the economic events considered to be possible rather than in terms of time as measured by the clock or calendar. Accordingly, the short run may be defined as a period too brief to permit full adjustment of all inputs in an industry to demand for the final product. Adjustment is especially likely to be incomplete if demand for the product or the production technology has recently changed markedly.[2]

A manager in a field of manufacturing is ordinarily confronted infrequently with long-run problems such as changing machines and

---

[1]This chapter focuses on private costs of production. Other costs may be incurred as a result of private decision making such as pollution. These are analyzed in Chapter 17.

[2]The distinction between short run and long run is due to Alfred Marshall. He summarized the former as follows: "To sum up then as regards short periods. The supply of specialized skill and ability, of suitable machinery and other material capital, and of the appropriate industrial organization has not time to be fully adapted to demand; but the producers have to adjust their supply to the demand as best they can with the appliances already at their disposal." (*Principles of Economics*, 8th ed. [London: Macmillan, 1930], p. 376).

processes, establishing programs for training labor, or altering plant capacity. He or she is confronted daily with the short-run problem of determining rate of output and perhaps prices to be charged for output and to be paid for inputs. As pointed out above, short- and long-run problems are intermingled and even difficult to classify. However, fruitful analysis requires simplification and a willingness to hold in *ceteris paribus* (i.e., assume to be unchanged) variables that in practice refuse to hold still as a favor to the analyst. A caution needs to be inserted here, as it was in connection with demand: the analyst should not assume constancy of a variable that could not conceivably remain constant because it is closely related to a variable that is permitted to change in magnitude in the analysis.

OPPORTUNITY COST

A most important concept in economics is "opportunity cost." This conceives of the true cost of any activity as consisting of the value of the best sacrificed alternative. The idea is basic since economics is the science of using scarce resources to satisfy unlimited wants as fully as possible. Resource owners must be paid prices at least as high as they could command in alternative employment opportunities. A successful bid for a resource and its employment in one type of economic activity denies its use for another product.

The opportunity cost idea fits the field of business economics especially well since it suggests the choice that managers must continually make among numerous opportunities for the use of available resources. These are so numerous that they can only be suggested: filling a position with one worker costs the firm the potential contribution of another at the same salary; choosing one location for a plant costs the advantages of another site; producing one product costs the income that could have been secured with an alternative product; even choosing to take a vacation costs the income that could have otherwise been earned.

Economic thinking focuses on present opportunities, sometimes in the form of capital values based on present expectations regarding the future. For example, ownership of stock in a corporation entails sacrifice of the opportunity of converting this asset into cash; consequently, the stock should not continue to be held unless the owner would be willing to buy it at today's market price. (Consideration needs to be given, however, to commissions, taxes, and the value of the owner's time in making transactions.) Similarly, if one is calculating the monthly cost of living in a house that is owned, the actual purchase price of the house is irrelevant to the calculation. The same is true of depreciation based on the actual cost. Instead, to operating and maintenance costs, insurance, and taxes, the homeowner should add interest on the present sales value and depreciation equal to the expected decline in sales value during the period for which the cost calculation is made.[3] The interest rate properly involved in the calculation is a rate attainable with equal risk in an alternate present investment of funds that could be withdrawn from the house by its immediate sale.

While this sort of opportunity cost thinking should be (and in large part actually is) at the heart of managerial decision making, it may sound strange to a student who has specialized in accounting. For tax purposes especially, definite accounting rules must be followed—rules such as evaluating a fixed asset at its actual cost less depreciation according to an acceptable formula. After a period of inflation and other typical economic changes, the book value of a commercial building is likely to be far below its actual sales value. In general, accountants are moving in the direction of incorporating evaluation of present opportunities in their accounts but are hampered by tax laws and traditional habits of thought.

The idea of opportunity cost can be illustrated by a simple chart, Figure 6–1. If two commodities A and B can be produced with resources available to a firm, the transformation curve TC can be considered to connect all possible output combinations. The company could, during the period, produce OT of good B and none of A, OC of A and none of B, or any combination lying on the curve, such as OM of A and OK of B. The slope of curve TC at any point measures the rate at which B must be sacrificed in order to produce more of A. This "marginal rate of transformation," or opportunity cost, applies to infinitesimal changes along the curve. Applying the idea to finite changes we could say that if point J is an actual combination being produced, the opportunity cost of turning out an additional TK units of B per period would be the OM units of A that could no longer be produced.

The slope of the transformation curve reflects the ability of resources to switch effectively from one product to the other. For example, some of the workers may be more skilled in producing A and other better at tasks associated with B. If the combination at H were being produced, the opportunity cost in terms of product B of increasing the output of A would be large because workers who are quite poor at producing A would have to be diverted from B. If all resources were equally well adapted to both goods, the transformation curve would be linear. Opportunity cost would be independent of relative output rates.

PRODUCTION FUNCTIONS

Anyone who is familiar with cookbooks has dealt with many production functions. For example, take this recipe for weiner schnitzel.[4] First it lists

---

[3]The depreciation cost may be negative if appreciation in value is expected. If a better speculative opportunity is seen by the homeowner, the opportunity cost of continuing to own the home includes the expected gain from the (sacrificed) better speculation less the expected gain in the value of the house.

[4]Julia Olden and Steve Sherman, *Dining in New Hampshire* (Canaan, N.H.: Phoenix Publishing, 1979), p. 109.

FIGURE 6–1   Transformation Curve—Illustrates Opportunity Cost

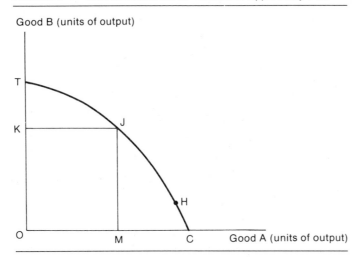

the factors of production: "1 lb. fancy veal (top round); 6 eggs, beaten; 1 box plain untoasted breadcrumbs; 1 lb. butter." Then it tells how to combine them so as to end up with a marketable (or at least edible) product: "Slice veal into thin steaks. Dip veal into beaten eggs, . . . etc." This technical know-how is the second requisite for a production function. In order to calculate the total costs of the weiner schnitzel, all that is necessary is to add the economic information of the price per unit of factor. Actually the recipe has not spelled out labor needs in terms of the cook's time or the cubic feet of gas required to "cook each side until it is golden brown." This completion of the factor list could come with experience. Clearly there are capital costs: a frying pan, cooking sheet, and refrigerator are mentioned, and an egg beater, bowl, and stove are implied. But the satisfaction of an urge for weiner schnitzel usually is achieved in the short run and these capital costs can be disregarded because they are fixed (and also negligible).

For the purposes of economic analysis this illustration is both too complex and too simple. It is too complex because there are so many factors: four materials, labor, gas, and several types of capital equipment. It is too simple in two important ways. First, it does not suggest alternative factor combinations that would produce the same output. For example, margarine might be substituted for butter, although for some weiner schnitzel buffs, there could be a question of product identity. In any case, a little labor and stale bread is a feasible substitute for boxed breadcrumbs.

The second oversimplification is that the production of only a single quantity of the product is provided for in the recipe. Actually the producer would like the production requirements for a range of product quantities. Cost curves incorporate costs of a series of volumes. While for

FIGURE 6–2   Production Isoquants—and Expansion
Paths

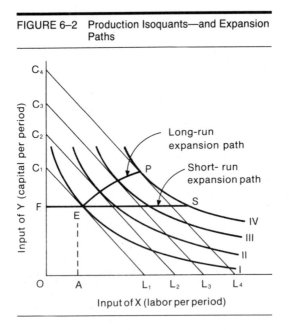

most recipes, including weiner schnitzel, doubling the material inputs
will double the outputs, there can be exceptions. Perhaps less than twice
the eggs, butter and breadcrumbs are needed for two pounds of veal. It is
unlikely that the cook's time or the gas consumed will be doubled. The
production function in Figure 6–2 includes isoquants for four different
volumes of production. It is necessary to deal with a more abstract model
for a less savory product than weiner schnitzel in further exposition.

THE TWO-INPUT, ONE-GOOD PRODUCTION FUNCTION

In order to understand the meaning of separating production possibilities
and costs into "short run" and "long run," it is useful to consider only one
good produced with two inputs. For example, in Figure 6–2, good A can
be considered to be produced with only labor and capital (both broadly
defined), the possible output being larger the greater the input of these
factors. Curves labeled I, II, III, IV are "production isoquants," referring
successively to larger outputs of A, each curve reflecting a particular
output attainable by use of the input combinations which it connects.

The curvature of any production isoquant reflects the possibilities of
substituting one input for the other without changing output. Isoquants
are concave upward reflecting, for example, the increasing technical difficulty of substituting labor for capital when the ratio of labor to capital is
already high. It is economically irrelevant to consider any part of the
isoquant that parallels either axis or "curls over" since additional quantities of one or both factors would then be required for the same output
without any savings in the amount of another factor.

Figure 6–2 also includes "isocost lines" C_1L_1, C_2L_2, C_3L_3, and C_4L_4, each connecting the input combinations purchasable by the firm for a particular outlay.[5] If no labor were hired, OC_1 would be the number of units of capital that could be purchased per period for a given outlay, OC_2 for a larger outlay, and so forth. Similarly, OL_1, OL_2, and so forth, could be hired for the same outlays if no capital were purchased. In practice, both resources would be hired, the objective of the firm being the attainment of maximum output for any given outlay. These maxima are found at the points of tangency with isoquants. Alternatively, the tangency points represent the minimum costs of producing a specified output. One should note that these tangency points represent the highest isoquant (greatest output) that is obtainable with the total cost represented by a given isocost line. Conversely, they represent the lowest total cost obtainable for a particular output as designated by its isoquant. At point E, where the output is represented by isoquant I, the input of capital is OF, and the input of labor is OA.

It is important to be clear about the role of relative factor prices in selecting the least-cost methods of production. The slope of each isocost line is $-P_L/P_c$.[6] The slope of each isoquant represents the marginal rate of substitution of capital for labor as one moves up the isoquant. At the tangency points these slopes are necessarily equal. In Figure 6–2, one can see that the prices per unit of capital and of labor are approximately equal since the quantities that can be purchased for each given outlay are equal ($OC_1 = OL_1$, $OC_2 = OL_2$, etc.).

The slope of the isocost line in this particular case is -1, and the least-cost method is that in which one unit of capital is substituted for one unit of labor with the output remaining the same. Above point E along isoquant I more than one unit of capital would be needed to replace a unit of labor in maintaining output. Clearly this would increase total costs since factor prices are equal. Should the price of labor increase, the slope of the isocost line would be greater (less labor would be purchased for a given outlay) and the economically efficient method would require more capital and less labor.

Line EP connects such points of tangency and can be called the "long-run expansion path." The implicit assumption is that any number of additional isoquants could have been drawn so that any combination of inputs along EP (or its extension in both directions) would be a possibility provided sufficient time is permitted for adjustment.

In the short run it is useful to assume that capital input is fixed (at OF) so that output can be increased only by increasing the use of labor.

---

[5]Each of these lines has the equation: Total cost $= P_LQ_L + P_cQ_c$, where P and Q represent the price and quantity of the factor denoted by the subscript.

[6]The student should recognize that the slope is the quantity of capital divided by the quantity of labor at the intercepts with the vertical axis and horizontal axis respectively, for example, C_1/L_1. The slope is negative: C declines as L increases.

Since one resource is fixed and hence its costs are fixed, short-run costs are minimized by allowing only the variable input to vary and using the least possible amount of this factor to produce a given output. This restricts the firm to the "short-run expansion path" FS. In this short-run situation when it is not possible to expand the plant, the firm will often be using more of the variable factor and less of the fixed factor than is called for by the long-run expansion path. Achievement of the output designated by isoquant IV in Figure 6–2 is clearly going to require total short-run costs in excess of those shown by isocost line C_4L_4 (the factor inputs called for are the coordinates of point S).

FIXED AND VARIABLE COSTS

Short-run cost curves useful in managerial decision making are related to the analysis of production possibilities in Figure 6–2. Corresponding to the fixed input of capital services and variable input of labor services along path FS are "fixed costs" and "variable costs" of production. The former are those that can be considered to be unaffected in their total by variations in the rate of use of existing capacity. The latter are those that vary in total with the rate of output.

Fixed costs from an economic point of view are quite different from those to which the study of accounting accustoms us. The reason for the difference lies in the need to ground economics on the opportunity cost idea. Consequently, the basic fixed costs of an enterprise consist of interest and "depreciation" on the present value of buildings and equipment. These cannot be avoided if the firm is to continue to own these assets during the period under consideration. These are opportunity costs because an alternative course of action would be the sale of the assets and the investment of the proceeds elsewhere. The interest rate that could then be secured on another investment of equal riskiness and liquidity is the one that is appropriate in the calculation of the interest cost. Depreciation as used in an economic sense is the expected loss in sales value over the period under consideration. This loss or change in market value is the result of changes in prices and the fact that the assets have lost potential service life due to wear and tear. It will be recognized that the principles are the same as those described earlier in connection with the cost of home ownership.

It is quite natural to think of interest that a firm pays on its debt as a fixed cost. While it is true that the interest paid may remain constant over long periods, it is not a fixed cost from the economic point of view. Once all interest on the present value of plant has been included in fixed cost, it would be double counting to include interest paid also on the bonds that were used in part to finance the purchase of fixed assets.

Certain other costs such as administrative salaries, fire insurance, and license fees are usually considered to be "fixed costs" from a short-run point of view. While important to the accountant, these can best be neglected from an economic point of view. They do not affect short-run decisions—there is no alternative opportunity open to the firm that has committed itself for a time to such costs. An exception would occur if the license, for example, could be sold. Then it would be similar to a plant that could be disposed of, and the interest lost by holding the license would be a fixed cost during the short period under analysis.

Variable costs are quite similar whether one takes an economic or accounting viewpoint. Labor costs, social security taxes, material costs, and costs of fuel and electric power vary with the rate of output and easily fit in with the idea of variable costs. They are clearly opportunity costs since funds currently expended on these items could alternatively be spent in other ways. Their prices reflect alternative uses to which the resources could have been put.

RELATIONSHIP OF COSTS TO PRODUCTION FUNCTION

It should be clear that costs of production will be influenced by the shape of the production function. In effect, the production function represents the technological relationships between the input factors and the way in which physical substitution can take place, that is, the exchange of additional machine-hours for labor-hours. The production function is drawn or formulated to illustrate technologically efficient resource combinations. The slope of a production isoquant is called the *marginal rate of substitution*. The interest of the economist or manager is to choose an input combination that considers not only technological efficiency but also economic efficiency. Hence, the tangency solution referred to above represents this idea by matching the marginal rate of substitution to the price ratio of the factors. But in the short run, when in the two-input model the quantity of one factor is fixed, expansion and contraction of output is not along the path of tangencies but follows the horizontal *FS* course in Figure 6–2.

The total cost of a particular output will be the sum of the fixed resource cost plus the variable cost. If variable costs increase in direct proportion to output, then total cost will be a linear function of output: $TC = FC + aQ$, where TC = total costs, FC = fixed costs, a = variable cost per unit, and Q = output. Figure 6–3 illustrates a cost curve of this type. Also shown are the unit cost curves associated with a total cost curve of this type. As is shown, average variable cost (AVC) and marginal cost (MC) are constant and equal to a which is the slope of the total cost curve. Marginal cost is defined as the addition to total cost as the result of an additional unit of output, or as the rate of change in total cost, that is, $\Delta TC/\Delta Q$. Average variable cost is total variable cost of a given output quantity divided by that quantity, TVC/Q. Average total cost or average cost is total cost divided by output. Clearly two dollar scales would be needed on the vertical cost axis to accommodate both total and unit costs. When quantity is 1,000, TC might be $10,000; average cost would be only

FIGURE 6–3   Total and Unit Costs—Linear Total Cost

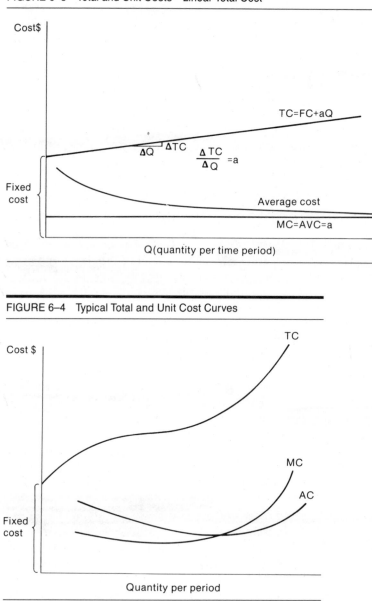

FIGURE 6–4   Typical Total and Unit Cost Curves

$10 and marginal cost would be lower. Because of this problem, no numbers are placed on the axes in Figure 6–3 and 6–4. The situation shown in Figure 6–3 in which variable costs vary proportionally is a special case that has wide applicability as a simplifying approximation and will be used later in a discussion of break-even analysis.

The usual expectation is that as more of a variable input factor is added to a fixed factor, output will first increase at an increasing rate, and then increase at a decreasing rate. This characteristic of the production function translates into total and unit cost curves of the general shapes indicated in Figure 6–4. This case is consistent with the hypothesis of eventually diminishing marginal returns—that is, the marginal product of added units of the variable factor will decline at some output. The declining portion of the marginal cost curve represents increasing marginal product, and the eventual rise in the marginal cost curve corresponds with diminishing marginal product or returns. In addition to reflecting the physical processes behind the production function, the variable cost curves may reflect factor prices that vary with volume. For example, a declining marginal cost curve could result from quantity discounts on materials and rising marginal costs from overtime premiums paid to labor at high outputs. However, the usual assumption underlying short-run cost curves in economics is that factor prices to the competitive firm remain unchanged as output changes.

Total cost in Figure 6–4 first increases at a decreasing rate and then at an increasing rate. This means that marginal cost first decreases until it levels, and then increases. Marginal cost thus varies inversely with marginal product of the variable factor. The necessary relationship between marginal and average cost is also illustrated in Figure 6–4. When marginal cost is below average cost, average cost is declining. When marginal cost is equal to average cost, average cost is constant. When marginal cost is above average cost, average cost is rising.

HYPOTHETICAL COST DATA

A short-run cost schedule for a factory is shown in Figure 6–5, the data being hypothetical and simplified in order to illustrate the basic points. Output is assumed to be capable of varying from 0 to 20 units per day, depending on how much is spent on variable inputs. Total fixed costs (column 2) remain at $32. These consist of interest and depreciation per day on the present value of the plant.

Total variable costs (column 4) rise continually as output increases, rising at first by decreasing increments and later by increasing additions. These increments are shown in column 8 as "marginal cost"—the cost added when one more unit is produced per period. (Marginal cost can be measured either as additional total variable costs or additional total costs.) This pattern of marginal cost is traceable to operation of the famous law of diminishing returns. In the low output range (one to six units), the efficiency of organization of production increases as more labor, materials, and other variable inputs are used in conjunction with the fixed plant. A better proportion is attained between fixed and variable inputs, and this shows up in the declining rate of increase in total variable costs.

FIGURE 6–5 Daily Cost Schedule for a Small Factory

(1) Output (units)	(2) Total Fixed Costs	(3) Average Fixed Cost	(4) Total Variable Costs	(5) Average Variable Cost	(6) Total of All Costs	(7) Average Total Cost	(8) Marginal Cost
1	$32.00	$32.00	$ 7.20	$ 7.20	$ 39.20	$39.20	$ 7.20
2	32.00	16.00	12.90	6.45	44.90	22.45	5.70
3	32.00	10.67	17.40	5.80	49.40	16.47	4.50
4	32.00	8.00	21.00	5.25	53.00	13.25	3.60
5	32.00	6.40	24.00	4.80	56.00	11.20	3.00
6	32.00	5.33	26.70	4.45	58.70	9.78	2.70
7	32.00	4.57	29.40	4.20	61.40	8.77	2.70
8	32.00	4.00	32.40	4.05	64.40	8.05	3.00
9	32.00	3.55	36.00	4.00	68.00	7.55	3.60
10	32.00	3.20	40.50	4.05	72.50	7.25	4.50
11	32.00	2.91	46.20	4.20	78.20	7.11	5.70
12	32.00	2.67	53.40	4.45	85.40	7.12	7.20
13	32.00	2.46	62.40	4.80	94.40	7.26	9.00
14	32.00	2.28	73.50	5.25	105.50	7.53	11.10
15	32.00	2.13	87.00	5.80	119.00	7.93	13.50
16	32.00	2.00	103.20	6.45	135.20	8.45	16.20
17	32.00	1.88	122.40	7.20	154.40	9.08	19.20
18	32.00	1.78	144.90	8.05	176.90	9.83	22.50
19	32.00	1.68	171.00	9.00	203.00	10.68	26.10
20	32.00	1.60	201.00	10.05	233.00	11.65	30.00

SOURCE: Albert L. Meyers, *Elements of Modern Economics*, 3d ed. (Englewood Cliffs, N.J.: Prentice-Hall, 1948), p. 158. Reproduced by permission.

Above a daily output of seven units, the factory is operating in the stage of diminishing marginal returns, which causes marginal costs to rise.[7]

Average variable cost can decline even after marginal cost begins to rise. This is apparent at outputs of eight and nine units. When average variable cost is at a minimum, it is equal to marginal cost. (This would occur between 9 and 10 units if units were divisible.) Average total cost continues to decline after average variable cost turns up (due to the influence of average fixed cost).

AVERAGE AND MARGINAL COST CURVES

It is usually more convenient to work with cost curves rather than a schedule. For many purposes the curves can be sketched without defining units along the axes. Figure 6–6, however, shows four cost curves that correspond with the data in Figure 6–5 except that units of output are assumed to be fully divisible rather than discrete. Average fixed cost (AFC) is of little importance except as a reminder of the source of high

---

[7]Increasing and decreasing marginal returns can be traced in a chart of the type shown in Figure 6–2. If each higher isoquant represents the same increment in output (e.g., if they were labeled 1, 2, 3, 4,— or 10, 20, 30,—), increasing returns to labor input would be reflected in decreasing distances between isoquants along path FS; farther to the right the distance between isoquants would increase, reflecting diminishing marginal returns.

FIGURE 6–6

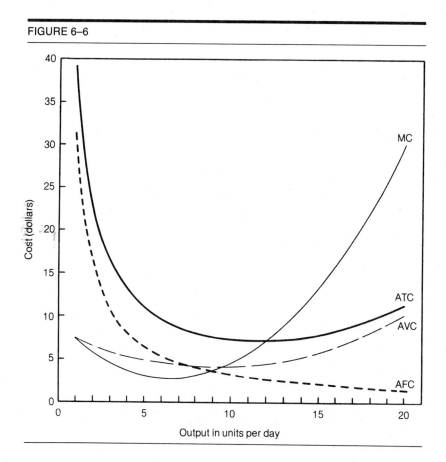

Output in units per day

cost per unit when fixed capacity is lightly utilized. Average variable cost is of some importance since it is usually better to shut down than to operate if price does not at least cover average variable cost.[8] Average total cost (ATC) is useful in gauging whether returns on capital tied up in fixed plant are adequate. The amount left to compensate for the use of capital consists of total revenue minus total variable costs. This residual is often called "cash flow," and this usage will be followed. Part of the cash flow can be considered to make up for depreciation in value of the plant. Any remainder permits interest to be earned on the plant.

While price minus average total cost is often referred to as "profit per unit," and total returns minus total costs is referred to as "profit," this differs from accounting profit. Accountants include interest on debt as a

[8]The qualification "usually" is inserted because it is not difficult to visualize many possible exceptions to the rule. For example, special shutdown and subsequent start-up costs may exist, costs may have to be incurred to rehire and retrain workers, or customers may be lost who could contribute to later profits.

cost, whereas economists include opportunity interest earnings. Account-ants compute depreciation on original cost according to permissible for-mulas, while expected change in market value of capital assets is in line with the economist's viewpoint.[9] The persistence of losses in the eco-nomic sense constitutes a signal to leave the industry, while economic profits tend to attract additional competition.

It should be noted that because of the opportunity cost viewpoint in economics, a high-cost firm is not necessarily an inefficient firm. Actually it may be unusually efficient in the sense of being able readily to produce other products. For example, if a skilled surgeon decided to try his hand at commercial fishing for a year, he would be a very high-cost fisherman because his time should be charged at the rate he could have earned as a doctor. If he is also a poor fisherman the cost per pound of his catch will be still higher! Similarly, a firm in a declining industry using ancient equipment may be economically efficient with low overall costs despite high labor inputs.

OUTPUT UNDER COMPETITIVE CONDITIONS

Under highly competitive conditions, market price is determined by sup-ply and demand: The individual firm cannot affect this price but does have the problem of adjusting its output rate to this price. The cost curves of Figure 6–6 are useful in understanding this adjustment.

The key curve is that of marginal cost. Ordinarily the firm should produce at a rate that equates marginal cost with the market price.[10] This follows logically from the definition of marginal cost as the *additional* cost of increasing the output. Since price of the product shows the added revenue from an extra unit of output, all units should be produced for which marginal cost is below price. The special case of Figure 6–3 in which marginal costs are constant over a wide range of outputs is no exception to this. When the firm reaches the fullest possible utilization of the fixed factor, the marginal cost curve becomes vertical, signifying that a greater output in the short run is impossible. It will then intercept the horizontal demand curve at the existing market price.

If price is temporarily below the lowest possible average variable cost, the firm should ordinarily cease production (except for additional consid-erations of the sorts already mentioned). Even if all variable costs are being met but price is below average total cost, continuation of the activity may depend upon an expectation of improvement. It is possible that steps should be taken immediately to alter production processes or to abandon the activity.

---

[9]Tax reform proposals being considered in the mid-1980s would substitute something like economic depreciation by using estimates of replacement rather than original cost.

[10]Marginal cost must be rising. If it is falling, the output is the *worst* possible since the firm will have produced all units that add more to cost than to revenue and none that add more to revenue than to cost.

ALL-OR-NONE DECISION

In the ordinary analysis of the relation of cost to output it is assumed that the competitive firm has complete freedom to adjust its rate of output and that it will choose the rate at which marginal cost equals price. This "short-run supply curve" is the marginal cost curve above and to the right of minimum average variable cost because this determines the optimum quantity to supply at any given price.

During a period of slack orders, management may instead be willing to consider an "all-or-none" offer from a buyer. There may be no options open to the producer except to reject or accept the offer. For example, a contract to produce 10,000 suits of a particular variety at $40 per suit may have to be considered even if the tailoring firm ordinarily can sell such garments at $50 each and has calculated standard costs including overhead at $47. Under such an all-or-none offer the average variable cost curve, rather than marginal cost, constitutes the supply curve.[11] That is, the offer is worth accepting if the average variable cost at that output rate is below $40 since this would leave some cash flow to apply against fixed costs. This offer should be turned down if AVC exceeds $40, because the $400,000 revenue would not even cover variable costs. There may, of course, be good reasons apart from immediate revenue and cost that would cause a firm to accept an offer that did not quite cover variable costs. An important reason might be labor turnover costs if present workers would otherwise be laid off. The offer also might be rejected even with AVC covered if there were expected to be adverse revenue consequences for future periods. Case 6–1 deals with an all-or-none decision.

ADAPTABILITY AND DIVISIBILITY OF PLANT

As a matter of convenience in drawing, curves depicting average total, average variable, and marginal costs are usually made markedly U-shaped. Geometric elegance and economic relevance are often at odds, however, and it should be recognized that many other shapes are quite possible in the real world.

Marginal cost is often approximately constant over a wide range of output. This would clearly be the case for a firm that purchases and resells commodities instead of manufacturing them. If all additional quantities of a good (say, TV sets) could be bought at the same price from the manufacturer, the retailer's marginal costs would be nearly the same regardless of the volume. The marginal cost curve would not be completely horizontal, however, because of economies and diseconomies of handling, storage, display, and selling.

---

[11]In one sense, marginal cost still governs the decision since the entire block of 10,000 suits constitutes one unit. Marginal cost per suit is total variable cost divided by 10,000; this is the same as variable cost per suit.

If attention is concentrated on producers of goods, it is useful to examine the concepts *adaptability* and *divisibility* as they apply to plant capacity.[12] A plant may be said to be *adaptable* to the extent that it is capable of being used with changing amounts of variable inputs. A piece of farmland, for example, is quite adaptable to different amounts of fertilizer and labor, while a steam shovel is highly unadaptable in that it can be used with only one operator at a time. Plant capacity is highly *divisible* when it contains a large number of identical machines—for example, 20 identical machines for producing concrete clocks, 50 nail-making machines, or 10 printing presses within a single establishment. Complete indivisibility exists when, for example, the plant consists of one long assembly line, each station of which is wholly dependent on the previous ones.

Divisible but unadaptable plants are common in manufacturing since many machines are built to operate at only one rate and require a fixed number of operators and specific amounts of material per time period. In this case, marginal costs are constant over a wide range of output. In order to secure more output, a greater number of machines is utilized, and each requires a fixed complement of labor, power, and materials; consequently, each one adds the same amount to cost as did the previous ones. Reduced output in this case is attained by shutting down a number of machines, and each one that is shut down reduces total variable cost by the same amount.

If plant capacity is indivisible but highly adaptable, a U-shaped marginal cost curve will result. Marginal costs will at first fall, as a better proportion is attained between the indivisible fixed plant and the variable inputs; but eventually, the proportions will become less compatible, and marginal costs will rise. This is the assumption on which Figure 6–6 is based.

STANDARD COSTS AND VOLUME VARIANCES

The primary source of cost data is likely to be a firm's cost accounting system. Standard costs are computed per unit of output with which actual costs incurred can be compared. These standards are based on assumed prices for factors, on the amount of inputs per unit of output, and on the volume of product being produced. Actual costs may differ from the standard because the price paid per unit of factor differs from that assumed in the standard, *price variances*, because less or more of inputs are used per unit of output, *efficiency variances*, and because the volume of output differs from the normal on which standard allocations were based, *volume variance*. Analyses of price variances may be helpful in assessing the performance of purchasing agents and of efficiency variances in assessing how well the production supervisor has done. Volume variances, how-

---

[12]See George J. Stigler, "Production and Distribution in the Short Run," *Journal of Political Economy*, June 1939, pp. 305–27.

ever, are most closely related to a subject of this chapter, short-run cost curves. The most important reason for variation in average cost with short-run volume has already been noted; as volume increases the fixed costs per unit fall. Before examining the significance of volume variance for decision making, it is worth looking briefly at the cost accounting process.

In assigning costs to units of product, the accountant distinguishes between direct costs that can be easily assigned to units of output and overhead costs that are difficult to identify with particular outputs and so are first charged to "overhead" or "burden" accounts. Such overhead costs can then be allocated to particular orders or products on criteria associated with direct costs such as direct labor-hours. This distinction between direct and overhead costs is not exactly the same as that between variable and fixed costs. Direct costs are usually variable since they are identifiable with particular units of output. Many overhead costs, such as managerial salaries, interest, or depreciation, are fixed in the short run and do not vary in total with output. Other overhead costs may tend to vary with output, although not necessarily proportionally. For example, electric power may roughly rise with output, but it is typically treated as an overhead cost since the identification of the particular output for which additional electricity is required may be difficult.

It can be quite misleading to use standard costs as a guide for decisions that affect volume. At higher volumes the fixed or semivariable overhead costs will be spread over more units and therefore will be less per unit. Using the higher standard costs associated with a lower normal volume will produce a negative volume variance, and actual average costs will be less than the standard estimates. The overhead can be said to be *overabsorbed*. At volumes lower than normal, it would be *underabsorbed*.

In order to make the most profitable decision, such as that on price that will affect the volume, the decision maker anticipates this over- or underabsorption of overhead. One way of doing this is *direct costing*, that is, comparing the revenues at different volumes with the direct costs involved. The output that will make the greatest contribution to overhead and profit is selected. This is effective when direct costs approximate variable costs. A second way is to prepare a flexible budget in which the actual variability of costs with volume changes is estimated in advance. Such a flexible budget, while more detailed as to cost items, is essentially the kind of cost schedule given in Figure 6–5, a tabular presentation of the cost curves. Case 6–3, the Nordon Case, illustrates this accounting approach.

BREAK-EVEN CHARTS

A frequently used method of comparing costs with possible revenue is the break-even chart that shows the output at which all costs will be covered at a particular price. Total costs are usually shown as in Figure 6–3 as $TC = FC + aQ$, where a is the marginal cost per unit and is equal

FIGURE 6–7 Break-Even Charts

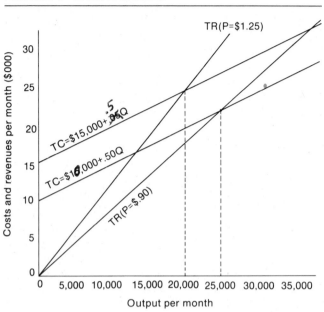

to the average variable cost. It is not necessary that *TC* be taken as linear, but for many firms with divisible plants, this is an appropriate simplification. The break-even output in the linear case is $Q = FC/(P - a)$ since $TR = PQ = FC + aQ$.

Figure 6–7 illustrates how break-even charts might be used to compare alternatives. The firm estimates fixed costs at $10,000 per month and alternatively at $15,000 a month if $5,000 is appropriated for an advertising program. Its marginal cost, equal to the *AVC*, is 50 cents. Total revenue curves are drawn for possible prices of $1.25 or 90 cents. The break-even output for the 90-cent price without advertising is 25,000 units, i.e., 10,000/(0.90 − 0.50), and for the $1.25 price is 20,000 units, i.e., 15,000/(1.25 − 0.50). The other break-even points can easily be worked out.

Two limitations of this tool should be recognized. First, no information on the actual demand is given. It may be very helpful to know that at the higher price with a significant advertising program, the break-even output is lower than at the 90-cent price. But actual market analysis must be made before a decision is justified. Second, the break-even point itself may not be of particular significance. Partly this is because the break-even chart is really a profit graph that compares revenues and costs at many outputs. Partly, in a truly short-run decision with limited opportunities, it is not necessary that the firm break even, that is, cover all the fixed overhead costs that are allocated to the product. It is better to produce when all the variable costs are covered with some contribution to meet fixed costs that would continue even if production were zero.

STATISTICAL COST ANALYSIS

Just as statistical analysis often proves useful in the analysis of demand, the statistical technique of multiple regression analysis is often useful in determining the type of cost structure that is present in a business. Of particular interest in pricing and output decisions is the knowledge of whether or not marginal cost is constant as in Figure 6–3 or rising in the relevant range as in Figure 6–4. Regression analysis may provide an answer to this question.[13]

One method of proceeding is to determine whether a linear cost function of the form $TC = a + bQ$, where a is fixed costs and b is variable costs as determined empirically, fits better than a curvilinear cost function. One possible curvilinear cost function might be $TC = a + bQ + cQ^2$, where a is fixed cost and b and c are the intercept and slope of a linear marginal cost curve. Since marginal cost is the slope or the derivative of TC, it would be $MC = b + 2cQ$ from this equation. If c were positive, the analysis would indicate a rising marginal cost curve.

OPTIMUM INVENTORY POLICY MODELS AND LINEAR PROGRAMMING METHODS

These two types of techniques that are concerned with short-run cost minimization are taken up in Cases 6–4 and 6–5, respectively. Inventories reflect the relationship between sales and production or purchases and thus involve short-run output decisions. The key variables, the size of inventory and its determinants, and the frequency and size of production orders require different types of models from those relating output per period to dollar costs.

Linear programming methods are concerned with cost minimization or profit maximization under constraints similar to the fixed factors in short-run economic decisions. They do require a fairly lengthy computational exposition. Therefore, the choice of this text (with due consideration to opportunity costs) has been to show graphically the principles involved in Case 6–5.

Case 6–1
Sunland Tailoring Company

The Sunland Tailoring Company manufactured men's suits and topcoats. Most of their output was sold to men's furnishings stores, department stores, and wholesalers, all of whom distributed the garments under their

---

[13]See J. Johnson, *Statistical Cost Analysis* (New York: McGraw-Hill, 1960), for a survey of a large number of industry studies of cost and for helpful information on methodology.

EXHIBIT 6–1A

Labor.	$25.00
Material.	22.00
Depreciation	3.50
General factory burden.	5.00
Administrative and selling expense	2.50
Total cost	58.00
Plus 10% markup.	5.80
Total.	$63.80

EXHIBIT 6–1B

Direct labor (all variable and because of high activity during usual vacation period overtime will add 10%)	$20.00 +2⁰⁰
Indirect labor (approximately 50% will vary with output).	5.00
Materials (quantity discounts should decrease this by 5%).	22.00
General factory burden (includes light, power, maintenance, factory supervision. Approximately 40% variable for this decision mostly because of increased maintenance)	5.00 +40%
Administrative and selling cost (no additional cost with sale made and top management salaries fixed)	2.50
Depreciation (100% fixed as sunk cost)	3.50

---

respective brand names. Sunland did no direct retail selling. From its origin as a tailor shop in 1924, the company had grown to a firm producing approximately 200,000 suits and coats per year.

Actual production of clothing in the plant was concentrated in a period of about nine months each year. Since the company produced no line of summer clothing, there was a period of three months, January through March, when the idle capacity was about 90 percent. During this period any needed repairs and renovations were made and a large part of the work force were given unpaid "vacations."

Sunland normally sold suits and coats at an average price of $63.80 each. The price was arrived at by adding approximately 10 percent to total cost per suit, as shown in Exhibit 6–1A.

In October 1985, the company received an inquiry from the manager of a large chain of department stores operating in the southwestern part of the United States, expressing interest in placing an order for 50,000 men's suits of various specified sizes, for delivery between April 1 and April 15, 1986. It was stated that the order would be confirmed if the price did not exceed $50 per suit.

The chief accountant recommended that the order be rejected. Unwilling to lose this business, the president of the company hired the services of a business management counsel, who prepared a new statement of costs per suit as shown in Exhibit 6–1B. The fee of the management counseling firm was $2,000.

Questions

1. Should the company accept the order for 50,000 suits? Explain which costs are relevant to the decision, and predict its effect on company profits in the short run.

2. Does average variable cost differ from marginal cost in this situation? Explain.

3. Whatever your decision was, cite some factors that might make the opposite decision wise.

CASE 6–2
Badger and Siegel

Badger and Siegel were two very small producers of a standardized product in a very competitive market. Both priced at the prevailing market price, and both desired to maximize profits. Both plants were about the same size and had a potential capacity of producing 10,000 units per year. Normally, however, both tended to operate at not over 80 percent of capacity, for unit variable costs increased rapidly for any extra production. This increase was caused by the fact that one stage of production required very skilled workmanship. These highly paid workers in consequence worked overtime when production exceeded 80 percent of capacity. Any production between 80 and 85 percent of capacity increased variable costs on this extra output by 10 percent. If production went above 85 percent and not over 90 percent, the *additional* units cost an *additional* 15 percent over the unit variable costs for outputs up to 80 percent. Any units produced over 90 percent of capacity cost 20 percent more than the basic variable costs. At 80 percent of capacity, Badger's unit fixed costs were $3. These costs in total did not change within the range of his production. For outputs through 80 percent capacity, his variable costs were $9 per unit. Siegel did not use quite as much machinery, and his costs at 80 percent capacity were as follows: unit fixed, $2; unit variable, $10.50. In 1959, the price had dropped from $12.60 to $12.40. At this price, Siegel was operating at a loss in 1963 when he was working at 80 percent of capacity.

Since Badger and Siegel were friends, Siegel asked Badger what to do under these circumstances. Badger told him that in such a case, he should forget fixed costs and watch variable costs only. Badger said that he watched his variable costs and continued production just so long as his additional costs did not exceed the selling price. Thus, if the price in the market was $12.40, Badger continued to increase output until his additional variable (marginal) costs approximated $12.40.

Siegel, however, insisted that since his costs at normal capacity were

$12.50 per unit, he could not possibly reduce his losses by forgetting his fixed costs. He insisted that average costs were the more significant.

In order to settle the argument, Badger and Siegel agreed that they would estimate their costs at various levels of production. They decided to start at 5,000, then estimate them at 7,000, 8,000, 8,500, 9,000, 10,000, and 11,000 units. For production between 10,000 and 11,000 units additional variable costs were estimated at double the level of 8,000 units.

Questions

1. Make this cost-output study for both Badger and Siegel, and indicate how many units each should produce.

2. Assume that there are 50 firms in the industry with Badger's costs and 50 with Siegel's costs. Plot the industry supply schedule.

3. What long-run changes of price and composition of this industry would you predict under the assumptions of pure competition? Assume that Badger and Siegel omitted opportunity interest from their calculation of fixed costs and that this approximated $2,000 for Badger and $8,000 for Siegel.

CASE 6–3
Nordon Manufacturing Company

Nordon Manufacturing Company calculated the following manufacturing costs for one of its two major products:

Materials (8 pounds "BC" at $1.50)	$12.00
Labor (3 hours at $5; 1 hour at $4)	19.00
Manufacturing expense (4 hours at $1)	4.00
	$35.00

The standard for manufacturing expense (overhead) was calculated at a rate of 80 percent of practical capacity from the flexible budget for manufacturing expense shown in Exhibit 6–3A. Expenses other than manufacturing are $8 a unit at the 80 percent rate ($6 fixed, $2 variable).

Questions

1. What will be the over- and underabsorbed manufacturing expense (volume variance) if operations are at 60 percent of practical capacity? At all other levels of operation? Illustrate graphically on an average cost chart and on a total cost chart.

2. Will a $44 price always result in profits?

EXHIBIT 6–3A   Manufacturing Expense Budgets by Level Period (one month)

			Percentage of Practical Capacity		
	60%	70%	80%	90%	100%
Standard hours*	5,625	6,562.5	7,500	8,437.5	9,375
Variables and semivariables:					
Assistant foremen (semivariable)	$ 600.00	$ 600.00	$ 900.00	$ 900.00	$ 900.00
Materials-handling labor (variable)	900.00	1,050.00	1,200.00	1,350.00	1,500.00
Repairman (semivariable)	400.00	400.00	600.00	800.00	800.00
Old-age benefit tax (semivariable)	39.00	41.25	51.00	56.25	58.50
Oil (semivariable)	180.00	180.00	224.74	224.74	224.74
Miscellaneous factory supplies (variable)	210.00	245.00	280.00	315.00	350.00
Repairs and replacement parts (semivariable)	400.00	400.00	490.00	550.00	550.00
Power and light (variable)	270.00	315.00	360.00	405.00	450.00
Total variables and semivariables	2,999.00	3,231.25	4,105.74	4,600.99	4,833.24
Fixed:					
Rent	1,950.00	1,950.00	1,950.00	1,950.00	1,950.00
Foreman	400.00	400.00	400.00	400.00	400.00
Materials storekeeper	300.00	300.00	300.00	300.00	300.00
Depreciation on machinery	416.66	416.66	416.66	416.66	416.66
Insurance on machinery and inventory	163.80	163.80	163.80	163.80	163.80
Taxes on machinery and inventory	163.80	163.80	163.80	163.80	163.80
Total fixed	3,394.26	3,394.26	3,394.26	3,394.26	3,394.26
Total manufacturing expense	$6,393.26	$6,625.51	$7,500.00	$7,995.25	$8,227.50

*For each unit of the product where output is being varied, four hours of direct labor are standard so that the charge is $4. Units produced at various operating rates: 60 percent, 1,406; 70 percent, 1,640; 80 percent, 1,875; 90 percent, 2,109; and 100 percent, 2,344.

3. Will a $42 price always result in losses?

4. Compute the marginal cost curve for output from 60 to 100 percent of capacity.

5. Nordon, which has been operating at 70 percent of capacity (1,640 units per month), with little prospect of a better rate in the next six months, has an opportunity to take a private-brand order for 3,000 units to be delivered at the rate of 500 per month at a price of $36.75 a unit. Assume no effect on other sales, and estimate the effect of accepting this order on Nordon's profits.

6. What advantage is there in working out expenses figures at several levels of output for pricing decisions? For operating control?

CASE 6–4
L. E. Mason Company and Optimal Inventory Policy

In the spring of 1979, the officers of the L. E. Mason Company of Boston, Massachusetts, were concerned about the inventory position of the company's Red Dot line of electrical conduit fittings. The Red Dot line consisted of approximately 180 different fittings made of die-cast aluminum.[14] The fittings were sold throughout the United States by manufacturers' representatives who took the goods on consignment in 20 warehouses. The company also maintained a factory warehouse in Brockton, Massachusetts, from which shipments were made to the field warehouses and also directly to some customers.

Prior to World War II the L. E. Mason Company was primarily engaged in the bronzing of baby shoes. This activity had led the company to the production by permanent molding of the bases upon which the baby shoes were mounted. With the advent of the war, supplies were no longer available for the bronzing of baby shoes, and the company used its facilities for the production of magnesium castings for incendiary bombs. During the war period the company acquired die-casting equipment. After the war the L. E. Mason Company converted to a proprietary line of gifts and housewares based on the die-casting process, did job-order die cast-

---

[14]Die casting is a manufacturing process in which molten metal is forced into a metal mold or die under pressure. A high-quality casting with excellent surface finish and dimensional accuracy may be produced. Castings are typically made of the lower melting point alloys of zinc, tin, lead, brass, aluminum, and magnesium. Dies are placed into a die-casting machine, which holds them in place with hydraulic pressure. The molten metal is forced into the cavity of the die under pressure. The machine releases the pressure on the die, and the casting is removed. The rate at which castings may be produced depends upon the size of the casting and the pressure required. Small items may be produced very rapidly in large volume through the use of multiple-cavity dies. The castings typically require only simple trimming, tapping, and inspection before packing. Dies may range in cost from a few hundred to several thousand dollars. Scrap may be remelted and used again.

ing, and resumed the bronzing of baby shoes; it decided upon producing the Red Dot line of electrical conduit fittings to make fuller use of its die-casting facilities. In 1979, its business was in three major categories: (1) the Red Dot line, (2) a line of die-cast gift items such as coasters and book ends (some bronzing of baby shoes), and (3) job-order die casting using customer-purchased dies.

Production and Inventory Control

Kenneth Sullo, chief engineer, stated that his methods of production planning, production scheduling, and inventory control for the Red Dot line were based upon four major criteria: (1) the annual sales forecast for the Red Dot line, (2) the necessary minimum inventory, (3) the desire to make economic production runs on the die-casting machines, and (4) the desire to maintain stable levels of production and employment to avoid the costs inherent in fluctuating production.

The first step in production and inventory planning after receiving the annual sales forecast for the Red Dot line from the sales department was to divide the forecast by 12 to obtain the expected average monthly sales in dollars. This dollar figure was converted into pieces by dividing average monthly dollar sales by the weighted average sales value of a single item to obtain the desired monthly production rate in pieces.

From past sales records, it was possible for Mr. Sullo to determine average monthly sales of each item in the line. These sales varied from almost zero for some items to many thousands of pieces for others. Sales patterns varied somewhat among the 20 warehouses; but the billing clerk, under the supervision of Mr. Sullo, was generally able to allocate the consigned merchandise to the field warehouses in a reasonably satisfactory manner. That is, localized shortages were relatively infrequent.

Inventory records of the field warehouses were maintained at the factory from daily sales reports by the manufacturers' representatives and from shipping records; these records, together with the main warehouse inventory records, were reported in total to Mr. Sullo on about the 10th of each month, accurate as of the 1st of the month. With this report, Mr. Sullo was able to see quickly which items were in short supply. Those items below a four-month supply were recorded on his production scheduling sheet for further consideration.

In general, Mr. Sullo allowed two weeks' time for trimming, tapping, other intermediate operations, and inspection. Therefore, items were scheduled for casting at least two weeks before their inventory was expected to reach the two-month minimum supply limit that is explained below. An item with two and one-half months' supply or less on hand at scheduling time was scheduled immediately. Others were scheduled so that production began two weeks before the inventory was expected to be at a two-month supply. Using a four-month supply as the cutoff for scheduling enabled Mr. Sullo to schedule monthly production in accordance with his two-month supply rule.

Minimum inventory levels were determined by Mr. Sullo on the assumptions that one week's supply was necessary in each of the field warehouses, that it took up to one week to receive sales information from the warehouses, and that shipping time was often as long as a week. An extra week's supply was added for safety, giving a one-month inventory in each of the field warehouses as an order point. An additional month's nationwide supply was desired in the factory warehouse to back up the field warehouses and for direct shipment to customers. Thus, the total minimum acceptable level of inventory was a two-month supply.

Through experience, Mr. Sullo found that high-volume items could get as low as one and one-half months' supply without causing great difficulty and that, paradoxically, slow-moving items could be troublesome when the total supply available was at a six-month or greater level. This he attributed to more difficult forecasting for the slow-moving items and to problems of distribution among the warehouses.

In Exhibit 6–4A, several items were taken from a typical monthly production scheduling form. Column 1 gives average monthly sales in pieces for the forecast period; column 2, the description or name of the item; column 3, the quantity in inventory in months with supply as of the first of the month; and column 4, the amount to be run (economic run) in pieces and months. Column 5 gives the number already available (cast and in process since the first of the month); column 6 gives the date to begin casting; column 7 gives the amount packed since the first of the month; and column 8, the date to begin packing.

From the items placed on the production schedule, Mr. Sullo scheduled an assortment that enabled monthly production to equal approximately one twelfth of expected annual sales, taking into account the current inventory levels of the items, the quantities already cast or in process, and any other information available.

An outage in the main warehouse could also cause alterations in the production schedule, depending upon the nationwide supply of the items and its distribution.

If the nationwide supply of the item was sufficient, Mr. Sullo might suggest that shipments be made among the warehouses instead of scheduling immediate production. In some cases, shifting among the warehouses was more costly than scheduling additional production; however, Mr. Sullo believed that this had educational value for the sales department and that employees would become more adept at estimating sales and distribution if they were unable to interrupt production schedules at will.

Economic production-run sizes on the die-casting machines were determined by Mr. Sullo on the primary criterion that it was desirable to run any setup on the machines for at least one three-shift day. Setting up the machines could take up to 15 man-hours in order to get proper temperatures and to obtain quality castings.

EXHIBIT 6–4A L. E. Mason Company Production Schedule (selected items)

(1) Average Monthly Sales	(2) Item	(3) On Hand, July 1 (months)	(4) Amount to Run		(5) In Process, July 12	(6) Start Casting Date	(7) Already Packed	(8) Start Packing Date
			Pieces	Months				
800	A	3.6	2,400	3		August 2		August 18
400	B	2.7	1,600	4		At once		July 21*
1,800	C	1.4	7,200	4	2,000	At once		At once
15,000	D	1.9	30,000	2	8,000	Running		At once
50	E	5.0	500	10		July 18		August 1

*Behind schedule, that is, less than two weeks allowed between packing and casting.

Current Situation

In the spring of 1980, the total inventory dollar value in the 20 field warehouses and in the main warehouse was a three-month supply of finished castings at current and expected sales volumes expressed in dollars. Estimated economic order quantities for approximately 60 slow-moving items revealed that these items alone accounted for about two thirds of the value of the three-month supply on hand. Mr. Sullo felt that he really should have a four-month supply on hand in order to service sales properly.

A Model for Determining Optimal Inventory Policy

In order to assess Mr. Sullo's inventory policy, the following inventory model is included for comparison to the present practices. For L. E. Mason which produces its own components, the essential component of reorder costs is the cost of setup time for production runs. It is not implied that this model is comprehensive enough to be the solution for Mason's inventory problems, but its use in comparison with present practices should suggest possible improvements.

A common problem facing many firms is the determination of an inventory policy that minimizes the total costs of carrying inventory. In the simplest case these costs consist of reorder costs and the variable costs of carrying inventory. Reorder costs vary with the number of orders placed, and the costs of carrying inventory vary with the size of the average level of inventory.

The inventory carrying cost is directly related to the average level of inventory. If an order is received on the first day of the month and is sold over the month so that none is on hand the last day of the month, the average amount on hand will be equal to the beginning amount plus the ending amount divided by 2. That is, if the order size is equal to Q, then the average inventory is given by

$$\frac{Q + 0}{2} = \frac{Q}{2}$$

If we let i represent the dollar interest and other costs of holding an item in inventory for one year, then the annual carrying cost of holding the average number of units in inventory will be $= iQ/2$.

The reorder costs will be a function of the number of orders per year. The number of orders per year will depend upon annual sales and the size of each order, or if $S =$ annual sales, then the number of orders will $= S/Q$. If the cost per order is equal to $\$b$, then the total ordering cost will $= \$bS/Q$.

The total inventory costs can now be expressed as the sum of these two costs or

$$TC = \frac{iQ}{2} + \frac{bS}{Q}$$

EXHIBIT 6–4B   Inventory Costs—Order Costs and Carrying Costs

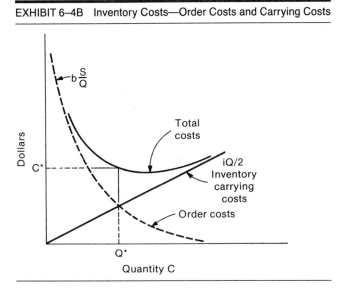

Exhibit 6–4B shows a graphic representation of the costs. Average inventory carrying costs increase as the size of the order increases, but the average costs of ordering decreases as the size of orders increases. Thus, the problem is to find the size of order that minimizes total inventory costs. This size is given by finding the minimum value of the expression above. Taking the derivatives with respect to Q and setting the resulting expression = 0 meets the first-order condition for a minimum:

$$\frac{dTC}{dQ} = \frac{i}{2} - \frac{bS}{Q^2} = 0$$

$$Q^2 = \frac{2bS}{i}$$

$$Q^* = \sqrt{\frac{2bS}{i}}$$

Thus, the optimal reorder size, Q^*, is given by the square root of $2bS/i$. That is, the optimum size orders vary directly with annual sales and reorder costs and inversely with inventory carrying costs.

In this simple formula an optimum order size can be determined. Most inventory systems are more complex and require more complicated variations of the model in order to optimize inventory costs. There are many books that deal with complex inventory problems.[15]

---

[15]See Thomas M. Whitin, *The Theory of Inventory Management* (Princeton, N.J.: Princeton University Press, 1953) as a pioneering study.

EXHIBIT 6–4C

	X	Y	Z
1979 average monthly sales (units)	1,000	25,000	100
Range of monthly sales (1979)	200–2,500	0–50,000	50–150
Hourly wage rate	$5	$5	$5
Inventory on hand (October 10)	2,200	15,000	100
Production rate	150/hr.	500/hr.	250/hr.
Material cost per unit	$0.625	$1.25	$0.375
Estimated annual cost of holding one unit in inventory	$0.075	$0.25	$0.05

Questions

1. Does Mr. Sullo's production control and inventory planning system lead to optimal decisions? If not, what modifications would you suggest?

2. Using the hypothetical information given in Exhibit 6–4C concerning items X, Y, and Z in the line, how many units would you schedule for production in the production period from October 10 to November 10? Use the inventory model as a starting point.

CASE 6–5
Linear Programming Methods—A Graphic Example

Although linear programming is strictly speaking a mathematical method for either maximizing or minimizing a linear function subject to a set of linear constraints, it has gained such widespread use and acceptance as a tool for business problem solving that it deserves inclusion in a book dealing with business or managerial economics. The exposition here will be concerned with some relatively simple applications of linear programming. The student who wishes to go further is referred to the books listed in the footnote below.[16]

An Example of a Linear Programming Problem
A building contractor is building a small subdivision and can build either brick or frame houses. He estimates that he will make a profit of

---

[16]Robert Dorfman, Paul Samuelson, and Robert Solow, *Linear Programming and Economic Analysis* (New York: McGraw-Hill, 1958); William Baumol, *Economic Theory and Operations Analysis*, 3d ed. (Englewood Cliffs, N.J.: Prentice-Hall, 1972); and George Hadley, *Linear Programming* (Reading, Mass.: Addison-Wesley Publishing, 1962).

EXHIBIT 6–5A   Resources and Requirements for House Construction

| Resources | Amount Required per House | | Amount Available |
	Frame	Brick	
Cement (bags)	20	35	280
Finish lumber (bd. ft.)	1,000	500	9,000
Man-hours	500	500	6,000
Bricks	0	4,000	24,000

$800 per house on the frame houses and a profit of $1,200 per house on the brick houses. He, naturally, desires to make the maximum amount of money he can. Since he is limited to these kinds of houses, his profit objective can be expressed algebraically as the equation:

$$\text{Profit} = \pi = 800F + 1{,}200B$$

where F is the number of frame houses and B is the number of brick houses. The $800 and $1,200 coefficients represent the profit contributions per frame or brick house. This equation is called the *objective function.*

Because of long lead times and higher prices if materials are ordered specially, the contractor desires to work with the material that he has on hand. To obtain additional raw materials would increase his costs and reduce the profit margins estimated above. The contractor sets out the requirements and available materials in a table that is reproduced as Exhibit 6–5A.

The requirements columns in Exhibit 6–5A are "recipes" for producing these types of houses, incomplete in that they concentrate only on the materials which are in limited supply. Any other materials required are assumed to cause no particular problems. Since supplies of these specific resources are limited, the use of a resource in the construction of a frame house precludes its being used in a brick house. These four resource limitations can be expressed as linear inequalities as below:

$$20F + 35B \leq 280$$
$$1{,}000F + 500B \leq 9{,}000$$
$$500F + 500B \leq 6{,}000$$
$$0F + 4{,}000B \leq 24{,}000$$

The first of these inequalities states that no more than 280 bags of cement can be used in building frame and brick houses; and therefore either 14 frame and no brick, 8 brick and no frame, or some intermediate combination of brick and frame houses that satisfies the equation $20F + 35B \leq 80$ can be built. To formally complete the structure of the problem, two additional constraints are required: $F \geq 0$ and $B \geq 0$). These are called the

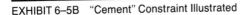

EXHIBIT 6–5B "Cement" Constraint Illustrated

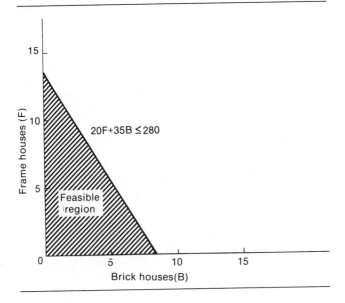

nonnegativity constraints and are designed to ensure that a formal solution does not suggest the production of a negative output. The formal problem now consists of three parts:

Objective function: Maximize $\pi = 800F + 1{,}200B$
Subject to
Resource
Constraints:

$$
\begin{aligned}
20F + 35B &\le 280 \\
1{,}000F + 500B &\le 9{,}000 \\
500F + 500B &\le 6{,}000 \\
0F + 4{,}000B &\le 24{,}000
\end{aligned}
$$

and

Nonnegativity constraints: $F \ge 0$
$B \ge 0$

A graph in this two-variable case provides a very simple and direct solution method and helps illustrate the concepts. Exhibit 6–5B shows the effect of the cement constraint on the solution possibilities. Numbers of brick and frame houses are shown on the axes of the graph. The non-negativity constraints are enforced in Exhibit 6–5B by indicating only zero or positive output of each type of house. The cement constraint line shows the combinations of the maximum number of houses of both kinds that can be produced given the cement constraint. Fewer houses than specified on the constraint line may be produced but would use less than the total supply of cement. The region enclosed by the axes and the

EXHIBIT 6–5C   Feasible Region—All Four Constraints

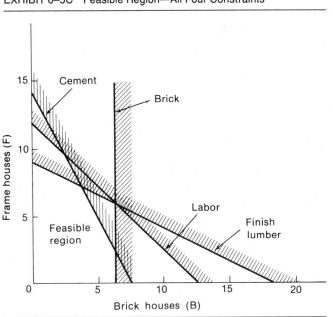

constraint line is known as the *feasible region*. This region will alter as the other constraints are taken into account.

In Exhibit 6–5C the feasible region designated by the cement constraint has been considerably reduced by the addition of further constraints. Each point in this region plus all the points on the boundary lines represent feasible combinations of frame and brick houses that can be built given the constraints of available resources. The contractor now wants to find, within the feasible region, the best, that is, most profitable, combination of houses he can build, using the objective function to define his profit possibilities.

In Exhibit 6–5D, the feasible region has been redrawn to show only those segments of the constraint lines that define the boundaries of the feasible region. As shown in Exhibit 6–5C, the constraint due to labor is not a restrictive constraint as it lies wholly outside the feasible region. The intersections of the constraint lines that define the feasible region are shown as points (B,F), identifying the numbers of brick and frame houses denoted by those intersections: for example, the intersection (6, 3.5) indicates 6 brick and 3.5 frame houses.[17]

---

[17]The reader may rightfully question the meaning of a possible solution which indicates that 3.5 houses should be built. A realistic solution to this specific problem requires that only complete houses be built. The text will ignore (for sake of ease of presentation) the unrealism of a solution that is not an integer, although there is in fact considerable literature and a methodology available to force integer solutions where they are required.

EXHIBIT 6–5D   Feasible Region and Equal Profit Lines Illustrated

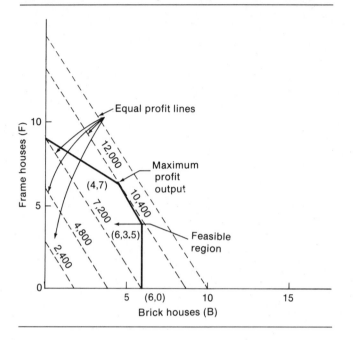

Shown in Exhibit 6–5D are several profit lines, each of which represents a set of combinations of brick and frame houses that, respectively, would yield profits of $2,400, $4,800, $7,200, $10,400, and $12,000. Lines representing higher levels of profit are at successively greater distances from the origin. The objective function

$$\text{Profit} = \pi = 800F + 1,200B$$

was used to derive the profit lines; and it is readily apparent that these lines have the slope

$$-\,^3/_2 = \frac{1,200}{800}$$

which reflects the ratio of profit contributions of brick and frame houses. Since $10,400 is the highest possible profit line that lies within the feasible region, it is evident that the greatest profit is attained by building four brick and seven frame houses. This point (4, 7), illustrates the general principle that maximum profit output will be found at either a corner or along a boundary of the feasible region. This reduces the solution to one of checking the corners and choosing the largest profit. In fact, solution methods for more complex problems are simply algorithms for doing just that and providing tests to see that a maximum truly has been reached. These methods, while not difficult, will not be discussed in this text.[18]

---

[18]See Baumol, *Economic Theory and Operations Analysis,* for a very good presentation of the *simplex* method.

EXHIBIT 6–5E   "Widget" Production with Fixed Proportion Processes

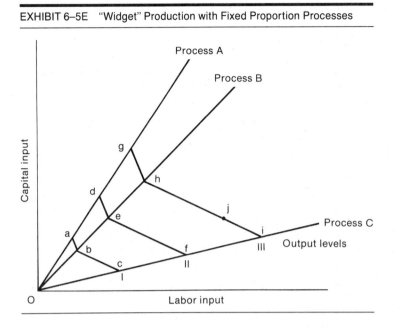

This profit-maximizing example has illustrated the basic concepts of linear programming. The same methodology can be applied when the objective is to minimize costs subject to certain specifications. The classic example of this type of problem is the so-called diet problem: minimization of total food cost, subject to constraints related to vitamins, caloric, and other food value inputs. Another example is the production of hot dogs which uses a variety of ingredients, some of which are subject to required minimum content. As long as the objective function and the constraints can be reasonably formulated as linear equalities or inequalities, linear programming is an effective solution method. Realistic problems may involve literally dozens of variables and constraints, requiring computer solutions.

Linear Programming and the Analysis of Production[19]

In Exhibit 6–5E, the axes again represent input factors as in Figure 6–2 in the chapter. However, in this case the production processes are assumed to require fixed proportions of the two input factors. Production, therefore, can take place only along the "process" rays that represent the allowable fixed proportion combinations of the input factors. In this diagram only three process rays are shown, indicating that there are only three technologically feasible production processes for "widgets." This

---

[19]This presentation is similar to that presented in many places in the literature. See particularly Robert Dorfman, "Mathematical, or 'Linear' Programming: A Non-Mathematical Exposition," *American Economic Review*, December 1953; and Baumol, *Economic Theory and Operations Analysis*, chap. 12.

assumption may be more realistic than the unlimited substitutibility of labor and capital shown in the production function in the text.

The three processes illustrated show the following input ratios: process A, three capital units for two labor units; process B, one capital unit for one labor unit; and process C, one capital for four labor units. Let points a, b, and c represent equal outputs of "widgets" using processes A, B, and C, respectively. Since each process utilizes fixed input proportions, doubled output is represented by points d, e, and f, each of which is twice the distance from the origin (O) along their respective rays as points a, b, and c. Points g, h, and i, likewise, are respectively three times the distance from O as points a, b, and c. Intermediate levels of output may be located in the same manner.

If a larger number of processes and several output levels were shown, the resulting diagram would bear a remarkable resemblance to the production function illustrated in the chapter, the difference being that in this case, production is limited to a finite number of specific processes which utilize the input factors in fixed proportions. Although the number of processes is finite, many combinations of these processes may be derived for a given output. For example, all points along the line segments (ab, bc, de, etc.) connecting equal levels of output on adjacent process rays denote the same output level as the points which are connected. However, production at these intermediate points requires use of a combination of the two adjacent processes, rather than one alone. Consider point j on line hi. Point j represents the same level of output of "widgets" as points h and i, but will use some ratio of units produced by both processes. Division of the output between processes B and C is determined by the way in which point j divides the line hi. The ratio of ji/hi indicates the proportion produced by process B and the ratio hj/hi indicates the proportion produced by process C. For example, if point j were ⅔ the distance from h, ⅔ of the output would be produced by process C and ⅓ by process B.

If there are no limitations on either labor or capital inputs, the total cost of a given output level can be minimized by finding the lowest possible isocost line that just touches a production "isoquant." This point, of necessity, will be either only on one process ray, or lie along the ray connecting two rays at the same output level. This solution is similar in nature to the tangency solution for least-cost output derived in the chapter. The slope of the isocost line is the ratio of the two factor prices. Since

$$TC = wL + mC$$

where w = the price of labor per unit L and m is the price of capital per unit C, then the isocost line is of the form

$$C = \frac{TC}{m} - \frac{w}{m}L.^{20}$$

---

[20]This slope intercept form of the equation says that if L is zero, $C = TC/m$, the y intercept and the slope is $-w/m$. This isocost line is found in exactly the same manner as the equal profit line was determined in the contractor example.

EXHIBIT 6–5F   Production with Fixed Proportion Processes
Limited Labor Input

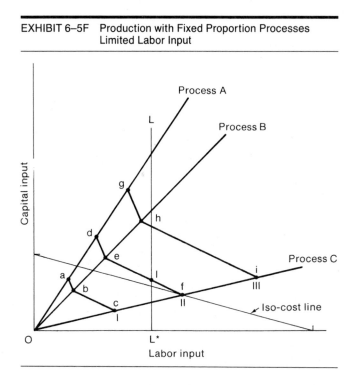

In Exhibit 6–5F, one isocost line is shown that indicates that the least costly way of producing output level II is using process C at level f.

If one or more factors are limited in supply, then the situation is analogous to the short-run economic analysis with a fixed input factor as discussed in the chapter. Exhibit 6–5F is the same as Exhibit 6–5E except that the labor input is limited to the amount shown by the vertical line LL*. With labor input constrained and with the desire to produce at output level II at minimum cost, the solution of Process C at level f is no longer possible. The lowest possible cost will be determined by the intersection of the fixed labor factor and the desired production level. This is at point I and will require the use of both process B and process C. (The proportions produced by each process are determined by the ratios: el/ef = proportion produced by C, and lf/ef = proportion produced by B.) It should be noted that point I lies on a higher isocost line than did point f since the fixed labor constraint prevented maximum utilization of the relative cost advantage of the more labor intensive process C.

Questions

1. Assume the widget firm whose production choices are illustrated in Exhibit 6–5E has a fixed capital input equal to the vertical distances indicated by the following letters. Show what process or processes would be used to achieve the three output levels. Note that some output level may be unachievable.

Capital Input	Production Process(es) to Achieve Output Levels		
	I	*II*	*II*
c			
a			
d			
h			
g			

2. A manufacturer makes two products, each requiring the following capacity in hours per unit:

Shop	Product		Available Hours
	X_1	X_2	
Foundry	6	6	500
Machine	3	5	420
Finish	5	2	250

Product X_1 brings in 40 cents per unit profit and X_2, 30 cents per unit.

a. Write the equations.

b. How many of each should the manufacturer produce?

c. What is his total profit?

7

Investment Decisions and Long-Run Cost

The rate of output is typically regarded in economic analysis as the crucial feature. But it is only one feature.

—*Armen Alchian*

Efficient management of a firm usually requires that consistent attention be paid to long-run affairs such as possible additions to capacity, changes in equipment, and alterations in products. Greatest freedom of choice in such matters exists when an activity is being planned since all opportunities are open (so far as they can be financed). At that point, all costs are variable. "Planning curves" or their analytical equivalents relating average costs to the scale of operation, and perhaps to location, are of interest to the business official trying to set up the most profitable operation.

In terms of the production isoquant chart shown in Figure 6–2 of the previous chapter, both types of input can be varied, and the long-run expansion path *EP* connects the lowest cost combinations of inputs for the attainment of various outputs. These depend on prices of factors as well as on engineering considerations.

The relation between short-run average cost curves for plants of various sizes and long-run average cost can be seen in Figure 7–1. In this illustration only five alternative sizes of plant are assumed to be technically possible due, for example, to the need to use some type of machine that is available only in one size. The five possible plants may be assumed to utilize one to five of these indivisible units of equipment. If the anticipated rate of output during the life of the plant is less than *OM*, it will be most economical to have the smallest size plant (for which $SRAC_1$ is the expected short-run average cost curve). If the expected rate is just a little more than *OM*, it would be possible to use the smallest size plant; but the next larger size plant, utilized at a relatively low rate, would give lower average cost. If anticipated output is between *ON* and *OS*, it will be desirable to build a plant of "optimum" size, associated with curve $SRAC_3$. A larger plant may encounter problems that will increase average costs. It is easy to conceive of a food-retailing store so large that clerks and customers would have to spend an undue amount of time stocking shelves and

FIGURE 7-1   Short-Run Average Cost from a Planning Viewpoint—Cost Depends on Scale of Operations

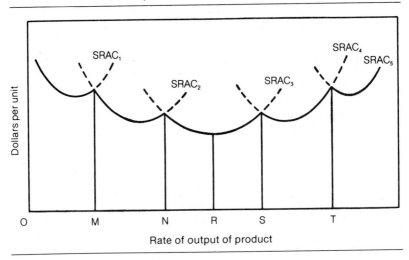

finding items. A manufacturing plant may be so large as to create unusually severe automobile, truck, and railroad congestion as well as problems of coordination and supervision within the facility. Curves $SRAC_4$ and $SRAC_5$ reflect the diseconomy of having excessively large plants. The problem of high costs due to undersized plants that are unable to make sufficient use of specialized machinery, skilled management, and division of labor is much more common. A shortage of capital—owned and borrowed—is especially likely to be the cause of small-scale, high-unit cost operation.

The solid line in Figure 7-1 can be called the *long-run average cost curve* since it shows the lowest possible unit cost of turning out any given output per period. This curve is often referred to as a *planning curve* since a firm never actually operates under long-run cost conditions but can use such an analytical framework in choosing the appropriate size of plant to construct. Under competitive conditions it is necessary for survival that unit costs be as low as possible so it is to be expected that the size of plant will be planned to make $SRAC_3$ the short-run average cost curve. Firms possessing monopoly power are also likely to choose plants that minimize unit costs, provided it is to their advantage to sell approximately the least-cost quantity per period. However, this condition may not exist. For example, the demand for electric power in a small and isolated community is likely to be insufficient to permit full economies of scale in production. Similarly, many firms have monopoly power in the production of patented items that they cannot sell at a rate sufficient to secure the cost advantages of large scale production.

In Figure 7-1, it was assumed that some sort of indivisibility of equipment permitted the plant to be built in only five alternative sizes. How-

FIGURE 7–2   Long-Run Average Cost—with Complete Divisibility

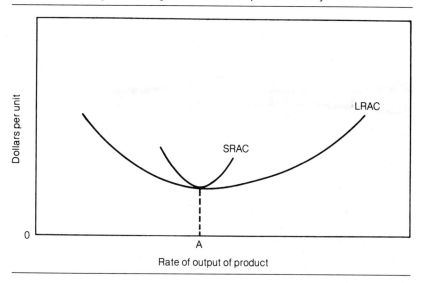

Dollars per unit

LRAC

SRAC

0

A

Rate of output of product

ever, it may instead be possible to build a plant of any desired size; and the long-run average cost curve then becomes a smooth curve, such as LRAC of Figure 7–2. This curve can be conceived as being tangent to all of the possible alternative short-run average cost curves when an unlimited number of sizes of plant is technically possible. It touches the *minimum* point of only one of these curves—SRAC in Figure 7–2.

Typically, in manufacturing and trade, industry sales per period are much greater than OA, the rate at which output can be produced at the lowest average cost by building plant to an optimal scale. In this planning situation a large number of plants, each of the best size, will be built. In the real world, large numbers of identically sized plants are seldom built at the same time. However, some examples can be seen in the fast-food franchise operations such as McDonald's. Usually, many firms will participate in the ownership of these plants, but any or all firms may control many plants. If, however, the advantages of large-scale production are such that the output of one plant of efficient size is a large fraction of the sales of the product in the entire market, it is clear that there will be room for only a small number of plants, and, consequently, only a small number of companies. A small city usually has only a few brickyards and a few "10-cent stores," for example.

FLEXIBILITY OF PLANT

The plant associated with curve SRAC in Figure 7–2 is large enough to take full advantage of economies of scale without being so large as to encounter diseconomies of size. Least-cost output is OA. There may, however, be considerable uncertainty as to the average rate at which it will subsequently be found desirable to operate. Or it may be clear that there will be a great deal of fluctuation in the rate of operation due, for example, to seasonality of demand. These circumstances may cause the businessperson to build a plant which is quite "flexible" in the sense that it can be operated at nonoptimal rates without greatly increasing the short-run unit cost.[1]

Flexibility can also be obtained by some substitution of labor for capital equipment. If the ratio of labor to capital is kept relatively high, a reduction in output can be effected without much increase in average cost by laying off workers or reducing hours of employment. (A machine that is owned or rented by the firm on a long-term contract cannot be "laid off" in order to reduce fixed costs.) To the extent that guaranteed wage plans are put into effect, however, the achievement of flexibility through the maintenance of a high ratio of labor to equipment is less feasible. Also, labor in which the firm has invested in the form of specific training is to some extent like capital equipment and cannot be laid off as economically as can unskilled labor.[2] This is due to the need to train a new worker if the trained worker does not return.

REPLICATION AND THE L-SHAPED LRAC FUNCTION

It should be recognized that for outputs beyond R in Figure 7–1 and A in Figure 7–2, the LRAC as drawn is essentially irrelevant for most firms. The firm can simply replicate plants of the most efficient size to meet larger production requirements. Case 7–5, "The Trend Toward Smaller Plants," gives examples of these possibilities of replication and suggests management and technological factors that can lead to smaller efficient plants.

Empirical evidence also strongly suggests that the LRAC functions for plants are nearly L-shaped. A fairly rapid decline in average costs occurs up to a minimum efficient scale, after which the LRAC tends to be flat thus suggesting the absence of diseconomies of scale for large outputs by the plant.

Stigler concluded that using the "survivor" technique (i.e., measuring the persistence of industry share over time by firms classified by the percentage of industry capacity they possessed) the minimum efficient scale (MES) for the production of steel ingots in the early 1950s was 2½ percent of industry capacity.[3] His study dealt with production by the

---

[1] Flexibility is more important when the commodity cannot be stored or is costly to store since withdrawals from inventory can be temporary substitutes for production.

[2] This idea was developed by Walter Y. Oi, "Labor as a Quasi-Fixed Factor," *Journal of Political Economy*, December 1962.

[3] G. J. Stigler, "The Economics of Scale, *Journal of Law and Economics*, vol. 1, no. 1 (October 1958), pp. 54–81

open-hearth or Bessemer process. Today the *MES* scale for ingots is lower with small electric furnace producers taking an increasing share of the market. The minimum efficient scale was found to be quite large in a study of electric power production by L. R. Christensen and W. H. Greene.[4] They found it at an output of about 20 billion kilowatt-hours a year with 97 out of 114 firms operating below this capacity. The ability to survive on the declining portion of the *LRAC* would reflect the regional monopoly nature of the industry with markets somewhat separated by high transmission costs.

SIZE OF FIRM AND COST

The planning curves shown in Figure 7–1 pertain to the variation in average costs as the scale of plant is altered. If the firm has only one plant and if most of its costs are production costs, the best size of firm will be governed almost entirely by the optimum size of the plant. If the firm is a multiplant organization, its optimum size may have little relation to the optimum scale of plant. (Large food-retailing companies, for example, are probably somewhat more efficient than smaller firms in this field, although individual plants [stores] are of moderate size.)

It may be necessary for a firm to be large in order to secure the efficient operations of its plants when the efficiency of each plant is related to the operation of the others. This seems to be the situation in the interstate bus business where plants (buses and terminals) are small, but where a large number of buses is needed in order to maintain regular schedules and where the terminals must be numerous if adequate common carrier service is to be provided. Up to a point, at least, a larger firm enjoys advantages in raising capital, in purchasing, in carrying on research, and in selling. These activities require for their most efficient performance certain specialized personnel, equipment, or procedures which a small firm may be unable to afford. (The possibility of hiring the services of experts who also serve other firms somewhat reduces the diseconomy of small size, however.) A large vertically integrated firm—one which owns plants at different stages in the production process—will probably have lower costs than a nonintegrated company if there is monopoly power at some of the earlier stages, since integration will make it possible to avoid paying monopolistic prices for materials. Unless the firm uses enough materials to make possible their production on an optimum scale, however, integration may be unprofitable. Use of part of the output and sale of the remainder may afford the integrated firm a chance both to avoid high-priced materials and components and to secure an adequate scale of output at the earlier stages.

---

[4]L. R. Christensen and W. H. Greene, "Economies of Scale in U.S. Electric Power Generation," *Journal of Political Economy*, vol. 84, no. 4 (August 1976).

LIMITED PRODUCTION RUN

The cost curves shown so far are based on the assumption that production of the good under consideration will continue indefinitely into the future. If it can be foreseen that it will be desirable, or may be desirable, to produce the item for a limited time only, the firm is likely to make a smaller financial commitment for specialized equipment and for specialized training of labor and management.

Suppose an airplane manufacturer has designed a new transport plane and is tooled up for production. A large expenditure will have been incurred for engineering, equipment, recruiting and training of labor, and perhaps for advertising and lobbying. As these sunk costs are divided among more units of output their average per plane will decline. This is one reason the company will hope to sell a large number of units. Another reason is that labor cost per unit diminishes because workers become more adept at their jobs as they continue to produce the same item and as "bugs" in the production process are removed. It was found during World War II that labor-hours per military airplane declined approximately 30 percent each time accumulated output doubled. If, for example, the first unit required 100,000 labor-hours, the second would take 70,000 labor-hours, the fourth would require 49,000 labor-hours, and so forth. This permitted dramatic reductions over time in the cost of planes which the armed forces found successful.

Under such conditions the rate of output per month or other time period is very likely to increase. But since a higher rate of output and larger total volume tend to have opposite effects on cost with a given size of plant, it is desirable analytically to assume that the monthly rate of output remains constant while the total production run is varied in amount. This is the implicit assumption in Figure 7–3.

Both average and marginal costs per unit decline as the production run becomes longer. The connection between the firm's ability to sell the item and to produce economically becomes especially close. Quantity discounts are likely to be used to increase total volume since additional sales result in lower costs. If the item is sold to a government agency, active lobbyists and "good connections" can have a similar importance.

In practice it may not be easy to distinguish between a succession of limited production runs and continuous production. If changes are made in the model that require some modification of equipment, part, but probably not all, of the cost reduction due to volume will be lost. Average and marginal cost curves may be similar to those of Figure 7–3 except for upward shifts occurring at the volumes at which model changes are made. If the model change is sufficiently drastic, the limited production run can be considered to be starting from scratch again.

Cost curves based on total volume produced, rather than on rate of output per time period, were introduced into economics by Armen Alchian. The basic idea that per unit costs decline as a plant turns out a

FIGURE 7–3   Limited Production Run—Average and
Marginal Costs Decline with Volume

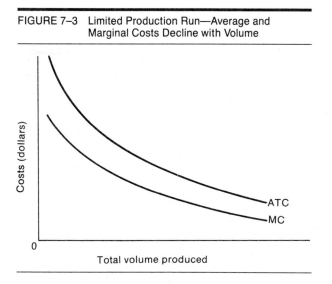

larger total volume of the same good had long been accepted in industrial
engineering and by many plant managers.

If cost curves are named for their originators, the traditional cost
curves can be called "Viner Cost Curves" while those of Figure 7–3 can be
called "Alchian Cost Curves." The latter can most easily be considered to
hold rate of output (e.g., per month) constant while changing the total
volume of the production run.

The relationship between Viner and Alchian curves can be seen most
readily in the propositions that follow. If an item is simple to produce,
there is no significant "learning curve" for workers and management. The
total volume produced then does not affect average and marginal costs. If,
however, the item is complex (such as a military airplane or an automobile), the length of the production run makes a great deal of difference. It
is useful for a complex good to think of the Viner Cost Curves as shifting
downward while learning is occurring. Once all learning has occurred,
the changes in unit and marginal costs are due exclusively to changes in
the rate of output. The Viner Cost Curves then begin to be significant. It
should be noted that while technology is impounded in *ceteris paribus* in
Viner Curves, it changes to some extent in the Alchian approach since
learning, shop organization, and tools change (for the better) with experience on a particular model.

VALUE OF EQUIPMENT

Whether continuous or limited production is being planned, business
executives are faced with difficult problems related to plant and equipment. For example, they must decide how much and what type of equipment to buy, whether it should be new or used, and when to replace old

equipment wholly or partially with new models. Regardless of the care with which calculations are made, judgment plays an important role.

The concept of capitalization is basic to this entire field. Capitalization is the mathematical process of finding the present value of a future stream of income. The calculation is simplest if this income stream is one without end—an income in perpetuity. Suppose a public utility company has paid a dividend of $5 per annum per share on its common stock for many years and will—as far as can be seen—continue to do so indefinitely. The market price of the stock should then depend almost entirely on the interest rate that is considered appropriate for this sort of investment.[5] (This percentage yield will be lower than on most stocks because of the relatively low risk of loss of interest or principal due to the stable nature of the company.) Suppose that the appropriate interest rate is 5 percent per year. The stock would then sell at about $100 per share. This is determined by the capitalization formula for a perpetual income, where P is the present value of a share, A is the anticipated income per annum, and i is the yearly market interest rate on investment of this quality:

$$P = \frac{A}{i}$$

The formula is appropriate only if no change is anticipated in either A or i. Suppose that A is expected to remain at $5 per year but that most buyers anticipate that interest rates in general will rise slightly in the near future. They would then be unwilling to pay quite as much as $100 per share, since they believe that by waiting a while, they can secure a little more than $5 a year on $100 invested in a security of this grade (or even in this same security). On the other hand, if there is a general expectation of a decline in interest rates, the stock should now sell at a little more than $100 a share. This simple capitalization formula is also applicable to the evaluation of a piece of land that is expected to yield a steady and perpetual income above taxes and all other costs. For example, the value of a piece of city land recently rented on a 99-year lease to a dependable firm that pays the owner a yearly rental of $10,000 would be $200,000 if, again, 5 percent were considered the appropriate rate of interest on such an investment. If the land changed hands at this price, the new buyer would, of course, receive a 5 percent return on the investment of $200,000, since this is just another view of the same problem.

The capitalization calculation is somewhat more complicated when the income will be received only for a finite number of years instead of in perpetuity. Income received today is more valuable than the same amount of income received a year from now because if it is received today, it can

---

[5]The market price is also affected by the number of dividends paid per year and by brokerage fees and transfer taxes, but these will have a relatively minor effect on market price and are disregarded for purposes of simplification. In periods of rapid inflation, the discount rate may considerably higher than in a period of expected stable prices. This is due to the loss in purchasing power of the stable dividend.

begin immediately to earn interest for the owner. Therefore, its additional worth is just the amount of interest that it will earn in a year. By the same token, income that is still a year away must be discounted—a year's interest must be taken away—in order to find its present value. If the income is more than a year away, it must be discounted more heavily.

Suppose that a merchant has a claim to three $1,000 payments that are due her one year, two years, and three years from today, respectively. She may wish to sell this claim in order to secure all of the cash immediately (from someone else who will look upon the claim as a suitable investment). The amount for which she can sell the claim depends on the risk that is deemed by potential buyers to be associated with the claim— that is, by the apparent degree of danger of nonpayment or slow payment of an installment when due.

The present value of this claim can be found from the formula:

$$P = \$1,000 \left(\frac{1}{1 + i} + \frac{1}{(1 + i)^2} + \frac{1}{(1 + i)^3} \right)$$

This formula discounts each successive payment more heavily. The first payment in now worth the sum that will build up to $1,000 in one year, without compounding the interest. The second payment is now worth the sum that will build up to $1,000 in two years, with interest compounded at the end of the first year; while the third payment is now worth the amount that would build up to $1,000 in three years if compounded at the end of the first and second years. Suppose i is 6 percent. The first $1,000 installment is now worth $943.40, the second installment is worth $890, and the third is worth $839.62. The entire claim is worth the sum of these amounts, or $2,673.02. This worth would, of course, be greater if the relevant interest rate were deemed to be less than 6 percent, and it would be lower if a higher discount rate were used. Also, the claim would be worth less today if a period shorter than a year were used for compounding interest. (See Figures 7–4 and 7–5 in this chapter for present value of a single payment of $1 in future years and of an annual payment of $1 at various interest rates.) The calculations in the present paragraph may be checked in Figure 7–4. It should be noted that the discount factor of 2.673 is found in Figure 7–5 so that it is not necessary to compute value of annual payments separately.

VALUE OF A MACHINE

The same sort of calculation may be used to determine the present value of a machine. In this case the annual income is the "quasi rent" derived from its productive contribution.[6] Annual quasi rent is found by deduct-

---

[6]This name was given by Alfred Marshall to the "income derived from machines or other appliances for production made by man" in *Principles of Economics*, 8th ed. (London: Macmillan, 1930), p. 74.

FIGURE 7–4 Present Value of $1

Years Hence	1%	2%	4%	6%	8%	10%	12%	14%	15%	16%	18%	20%	22%	24%	25%	26%	28%	30%	35%	40%	45%	50%
1	0.990	0.980	0.962	0.943	0.926	0.909	0.893	0.877	0.870	0.862	0.847	0.833	0.820	0.806	0.800	0.794	0.781	0.769	0.741	0.714	0.690	0.667
2	0.980	0.961	0.925	0.890	0.857	0.826	0.797	0.769	0.756	0.743	0.718	0.694	0.672	0.650	0.640	0.630	0.610	0.592	0.549	0.510	0.476	0.444
3	0.971	0.942	0.889	0.840	0.794	0.751	0.712	0.675	0.658	0.641	0.609	0.579	0.551	0.524	0.512	0.500	0.477	0.455	0.406	0.364	0.328	0.296
4	0.961	0.924	0.855	0.792	0.735	0.683	0.636	0.592	0.572	0.552	0.516	0.482	0.451	0.423	0.410	0.397	0.373	0.350	0.301	0.260	0.226	0.198
5	0.951	0.906	0.822	0.747	0.681	0.621	0.567	0.519	0.497	0.476	0.437	0.402	0.370	0.341	0.328	0.315	0.291	0.269	0.223	0.186	0.156	0.132
6	0.942	0.888	0.790	0.705	0.630	0.564	0.507	0.456	0.432	0.410	0.370	0.335	0.303	0.275	0.262	0.250	0.227	0.207	0.165	0.133	0.108	0.088
7	0.933	0.871	0.760	0.665	0.583	0.513	0.452	0.400	0.376	0.354	0.314	0.279	0.249	0.222	0.210	0.198	0.178	0.159	0.122	0.095	0.074	0.059
8	0.923	0.853	0.731	0.627	0.540	0.467	0.404	0.351	0.327	0.305	0.266	0.233	0.204	0.179	0.168	0.157	0.139	0.123	0.091	0.068	0.051	0.039
9	0.914	0.837	0.703	0.592	0.500	0.424	0.361	0.308	0.284	0.263	0.225	0.194	0.167	0.144	0.134	0.125	0.108	0.094	0.067	0.048	0.035	0.026
10	0.905	0.820	0.676	0.558	0.463	0.386	0.322	0.270	0.247	0.227	0.191	0.162	0.137	0.116	0.107	0.099	0.085	0.073	0.050	0.035	0.024	0.017
11	0.896	0.804	0.650	0.527	0.429	0.350	0.287	0.237	0.215	0.195	0.162	0.135	0.112	0.094	0.086	0.079	0.066	0.056	0.037	0.025	0.017	0.012
12	0.887	0.788	0.625	0.497	0.397	0.319	0.257	0.208	0.187	0.168	0.137	0.112	0.092	0.076	0.069	0.062	0.052	0.043	0.027	0.018	0.012	0.008
13	0.879	0.773	0.601	0.469	0.368	0.290	0.229	0.182	0.163	0.145	0.116	0.093	0.075	0.061	0.055	0.050	0.040	0.033	0.020	0.013	0.008	0.005
14	0.870	0.758	0.577	0.442	0.340	0.263	0.205	0.160	0.141	0.125	0.099	0.078	0.062	0.049	0.044	0.039	0.032	0.025	0.015	0.009	0.006	0.003
15	0.861	0.743	0.555	0.417	0.315	0.239	0.183	0.140	0.123	0.108	0.084	0.065	0.051	0.040	0.035	0.031	0.025	0.020	0.011	0.006	0.004	0.002
16	0.853	0.728	0.534	0.394	0.292	0.218	0.163	0.123	0.107	0.093	0.071	0.054	0.042	0.032	0.028	0.025	0.019	0.015	0.008	0.005	0.003	0.002
17	0.844	0.714	0.513	0.371	0.270	0.198	0.146	0.108	0.093	0.080	0.060	0.045	0.034	0.026	0.023	0.020	0.015	0.012	0.006	0.003	0.002	0.001
18	0.836	0.700	0.494	0.350	0.250	0.180	0.130	0.095	0.081	0.069	0.051	0.038	0.028	0.021	0.018	0.016	0.012	0.009	0.005	0.002	0.001	0.001
19	0.828	0.686	0.475	0.331	0.232	0.164	0.116	0.083	0.070	0.060	0.043	0.031	0.023	0.017	0.014	0.012	0.009	0.007	0.003	0.002	0.001	
20	0.820	0.673	0.456	0.312	0.215	0.149	0.104	0.073	0.061	0.051	0.037	0.026	0.019	0.014	0.012	0.010	0.007	0.005	0.002	0.001	0.001	
21	0.811	0.660	0.439	0.294	0.199	0.135	0.093	0.064	0.053	0.044	0.031	0.022	0.015	0.011	0.009	0.008	0.006	0.004	0.002	0.001	0.001	
22	0.803	0.647	0.422	0.278	0.184	0.123	0.083	0.056	0.046	0.038	0.026	0.018	0.013	0.009	0.007	0.006	0.004	0.003	0.001	0.001		
23	0.795	0.634	0.406	0.262	0.170	0.112	0.074	0.049	0.040	0.033	0.022	0.015	0.010	0.007	0.006	0.005	0.003	0.002	0.001			
24	0.788	0.622	0.390	0.247	0.158	0.102	0.066	0.043	0.035	0.028	0.019	0.013	0.008	0.006	0.005	0.004	0.003	0.002	0.001			
25	0.780	0.610	0.375	0.233	0.146	0.092	0.059	0.038	0.030	0.024	0.016	0.010	0.007	0.005	0.004	0.003	0.002	0.001	0.001			
26	0.772	0.598	0.361	0.220	0.135	0.084	0.053	0.033	0.026	0.021	0.014	0.009	0.006	0.004	0.003	0.002	0.002	0.001				
27	0.764	0.586	0.347	0.207	0.125	0.076	0.047	0.029	0.020	0.018	0.011	0.007	0.005	0.003	0.002	0.002	0.001	0.001				
28	0.757	0.574	0.333	0.196	0.116	0.069	0.042	0.026	0.020	0.016	0.010	0.006	0.004	0.002	0.002	0.001	0.001	0.001				
29	0.749	0.563	0.321	0.185	0.107	0.063	0.037	0.022	0.017	0.014	0.008	0.005	0.003	0.002	0.002	0.001	0.001					
30	0.742	0.552	0.308	0.174	0.099	0.057	0.033	0.020	0.015	0.012	0.007	0.004	0.003	0.002	0.001	0.001						
40	0.672	0.453	0.208	0.097	0.046	0.022	0.011	0.005	0.004	0.003	0.001	0.001										
50	0.608	0.372	0.141	0.054	0.021	0.009	0.003	0.001	0.001	0.001												

FIGURE 7–5 Present Value of $1 Received Annually for n Years

Years (n)	1%	2%	4%	6%	8%	10%	12%	14%	15%	16%	18%	20%	22%	24%	25%	26%	28%	30%	35%	40%	45%	50%
1......	0.990	0.980	0.962	0.943	0.926	0.909	0.893	0.877	0.870	0.862	0.847	0.833	0.820	0.806	0.800	0.794	0.781	9.769	0.741	0.714	0.690	0.667
2......	1.970	1.942	1.886	1.833	1.783	1.736	1.690	1.647	1.626	1.605	1.566	1.528	1.492	1.457	1.440	1.424	1.392	1.361	1.289	1.224	1.165	1.111
3......	2.941	2.884	2.775	2.673	2.577	2.487	2.402	2.322	2.283	2.246	2.174	2.106	2.042	1.981	1.952	1.923	1.868	1.816	1.696	1.589	1.493	1.407
4......	3.902	3.808	3.630	3.465	3.312	3.170	3.037	2.914	2.855	2.798	2.690	2.589	2.494	2.404	2.362	2.320	2.241	2.166	1.997	1.849	1.720	1.605
5......	4.853	4.713	4.452	4.212	3.993	3.791	3.605	3.433	3.352	3.274	3.127	2.991	2.864	2.745	2.689	2.635	2.532	2.436	2.220	2.035	1.876	1.737
6......	5.795	5.601	5.242	4.917	4.623	4.355	4.111	3.889	3.784	3.685	3.498	3.326	3.167	3.020	2.951	2.885	2.759	2.643	2.385	2.168	1.983	1.824
7......	6.728	6.472	6.002	5.582	5.206	4.868	4.564	4.288	4.160	4.039	3.812	3.605	3.416	3.242	3.161	3.083	2.937	2.802	2.508	2.263	2.057	1.883
8......	7.652	7.325	6.733	6.210	5.747	5.335	4.968	4.639	4.487	4.344	4.078	3.837	3.619	3.421	3.329	3.241	3.076	2.925	2.598	2.331	2.108	1.922
9......	8.566	8.162	7.435	6.802	6.247	5.759	5.328	4.946	4.772	4.607	4.303	4.031	3.786	3.566	3.463	3.366	3.184	3.019	2.665	2.379	2.144	1.948
10......	9.471	8.983	8.111	7.360	6.710	6.145	5.650	5.216	5.019	4.833	4.494	4.192	3.923	3.682	3.571	3.465	3.269	3.092	2.715	2.414	2.168	1.965
11......	10.368	9.787	8.760	7.887	7.139	6.495	5.988	5.453	5.234	5.029	4.656	4.327	4.035	3.776	3.656	3.544	3.335	3.147	2.757	2.438	2.185	1.977
12......	11.255	10.575	9.385	8.384	7.536	6.814	6.194	5.660	5.421	5.197	4.793	4.439	4.127	3.851	3.725	3.606	3.387	3.190	2.779	2.456	2.196	1.985
13......	12.134	11.343	9.986	8.853	7.904	7.103	6.424	5.842	5.583	5.342	4.910	4.533	4.203	3.912	3.780	3.656	3.427	3.223	2.799	2.468	2.204	1.990
14......	13.004	12.106	10.563	9.295	8.244	7.367	6.628	6.002	5.724	5.468	5.008	4.611	4.265	3.962	3.824	3.695	3.459	3.249	2.814	2.477	2.210	1.993
15......	13.865	12.849	11.118	9.712	8.559	7.606	6.811	6.142	5.847	5.575	5.092	4.675	4.315	4.001	3.859	3.726	3.483	3.268	2.825	2.484	2.214	1.995
16......	14.718	13.578	11.652	10.106	8.851	7.824	6.974	6.265	5.954	5.669	5.162	4.730	4.357	4.033	3.887	3.751	3.503	3.283	2.834	2.489	2.216	1.997
17......	15.562	14.292	12.166	10.477	9.122	8.022	7.120	6.373	6.047	5.749	5.222	4.775	4.391	4.059	3.910	3.771	3.518	3.295	2.840	2.492	2.218	1.998
18......	16.398	14.992	12.659	10.828	9.372	8.201	7.250	6.467	6.128	5.818	5.273	4.812	4.419	4.080	3.928	3.786	3.529	3.304	2.844	2.494	2.219	1.999
19......	17.226	15.678	13.134	11.158	9.604	8.365	7.366	6.550	6.198	5.877	5.316	4.844	4.442	4.097	3.942	3.799	3.539	3.311	2.848	2.496	2.220	1.999
20......	18.046	16.351	13.590	11.470	9.818	8.514	7.469	6.623	6.259	5.929	5.353	4.870	4.460	4.110	3.954	3.808	3.546	3.316	2.850	2.497	2.221	1.999
21......	18.857	17.011	14.029	11.764	10.017	8.649	7.562	6.687	6.312	5.973	5.384	4.891	4.476	4.121	3.963	3.816	3.551	3.320	2.852	2.498	2.221	2.000
22......	19.660	17.658	14.451	12.042	10.201	8.772	7.645	6.743	6.359	6.011	5.410	4.909	4.488	4.130	3.970	3.822	3.556	3.323	2.853	2.498	2.222	2.000
23......	20.456	18.292	14.857	12.303	10.371	8.883	7.718	6.792	6.399	6.044	5.432	4.925	4.499	4.137	3.976	3.827	3.559	3.325	2.854	2.499	2.222	2.000
24......	21.243	18.914	15.247	12.550	10.529	8.985	7.784	6.835	6.434	6.073	5.451	4.937	4.507	4.143	3.981	3.831	3.562	3.327	2.855	2.499	2.222	2.000
25......	22.023	19.523	15.622	12.783	10.675	9.077	7.843	6.873	6.464	6.097	5.467	4.948	4.514	4.147	3.985	3.834	3.564	3.329	2.856	2.499	2.222	2.000
26......	22.795	20.121	15.983	13.003	10.810	9.161	7.896	6.906	6.491	6.118	5.480	4.956	4.520	4.151	3.988	3.837	3.566	3.330	2.856	2.500	2.222	2.000
27......	23.560	20.707	16.330	13.211	10.935	9.237	7.943	6.935	6.514	6.136	5.492	4.964	4.524	4.154	3.990	3.839	3.567	3.331	2.856	2.500	2.222	2.000
28......	24.316	21.281	16.663	13.406	11.051	9.307	7.984	6.961	6.534	6.152	5.502	4.970	4.528	4.157	3.992	3.840	3.563	3.331	2.857	2.500	2.222	2.000
29......	25.066	21.844	16.984	13.591	11.158	9.370	8.022	6.983	6.551	6.166	5.510	4.975	4.531	4.159	3.994	3.841	3.569	3.332	2.857	2.500	2.222	2.000
30......	25.808	22.396	17.292	13.765	11.258	9.427	8.055	7.003	6.566	6.177	5.517	4.979	4.534	4.160	3.995	3.842	3.569	3.332	2.857	2.500	2.222	2.000
40......	32.835	27.355	19.793	15.046	11.925	9.779	8.244	7.105	6.642	6.234	5.548	4.997	4.544	4.166	3.999	3.846	3.571	3.333	2.857	2.500	2.222	2.000
50......	39.196	31.424	21.482	15.762	12.234	9.915	8.304	7.133	6.661	6.246	5.554	4.999	4.545	4.167	4.000	3.816	3.571	3.333	2.857	2.500	2.222	2.000

ing from the value of the annual product of the machine all variable costs (labor, materials, fuel, etc.) incurred in the same process. No deduction is made, however, for depreciation on the machine or for interest. The term *cash flow* is often used in this connection in place of quasi rent. While it brings to mind approximately the correct picture, this term is not an entirely accurate one because in a given year the inflow of funds may take the form of increases in accounts receivable, reductions in liabilities of the firm, or some other change in noncash accounts. In the subsequent discussion the term *cash flow* will be utilized because of its widespread use.

Suppose a machine has three years of productive life remaining and that at the end of that time, it will have no scrap value. Assume also that (like an electric light bulb or, perhaps, a TV picture tube) it gives satisfactory service until it expires, rather than gradually running down or requiring ever-increasing maintenance expenditures. If the product turned out by the machine is worth $4,000 a year and variable expenses of $3,000 a year are incurred in its operation, the machine has a present value of $2,673.02, if a 6 percent rate is used in discounting. (This is the same calculation as made previously—a neat trick that saves the writers a bit of time.)

Usually, a machine will have scrap value or trade-in value at the end of its productive life. This requires only the modification of adding in the discounted value of this last-ditch contribution of the machine. The scrap value is assumed to be realized as soon as the last output is sold (at the end of the nth year). Letting Q stand for cash flow received at the end of each year and S for scrap value, the formula for the present value of a machine is:

$$P = \frac{Q_1}{1 + i} + \frac{Q_2}{(1 + i)^2} + \frac{Q_3}{(1 + i)^3} + \cdots + \frac{Q_n}{(1 + i)^n} + \frac{S}{(1 + i)^n}$$

The cash flow need not be the same each year. (If it were, A would be the designation as used in the present chapter.) Normally, it will decrease with time as maintenance and repair expenses connected with the aging machine increase. It is implicitly assumed, however, that the cash flow is maximized each year by operation of the machine at the output rate where marginal cost equals marginal revenue. It has been pointed out that a plant is operated optimally only when marginal revenue and marginal cost are equated, and the same is true of an individual machine. The correct present value of the machine can only be derived on the assumption that its earnings will be maximized through correct management.

It should be realized that regardless of the arithmetical care with which the present value of a machine is calculated, much uncertainty is present in the calculation. The cash flow will be affected by the price of the output, by prices which will be paid for materials, labor, and so forth, in the future, and by possible breakdowns of the machine itself. Its scrap or trade-in value is probably not definitely ascertainable if the machine has a number of years of life remaining. Also, the selection of the interest rate to be used in discounting requires much information and judgment. Usually, it is correct to utilize an interest rate which reflects the market-determined rate at which the firm could lend its money, the degree of risk being the same. More on the proper choice of an interest rate representing the cost of capital is in the following chapter.

DECISION TO PURCHASE A MACHINE

Estimating the worth of a machine involves difficulties but must somehow be accomplished, at least roughly, if a rational decision to purchase or not to purchase a machine is to be made. Once the present value (P) has been determined, it is only necessary to compare this with the cost of the machine. If its value is less than its cost, it should not be purchased; if its value is equal to its cost, it is a matter of indifference whether it is purchased, since funds invested in the machine will bring the same return as they could earn in an alternative investment. This assumes that sufficient funds are available and there are not other, more attractive uses for the funds. The subject of capital budgeting is considered in the next chapter.

If (P) exceeds the cost of the machine, it means that according to the best calculation that can be made, the returns from the machine will more than cover all variable costs, depreciation on the machine, and an "opportunity" interest return on the capital tied up in the machine. The investment then appears to be a good one, and management is likely to buy the machine (unless a still better one is available for the job). Sales opportunities may be such that additional machines would also be expected to have a present worth greater than their cost. In this event, management should purchase additional machines as long as the value added by another machine to the present value of the whole stock of machines exceeds the cost of the machine. In this calculation, account must be taken of the fact that each machine that is added may lower the present value of the earlier machines by lowering the market price at which the output can be disposed of. It is also possible that "quantity discounts" can be secured on larger orders for machines, and this further complicates the calculation. These complications are greater than those we wish to address in this partial treatment of a difficult subject.[7]

---

[7]A classic that should be studied by the reader desiring a thorough training in this subject is Friedrich A. and Vera C. Lutz, *The Theory of Investment of the Firm* (Princeton: Princeton University Press, 1951). Such problems as optimum productive techniques, optimum size of firm, optimum length of life of equipment, and optimum method of finance are treated mathematically. More practical treatments can be found in textbooks in financial management and engineering economics.

SHOULD A NEW MODEL BE PURCHASED?

Management faces a slightly different sort of investment decision when confronted with the problem whether to replace a machine that is still usable with a new, improved model. The problem is similar to that of the opulent family that has to decide each year whether to buy a new-model automobile or to continue to drive the "old" car. (The firm is more likely than the household to make a rational decision, however.) The development of a dramatically altered model, such as a jet-propelled airliner or an atomic-powered ocean liner, can bring this question forcibly before a great many firms at the same time.

It would seem at first glance that a new type of machine that becomes available should be purchased if it will lower the unit cost of production. If investment has already been made in one machine, however, it is often correct to compare the *variable operating costs* per unit using the old machine to the *total cost* per unit using the new machine. Costs that are already sunk should not enter into decisions regarding new steps to be taken or avoided. They are bygones that should remain bygones.

This comparison is not correct, however, to the extent that sunk costs are really not lost because they can be partially recovered through the sale or trade-in of the old machine. As long as average variable operating costs using the old machine are below the selling price of the product, it can continue to yield an annual cash flow. If this cash flow is sufficient to cover interest on its own scrap value plus interest on the difference between the value and cost of a new machine, use of the old machine should be continued.[8]

Like most calculations involving interest, the appropriateness of this formulation is not easy to see. The following may help. If the old machine is continued in use, the firm sacrifices during each time period the interest which could otherwise be earned on its market value. This is one cost of keeping the old machine. Also, by retaining the old machine, the firm sacrifices interest income on the difference between the present value and the cost of the new machine. This interest would actually be secured from the cash flow which would be returned by the new machine over time. If the new machine is markedly superior to the old one, this will be a large item and will make it desirable to replace the old machine with the new one immediately. If, however, the new machine is only a slight improvement over the old one, this will not be a large amount. If that event, it is quite possible that for some years to come, the annual cash flow returned by the old machine will exceed the sum of the annual interest on its disposal value and the annual interest on the difference between value and cost of a new machine. Eventually, of course, the old machine should be replaced, but premature replacement by a model which is only slightly better is both common and uneconomical.

---

[8]This formulation is given by Lutz and Lutz, *Theory of Investment of the Firm*, pp. 113–14.

ALTERNATIVE FORMULATION OF REPLACEMENT CRITERION

The complex-sounding considerations that have been set forth for deciding rationally between retaining and replacing old machinery can be restated in a somewhat simpler way. *Average cost* of a product turned out by the machinery should be defined in economic terms rather than in accounting terms. Ordinarily, the accountant considers average cost to be made up of variable cost per unit and fixed cost per unit, including in the latter depreciation based on the original cost of the asset. However, it will seldom happen that the market or trade-in value of an old machine will exactly equal its original cost less depreciation as charged off on the books from the time of acquisition to the time at which a decision to keep or replace is to be made.

A direct comparison of the average cost of production using the new machine and using the old machine may be appropriate if three things are done: (1) average cost of producing with the old equipment must include depreciation based not on original cost but on expected decline in market value; (2) interest must be added in as a cost, with its amount being computed on the cost and market value, respectively, of the new and the old equipment; and (3) the average cost calculation using both old and new equipment must be made in each case for the expected optimum output, that is, where marginal cost equals marginal revenue. This may not be the same output in both cases. If it is expected that demand will fall off, replacement of the old machinery becomes less desirable, since a reduction in output will raise average cost of output more sharply for the new machinery than for the old. This is due to the higher fixed costs that will be associated with the new equipment.

In summary, the decision whether to replace existing machinery with new machinery usually cannot be made simply by comparing average cost of production as likely to be calculated by an accountant. Capital will have been sunk in the old equipment, but this historical event is irrelevant to a present decision except to the extent that capital could now be recovered by selling or trading in the old machinery. This requires an economist's calculation of average cost of production using the old machinery. In addition, interest must be included as a cost of production. This is normal procedure for the economist but not for the accountant, except where the interest payment is explicit. Also, the average cost of production using either old or new equipment will depend on the rate of production; consequently, not a single average cost but instead an *average cost curve* should be computed for output from both old and new machinery. The optimum rate of output that is anticipated for each of the two productive processes then determines an average cost for each, and these averages can be directly compared to judge whether replacement is desirable. If *none* of the capital sunk in the old machinery can be recovered by its sale or trade-in, the relevant comparison is simply average cost at the expected output with the new machine versus average variable cost at the expected rate of output using the old machine. Interest and depreciation are elements in the former but not in the latter.

REVENUE CONSIDERATIONS

In the preceding discussion, it is implicitly assumed that the revenue received by the firm will be the same whether or not old equipment is replaced. Frequently, however, a better product is turned out by the new equipment, and income is thereby increased. This is especially easy to see in the case of new transportation equipment that will attract customers through greater speed, convenience, and so forth. When revenue is affected, the replacement calculation is more difficult than was indicated by the suggested comparison of average cost of production with new and old equipment. Instead, for the rate of operation expected in each case, net earnings after income taxes must be compared, total income being computed by multiplying output by price per unit and total cost being computed by multiplying output by adjusted cost per unit. (The income tax is computed with the use of accounting costs as permitted for tax purposes, and these will differ from the costs just mentioned.)

The preceding discussion can be reduced to the rather obvious statement that old equipment should be replaced by new equipment if annual net income after taxes can thereby be increased. It should be noted, however, that the relevant net income as computed for the alternative of retention of old equipment involves the basic economic concept of disregarding sunk costs based on *previous* decisions. Instead, only *present* alternatives are involved, since average cost is derived in part from the present disposal value of old equipment. In some cases, another firm can make especially good use of second-hand equipment (due perhaps to a very limited capital budget), and in such a case the firm that owns such equipment may have an especially good opportunity to modernize its own plant.

The foregoing discussion of equipment replacement criteria aids in the understanding of long-run cost curves such as those of Figure 7–1. First, it emphasizes that these are planning curves prior to commitment of any resources to the activity. If, instead, the operation is already an active one, the relevant planning involves a comparison of average costs per unit of output attainable with new and existing equipment. Second, it should be noted that demand is usually assumed to be independent of cost, although this is not always true (e.g., commercial aircraft). And lastly, it becomes evident that while cost curves can be drawn without considering demand, production processes will not actually be established unless prospective sales are sufficient. This is why good schools of engineering usually require that students study some economics.

DETERMINATION OF LONG-RUN COST (PLANNING) CURVES

The remaining problem of assigning long-run costs to a unit of output is essentially one of determining the appropriate capital costs where the capital costs are functions of time, not output. For long-run decisions, business management is geared to thinking of the yearly periods for which financial statements are prepared. In order to estimate the appropriate annual cost associated with various capital inputs, the present value formulas can be solved for A, a uniform annual cash flow, as follows:

For perpetual life: $A = Pi$

For life of n years: $A = P / \left(\dfrac{1}{1 + i} + \dfrac{1}{(1 + i)^2} \cdots \cdots \dfrac{1}{(1 + i)^n} \right)$

P is the present worth or value of the capital equipment measured by the market, that is, the price that the firm would pay for new equipment or the price it would receive for owned equipment. The values of

$$\left(\frac{1}{1 + i} + \frac{1}{(1 + i)^2} \cdots \cdots + \frac{1}{(1 + 1)^n} \right)$$

are given in Figure 7–5. The student will note that these will be divided into P to get an annual capital cost, the amount needed to recover the initial capital cost plus interest at rate i on the cost balance not yet recovered. For this reason

$$1 / \left(\frac{1}{1 + i} + \frac{1}{(1 + i)^2} \cdots \cdots + \frac{1}{(1 + i)^n} \right)$$

is often called the *capital recovery factor*. Probably the clearest way to show the determination of the planning curve is to work out the following illustrative example:

Tinker Assembly is planning a new plant and wishes to construct a long-run cost curve relating average costs to volume to use in conjunction with a demand study to select the proper size. It has the three technologies: L, S, and M. In each case, fixed costs for administration, etc., are estimated at $50,000, equipment life is estimated at 20 years, and i is 10 percent. All can produce up to 500,000 units (X = units). An additional cost is the $100,000 market value of its land that will be used for the plant.

Plant	Initial Investment	Operating Costs	Plant Capacity
L	$3,000,000	$1X	500,000
M	2,000,000	1.4X	400,000
S	1,000,000	2X	300,000

Estimate for what range of outputs each plant curve would constitute the LRAC and construct the curve.

Since land is not a depreciable asset, its annual cost for all three alternatives can be worked out using $A = Pi$ or $10,000 = 100,000(.10)$. Figure 7–5 gives the value of $1 received annually for 20 years as 8.514, so that $A = P/8.514$ is equal to the amount of capital recovery needed each year. This can be calculated as $352,360 for plant L, $234,907 for plant M, and $117,454 for plant S. The average (unit) cost curves for the plant can now be estimated as follows:

$$AC_L = \$412,360/x + 1$$
$$AC_M = \$294,907/x + 1.4$$
$$AC_S = \$177,454/x + 2$$

By setting the $AC_S = AC_M$, the range of output over which plant S represents the low cost alternative can be determined as from 0 to 195,755 units. The range for plant M will be from 195,755 to the output at which M's costs are equal to L's, or 293,635; plant L will have the lowest unit costs for outputs greater than 293,635.

The average costs for the three plants at outputs ranging from 50,000 to 600,000 are shown in Figure 7–6 with the lowest cost figures in italics. Each of the columns gives the necessary data for drawing the plant curves, which are designated SRACs in Figure 7–7. Once the decision has been made on which plant to build, the capital input becomes fixed, so the designation of short run becomes appropriate. For that range of output for which a particular plant has the lowest costs, its curve is shown as a solid line, and these solid segments constitute the LRAC or planning curve. Figure 7–7 represents the case of indivisibility previously shown in Figure 7–1, since capital investment was assumed possible only in blocks differing by $1 million.[9]

Instead of using the present value tables, annual capital costs could have been calculated as the sum of the annual straight-line depreciation and interest on the average investment in capital equipment. This method brings out the dual aspect of capital recovery costs: the allocation of the original cost of capital over its economic life span and the opportunity cost of losing the use of the financial resources tied up in the particular project for other purposes. For plant L in this example, the straight-line depreciation would be $150,000 (the cost, $3 million, minus the salvage, zero, divided by the estimated life, 20 years). The interest on average investment would be $150,000 (the initial investment of $3 million minus

---

[9]The case of complete indivisibility could be represented by a production function such as the following: Output = H (Labor)^b (Capital)^c (Land)^d, where H is the technological and scale-coefficient that will adjust the product of inputs to units of output. If the sum of the exponents b, c, and d is greater than one, LRAC will fall with output; if equal to one, the LRAC will be horizontal, and if less than one, LRAC will rise. In each case fixed prices for inputs are assumed.

FIGURE 7–6 Average Costs for Three Plants, Tinker Assembly

Output (units)	Plant S	Plant M	Plant L
50,000	$5.55	$6.30	$9.25
100,000	3.77	4.35	5.12
195,755	2.91	2.91	3.11
200,000	2.89	2.87	3.06
293,635	2.60	2.40	2.40
300,000	2.59	2.38	2.34
400,000	2.69*	2.16	2.03
500,000	2.79*	2.19*	1.82
600,000	2.90*	2.26*	1.85*

*Additional administrative and higher variable costs are assumed for second-shift operations beyond given capacity.

FIGURE 7–7 Plant Cost Curves and *LRAC* for Three Possible Plants of Tinker Assembly

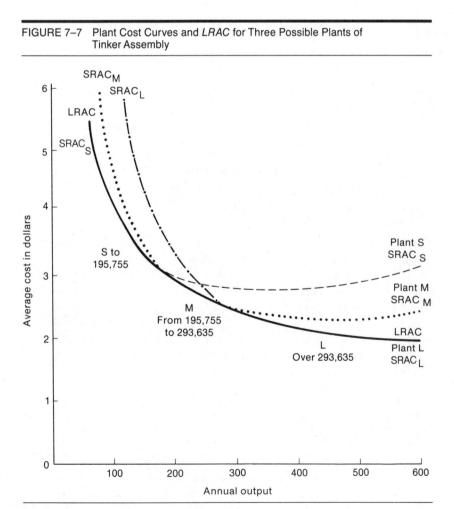

the final investment with salvage value of zero, averaged by dividing by 2 and multiplying by the interest rate).[10]

This annual capital cost of $300,000 (or $307,500 if the footnote procedure is followed) is less than that obtained by using the present value tables. This is because the bulk of equal annual payments in the early years goes for interest (in the later years, more is paid on principal). Thus, depreciation is initially slower than the straight-line rate, and the average investment is therefore greater than one half the initial minus final investment. Mortgage-holding houseowners are familiar with the fact that halfway through the mortgage term more than half of the original indebtedness remains.[11]

CASE 7–1
The Use of Interest Rate Formulas by Managers and Engineers

The purposes of this case are:

1. To gather in one place the important interest rate formulas used in financial economics using a notation useful for manager and engineer.
2. To give a sample problem for each formula and indicate how the tables in Figures 7–4 and 7–5 are sufficient for their solution. Answers are given so students may check their understanding of the methods and formulas involved.

Cash flows from alternative investments both in financial and physical assets can take many forms. For decision making, they must be made comparable. The essential problem is that as long as there are opportunities to receive interest on resources invested, dollars received or paid in different time periods have different worths. Specifically, one dollar one year in the future is worth only $1/(1 + i)$ since in a year one dollar at interest will become equal to $1 + i$ dollars. See Figure 7–4 for discount factors associated with various interest rates and years in the future.

There are basically three ways in which comparability may be

---

[10]With the convention, usual in engineering economic analysis, of charging all expenses at the end of the period, the first year's investment would be $3 million and the last year's investment would be $150,000 (one year's depreciation), so that the average investment would be $1,575,000. Ten percent for interest would equal $157,500.

[11]This can be simply illustrated by a two-year, 10 percent mortgage for $10,000. Annual payments can be computed from Figure 7–5 as about $5,760 ($10,000/1.736). Interest in the first year is $1,000 so the principal repaid is $4,760, leaving $5,240 to be repaid in the second year.

achieved. First, all costs and benefits in a cash flow can be converted to an equivalent single sum, usually at time zero, and thus termed present worth and designated P. Occasionally a future year will be selected as the base year for comparison and the single-figure equivalent is designated F.

Second, all costs and benefits can be converted to a uniform annual series covering the life of a project. The annual figure for such a series running from years 1 to n is designated A.

Third, an interest rate i may be calculated so as to reduce the net present worth of a cash flow to zero. This interest rate is the rate of return, and generally the project will be justified if the rate of return exceeds or equals the interest rate given as the cost of capital.

In order to calculate equivalent sums or series, the following interest rate formulas are used. Their names are given in brackets.

1. $P = F (1 + i)^{-n}$

See Figure 7–4 (single payment present worth factor).

2. $F = P (1 + i)^n$

See Figure 7–4. Use reciprocals (single payment compound amount factor.).

3. $P = A \left(\dfrac{(1 + i)^n - 1}{i(1 + i)^n} \right)$;

the last term is an algebraic consolidation of the series: $(1 + i)^{-1} + (1 + i)^{-2} \ldots (1 + i)^{-n}$. See Figure 7–5 (uniform series present worth factor.).

4. $A = P \left(\dfrac{i(1 + i)^n}{(1 + i)^n - 1} \right)$;

the reciprocal of 3. Values are reciprocals of Figure 7–5 (uniform series capital recovery factor).

5. $F = A \left(\dfrac{(1 + i)^n - 1}{i} \right)$;

note this differs from 3 by being multiplied by $(1 + i)^n$ to convert P to F. Use Figure 7–5 and reciprocals of Figure 7–4 (uniform series compound amount factor).

6. $A = F \left(\dfrac{i}{(1 + i)^n - 1} \right)$;

the reciprocal of 5. Use reciprocals of Figure 7–5 times Figure 7–4 (uniform series sinking fund factor).

Note that in the special case when n is equal to infinity, formula 3 would simplify to $P = A/i$. This is usually called the capitalization formula. Formula 4 under this circumstance would become $A = Pi$, establishing the uniform annual payment over an infinite time equal to a present sum.

The "functional notation" commonly used to refer to the formulas or equivalence factors above is the following: 1. P/F, i, n); 2. (F/P, i, n); 3. (P/A, i, n); 4. (A/P, i, n); 5. (F/A, i, n); 6. (A/F, i, n). These are read as follows using 1 as an illustration: Wanted P, given F, at interest rate i, for n periods. Their use is illustrated in the problems on the following page.

1. Uncle Peter wishes to make a present deposit that will provide his newborn nephew $50,000 at age 18. What should be the deposit if the interest rate is 6 percent? F = $50,000 (P/F, 6 percent, 18).

2. How many people will inhabit India in 1989 if the annual death rate per 1,000 continues at 16 and the annual birth rate at 36? The 1979 population was 667,000,000. P = 667,000,000 (F/P, 2 percent, 10).

3. Mr. Newly Retired wishes to purchase a 20-year annuity giving him annual payments of $15,000. What prices should the annuity company charge at an interest rate of 6 percent? P = $15,000 ($P/A$, 6 percent, 20).

3a. United General American Corporation is making an offer for the QXZ Corporation whose earnings of $1 million a year are assumed to last indefinitely or in perpetuity. What would it pay if the interest rate was 15 percent? A = 1,000,000 (P/A, 15 percent, ∞).

4. What are the minimum annual savings that would justify paying $50,000 for a machine with an expected life of 10 years if the required rate of return is 14 percent? P = $50,000 (A/P, 14 percent, 10).

5. Every December for 20 years Melissa Brown has deposited $100 in a 6 percent savings account. Assuming interest is compounded annually, what is her balance immediately after the last deposit? A = $100 (F/A, 6 percent, 20).

6. Kurt Waldschneisser has an option to purchase a tract of timberland for $100,000. He plans to exercise it five years from now. What sum should he set aside at the end of each of the five years at interest of 8 percent to have an amount equal to the purchase price? F = $100,000 (A/F, 8 percent, 5).

The answers to the above are: 1. P = $17,500; 2. F = 813,415,000; 3. P = $172,050; 3a. P = $6,666,667; 4. A = $9,586; 5. F = $3,676; 6. A = $17,055. These answers used tables and differ slightly from formula answers because of rounding. A suggested problem is to work out with interest rates 2 percent higher in each case.

CASE 7–2
Problems in Capital Investment

In order to evaluate an investment decision or a set of investment alternatives, the first step is to spell out on a time scale the flow of costs and benefits. This is done for the first two problems and left to the student for part C.

All items may not literally represent inflows or outflows of cash, but they are assessed a monetary value. The usual convention in engineering economics is to date all flows at a year's end so the time scale is generally set up to run from zero with the years numbered through the end of the project. Costs and benefits may be distinguished either by opposite signs ($-$ and $+$) or by upward and downward pointing arrows as convenient to the problem.

A. Ajax, Inc.

For example, a firm considers two alternatives: (a) to use an existing machine with current sale value of $5,000 and average annual labor and maintenance costs of $10,000 for five years, with salvage estimated at $1,000; (b) to purchase a new machine for $25,000, estimated life of 10 years, with salvage value of $3,000, and annual labor and maintenance costs of $5,000 a year. Which alternative will minimize annual costs at an interest rate of 15 percent?

Years					
Years	0	1–5	5	6–10	10
Alternative A	$ 5,000	$10,000	–$1,000	Not defined	
Alternative B	25,000	5,000	—	$5,000	–3,000

In this minimization of cost problem with output assumed fixed, most figures are costs. It is more convenient to use the minus sign for benefits. In the many cases where benefits and costs vary, positive figures would represent benefits.

B. Timberlands

An owner considers devoting land for timber with initial planting costs of $5,000, $1,000 a year for taxes and other expenses for 50 years, net revenues from selling pulpwood in the 30th year of $20,000 and from timber sales in the 50th year of $125,000. The alternative is to sell the land for $10,000 and the relevant interest rate is 8 percent. Should he plant timber?

Years				
Years	0	1–50	30	50
Cash flow	–$5,000	–$1,000	$20,000	$125,000

C. The Energy-Saving Lamp

"In General Electric's 100th anniversary year we announce this 8-foot lamp that will give you fluorescent lighting efficiency you never had before. . . . Watt Miser II Slimline produces an average of 19% more lumens per watt than G.E.'s standard 8-foot lamps you may be using now. So you use up to 20% less energy with only slight loss of light." (GE ad in March 1978)

Questions

1. Under the following assumptions, what is the maximum price that could be charged for the new lamp so its purchase would yield a pretax annual return of 30 percent to the customer? (The alternative is purchase of old-style lamp.)

    18,000—hours average life for new and old lamps.
     3,600—hours average annual use of old and new lamp.
        60—wattage of new lamp.
        72—wattage of old-style lamp to give same light.
     $1.60—price per old-style lamp (when used in quantity).
       3.5¢—price per kilowatt-hour.

2. Why would a price this high be unlikely?

3. Would there be any economical use for old lamps now on hand were the Miser II price set at $2.50? Explain briefly.

D. Why IRAs Are Popular

As an added incentive for saving, the 1981 tax bill permits all workers to place up to $2,000 a year in an Individual Retirement Account (IRA). The $2,000 is deducted from current taxable income, and no current taxes are paid on interest accumulations. A modest penalty of 10 percent in addition to regular income tax must be paid for withdrawals before age 60 when all withdrawals are taxed as made. Take i as 10 percent in a, b, and d.

1. If you start an IRA at age 30 and continue to pay $2,000 a year through age 59 (30 years), how much will your IRA have accumulated with $i = 10$ percent?

     (A) $18,500   (B) $60,000   (C) $99,000
                  (D) $227,000   (E) $329,000

2. What equal annual amount can then be withdrawn for 25 years (you may depart this mortal realm at age 85)?

     (A) $13,200   (B) $25,000   (C) $32,900
                  (D) $36,250   (E) $50,000

3. Assuming your marginal rate of taxation is 40 percent after age 30, only $1,200 ($2,000 − tax of $800) would be available without an IRA. The effective interest rate is only 6 percent (since 40 percent of the 10 percent interest will be taxed.) What would the non-IRA accumulation be after 30 years?

     (A) $36,000   (B) $60,000   (C) $ 94,870
                  (D) $227,000   (E) $329,000

4. One reason that it is difficult to be sure that IRAs will increase saving is that less has to be saved to reach a particular savings goal. What would be the needed annual IRA payment to reach the accumulation in (C) above?

(A) $400   (B) $577   (C) $655

(D) $1,200   (E) $2,000

5. While IRAs are popular and useful, it is important also to analyze the propriety of advertising the promise that you will be a millionaire (or at least half a millionaire) when you retire. Why can this sort of claim be misleading?

Answers are 1(E); 2(D); 3(C); and 4(B)

Show how they are arrived at.

CASE 7–3
Robbins Manufacturing Company

Many products can be made either in factories that use automatic machines or in plants using hand assembly by semiskilled workers. Robbins Manufacturing Company, after considerable study, found that it could build any one of three plants: the largest, an almost completely automatic factory; an intermediate one, utilizing an assembly line with some automatic machinery; or the smallest, relying heavily on hand assembly. Estimated costs of producing one type of electronic circuit under these three assumed plant conditions were as shown in Exhibit 7–3A. The life of the equipment was estimated at 10 years; a pretax interest rate of 15 percent was taken as the cost of capital.

EXHIBIT 7–3A

	Plant A Automatic	Plant B Assembly Line	Plant C Hand Operating
Unit costs:			
Materials . . . . $	2.00	$ 2.00	$ 2.00
Direct labor.	0.30	0.60	1.00
Plant and equipment cost	1,000,000.00	300,000.00	125,000.00
Maintenance and overhead:			
Fixed portion	50,000.00	30,000.00	20,000.00
Variable costs per unit	0.20	0.25	0.40
Annual output capacity (units)*	1,000,000.00	500,000.00	250,000.00

*For outputs greater than the annual capacity of any plant, these plants and their costs would simply be duplicated.

Questions

1. Construct the planning curve *(LRAC)* for Robbins by first calculating lowest cost at outputs where plant A's costs = plant B's costs; plant B's costs = plant C's costs; 50,000 units; 125,000 units; 500,000 units; and 1 million units of output.[12]

2. Assume demand and cost analysis has estimated the most profitable output at 500,000 sold at a price of $3.50. Which if any plant should be built?

3. Assume Robbins has already built plant C (which has no recoverable market value). Its annual sales are expected to continue to be 100,000 at a price of $3.70, with no prospect of improving profitability by different pricing. Should it continue production? If so should it use plant C or build another plant?

CASE 7–4
Productivity in Air-Conditioning and Related Industries*

This case illustrates the changing labor requirements in industrial production and some problems in measuring productivity.

The manufacture of air-conditioning and refrigeration equipment and warm air furnaces involves the production of heat transfer apparatuses for residential, commercial, industrial, and other applications. The industry's output more than doubled from 1967 to 1973, aided especially by greater use of air conditioners in motor vehicles and by exports. Growth slowed sharply after 1973.

Investment by the industry in plant and equipment was strong in the 1967–73 period but diminished along with output after 1973. The investment has included many laborsaving devices, causing output per employee-hour to rise about 30 percent from 1967 to 1982.

Improved productivity in the fabrication of air-conditioning equipment components is exemplified by the coil manufacturing process. The refrigerant is pumped through the coil to absorb heat from the surrounding space. The coil originates as tubing on a large roll. In the more advanced shops the rolled tubing is automatically straightened, cut to length as specified in, and controlled by, a taped program, and automatically bent to the shape of a U (or hairpin). This operation has come to be performed by one person, where about a decade ago, four persons were required to shear the tube manually and insert it into a bending device.

---

[12]For uniformity it is suggested students use the capital recovery factor (reciprocals of Figure 7–5) to get annual capital costs. Interest at 20 percent will result in approximately the same results with the straight-line depreciation plus average interest method.

*SOURCE: Based on Horst Brand and Clyde Huffstutler, "Productivity in Making Air Conditioners, Refrigeration Equipment, and Furnaces," *Monthly Labor Review*, December 1985.

The cutting of steel, a large-scale operation in the bigger shops, has also become progressively more automated. The cutting and punching of steel is often still done by an operator using templates and judging by sight how to minimize waste in laying them out. Templates and operator judgment have begun to be replaced by computer-instructed cutting machines, where the computer calculates the most economical distribution of cuts. The computer memory also records odd pieces of steel that might be used in future work. With template labor and layout estimation by an operator eliminated, five times as much steel may be processed in the same period as previously. Also, material savings of up to 60 percent are expected.

The occupational composition of the industry's employment is not expected to change very much during the 1980s except for growth in the proportion of engineers, engineering and science technicians, and computer specialists. Employment in these occupational categories has been projected by the Bureau of Labor Statistics to rise 27 percent between 1980 and 1990, compared with a 15 percent increase in the industry as a whole.

Questions

1. Output per employee increased at an annual rate of 5.1 percent in the 1967–73 period. What do you regard as the main reasons for this gain?

2. In drawing cost curves, the economist usually assumes that some variables are "impounded in *ceteris paribus*" that did not actually remain constant in this industry in the 1967–73 period. Explain.

3. Use your imagination and general knowledge to describe other industries or activities where computers will increasingly replace skilled or semiskilled employees.

CASE 7–5
The Trend Toward Smaller Plants

American manufacturers have traditionally been impressed with "economies of scale" inherent in the use of large plants. Economists' "long-run cost curves" pertaining to plants often show an upturn after a certain size but only after a long and substantial decline from left to right as they too tend to be impressed with economies of scale. Lately there has been more skepticism about the universality of economies of large-scale production. Numerous manufacturers have recently built smaller plants and/or divided existing facilities into smaller units.

Examples are General Electric's Aircraft Engine Business Group which once concentrated production in two very large plants and has shifted to eight smaller "satellite" plants.[13]

AT&T has shut down large assembly lines at its former Western Electric Co. subsidiary—now AT&T Technologies Inc.—and has set up smaller automated facilities.

Kollmorgen Corporation, a producer of printed circuit boards, small industrial motors, and other products, created five separate product groups, each with a manager utilizing his own sales force and production capacity. Main goals were to emulate the flexibility of "Mom and Pop" operations where communication among advertising, sales, and production people is usually not a major problem.

In part, the trend toward smaller plants is designed to reduce the feeling of unimportance on the part of a worker in a huge assembly line operation by making him or her a member of a team with a considerable amount of autonomy. (Refer to Case 9–2, "Combating Worker Alienation," for some detail on this modern trend.)

In part, the move toward smaller plants in many industries is due to the rapidity of technological change and the need to compete with imports. If a plant runs the risk of becoming obsolete within a few years, it is better not to have a large investment in the facility. Customized products tend to require shorter assembly lines that can be quickly adjusted to new specifications.

Questions

1. Frequently, firms have built large plants in rural areas in order to use cheaper land and workers who tend to be handy with tools. They often have to attract workers from a wide surrounding area.

   What are some industries that you believe should still follow this practice rather than that emphasized in this case? Why?

2. Summarize what you regard as important reasons for locating "high-tech" plants in more urban areas and building to a smaller scale.

3. It is important not to confuse economies and diseconomies of large firms and economies and diseconomies of large plants. While this case deals with large plants, why are large firms (like IBM) likely to have relatively large plants?

4. How does rapid technological progress affect optimum plant size in an industry?

5. In the ordinary cost curves used in economic theory, technology is held constant. Another variable, for some complicated items, such as aircraft, is the "learning curve." Comment on the problem of drawing cost curves when rate of output, cumulative output, and technology are all independent variables.

---

[13]As stated by Albert Gore in *Business Week*, October 22, 1984, in an article "Small Is Beautiful Now in Manufacturing." Some of the other information in this case comes from Gore's article.

CASE 7–6
The Learning Curve and Military Aircraft

If the additional labor input per unit declines by a given percentage with each doubling of output as the production run is lengthened, the following mathematical expression is appropriate: $C = aQ^b$, which could be expressed as the linear-log relation, $\log C = \log a + b \log Q$. C represents the additional input of the Qth unit in the production run; and a is the labor input for the initial unit. An easy way to estimate the additional input required for any Q would be to plot two observations of P and Q on double-log paper, and b would be the negative slope of the learning curve representing the decline in $\log C$ as output increased.

In the example for military airplanes given in the text, the rate of decline in labor input as output doubled was observed as 0.30. This is often called the "learning rate," and could be expressed as $1 - a$ $(2Q^b/aQ^b)$. (The numerator of the fraction is the C for double the output in the denominator.) Simplifying, we have $0.30 = 1 - 2^b$, and solving, we find the b appropriate to this illustration is $- 0.51457$. The airplane example estimated the labor input for the initial plane as 100,000, the value of a in the formula. The estimate for two planes was 70,000 and for four planes 49,000.

Questions

1. Use the formula to confirm that it gives these results for one, two and four planes.

2. Estimate the labor input for the 10th and 100th planes of a production run of military aircraft.

3. Why might you have greater confidence in the estimate for the 10th rather than the 100th plane?

8

Capital Budgeting and Financing

There are always alternatives to an investment proposal, and a systematic analysis of the alternatives is the benchmark for estimating both the investment and the earnings of a capital project.

—*Joel Dean*

In the previous chapter, it was pointed out that investment in capital equipment can rationally be made if its calculated present value exceeds its present cost. It is obvious that fairly long-term forecasting is required in order to compute the present value, since this is the discounted value of cash flows expected to accrue over the entire useful life of the machine (or other form of capital good). If the investment in question is an apartment building with an expected useful life of 50 years, for example, the forecast of rental returns must be made for a period of half a century. Fortunately, the most distant expected cash flows are discounted so heavily that they are not very significant in the calculation of present value, while the near-future returns, which are easier to estimate, have more weight in the calculation.

In order to calculate net present values, not only are long-term forecasts necessary but adequate estimates of the cost of capital are required. Cost-of-capital questions are particularly important when there are many competing capital investment projects that may be undertaken but only limited capital funds are available.

This chapter will, first, refine our previous analysis to look at the cash flows of an investment project after taking into account corporate income taxes. Second, it will look at the derivation of the demand curve for capital investment for a firm. This is the heart of a capital budgeting process in which a firm considers all of the projects that might enter its investment program for a period such as a year. Third, it will examine the computation of the cost of capital by a firm and relate this to the concept of a supply schedule or curve for capital funds. Fourth, the chapter will briefly tackle capital budgeting problems in a period of high general inflation if it recurs. Fifth, a special type of investment decision encountered lately in hostile takeovers of corporations is given preliminary attention.

AFTERTAX CASH FLOWS

In Chapter 7, investment decisons were based on cash flows without deductions for personal and corporate income taxes. This is a generally tolerable preliminary procedure with the use of an interest rate raised to levels adequate to compensate for such taxes. However, in this chapter on capital budgeting with multiple alternatives whose rates of return will be influenced somewhat differently by tax rates and with several sources of capital having varying tax treatments, it is desirable to consider aftertax flows.

The major tax to be considered is the corporate income tax, which in illustrative examples is taken at the marginal rate of 40 percent, a figure easy for calculations and one recommended by many tax experts. Nonincome taxes such as the investment credit and real estate taxes are assumed to have figured in pretax flows.

On investments with lives so long as to be taken as infinite, the effect of the corporate tax for profitable corporations is to reduce all noncapital flows, both revenues and costs, by the percentage of the tax. The rate of return is reduced by the same percentage for investments with unlimited life. For example, a $1,000 investment yielding $500 worth of labor savings in perpetuity would have its annual savings reduced to $300 by a 40 percent tax and its rate of return from 50 percent to 30 percent, a 40 percent reduction. If the company were permitted to charge the $1,000 initial investment as a cost, it would reduce its taxable profits by $1,000 for a tax saving of $400 and would have maintained its 50 percent return, now $300 a year on a net initial investment of $600.

In fact, the government does not permit corporations to write off capital investments immediately. Corporations may charge off annually over the life of the asset a fraction of the initial cost of the capital asset. This annual depreciation times the the marginal tax rate can be termed the *depreciation tax shield*. In order to convert a pretax cash flow to an aftertax cash flow, two adjustments are necessary: $(1 - t)$(noncapital revenues and costs) plus tD, where t denotes the tax rate and D represents depreciation in a particular period.

The key to how greatly aftertax rates of return on investment will be reduced from those before taxes is the rapidity with which outlays for investment can be charged as costs for tax purposes. In other words, how early in the cash flow can the depreciation tax shield be used to reduce taxes. Figure 8–1 illustrates this along with the computations involved in getting aftertax cash flows using straight-line, double-declining balance, and sum-of-the-years'-digits depreciation. The details of the methods and the calculations are discussed in notes to Figure 8–1. Items 1 and 2 show that when no depreciation is charged the rate of return is reduced by the full percentage of the tax. A comparison of the before-tax flow in item 3 with the aftertax flow in item 4 where straight-line depreciation is used for calculating the tax shield shows that a 40 percent tax reduced the rate

---

FIGURE 8–1 Cash Flows and Rate of Return, before and after Tax, for Laborsaving Equipment ($1,000 = P [cost]; $500 = A [annual savings]; effective tax rate, 40 percent)

Years:	0	1	2	3	4	5	6 to Inf.	P/A	r
1. Infinite life, before tax	−1,000	500	500	500	500	500	500	2.000	50%
2. Infinite life, after tax $(1-t)A$.	−1,000	300	300	300	300	300	300	3.333	30
3. Five-year life, before tax ...	−1,000	500	500	500	500	500	—	2.000	40
4. a. Five-year life, aftertax $(1-t)A$	−1,000	300	300	300	300	300	—	—	—
b. Straight-line depreciation tax shield (tD)	—	80	80	80	80	80	—	—	—
c. Aftertax $(4a + 4b)$	−1,000	380	380	380	380	380	—	2.632	26
5. a. Five-year double-declining-balance depreciation	—	400	240	144	108	108	—	—	—
b. Depreciation tax shield (tD)	—	160	96	58	43	43	—	—	—
c. Aftertax $(4a + 5b)$	−1,000	460	396	358	343	343	—	—	—
d. Discounted aftertax flow .	−1,000	359	242	171	128	100	—	—	28
6. a. Five-year sum-of-the-years'-digits depreciation	—	333	267	200	133	67	—	—	—
b. Depreciation tax shield (tD)	—	133	107	80	53	27	—	—	—
c. Aftertax $(4a + 6b)$	−1,000	433	407	380	353	327	—	—	—
d. Discounted aftertax flow .	−1,000	338	248	181	132	95	—	—	28

1. In items 3 and 4c, r was found by scanning the row for five years in Figure 7–5 until the approximate P/A was located.

2. Straight-line depreciation, item 4. Annual depreciation (D) equaled (original cost − salvage)/estimated life. In this case, D = 200, and the tax shield was 40 percent of this.

3. Double-declining-balance depreciation, item 5. The original cost minus accumulated depreciation is the balance that is multiplied by 2/n, the double of the 1/n used in straight-line depreciation. When the depreciation calculated this way becomes less than the straight-line amount over the remaining life, the latter is used. In item 5a, the balance of 3.216 after year 3 divided by the two years' remaining life gives $108 for years 4 and 5. The r of 28 percent was arrived at since the sum of the aftertax flow of 5c was reduced to the zero sum of 5d when years 1 through 5 were discounted by an interest rate of 28 percent using Figure 7.5.

4. Sum-of-the-years'-digits depreciation, item 6. For n = 5, the sum equals 15 (1 + 2 + 3 + 4 + 5). The original cost less salvage is multiplied by a fraction in which the numerator is the years of life remaining and the denominator is the sum calculated this way. Here the rate of return is a little less than 28 percent as the discounted aftertax flow in item 6d is slightly negative.

---

of return by 35 percent (40–26)/40. Each of the methods of accelerated depreciation worked out in items 5 and 6 of Figure 8–1 keeps the reduction down to about 30 percent, (40–28)/40.

Clearly firms have an interest in using accelerated depreciation methods for tax purposes. They will also find that keeping their estimates of the life of an asset as low as the Internal Revenue Service will permit enhances the rate of return by getting tax reductions earlier, which allows reinvestment of the tax savings. There is a particular advantage in incurring expenses that can be immediately used to reduce income taxes, and that at the same time produce assets of long-run significance, for example, the product reputation purchased by advertising. The government has used incentives such as the investment credit to allow corporations to get early tax reductions as an encouragement for capital formation. Many economists suggest that reducing or eliminating the corporate income tax would provide a sounder stimulus for investment by increasing aftertax rates of return. Tax laws can change radically, so the student is encouraged to try to follow major alterations and appraise their effects.

THE DEMAND FOR CAPITAL FUNDS BY A FIRM

By calculating the rates of return for capital projects that could be undertaken during a particular time period, a demand curve for capital funds can be constructed as in Figure 8–4. The vertical axis is the expected rate of return; the horizontal axis is the cumulative demand for funds and shows the amount of investment that will have a rate of return greater than or equal to particular rates of return. In accumulating the demand for funds, the investments are taken in order of their expected rates of return from the highest to the lowest. As in Figure 8–1, the procedure is to seek the interest rate that will make the net present value of the present cost and the future aftertax flows equal to zero. Symbolically, find the i that will make $NPV = 0$ in the following formula.

$$NPV = -P + \frac{F_1}{(1 + i)} + \frac{F_2}{(1 + i)^2} \cdots + \frac{F_n}{(1 + i)^n}$$

where P is equal to the present cost and the F's represent cash flows in the years of the subscripts. Obviously, the estimating process would be greatly shortened if the future flows were uniform and A could be substituted for the F's.

The lower the cost of the project, the higher r becomes for any given cash flow. This rate is sometimes called the "internal rate of return" or the "marginal efficiency of capital." If the annual rate of return calculated in this way exceeds the annual rate of cost of capital to the firm, the investment promises to be an acceptable one. The two approaches—computation of NPV and comparison of the annual rate of return with the annual cost of capital to the firm—are similar, except in certain cases involving large negative cash flows in later years. They are similar because present value will exceed present cost for any project that promises an internal rate of return in excess of the rate of cost of capital. Large negative cash flows in later years may cause the above equation to have multiple solutions. In most cases, however, identical decisions would result under either approach. It should be noted, however, that net present value assumes that cash inflows are reinvested at the cost of capital and the use of internal rate of return assumes that these inflows earn the internal rate of return. It is possible, however, that as cash inflows are received, there are no investment opportunities available to the firm that would yield a return as great as the so-called internal rate of return.

In a "going" company the very highest rate of return may often come from replacement of a machine or other capital asset that is crucial to the

FIGURE 8–2   Demand for Capital Funds by a Firm

Project	Expected Rate of Return	Cost of Project ($ millions)	Cumulative Demand for Funds ($ millions)
A	50%	$ 5	$ 5
B	46	4	9
C	35	10	19
D	24	6	25
E	15	2	27
F	10	10	37
G	8	3	40
H	6	12	52

continued use of other equipment that is on hand. Other promising projects may involve expansion of capacity for a product already being produced (e.g., doubling the size of a motel), acquisition of capacity for turning out wholly new products (perhaps by purchasing other companies), acquisition of earlier or later stages in the production-distribution process, or some other activity.

A hypothetical demand schedule for capital funds is shown in Figure 8–2. The arbitrary cutoff point in this schedule is 6 percent; usually a large number of additional projects could be listed at low rates, but these have little prospect of becoming actualities. An implicit assumption made in compiling this sort of schedule is that each project is independent of those that rank lower. Otherwise, it would not be possible to adopt only projects above any desired point without an effect on the expected rate of return. Projects need not be independent of those which rank higher, since it is assumed that all projects down to the actual cutoff point will be carried out. An investment project that depends on one lower in the scale is not really a separate project and should be combined with the lower one and the combination entered at the appropriate place.

An interesting application of the rate of return approach is in the analysis of a decision in which a firm has several options as to the level of capital investment. For example, the following levels of capital investment (P) are associated with varying amounts of aftertax laborsavings (A). The relevant r's are worked out for incremental investments. For simplicity in this case, A has been taken as infinite so $\Delta A/\Delta P = r$.

	P	A	ΔP	ΔA	r	Cumulative Demand for Funds
A	100	30	100	30	30%	100
B	200	50	100	20	20	200
C	300	60	100	10	10	—
D	400	80	100	20	20	—
D–B	—	—	200	30	15	400

The last two columns give the investment totals to be incorporated into the demand curve. It should be noted that alternative C would not be profitable even at a cost of capital of less than 10 percent since going ahead with D as shown by incremental return to D–B yields a greater return, and so the relevant increments for capital budgeting analysis are A, B–A, and D–B.

SUPPLY OF CAPITAL FUNDS

Concepts involved in an accurate statement of the nature of the supply of capital funds to the firm are more difficult than the concepts on the demand side. The supply curve of funds must be considered to be a curve of the "cost of capital" expressed as an annual interest rate. As long as investment projects promise to yield higher internal rates of interest than the cost-of-capital funds, they should be carried out. The cost of capital to a firm is complicated by the fact that funds for capital investment may come from a variety of sources and have specific costs which differ from the overall cost of capital.

SOURCES OF FUNDS

The corporation obtains funds from internally generated sources and may obtain additional funds through outside equity and/or debt financing. Annual depreciation charges by a firm represent (very roughly) the conversion of the firm's fixed assets into liquid or near liquid assets. The depreciation charges themselves are not a source of funds. Rather, they are revenue brought in by the operations of the firm that build up liquid assets; depreciation charges prevent these assets from being paid out as dividends or income taxes. To the extent that these assets are liquid (rather than being in the form of slow-moving accounts receivable, for example), they can be expended for capital goods in a given year in furtherance of the firm's investment program. Similarly, profits earned and retained by the firm during a given year are usually at least partially available for investment. However, this may not always be the case. If the year's profits show up on the balance sheet as a diminution of liabilities rather than as an increase in assets, no actual funds will have been made available for investment, although it may then be easier to borrow again in order to secure capital assets. If additional equity capital has been raised by selling stock during the year, funds will have been made available for investment. The same is true if bonds have been sold or if short-term borrowing from banks has been increased.

COST OF CAPITAL FROM SPECIFIC SOURCES

For decision making, the relevant costs of capital are future costs, not current or past costs. However, since a firm obtains capital funds from many sources, it is usually not wise to attempt to associate a particular source of funds with a particular capital expenditure outlay. Use of the specific cost of a particular source of capital funds is not wise because increasing the amount of equity funds may result in higher or lower debt costs and hence change the overall cost of capital. Thus, all changes in capital costs should be included, not just those directly associated with a particular source of funds.

In the following sections, costs of capital from specific sources will be discussed first, followed by a discussion of the overall cost of capital. In discussing specific costs, it is implicitly assumed that the mix of debt and equity sources of funds will remain approximately the same.[1]

COST OF DEBT

The cost of long-term debt or bonds when the firm receives the face value of the bonds or notes is the interest rate adjusted for the fact that interest is tax deductible. This cost can be expressed as:

$$i_D = (1 - t) R$$

where t is the marginal tax rate and R is the coupon interest rate. Thus, with a marginal tax rate of 0.4 and a coupon rate of 9 percent, $i_D = 5.4$ percent.

In many cases, bonds are sold at more or less than their face amount resulting in a premium or discount that either lowers or raises the effective interest rate. In order to calculate the tax-adjusted effective interest rate, the present value formula is used with P representing the price received per $100 of bonds, and A is taken as $(1 - t)R$ expressed in dollars. Years to maturity is n, and in year n, an additional $100 must be paid. For example, in 1980, a firm receives $900 for each bond which is a promise to pay $1,000 in 1990 with a coupon rate of 8 percent. At a corporate tax rate of 40 percent, the effective interest rate is found by solving for i in the following cash flow:

$$0 = \$90 - 4.80 \left(\frac{1}{(1 + i)} + \frac{1}{(1 + i)^2} \cdots + \frac{1}{(1 + i)^{10}} \right) - \$100 \frac{1}{(1 + i)^{10}}$$

The student should check using Figures 7–4 and 7–5 to confirm that an interest cost of slightly more than 6 percent has been incurred.

COST OF PREFERRED STOCK

In recent years, preferred stock has been somewhat in disfavor among corporations seeking investment funds. This is partially because it imposes a debt-like obligation to pay dividends that are not tax deductible.

---

[1] An excellent introduction to the capital structure problem is given by Burton G. Malkiel, *The Debt Equity Combination of the Firm and the Cost of Capital: An Introductory Analysis* (Morristown, N.J.: General Learning Press, 1971).

Even though they are not required, as is interest on debt, dividends are a must if a firm is to successfully issue preferred stock. It is usual to treat dividends on preferred stock as a perpetual requirement; thus, the cost can be expressed as:

$$i_P = D/Q_0$$

where D is the annual dividend and Q_0 is the proceeds of the issue.

COST OF COMMON STOCK

Equity costs are the most difficult costs to evaluate. One reason is that in order to determine the cost of equity, it is necessary to venture into that highly tentative area of knowledge—the valuation of common stocks. The discussion here will stress the approach proposed by Myron J. Gordon.[2] There is, however, no general agreement that this particular model is the last word on valuation.

The fundamental problem in the determination of the cost of capital on equity is ascertaining the risk premium over the riskless interest rate. Various approaches relate some measure of returns on a share of stock to its market price. One measure relates current earnings per share times a growth factor to the current market price per share.[3] With no future growth assumed, this measure would simply be the reciprocal of the price-earnings ratio.

A second measure attributed to J. Fred Weston uses beta analysis to determine explicitly the appropriate premium to add to the return on a riskless investment. The beta coefficient reflects the industry characteristics and management policies as perceived by investors, and it measures the volatility of particular returns relative to the returns on a broad market index of securities and real assets.[4]

The approach associated with Myron Gordon is based on the concept that the present worth of a stock is the expected value of the entire flow of income to be derived from owning that stock. Dividends are assumed to be the primary income that stockholders receive from stock ownership. Future dividends from year zero to infinity are thus discounted by a market interest rate, i_E, for the risk class in which the company falls. A

---

[2]Myron J. Gordon, *The Investment, Financing, and Valuation of the Corporation* (Homewood, Ill.: Richard D. Irwin, 1962).

[3]The formulation $i_E = \dfrac{EPS(1 + g)^3}{MP}$ is given in John J. Hampton, *Financial Decision-Making* (Reston, Va.: Reston Publishing, 1976), p. 306. The letter g is the annual growth rate expressed as a percentage, and cubing $(1 + g)$ implies that the shareholders are interested in the profit level three years from now, admittedly an arbitrary assumption.

[4]The whole of chap. 2 and pp. 290–93 of J. J. Clark, M. T. Clark, and P. T. Elgers, *Financial Management, A Capital Market Approach* (Boston: Holbrook Press, 1976) are devoted to beta analysis and its use to estimate the cost of capital. The cost of capital is the rate of return on a riskless investment plus beta times the risk premium implicit in the expected return on the broad index of assets.

risk class is a group of firms viewed by the market as having the same risk characteristics, that is, probability distributions of expected dividends. If the same dividend is expected to be paid forever

$$i_E = \frac{D_0}{P_0}$$

where D_0 is the current dividend per share and P_0 is the current price. If the dividends are expected to grow by a constant percentage, g, it can be shown algebraically that

$$i_E = D_0/P_0 + g$$

or that the cost of capital is equal to the current dividend yield plus the growth rate.

In order to use this cost of equity capital measure, estimates must be made of growth rate, and the user must be willing to accept the assumption of a constant compound growth rate.[5] For example, given a stock currently paying a $2.50 dividend, which is expected to grow at a rate of 5 percent, and whose market price is $50, the cost of equity capital is computed as

$$i_E = \frac{2.50}{50.00} + 0.05 = 0.10, \text{ or } 10 \text{ percent}$$

Several questions are raised by this model. First, how valid is its emphasis on dividends; there are many companies that pay no dividends, yet their stocks trade at high price-earnings ratios. The second question involves the assumption of constant growth which was discussed briefly above. Third, the implicit assumption of a constant market rate of discount must be questioned. The problems can be recognized here, but the student should look to his or her course work in finance for some of the approaches to these problems.

Most companies make a choice between paying large dividends or retaining most of the profits in business. The question of an optimal dividend policy is another interesting one that must be deferred to some other book or course.[6] Investors who buy stock that pays no dividends must expect to sell the stock in the future to some other investors at a higher price even though there are no current dividends. Underlying these trans-

---

[5]Other growth stock models are discussed in Paul F. Wendt, "Current Growth Stock Valuation Methods," *Financial Analysts Journal*, March–April 1965.

[6]See, for example, Irwin Friend and Marshall Puckett, "Dividends and Stock Prices," *American Economic Review*, vol. 54 (September 1964); John Lintner, "Distribution of Incomes of Corporations among Dividends, Retained Earnings, and Taxes," *American Economic Review*, vol. 46 (May 1956); Merton H. Miller and Franco Modigliani, "Dividend Policy, Growth, and the Valuation of Shares," *Journal of Business*, vol. 34 (October 1961); Alexander A. Robichek and Steward C. Myers, *Optimal Financing Decisions* (Englewood Cliffs, N.J.: Prentice-Hall, 1965); and James E. Walter, *Dividend Policies and Enterprise Valuation* (Belmont, Calif.: Wadsworth, 1967).

actions must be a belief that some time in the future the corporation will begin to pay dividends. Formally, however, the only element that would enter in the valuation model for such a corporation would be the liquidation or terminal value. In the formal equation for the cost of equity capital, the firm might substitute the average return that investors might expect to make from market price appreciation.

While the assumption of constant growth may be troublesome, most other assumptions about growth patterns are also troublesome. Often companies grow at high rates in their early years and experience slower growth in their later years. Specific growth assumptions can be used in the valuation model outlined above. While these alternative growth assumptions are more cumbersome to work with, computers make the solution of such an equation a relatively simple matter.

Several writers have suggested that since the distant future is more uncertain than the near future, the market rate of discount should be increased for the distant future. A problem is to determine the appropriate adjustment rates to apply. It is more desirable to build the risk elements directly into your analysis rather than to make an arbitrary adjustment of the market discount rate. There are a number of books and articles dealing with the treatment of risk and uncertainty in capital expenditure decision problems.[7] Unless there is a radical change in the kind of assets that the firm employs, it seems reasonable to assume that it remains in the same risk class and therefore has a relatively constant cost of equity capital.[8]

COST OF INTERNALLY GENERATED FUNDS

Funds for investment may be generated internally in a number of ways. Earnings may be retained in the business rather than paid out in dividends. Balances may accrue through the reduction in the level of accounts receivable, or from an increase in the amount of accounts payable (which does not increase costs through lost discounts). Also, funds may be retained through a reduction in accounting profits and taxes due to the noncash depreciation expenses charges that prevent the payment of taxes and dividends.

These internally generated funds are the largest source of funds available to corporations for new investments. Even though they do not cause an entry on the books to express their costs, it would be a grave mistake to regard them as free. Investments made from internally generated funds

---

[7]See David B. Hertz, "Risk Analysis in Capital Investment," *Harvard Business Review*, January–February 1964; and Wilbur G. Lewellen, *The Cost of Capital* (Belmont, Calif.: Wadsworth, 1969).

[8]Another approach to the cost of equity capital is by use of the capital-asset pricing model developed by William F. Sharpe, "Capital Asset Prices: A Theory of Market Equilibrium under Conditions of Risk," *Journal of Finance*, vol. 19 (September 1964). See James C. Van Horne, *Financial Management and Policy*, 3d ed. (Englewood Cliffs, N.J.: Prentice-Hall, 1974).

at returns below the firm's market rate of discount would reduce the average return on the firm's assets and lower the market value of the firm. Such a policy would reduce the well-being of the stockholders and would certainly be unwise. These funds therefore should earn at least the cost of capital.[9]

OVERALL COST OF CAPITAL

Use of the proportions of the capital represented by the various classes of securities as weights in determining the cost of capital has been suggested by several authors. However, some have suggested using the book value of the securities while others have suggested using market value. Book value weights can lead to inconsistent estimates since market values were used in computing the specific costs of capital for each source. Book value for equity may seriously understate the proportion of equity in the capital structure. Market value weights also have some difficulties. They may appear quite different from the book value, and investors may perceive the capital structure to be that implied by the book value figures. Such observations may alter the risk perceptions of investors and may change their valuation of the stock. Also, market prices are subject to greater variation than book values and may fluctuate widely making the appropriate weights difficult to choose.

The example shown in Figure 8–3 indicates the procedure for computing the weighted average cost of capital using either book or market value weights. The balance sheet shows debt of $300,000 and equity of $700,000. However, the market values are $250,000 and $1 million, respectively. The computations indicate a weighted average cost using book value weights of 7.9 percent but a cost of 8.6 percent when market values are used. Where possible, market value weights should be used but care must be taken not to have extreme market fluctuations unduly influence the computations.

CAPITAL STRUCTURE

All of the foregoing discussion of the cost of capital has been under the assumption that the capital structure—proportion of debt and equity— was unchanged. As with the other areas discussed, there is considerable controversy over the effect of changing capital structure upon the cost of capital. Modigliani and Miller have shown that under certain assumptions the average cost of capital will remain unchanged with varying

---

[9]Funds available because of depreciation should be taken at the overall cost of capital and retained earnings at the cost of common stock according to Hampton, *Financial Decision-Making*, p. 308. J. J. Clark et al. in *Financial Management* qualifies this by taking the proportion left to the average shareholder after paying income taxes on dividends and incurring brokerage costs to reinvest (pp. 246–47).

FIGURE 8–3

CFW CORPORATION
Book and Market Value Weights
Cost of Capital Computations
Balance Sheet

Assets		Liabilities	
Cash and plant	$1,000,000	Long-term debt	$ 300,000
		Common stock	700,000
Total assets	$1,000,000	Total liabilities	$1,000,000

Market value of debt . . . . $ 250,000
Market value of stock 1,000,000
Specific cost of debt, 3.00% $= i_D$
Specific cost of equity, 10.00% $= i_E$

COSTS OF CAPITAL

	Book Value Weights	Market Value Weights
Proportion debt	0.3 × 3.00 = 0.9	0.2 × 3.00 = 0.6
Proportion equity	0.7 × 10.00 = 7.0	0.8 × 10.00 = 8.0
Cost of capital	7.9%	8.6%

proportions of debt and equity. Others have questioned this analysis primarily on the validity of the assumptions and have shown that violations of their assumptions lead to the more traditional view that an appropriate use of debt can reduce the average cost of capital. Thus, the analysis in this chapter has assumed that the optimal capital structure has been found and that additional financing will maintain this structure. In practice, there are periodic departures from optimum capital structures as firms issue first debt and then equity capital to obtain new funds for capital investment.[10]

SUPPLY SCHEDULE FOR CAPITAL FUNDS

The supply schedule for capital funds should relate the average and marginal cost of capital and increasing quantities of capital funds. Within fairly wide ranges, the cost of capital to a firm may be fairly constant. A number of scholars have suggested, however, that as the amount of funds sought increases the average cost of capital rises.[11] The shape and position of the curve will depend upon the size and risk class of the corporation. Figure 8–4 shows three possible supply schedules for capital funds on the

---

[10]See Modigliani and Miller, "The Cost of Capital . . ."; and for the traditional view, Eli Schwartz, "Theory of the Capital Structure of the Firm," *Journal of Finance,* vol. 14 (March 1959).

[11]James S. Duesenberry, *Business Cycles and Economic Growth* (New York: McGraw-Hill, 1958).

FIGURE 8–4 Demand and Supply of Capital Funds

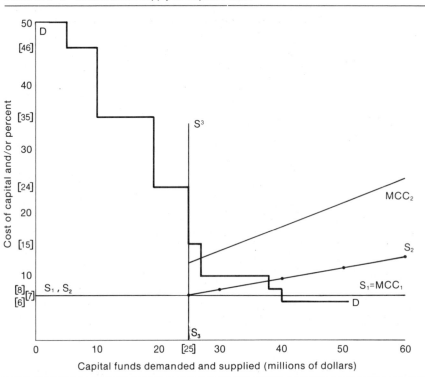

Capital funds demanded and supplied (millions of dollars)

graph of the demand for investment funds derived from a schedule such as that given in Figure 8–1. The flat segment of S_1 and S_2 would represent the funds available at a constant average and marginal cost from internal and external sources. The rising segment of S_2 suggests that above some amount, the market is unwilling to supply funds at the same price to this firm. Perhaps this reflects a market judgment that the firm cannot manage additional investment projects at this time and that it should undertake fewer projects.

S_3 would be a strict rationing situation in which a firm was unable or unwilling to get capital funds beyond $25 million. The firm might be reluctant to seek equity funds because of the interest of its entrepreneurs in maintaining capital control. Potential creditors may be unavailable because of high risks.

The firm should invest only in those projects in which the additional return on investment is equal to the additional cost of capital. In Figure 8–4, the intersection of the supply and demand schedules determines the optimum amount of investment in the case of S_3 (where marginal costs become infinite beyond $25 million) and S_1, where the marginal and average costs of capital are equal. For S_2, a marginal cost of capital curve,

MCC_2, must be drawn. For example, S_2 indicates the \$25 million can be raised at a 7 percent cost of capital and \$30 million at 8 percent. The annual cost of the additional \$5 million is \$650,000 (\$2.4 million minus \$1,750,000) or 13 percent; in constructing MCC_2 the 13 percent is plotted at the midpoint of the interval, \$27.5 million. The investment called for is \$25 million with S_3, \$27 million (not \$37 million) with S_2, and \$40 million with S_1.

DEALING WITH INFLATION

By the early 1980s, the United States had had over a decade of increases in the general price level at rates of from 3 percent to low double-digit levels per year. It had become clear that in measuring future cash flows the dollar was a steadily contracting unit of measurement. The inflation rate was much lower in the mid-1980s but may, of course, rise again.

The following procedures are recommended in capital budgeting problems for dealing with expected inflation. First, the benefits and costs coming from investment in capital goods should be expressed in dollars of constant purchasing power. The most convenient measuring rod will usually be dollars of present or year 0 purchasing power.

Second, if prices of particular goods or factors are forecast to rise more or less than the measures of the general price level, allowance should be made for this in the cash flow. For example, if oil prices were forecast to jump 8 percent in years 1 and 2 and then move consistently with an overall inflation rate of 5 percent, 3 percent rises would be incorporated in those years with no further increases over the life of the project.

Third, the relevant cost of capital is the monetary cost of capital less the inflation rate. In the face of an unexpected inflation rate of 5 percent, a calculated cost of capital of 13 percent would represent a real cost of capital of 8 percent.

The alternative procedure is to incorporate all anticipated price changes into the cash flows including those reflecting the movement of the general price level. Then the monetary cost of capital, 13 percent, for example, would be used to discount the cash flows of future years. The errors that must be avoided are the use of the monetary cost when future flows are expressed in constant-value dollars of the present or the use of real costs of capital when inflation is built into the future cash flows.

NEW ERA OF CORPORATE TAKEOVERS

Investments mentioned in this chapter are of a conventional kind. In the mid-1980s, a dramatic development has been the "takeover game" where investments in selected corporations often result in immediate, very large gains to the successful promoters. Corporate raiders such as T. Boone Pickens have become almost as well known to the public as Larry Bird and William ("The Refrigerator") Perry.

Oil companies have been favorite takeover targets, ending the independent existence of Gulf Oil, Cities Service, and some other large firms in the industry. In part, the underlying idea is that it is often cheaper and quicker to acquire oil and gas in the New York Stock Exchange than to acquire it by drilling. Researchers for the takeover specialists study corporations in depth, looking especially for situations where management is not making good use of its resources, including such reserves. After secretly acquiring a substantial block of stock, the raider may publicly offer a higher-than-market price for outstanding shares, bringing on a dramatic rise in the price of the stock of the target firm.

Stockholders in targeted corporations may reap large capital gains, especially if original offers are raised by the takeover specialists or by counteroffers of a firm resisting takeover. Arbitragers will seek to make a profit by buying quickly if the price that is offered by either party exceeds current market price. Even if the takeover does not finally take place, the attempt can provide millions of dollars in capital gains to the raider and others, along with some capital losses and losses of executive positions. A new era of mergers has resulted (in part) from this type of activity, which will be described in greater detail in a later chapter.

CASE 8–1
Problems in Capital Budgeting

1. The XYZ Company has several available investment opportunities with outlays and aftertax cash inflows as shown in Exhibit 8–1A.
   a. Compute the internal rate of return on each project.
   b. Plot the investment demand schedule.
   c. If the cost of capital to XYZ is 10 percent, which projects should be undertaken?
2. The balance sheet of ABC Corporation is given below. ABC has been growing at the rate of 7 percent per year and currently pays a dividend of $2 per year, which is expected to increase by the same 7 percent.

ABC CORPORATION
Balance Sheet

Assets		*Liabilities*	
Plant	$1,000,000	Long-term debt	$ 500,000
		Common stock	500,000
Total assets	$1,000,000	Total liabilities	$1,000,000

EXHIBIT 8–1A

		Cash Inflow by Year				
Project	Outlay	1	2	3	4	5
A	.$ 50,000	15,000	15,000	15,000	15,000	15,000
B	75,000	25,000	25,000	30,000	35,000	35,000
C	100,000	75,000	25,000	20,000	15,000	10,000
D	15,000	5,000	5,000	5,000	5,000	0
E	90,000	25,000	20,000	20,000	20,000	20,000

a. If the market price of the stock is currently $75 with 10,000 shares outstanding, what is the cost of equity capital?

b. The company's earnings are such that its marginal tax rate is 0.44 and it can issue new bonds with a coupon rate of 10 percent. What is the cost of debt capital?

c. What is the average cost of capital if new stock and bonds are going to be issued so that the proportions of debt and equity remain the same when valued at book? At market, assuming the current debt has a market value of $450,000?

d. (Optional) Using the annual reports of several corporations, compute the average cost of capital. How does the cost of capital for a utility compare to an industrial? Use both book and market value weights.

3. The NPQ Company is considering a replacement machine that costs $9,500 and will save $2,600 a year in labor costs. Its cost of capital criterion is 10 percent after taxes. After five years' economic life, the value of the new machine is estimated at $2,000. The present equipment has zero book value and can be scrapped at a price equal to installation costs for a new machine. Assume a tax rate of 40 percent and show that replacement is justified only if accelerated depreciation (either sum-of-the-years' digits or double-declining balance is used).

CASE 8–2A _____
The Paragon Parking Lot

In 1980, Mrs. Hodgkins was considering the development of vacant land she held in a small southern city. She had just received an offer of $400,000 for the land that was being used for the Paragon parking lot. Her alternatives were to sell, to keep the parking lot, or to build an office building from one to five stories high (five stories were the limit permitted by local building codes).

EXHIBIT 8–2A

	Estimated Total Investment	Estimated Net Annual Cash Flow from Property
Selling parking lot	–0–	–0–
Keep parking lot	$ 400,000	$ 44,000
One-story building	800,000	120,000
Two-story building	1,100,000	144,000
Three-story building	1,500,000	200,000
Four-story building	1,750,000	210,000
Five-story building	2,000,000	240,000

The following estimates in Exhibit 8–2A were developed for a 40-year period at the end of which $800,000 was taken as the value of the property for all alternatives in which she kept the land (land was expected to appreciate and while a larger building might be worth more, its demolition costs for a different use would also be greater). All dollar estimates were in constant (1980) dollars. At this point, a pretax analysis was deemed sufficient.

Questions

1. Compute rates of return on incremental investment, discarding alternatives that are irrelevant, at any cost of capital, and arrange as a demand curve for capital.

2. What alternative should be selected at a real cost of capital of 10 percent?

3. Assume that in 1980 bank financing was available for construction costs at 12 percent for 40 years. The expectation was that inflation would average 5 percent or more for the period. Would this tend toward modifying the decision in question toward more or less intensive development of the site? Explain.

CASE 8–2B
How Much Insulation?

In part A, Paragon Parking Lot, the demand for capital (MEC) was described incrementally. In this case, MEC is continuous and obtained by taking the first derivative of the estimated total productivity function. The total productivity of dollars invested in insulation (X) can be measured by the annual dollar savings in energy costs (A).

Assume the relationship is $A = 0.4X - 0.00005X$ at given prices for energy and insulation for a particular small structure. For practical purposes, the life of the investment in insulation can be taken as infinite.

Questions

1. What is the equation for the marginal productivity of insulation (which is the marginal efficiency of capital since it shows the annual rate of savings per additional dollar of invested insulation)?
2. What investment should be made if i = 12 percent; if i = 5 percent?
3. Show the solutions diagramatically with the *MEC* expressing the demand for investment and horizontal supply curves at interest rates of 12 percent and 5 percent.
4. What would be the rate of return on an investment of $4,000? Even though this is greater than i = 12 percent (or even 8 percent), explain carefully why it is not economically justified.

CASE 8–3
The Component Manufacturing Company

The Component Manufacturing Company, located in Oakland, California, was a medium-sized producer of parts for the aircraft industry. Prior to 1958, operations were conducted at four plants scattered throughout the city of Oakland.

The dispersion of these plants had been a matter of vital concern to the board of directors for some time. Costs had been rising rapidly and had begun to endanger the competitive pricing position of the company. The board felt that the consolidation of operations under one or possibly two roofs could do much to alleviate the situation.

So, in the spring of 1958 the company entered into a contract with the Acme Construction Company to build a plant on a site in the city of Stockton, 60 miles from the Oakland plants. The financing was arranged through the company's bankers acting as intermediaries with a financial holding company. Under the terms of the deal, the Component Manufacturing Company entered into a 17-year lease agreement with a $250,000 "buy-back" provision. It was contemplated that the transfer of manufacturing facilities and operations would be conducted in phases, with the final move occurring by 1964.

The first section of the new plant was completed, and operations commenced in August of 1960. It had now become apparent that it was not feasible to transfer all operations to this plant. Certain administration and sales functions were better coordinated in Oakland. In addition, it was discovered that the disposal of waste from plating operations could not be handled without a major capital expenditure. So the long-range policy now became firmly established as envisioning a two-plant operation.

To implement this objective, a new plant, contiguous to a super-highway leading to Stockton, was leased for a 10-year period in December of 1960.

Between 1960 and 1962, the company suffered severe losses due to quality problems in the field, training costs at the new plant, and a heavy litigation claim. As a result, the company had a $400,000 carryforward loss for tax purposes.

By now, operations were conducted in three plants:

Plant 1—Owned by the company, encumbered with a $200,000 mortgage. Fully depreciated as war facility. Located in Oakland in generally undesirable area.

Plant 2—Leased in December, 1960. Approximately eight years of lease remaining. Located in Oakland.

Plant 3—Lease commenced in August of 1960 to continue for 17 years. Located in Stockton.

In September of 1962, the company received an offer of $200,000 for plant 1. The offer was considered quite substantial, considering the general deterioration of real estate values in the neighborhood. Further, acceptance would enable the company to consolidate operations into two plants.

However, before the consolidation could be accomplished, an extension had to be built on plant 2. The treasurer, R. C. Baker, was directed to negotiate this possibility with the owners of the plant. He was further directed to make a thorough study of the cost and cash flow implications of the sale.

The owners of plant 2 would make the necessary extensions at an annual rental of $48,000, provided Component Manufacturing Company agreed to an extension of the lease to 10 years.

Mr. Baker realized that the tax carryforward position of $400,000 would be very important in the cash flow analysis. Selling the building now would result in a $200,000 capital gain, since the plant was fully amortized. Capital gains would be applied to an ordinary loss, and the company would lose 25 cents on the dollar (assuming a tax rate of 50 percent for ease of calculation). This loss would amount to $50,000. If the building were not sold, it would take two years to use up the loss carryforward.

On the basis of these preliminary considerations, Mr. Baker decided to analyze two alternatives: (1) sale of the plant immediately and (2) sale of the plant in two years.

Exhibits 8–3A, 8–3B, and 8–3C were prepared by Mr. Baker's staff with the assistance of the industrial engineering department to facilitate the analysis of the move accompanied by immediate sale of plant.

Exhibit 8–3A shows the estimated cost savings from consolidation on a pro forma basis. Exhibit 8–3B is the schedule of capital requirements. Depreciable items are separated from moving costs to facilitate cash flow

EXHIBIT 8–3A   Sale of Building and Move Proposal: Analysis of
Cost Savings

	Present Cost	Proposed Cost
Rent	—	$48,000
Taxes and insurance	$15,200	7,000
Heat	6,800	4,500
Power, light, and water	9,400	8,000
Guards	12,000	4,000
Porters	12,000	9,000
Building repair	4,000	1,000
Parking	900	3,900
Interest	12,000	—
Maintenance	16,200	2,500
Total operating cost	$88,500	$87,900
Gross cost saving		$ 600
Additional savings:		
Labor rate revision		9,000
Trucking costs		6,000
Plating maintenance reduction		4,000
Companywide improved efficiency		10,400
Net savings from move		$30,000

EXHIBIT 8–3B

COMPONENT MANUFACTURING COMPANY
Schedule of Capital Expenditures

Item	Amount
Depreciable items:	
Plating department	$43,000
Switchboard	5,000
Laboratory equipment	1,000
Electric wiring	5,000
Total depreciable items	54,000
Moving costs:	
IBM	4,000
Level plating floor	2,000
Clean up plant 1	2,000
Office	3,000
Model room	2,000
Miscellaneous and extras	3,000
Total moving	16,000
Total expenditures	$70,000

computations. Exhibit 8–3C shows the cash flow generated by the move
to the addition.

The greatest concern of Mr. Baker in delaying the sale until the end of
the second year (payment of capital gains tax would be delayed another

---

EXHIBIT 8–3C   Cash Flows for Move Assuming Immediate Sale of Old
Plant and Repayment of Mortgage

	Year 0	Years 1–10
Before-tax cash flow	$(70,000)	$30,000
Aftertax cash savings		15,000
Add depreciation tax shield		
(0.50 × $5,400); 0.50 exp. for year 0	8,000	2,700
Aftertax cash flow	$(62,000)	$17,700

EXHIBIT 8–3D   Net Aftertax Cash Flow Advantage of Delayed Sale of Old Plant*

	Year 1	Year 2	Year 3	Total A
Price of $200,000	$(12,000)	$88,000	$(38,000)	$38,000
Price of $150,000	(12,000)	38,000	(25,500)	500
Price of $100,000	(12,000)	(12,000)	(13,000)	(37,000)

*Note of explanation: Regardless of price, $12,000 of mortgage interest in year 1 would be paid when estimated normal profits are nontaxable. In Year 2, taxes of $100,000 on profits of $200,000 would be avoided since a tax carryforward position of $212,000 is still available; this saving is reduced by $12,000 interest. In year 3, 25 percent capital gain tax must be paid but $24,000 of tax carryforward is still available to offset $12,000 of taxes on normal profits. If the company receives a lower price, the tax gains are reduced by the amount needed to pay off mortgage out of other funds. This reduction is put at end of year 2 and smaller capital gains tax is shown in year 3.

year) was the possibility of getting less than $200,000 for the plant. Exhibit 8–3D shows cash flows for the delayed sale at three prices: $200,000 considered a 60 percent probability; $150,000, a 30 percent probability; and $100,000, a 10 percent probability. Because of the risks involved, Mr. Baker felt the expected value of the possible tax savings less the additional interest and loss on the $200,000 needed to pay off the mortgage should be discounted at 12 percent.

Question

1. Consider the conversion decision and the sell now or later decision as separate decisions and analyze each. What actions should the firm take? What qualifications are necessary?

CASE 8–4
That First House: Inflation, Interest, and Taxes

Purchasing a house represents an investment very much favored by American values as reflected in the tax laws that do not require the declaration of the nonmonetary income received from housing services but permit the deduction of the major expenses such as mortgage interest and real estate taxes. Let us follow the fortunes of a young couple through this housing investment.

1. Three years after leaving college they purchase an $80,000 house and take out a 30-year mortgage for $72,000 at an annual interest rate of 12 percent. (In the A given P formula, use $i = 1$ percent and $n = 360$). Their monthly payments are: _____.

2. They are transferred after five years and must sell the house. The present value of what they will owe is then: _____.

3. The value of their house has appreciated by 5 percent a year and is then: _____.

4. Their original equity of $8,000 has now increased to _____ (take off the real estate broker's fee of 6 percent of the selling price to get your answer).

5. They breathe a sigh of satisfaction and give thanks for inflation (assume the rise in the price was equal to that of the general price level) since without the price rise their initial equity would have been reduced to _____ after the sale.

6. Their interest payments came to a total of _____ during the five-year period. Under 1985 tax laws, their taxes would have been reduced by their marginal income tax rate times this amount.

7. They recognize that much of what they paid in interest was not real interest but compensation to the lender for the fact that it received only _____ dollars of the worth it loaned when they paid the principal due at the end of five years. Their increase in real equity is largely due to the decline in the real value of their debt.

8. They have paid for this reduction in real value of their debt insofar as the rise in the price level was anticipated with an inflation premium of 5 percent in their 12 percent interest rate. The government under 1985 law would have helped them out by reducing their income taxes by their tax rate times the total interest, including the inflation component that reduced the real value of their debt. The tax reform proposals of the Treasury Department in 1984 called for allowing interest deductions from taxable income only to the extent that the interest rate exceeded the inflation rate. Similarly, interest would be taxable to the recipient only to the extent that the interest rate exceeded the inflation rate. For example, an individual paying a 5 percent interest rate would not pay any income tax if the inflation rate were 5 percent. Assume a relevant tax rate of 0.30. The current dollar amount of their interest (see Question 6) that was offset by taxes under 1985 law would be _____. Under the tax reform proposals, the offset, assuming 5 percent inflation would be approximately _____.

9

Employment of Human Resources

> The declining marginal product of the variable service can be attributed either to an increasing quantity of the variable service relative to the fixed service or to a decreasing quantity of the fixed service relative to the variable service.
>
> —George J. Stigler — V. of Chicago

Payments for labor services usually make up the largest part of a firm's variable costs. This proportion varies greatly between products, however. Near one extreme is an electric power generating facility where few persons except an occasional skilled attendant can be seen. At the other extreme is the business of gathering unusual sea shells (before the tourists have awakened) by workers who need only ordinary buckets as their capital equipment. With development of improved technology the proportion of the labor force in professional and skilled manual occupations is increasing quite dramatically.

Since a great deal of investment in the individual is required to turn out an engineer, an astronaut, or even a competent automobile mechanic, economists have begun to consider *human capital* to be a factor of production. The term *labor* is becoming less appropriate as a general designation for the human agent. When the term is used, it is at least important to keep in mind the tremendous diversity of abilities covered. For analytical purpose it is usually necessary to consider only one reasonably homogeneous type of labor at a time. This approach is similar to the simplification involved in analyzing the single product firm. Usually the principles involved are similar for all the products actually turned out by a firm and for all the types of labor it actually employs.

MARGINAL PRODUCTIVITY OF LABOR

Output and input decisions are made simultaneously in response to the price-cost situation in which the firm finds itself. They are parts of the same optimizing process that the decision makers of the firm are conceived to follow. For the purpose of analytical simplicity, however, it is best to consider output and input decisions separately; consequently, the input side is concentrated upon in this chapter.

A unit of labor will be hired by an entrepreneur only if the value of its product is believed to be at least as high as its cost. *Value and cost* are usually measured in monetary terms, although rational calculation may also involve nonpecuniary considerations. For example, a business executive may hire his indolent father-in-law as a way of getting some work out of him if he would have to support him anyway.

Judging the contribution of a worker is complicated by the fact that usually he or she is employed along with capital equipment, materials, supplies, electric power, and other factors. A worker cannot profitably be paid a wage out of income that is actually attributable to other inputs. The marginal productivity approach offers a logical way out of the dilemma. If all other inputs are held constant, the increase in output that would occur if one more unit of labor is hired constitutes the product attributable to that unit. Since all units of labor are considered to be interchangeable, any one of the units hired can properly be considered to be contributing this same marginal product. If employing one more worker necessarily entails adding other inputs, such as supplies, the net marginal productivity of labor can be calculated if the cost of this ancillary additional input is deducted from the value of added output. For the purpose of simplification, it is usually sufficient to assume all other inputs to be strictly fixed in quantity and to consider only labor to vary in amount.

This is the procedure used in Figure 9–1. The quantity of capital utilized by the hypothetical plant is not shown explicitly but is assumed to be constant while labor input per month can vary from 2 to 10 units. The plant's production function is reflected in the relation between the fixed capital input, the variable labor input, and the total output shown in column 2. Column 3 shows the marginal physical product of labor, which is simply the increment in total output per month as labor input is increased by one unit. (If labor increments were not exactly one unit in each line of the table, it would be necessary to divide the change in number of units of output by the change in labor input.)

If 6 units of labor were employed, for example, the marginal physical product would be 36 units. This output should not be thought of as the product of the "last worker" or the "sixth worker" but as the amount of product imputable to any one of the six workers employed. Translated into value terms it consequently represents the maximum amount the firm can profitably pay per month to any one of the six workers.

The translation of physical product into monetary terms is shown in columns 4 and 5. The firm is assumed to be able to sell any output it wishes at a price of $20 per unit. This means the company is assumed to be too small to affect price by its own actions—it sells in a perfectly competitive market. Value of the marginal product is found by multiplying marginal physical product by $20.

If it is further assumed that the firm is also a price taker (rather than price maker) in the labor market, how much labor should it hire? The answer depends on the monthly wage rate it must pay, and this depends

FIGURE 9–1   Computation of Value of Marginal Product

(1) Labor Input per Month	(2) Total Output per Month	(3) Marginal Physical Product	(4) Price of Output	(5) Value of Marginal Product
1	25	25	$20	$500
2	53	28	20	560
3	84	31	20	620
4	118	34	20	680
5	155	37	20	740
6	191	36	20	720
7	226	35	20	700
8	259	33	20	660
9	285	26	20	520
10	305	20	20	400

on the entire supply-demand situation in the labor market for the kind of labor needed. Suppose the prevailing wage rate is $600 per month. Eight workers appears to be the optimum input. Value of the marginal product at this employment level is $660, but if another worker were hired, the addition to the firm's revenue would be only $520 while the addition to wage cost would be $600.

It can be said that optimum input of labor is eight units per month provided it is considered to be worth operating at all. Total revenue from the product will be $5,180 per month (259 × $20) while the total wage bill will be $4,800, leaving $380 to cover other costs. As indicated in Chapter 6, these costs are (in a simplified explanation) interest and depreciation on the selling value of the plant. If the $380 is not sufficient to cover these costs, the indication is that another use of the firm's plant (perhaps the production of a different product) would be better. If the outlook is for near-future improvement of the price-cost situation for the present product, a switch to another product or disposal of the plant is less likely.

Not all of the information needed for a rational input decision is given in Figure 9–1. All that can be said with certainty is that if a decision is made to turn out the product under consideration and the wage rate is $600 per month, eight units is the best number of units of labor to employ. Other decisions such as whether to switch products, install new equipment, or to sell out altogether require additional information, and some of the relevant principles are stated elsewhere in this book. However, if the prevailing wage rate were $800 per month rather than $600, it can be inferred directly from Figure 9–1 that it would be more economical to shut down. This is because the total value of the product would not be so large as the wage bill at any level of labor input. (In terms of output analysis, the average variable cost would be above the price of the product at all possible output rates.)

Figure 9–1 (like all tables) incorporates finite steps, whereas a diagram such as Figure 9–2 permits consideration of infinitely divisible inputs.

FIGURE 9–2   Optimum Input of Labor—Where *VMP* Equals
Wage Rate

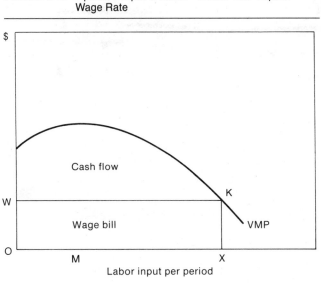

Assuming that it is desirable to operate the plant, optimum labor input is
OX at wage rate OW.[1] The total wage bill per time period is OWKX. Since
total value of the product is the entire area under the *VMP* curve, the area
remaining after deduction of OWKX represents the cash flow available to
meet interest, depreciation, and other fixed costs and—if the situation is
especially favorable—to yield an excess return above other alternatives to
owners of the firm.

As stated in the title quotation by George Stigler, a recent Nobel Lau-
reate, declining marginal product is really a matter of proportionate use
of variable and fixed inputs. If the two inputs are called "labor" and
"capital," a curve such as that of Figure 9–2 implies that capital is held
constant while labor is varied. But an increase in labor per unit of capital
is at the same time a decrease in capital per unit of labor. The rising
portion of *VMP* can consequently be attributed to use of too little labor for
the capital used or, alternatively, use of too much capital for the labor
applied. This can be of practical use. If the plant is divisible (that is, can
be used in part), a more efficient operation can sometimes be secured by
shutting down part of the plant. For example, if for some reason, only a
few hired hands are available, a farmer can have them work on only part
of the acreage letting the rest lie unused, thus securing more output than
could be secured by spreading the workers over the whole farm.

---

[1]The *VMP* curve must be falling rather than rising. If the wage rate and *VMP* were
equated in the rising portion of *VMP*, labor input would be the worst rather than the best.
This is because all units would be hired where the wage was higher than contribution to
revenue and none would be hired that added more to revenue than to the wage bill.

The rising, then falling *VMP* curve of Figure 9–2 implies indivisibility of the fixed factor—it must all be utilized. Increasing marginal product of labor is attained as better proportions of inputs, variable and fixed, are secured. Maximum *VMP* is reached at labor input *OM*. This is not the optimum input of labor, however, since this is found in the stage of diminishing marginal product and depends on price of the product and the wage rate.

FIXED PROPORTIONS

Frequently the production function is quite different from those incorporated in Figures 9–1 and 9–2, involving fixed rather than variable proportions between labor and capital. The assumption of fixed proportions may be appropriate to both short-run and long-run analysis. In the latter, fixed proportions can occur if labor and capital are altered proportionally.

Suppose an apparel plant is equipped with 10 identical sewing machines, each utilizing one operator. The curve depicting value of the marginal product will consist of 10 dots at the same height, as in Figure 9–3. This is because each operator-machine combination will add the same amount of product per time period. Diminishing returns do not set in.

If the prevailing wage rate is *OW*, it appears likely with a competitive product market that 10 operators will be employed in the production, but, as indicated earlier, this is not necessarily true if we consider a product switch or sale of the plant to be possible as a short-run action. While each machine will yield a return above the wages of its operator, the information given in the chart is not sufficient to tell us whether another product (perhaps bathing suits rather than dresses) should be turned out or whether the entire plant should be sold or leased to someone else. Modern technology probably makes short-run fixity of input proportions more common.

MONOPOLIST'S DEMAND FOR LABOR

Only a minor modification of the marginal productivity concept is needed if the firm is a monopolistic rather than competitive seller of output. As a monopolist hires more labor, the rate of output will increase and this will lower the price at which the product can be sold. This effect of amount of input on price of output must be taken into account in a rational decision as to how much labor to employ.

In the situation depicted in Figure 9–2, the down-sloping portion of the *VMP* curve reflects operation of the law of diminishing returns. If the firm sold in a monopolistic rather than competitive market, an additional factor—the law of demand—would reinforce the law of diminishing returns; that is, price and marginal revenue from output would decline as input increased. The resulting curve is usually called *marginal revenue product*. Mathematically:

$$MRP = MPP \cdot MR$$

FIGURE 9–3 Fixed Input Proportions—Diminishing Returns Are Absent

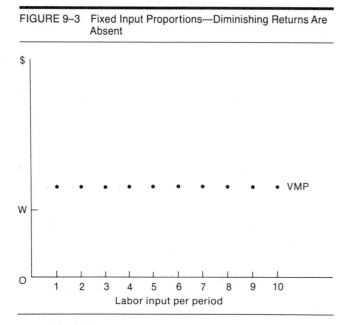

(whereas under competitive selling *VMP* equals *MPP* times price of output). Assuming that the monopolistic seller is nevertheless a competitive buyer of labor, optimum input would be determined as in Figure 9–2, the only difference being that a *MRP* rather than *VMP* curve would be the demand curve. It should be kept in mind that the analysis of Figure 9–2 assumes that one factor (e.g., the amount of land) is kept fixed in amount and only one variable input is used. Alternative assumptions can be made, but the analysis can quickly gain more in complexity than it gains in predictive power.[2]

MONOPSONY

If a firm is the only buyer of a particular type of labor in a market, it is said to be a monopsonist in that market. Even if there are several firms that hire labor but act in unison in their employment practices, the monopsony analysis is applicable. Actually, monopsony power in local labor markets is not very prevalent in the United States according to a careful study made some years ago.[3] This is not to say that it is always unimportant. There has been a tendency in recent years to locate manufacturing

---

[2]In the analysis of fixed proportions, as in Figure 9–3, the dots would be labeled *MRP* if the output were sold monopolistically and would decline from left to right due to the lower price at which higher output would have to be sold.

[3]Robert L. Bunting, *Employer Concentration in Local Labor Markets* (Chapel Hill: University of North Carolina Press, 1962).

FIGURE 9–4 Computation of Marginal Factor Cost

Labor Input per Hour	Wage Rate per Hour	Total Labor Cost per Hour	Marginal Factor Cost per Hour
1	$4.00	$ 4.00	$4.00
2	4.10	8.20	4.20
3	4.20	12.60	4.40
4	4.30	17.20	4.60
5	4.40	22.00	4.80
6	4.50	27.00	5.00
7	4.60	32.20	5.20
8	4.70	37.60	5.40
9	4.80	43.20	5.60
10	4.90	49.00	5.80

plants in rural areas to get away from urban congestion. Such a plant may be the only large employer within a substantial geographic area and hence possess monopsony power.

Just as a monopolistic seller must consider the effect of output on the price at which it can sell, the monopsonist must consider the effect of purchases on the price at which it can buy. (This contrasts with the situation facing a customer in a grocery store who pays the same price per pound of shrimp no matter what quantity she buys.) The supply schedule of labor to a monopsonist is up-sloping, reflecting the fact that higher wage rates will cause more persons to be willing to supply their labor. In the case of a plant located in a rather isolated area, a higher wage will cause people to drive longer distances to and from work and will consequently increase the amount of labor supplied.

Corresponding to the important concept of marginal revenue to the monopolist is the idea of marginal factor cost to the monopsonist. Computation of marginal factor cost is shown in Figure 9–4. Suppose the monopsonist were hiring five workers at $4.40 per hour. If a sixth person were hired, he or she would be available at $4.50 per hour. However, all workers would then have to receive $4.50 per hour to avoid a serious morale problem. Thus, the actual extra cost (marginal factor cost) of a sixth worker is $5 even though he or she is paid only $4.50. It is not necessary to think in terms of movements from one employment level to another. Rather the various employment levels can be thought of as alternatives at a point of time, as seen by the employer.

The situation of a firm that buys labor monopsonistically is shown in Figure 9–5. The contribution of labor is labeled VMP or MRP according to whether the firm is assumed to sell output competitively or monopolistically. Optimum input is OX units of labor per period, determined by the equality of MFC and VMP (or MRP). That is, the monopsonist should hire all workers that add more to income than they add to labor cost, but no workers who add more to labor cost than to income. In Figure 9–5, the wage rate paid will be OW, located on the labor supply curve at the

FIGURE 9–5 Optimum Input for a Monopsonist

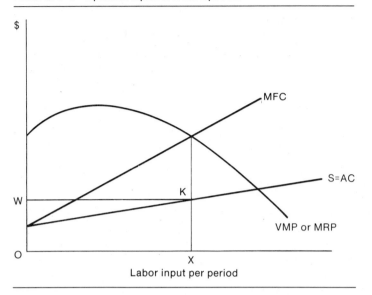

optimum input level. The wage bill will be *OWKX*, and the remaining area under the *VMP* (or *MRP*) curve to the left of *X* measures "cash flow" under the simplified assumption that labor is the only variable input. This is because the total area under *VMP* (*MRP*) measures total revenue. Under monopsony, *VMP* or *MRP* should not be called a demand curve since the wage rate actually paid will not be on this curve.[4]

BILATERAL MONOPOLY

When a single seller of labor or of a product deals with a single buyer, the situation is known as *bilateral monopoly*. Although bilateral monopoly occurs in industrial markets (as when an automobile company buys the entire output of a parts maker and cannot deal with any other firm), it is of greater importance in unionized labor relations. A large company or group of firms may be considered to be monopsonistic in dealing with a monopolistic union selling labor, especially when one labor contract applies to all the firms and workers. The outcome is not theoretically determinate but depends on relative bargaining power. Both sides have strengths and weaknesses that will affect the f.nal outcome regarding wage rates, working conditions, and fringe benefits.

Labor unions will have their bargaining power increased by such

---

[4]A useful rule to remember is that the monopolist has no supply curve for output and the monopsonist has no demand curve for input.

factors as: (1) substantial fixity of proportions between labor and expensive capital equipment, (2) large profits being made by firms, (3) strong and inelastic demand for the product, (4) large reserves in union treasuries, (5) unemployment insurance paid by government agencies during strikes, and (6) difficulty of transferring operations to another locality.

Company bargaining power is increased by such factors as: (1) large and durable inventories of the final product, (2) ability to reduce the use of labor relative to capital, (3) large reserve funds, (4) possibility of transferring operations to nonunion localities, and (5) political officials opposed to paying unemployment insurance to striking workers. These lists are, of course, not exhaustive.

RIGHT-TO-WORK LAWS

The Taft-Hartley Act amendments to the National Labor Relations Act, passed in 1947, outlaw the "closed shop"[5] but permit the "union shop"[6] except where the individual states pass right-to-work laws. These state laws are permitted by the famous Section 14(b) of the Taft-Hartley Act. They permit workers to join unions only if they wish to do so, even where collective bargaining takes place involving a unit in which they work.

To date, 21 states have enacted right-to-work laws under authorization of Section 14(b), or by constitutional amendment, or both.[7] Due in part to their right-to-work laws, North Carolina and South Carolina have fewer than 10 percent of nonfarm workers in labor unions. This appears partly to account for the great success these states have had in attracting foreign investment. In 1975, South Carolina attracted $300 million in foreign capital, bringing total foreign investment in that state's manufacturing facilities to over $1.43 billion and providing employment for 19,300 of its residents.[8] Michelin, the important French tire company, has three plants in South Carolina. As shown in Case 9–1, foreign imports and investment are of great concern to unionized rubber workers, as is the establishment of domestic tire plants in nonunionized areas. It is not surprising that the right-to-work laws have been, and will continue to be, the subject of bitter legislative battles, both nationally and in the states. Idaho is the latest right-to-work state, as both houses of the legislature overrode a veto by the governor in January 1985.

---

[5]This requires that a job-seeker be a member of the union in order to be eligible for hiring and maintain that membership in order to retain the job.

[6]This means that the worker need not be a member of the union at the time of hiring but must join within a specified period to retain the job and must maintain membership.

[7]Alabama, Arizona, Arkansas, Florida, Georgia, Idaho, Iowa, Kansas, Louisiana, Mississippi, Nebraska, Nevada, North Carolina, North Dakota, South Carolina, South Dakota, Tennessee, Texas, Utah, Virginia, and Wyoming. The Territory of American Samoa also has such a law.

[8]Lloyd Shearer, *Parade*, February 13, 1977. The article uses material published in the *Vanderbilt Journal of Transnational Law*, written by Paul S. Dempsey.

MINIMUM WAGE RATES

Since passage of the Fair Labor Standards Act in 1938, the federal government has set minimum wage rates for jobs in "interstate commerce." Coverage has been greatly expanded since that time so that in addition to manufacturing, mining, and wholesaling, such activities as retailing, restaurants, hotels and motels, hospitals, laundries, construction, taxicabs, agriculture, and domestic service are covered. This follows the tendency of the federal government, aided by the courts, to regard almost all economic activity as interstate commerce.

Since 1966, Congress has legislated schedules of future increases in the minimum wage rather than following the previous practice of covering just a year at a time. The law signed November 1, 1977, by President Jimmy Carter, covering about 52 million workers, established the following schedule.[9]

	Minimum Wage Rate (per hour)	
Effective Date	Nontipped Employees	Tipped Employees
January 1, 1978.	$2.65	$1.33
January 1, 1979.	2.90	1.60
January 1, 1980.	3.10	1.86
January 1, 1981.	3.35	2.01

The minimum wage increases were about in line with the inflation rate that was anticipated by the U.S. Department of Labor. Since wage rates are costs as well as incomes, the schedule itself contributed to inflation. A significant feature of the schedule is that tips are counted to a decreasing extent as meeting minimum wage requirements. Employers of tipped personnel previously had to pay 50 percent of the minimum wage but 60 percent beginning in 1980.

The analysis of this chapter can constitute a framework for predicting probable effects of increases in the legal minimum wage either at the federal level or by the states that have such laws. Most employers are not directly affected because they already pay more than the minimum. Employers of skilled or professional persons are in this category. Employers of low-skilled persons are likely to be more selective in their hiring practices and to lay off the poorer workers who have marginal revenue productivity below the legal minimum wage. Minority groups especially tend to suffer increased unemployment as their power to compete with majority groups (who may be favored by most employers) is diminished since a floor is put on the wage at which they can offer to work.

---

[9]As shown in Peyton Elder, "The 1977 Amendments to the Federal Minimum Wage Law," *Monthly Labor Review*, vol. 101 (January 1978), p. 9.

If the *VMP* or *MRP* curve is completely inelastic due to the need to use labor in fixed proportions to equipment, the firm may not change its employment in the short run in response to a higher minimum wage but will attempt to automate to a greater extent over time. For example, elevator operators may receive wage increases and suffer no employment losses in the short run but will face greater danger of being replaced eventually by automatic elevators. Companies that have some leeway in their processes, such as chain food stores, are likely to make immediate laborsaving adjustments such as reducing the number of bag boys and girls employed. (Chain food stores will also have an incentive to consider more automated checkout systems.) In agriculture, a higher minimum wage tends to induce a substitution of weed killers, fertilizer, and machinery for hand labor. Many "cotton choppers" in Mississippi and Louisiana were fired when the federal minimum wage was extended to cover large farms since it became cheaper to substitute chemical weed killers for their labor. (Cotton choppers dig out the roots of cotton plants after the harvest.) The federal minimum wage was not increased during the first term of Ronald Reagan—an aspect of "Reaganomics" that is usually overlooked.[10] To have kept up with the more moderate rate of inflation, a 1985 minimum of $4 would have been necessary.

DAVIS-BACON ACT

The Davis-Bacon Act has been in effect even longer than the minimum wage law, having been enacted in 1931. It directly affects contractors performing construction work for the federal government by requiring that workers be paid wages "prevailing" in the community where construction takes place. Like the minimum wage law, the Davis-Bacon law receives strong union support.

A difficult administrative problem for the Department of Labor is finding out what wage rate actually "prevails" in any particular area. In practice, this is often the rate paid to union workers in the general area, in part because these are easier to acquire.

The administrative problem is aggravated by the existence of over 3,000 civil subdivisions in the United States and by the fact that any one project may employ workers in 20 or 30 classifications.[11]

---

[10]Numerous statistical studies have been made of employment effects of minimum wages. For example, J. M. Peterson, "Employment Effects of Minimum Wages, 1938–1950" (Ph.D. dissertation, University of Chicago, 1956); H. M. Douty, "Some Effects of the $1.00 Minimum Wage in the United States," *Economica*, May 1960; M. R. Colberg, "Minimum Wage Effects on Florida's Economic Development," *Journal of Law and Economics*, October 1960; and Yale Brozen, "The Effect of Statutory Minimum Wage Increases on Teen-Age Employment," *Journal of Law and Economics*, April 1969.

[11]John P. Gould and George Bittlingmayer, *The Economics of the Davis-Bacon Act* (Washington, D.C.: American Enterprise Institute for Public Policy Research, 1980), p. 14.

The General Accounting Office has reported that the prevailing wage determinations have been too high. For example, the Department of Labor for a time used wage rates in commercial construction (which is more dangerous) as appropriate for residential construction. GAO concluded that "after nearly fifty years, the Department of Labor has yet to develop an effective program to issue and maintain accurate wage determinations and it may be impractical to ever do so."[12]

The law raises the cost of construction and repairs to which the federal government or the District of Columbia is a party. Nonunion employers have more difficulty in getting federal contracts since they must usually pay union wage rates.

The strong lobbying support received by Davis-Bacon in spite of much criticism illustrates the difficulty of eliminating programs that have adverse effects on organized groups. This is the major reason for the difficulty of reducing yearly federal deficits. Indirectly it shows the folly of such ideas as "equal pay for comparable work." Substitution of administrative determinations for market determination causes almost unlimited problems and provides a tremendous bonanza to the legal profession.

TRAINING OF WORKERS

In recent years there has been great interest in the idea of investment in the individual as a way to build "human capital" that returns interest to the worker in the form of enhanced future earnings. T. W. Schultz and Gary Becker are the best-known recent contributors to the field, although the general idea is an old one.[13] The emphasis here will be on some of the implications of human capital theory for the firm.

One of the important areas is the training of employees. The more specific the training to the particular needs of a firm, the more likely the firm is to pay for the training; the more general the training the more likely it is that the individual or government will undergo the cost. The reason is simple. If, for example, a firm pays for a secretarial course for its employees, many are likely to leave the firm after their secretarial capabilities have been built up because there are many places they can work. The company will probably lose much of its investment. If, however, workers are trained to run nylon spinning equipment, the skill acquired cannot often be sold to another company and hence the investment in training is likely to pay off to the company that provides it. Monopsony power in a labor market increases the probability that training of a fairly general nature can usefully be provided by a firm because employment

---

[12]U.S. General Accounting Office, *The Davis-Bacon Act Should Be Repealed*, 1979, letter of transmittal of the Comptroller General.

[13]See especially T. W. Schultz, "Investment in Human Capital," *American Economic Review*, March 1961; and Gary S. Becker, *Human Capital* (New York: Columbia University Press, 1975).

alternatives are scarce. In a "company town" the dominant company may even find it worthwhile to pay for the improvement of reading and arithmetic skills of employees as they would have to leave town to find other substantial employment.

Similarly, although it is usually felt to be wiser to spend money on training young workers in skills specific to a company, it should be kept in mind that their intercompany mobility is greater. This can make investment in older, less mobile employees more desirable than consideration only of the number of years of working life remaining would suggest. Also company-paid programs for training of executives are often worthwhile because the turnover of executives tends to be low. Although the acquisition of general skills (computer programming may qualify) is desirable from the viewpoint of the employee in that it opens up many alternatives for employment, specific training has its values. The employee tends to receive a higher wage than could be earned elsewhere and has greater job security because he or she will probably be retained in a temporary business slump. If the employee is lost to the firm, it will have to invest in the training of a replacement. From the firm's point of view, specifically trained labor is a sort of fixed capital, and even if the original investment in training is not currently providing the firm a suitable rate of return, there is special incentive to continue to employ the worker.[14]

WORKER ALIENATION

One of the famous early descriptions of a factory assembly line is found in Adam Smith's *Wealth of Nations:*

> One man draws out the wire, another straights it, a third cuts it, a fourth paints it, a fifth grinds it at the top for receiving the head; to make the head requires two or three distinct operations; to put it on is a peculiar business, to whiten the pins is another; it is even a trade by itself to put them into the paper, and the important business of making a pin is, in this manner, divided into about eighteen distinct operations which in some manufactories, are all performed by distinct hands, though in others the same man will sometimes perform two or three of them.[15]

The extreme specialization and repetitiveness of the assembly line is well suited to many workers who do not like the bother of learning new skills. It may even suit some imaginative people who can think about other things much of the time because a well-learned routine requires little thought. For the most part, however, an increasingly well-educated working force becomes alienated from jobs that involve routine and repetition. This has led recently to great interest in ways of rearranging work. In some cases it is possible to organize "teams" of workers that perform all of the operations required to turn out a product, with frequent changes

---

[14]This line of analysis was first developed carefully by Walter Oi, "Labor as a Quasi Fixed Factor of Production" (Ph.D. dissertation, University of Chicago, 1961).

[15]Adam Smith, *The Wealth of Nations*, Modern Library Edition, 1937, pp. 4–5.

in job assignments and with supervisory autonomy. Team members usually willingly fill in when someone is temporarily absent from the job. Where a real *esprit de corps* has been established, productivity has risen markedly.

The Saab automobile plant in Sweden has had encouraging success with new plant and work organization techniques in which production workers (1) are included in development teams, (2) help rebalance jobs, (3) inspect for quality, (4) are responsible for care of equipment they use, and (5) are urged and enabled to learn several jobs. Results have been sufficiently impressive to cause Saab to apply the ideas to a new engine plant opened in January 1972.[16]

To some extent the steps being taken to decrease worker alienation can be interpreted as methods to give the workers greater "property rights" in their jobs—that is, to make it easier for them to appropriate both pecuniary and nonpecuniary gains from good performance. For example, if truck drivers are assigned to a particular truck to drive rather than being rotated daily to any one of a fleet of trucks, they are certain to be more interested in its maintenance since they can personally benefit from this effort. Also, team workers who perform different kinds of jobs can more easily develop the professional attitude needed to become a company executive. Their personal investment in human capital is facilitated.

To a limited degree some American firms are moving toward the worker-management system that is a feature of industry in Yugoslavia. In that country, workers' councils have jurisdiction over many aspects of employment, investment, and profit distribution and can even fire the managers. Their wage consists of a fixed sum plus a share in profits. Although production capital is socially owned in all but small enterprises, workers are given a virtual property right in the capital utilized by their own companies which have to compete with other domestic and foreign enterprise for sales.[17] "Capitalistic" firms that take special steps such as subsidizing stock ownership by employees (Sears, Roebuck is an outstanding example) or delegating some managerial power to production teams are somewhat similarly trying to prevent worker alienation from the job. Where financially ailing companies such as Weirton Steel have been purchased by employees, alienation may prove to be less likely.

EXECUTIVE INCENTIVES

Although the corporation can be viewed historically as a device by which management has been largely separated from ownership, much of the criticism often heard along this line is unjustified. Many owners of capital

---

[16]Richard E. Walton, "How to Counter Alienation in the Plant," *Harvard Business Review*, November-December, 1972, p. 80.

[17]See, for example, George Macesich, *Yugoslavia: The Theory and Practice of Development Planning* (Charlottesville: University Press of Virginia, 1964); and *World Banking and Finance* (New York: Praeger, 1984), pp. 118–20.

do not want to be concerned with management, and officials in a given field may prefer to invest in other areas. Still there is good reason to attempt to secure a partial remarriage of management and ownership in order to give officials a greater incentive to build up profits.

One such device is the supplementing of salaries with stock options. Such options give the right to buy a specified amount of the corporation's unissued stock at a specified price over a designated period of time. If the market price rises, the holder can still purchase the stock at the stated price. If it falls sufficiently in price, the executive will not exercise the option. If the executive does acquire the stock, he or she may end up with a capital loss. In the past few years stock options have lost in popularity among corporations officials because of less favorable income tax treatment.

Executive incentive plans usually are based on either a straight percentage of net income or on a percentage of profits when profits exceed a designated rate of return on invested capital. Like all formulas these have problems. If bonuses are based on a fixed percentage of net income, they are paid even when profits fall off sharply, so long as they are positive, and even if poor decisions were responsible. Bonuses are sometimes based on planned rather than actual profits, being paid only when the plan is achieved or surpassed. This, however, provides an incentive to keep profit plans as low as possible, much as the Soviet production manager is happier with a centrally planned output that is easy to surpass. Or executive bonuses may be paid for improved company performance relative to the industry. This can encounter problems of defining the industry, especially when product mixes change. According to a leading authority in the field, about two thirds of listed companies have incentive plans for executives.[18]

Virtually every large company in the automotive, retail chain, department store, electrical appliance, office equipment, textile, chemical, and pharmaceutical industries has an executive incentive program. Relatively few are found in public utility, banking, mining, railroad, or life insurance companies.

Bonus plans for executives are more likely to be successful when company results depend heavily on frequently made decisions regarding production, buying, selling, style changes, and the like. They are not needed when results depend mainly on general economic conditions, population movements, actions of regulatory commissions, or on pure chance.[19]

---

[18]Arch Patton, "Why Incentive Plans Fail," *Harvard Business Review*, May–June, 1972, p. 59. Much of the material in this section has been derived from his article.

[19]Alfred Marshall, whose work still profoundly affects economics, attributed the incomes of successful men to a combination of chance, environment, opportunity, a good start in life, capital invested in their special training, hard work, and rare natural gifts. The last named can provide "a producer's surplus or rent." Alfred Marshall, *Principles of Economics*, 8th ed. (London: Macmillan & Co., Ltd., 1930), p. 577.

CASE 9–1
Union and Nonunion Rubber Plants (March, 1979)*

BILATERAL Monopoly

A sprawling tire plant in the rolling tobacco country here (Wilson, North Carolina) will strongly influence the labor negotiations just getting under way in the rubber industry. Yet the facility, owned by Firestone Tire & Rubber Company, isn't even unionized.

This clean, highly mechanized plant, which got up to capacity production just two years ago, makes only radial passenger-car tires. But it does that very efficiently indeed; it pours out 15,000 tires a day, or 5.5 million a year.

Some 1,200 production workers, divided into four production crews, operate the plant seven days a week, 24 hours a day. It closes only two days a year, Christmas Eve and Christmas Day. All the employees are on salary. And they have shown so little interest in joining a union that they haven't even voted on the issue yet.

The United Rubber Worker Union's contracts with the four leading tire producers expire at midnight, April 20, 1979, and bargainers are in the preliminary stages of negotiating new agreements. But for the first time since the 1930s, the so-called master contracts with Firestone, Goodyear Tire and Rubber Co., Uniroyal Inc., and B. F. Goodrich Co. cover less than half of the nation's tire-production capacity.

* * * * *

The URW isn't the only union feeling a decline in bargaining muscle because of expanding nonunion operations. The United Mine Workers, for instance, now represents workers mining only about half the nation's coal, down from about 70 percent five years ago. And hundreds of manufacturing plants making everything from heavy machinery to household appliances are being opened in small cities and rural areas, often in the South and Southwest, without union representation. Nationally less than a quarter of nonfarm workers belong to unions, down from about a third 20 years ago, according to government statistics.

Many older tire and rubber-products plants in Akron that were under the master agreements have been sharply curtailed or closed down, the victims of obsolescence of the multistory facilities themselves and of high labor costs built into operations through 40 years of union contracts. Nobody makes automobile tires in Akron anymore and the last truck tire operations are threatened. In other areas, some of the newer plants that the union has managed to organize have separate contracts outside the master agreements.

* * * * *

---

*SOURCE: Extracted from Ralph E. Winter, "Nonunion Rubber Plants Help Lift Hopes of Averting Strike in Current Labor Talks," *The Wall Street Journal*, March 16, 1979, p. 42, with permission.

Another complication involves the growing competitive threat from imports; they rose last year to about 17 million tires, up 45 percent from 1975 and nearly double the 8.7 million of 1970. Michelin, the big French tire maker, is pushing to expand its market share with a combination of imports and tires made in nonunion U.S. plants. The Big Four says this competition also limits the wages and benefits that they can afford.

Questions

1. Using information in the case and in the body of the chapter, explain why the labor unions are violently opposed to right-to-work laws.
2. Why may officials of some tire companies have ambivalent feelings about these laws?
3. What is the present status of unionization in the tire industry?
4. Explain why the same congressmen who vote favorably on bills raising federal minimum wages probably oppose right-to-work laws.
5. Why do many workers, who would probably receive higher wage rates if their plants were unionized, still prefer nonunion plants?
6. How is bargaining power of the parties affected by the possibility of diverting production to nonunion tire plants?

CASE 9–2 _____
Combating Worker Alienation*

In a famous moving picture, *Modern Times*, Charlie Chaplin satirized the assembly line. After turning the same bolt on successive units of a product all day, he walked out on the street still going through the same bolt-turning motions in a way possible only for a master pantomimist.

In recent years, especially, there has been an increasing tendency for blue- and white-collar workers, and to some extent middle managers, to dislike their jobs and resent their bosses. There is less concern about the quality of their product—as suggested by the epidemic of new automobile recalls for correction of defects.

Henry Ford once stated that what the typical worker wants is a job where he does not have to think. Employees today are better educated and accustomed to a considerable amount of convenience and even luxury when off the job. Their organizational commitment is increasingly influenced not just by income and security but by the quality of the work experience itself.

---

*SOURCE: Information for this case is from Richard E. Walton, "How to Counter Alienation in the Plant," *Harvard Business Review*, November-December 1972, pp. 70–81, with permission.

Unfortunately, it is more difficult to rearrange work procedures to relieve monotony in the automobile plants and other plants with complex assembly lines than it is in the production of technically simpler products. Nevertheless, such companies as Saab-Scandia and Volvo in Sweden have made major efforts to redesign production processes to counter job alienation. At Saab, the following has occurred:

1. Production workers are also made members of development groups.
2. Responsibility for in-process inspection has been shifted from a separate quality inspection unit to the production workers themselves.
3. Workers take care of their own equipment instead of this being the responsibility of special mechanics.
4. Workers are encouraged to learn several jobs rather than one specialized task in the assembly.

At a new Volvo plant, teams of 15 to 25 men are assigned responsibility for particular sections of a car, such as the electrical system, brakes and wheels, and so forth. Within teams, members decide how to allocate tasks. Buffer stocks between work teams allow variations in the rate of work without greatly affecting output of the final product. The revised production setup will cost about 10 percent more than a conventional car plant, but the Volvo management expects this outlay to be more than made up by the greater satisfaction workers find in their jobs.

In the United States, a well-known experiment in work rearrangement to promote employee satisfaction has taken place at a Gaines pet food plant. In 1968, the company was planning an additional plant at a new location. The existing facility was encountering problems of worker alienation, and it was decided to attempt to counter these problems at the new plant. The new plant was designed both to accommodate changes in the expectations of workers and to utilize knowledge developed by the behavioral sciences. Nine key features were incorporated in the plant design:

1. Work groups are autonomous. Teams are given responsiblity for large segments of the production process. The teams assign workers to tasks, and these are often rotated.
2. Inspection of product and maintenance of equipment are kept within the team.
3. Every set of tasks is designed to include some actions requiring judgment and skill.
4. Pay increases are geared to the mastering by an employee of an increasing number of jobs within a team and then in the plant.
5. Team leaders replace the usual use of specialized supervisory personnel.
6. Production decisions can be made at team levels because economic information and business decision rules are provided at the team level.

7. Rules for plant management were not prespecified but were allowed to evolve from experience.
8. Differentiating status symbols are avoided. For example, a common decor is used throughout the plant.
9. Management is committed to assess both productivity and employees' satisfaction on a continuing basis.

Early results indicated considerable success. Seventy employees rather than the originally estimated 110 are able to man the plant. Fewer quality rejects and lower absenteeism reduced variable costs. Safety was up, and employee turnover down.

Operators, team leaders, and managers alike have become more involved in their work and also have derived more satisfaction from it. For example, when asked what work is like in the plant and how it differs from other places they have worked, employees typically replied: "I never get bored." "I can make my own decisions." "People will help you; even the operations manager will pitch in to help you clean up a mess—he doesn't act like he is better than you are."

Questions

1. Do you believe that similar innovation would be more difficult, or less difficult, in an old plant?
2. How does size of the work force affect the possibilities of productive innovations along the lines followed by the pet food plant?
3. The Gaines plant was not unionized. How would unionization be likely to affect the outcome of a similar attempt at innovation?
4. Name another type of product where somewhat similar innovation might be useful. Name another product where it is unlikely to work well. Justify your answers.
5. Adam Smith said that "specialization is limited by the extent of the market." What other factors may limit the efficiency of specialization?

CASE 9–3
Discrimination and Employment

A managerial problem of considerable dimension is how to avoid discrimination on grounds of race, sex, and age; and particularly how to comply with legislation and administrative rulings that followed the Civil Rights legislation of 1964 forbidding race and sex discrimination.

That women and nonwhites (preponderantly blacks) have been increasing their relative participation in more prestigious occupations is shown in Exhibit 9–3A.

EXHIBIT 9–3A   Employed Persons by Sex, Race, and Occupation

	1971			1981		
	Number Employed (000s)	Percent		Number Employed (000s)	Percent	
		Female	Nonwhite		Female	Nonwhite
Total...................	82,153	38.0	10.6	100,397	42.8	11.4
Professional, technical, kindred total..........	11,538	39.3	7.2	16,420	44.6	9.9
Accountants...........	720	21.7	4.3	1,126	38.5	9.9
Engineers	1,111	0.8	3.4	1,537	4.4	7.3
Lawyers and judges	322	3.8	1.9	581	14.1	4.6
Teachers, except college...	2,852	70.0	9.2	3,197	70.6	10.1
Managers and administrators, except farm total.......	8,081	17.6	4.0	11,540	27.5	5.8
Bank officers and financial managers	430	19.0	2.6	696	37.5	5.5
Craft and kindred workers total...............	10,867	3.6	6.9	12,662	6.3	8.5
Carpenters............	1,052	0.5	5.9	1,122	1.9	5.8
Laborers (except farm) total..	4,242	6.0	20.2	4,583	11.5	16.5
Construction laborers.....	948	0.5	22.4	825	2.2	15.8

SOURCE: *Statistical Abstract of the United States, 1982–83,* Table No. 651.

EXHIBIT 9–3B   Participation and Employment Ratios by Race, Sex, and Age

	1960	1965	1975	1982	1984
Participation rates in civilian labor force:					
White 58.8		58.4	60.4	64.3	64.6
Black and other 64.5		62.9	60.2	61.6	62.6
Black..............................n.a.		n.a.	59.9	61.0	62.2
Employment/population ratios:					
White 55.9		56.0	57.4	58.8	60.5
Black and other 57.9		57.8	54.1	50.9	53.6
Black..............................n.a.		n.a.	53.7	49.4	52.3
Unemployment rates:					
White 5.0		4.1	5.1	8.6	6.5
Black and other 10.2		8.1	10.0	17.3	14.4
Black..............................n.a.		n.a.	10.4	18.9	15.9
Participation rates by race and sex:					
Males, White 83.4		80.8	80.3	77.9	n.a.
Black and other.................83.0		79.6	74.7	70.1	n.a.
Females, White 36.5		38.1	43.3	51.9	n.a.
Black and other 48.2		48.6	48.7	53.7	n.a.
Participation rates by sex and age:					
Males, 45–54.......................95.7		95.6	92.3	91.2	n.a.
55–64.......................86.8		84.6	79.5	70.2	n.a.
65 up 33.1		27.9	23.3	17.8	n.a.
Females, 45–54.....................49.8		54.4	53.5	61.6	n.a.
55–64.......................37.2		41.1	41.8	41.4	n.a.
65 up 10.6		10.0	8.8	7.9	n.a.

n.a. = not available.

SOURCES: *Economic Report of the President, 1985,* Table B32–33; and *Statistical Abstract of the United States, 1984,* Table 671; 1975, Table 543.

However, in terms of civilian labor force participation rates (the percentage of the total civilian noninstitutional population over 16 either working or seeking work) and employment-population ratios (which take into account unemployment), the trends by race diverge sharply from those of sex, as shown in Exhibit 9–3B.

Questions

1. What evidence is there in these exhibits that direct discrimination in employment has increased or decreased?
2. How might the following social and political developments be related to the data of this case:
   a. The tenfold increase in transfer payments by government between 1965 and 1984 from $40 billion to over $400 billion annually. (This amounts to more than a tripling in real terms. Most of the increase was in social security and government pensions.)
   b. Affirmative action programs; a somewhat higher ratio of the minimum wage to average wage (near 50 rather than 40 plus) from 1966 to 1981; labor legislation discussed in the chapter such as "right-to-work" laws.
   c. The baby boom from the late 1940s through the mid 1960s; the upward shift in the overall unemployment rate from an average of 4.6 percent in the 1965–74 decade to 7.7 percent from 1975–84; the relatively high birth rates for nonwhites.
3. Data on the median weekly earnings of full-time wage and salary workers indicates that the nonwhite/white ratio rose from 0.74 to 0.81 in the 1970s while the female/male ratio was fairly constant at 0.62. (A revised series showed the black/white ratio at 0.81 and the female/male ratio at 0.65 in 1981.) How do the data in the exhibits help explain the smaller change in the female/male ratio as compared with the black/white ratio?

CASE 9–4
Collective Bargaining in the Basic Steel Industry*

The Steel Industry Coordinating Committee, representing nine major steel companies, began negotiating with the Basic Steel Industry Conference of the United Steelworkers of America (USA–AFL–CIO) on February 5, to replace contracts expiring on August 1, 1980. The nine major companies, which employ about 286,000 workers, are: U.S. Steel Corp., Bethlehem Steel Corp., Jones and Laughlin Steel Corp. (subsidiary of LTV), Republic

---

*SOURCE: Extracted from U.S. Department of Labor, Bureau of Labor Statistics, May 1980, Report 603.

Steel Corp., Inland Steel Corp., National Steel Corp., Armco Corp., Wheeling-Pittsburgh Steel Corp., and Allegheny-Ludlum Industries, Inc. Another 169,000 workers are employed at smaller companies under the agreement. Negotiations will cover workers employed at iron ore mines and those engaged in steel production, fabrication, warehousing, and transportation, and will serve as a pattern for steel companies not included under the basic agreement as well as companies in other industries. Total production and nonsupervisory employment in basic steel (SIC 331) is around 549,000.

The basic steel industry has undergone a sharp contraction since the current contract was signed in 1977. Full and partial plant closings have cost 35,000 jobs and reduced U.S. production capacity by 5 million tons. Foreign competition has increased over the years and is expected to become even more vigorous. An overriding problem is the U.S. industry's dependence on outdated mills. Large sums of money are needed to make the existing plants competitive and to clean them up so that they will meet stringent environmental standards. However, given the industry's low profits, steel executives are putting available funds into other fields, such as chemicals, banking, aluminum, and construction. In addition, although some effort is going toward improving the overall management and organization of steel operations, the strategy is aimed primarily at curtailing unprofitable and marginal fabrication operations. Most of the 16 plant closings announced by U.S. Steel at the end of 1979, which will eliminate 13,000 more jobs, include plants in this category.

The profit outlook is not expected to improve in 1980, and more plant closings are anticipated. The U.S. Department of Commerce has predicted a 5 percent drop in domestic shipments from the 100 million tons sold in 1979 and a 3.8 percent decline in employment. This projection was based on an expected decline in domestic automobile production, consumer preference for smaller cars, a sluggish construction industry, and lower demand from the appliance and container industries.

Given its poor financial situation, the steel industry is seeking government assistance through greater protection of imports, faster depreciation on plant and equipment, and relaxation of environmental regulations. The U.S. Steel Corp. has filed an antidumping suit against seven European countries to back up its demand for government aid against imports.

Negotiations for 10 major steel companies (Youngstown Sheet and Tube Co. has since merged with Jones and Laughlin) were completed by April 9, 1977, 11 days before the April 20 arbitration deadline. Bargaining demands reflected the union's increasing concern over dwindling employment in the industry.

Employees with 20 years or more of continuous service received greatly increased benefits under the Employment and Income Security Program, which incorporated many of the union's demands aimed at protecting members from unplanned loss of income. The most significant feature of this program was the "rule-of-65" pension option. Under its terms, long-service employees who are affected by shutdowns, extended layoffs, or disabilities may retire and obtain a $300 pension supplement in addition to their regular pension if their age and continuous years of service total 65, provided the company fails to offer suitable long-term employment as an alternative. The program also guarantees supplemental unemployment benefits (SUB) if these workers are laid off, and it adds 52 weeks of coverage for those who do not qualify for an unreduced pension. Other provisions include increased short-week benefits, extended sickness and accident benefits, and a guarantee under the earnings protection plan to employees reassigned to lower rated jobs of at least 90 percent (from 85) of their former base period earnings.

Questions

1. Many economists would say that the serious troubles of the American steel industry are the fault of the industry itself and the USA–AFL–CIO. Whether you agree or not, state the arguments in favor of this belief.
2. Have steel industry executives been plowing back most available capital into plant improvements? Secure some pertinent information for the period since 1980 to improve your answer.
3. What effect is the "rule of 65" likely to have on the level of skill of steel industry labor?
4. Why do the steel unions insist on industrywide collective bargaining? Are regional effects somewhat similar to those of the federal minimum wage law and the Davis-Bacon Act? How?

CASE 9–5
How the Government Measures Unemployment*

Early each month, the Bureau of Labor Statistics of the U.S. Department of Labor announces the total number of employed and unemployed workers in the United States for the previous month along with many characteristics of such persons. These figures receive wide coverage in the press and on radio and television.

Some people think that to get these figures the government counts every unemployed person each month. To do this, every home in the country would have to be contacted just as in the population census every 10 years. This procedure would cost too much and take too long. Besides, people would soon grow tired of having a census taker come to their homes every month, year after year, to ask about job-related activities.

---

*SOURCE: Extracted from U.S. Department of Labor, Bureau of Labor Statistics, 1977, Report 505.

Since everyone cannot be counted each month, a sample called the Current Population Survey (CPS) is taken to discover who in the country is employed or who is looking for work. First, a sample of independent cities and counties or groups of counties is chosen from the 3,146 counties and cities in the country. The Bureau of the Census designs and selects the sample of 461 areas which includes 923 counties and independent cities in every state and also the District of Columbia. The sample is designed to reflect urban and rural areas, different types of industrial and farming areas, and the major geographic divisions of the country in the same proportion as they occur in the Nation as a whole. Each of these 461 areas is subdivided into enumeration districts of about 350 households. The enumeration districts, in turn, are divided into smaller clusters of about four dwelling units each, through the use of lists of addresses, detailed maps, and other sources. Then, the dwelling units to be surveyed are chosen statistically, and these households are interviewed. About 47,000 households are eligible for interview—or about 1 in every 1,500 throughout the country.

Each month one fourth of the households in the sample are replaced so that no family is interviewed more than four consecutive months. This practice avoids placing too heavy a burden on the families selected for the sample. After a household is interviewed for four months, it is dropped for eight months and then is interviewed for four more months before being dropped from the sample for good. This procedure also results in continuity of data for month-to-month and year-to-year comparisons.

Because a sample is not a total count, the survey may not produce results exactly the same as could be obtained from interviewing the total population. The chances are 90 out of 100 that the estimate of unemployment from the sample is within 185,000 of the figure obtainable from a total census. Since monthly unemployment totals have ranged between about three and eight million in recent years, the possible error resulting from sampling is not large enough to distort the total unemployment picture. Before each monthly survey, experienced workers are given two to three hours of home study materials. At least three times a year, interviewers convene for daylong training and review sessions, and at least once a year they are accompanied by a supervisor during a full day of interviewing to determine how well they carry out their assignments.

Beginning in 1978, the number of households in the sample was expanded to 55,000 when a supplementary sample increasing the reliability of state and area labor force data was added to the regular CPS sample. After this expansion, annual average unemployment estimates for each of the 50 states is now available from the CPS.

What Do Unemployment Statistics Mean?

The survey of households is designed so that every civilian age 16 years or over who is not in an institution such as a prison or mental hospital is classified as either employed, unemployed, or not in the labor force.

Each person is counted and classified in only one group. The sum of the employed and the unemployed constitutes the civilian labor force. Persons not in the labor force combined with those in the civilian labor force constitute the total civilian noninstitutional population 16 years of age and over.

Who Is Counted as Employed?

Not all of the wide range of job situations in the American economy fit neatly into a given category. For example, people are considered employed if they did any work at all for pay or profit during the survey week. This includes all part-time and temporary work as well as regular full-time year-round employment. Persons also are counted as employed if they have a job at which they did not work during the survey week because they were on vacation, ill, involved in an industrial dispute, prevented from working by bad weather, or taking time off for various personal reasons.

Who Is Counted as Unemployed?

Persons are unemployed if they have actively looked for work in the past four weeks, are currently available for work, and, of course, do not have a job at the same time. Looking for work may consist of any of the following specific activities:

Registering at a public or private employment office.

Meeting with prospective employers.

Checking with friends or relatives.

Placing or answering advertisements.

Writing letters of application.

Being on a union or professional register.

Sometimes questions are raised as to the advisability of including among the unemployed persons such as teenagers, married women, and others who are not usually the family's main breadwinner. The point is made that for the family, unemployment of the main breadwinner is more important than unemployment of any other member of the family.

This view ignores some very fundamental changes that have occurred in lifestyles and attitudes toward work. For example, the "typical family" of a working husband, a wife who is not in the labor force, and one or more children accounts for fewer than one out of every five American families. Someone other than the husband is the *primary earner* in about *one fourth* of the families that include a husband and a wife. Nearly one fifth of the unemployed wives are in families where no one is working.

Today, over 30 percent of all workers are married women and teenagers. They are counted as employed when they contribute to the total productive effort of the nation. Otherwise, there would be no way to measure the total amount of labor resources the economy is using. If persons are counted as *employed* when they have a job, they must be counted as *unemployed* when they have no job and are searching for one; otherwise, the measurement of unemployment loses much of its meaning and a very important indication of business conditions is lost. Unemployment statistics are intended to count unutilized available labor resources rather than persons who are suffering a hardship.

As suggested in the previous section, employment and unemployment change during the year as a result of holidays, vacations, harvest time, changing seasons, shifts in industry production schedules, and similar occurrences. Often it is difficult to tell whether developments between any two months reflect changing economic conditions or merely normal seasonal fluctuations. To compare employment and unemployment data for any two months accurately, a statistical technique called seasonal adjustment is used.

When a statistical series has been seasonally adjusted, data for any month can be meaningfully compared with data for any other month or with an annual average. One of the most important seasonally adjusted figures that is published monthly is the unemployment rate, which is total unemployment expressed as a percent of the civilian labor force. Typically, the unadjusted rate is 10 to 20 percent higher in February and 10 to 20 percent lower in May than the annual average. When the rate is seasonally adjusted and when the employment situation has no changes except those that are purely seasonal, then the rate will be exactly the same from one month to the next. On the other hand, if changes occur in the underlying employment situation in addition to seasonal movements, these changes will show up as a rising or declining trend in the seasonally adjusted unemployment rate.

Questions

1. As a manager in the BLS concerned with the accuracy of your sample, what steps could you take to reduce any tendencies of your interviewers to skip interviews and simply fill in the forms themselves? Consider the possible pressures faced by interviewers and suggest ways to alleviate them.

2. The American underground economy is said to be one of the large economies in the world. What is the relevance to the published employment and unemployment data?

3. How might means-tested transfer payments (especially Aid to Families with Dependent Children) affect the accuracy of employment figures?

CASE 9–6 _____
How High a Minimum Wage?

In spring of 1977, the Coalition for a Fair Minimum Wage was vigorously lobbying for a minimum wage of $3 an hour to replace the then current

$2.30; each January 1 the minimum would be adjusted to 60 percent of average weekly earnings in manufacturing. The counterproposal of the Carter administration was $2.50, with a 50 percent ratio to average weekly earnings in manufacturing delayed a year (some economists within the administration had opposed any increase in view of unemployment and inflation problems).

The $2.50 proposal is "shameful," declared George Meany, president of the AFL–CIO. The 50 percent criterion "would guarantee that the nation's minimum-wage workers will be permanently locked in poverty." (This apparently is a reference to the $5,500 annual income estimated for a family of four to exceed the poverty level.) Just to restore the 1974 purchasing power of the minimum wage ($2 an hour then), $0.33 would be needed, and this "buying power is essential to economic recovery."

Most economists would probably agree with economist Andrew Brimmer, who concluded, "As the statutory minimum wage has risen, the adverse impact on the level of employment has become progressively noticeable. This is especially true in the case of young unskilled workers—and particularly among black teenagers." (The application in the United States of the same minimum wage to the young is not typical practice in western economies.) The actual legislation passed made the minimum $2.65 in 1978, $2.90 in 1979, $3.10 in 1980, and $3.35 in 1981, as shown in the text of Chapter 9 for untipped employees.

In the first term of the Reagan administration, no change was made in the minimum wage though a Reagan initiative to set a youth minimum of about $2 was defeated.

Data for selected recent years are as follows:

Year	CPI	Average Hourly Private Earnings*	Minimum Wage Rate	Unemployment Rates (Percentages)			
				Ages 16–19		All Ages	
				White	Nonwhite	White	Nonwhite
1956	81.4	$1.80	$0.75	11	18	3.6	8.3
1961	89.6	2.14	1.00	16	28	6.0	12.4
1966	97.2	2.68	1.40	11	25	3.3	7.3
1976	170.5	4.86	2.30	17	37	7.0	13.1
1979	217.4	6.16	2.90	14	34	5.1	11.3
1982	289.1	7.67	3.35	21	44	8.6	17.3

*Production or nonsupervisory workers in private nonagricultural industries.

Questions

1. Should an employer have the right to pay (and an employee to work at) a rate lower than that sufficient to maintain a family of four above the poverty line? Why or why not? (By 1983, the poverty line was about $10,000.)

2. Why should job opportunities for teenagers, particularly black, be most affected by higher minimum wages?

3. Do you believe that aggregate "buying power" is increased when the legal minimum wage is increased? Why or why not?

4. What do you believe is the main argument used by legislators who oppose a lower minimum wage for teenagers?

5. In hiring bag boys and bag girls, why is nepotism likely to increase as the minimum wage increases?

10

Plant Location—Domestic
and Multinational

> In every site-selection, a balancing is involved among all factors, demand
> and cost. No theory is general which abstracts from either.
> —Melvin L. Greenhut

Although the problem where to locate a new plant arises infrequently for
most firms, it is clearly a matter of great importance whenever it must be
faced. Economic consultants are often brought in to study alternative
locations and to advise management on this subject. While company officials are usually expert in day-to-day operations of the firm, they may feel
much less at home with the problem of finding an optimum location,
since this involves such questions as the relative availability and cost of
labor, capital, and materials at various places at which they may have had
no business experience. Executives employed by large retailing chains are
more likely than most officials to be in close touch with locational problems because of the frequency with which new outlets are established.
There is seldom only one suitable location for a plant; instead, numerous
locations are likely to be satisfactory, though some may be decidedly
better than others. Some locations are so poor that their selection alone
would ensure failure.

NONPECUNIARY FACTORS IN LOCATION

Most theorizing about the behavior of firms assumes that the goal of management is to maximize the excess of receipts over costs during a period
of time (or, more accurately, the present value of such net receipts). Economists are paying increased attention, however, to nonpecuniary gratifications and costs as a motivating force in decisions, and this seems to be
true also for locational decisions. A plant may be located so as to be
convenient to the home of the owner even if this would not otherwise be
considered the best site. Or plants may locate near such cities as New
York, New Orleans, or San Francisco for the convenience of executives
and visitors interested in urban divertissement. In other cases an urban

location is carefully avoided because of city problems. Frequently, plants are located in Florida, Arizona, or California, for example, because of favorable climatic conditions that may be sought by officials. Pecuniary and nonpecuniary motivations become intermixed, however, when favorable climate also makes it possible to pay lower wages or salaries to employees or to secure better personnel at any given rate of pay.

Personal considerations are more likely to be important in the location of plants belonging to small firms than to those of large, multiplant companies. Questionnaire studies of reasons for locational decisions are quite popular, but special care must be taken with respect to evaluating responses dealing with personal considerations. One reason is that factors that appeal to the owner or manager may also affect costs or receipts by appealing also to employees or customers.[1] Another reason is that a business executive may not be willing to leave the home community but in locating a new enterprise there the executive will select one that is compatible with that location. The executive's response may then fail to emphasize the basic economic factors that made the location favorable.[2]

COST

In location theory, main emphasis is usually given to the cost side. The most favorable location for production is often said to be at the place where the unit cost of gathering materials, processing them, and delivering the finished product is minimized. This formulation is somewhat vague because it does not say *how many* units are produced and sold. Nevertheless, it is a useful approach for a large class of locational decisions where demand is large in relation to the output of a plant of economical size so that the main problem is one of producing at low cost.

A simple chart that usefully emphasizes some of the key variables is shown as Figure 10–1. This pertains to a plant turning out a single product made of one important raw material and sold in a single market. Processing costs, consisting of such expenses as wages, utility charges, depreciation of plant and equipment, and rent on land, are included in the line labeled P. Since these vary with the rate of output, the line pertains to an expected long-run average rate of production. Processing costs are apt to be higher in urban locations due to higher land values and wage rates. Since it is assumed that the market is an urban area, the P line is highest at that end of the chart. Material-gathering costs (G) per unit of output are lowest if the plant is located at the material source (e.g., a paper mill near the forest) and highest if the material must be brought all the way to the market before manufacture. The cost of transportation per

[1]Melvin L. Greenhut, *Plant Location in Theory and in Practise* (Chapel Hill: The University of North Carolina Press, 1956), chap. 7.

[2]This is pointed out in Hugh O. Nourse, *Regional Economics* (New York: McGraw-Hill, 1968), p. 10.

FIGURE 10–1   Optimum Location in a Simple Case (material source
                provides lowest costs)

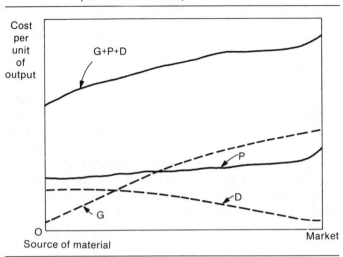

mile is assumed to diminish with distance—a common feature in railroad
rates, for example.

The D line pertains to the cost per unit of transporting the finished
good to market. This is lowest if the plant is located at the market (e.g., a
soft drink plant in a city) and higher if the plant is located farther from
the market.

The top line, found by vertical addition of P, G, and D, should indicate
the lowest cost location—at the material source as Figure 10–1 is drawn.
The principal determinant of the best location is usually the relative
change in height of curves G and D over the range between material source
and market. That is, if curve G rises more than curve D falls over this
range (as it does in Figure 10–1), location at the material source is apt to
be more economical; if curve D had declined relatively more, location at
the market would probably have been indicated. These locational forces
can, of course, be overcome by processing advantages of other locations.
For example, a town between the material source and market may have
an especially favorable labor supply situation, a river to provide essential
cooling or transportation, or other decisive advantage.

Suppose the material source and the market are 500 miles apart. The
amount of raw material per unit of product may be an important determinant of the relative change in the G and D curves over the 500-mile
distance. If 10 pounds of material were needed to make 1 pound of finished product, the material gathering cost curve would go up much more
than the product delivery cost curve would decline. That is, the cost of
transporting 10 pounds of material 500 miles would probably greatly
exceed the cost of moving 1 pound of product the distance. The smelting
of most ores, the ginning of cotton, the crushing of cane sugar, the produc-

tion of fruit juices, and the canning of crab meat, tuna, and salmon are examples of "weight-losing" processes where it would be uneconomical to locate near the market, since this would mean incurring heavy transportation expenses on substances that are wasted or burned up in processing. A dramatic example of extreme weight loss is found in the processing of gold-containing ore, where almost all of the weight is lost. This processing takes place, of course, right at the mines.

MARKET ORIENTATION

In other cases, it would cost more to move the finished product a long distance than it costs to move the material(s) the same distance. This promotes location at the market. An example is the baking industry. Flour and other components can be transported quite cheaply to the city; but bread, pies, and cakes are costly to transport. Also, the need for freshness reinforces the desirability of urban location. The farm machinery industry tends to locate in farming areas rather than near steel mills and other sources of components because such bulky machinery is expensive to transport compared with components. The same force has led to the establishment of regional automobile assembly plants, especially by General Motors and Ford. The form, perishability, and unit value of finished products have a great influence on freight rate, and hence on location. For example, the waste space necessarily involved in transporting cans and bottles fosters their production near the market rather than near sources of materials.

Products that use "ubiquitous" materials—those that are available nearly everywhere—tend to locate at the market. In terms of Figure 10–1, the principal raw material source and the market are the same place (the market) so that no other location need be considered. Such products as soft drinks and ice are manufactured in cities, since it would be uneconomical to transport the water incorporated in these commodities very far. At the same time, such manufacturing is usually not carried on in the very heart of cities because the competition of other uses (clothing stores, drugstores, banks, etc.) makes rental costs in central areas excessive for businesses that do not sell directly to large numbers of consumers. Sulfuric acid, an extremely important industrial material, is produced near the market. The production process adds weight, and the expense of long-distance transportation of a corrosive substance is relatively high. The construction industry is obviously extremely market oriented.

Location near the market is also promoted by the production of "style goods." The demand for such products as ladies' hats and dresses is so capricious that producers must be ready to alter the nature of their output on short notice. By locating in such cities as New York, Miami, and Los Angeles, style goods producers are able to reduce inventory losses by keeping their fingers on the pulse of demand. The locational importance of this factor has been somewhat reduced by the utilization of high-speed air transportation for style goods.

LOCATION AT BOTH ENDS

Where the principal raw material loses very little weight or where the higher transportation rate on the finished product quite closely compensates for the lower weight of the finished product, it may make little difference whether processing takes place near the raw material source or near the market. In terms of Figure 10–1, the G and P curves would rise and fall about the same distance so that the $G + P + D$ curve might be at about the same level at the market and at the material source. An example is the oil-refining industry, which has processing facilities both near the oil fields and near the large cities. The utilization of a very large part of the crude oil for a great variety of products means that processing is not greatly weight losing; consequently, oil may be refined at the market. At the same time, the finished products are economically transportable (by pipeline, tank car, and tanker, for example), so that processing at the source is also feasible.

The slight weight-losing property of wheat when milled into flour is quite closely compensated by the higher transportation rate for flour. Consequently, flour milling occurs both near the wheat fields and near the markets. Changes in the relative cost of transporting wheat and flour can quickly alter the relative desirability of milling near the material source or near the market.[3]

MILLING-IN-TRANSIT PRIVILEGE

There is a tendency for location to be most economical either at the source of the principal material or at the market due to the downward concavity of curves G and P in Figure 10–1—that is, to the fact that freight rates usually increase less than proportionally with distance. While a location between the material source and the market would secure some of this advantage of rate "tapering" with distance for *both* the material and the product, it would not secure so great a *total* advantage in transfer cost as location at either end. To offset this tendency, the railroads frequently grant "transit" privileges, under which a through rate is paid on both the raw material (e.g., grain) and the finished product (e.g., flour). This is usually the rate applicable to the raw material. The through rate replaces the combination of rates that would otherwise be charged; that is, it neglects the fact that a stop is made for purposes of processing.

In terms of Figure 10–1, the transit privilege would cause $G + P$ to be horizontal over the entire range. As a consequence, any location between

---

[3]D. Phillip Locklin, *Economics of Transportation*, 7th ed. (Homewood, Ill.: Richard D. Irwin, 1954), p. 61, points out that the relationship between transportation rates on wheat and flour has at times determined whether flour to be consumed in Europe should be milled in the United States or abroad. Shipping rates for wheat and flour on the Great Lakes greatly affect the desirability of milling flour for the eastern markets in the Midwest or the East.

the source of the material and the market would be equally feasible from a transportation point of view. It should, however, be noted that from a *social* point of view the transit privilege is not desirable in that more resources must be devoted to transportation to the extent that location is artificially influenced by this sort of rate. That is, if the concavity of the G and P curves is consistent with the actual cost savings due to long hauls, the transit privilege, by causing G + P to be horizontal, distorts "natural" patterns of location. It would also tend to hold down land values at the material source and at the market, and to increase land values at intermediate points.

Transit privileges apply to a large number of commodities and to quite dissimilar forms of processing. Shippers of livestock may use the privilege to rest their stock and to test the possibilities of local sale. Soybeans and cottonseed may be converted into oil and meal under this rate system. Lumber products may be milled, iron and steel stopped for fabrication of certain kinds, and agricultural products stopped for storage under the transit privilege.

MULTIPLE SOURCES OF MATERIALS

Frequently, a manufacturing process uses two or more materials in large quantities. When both are weight losing in the process, the optimal location may be between the principal sources of these materials. If one of the materials—for example, fuel—is more weight losing than the other, this material will tend to exert more influence on the minimum transfer cost location. At the same time, the attraction of the market may also be significant.

The steel industry provides an interesting example of this situation. It is also an extremely important example because of the attraction of steel itself to a great variety of steel-using manufacturing activities.[4] Steel plants are usually located between deposits of coking coal and iron ore. Much the greater influence has been exerted by coal, in part because of low-cost water transportation available on the Great Lakes for ore from the Lake Superior region and on the eastern seaboard for imported ore. The market exerts perhaps an even greater influence than fuel, especially since cities are the main source of the scrap used in steelmaking. That is, the best markets are also important sources of an important material. Economies recently introduced in the use of coal in blast furnaces have somewhat diminished the attraction of fuel as a locational factor for steel mills and have increased the relative locational pull of the markets.

---

[4]According to Richardson Wood, "Where to Put Your Plant," *Fortune*, July 1956, p. 101, the existence of the steel belt stretching from Buffalo and Pittsburgh to Detroit and Chicago is the main reason why 70 percent of the industrial labor force of the country was found in less than 10 percent of the nation's territory. In recent decades, however, manufacturing employment in the steel belt has declined relative to that of the rest of the nation.

PROCESSING COSTS

In many industries, transportation is not highly significant, constituting but a small part of the total cost of putting the product into the hands of the consumer. Improvements in highways and transportation technology are tending to increase the number of such industries. This may lead to the establishment of a relatively small number of large plants designed to serve national or even international markets. Examples of such commodities are typewriters, clocks and watches, razor blades, and bobby pins. For such goods the location that minimizes processing costs is apt to be optimal.

If labor were perfectly mobile between different geographical areas, regional differences in wage and salary rates would not be an important factor in plant location.[5] Under this assumption, workers would move until no further advantage in terms of real wages could be secured. (If this is to be strictly true, real wages must be considered to reflect—as positive or negative items—such factors as climate, cultural advantages and disadvantages, traffic congestion, and recreational opportunities.) In the real world, however, some types of labor are slow to move in adequate numbers. This is a basic reason for the "farm problem" and for the low earnings of many families in such areas as the Appalachian South. Well-educated persons tend to be much more mobile, however.

The existence of regional differences in the wages of equally productive workers may exert a powerful locational pull in industries where labor costs are a large part of total processing cost. Many textile and woolen mills have moved to the South and to Puerto Rico to take advantage of lower wage rates. The shoe industry has shown a tendency to establish plants in small communities, especially to utilize female labor. Frequently, firms that move to low-wage areas to take advantage of this cost saving are careful to conceal the fact, in view of the rather general feeling that there is something reprehensible in this sort of action. Actually, the only way in which low-wage areas can rapidly improve their economic lot is through the increase in capital in relation to labor. Each plant that is located to take advantage of relatively low-cost labor helps raise the real income of workers in that area.

There is, however, much resistance to the "natural" process of permitting relative labor surplus areas to attract industry by paying lower wages. Labor unions attempt to equalize wage rages throughout the country by means of industrywide collective bargaining and by pressing politically for an ever higher and broader federal minimum wage. They are joined in these efforts by congressmen and some business executives from high-wage areas who fear the competition of lower wage areas. Paradoxically, the federal government tends to price many low-productivity persons out of the labor market by raising legal minimum wage rates while operating

---

[5]"Perfect mobility" does not necessitate a readiness of *every* worker to move. It implies only such readiness on the part of a sufficient number of laborers to equate wage rates for a given type of work at different places.

programs designed to employ persons of low skill. A great many state and local programs, many providing subsidies, attest to the tremendous interest in attracting new industry. While manufacturing facilities are usually more spectacular, local unemployment can also be relieved by bringing in wholesale, retail, recreational, and government facilities.

LAND RENT

The purchase price that must be paid by a firm for the land on which it erects a plant—or alternatively, the rent that must be paid on a long-term lease for the use of land—may be an important locational factor. For convenience, we shall speak of the rent on land, since this keeps the cost on an annual or monthly basis comparable to wage and interest payments.

Land rent, like the return to any factor of production, arises from its value productivity. This productivity stems from the fertility of the soil in agricultural uses, from the minerals that it may contain, and from its location, especially with respect to markets. The last named factor is of principal importance in location theory.

A German economist, Johann Heinrich von Thünen,[6] was the first to describe the pattern of land use and rents that would tend to evolve from the unhampered workings of the price system. He considered a large town in the middle of a wide plain, where the land was everywhere of equal fertility. The plain was assumed to be isolated from other places of economic activity by a wilderness. The town was considered to supply the farmers with manufactured items in exchange for raw materials and food.

Von Thünen concluded that the rent of land would decline with its distance from the town. Within a circle nearest the town, such commodities as green vegetables and milk would be produced. Intensive cultivation of forest lands for fuel and building materials would take place in the next circle. Such activities as grain and cattle raising would occur in the outer circles. In the most remote zone, the most extensive land use— hunting—would take place. The basic principle is that different uses of land vary in their ability to bear rental costs relative to transportation costs. Such items as milk and vegetables are perishable and are transported to market frequently. They are better able to stand high yearly rental costs than the high yearly transportation costs that would be associated with more distant hauls to market. Grains, on the other hand, are transported to market less frequently and in larger lots, so they can better bear high transfer costs than high land rents. The aim of each user of land is to minimize the sum of land rental and transportation charges per time period.

Although based on highly abstract assumptions, the von Thünen theory discloses factors that are of importance both for agricultural and industrial location. If fertility, land contours, and other natural features are

---

[6]*Der Isolierte Staat in Beziehung auf Landwirtschaft und Nationalökonomie,* 3d ed. (Berlin: Schumacher-Zarchlin, 1875).

fairly uniform, rent per unit of land tends to decline with distance from the market. Since this decline is due basically to the cost of transportation from plant or farm to the market, any change in the structure of transportation charges tends to affect land rents. It was pointed out earlier that the milling-in-transit privilege tends to increase land rents at points more remote from the market and material source by giving the same through rate from material source to market regardless of where processing actually takes place. A general increase in freight rates tends to increase rental values near the market and to decrease the value of the more remote sites. Von Thünen's pattern of location of various activities can still be observed, although it tends to become less obvious as population centers become less isolated.

DEMAND AS A LOCATIONAL FACTOR

Although location theory tends to emphasize cost of transporting raw materials and final products and variations in labor cost from place to place, many locational choices are based more importantly on demand. This is clearly true where convenience to the buyer requires a downtown or shopping center location for jewelry stores, banks, clothing stores, or theaters.

For industrial plants the demand factor is often difficult to separate from that of transportation cost on final products. A plant locating in a rapidly growing urban community is likely to be choosing a transportation cost minimizing site if its product is weight gaining in nature. Still, total demand may also be greater because buyers can easily visit the plant and because there are advertising and other sales values in being a local firm. The demand factor does not, of course, dictate location only in the large markets. A firm may be better advised to locate in a market of limited size where it is an important supplier than in a much larger market where the number of competitors is also large and where profit possibilities are easier to detect.

The rate of growth of a local market appears to be a particularly important locational determinant. Rapid growth of population and income provides much protection to existing firms because new rivals must enter at a rapid rate in order to reduce the sales volume of earlier entrants. This was an outstanding reason given by business executives for selection of South Florida for new manufacturing facilities.[7]

DEMAND INTERDEPENDENCE

Some useful location theory bears a strong resemblance to price theory in oligopolistic markets in that close rivals may react to one another's deci-

---

[7]M. L. Greenhut and M. R. Colberg, *Factors in the Location of Florida Industry* (Tallahassee: Florida State University, 1962), p. 66.

sions. The substantial, and sometimes prohibitive, cost of relocation, however, usually means that a new entrant will give more consideration to the location of an existing plant than owners of an existing plant will give to reacting locationwise to a new rival's choice.

Because of the large number of possibilities with respect to the nature of price competition, costliness of changing location, and assumptions that a firm may make as to rivals' reactions, it is necessary to specify clearly the set of assumptions on which any theory of locational interdependence is based. It is also a convenient simplification to consider the market to lie along a straight line rather than having a circular, hexagonal, or irregular shape, as it usually would have in reality. Despite this simplification (or rather *because* of this simplification), it is possible to see some interrelationships of real-world significance.

The following assumptions make possible the study of a simple model of locational interdependence:

1. The market is linear and bounded at both ends.
2. At each point, there can be only one delivered price. The total amount purchased at that point is sold by the firm with the lower delivered price. The lower the delivered price, the greater the physical volume of sales.
3. There are two rival firms, A and B, selling the same product.
4. Marginal costs are constant, so that the desirability of increasing sales is not limited by rising production costs.
5. Freight rates per unit mile decline uniformly as the haul increases.
6. Sales are made on a FOB mill basis, so that delivered price at any point is equal to the mill price plus freight.
7. Each plant can be moved to any point, without cost.

Figure 10–2 represents the linear market by the distance CD.[8] If a mill is located at point A, the FOB mill price is AM; delivered prices to left and right of A are shown by the lines MP and MR, respectively. These price lines are drawn concave downward, to reflect the tapering rates with distance. If a mill is located at point B, the mill price is similarly represented by BN, and delivered prices by NR and NQ. Points F and G represent the highest price at which any sales can be made. It is clear that if demand curves are similar and downsloping at all points in the market, greater quantities will be sold near the mills than at a distance, but it will pay to make additional sales which can be secured, since the consumer is assumed to pay the freight.

If it is assumed that a single firm owns both plants—that is, that the firm is a monopolist in the market—it is not difficult to see that the locations A and B are optimal. These locations are at the quartiles, so that distances CA, AS, SB, and BD are all equal. Maximum sales could be

---

[8]Chart and analysis are a modification of Arthur Smithies, "Optimal Location in Spatial Competition," *Journal of Political Economy,* June, 1941, p. 426.

FIGURE 10–2 Optimum Locations for Two-Plant Monopoly (fall at quartiles A and B)

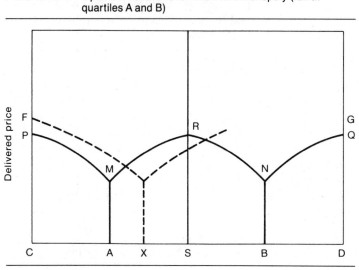

secured by these locations, since lower average delivered prices can be charged than with any other locations. This can be seen by considering what the situation would be if plant A were closer to S than is now shown. Suppose it were located at point X, plant A could then undersell plant B in the territory just to the right of S (as indicated by the dotted price line), but this would not help the firm, since it owns both plants. To the left of A, plant A would sell less than before because delivered prices (as shown by the dotted line) would be higher. While the same amount as before could be sold between A and X, the decreased sales to the left of A would cause a diminution in total sales. The firm would, consequently, be better off with its plants at the quartiles.

COMPETITION IN LOCATION

If the two plants are owned by separate companies and if each firm believes that the other will match both its price and its location, the quartiles will again be the equilibrium location. Suppose that plant A considers a move to the center of the market in an effort to control a greater territory. Under this assumption the locator would know immediately that plant B would also move to the center. If the moves were made, both firms would then still control only half the market (as before) but would have diminished sales, since the long hauls toward C and D would reduce the quantities which buyers would purchase. The best thing for both plants to do would be to stay at the quartile locations, since they would anticipate poor results from any movement toward the center.

Under altered assumptions as to rivals' reactions, the quartiles will no longer be the likely locations. If each competitor erroneously believes sales can be increased in his or her sales territory by moving closer to the center because a rival will not change location, both the competitor and the rival will locate closer than the quartiles to the center. Plant A, for example, may first move from A to X. This will cause plant A to take sales away from plant B, which will move a comparable distance toward S, or even farther (that is, the belief that plant B would "stay put" turns out to be erroneous). Plant A will then locate symmetrically, or go even closer to the center. Where the move toward the center will stop depends on how quickly the competitors revise their original expectation of locational independence as they notice declining sales brought on by the rival's movements. Once they have moved toward S, locating at equal distances on either side, they will not retreat to the quartiles, since each would fear that the other would not also move away from the center. The wisest thing for the firms to do would be to come to a cartel-like agreement to move back to the quartiles. In this case a monopolistic agreement as to location (but not as to mill price) would be socially beneficial.

LOCATION ALONG A HIGHWAY

Those great modern institutions—the automobile and highway—create numerous interesting locational problems. In this case the buyers transport themselves to the goods offered by the gift shop, restaurant, filling station, motel, or other roadside facility. The most important consideration is locating and advertising in such a way as to stop a sufficient number of cars. Location at or near the intersection of highways may be advantageous not only because of the greater number of cars passing such a point but also because of the lower speeds which the intersection imposes on drivers.

Gift shops that also sell candy, soft drinks, and other items of interest to motorists often locate along a long stretch of highway well away from all other structures. This permits the economical purchase or lease of a substantial plot of land with ample parking space. Where the highway is divided or where it is a heavily traveled two-lane road, most cars will stop only on the right-hand side of the road. This may make it important to measure the flow in both directions before arriving at a locational decision. A gift shop located along a barren stretch of road will usually advertise heavily for many miles in order to build up demand. In this situation the optimal strategy for a competitor is to locate on the same side of the road but at a point that will be reached a little sooner by the traffic stream. This permits the invader to take over part of the demand that the other firm's advertising has built up. Adoption of a quite similar name for the shop (Jones' Gift Shop versus Jane's Gift Shoppe) and the handling of similar commodities are also useful. If the first firm then adds a shop on the other side of the highway some miles away, the rival firm can again set up a shop near to it, but reached sooner by the stream of traffic. While the first firm might retaliate by erecting a third facility in front of its rival, this may not be economically feasible, since aggregate capacity could easily become too large for the market. Relocation of an existing shop and associated advertising is costly, so a situation of being outflanked by a new rival is apt to be serious.

It is well known that motels and restaurants are complementary facilities, each increasing the demand for the other. To a lesser extent, theaters, bowling alleys, and drugstores exert useful complementarity. A location either close to or one day's drive from a tourist center such as Disneyland in California or Walt Disney World in Florida is especially attractive to motels. Unfortunately for some investors, new interstate highways can extend the distance typically covered in one day as well as causing much traffic to bypass motels on older roads.

AGGLOMERATION OF SELLERS

Location theorists make frequent use of the term *agglomeration* in referring to the tendency of firms or plants to locate adjacent to one another. A principal motive in agglomerating is the saving of transfer costs between facilities. An extreme example is location of a can producing plant next door to a soup company, with conveyor belts transporting the cans between the plants. One reason for the growing popularity of industrial parks is the ability of some firms to cooperate with others because of proximity. Technical personnel, for example, may be able more easily to communicate regarding common problems.

Modern shopping centers, which include stores selling items that customers are likely to buy on the same trip, demonstrate vividly the advantages of agglomeration. The same is true of a wholesaling center such as the huge Merchandise Mart in Chicago. Well informed and alert buyers are able to compare available merchandise more easily on a single trip. It is interesting, however, to note that life insurance companies do not agglomerate in order to help the consumer secure the best buy. They prefer, in fact, to do business as far away as possible from competitors, namely, right in the homes of prospective buyers.

MULTINATIONAL BUSINESS

When firms establish plants on foreign soil, the locational forces already described apply but their relative importance is altered and some new considerations come into play. Multinational corporations have grown rapidly in number and size in recent years. They are, however, not a new idea. Such enterprises as the East India Company, the Virginia Company, and the Massachusetts Bay Company operated as multinational companies as early as the 17th and 18th centuries. In the United States, multinational companies existed as early as the 1850s.[9]

---

[9]National Association of Manufacturers, *U.S. Stake in World Trade and Investment*, (1972), p. 2.

FIGURE 10–3   Largest U.S. Industrial Corporations in 1983

Fortune*	Sales ($ billions)	Forbes†	Market Value ($ billions)
Exxon	88.6	IBM	74.5
General Motors	74.6	Exxon	31.6
Mobil	54.6	General Electric	26.7
Ford Motor	44.5	General Motors	23.4
IBM	40.2	Standard Oil, Indiana	14.8
Texaco	40.1	Eastman Kodak	12.6
E. I. du Pont	35.4	E. I. du Pont	12.4
Standard Oil, Indiana	27.6	Shell Oil	12.4
Standard Oil, California	27.3	Standard Oil, California	11.8
General Electric	26.8	Mobil	11.7
Gulf Oil	26.6	Standard Oil, Ohio	11.1
Atlantic Richfield	25.1	Atlantic Richfield	10.8
Shell Oil	19.7	Hewlett-Packard	10.6
Occidental Petroleum	19.1	Minnesota Mining & Mfg.	9.7
U.S. Steel	16.9	Procter & Gamble	9.5
Phillips Petroleum	15.2	Texaco	9.3
Sun Company	14.7	Philip Morris	9.0
United Technologies	14.7	GTE	8.3
Tenneco	14.4	Johnson & Johnson	7.8
ITT	14.2	Ford Motor	7.8

*Fortune, April 30, 1984.
†Forbes, April 30, 1984.

Multinational corporations are usually large companies that are likely to be listed in the "*Fortune* 500" and high on the lists published by *Forbes*.[10] The 20 largest U.S. Industrial Corporations (*Fortune*, according to sales volume) are shown in Figure 10–3. The list is somewhat different when firms are ranked according to market value as in the *Forbes* list, also shown in Figure 10–3. The top 10 (*Fortune*) corporations are on both lists, but there is much less similarity below that number.

It should be kept in mind that these are manufacturers only. American Telephone & Telegraph—before divestiture—ranked above Exxon in value of assets. Bank of America and Chase Manhattan stand very high in asset value. Sears, Roebuck leads in retail sales and is seventh in market value.

The large multinational industrial companies are not all American based. Such firms as Royal Dutch/Shell, British Petroleum, Unilever, Phillips, Siemens, Volkswagen, Toyota, and Nissan have facilities in the United States and other nations away from home. In 1984, a record 39 Japanese companies located factories in the United States. Automobile manufacturing stands out. For several years, the Nissan Motor Manufacturing Corporation has been operating in Smyrna, Tennessee (a right-to-work state). (See Case 10–1.) General Motors has a joint venture with Toyota in Fremont, California, and Toyota has plans to build plants in the United States and Canada. Mazda Motor Corporation is planning to build

---

[10]*Forbes* also lists the 500 largest corporations according to total assets, market value, and profits.

cars near Detroit in 1987. Automobile engines and parts and machine tools rank high among goods produced in foreign-owned plants located in this country. Imports from Japanese, German, and other firms located abroad also loom large in cars, engines, parts, machine tools, and many other items as shown by our huge foreign trade deficit.

We are usually better informed about large industrial companies than about those that provide direct services. However, the percentage of GNP produced within the service sector is larger and is growing steadily. In 1948, 54 percent was accounted for by services; by 1981, the proportion was about two thirds. From 1948 to mid-1983, the number of U.S. workers producing manufactured goods rose from 15.6 million to 18.6 million, but employment in services more than tripled from 20.9 million to 66.2 million workers.[11] (These figures necessarily leave out the large underground economy that exists in both production and services.) Banking, construction/engineering, franchising and leasing, advertising, and insurance are especially important international service activities, often carried out by U.S. firms that can be called "multinational."[12]

CASE 10–1
Nissan in Tennessee

An earlier case (9–2) emphasized the steps taken in Sweden, especially, to reduce worker alienation and to increase productivity. The Japanese have taken additional steps along these lines. The Nissan truck plant in Smyrna, Tennessee, utilizes Japanese innovations, modified in some cases to meet American traditions.

Nissan uses local labor but screens applicants carefully. The state of Tennessee made the first cut on 130,000 applications that came in for the 2,000 or so jobs the plant has generated so far.[13] Nissan also conducted interviews and insisted that potential employees take relevant courses at their own expense without assurance of subsequent employment.

Outstanding features related to workers at the Nissan plant include:

1. A sense of equality, promoted by the boss wearing the same uniform as production workers and having the same parking and cafeteria privileges.
2. An acquisition of some of the Japanese work ethic by means of workers' visits to Japan.

---

[11]Jonathan D. Aronson and Peter F. Cowhey, *Trade in Services* (Washington D.C.: American Enterprise Institute for Public Policy Research, 1984), p. 41.

[12]Ibid, p. 9.

[13]James Cook, "We Started from Ground Zero," *Forbes*, March 12, 1984. This article is one of many that have appeared on this subject.

3. Pay according to the number of relevant skills acquired by a worker.
4. Rotation of jobs.
5. Maintenance of one's own equipment.
6. Payment by a worker of his or her own health insurance.

The plant itself engages in assembly of trucks, utilizes modern automation, and depends on both U.S. and Japanese parts. A "just in time" inventory policy is followed to the extent that is possible for a plant that gets parts from all sections of the United States and from Japan. Tight scheduling and optimum means of transportation reduce the cost of carrying inventories.

Questions

1. What locational advantages do you believe were secured by Nissan in choosing the site of their U.S. plant? (Reference to other parts of the book and to available articles should improve your answer.)
2. How do "economies of scale" affect Nissan's decision to buy rather than produce most of the needed parts?
3. How are Nissan's costs reduced by the ability of many workers to perform several different tasks along the assembly line?
4. Many workers in the Detroit auto plants have shown great resentment against owners of Japanese cars. How does the new trend demonstrated by Nissan and also by Honda (at Marysville, Ohio) tend to diffuse the resentment?
5. Damaging strikes are uncommon in Japan. Do you believe this advantage will also accrue to Nissan in Smyrna, Tennessee?

CASE 10–2
Reed, Waite, and Gentzler

The firm of Reed, Waite, and Gentzler had for many years been engaged in the production and distribution of a line of work clothes sold under the brand name "RWG." The line consisted primarily of denim overalls and jackets, denim trousers (more popularly known as "blue jeans"), cotton twill trousers and shirts, and plain cotton trousers and shirts. A line of work hosiery was also included. These products were sold nationally, and the line was well known and popular. They were sold by department stores, chains, and specialty shops, and in smaller towns and villages were found in the "dry goods" stores.

The company operated three plants to supply its market. The shirt factory was located in a city of approximately 80,000 population in New

Hampshire. The trouser factory was located in a suburb of Philadelphia, Pennsylvania. This factory produced trousers, overalls, and jackets. The hosiery mill was located in central Pennsylvania in a community of about 110,000 population. The executive and sales offices of the firm were located in New York City. Sales offices were also maintained in Chicago and Los Angeles. The location of headquarters in New York City was dictated by the long-established custom in the trade of buyers converging upon New York. There had been some modification of this practice since 1947; for this reason, sales offices had been opened in both Chicago and Los Angeles.

Like practically all industries in the postwar period, the textile industry had expanded to meet both accumulated demand and new demand resulting from population increases. It appeared, however, that the industry as a whole suffered from chronic excess capacity, which was reflected in keen price competition. A large part of the industry was affected by frequent style changes that, at the manufactured clothing level, sometimes resulted in drastic price cutting. Firms whose products were sensitive to these factors found it essential to maintain locations where such changes in demand could be most quickly perceived. The so-called work clothes, while not subject to such frequent style changes, were nevertheless highly competitive. There were several large firms competing with Reed, Waite, and Gentzler, as well as a number of smaller firms serving regional and local markets.

In addition to the production of RWG-brand clothes, the company produced a number of private brands under contract with department stores and chains. The capacity of the company's plants was, therefore, geared to a demand consisting of RWG products plus private brands produced under contract. Placing of orders for private brands by purchasers was usually handled by competitive bidding. Securing such contracts was almost entirely a problem of competitive costs. Reed, Waite, and Gentzler experienced no more than the usual problems associated with the sales estimates of its own brands of clothing. Production of RWG clothing was planned according to sales estimates plus inventory control, and the balance of capacity was filled to the greatest possible extent by production of private brands. Certain items of work clothing—such as blue jeans, blue cotton shirts, olive-drab twill trousers, and olive-drab cotton and twill shirts—were considered staples. These items could be produced for inventory when there was stability in the market for finished goods. Materials and labor were the two largest components of production. Instability in the finished goods market, however, seriously complicated the inventory problem.

Until 1950, Reed, Waite, and Gentzler had been fairly successful in obtaining sufficient contracts for private brands to keep the trouser factory near Philadelphia operating at or near rated capacity. Early in 1950, there was some noticeable idle capacity that had caused a reduction in the labor force. The outbreak of the Korean War in June of that year had resulted in the procurement of some military contracts that kept the plant occupied until April of 1951. Again, idle capacity began to appear. A similar situation existed among competitors of the company. This condition was reflected in keener competition for bids on private-brand production. Reed, Waite, and Gentzler were unsuccessful bidders on several contracts that they had obtained on many occasions in the past. The company reduced its bids on future contracts but still lost several to its competitors. On the latest contracts that had gone to competitors, the firm felt that it had submitted the lowest possible quotations consistent with its costs of operations. The loss of these contracts was also causing the unit costs of its own brands to rise to such an extent that competition was jeopardizing the market for RWG clothing.

An investigation of the problem was undertaken, and the following facts were revealed:

Labor costs. It was easily and quickly determined that the labor costs of Reed, Waite, and Gentzler were higher than the costs of several of its larger competitors. Philadelphia had long been known as a "needle trades" city. During the time that a large part of the total labor force of the area had been engaged in the needle trades, the level of wages for the area as a whole had been strongly influenced by wages in the trade. While the supply of labor was adequate, there was little demand on the part of other industries to put upward pressure upon wage rates. The clothing industry had long been unionized except for a number of very small firms, so that the wage structure for the community as a whole had remained fairly stable, although it had tended upward. With the growth of "hard goods" industries in the Philadelphia area, however, the needle trades workers had become a proportionally smaller part of the labor supply, and their influence upon the wage structure had diminished accordingly. The growth of the area as an industrial center during and following World War II had diminished the influence of the trade even further. It was now quite apparent that the rise in wages of textile workers was influenced by the labor demands of other industries rather than exerting an influence upon them. To some extent the pressure of textile workers' unions was an effort to maintain their wage level consistent with that of the area. In the postwar period, growth of new industries and expansion of older ones had placed heavy demands upon the labor supply, in spite of a large population increase in the area.

The same situation existed in other textile areas of the Northeast. This was not true in all areas, however. In some isolated New England textile areas, this condition had not developed, so that some textile mills were able to enjoy a wage advantage due to the local situation. Of greater effect, however, were the differentials in wages within the clothing industry itself. During the decade of the 30s, there had begun a migration of the textile and clothing industry to the southern part of eastern United States. Some of the firms that had relocated in the Carolinas, Georgia, Tennessee, and Alabama were experiencing lower wage scales than plants of the same firms in the north. To some extent, this was because many of the workers in southern plants were not organized by labor unions, and the effects of local labor-supply situations permitted lower wages. The unions had undertaken the organization of southern workers; but even where some workers were organized, there were still wage differentials as compared with the North.

Productivity. Of equal, if not greater, importance was the differential in productivity between southern and northern mills. While the differentials varied between plants and regions, it was clear that productivity was greater, on the average, in southern than in northern plants. Some of this greater productivity could be traced to more modern plants and equipment, but there were also indications that some was due to the workers themselves. In the North, productivity had actually declined with the growth of more restrictive practices negotiated by collective bargaining.

Materials. There appeared to be little differentiation in material costs between the two regions. In some cases of individual bargaining between clothing manufacturers and individual mills there was some shading of prices, but the general practice of price quotations on wide regional bases tended to prevail. There was, however, one notable exception on the Pacific Coast. This area was accessible to Japanese mills, and many kinds of cotton finished goods could be obtained more cheaply than in the eastern United States, although there was some tariff protection.

Markets. Analysis of sales of Reed, Waite, and Gentzler on a regional basis indicated that there had been a considerable shift in the past 25 years. For many years the firm had marketed the greater share of its output in the East, the Northeast, and the Midwest, and since 1947 had moved to the Pacific Coast. The rapid growth of chain stores in smaller cities and towns in rural areas had enabled the company to grow into a national market. With the growth in the production of private brands the output of the firm was further diffused. The chief markets at present were the Atlantic seaboard, the upper Midwest and the Mississippi Valley, and the Pacific Coast. The company had always sold its merchandise FOB factory. This practice should perhaps be examined, since transportation to the Pacific Coast was an important factor on RWG brands. On private brands, transportation had become more important with the population shift to the Pacific area.

Following this investigation, the company considered the relocation of the trouser factory from Philadelphia to a point that would improve the company's competitive position. Three locations—designated as cities A, B, and C—were suitable as possible choices. Location A was a city of about 55,000 population in western Tennessee. This city was provided with adequate rail and highway transportation and was within a radius of 200 miles of several textile mills producing the kinds of finished cotton goods used by the trouser factory. Currently, there was in this city a firm producing inexpensive women's dresses. There were also several small firms assembling light electrical goods, and there was a soap factory. The nearest city of comparable size was 83 miles distant. Surrounding city A was an agricultural area of near-marginal productivity. The city streets, water supply, and similar services were considered adequate for the needs of the immediate future. There was no indication that the city would experience any considerable growth within the next 10 to 20 years. Land was available both within the city and just outside the city limits. The trouser factory in Philadelphia currently employed about 450 persons. It was believed that this number of workers could be recruited from the present population of city A without serious effect upon the existing labor supply.

Location B was in northeastern Mississippi in a city of approximately 18,000 in an area served by the Tennessee Valley Authority. At present, there was a small hosiery mill located there, as well as a meat-packing firm, a mirror factory, a lumber mill, a small electronics plant, and two canneries. City B was located on the main line of the Illinois Central Railroad and was served by two arterial highways. This city, in contrast to the others, had been actively engaged in a program of attracting industry and was prepared to offer a number of concessions as to land and taxes. In three instances the city had bonded itself to erect the buildings, and it had leased the buildings to the firms currently occupying them. Upon learning of the interest of Reed, Waite, and Gentzler, similar approaches had been made. City B, however, had grown rapidly within the past 10 years. Its population had increased almost 4,000 within that period, and there were indications that growth would continue, but perhaps at a less rapid rate. About 22 miles distant was another city of 12,000 population; and Memphis, Tennessee, was 125 miles away. Jackson, the capital of Mississippi, was at a distance of 92 miles. An extensive program of street paving, sewer construction, and school building had been projected, but only the early stages had been completed. The area immediately surrounding the city was agricultural, and there appeared to be noticeable migration from this area into city B.

Location C was in Georgia, about 15 miles from Atlanta. City C was also well located as to rail and highway transportation. Since the end of World War II, however, the countryside between city C and Altanta had developed to such an extent that highway travel between the two areas was regulated by traffic lights and highway patrols. Nearer Atlanta were large housing developments. Toward city C, there were both housing and industry. The population of city C was approximately 24,000 and was still increasing. To relieve the traffic congestion, a new superhighway had been planned and approved for construction between city C and Atlanta. A number of firms had located their plants in city C in the past 10 years, and several more were currently interested. Beyond city C the area was agricultural. There was evidence of union activity in city C, and many firms in Atlanta and city C were now organized. Where comparisons could be made, there still appeared to be lower unit costs in city C than in plants in the North performing similar operations with organized labor. There was little doubt that the facilities of city C would require improvement and expansion within the next five years.

EXHIBIT 10–2A   Comparison of Actual and Estimated Costs of Denim Trousers
(per dozen)

Item	Philadelphia	City A	City B	City C
Materials.	$ 3.13	$ 3.14	$3.13	$ 3.11
Labor	3.21	1.53	1.49	2.04
Waste	0.59	0.61	0.60	0.60
Factory overhead*	4.08	2.97	2.27†	2.74
Indirect labor	2.01	1.62	1.65	1.81
Administration expense	0.40	0.41	0.41	0.41
Total cost	$13.42	$10.28	$9.55	$10.71

*Includes amortization of new plant; does not include book value of Philadelphia plant.
†City B proposed certain tax and land concessions, which are taken into account.

EXHIBIT 10–2B   Average Railroad Freight Rates to Selected Cities from Philadelphia
and Proposed Locations (per dozen)

	Freight Rates—			
Destination	From Philadelphia	From City A	From City B	From City C
New York.	$0.39	$1.01	$1.14	$0.39
Chicago	0.86	0.99	0.99	0.86
Los Angeles.	1.52	1.31	1.49	1.52

Exhibit 10–2A shows costs of producing blue denim trousers at the Philadelphia factory as compared with costs at the three proposed locations. Costs in the proposed locations are estimates based upon surveys of the areas. Exhibit 10–2B shows the railroad transportation cost from the various points per dozen pairs of blue denim trousers. While these costs are not paid by Reed, Waite, and Gentzler, they are part of the delivered cost to the purchaser and thus are a competitive element of delivered price.

The market for Reed, Waite, and Gentzler is divided approximately as follows: 40 percent is sold in the Atlantic seaboard division, 50 percent in the Midwest and the Mississippi Valley, and 10 percent in the Far West and Pacific Coast region.

Questions

1. Which location would you recommend? Why?
2. Is the present lowest cost location always the best? Elaborate.
3. How would industrywide collective bargaining with labor affect the location of firms like Reed, Waite, and Gentzler?
4. What considerations other than those explicitly taken up in the text may influence the choice of a new location for the trouser factory?
5. What influence, if any, might the following laws have on the location of RWG? Fair Labor Standards Act; Taft-Hartley Act; and Davis-Bacon Act.

CASE 10–3
Dow Chemical in Europe*

Dow Chemical has shown that it is possible to make money as a basic chemical producer. In 1967, with total sales of $1.4 billion, Dow was the only large American chemical producer to show an upturn in profits, which reached $131 million, and in 1968 it bettered that record. In building up its European business, which now runs to $250 million, Dow was careful to establish strong marketing positions through exports before investing too heavily abroad. Such exports included both ethylene oxide and styrene, which goes into the making of the plastic polystyrene. With these selling positions established, Dow set up a manufacturing complex at Terneuzen, Holland, on the Schelde River near Antwerp, where it now makes most of the products it formerly shipped from the United States. For some years Dow has relied on European sources for its basic feedstocks such as ethylene and benzene, but this dependency is ending. This year the company will bring on stream a $60 million cracker at Terneuzen that will supply all of its current needs, and more besides. It will buy naptha from the oil companies, but in other respects it will be self-sufficient.

Dow, in short, has accomplished the "backward integration" toward petroleum that Carbide hesitated to try. Dow is confident about its prospects precisely because it has paid so much attention to broadening its markets. "The point about a modern cracker," one of its experts explains, "is that it throws off not one product but many—ethylene, of course, but also benzene and propylene. If you can use only one of those products, backward integration does not pay. But if you can use all of them, as we can, there is a very considerable cost saving." In addition, Dow has wangled a long-term contract from the big Belgian company, Solvay, for its excess ethylene.

Questions

1. Why do multinational companies usually start as domestic firms and branch out later?
2. What are some common dangers in backward integration? Why may they be of particular concern to a firm operating away from its home country?
3. Why is backward integration likely to pose special problems when the earlier stage turns out many joint products, as in petroleum cracking?
4. What effect should the expansion of the European common market have on Dow's European market?
5. The American dollar has appreciated sharply against European currencies in recent years. How should this affect the desirability of establishing production facilities by firms such as Dow Chemical in Europe?

---

*SOURCE: Selected portions of an article by John Davenport, "The Chemical Industry Pushes into Hostile Country," *Fortune*, April 1969. Reprinted with permission.

CASE 10–4
Pepsi-Cola for Vodka*

The Pepsi-Cola story actually started back in 1959 when we attended a U.S. exposition in Moscow where we were asked to dispense Pepsi-Cola. We started negotiations at that time. In fact, I went into one of their bottling plants during that period. . . . During a reception with the Soviets, Kosygin was talking to me and said he understood that I wanted to trade Pepsi-Cola for vodka. The transaction was actually completed in about 15 minutes at the reception.

It took then about six months of negotiations to put that conversation down on paper, and, as you know, the announcement was made over a year ago last fall.

The plant opened in Novorossisk in May of this year. We had our board of directors attend the meeting. Pepsi-Cola is now being sold throughout the Black Sea resort area.

The plant is turning out to be very successful. It is totally operated by the Soviets. Fortunately they are selling all they can produce and I think there are opportunities that we are going to end up opening additional plants.

As far as the vodka is concerned, in the United States, we are running ahead of the projections that we originally made. The transaction, as you perhaps have read in the papers, balances off over a five-year period. They agreed to buy as much Pepsi-Cola as we buy vodka. They pay dollars for the concentrate, we pay dollars for the vodka.

The transaction can be out of balance anytime during this five-year period. But at the end of the five-year period it must balance.

Why did this occur? I think that there are several things that happened that permitted this type of transaction. Number 1 was the improvement in our relations. Without improved political relations this obviously would have been impossible.

Number 2, the Soviets do not have a national drink, despite what some people think. They have a product called kvass. It is only sold in the Russian Republic. Their products do not have shelf life. They cannot ship them from many parts of the country. Of course, they can with our product.

Another reason I think is the problem they have had with alcoholism which they are very open about. They want to try to do something to correct this problem.

---

*SOURCE: Selected testimony of Donald Kendall, president of PEPSICO, before the Senate Committee on Foreign Relations, "Multinational Corporations and United States Foreign Policy," Pt. 10, Hearings before the Sub-Committee on Multinational Corporations (Washington, D.C.: U.S. Government Printing Office, 1975), pp. 189–90.

Questions

1. Contrast the locational determinants of a plant producing a soft-drink concentrate and the plants which bottle and distribute the soft drink.
2. Theoretically, what locational determinants should affect the production of kvass compared with the bottling of Pepsi-Cola?
3. What advantages do you see in the barter-like arrangement regarding vodka and Pepsi-Cola?
4. Coca-Cola has recently "matched" Pepsi-Cola by entering into arrangements with the Peoples Republic of China. Look up recent references to this activity and describe the nature of these arrangements.

11

Price Determination under Competition

Actual competition is undoubtedly very imperfect, but the degree of imperfection is quite as easily over- as under-estimated.
—*Frank H. Knight*

As suggested in the above quotation from Frank H. Knight, most firms have some degree of power to determine the prices at which they will sell (and sometimes at which they will buy). Still, competition is the most persistent force the businessperson must face every day. For this reason most economists place great emphasis on the competitive model of price determination since the model spells out in detail the consequences of this great force on prices, output, input, number and size of firms and plants, resource allocation, and many other important variables. At the same time, anyone with something to sell prefers to be a monopolist because it is more profitable. Consequently, models of competitive and monopolistic behavior together capture much of the essence of what is going on in the business world, although (or rather *because*) the models are simplified and not wholly in accord with any specific real situation. All theory is abstract, and the student should not shrug it off as "unrealistic." At the same time, he or she must learn not to apply a model to a situation that it is wholly unsuited to explain, for example, treating the OPEC cartel as a perfectly competitive organization.

A wide range of firms can usefully be analyzed "as if" they are perfectly competitive since they are guided strongly by this force. As stated by Milton Friedman, "Complete 'realism' is clearly unattainable, and the question whether a theory is realistic 'enough' can be settled only by seeing whether it yields predictions that are good enough for the purpose in hand or that are better than predictions from alternative theories."[1]

VERY SHORT-RUN PRICE DETERMINATION

Following the great Cambridge economist Alfred Marshall, it is common to distinguish between the "market period," the "short run," and the "long

[1] Milton Friedman, *Essays in Positive Economics*, "The Methodology of Positive Economics" (Chicago: The University of Chicago Press, 1953), p. 41.

run," even though, as he recognized there is no hard and sharp line between these analytical periods.[2] The market period or "very short run" pertains to the pricing of existing inventories of goods since the period is too short to permit production. The analysis is useful for perishing goods, for durables no longer being produced, and for goods such as housing where the accumulated supply is large in relation to the rate of production.

FIXED SUPPLY WITHOUT RESERVATION PRICES

We usually think about such goods as bananas, fresh strawberries, and cut flowers as perishables. In theory, they have a vertical supply curve in the very short run since there is a fixed amount on hand and the seller, while hoping for a high price, should be ready to offer the goods for sale at a low price in preference to letting them spoil. Often this behavior can be observed in retail markets, especially on Saturday evening if the store will be closed on Sunday. The manager who does not cut prices to salvage some sales of perishables may be less than alert. Figure 11–1 illustrates the situation for a perishing good that is (temporarily) fixed in supply. A much higher price is secured by the seller if the demand is D_1 rather than D_2. But it is better to sell at a low price (OP_2) than to let the commodity spoil.

The fixed supply case is applicable to much more than items we usually consider perishable. Services rendered by motels and hotels, parking lots, theaters, and stadia are perishing in that once the structures are built (and the attractions, if any, are scheduled), available spaces are wasted if not used. The structures themselves endure, but a given day's demand is lost to the extent that customers are lacking. It is likely to be more difficult, however, to cut a price late in the day to stimulate sales than it is for perishing foods, especially because more complaints will probably be secured from those who feel discriminated against.

Vertical very short-run supply curves can exist also if the motivation of suppliers is nonpecuniary. Sandlot baseball teams often supply entertainment because they wish to play even at zero price. The amount of money they raise by passing a hat depends on the number who watch and their generosity. Charitable and religious services are often provided on a similar voluntary basis, although a degree of compulsion may be present.

The fixed supply case can also arise because of government regulation. Passenger service may be required on a railroad route that would otherwise be abandoned. Even if passenger fares are regulated, the actual price received per space provided depends on demand, that is, on the number of passengers carried. Similarly, the supply of broadcasting

---

[2]Alfred Marshall, *Principles of Economics* (London: MacMillan, 1930), p. 379. Marshall also analyzed very long-run or secular movements of prices.

FIGURE 11–1   Fixed Supply—Perishing Good

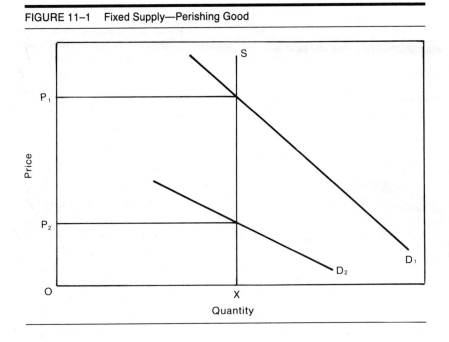

services is perfectly inelastic for a station on a regular schedule, and the price received per hour depends on the amount of advertising sold. In the fixed supply case, competitive price can be considered to depend primarily on demand (although the location of the supply curve is also a factor).

FIXED SUPPLY WITH RESERVATION PRICES

If the problem under consideration is competitive pricing of an existing stock of a durable good (e.g., houses, oriental rugs, automobiles, or rare coins), the very short-run supply curve is not vertical.[3] Owners of such goods will have "reservation prices" below which they will not offer units for sale. For reproducible goods such as houses and cars, the cost of reproducing the same or a somewhat equivalent item will greatly influence the price below which an owner will not sell. For famous paintings, rare coins or stamps, or Ming vases, satisfaction of ownership is important in determining reservation prices. Different individual owners will have differing reservation prices for the same good but altogether their attitudes determine the shape of the very short-run supply curve. At higher prices

---

[3]It can, however, be made vertical by means of a special definition used first by Philip H. Wicksteed and Herbert J. Davenport. They included possessors' desires to retain their own goods in the demand curve rather than reflecting their reservation prices in the supply curve. This view is often useful in economics, as in analysis of the "demand for money."

FIGURE 11–2   Fixed Supply—Durable Good

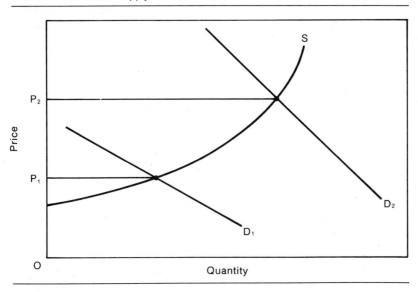

more units will be offered for sale. At a sufficiently high price virtually the entire stock would be available to new buyers.

The competitive supply-demand situation for a durable good in fixed supply is illustrated in Figure 11–2. The supply curve does not start at a zero price as it will be affected by such factors as cost of reproduction (of a somewhat similar good), satisfaction of ownership, and speculative motives. The extreme right-hand portion cannot have an abscissa larger than the available supply. As would be expected, the addition of demand curve D_1 provides a market period price OP_1.

A very important phenomenon for this situation is the shift of demand over time. Usually this is a rightward shift due to such factors as population growth, rise in real incomes and wealth, and inflation in the general price level. Curve D_2 reflects an increase in demand over time when the supply curve is assumed to be fixed. (Actually, S would probably move to the left to reflect higher reservation prices and perhaps some disappearance of the good due to fire, etc.) Case 11–1, "Prices in Philately," based on actual catalog prices of stamps that are popular with collectors, reflects the fixed supply case for a durable commodity when the demand moves up over time.

Some speculators and investors rely heavily on this common phenomenon. Good waterfront property is (nearly) limited in supply making capital gains dependable for those who correctly anticipate growth in demand (and who do not pay a price that already fully reflects future growth).

RATIONING OF SEASONAL OUTPUT

Agricultural commodities tend to be harvested periodically, for example, in the fall, and the supply must be allocated not only among competing buyers but also made to stretch out until the next harvest. In "capitalist" economies this is accomplished by the free movement of prices. In general, if a crop is being used up too rapidly, shortages at existing prices will cause those prices to be bid up, slowing down the rate of consumption. If prices are temporarily too high, surpluses will cause prices to be reduced, speeding the rate of use. Speculators in the grain markets are vital to the constant adjustments in price, as they see developing shortages or surpluses. A more even flow of the crop into consumption (including reprocessing activities) is effected by the price system.

A supply-demand picture of such rationing over time can be drawn if some simplifying assumptions are made. Suppose the relevant very short run is one year but that the demand curve of Figure 11–3 is applicable to a four-month period only. The demand curve for each of the three four-month periods is assumed to be the same.[4]

The total crop, harvested once a year, is represented by OT. Sellers would offer quantities along S_1 in the first period. Actual price is P_1, where the (four-month) demand curve crosses, and sales are OX_1. Due to storage and interest costs of carrying the remaining inventory $(OT - OX_1)$, reservation prices will normally be higher in period 2 and price will be higher at OX_2. The smallest amount $(OT - OX_1 - OX_2)$ will be available for period 3. The vertical supply curve S_3 indicates that all of the remaining quantity must be disposed of in the last four-month period since no inventory carryover is assumed. Sales in this period will be OX_3; price will be OP_3.

As is usually the case, the real world is more complicated than the theoretical model. The rationing function of price for a periodically produced crop for which there is an organized market takes place heavily through the sale and purchase of futures contracts. The buyer of March oats, for example, agrees to accept delivery of a specified amount of this commodity in that month, while the seller agrees to make the delivery. (Recall from Chapter 2 that a given contract usually changes hands many times before the delivery date.) Since there is a fairly close relationship between futures and cash prices, the futures transactions will also affect cash prices at which processors and others can buy the commodity. The processors' costs will affect the price of oatmeal, for example, and thus affect final consumers. Upward pressure on future prices will tend to slow utilization of the existing stock while downward pressure will speed use.

---

[4] The authors have benefited from a somewhat similar discussion by Richard H. Leftwich in a widely used microeconomics textbook, *The Price System and Resource Allocation*, 4th ed. (Hinsdale, Ill.: Dryden Press, 1970), pp. 179–81.

FIGURE 11–3   Rationing of Seasonal Crop

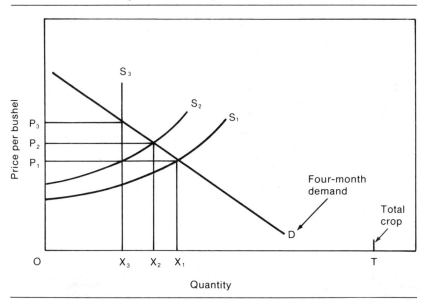

Speculators who engage in arbitrage will also tend to assure the proper differential in prices between markets in different places and even between markets in the same city, such as the Chicago Board of Trade and the Chicago Mercantile Exchange, since corn is traded on both exchanges.

SHORT RUN AND LONG RUN UNDER COMPETITION

The short run is an analytical time period within which the firm can alter its output from existing plant capacity but cannot change this capacity. The long run is a period sufficiently long to permit changes in capacity and the entry or exit of new companies. A great many real-world situations can best be analyzed in a side-by-side chart where short-run adjustments of a competitive firm and the entire industry are shown along with long-run adjustments by both.

Figure 11–4 is such a chart. The competitive industry is first assumed to be in both short-run and long-run equilibrium with price at OP_1 and output per period at OA. Curve S_1 is the industry's short-run supply function; and LRS, which is drawn horizontally, shows that the industry is one of "constant cost" in the long run in the sense that if enough time is considered to elapse, any quantity—large or small—can be produced at the same unit cost. This, in turn, means that prices of productive inputs will be unaffected by the size of this industry and that such adverse factors as congestion will not set in as the industry expands in size.

FIGURE 11–4   Decline in Demand—Causes Short-Run and Long-Run Adjustments

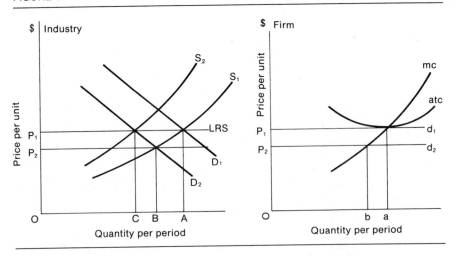

The initial equilibrium price and output are determined by the intersection of D_1, S_1, and LRS. The firm on the right is a "price taker" being too small to affect industry price. It does possess the power to determine its own output, which will be Oa, at the intersection of its own demand curve d_1 and its own marginal cost curve mc. That is, the firm will turn out all units that add less to its costs than they can be sold for.

Next suppose demand for the product of this industry suddenly declines to D_2. An immediate reduction of price to OP_2 and of industry output to OB would occur. The firm would react to the lower price by reducing its output to Ob. (This sort of action by all firms is what reduces industry output to OB.) This firm, and the others, will now be suffering economic losses as shown by price being below average total cost (since atc includes a return on capital equal to the best alternative employment of the capital). Some firms will leave the industry.[5] A new full equilibrium will be established when enough firms leave the industry to shift the short-run supply curve to the position of S_2 with output OC but with price restored to the original level OP_1. Assuming that the firm on the right is one that survives, its output should gradually increase from Ob back to the original amount Oa as other firms leave and price returns to the level determined by LRS.

The analysis can readily be modified to show the effect of an increase in demand or a change in the level of the LRS curve. Perhaps the main lesson to be learned is that a change in demand in a competitive industry,

[5]It is not easy to specify which firms will leave. In general, those with better alternative uses of capital and entrepreneurial talent and those with more pessimistic expectations regarding this industry will be among those who exit. The technically less efficient firms are also likely to leave.

FIGURE 11–5   Price Ceilings and Floors

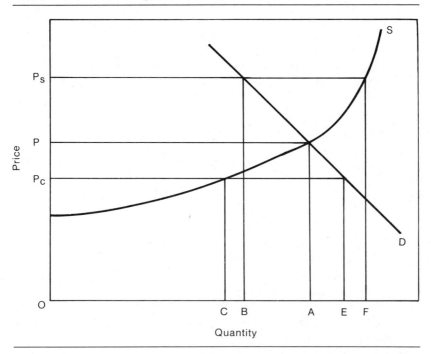

ceteris paribus, will often cause only a temporary upward or downward change in price.[6]

Models that show how competition works can easily be modified to show the consequences of government controls on prices. Figure 11–5 portrays a competitive industry in the short run. Competitive price is *OP,* with sales per period of *OA.* If government authorities set a legal maximum price at a lower level such as *OP$_c$* amount demanded, *OE,* will exceed amount supplied, *OC.* If, instead, government supports the price at level *OP$_s$,* amount supplied *OF* will exceed amount demanded (in the private market) *OB.* This simple chart predicts many consequences of government intervention that are readily observable.

RENT AND OTHER PRICE CONTROLS

Rent controls were first introduced to Britain in 1915, prohibiting land-lords to charge rents higher than those in effect in August 1914, when

---

[6]If the *LRS* curve is upsloping (due to higher input prices or to congestion or pollution as the industry expands), an increase in demand will bring a higher price even in the long run. A downsloping *LRS* curve will have the opposite effect. The student is urged to draw charts for the various possible situations.

World War I broke out.[7] Since 1972 nearly all unfurnished rented property has been rent controlled. One result has been a greater shortage of unfurnished, compared with furnished, apartments. Landlords in Britain have also had to compete with low-cost public housing for which the wait is typically several years.

Paris is among the European cities with a long history of rent controls. Apartments are extremely difficult to secure. Huge (illegal) bonuses accompany the acquisition of rental units. The situation has been made even worse by the withdrawal of apartments and undermaintenance where owners feel they have insufficient economic incentive to keep up their buildings.

New York City rents were controlled early in World War II by the federal government. The state took over its administration in 1950, and the city became the administrator in 1962. In 1975, city officials conceded that rent control cost the loss of some 30,000 dwelling units annually.[8] Even in good neighborhoods, abandoned buildings have sometimes been used as garbage dumps by other New Yorkers. In the terms of Figure 11–5, rent control causes a shift over time of the supply curve to the left, increasing the shortage.

General price control, applying to a great many goods and services is less common in the United States but has been imposed during wartime and under the Nixon administration. (Nixon price control is described in the next chapter—Case 12–1—as it was sometimes regarded as a way to curb monopoly pricing.) The previous analysis applies to each commodity that is controlled if the price is actually held below the equilibrium level. Unable to raise prices overtly sellers tend strongly to substitute other ways of raising their income. These include reducing quality or convenience to buyers, eliminating discounts or free delivery, selling to buyers who can offer a reciprocal advantage, and a host of other means. The National Recovery Administration's list of ways to cut prices (shown in Case 12–2) in subtle ways applies in part (in the opposite direction) to ways to get around price controls. In World War II, consumers were issued ration tickets for groceries, gasoline, and other goods as a way of diminishing the favoritism that sellers can show in allocating items in short supply.

Economists feel that the gasoline shortages in the summer of 1979 were due in large part to the use of price controls in the United States, although the trouble had its origin in the curtailment of oil exports from Iran. Canada and Mexico, without such controls, did not experience gasoline shortages.

---

[7] Robert L. Schuettinger and Eamonn F. Butler, *Forty Centuries of Wage and Price Controls* (Washington, D.C.: Heritage Foundation, 1979), p. 87.

[8] Ibid., p. 88.

PRICE SUPPORTS

The consequences of supporting prices above their equilibrium level (OP_s in Figure 11–5) is dramatically revealed in agriculture. For over half a century, an extensive and ever-changing farm program has been in effect. There is, perhaps, more justification for governmental interference on behalf of producers than in most segments of the economy since fluctuations in farm prices and incomes are especially severe. Improved technology in agriculture has increased supply faster than demand has grown, and the number of farmers has declined steadily. (See Figure 3–1 which shows the decline in farm population.)

Among the concepts that have entered into the federal farm program is the "parity" idea. The ratio of farm prices received to the prices farmers must pay for things they buy, as it existed in the base period 1910 to 1914 (revised to later years for some products) is supposed to represent "full parity" for farmers. Innumerable arguments have occurred about the percent of parity to be used in various years, although the concept is obviously without much meaning. Different rates of technological progress and changing prices and availability of imported goods clearly upset any rationale for "parity."

The farm program has long been a complex mixture of loans and cash payments, often depending on acreage restrictions to reduce the federal liability. "Nonrecourse" crop loans are the basic price-support mechanism. After the harvest the federal government can lend to a farmer at a rate set by the U.S. Department of Agriculture under congressional guidelines. If the farmer can sell for more than this amount, he is free to do so and the federal government has no recourse to collect the loan but keeps the crop instead.

In 1983, the government bought 12 percent of all dairy products. The accumulated amount stored away in 1985 was 17 billion pounds of butter, cheese, and dried milk. Government-owned products in storage also included 1 billion bushels of wheat and 650 million bushels of corn.[9] The farm program is widely criticized, but its momentum is difficult to reverse due to strong lobbies, congressional supporters, and protests of farmers who fear they will be even further squeezed if the supports are weakened.

Part of the problem derives from the encouragement that was given to farmers by government and bankers to expand and produce, especially in the 1970s. Since then, U.S. exports of agricultural products have fallen due to the recession of the early 1980s, the huge foreign debt of many of the poorer countries, and the great rise in the international value of the dollar. (In late 1985 the dollar was slipping somewhat in value, however.)

---

[9]"Real Trouble on the Farm," *Time*, February 18, 1985, pp. 26–27.

SUMMARY OF IMPLICATIONS OF THE COMPETITIVE MODEL

The strength of the economist's model of pure or perfect competition does not lie in its close fit to reality but in its ability to isolate and emphasize so many of the powerful forces that actually affect consumers, firms, industries, and the economy. By showing these forces in detail, the model also helps us understand the effects of public and private restraints on competition. Some of the main lessons follow.

1. Market or very short run. If we are studying a situation where production does not take place, supply will be completely or largely inelastic. Original cost is not relevant, although cost of reproduction may have an effect on reservation prices. If the good is perishing, it is better to secure a low price than none at all. If the good is durable, it may be possible to realize very large capital gains by holding it over a substantial period of time when demand grows due to economic development, population growth, etc.

2. Short run. In the short run, facilities can usually expand their rate of output by hiring more labor or working overtime and using more other inputs such as materials and power. Higher prices stimulate an increase in output while lower prices do the opposite. In economics, the relevant costs are "opportunity costs" of inputs. If these cannot be met, the firm is producing the wrong good (or perhaps at the wrong place) and should reappraise the situation, perhaps even selling out. In the short run, fixed costs should be disregarded as nothing can be done about them. Marginal costs, based on variable costs, play a key role in determining optimum output. This output is found where marginal cost equals price. Price is determined by overall supply and demand in the industry, not by the individual competitive firm.

3. Long Run. As Alfred Marshall stated, "Of course there is no hard and sharp line of division between 'long' and 'short' periods." Still, the relatively long-run implications of the competitive model are even more important than those derived from a short-run view.

If demand for the product of a competitive industry increases (more than momentarily), new firms will enter the industry to try to capture some of the returns if they are abnormally high. The new firms and plants will tend to be of a size that has proved to be economically efficient. As new firms enter, prices will decline, and economic profits will fall until only opportunity costs are met. (These costs, however, include a "normal" or "alternative" return on capital and labor—zero economic profit is not a desperate situation.)

If, instead, demand for a good declines, prices will fall, opportunity costs of many firms will not be met and some will leave the industry. The ones that exit will be the "inefficient" ones. "Efficiency" does not pertain just to technical matters but also to alternative opportunities. Rather paradoxically, a high-cost firm may be a technically efficient one with good alternatives, since this raises its opportunity costs. With a decline in industry demand, the firms with the best alternatives should be among those that exit. Firms that last out the adjustment should eventually secure normal returns again.

GOVERNMENT INTERFERENCE WITH PRICES

A good rule is that when government wants to alter income distribution or seeks other social goals, it should do so without upsetting the working of competitive prices. Rent controls, at least initially, benefit some tenants at the expense of landlords (who may or may not be wealthier). The effects will also be to cause a shortage of rental units and long-term undermaintenance, abandonment, and underbuilding of new units.

More general control of prices will cause shortages, promote black markets, and foster favoritism. A large and highly imperfect rationing system may be established. Nevertheless, governments from the times of Hammurabi and ancient Egypt, 4,000 years ago, to the present have attempted often to fix prices and wages. The Edict of Diocletian in A.D. 301 even included the death penalty for exceeding the maximum prices at which some necessities could be sold.[10]

Diocletian, at least, did not prevent prices from falling, as is now common. Our complicated farm program has placed the U.S. government into the storage business on a large scale, without solving many farm problems. Largest benefits have accrued to the largest farms.

CASE 11–1
Prices in Philately*

Millions of collectors and many stamp dealers in the United States rely heavily on *Scott's Standard Postage Stamp Catalogue*, which describes and gives prices of over 200,000 stamps in its recent annual editions. After stating that "condition is the all important factor of price," the Scott *Catalogue* goes on to explain its prices as follows:

> The prices appearing in this Catalogue were estimated after careful study of available wholesale and retail offerings together with recommendations and information submitted by many of the leading philatelic societies. These and other factors were considered in determining the figures

---

[10]Schuettinger and Butler, *Forty Centuries of Wage and Price Controls*, p. 23.

*SOURCE: Philately is defined as the "collection and study of postage stamps . . . usually as a hobby" (*Webster's New World Dictionary* [Cleveland: World Publishing Co., 1957]).

which the editor considers represent the proper or present basis for a fine specimen when offered by an informed dealer to an informed buyer. Sales are frequently made at lower figures occasioned by individual bargaining, changes in popularity, temporary over-supply, local custom, the "vest pocket dealer," or the many other reasons which cause deviations from any accepted standard. Sales at higher prices are usually because of exceptionally fine condition, unusual postal markings, unexpected political changes or newly discovered information. While the minimum price of a stamp is fixed at 2 cents to cover the dealer's labor and service cost of assorting, cataloguing and filling orders individually, the sum of these list prices does not properly represent the "value" of a packet of unsorted or unmounted stamps sold in bulk which generally consists of only the cheaper stamps. Prices in italics indicate infrequent sales or lack of adequate pricing information.[11]

The Post Office Department at periodic intervals issues *Postage Stamps of the United States,* which gives fuller details on each U.S. stamp and gives the quantity issued for all commemoratives and airmail stamps. Exhibits 11–1A, 11–1B, and 11–1C give the quantities issued and catalog prices of canceled stamps for three groups of stamps that could be considered "blue chips" because of the wide popularity of U.S. commemoratives and airmails. More recent U.S. commemoratives probably have limited chances of appreciation because of the large quantities issued, usually 120 million, and the very substantial purchases by collectors. Mint commemoratives have been made freely available to all who desired them for a year or two after issue at the U.S. Philatelic Agency. Government policy has also been against allowing the great enhancement of value through the discovery of important errors. When faulty sheets of the Dag Hammarskjöld issue were discovered in 1962, the Post Office Department reissued the error for purchase by all who desired it. Thus, the spectacular price appreciation of the best-known U.S. error, the inverted airplane in the tricolored 24-cent issue of 1918, seems unlikely to be repeated.

Since World War II, the Post Office Department has issued stamps in steadily increasing numbers. From 1950 to 1959, 151 regular stamps were issued; the number increased to 247 in the 1960s, 415 in the 1970s, and to 244 from 1980 to June 1983. Two recent sheets of state flags, and state's birds and flowers, included 50 varieties for a single issue.

Questions

1. What is the general relationship between price and the quantity issued? What are possible explanations for the price not varying proportionally (though inversely) with the quantity issued?

2. Are the changes in prices between 1949 and 1984 best explained by shifts in supply or demand, or both? Show diagrammatically.

---

[11]*Scott's Standard Postage Stamp Catalogue* (New York: Scott Publications, 1962), p. v.

EXHIBIT 11–1A   Quantity Issued and Catalog Prices of the U.S. Columbian Exposition
Issue—1893

Denomination	Quantity Issued (000s)	Scott Catalogue Price, 1949	Scott Catalogue Price, 1962	Scott Catalogue Price, 1974	Scott Catalogue Price, 1978	Scott Catalogue Price, 1984*
$0.01......	449,196	$ 0.03	$ 0.10	$ 0.15	$ 0.15	$ 0.25
0.02......	1,464,589	0.02	0.05	0.06	0.06	0.06
0.03......	11,501	1.10	2.50	6.00	7.75	15.00
0.04......	19,182	0.35	0.85	2.25	3.50	5.50
0.05......	35,248	0.40	1.00	2.50	3.75	7.00
0.06......	4,708	1.85	3.25	7.00	9.00	20.00
0.08......	10,657	0.50	1.00	2.65	3.50	7.50
0.10......	16,517	0.45	0.85	2.25	3.70	6.50
0.15......	1,577	5.00	7.50	20.00	30.00	65.00
0.30......	617	8.00	13.00	30.00	48.00	90.00
0.50......	244	11.00	17.50	45.00	65.00	140.00
1.00......	55	36.00	50.00	150.00	250.00	575.00
2.00......	46	30.00	50.00	140.00	225.00	800.00
3.00......	28	57.50	90.00	250.00	400.00	900.00
4.00......	26	70.00	110.00	350.00	550.00	1,300.00
5.00......	27	77.50	220.00	400.00	650.00	1,500.00
Total ...		$299.70	$567.60	$1,407.86	$2,249.41	$5,431.81

*For canceled stamps.

SOURCES: *Scott's Standard Postage Stamp Catalogue* (New York: Scott Publications, 1949, 1962, 1974, 1978); and *U.S. Postage Stamps, 1847–1957* (Washington, D.C.: U.S. Government Printing Office, 1957).

3. Assess American stamps as an investment vehicle by considering:
   a. A serious collector of modest means who assembled the "collector's port-folio" of the relatively low-priced stamps listed in Exhibit 11–1B and the definitive airmails listed in Exhibit 11–1C (all but the inverted airmail and Graf Zeppelin stamps). Assume that such a collector bought at cata-log and could sell at two-third's catalog;
   b. An individual who bought the higher priced Columbian and Graf Zep-pelin issues for possible financial gain. Deduct 15% from catalog price in selling.

	1949	1962	1974	1978	1984
a. Collector's portfolio...............	$ 47	$ 91	$ 201	$ 289	$ 520
Less one third in selling............	31	61	134	193	342
b. Columbian-Zeppelin...............	410	748	1,868	3,024	7,882
Less 15% in selling...............	348	635	1,588	2,570	6,700
c. GNP deflator*...................	58	69	106	140	215

*Base is 1972=100 and is for years before catalogue year (1948, 1961, 1973, 1977, and 1983) to correspond with catalog publication dates.

Calculate the annual rate of return to nearest percentage of the two portfolios and compare with the annual change in price level indicated by the GNP deflator to estimate the real rate of growth. A quick way of doing this is to make use of the first PV table.

EXHIBIT 11–1B Quantity Issued and Catalog Prices of Selected U.S. Commemorative Stamps of the 1920s

Date	Issue	Denomi-nation	Quantity Issued (000)	Scott Catalogue Price, 1949*	Scott Catalogue Price, 1962*	Scott Catalogue Price, 1974*	Scott Catalogue Price, 1978*	Scott Catalogue Price, 1984*
1920	Pilgrim Tercentenary	$0.01	137,978	$ 0.20	$ 0.50	$ 1.20	$ 1.75	$ 3.00
1920	Pilgrim Tercentenary	0.02	196,037	0.12	0.35	0.80	1.50	2.25
1920	Pilgrim Tercentenary	0.05	11,321	2.50	4.50	8.50	11.50	17.00
1921	Harding Memorial	0.02	1,459,487	0.03	0.06	0.08	0.08	0.10
1921	Harding Memorial (imperforate)	0.02	770	1.10	1.50	1.75	2.50	5.30
1921	Harding Memorial (rotary press)	0.02	99,950	0.10	0.20	0.50	0.75	2.00
1924	Huguenot-Walloon Tercentenary	0.01	51,387	0.25	0.55	1.50	2.75	5.00
1924	Huguenot-Walloon Tercentenary	0.02	77,753	0.20	0.50	1.25	2.00	3.50
1924	Huguenot-Walloon Tercentenary	0.05	5,659	2.75	4.50	8.50	13.50	22.50
1925	Lexington-Concord.	0.01	15,615	0.30	0.60	1.65	3.00	5.25
1925	Lexington-Concord.	0.02	26,596	0.45	1.15	3.00	4.50	7.50
1925	Lexington-Concord.	0.05	5,349	2.00	3.00	8.00	13.50	20.00
1925	Norse-American.	0.02	9,105	0.60	1.10	2.00	2.50	5.00
1925	Norse-American.	0.05	1,901	3.00	5.50	9.00	12.50	12.50
	Subtotal value.			13.60	24.01	47.73	72.33	110.90
1929	Nebraska issue	0.01	8,220	0.12	0.22	0.65	1.00	2.00
1929	Nebraska issue	0.015	8,990	0.10	0.20	0.80	1.20	2.25
1929	Nebraska issue	0.02	73,220	0.05	0.15	0.30	0.45	0.85
1929	Nebraska issue	0.03	2,110	0.50	1.10	3.50	5.50	8.75
1929	Nebraska issue	0.04	1,600	0.75	1.60	3.75	5.75	11.00
1929	Nebraska issue	0.05	1,860	0.80	1.60	4.00	6.25	13.50
1929	Nebraska issue	0.06	980	2.75	4.00	7.00	12.50	19.00
1929	Nebraska issue	0.07	850	1.50	3.00	6.00	8.50	15.00
1929	Nebraska issue	0.08	1,480	1.50	4.50	9.00	13.50	22.00
1929	Nebraska issue	0.09	530	3.75	5.25	9.50	14.00	25.00
1929	Nebraska issue	0.10	1,890	2.50	4.00	8.50	13.00	17.50
	Subtotal value.			14.32	25.62	53.00	81.65	136.85
	Total value.			$27.92	$49.63	$100.73	$153.98	$247.75

EXHIBIT 11–1C Quantity Issued and Catalog Prices, U.S. Airmail Stamps, 1918–1930

Date	Issue	Denomination	Quantity Issued (000s)	Scott Catalogue Price, 1949*	Scott Catalogue Price, 1962*	Scott Catalogue Price, 1974*	Scott Catalogue Price, 1978*	Scott Catalogue Price, 1984*
1918	Definitive first issue	$0.06	3,396	$ 2.00	$ 5.00	$ 12.00	$ 18.50	$ 40.00
1918	Definitive first issue	0.16	3,794	4.50	9.50	21.00	27.50	50.50
1918	Definitive first issue	0.24	2,135	4.00	8.00	20.00	25.00	60.00
1918	Definitive first issue (center inverted)	0.24	0.1	3,500.00	10,000.00	35,000.00	45,000.00	120,000.00
1923	Definitive	0.08	6,415	1.40	2.75	7.00	12.00	22.50
1923	Definitive	0.16	5,309	4.00	8.50	21.00	25.00	50.00
1923	Definitive	0.24	5,286	2.25	4.75	12.50	18.50	40.00
1926–27	Definitive	0.10	42,093	0.04	0.15	0.25	0.40	0.50
1926–27	Definitive	0.15	15,597	0.20	0.50	1.20	2.25	2.75
1926–27	Definitive	0.20	17,616	0.12	0.40	1.00	1.85	2.25
1927	Definitive (Lindbergh)	0.10	20,379	0.15	1.00	1.85	2.35	3.00
1928	Definitive	0.05	106,888	0.05	0.20	0.50	0.50	0.65
1930	Definitive	0.05	97,641	0.04	0.15	0.40	0.40	0.45
1930	Definitive (rotary 1931)	0.05	57,340	0.04	0.15	0.35	0.35	0.50
1930	Graf Zeppelin	0.65	94	18.00	35.00	90.00	150.00	450.00
1930	Graf Zeppelin	1.30	72	35.00	50.00	135.00	275.00	800.00
1930	Graf Zeppelin	2.60	61	57.50	95.00	235.00	450.00	1,200.00
	Total value (excluding 24¢ inverted)			$129.29	$221.05	$559.05	$1,009.60	$2,723.10

*For canceled stamps except center-inverted 24-cent stamp, which exists only uncanceled and whose price is quoted in italics in the Scott catalogue.
SOURCES: *Scott's Standard Postage Stamp Catalogue* (New York: Scott Publications, 1949, 1962, 1974, 1978, 1984); and *U.S. Postage Stamps, 1847–1957* (Washington, D.C.: U.S. Government Printing Office, 1957).

4. Another popular way that some collectors have sought to invest in stamps is to buy sheets of 50 of current commemoratives at face value. For example, one could have purchased 100 sheets of a 1949 3-cent commemorative for $150. In 1974, although the stamps catalogued at 10 cents apiece, they might have been sold to a dealer for 3½ cents. Why would this investment have been the least attractive?

5. Consider whether the post office's policies toward commemoratives is the position of an enlightened monopolist, i.e. one that does not maximize profits.

CASE 11–2
Moscow's Taxi Business*

Angered by sharp increases in fares, Muscovites have deserted the city's taxicabs in the first major consumer boycott in memory in the Soviet capital.

Taxi drivers who once cruised the streets bestowing rides on customers who begged and bribed for lifts now line up by the score at taxi stands hoping for passengers.

The state-controlled taxi monopoly said the increases, which went into effect April 1, were justified by better service. It now costs the equivalent of 41 cents to travel a mile, double the old rate. The basic fee for starting a trip has also risen, from 13 to 26 cents.

New York taxi rates went up last month to 75 cents for the first seventh of a mile and a dime for every seventh after that. But the average Soviet wage is $199 a month.

The government-controlled press has carried no complaints about the fare hikes and the consumer boycott is not organized. It apparently is the result of thousands of individual Muscovites deciding a ride in one of the city's 14,600 cabs is just not worth the price.

Subway prices remained unchanged at about 6 cents a ride, roughly the same as bus, trolley, and train fares.

"The drivers didn't ask for this," one cabbie said. "We normally get to keep a third of the money we take in, with a minimum pay for us of 180 rubles ($237) a month."

"The management is worried too. They're going to have trouble getting drivers. People will go away to trucking firms where they can make a lot more money."

---

*SOURCE: Selected portion of an AP release, "Moscow Riders Boycott High Cost of Cabs," as published in the *Florida Times Union*, April 6, 1977.

Moscow taxis were carrying about 600,000 passengers a day, but have long been known for uneven service. Drivers frequently demanded extra money for longer trips, and scores of the boxy taxis frequently idled outside leading hotels while drivers bargained with customers over fares.

"It would be a mistake to claim that everything is perfect in our work," Moscow taxi chief Leo A. Yakoviev said in a recent newspaper interview.

Questions

1. Draw a chart to illustrate that the Moscow authorities apparently set taxi fares above the equilibrium price.
2. What are the principal factors that affect elasticity of demand and of supply for Moscow cabs? Consider both short-run and long-run aspects.
3. What is the nature of markets where bargaining over price is likely to be utilized? Why is this practice likely to be quite annoying in the taxi business?
4. Under some conditions potential taxi riders wave paper money at cab drivers in order to increase their chance of being picked up. What supply-demand conditions are likely to bring about this situation?
5. Free markets and free men tend to go together. What connection is suggested in the case?

CASE 11–3
Even the Cows Are Laughing

The dairy industry with its paraphernalia of import quotas, regional market orders, distinction in prices between fluid and surplus milk, and difficulties in entry and particularly in exit does not fully qualify as a model of perfect competition. But the individual farm has negligible power to affect the price it receives (outside of modest butterfat or protein premiums).

The particular type of controls in effect in the late 1980s may vary somewhat from those of this case. It seems predictable, however, that despite enormous government stores of dairy products, the goverment will set some sort of price floor. The static or slightly declining demand for milk products, together with technological developments that were increasing the productivity of cows, and thus the optimum scale for farms, kept downward pressure on the equilibrium price.

The Dairy Production Stabilization Act of 1983 was passed in November with the hope that it would reduce milk output by 10 percent and thus prevent the accumulation of further dairy surpluses. From many farmers' point of view, it prevented a drastic drop or abandonment of supports that would allow the price of milk to drop to an unprofitable $10 per hundredweight. From the consumer point of view, it would halt the rise in milk prices. The government hoped to cut budgetary outlays for supports and surplus management.

In the spring of 1984, it seemed clear that the great majority of dairy farmers made the managerial decision that despite the apparent attractions of getting $10 a hundredweight for not producing up to 30 percent of their 1982 production (or average of 1981–82 production), they would opt out of the paid output reduction feature of the program and rely on the guaranteed price floor.

As a close approximation, the guaranteed price may be taken as $12 with a scheduled reduction to $11.50 if surpluses continue to accumulate. Assume short-run marginal costs of production averaged about $5. These are mostly for feed and would vary between farms depending on the proportions of fodder grown and purchased, and the productivity of the cows per unit of feed. The MC would rise with output because of probable increases in amounts of purchased grain and the continued use of less efficient cows.

The reason for Senator Dole saying, "This program is so bad, that even the cows are laughing" is that the prospective cutbacks amounted to only 5.4 billion pounds (about 3 percent of the 15-month production), and 2 billion of these had already been made for other reasons. Clearly, the majority of cows who continued to live rather than be converted to hamburger were happy.

Questions

1. At this point, construct industry supply and demand curves with the equilibrium price estimated at $10. Show diagrammatically the gap to be closed by the production reduction program *at effective support prices of $12* (about 10 percent of total production).

2. Show that on the basis of marginal analysis for a typical farmer, the cutback of the full 30 percent would be the apparent profit maximizing decision since the opportunity costs for levels of production of over 70 percent of the 1982 base have been greatly increased by the $10 for the nonproduction option.

3. Some farmers rejected the program because their 1983 production substantially exceeded the 1982 or 1981–82 base. Take as an example a farmer who had produced 20 percent more in 1983 than in the base year and show that the contribution to fixed costs and overhead would be less under the crop reduction program than by maintaining 1983 output. (Other farmers rejected the program because they needed the maximum cash flow to pay indebtedness and they produced virtually all of their feed. Others expected to average above the support price because a favorable location enabled them to sell most of their product at higher fluid milk prices.)

4. Probably the most important reason for nonparticipation was that the Dairy Production Stabilization Act of 1983 was a temporary 15-month program that required farm managers to make decisions with long-run implications.

Any substantial reduction in production required culling the herd (minor cutbacks might be made by smaller food rations perhaps combined with less frequent milking). A plan for production reduction had to include culling plans. (For obvious reasons, a farmer was not permitted to sell or lease a superior milking animal to a friend). For farmers with marginal cows where value was about equal to the slaughter price of $500, this posed no problem. But to sell a good milker worth $2,000 for the meat price and then be faced with the problem of replacement when the program expired changed the relevant marginal analysis. Show, numerically, why the analysis in part 2 would be altered if good milkers with the potential of 20,000 pounds production of milk a year had to be culled to achieve the production reduction under the assumption the farmer plans to resume normal or increased production in 1985.

12

Monopolistic Pricing

If P = price and C = marginal cost, then the index of the degree of monopoly power is $\dfrac{P - C}{P}$.

—*Abba P. Lerner*

As stated in the previous chapter, every seller wants to be a monopolist because it is profitable. But monopoly is not a guarantee that profits will be made. For example, thousands of patented items, many of them very ingenious, are never produced in spite of the monopoly power conferred by law because the demand-cost situation does not appear to be sufficiently favorable or because the necessary entrepreneurial talent is lacking.[1] In a private enterprise system, a basic role of government is establishing and enforcing a body of rules to frustrate the more harmful acts resulting from the universal desire to monopolize. Almost needless to say, those who wish to monopolize use their political power to reduce the effectiveness of antimonopoly forces.

The formula due to Abba Lerner, shown at the beginning of the chapter, captures much of the problem of monopoly as seen by the economist. Monopoly can be said to "drive a wedge" between price and marginal cost—that is, the monopolistic seller can mark up price to a point above his marginal cost. Lerner's index expresses this markup as a percentage of price. He considered this index to be superior to the mere counting of the number of firms in an industry because a firm controlling 100 percent of a commodity with a highly elastic demand (due to very close substitutes) has insignificant monopoly power. On the other hand, a "partial monopoly" of a commodity for which the demand is quite inelastic may be able to raise price sharply by reducing output.[2] At the heart of the problem of defining monopoly carefully is the difficulty of defining a commodity. Substitutability of one good for another, rather than physical

---

[1] A very simple illustration is a burglar alarm featuring the automatic discharge of a blank cartridge when the window is opened. The demand would probably not be sufficient since a house guest wanting some fresh air at night might instead get a heart attack.

[2] Abba P. Lerner, "The Concept of Monopoly and the Measurement of Monopoly Power," *Review of Economic Studies*, June 1943, pp. 157–75.

similarity, is basic. Thus, a hot-dog sandwich at a football game is not really the same good as a similar sandwich on the outside even if it happens to be made just as well.

Where competition is not likely to be an effective regulator of price, as in the case of local electric power production and sale, monopoly may be socially preferable if there are safeguards. Alternative institutional arrangements such as private ownership with public regulation of rates, cooperative ownership, public ownership either with or without regulation by a separate public commission are all possibilities. Selection of the best institutional framework within which to let monopoly operate can make it less objectionable socially.

An interesting example of this idea can be found in the situation of retail liquor stores. In this country it is usually the state or local practice to license such stores, thus holding down their number and securing some public revenue. However, license fees are not closely related to size, profitability, or area within which other stores are excluded. Persons with the political connections to secure licenses at nominal cost from public authorities can often resell the licenses for many times their cost. Indeed, some men are more interested in selling licenses than in the business itself. Alternatively, they may be able to secure monopoly profits from operating the stores. The basic problem is that a valuable business privilege is conferred by representatives of the public at low prices or even at no cost whatever. Since rationing of licenses is not performed by the price system, political favoritism, nepotism, country club or church membership, bribery, or other factors enter as substitutes in their allocation. Scandals connected with the awarding of lucrative television channels dramatize this situation from time to time. The best solution appears to be extension of the price system to the allocation of liquor licenses, television and radio broadcasting privileges, bank charters, and many similar rights. Rights could be awarded in auctions to the highest bidders, thus siphoning off in public revenue a large part of the monopolistic gain that is often available in such fields. Numerous difficulties are inherent in setting up such auctioning schemes—especially in renewing rights—but important social gains, now seldom reaped, are available.

OTHER SOURCES OF MONOPOLY POWER

In addition to licenses and exclusive franchises, firms may secure monopoly power from patents and copyrights, from exclusive locations, from control of raw materials, from well-known brand names or trademarks, from membership in a cartel, from political connections, from agreements with rivals, and in other ways. Workers can secure monopoly power through unionization; professional associations often do so through unduly restrictive licensing and educational practices. (See Case 12–3.) In spite of some check on business firms provided by the federal antitrust laws, as described in Chapter 18, government at all levels appears to do much more to establish and support than to curb monopolistic practices.

FIGURE 12–1   Monopoly Demand—and Marginal Revenue

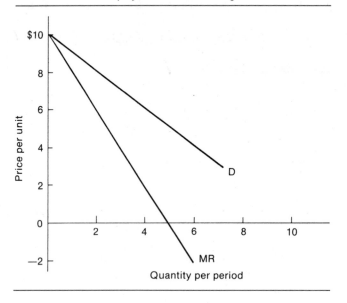

MONOPOLY DEMAND

Whatever the source of monopoly power, its distinctive theoretical feature is a downsloping demand curve facing the individual firm. This allows the firm to have some choice as to what price to charge. Although a downsloping demand curve implies that some substitution of other goods and services for the one under consideration will occur if price is increased, the monopolist is faced with a demand curve that is not affected by rivals' immediate reactions to his price. This can occur because rivals are so remote (e.g., the local power company has no close rival) or because the firm constitutes only a small part of the (broadly defined) industry. For example, a firm manufacturing ballpoint pens may have a distinctive name that it advertises but may not be important enough in the entire pen industry to cause rivals to react to any price change. This situation is often called *monopolistic competition,* although analytically it is difficult to separate clearly from monopoly. In both cases the demand curve facing the firm is downsloping from left to right, but under "monopolistic competition" the slope may be less steep and entry of new firms producing close substitutes may make long-run profits less dependable.[3]

---

[3]See Edward H. Chamberlin, *The Theory of Monopolistic Competition,* 6th ed. (Cambridge: Harvard University Press, 1950). A leading critic of monopolistic competition as a separate field of theory is George J. Stigler, "Monopolistic Competition in Retrospect," *Five Lectures on Economic Problems* (New York: Macmillan, 1949).

MARGINAL REVENUE

A distinctive feature of monopoly analysis is the importance of marginal revenue. Like other marginal concepts in economics, this is the rate of change of an associated total. Marginal revenue is the rate of change in total revenue as sales are altered by a unit (strictly, an infinitesimal unit) per time period. For a competitive firm this is the same as price of the product, but for a monopolist marginal revenue is less than price. This can be seen most easily by considering the following extremely simple demand schedule:

Price	Quantity Demanded	Total Revenue	Marginal Revenue
$10............	0	$ 0	$—
9............	1	9	9
8............	2	16	7
7............	3	21	5
6............	4	24	3
5............	5	25	1
4............	6	24	−1
3............	7	21	−3

Since the quantity changes by one unit from one row to the next lower one, marginal revenue is simply the change in total revenue as an additional unit is demanded. (If quantity increased by more than one unit at a time, the increase in revenue would be divided by the increase in quantity.) Suppose the monopolist knew the demand situation perfectly. He would know that by charging $9 he could sell one unit per period and that if he charged $8 instead, his gain in revenue would be the $8 secured for the second unit less the $1 cut in income from the first unit (since it will be sold at $8 instead of $9.) Hence, marginal revenue of $7 is below the price of $8. The demand schedule and the associated marginal revenue schedule must be understood to represent alternatives at a point in time rather than a series of sales at different prices. What price is actually best from the monopolist's point of view depends on cost and other conditions that will be discussed later.

The foregoing simple demand and marginal revenue schedules are shown graphically in Figure 12–1. Since the demand curve is linear, the marginal revenue curve is also a straight line (with twice as steep a slope). For graphical convenience, units are assumed to be infinitesimal rather than finite in size.

MONOPOLY PRICE FOR EXISTING SUPPLY

The simple demand-marginal revenue tools described above lead immediately to useful analysis of some situations in which monopoly pricing

FIGURE 12–2 Monopoly Pricing—of Existing Supply

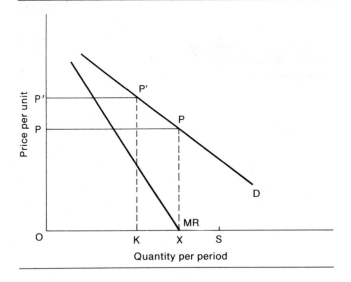

occurs. Suppose there are *OS* seats or spaces available in a stadium or parking lot and that the owner wishes to charge a single profit-maximizing price. Assuming monopoly power, the demand curve facing the seller would be downsloping, as in Figure 12–2. What price should be charged? The answer is *OP*, which is the price at which demand is of unitary elasticity. Sales would be *OX* seats or spaces, where MR equals zero. It is implicitly assumed that it costs nothing extra to allow additional persons or cars to use the existing facilities—which is close to the actual case. Unsold spaces would be *XS* in amount, since it would "spoil the market" to sell all available spaces.

If the existing supply were much smaller, *OK*, the seller would fill the stadium or parking lot and charge *OP'*. This analysis is approximately relevant for a cartel such as in coffee growing. Favorable growing conditions or inability to control productive efforts of individual coffee growers may easily result in a crop (such as *OS*) that is too large for the good of the industry as a whole. Huge bonfires have been used as a way of destroying the excess coffee *(XS)*. In other years, no destruction of supply is needed. The above monopoly analysis is not fully applicable if the commodity under consideration is durable, even though fixed in amount. Price policy must then take into account foregone interest and possibly depreciation, maintenance, and storage costs if the existing stock is not sold immediately. The industry must also contend with "cheating" where some growers are able to receive a higher price for their *entire* crop.

FIGURE 12–3 Monopolistic Optimizing—in Short Run

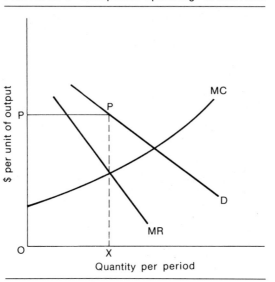

SHORT-RUN OUTPUT AND PRICES

If it is assumed that the monopolist can adjust the rate of production from
existing capacity to meet conditions on the demand side, marginal cost
must be equated to marginal revenue in order to optimize output and
sales. The most profitable single price at which this output can be sold is
found at this quantity on the demand curve.

Figure 12–3 is a graphic representation of short-run output and price
determination under monopolistic market conditions. Optimum output is
OX, where MC = MR.[4] If the monopolist stopped short of this output, he
or she would not be maximizing profit because some additional units
would add more to revenue than to cost (MR > MC). If output were greater
than OX, some units would be adding more to cost than to revenue (MC
> MR). The difficult problem of inventory policy, which exists whenever
output and sale need not be simultaneous, will be omitted from consideration here. Consequently, output and sales per period are considered to
be equal.

Upward or downward shifts in demand and costs will require output
and price adjustments by the monopolist. If entry into the same, or closely
related, markets is difficult, demand is less likely to be eroded even over
a long period of time.

---

[4]This is a sufficient condition provided it is worth operating at all. As the chart is
drawn it is probably worth operating since total variable cost is the area under the MC
curve at quantity OX, and this amount is well below total revenue.

LONG-RUN ADJUSTMENTS

A firm with monopoly power may be maximizing immediate profits but may still be producing on a scale that is too small or too large in view of demand. For example, a motel firm with an advantageous and exclusive location on an interstate highway may be optimizing its situation with respect to the existing facility but be too small to be doing so in a long-run sense. Even assuming that demand will not increase, long-run marginal cost may be below marginal revenue at the existing rate of use, calling for expansion of the facility. The cost of the additional resources needed to construct and operate the new motel units would then be below the additional revenue derivable from the expenditure.

A monopolistic firm in an optimum short-run position but with too small a plant is portrayed in Figure 12–4. While SRMC is equated to MR at output OX, greater profits could be secured through expansion of capacity since LRMC is below SRMC and MR at output OX. If needed expansion is carried out, OX' will be the optimum output and OP' the optimum price. The expansion will shift the short-run marginal cost curve to the right to the position of SRMC'. At output OX' the firm is producing the best output from both a short-run and long-run point of view.

The student may wonder how long-run marginal cost at output OX can be lower than short-run marginal cost when LRMC pertains to *all* resources needed to expand output, while SRMC involves only the short-run variable resources required. That is, such items as opportunity interest on investment and depreciation per time period on new plant are included in LRMC but not in SRMC. The answer is that there are assumed to be substantial economies of scale obtainable by having greater capacity. Marginal costs of labor, electric power, materials, and other short-run variable inputs might fall substantially due to the expansion of capacity, and this reduction can exceed the additional costs attributable to the augmented fixed factor.

CARTELS

The analytical apparatus applicable to a single monopolistic seller is useful also for a combination of firms acting in concert to restrict competition. Such a combination is called a cartel by economists, although many business executives acting legally or illegally to fix noncompetitive prices would be surprised to find the word applied to their own fields. The more spectacular cartels have been international in scope, especially in chemicals and allied products. However, cartel prices are the rule for haircuts within urban areas and are common for dry cleaning, milk, physicians' services, legal services, major brands of gasoline, and some other goods and services.

Cartels that operate over broad geographic areas may allot exclusive marketing territories or assign sales quotas to member firms. It is probably more commonly the case that the cartel fixes price and permits firms to

FIGURE 12–4 Monopolistic Optimizing—May Call for Plant Expansion

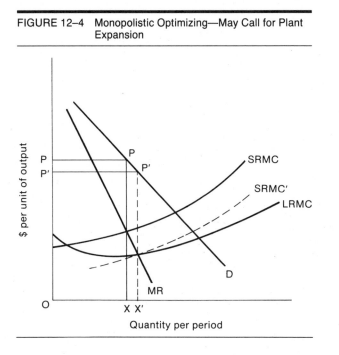

compete for sales. Cartel arrangements are difficult to maintain. Usually "chiseling" generates strains that bring down price or even cause the complete collapse of monopolistic agreements. A basic reason for the strains is that the cartel-determined price usually best fits the needs of a dominant firm, or pleases "representative" companies but is quite poor for some of the firms. Periods of economic recession are especially likely to create disunity by increasing unused capacity. The OPEC cartel has yielded enormous profits, but disunity in the face of an oil glut has reduced its power.

Figure 12–5 pertains to a single firm subject to a cartel-determined price OP_c. The demand curve is of the "rivals do not match" variety, reflecting potential sales by the firm that is under consideration provided that other cartel members hold strictly to the cartel price. The firm of Figure 12–5 has both short-run and long-run incentives to reduce price below OP_c, provided management does not believe its actions will provoke retaliation. (This belief is more likely to be realistic for a relatively small firm.) The immediate establishment of price at P_o, with output and sales of OB, would be better for this firm than the cartel price P_c and sales OA. This is because marginal revenue exceeds SRMC at output OA. However, the firm also has an incentive to add to its capacity because even at price P_o long-run marginal cost is below marginal revenue. Full adjustment—if the firm can get away with it—requires enough expansion to make SRMC' the short-run marginal cost curve, output and sales OC, the price P_o'.

FIGURE 12–5 Incentive to Chisel in a Cartel, Short Run and Long Run

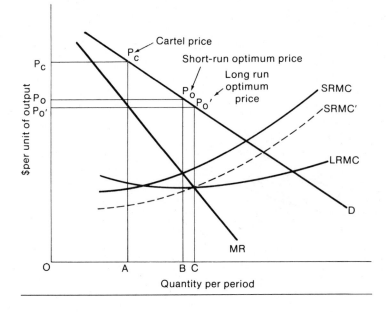

If the firm does not want overtly to violate the cartel price, there are many possibilities for making concessions of a sort less likely to bring retaliation. Some of these devices are special installation and service to customers, money-back guarantees, trading stamps, premiums, high trade-in allowances, entertainment of buyers, and reciprocal purchases at favorable prices.[5] One or more members of a cartel may increase its share of the market so greatly by means of overt or covert price cuts that the more loyal members will cut price or increase concessions to buyers. The process of cartel dissolution may be hastened by the entry of new sellers who remain outside the organization, as some oil-producing nations have done.

The strong arm of government is often enlisted by sellers to strengthen cartel policy. During the depression of the 1930s, the National Recovery Administration encouraged cartel pricing as a (misguided) way of halting price deflation. Even today milk prices are commonly fixed under either federal or state agreements; federal fair trade laws (in periods when they are constitutional) permit manufacturers to set retail prices; and state laws often permit makers of drugs, sporting goods, and other items to make collective decisions on prices. Police power, paid for by the public, is thus enlisted to prevent price cutting, which would aid the public.

---

[5]See the excellent list compiled by the National Recovery Administration in Case 12–2.

GOVERNMENT REGULATION

It has long been public policy in the United States to regulate public utility and transportation rates on the grounds that "natural monopolies" exist that will otherwise be able to earn exorbitant profits. Most economists believe that electric power companies clearly fall in the category of firms that should be regulated.[6] Decreasing long-run cost (as scale of plant increases) can make it technically undesirable for more than one company to furnish the service. An exclusive franchise, secured at nominal cost from public authorities, can make the venture highly profitable. The common compromise is to allow monopoly but to give appointed or elected commissioners power over rates, accounting practices, and other aspects of the operation. It is not clear that the whole process is successful since commissioners are usually more in tune to the desires of the companies than those of the public. Prices of many public utility stocks have increased so much in the past quarter century that the long-run effectiveness of commissions in curbing monopoly profits is questionable. (Utility stocks are frequently "split" in order to reduce their price and not call attention to long-run profitability.)

Once initiated, regulation is difficult to abandon because many investments and other economic decisions are based on situations engendered by the regulation. Also, many well-paid positions are based on the need of both government and firms to acquire detailed knowledge of legal and economic aspects that affect negotiations between regulators and the regulated.

Railroads have been subject to public regulation since the Act to Regulate Commerce of 1887. The most basic provision required that railroad rates in interstate commerce be "just and reasonable." In addition, the Interstate Commerce Commission has had far-reaching jurisdiction over mergers, abandonments, service, and accounting methods in the railroad industry. Since 1980 there has been much deregulation based on academic and other criticism. The low rate of return, particularly for Northeastern railroads has been due in part to excessive regulation. Railroads must perform as an integrated system, so that strong and progressive railroads are dependent on weaker and less well-managed roads. The trend toward deregulation will probably result in railroad mergers producing strong north-south and east-west organizations. There has been an easing of restrictions on rail-affiliated motor carriers and abandonment of track.

Similarly, regulation of the interstate trucking industry has been reduced, especially since the Motor Carrier Act of 1980. Entry into the industry has been eased, although this remains a controversial matter.

---

[6]There are doubters among the best economists, however. George Stigler and Claire Friedland, "What Can Regulators Regulate? The Case of Electricity," *Journal of Law and Economics,*" October 1965, stress that long-run monopoly power is small in this field and that quality of service remains an important variable that is hard to regulate.

Earlier regulations of the ICC sometimes fostered very uneconomical practices, such as trucks being required to remain empty on the backhaul along certain routes.

For many years, Greyhound and Trailways were virtually duopolists in the interstate bus business in the South, Southwest, and some other areas of the country. Since these companies have their own terminals, much duplication of investments could occur in a highly competitive system. The only prominent discounts were those intended to attract passengers from other modes of transportation. Greyhound and Trailways usually had identical fares.[7] Recently there has been some head-to-head competition between these companies and some new entrants, as well as expansion of routes by the big two. Some rural communities, however, have lost their bus service.

AIRLINE DEREGULATION

The most spectacular deregulation has occurred in the airline industry. For many years the Civil Aeronautics Board minimized direct competition by controlling fares and routes. New routes were sometimes sought solely to deny them to other air carriers. Increases in fares were usually approved, but fare cutting was subject to hearings and charges by competitors of predatory pricing and discrimination.[8]

With political support from both major parties, the CAB administrators themselves, especially an economist, Alfred Kahn, effected substantial deregulation even before the Airline Deregulation Act of 1978. Since then the CAB has been abolished, fares are determined by the airlines, and numerous small airlines have entered the field.

Deregulation has ended or diminished many of the problems in a way that economic theory would suggest. When fares cannot be reduced as a competitive weapon, nonprice substitutes in such forms as free or low-cost drinks, pretty stewardesses, and lounges in airports tend to be utilized. With extensive deregulation of railroads, trucking, airlines, and buses, public utility regulation remains as the principal example of continuous control over prices and other matters for very important products.

GEOMETRIC ANALYSIS OF REGULATION

The courts have laid down the principle that regulated firms are entitled to a "fair return on the fair value" of their property. Both types of "fairness" have been extremely controversial and have generated an enormous amount of paper work and expert testimony in rate hearings. A fair annual rate of return to an electric utility company is obviously well below that

---

[7]Elizabeth A. Pinkston, "The Rise and Fall of Bus Regulation," *Regulation*, September/December 1984, p. 47.

[8]Sheldon Richman, "Setting the Airlines Free," *Inquiry*, June 1982, p. 16.

FIGURE 12–6 Possible Goals in Utility Pricing

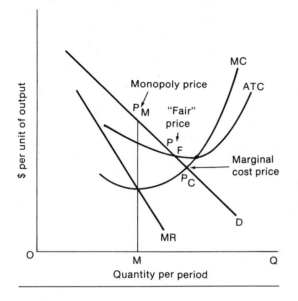

of highly risky fields where principal can easily be lost in a bad period. But exactly what level is appropriate? A common (but still nebulous) view is that it should permit the company to compete successfully in the capital markets. "Fair value" is usually based on some combination of original cost and cost of reproduction, but the details of calculation are manifold and controversial. If original cost is used as the sole basis, investors in utility stocks will not secure the capital gains from inflation and growth that usually benefit other investors. If reproduction cost were the sole basis, there are knotty questions about such matters as land cost in a hypothetical present purchase and present cost of items that are no longer manufactured.

In a general way, some dilemmas of regulation by commission are illustrated in Figure 12–6. If the company were unregulated and interested in maximizing immediate profits, it would charge a monopoly price MP_M (we are disregarding possibilities of quantity discounts). A utility commission trying to follow the "fair return on fair value" dictum would set price at P_F, or at average cost, since the ATC curve should include an alternative return on investments of similar riskiness. However, there is also some merit in price P_C, where the marginal cost curve crosses demand because once the plant capacity is built it can be argued that best use is made of the plant when all units are turned out that could sell at a price that covers only the value of *additional* resources required in production. In the situation pictured in Figure 12–6, interest and depreciation on capital could not be covered at price P_C without a government subsidy (or conceivably by voluntary contributions from users). This makes marginal cost pricing an unlikely actual policy of commissioners.

As already implied, the simple graphic analysis of Figure 12–6 omits many of the variables that would be of real-world importance. If the firm sells electric power, it may use a system of quantity discounts as a means of increasing profits. Buyers with less short-run and long-run elasticity of demand will be charged more than those who have a better opportunity to switch to substitutes. Low rates to large users also secure fuller utilization of electric generating capacity. Also, off-daily peak and off-season rates may be lower as a way of smoothing use of existing capacity over time. A certain amount of quality deterioration can be allowed to occur by a utility company as a way of cutting costs or as a way of dramatizing its alleged need for more revenue. Recently, some electric companies have gone to an "inverted" rate structure, where the rate per kilowatt-hour increases after a specified usage. The "energy crisis," now over, still serves as an excuse for this type of rate.

CASE 12–1
Nixon Price Controls*

An unusual experiment in direct controls was announced by President Nixon on August 15, 1971. The main provision of the executive order was that for a period of 90 days prices, wages, rents, and salaries were to be held at levels no higher than existed in the previous 30-day period. At the end of the 90-day period, Phase II went into effect. A Pay Board and Price Commission were established. The former was supposed to limit average annual wage increases to 5.5 percent, and the latter hoped to reduce the rate of price inflation to 2.5 percent per year compared with an actual 6 percent the previous year.

Organized labor soon decided that the actual effect of Phase II was to hold down wage rates while "permitting profits to soar." On March 22, 1972, the AFL–CIO members resigned from the Pay Board, making it necessary to restructure the group. The already burdened Internal Revenue Service was charged with the task of policing millions of small businesses. The Pay Board and the Price Commission dealt mainly with big corporations and major wage contracts, trying to keep increases within stabilization boundaries. In order to ease the administrative problem, small businesses and governments with 60 or fewer employees were freed from wage and price controls in early May 1972. The action was justified

---

*SOURCE: Cost of Living Council, *Economic Stabilization Program Quarterly Report*, covering the period October 1, 1973, through December 31, 1973.

on the dubious theoretical grounds that the large companies tend to exert price discipline over the small ones.

Phase III, a greatly relaxed program of control, was instituted January 11, 1973. Voluntary restraints were to replace mandatory ones. Self-administration by businesses and unions was supposed to keep price increases in line only with cost increases and to keep wage increases in line within the 5.5 percent guideline. Three "problem areas"—food, health care, and construction wages—were kept under mandatory controls. A construction industry stabilization committee was established.

By the spring of 1973 it was clear that the program was not working as such items as precious metals, copper wire, and transformers rose wildly in price. Food prices rose rapidly, soybeans rising so much in price that exports were curtailed, much to the dismay of the Japanese who rely heavily on the United States for this commodity. As a stop-gap measure in preparation for a renewed mandatory effort in Phase IV, prices were frozen on June 13, 1973, with the freeze being for a maximum of 60 days. The freeze was to apply to food after the first processing, but it also affected poultry, fruit, and vegetable growers since they were unable to sell at profitable prices to processors who were caught in a price-cost squeeze.

Phase IV Controls

Disruptions of supply proved to be so severe that the 60-day price freeze on food and health care lasted only 36 days. The price freeze in the rest of the economy was allowed to last until August 12, 1973, when Phase IV was to take effect. Beef prices were to remain frozen until September 12, 1973.

The basic rule of Phase IV was that prices were to be permitted to rise only as much as business costs went up. This was similar to Phase II rules except that further markups above cost increases were to be disallowed.

The fourth quarter of 1973 demonstrated forcibly the types of problems inevitably faced by government when it attempts to control prices in a comprehensive way. During Phase IV more recognition was given to the very different problems produced by different conditions in the various sectors with such fields as petroleum, chemicals, steel, paper, food, and health services posing especially difficult problems. Also during this period of Phase IV there was a movement out of wage and price controls, with actions occurring such as decontrol of fertilizer, some nonferrous metals, portland cement, and automobiles.

Heavy international demand for many basic materials increased the pressures on price control agencies. This was stimulated by a large decline in the international value of the American dollar. The consequence was formation of a two-tiered pricing system as the controls program did not permit domestic prices to increase at the same rate as foreign prices. The resultant increase in exports of many products reduced available domestic supplies. The increase in the spread between world prices and

---

EXHIBIT 12–1A   Price Spread for Nonferrous
Metals

Excess of World Price over U.S. Price

Material	Jan. 1, 1973	Nov. 30, 1973
Aluminum	18%	38%
Copper	None	65
Lead	None	45
Zinc	1%	332

EXHIBIT 12–1B   Manufacturing and Service Exceptions by Issues, October 1–
December 31, 1973

Issue	Number of Requests
1. Requests to increase prices without the requisite cost justification	23
2. Requests for base period profit margin adjustment	16
3. Requests for price relief to permit a firm to continue to manufacture products in short supply whose prices, under Phase IV regulations, do not justify the continued allocation of corporate resources as a result of insufficient return on investment	14
4. Requests to amend the base price or base cost period	11
5. Requests to pass through cost increases on raw materials immediately without cost justification	10
6. Request for relief from Special Rule No. 1 which prohibited price increases on nonflat rolled steel products and noncarbon sheet and strip steel	10
7. Requests for a separate entity treatment for divisions or subsidiaries in a loss position in order to permit a greater than dollar-for-dollar pass through of cost increases	10
8. Requests for adjustment in productivity factor	4
9. Requests that would allow the purchase of and sale of raw or partially processed materials in scarce supply at prices higher than those allowed under the Phase IV regulations	4
10. Requests that would allow firms to increase prices without prenotification . .	3
11. Requests for relief from the limitations to the maximum price increase that may be implemented on any one item	2
12. Requests for treatment under the Small Business Exemption	1
13. Requests for relief from the provisions of Special Rule No. 2 which permitted price increases for tires and tubes equal to one half of the otherwise cost-justified amounts	1
	109

U.S. prices for nonferrous metals is shown in Exhibit 12–1A. U.S. prices
were held down by means of requiring strict cost justification for price
increases. The pressure buildup was reflected in four actions announced
by the Cost of Living Council on December 6, 1973.

1. The prices of lead, zinc, and lesser nonferrous metals such as tin,
   platinum, and bismuth were exempted from controls.
2. Most nonferrous scrap metals were also exempted.
3. Primary aluminum producers were permitted to use the Phase II

EXHIBIT 12–1C Decisions of Cost of Living Council and Internal Revenue Service Combined, Phase IV, August 12–December 31, 1973

		Number of Decisions		
Sector	Total	Full Approval	Part Approval	Full Denial
Durable goods manufacturing	2,163	1,560	521	82
Nondurable goods manufacturing.	2,019	1,484	478	57
Nonmanufacturing	182	143	30	9
Total	4,364	3,187	1,029	148

base price of 29 cents per pound compared with the Phase IV base price of 25 cents per pound.

4. Primary copper producers were permitted a base price of 68 cents per pound compared to the recent price of 60 cents per pound.

During the difficult October 1–December 31, 1973, period the Cost of Living Council received an increased number of requests for exceptions. Exhibit 12–1B shows the "issues" involved in these requests by the manufacturing and service sector.

The difficulty that price control agencies have in denying applications for price relief is shown by the data of Exhibit 12–1C.

Questions

1. If "cost justification" is required for price increases by U.S. metal producers, why are domestic prices likely to fall below world prices? (Consider the role of demand in price determination.)

2. Comment carefully on the "issues" shown in Exhibit 12–1B. One problem in control is the difference between accounting cost measurement and the more relevant ideas of economic cost. Comment on this problem.

3. Why is it practically inevitable that most applications for price relief be approved rather than denied?

4. Write a few paragraphs summarizing the work of a system of uncontrolled prices emphasizing the informational advantages possessed by decentralized decision makers.

CASE 12–2 _____
Hundreds of Ways to Chisel on Price

Under the NRA codes, business executives were frequently forbidden to cut prices. As a result, numerous forms of evasion sprang up. The following list of concessions designed to influence sales was prepared by the Division of Industrial Economics of the National Recovery Administration:

1. Concessions primarily related to the time of buyer's payment:
   Discounts.
   "Terms" and "conditions" of sale or payment.
   Credit practices.
   Credit terms.
   Cash discounts.
   Periods of free credit.
   Interest rate beyond free credit period.
   Datings.
   Seasonal datings.
   Installment sales.
   Deferred payment.
   Anticipation of bills.
   Sales to delinquent accounts.
   Sales not contingent upon buyer's credit standing.
   Payment due when money received from other sources.
   Retained percentages.

2. Concessions primarily related to risks of buyer:
   Guarantees.
   Price guarantees.
   Contracts for deferred delivery not subject to price change.
   Price offer not subject to change.
   Advance notification of price change.
   Delaying acceptance of order.
   Options.
   Agreements indefinite as to time or quantity.
   Offers without time limit.
   Offers not expiring within specified period of time.
   Offers without withdrawal provisions.
   Guarantees against defective goods.
   Product guarantees.
   Product guarantees against other than defective merchandise.
   Uniform product guarantees specified in code.
   Guarantees in excess of manufacturer's warranty (distributing and fabricating codes).
   Maintenance guarantees.
   Adjusting incorrect shipments.
   Accepting return of merchandise.
   Accepting return of obsolete, discontinued, or "unsalable" merchandise.
   Exchanging merchandise.
   Accepting return of other than defective merchandise.
   Repurchase agreements.
   "Money-back" agreements.
   Sales subject to trial.
   Sales on approval.
   Shipments without order.

Sales on consignment or memorandum.
Storing goods with customer.
Display for direct sale in customer's store.
Renting or leasing industry products.
Resale guarantees.
Agreeing that payment be governed by sales of secondary product.
Accepting orders for specific jobs before customer secures award.
Guaranteeing accounts due customer.
"Compensation of customer for business losses."
Unilateral agreements (buyer not bound).
Contracts containing penalty clauses.
Contracts not subject to adjustment necessitated by noncontrollable factors.
Assuming liability for nonperformance caused by noncontrollable factors.
Assuming liability for damage to buyer's drawings or equipment caused by noncontrollable factors.
Assuming liability for errors in plans or specifications furnished or approved by buyer.
Assuming liability for consequential damages.
Assuming liability for patent infringement.
Failure to give advance notice of discontinued lines.

3. Concessions primarily related to supplying additional goods:[9]
Any gratuities.
Free deals.
Premiums.
Sales of other or additional goods at reduced prices.
Combination sales.
Combination offers.
Coupons.
Samples.
Scrip books.
Prices.
Sales promotion awards.
Containers.
Special containers.
Labels.
Special labels.
Special equipment.
Accessories.
Certain advertising material.
Display materials.
Printed matter (other than advertising material).

4. Concessions rendered buyer through use of seller's employees or property:
Any unusual service.
Providing sales help.
Demonstrating.

---

[9]To modernize this list, it is important to add trading stamps!

Estimating.

Furnishing drawings.

Furnishing plans and specifications.

Furnishing surveys and formulas.

Installation and erection.

Inspections.

Furnishing unusual processing services specified in codes.

Stamping or markings.

Repair and maintenance.

Reconditioning.

Engineering services.

Handling.

Crating or packing.

Repacking.

Delivery service by seller's trucks.

Warehousing and storage.

Lending of equipment.

Permitting retention of trade-in equipment.

5. Concessions rendered buyer through financial assistance or favors:

Favors.

Entertaining.

Patronizing publications in which buyer is interested.

Participating in group showing.

Gifts.

Gifts to organizations (in which buyer is interested).

Paying buyer's personal expenses.

Paying permit or inspection fees of buyers.

Paying customer's insurance.

Paying customer's advertising expenses for products other than member's.

Assuming reversed telephone or telegraph charges.

Assisting customer to obtain used products for trade-ins.

Assisting customer to find purchaser for used products.

Subsidizing or financing buyer.

Employing customers, employees, relatives, associates.

Purchase of buyer's capital stock.

Financing payments due customers.

6. Concessions related to manner and/or time of shipment:

Split shipments.

Shipments smaller than specified minimum.

Tolerance in time of shipment.

Deferred delivery.

7. Concessions through payment or diversion of commissions or fees to customer:

Payment of commissions or fees by members to buyers.

Payment of commissions or fees by members to other than bona fide or controlled sales representatives.

Payment of commissions or fees by members to purchasing agents compensated by buyers.

Payments of commissions or fees by agents of members to buyers.

Splitting of commissions or fees by agents of members with agents of buyers without buyer's knowledge.

Splitting of commissions or fees by members or their agents with buyers or their agents.

Payment of brokerage to other than bona fide brokers.

8. Concessions through allowances or payments for value rendered by buyer:

Allowances

Trade-in allowances.

Advertising allowances.

Catalogue allowances.

Distribution service allowances.

Container allowances.

Installation allowances.

Allowance for further processing.

Maintenance or repair allowance.

Rental allowances for space hired.

Allowances on supplies furnished by purchaser for production of product ordered.

Carriage allowances when buyer receives goods at factory.

Allowance for special service.

Label allowances.

Purchasing from buyer.

Renting from buyer.

9. Concessions through acceptance of competitor's materials from buyers:

Exchange of own for competitor's products.

Purchase of competitor's products from customer.

10. Concessions through sale of substandard or obsolete goods:

Sale of seconds.

Sale of used goods.

Sale of damaged goods.

Sale of rebuilt or overhauled goods.

Sale of demonstrators.

Sale of obsolete goods.

Sale of discontinued lines.

Willful manufacture of substandard products.

Sale of returns.

Sale of scrap.

Sale of chaff.

Sale of culled goods.

Sale of surplus stock.

11. Concessions granted during performance contrary to provisions of agreement:

Rebates.

Departure from credit of contract.

Settlement of old accounts at less than full value.

Permitting improper deductions when buyer remits.

Permitting buyer's cancellation or repudiation.

Substitution of higher quality or greater quantity of goods.

Substitution of new contract at lower price.
Receipting bills before payment.
Extending or exceeding contract.
Collateral agreement not to enforce part of contract.
Departure from delivery date of contract.
Retroactive settlement or adjustments.

12. Acceptance of forms of payment in which concessions may be concealed:
Accepting securities.
Accepting buyer's capital stock.
Accepting goods from buyer.
Accepting real or personal property.
Accepting negotiable instruments.
Accepting other than lawful money.
Accepting credit transferred from one buyer to another.
Selling for customer account and accepting proceeds for credit.
Accepting form of payment other than specified in code.
Accepting rental payments as part payment on purchases.
Accepting deposit made to another manufacturer.
Assignments (of receivables, etc.).

13. Types of agreements, offers, invoicing, etc., by means of which concessions may be concealed:
Oral agreements.
Oral offers.
Oral appraisals.
Oral orders.
False billing.
False orders.
False receipts.
False agreements.
False offers.
Delayed billing.
Misdated invoices.
Misdated contracts.
Misdated orders.
Misdated offers.
Misdated receipts.
Invoices omitting terms of sale.
Invoices omitting date of shipment.
Invoices omitting specifications.
Invoices omitting other specified detail.
Agreements omitting terms of sale.
Agreements omitting date of shipment.
Agreements omitting specifications.
Agreements omitting other specified detail.
Offers omitting terms of sale.
Offers omitting date of shipment.
Offers omitting specifications.
Offers omitting other specified detail.
Orders omitting terms of sale.
Orders omitting date of shipment.

Orders omitting specifications.
Orders omitting other specified detail.
Split billing.
Lump-sum offers.
Unitemized billing.
Orders not subject to member's acceptance.
Auction sales.
14. Types of agreements, offers, invoicing, etc., primarily designed to prevent the concealing of concessions:
Uniform contract form.
Uniform order form.
Uniform bid or quotation form.
Standard invoice form.
Standard leasing form.
Form of contract.

Questions

1. What is the general significance of the extensive NRA list to the problem of maintaining a cartel price? Explain in some detail.

2. The list is also relevant to the opposite problem—government price control to attempt to hold down prices. Explain by referring to the problem of renting an apartment under rent control.

CASE 12–3
Medical Advertising*

The Broward County Medical Association, a Florida corporation with its office and principal place of business in Fort Lauderdale, signed a consent agreement after the Federal Trade Commission initiated an investigation into certain of its acts and practices. This consent order was an admission by the BCMA of all the jurisdictional facts set forth in the complaint. It did not constitute an admission that the law had been violated but was signed for settlement purposes only.

The complaint included the following: the BCMA has acted in combination with at least some of its members "to foreclose, frustrate, and eliminate competition among medical doctors in Broward County" by:

a. Prohibiting its members from truthfully advertising their fees and services.

b. Coercing individual members into abandoning their efforts to advertise truthfully in these regards.

---

*SOURCE: Case is from Federal Trade Commission, *Decisions, Findings, Opinions, and Orders,* January 1, 1982–June 30, 1982, No. 99. Docket C-3091, Complaint June 28, 1982–Decision June 28, 1982.

    c. Adopting and implementing written and unwritten codes of ethics that prohibit efforts by its members to advertise truthfully with respect to such matters as fees and services, whether there is Medicare assignment of benefits, whether credit cards are accepted, professional training and experience, and knowledge of languages other than English.

    d. Publishing statements by some of its officials that advertising is unethical and threatening disciplinary action against members who advertise, including advertising in the Yellow Pages of telephone directories.

The FTC investigation was carried out under section 5 of the Federal Trade Commission Act of 1914 which declared unfair methods of competition or unfair or deceptive acts or practices to be illegal.

The consent agreement required that each new member of the BCMA be furnished a copy of the complaint and the Order, that the Order be given as much prominence in the BCMA Record as feature articles, and remove from its *Code of Ethics*, its constitution, and bylaws any policy statement inconsistent with the Order. Further, the BCMA was required to make periodic written reports to the Federal Trade Commission detailing its actions to comply with the consent agreement.

Questions

1. What is the basic motivation of a medical association or society when it suppresses advertising beyond the mere listing of names, specialties, and addresses?
2. Why is "Medicare assignment" and knowledge of a foreign language especially important in South Florida?
3. Conduct research in order to determine how much restriction of medical advertising exists in your own state or Province.
4. Also investigate and describe the relation of medical associations or societies to Blue Cross/Blue Shield medical insurance.

CASE 12–4
De Beers and the CSO*

In early 1985, Harry Oppenheimer stepped down as Chairman of De Beers Consolidated Mines. Ltd., to end a family stewardship extending from the

---

*source: The quoted *Fortune* article is in the September 6, 1982, issue. The Epstein citations are from "Diamonds Are Not Forever," *Penthouse,* June 1983. Mr. Thompson is quoted from the *New York Times,* March 3, 1985. Part of this case is reprinted from Forbush and Menz, "Study Guide and Problems to Accompany *Economics* by Lipsey, Steiner, and Purvis," 7th ed. (New York: Harper & Row, 1984).

late 19th century. Through its subsidiary in London, the Central Selling Organization (CSO), De Beers controlled over 80 percent of the world's diamond trade. It had been perhaps the world's most successful long-lived cartel but had faced difficulties after 1980 when De Beers' profits had peaked at $1.1 billion and its stock price was $12 a share. The resolution of some of these problems is described below.

But difficulties for Oppenheimer's successor, Julian O. Thompson, remained as the low 1985 stock price of $5.50 a share indicated. He stated "what the whole diamond industry needs is continuity to bring the business through a very difficult time." He explained the lure of the gems in terms of beauty and their gift-giving symbolism as much of the durability of their value—"We have never sold diamonds as investments per se." Neither has De Beers ever lowered their prices, preferring to stockpile rather than to devalue the product. Particular problems were the continued high interest cost of keeping stockpiles off the market and of maintaining a relationship with the Soviet Union under which the Russians did not compete in the rough diamond market but had in 1984 sold large quantities of polished stones on the Antwerp market.

A long-term threat was the competitively produced man-made gem, the cubic zirconium, which had been perfected to be virtually indistinguishable in appearance from the diamond. The antiapartheid movement in the United States, by far the largest market for small diamonds, could give De Beers little comfort. While the stated policies of De Beers were for integrated mines where workers could live nearby with their families, South African authorities allowed no more than 3 percent of black mine laborers to be permanent residents.

In September 1982, less than two years after De Beers posted a record of $2.8 billion in sales of diamonds and $1.1 billion in profits, *Fortune* ran an article entitled "De Beers and the Diamond Debacle." Another commentator, Edward J. Epstein, was more flamboyant, stating, "The cartel has lost control of the diamond market and the final collapse of diamonds is months not years away."

The economic issue was whether De Beers, as the dominant firm in an international cartel, the CSO, or Central Selling Organization, could keep the quantity demanded and quantity supplied in equilibrium at prices far above the cost of production.

From the late 19th century, when De Beers controlled the only abundant source of diamonds in the "volcanic" pipes of South Africa, De Beers was successful in contracting to buy up the output of new producers, mostly in neighboring countries. Demand grew quickly, largely because young American males lived up to the expectation that intended brides should be furnished with bestoned rings as demonstration both of depth of affection and financial competence.

Strategies for maintaining prices and profits varied with outside influences. It was necessary to shut down production for four years in the Great Depression and to stockpile the output of outside producers. A major postwar problem was the entry of Russian supplies. While the Russians were willing to sell through the CSO, by 1981 the Siberian mines were accounting for nearly one quarter of the CSO supplies, a share that otherwise would have been available to African producers. A fortunate development was the successful introduction into Japan of the American engagement ring. With the help of a massive De Beers advertising campaign, the proportion of Japanese brides receiving diamond rings increased from 5 percent in 1967 to 60 percent in 1977.

The cause of the proximate crisis in the 1980s was the arrival on a large scale of the investor/speculator who fancied diamonds with their long record of gradual price appreciation as an appropriate source of profit during times of inflation. The price of a one-carat, quality diamond was bid up from its level of a few thousand dollars in the early 1970s to over $60,000 in 1980. This high price proved unsustainable since the profitability of holding diamonds depended upon continued annual appreciation by at least as much as the high interest rates of the time. Despite the accumulation by De Beers of $1.4 billion in diamond inventories and cutbacks in production, the price plummeted to the $8,000–$18,000 range in the early 1980s and speculative demand, which represented about one quarter of the total demand, evaporated. A new Australian discovery increased prospective supplies by 25 million carats a year. Fortunately for De Beers, most of the output promised to be in industrial diamonds and De Beers was able to contract for all but 5 percent of Australian diamond production.

In the early 1980s, De Beers was hopeful of increasing the market for the larger stones with advertising based on the slogan " . . . a diamond of a carat or more, there's only one in a million." (In 1981, the average diamond in an engagement ring weighed only 0.29 carats; it had been 25 percent bigger five years before.)

Fortune felt De Beers might have the resources to restore the status of the diamond as a precious stone whose value would gradually appreciate. In contrast, Epstein concluded that "as De Beers realizes it can no longer afford its multi-billion dollar illusion of scarcity, diamonds will be recognized for what they are—brilliant, glittering, and exceedingly common pebbles." The stock market of mid-1983 (when the Dow-Jones average was at a peak of about 1250) took the middle ground: De Beers stock was selling on the over-the-counter market at $9, substantially over its 1982 low of $4.

Under the heading "Restored Luster," The *Wall Street Journal*, July 7, 1983, expressed guarded optimism for the De Beers-led cartel, though the production cuts were deep and painful. It felt the rough treatment of Zaire (who left the cartel) would keep other African producers in line. De Beers helped drive the prices of industrial diamonds (Zaire's specialty) down by two thirds. Zaire then decided to rejoin the CSO. It also speculated that the Soviet Union, a major independent producer, would opt for long-run price stability at high prices over independent action that would maximize production and possibly be more lucrative in the short run. Finally, De Beers had increased its own prices by modestly more than the CPI rise in 1973–85 and never cut the official cartel price even during the speculative decline.

Questions

1. Draw an appropriate monopoly pricing model for De Beers and the CSO. The MC should be low relative to the price but would eventually rise at high quantities.

2. Illustrate the temptation to "chisel" on price by members of the cartel, particularly if they are convinced that De Beers will follow a policy of maintaining real price.

3. Does an attempt to maintain real price (i.e., allow the prices to go up by roughly the amount of inflation) seem to be an appropriate long-run policy for De Beers?

4. Show what happened to the demand for diamonds when speculators came in expecting higher prices; what happened when it became clear that increases in prices produced by speculation could no longer be maintained?

5. The diamond cartel has been successful far longer than any other international cartel. How might the nature of the product help in maintaining the cartel? How might it eventually hurt, especially in view of the decline in birth rates in the United States, Japan, and other developed countries?

6. How well De Beers has done in restoring the mystique of "a diamond is (valuable) forever" might be judged by comparing its present stock price relative to that of the Dow Jones with the figure given for 1985. Check it (you will find De Beers in the NASDAQ listings).

CASE 12–5
Selected Problems in Monopoly Pricing

A. The Proverbial Ever-Flowing Spring

1. A firm owns a roadside spring with a flow of 10,000 gallons a day. The public perceives the water as unique. The daily demand may be estimated as $P = \$5 - 0.0005Q$. All costs are fixed (customers bring their own containers). What is the profit-maximizing price and quantity?

2. Rumors spread about the curative powers of the water for hangnail, herpes 2, and hepatitis B so that the demand shifts to $P = \$12 - 0.0005Q$. What should the price now become?

B. Contrasting Monopoly with Competition

The data below relate to a monopolist and the daily quantities of its product:

Output	Total Cost	Price	Quantity Demanded	MR
0	$20	$20	0	0
1	24	18	1	18
2	27	16	2	24
3	32	14	3	
4	39	12	4	
5	48	10	5	
6	59	8	6	

1. Calculate the profit maximizing price and output.
2. Now assume competition and a market price of $9. What is the best output for the short run? Make a long-run prediction.

C. OPEC as the Not So Dominant Firm

Assume these are approximations of the estimates that have faced OPEC in their 1985 meetings:

The supply curve for non-OPEC nations could be approximated by the formula $Q = 25 + 0.4P$, where Q equals millions of barrels per day and P = price per barrel in dollars; the demand curve for world oil is approximated by $Q = 70 - 0.6P$; the marginal cost of OPEC is taken as a constant at $10 (this $10 includes an opportunity cost of the discounted present value of future recovery as well as the low out-of-pocket costs); the OPEC nations have a capacity of 30 million barrels per day and have run into difficulties restricting output to 16 million per day.

1. Calculate the price OPEC should charge and the quantity it should produce on the basis of this data. Remember the demand for the dominant firm is simply the world demand less the estimated supply of others.
2. Contrast this with 1980 when OPEC produced 30 million barrels and the price approached $40. A world demand of $85 - 0.6P$ and supply for non-OPEC oil of $15 + 0.4P$ are consistent with this price and quantity. Show diagrammatically what occurred using the short-run supply and demand curves for 1980 and 1985.
3. Why is a cartel like OPEC in a weaker position than a single unitary firm?

13

Price Discrimination and
Price Differentials

> The act of selling the same article, produced under a single control, at different prices to different buyers, is known as price discrimination.
> —*Joan Robinson*

Discrimination is one of those words in the English language that has both highly favorable and unfavorable connotations. Contrast the following: Mr. Johnson is a man of quick mind, impeccable tastes, and keen discrimination; Mr. Robinson advocates discrimination on grounds of race, religion, and national origin. Mr. Johnson's discrimination, an ability to perceive and act on distinctions, seems praiseworthy; Mr. Robinson's discrimination, with implications of unjust favoritism in treatment of people entitled to equal treatment, is condemned. The economist's view of price discrimination initially is a neutral one. The usefulness of price discrimination depends on whether it contributes to or detracts from the achievement of such goals as efficiency in the allocation of resources. The current legal view starts out by making it unlawful "to discriminate in price between different purchasers of commodities of like grade and quality" and in effect embraces the adverse concept of discrimination, but it then goes on to indicate it is only those differentials that will probably have adverse effects on competition or competitors that are discriminations that will be considered unlawful.

PRICE DIFFERENTIALS AND DISCRIMINATION

The existence of a price differential is neither a necessary nor a sufficient condition for the presence of price discrimination, which also depends on costs. Before 1973, when the Organization of Petroleum Exporting Countries (OPEC) was not powerful, the oil industry was fairly competitive and regular gasoline usually sold for less than 40 cents per gallon in the United States. Filling stations often sold a composite product consisting of gasoline, trading stamps (or direct premiums of low value), and a chance in a lottery. While no price differential existed, the economist would detect price discrimination since some motorists were interested only in the gasoline while others also made use of the stamps or premiums and/or carefully watched the winning lottery numbers. (The usefulness of lotteries in bringing back customers has recently made them popular in the grocery business.)

Similarly, persons who buy merchandise for cash are usually discriminated against compared with credit card buyers in that there are extra costs to the seller associated with the latter. A limited number of sellers now are offering discounts for cash purchases as a way of eliminating or reducing the discrimination (and attracting custom). The basic theoretical point is that price discrimination among persons who buy from a given seller exists when price differentials are not equal to the difference in marginal cost of serving customers.

The strong move toward self-service gasoline pumps has provided a handy new device for discriminatory pricing in that self-service gasoline is often reduced in price by more than the cost saving to the station. In part, this pricing system derives its usefulness to sellers by making it possible to display clearly only the lowest price. In part, it is price discrimination in favor of younger motorists who are more likely to be willing to pump their own gasoline, check the oil, etc. The lower average income of persons interested in self-service fits well the theory that profits can be increased by charging lower prices in submarkets where demand is more elastic.

ELEMENTS OF MONOPOLY AND MARKET IMPERFECTION AS REQUISITES FOR DISCRIMINATION

The conditions of equilibrium under competition are those under which price discrimination is impossible. Only one price known to all buyers and sellers exists for a product. Each firm is confronted by a horizontal demand curve at the going price that constitutes its MR. Only when the demand curve is downward sloping to the right as in monopoly does the firm have price options. The use of this perfectly competitive model has led to useful predictions for many markets in which its assumptions are only approximated. So far as price discrimination is concerned, the competitive model's usefulness is in highlighting the departures from it that make discrimination possible; lack of knowledge of prices by consumers; real or imagined distinctions in product quality that make some people willing to pay more than others for a product; dispersion of producers and consumers over geographical space that results in disparities in the additional costs of serving particular customers; the existence of selling costs that reflect possibilities of shaping people's demands toward a particular product; and unlike size and importance of buyers.

SEPARATION OF MARKETS AS A REQUISITE
FOR PRICE DISCRIMINATION

If price differentials are going to be used, separation of the markets for which the different prices are to be charged is essential. This separation involves two elements: first, a decision upon the classifications of customers who will receive the different prices; and second, cost barriers between the markets that will prevent the resale of lower priced units in higher priced markets. This latter provision is, of course, unnecessary if the products are personal services that could not be resold. The used tonsillectomy and appendectomy markets are nonexistent.

In the next section it will be pointed out that for price discrimination to be profitable, the elasticities of demand for the product must be different between the classification of customers that is to receive a higher price and the one that is to receive a lower price. It is worth keeping this point in mind in this discussion of the basis on which markets might be separated. For example, the vendor of a hair shampoo might establish a higher price for blondes as against brunettes. Although this distinction would make it possible to identify the customers (the identification may change from day to day; in this day, "only the hair dresser knows for sure"), there is no reason to think that the basic demands of these groups for shampoos differ in price elasticity. The only justification for a differential in this case would be a difference in cost of production and distribution of the product for different customers. The following list is representative of criteria that reflect classifications based on either a different value of service or a different cost of providing the product or services.

1. Apparent income or wealth of buyer. The man or woman who drives a large car may be charged more for an identical repair job than the owner of a more modest vehicle. The sale of a larger house typically involves a larger commission to the real estate agent since these fees are usually computed at a percentage of sales price and may not reflect an increased effort on his or her part. Medical doctors, particularly surgeons, may discriminate in price on the basis of income, or a higher fee may be charged if the patient has medical insurance.

2. Time of purchase. Prices are frequently different to those who buy at various times of the day or at different seasons of the year. As later discussion and the Urban Electric case (13–2) indicate, the cost to firms may differ greatly depending upon the time the product is offered. Electric utilities now typically have lower demands in the winter so that current could be provided for heating with a very small additional cost, whereas electricity used for air conditioning would necessitate an increase in plant with capital costs to the company. The telephone companies similarly face a daytime peak and are willing to offer low long-distance rates at night when excess capacity is available and additional costs are very small.

3. Quantity purchased by individual buyer. There are obvious packaging and distribution economies in the sale of multiple units at once, and quantity discount structures may be primarily tailored to match the marginal costs involved in transactions of a different size. As long as the difference in price is reflected in such cost differences, such discounts would be nondiscriminatory. Differences in the intensity of demand may also be reflected. Large customers may well be able economically to manufacture the good or service for themselves; for example, a large industrial firm could choose to generate its own electricity. Thus, the seller may be tempted to offer the services at a differential greater than his or her cost savings. Such price differences as are not justified by cost differences may be challenged under the Robinson-Patman Act.

4. Age or other personal characteristics of buyers. Youthful and aged persons sometimes receive lower prices than those of intermediate ages. In part, this is a way of discriminating according to purchasing power since incomes tend to be lower among the young and the old. The price of motion pictures and rates in amusement parks exemplify discrimination in favor of children. Group life insurance plans, when they provide for payment of the same premium by persons of all ages, discriminate in favor of the older participants for whom mortality rates are higher. The airlines have introduced family fare plans that permit wives and children to accompany the head of the family at reduced fares. Complete market separation may be impossible in some of these cases; a small 14-year-old may receive the 12-year-old price; the executive's secretary could receive the family discount.

5. Newness of customer's business. Remarkable price concessions have been made by magazines to enlist new subscribers who presumably have not built up habits favorable to using the particular publication. Graduate students often receive lower subscription rates on professional journals than do regular buyers. On the other hand, long-time customers may receive informal concessions from dealers to whom they are well known. Such informal concessions have helped neighborhood appliance dealers to compete on price with discount or mail-order houses.

6. Use of the commodity. A leading illustration of this method or market separation has occurred in the milk market. Class I, or fluid milk—that is, milk that is sold as fresh bottled milk—commands a higher price than Class II, or surplus milk, which is used for processed milk products such as ice cream, evaporated milk, and dried milk powder. Since the milk is identical, this kind of price discrimination requires record keeping by the milk dealers and processors and has usually been successful only when aided by government regulation. The apparatus required for this type of discrimination emphasizes the first requisite for price discrimination, that is, an element of monopoly power.

7. Location of buyer. The geographic separation of buyers often provides a convenient basis for price discrimination. Local producers of products with substantial transportation costs enjoy a cost advantage with customers located nearer their plants than that of any competitors. They may well be able to realize a higher effective price at their mills from these customers than they could from shipments to distant buyers on which they must absorb freight. Later in the chapter the discriminatory aspects of "basing-point" pricing will be discussed. Geographic location as a basis for discrimination is apparent in many international transactions. Producers in one country may sell their product abroad at lower prices than in the domestic market. When a foreign country encourages this process, Americans have termed it "dumping," but the agricultural policies of the United States frequently use a two-price technique with the lower foreign price being designed to get rid of undesired surpluses.

8. Market function.   The company may choose to sell a commodity at different prices depending upon the economic function that the customer serves. Spark plugs sold to automobile manufacturers as original equipment carry lower prices than those sold to wholesale distributors. The price to wholesalers may be lower than sales made directly to retailers.

9. Product quality as a method of market separation.   Strictly speaking, the price differentials and price discriminations that have been discussed refer to identical products. A very similar strategy to that of price discrimination is to seek to appeal to different segments of the market by offering products that differ slightly in quality but substantially in price. For example, the manufacturer of a branded aspirin could sell it at a high price to those customers who desired the additional assurance of a quality reputation. At the same time it could bottle the identical aspirin and sell it to a drug or grocery chain at a very much lower price. Case 13–4 takes up the important problem of generic and brand name drugs. The price differential would be quite evident; whether or not economic price discrimination existed would have to be established by a difficult calculation as to the marginal costs of advertising. Many consumers are familiar with the various options they have in purchasing automobiles or appliances, options that range from a "stripped" model to a highly deluxe model. Frequently, the markup of price over cost is significantly less for the stripped model that incorporates the same basic mechanism as the more luxurious lines. Such models allow the manufacturer both to attract the unusually price conscious among the public and to establish a promotional price that will bring many customers into the store. In the less ethical uses of this strategy, the stripped model may be considered "nailed to the floor." The salesperson is expected to trade the customer up to higher priced models by stressing the desirable extra features.

PERFECT PRICE DISCRIMINATION

It is instructive to consider the extreme case of "perfect" price discrimination in order to understand the motivation behind more practicable

FIGURE 13–1 Perfect Price Discrimination Contrasted with Single
Monopoly Price

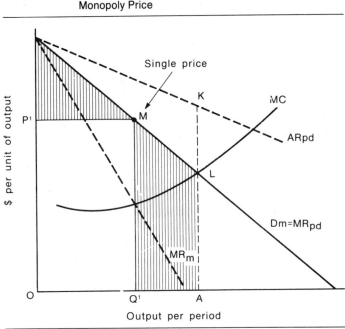

schemes of discrimination. Whereas the usual assumption employed in
the economic theory of monopoly is that the *single* most profitable price
under existing conditions is charged, the notion of perfect price discrimination is that every unit be sold at a *different* price and that this be the
highest price at which that unit will be purchased.

The usual geometrical demonstration of perfect price discrimination
is given in Figure 13–1, which contrasts it with one-price monopoly pricing. It should be noted that the demand curve becomes the marginal
revenue curve under perfect discrimination. This follows from the assumption that each unit sold is independent of the others; that is, to sell
an additional unit, monopolists do not have to take a lower price on the
earlier units. Whatever price they get for a particular unit adds exactly
that amount to their revenue. The average revenue curve lies above the
marginal revenue curve, since whatever quantity is considered along the
horizontal axis, the earlier units in this quantity will bring a higher price
than the later ones and hence will hold the average price above the price
at the margin. Maximum profit is secured by selling OA units, where
marginal cost equals marginal revenue. Further sales would not be profitable because more would be added to cost than to revenue. Total revenue
would amount to OA times AK.

Total revenue under perfect discrimination is also equal to OP_1MQ_1,
the revenue under single-price monopoly, plus the shaded areas. The
vertically shaded area to the left of M represents the additional amounts

paid for units that would have been sold at price M under a one-price system. The shaded area to the right of M is revenue from units that could not be sold profitably under a one-price system.

It should be noted that perfect price discrimination is a theoretical model that is virtually impossible to follow fully in an actual sales situation. Still, it demonstrates vividly how additional revenues can be secured if it is possible to charge different prices for different units of output according to the maximum that anyone will pay. Each unit is sold for the highest price that the "traffic will bear."

Substantial approaches to perfect price discrimination may be found in an oriental bazaar and in the retail automobile market, when the seller is willing to spend time to determine the best price she can get. (In the case of the automobile this may hinge primarily on the trade-in price of an old car.) Although a bazaar is highly competitive in general, any particular vendor has a certain amount of monopoly power if the buyer is not fully informed regarding quality and alternative prices, and the poorly informed tourist may consequently pay a high price. The well-informed buyer may pay a price as low as the seller's marginal cost, as indicated by the theoretical model. Another case in which the perfect discrimination model is instructive may be that of patented capital equipment. A manufacturer may set up a schedule of charges based on the savings made possible with the equipment. In order to avoid the resale problem, the manufacturer may have to lease rather than sell the equipment.

A theoretical problem with no easy answer is involved in the theory of perfect price discrimination. Although Figure 13–1 identifies an optimum single price as well as the numerous prices under perfect discrimination, the illustration is approximate only. The *same* demand curve cannot be used for showing both pricing policies because more purchasing power is extracted from buyers when there is price discrimination. This will decrease the demand facing other sellers to a greater extent than if a single price had been charged. For example, a strong bargainer among sellers in a bazaar could reduce the sales of other vendors by his large take from naive tourists. This is part of the difficult *ceteris paribus* problem in all economic theory, namely, what to hold constant when engaged in any particular analysis.[1]

Instead of attempting to charge the maximum that the demand will bear for each unit, the firm with some monopoly may divide customers by some identifiable characteristics. Examples are adults and children in a theater, city slickers and "good ole boys" in Georgia, or women and men applying for credit. To a lesser extent, the *ceteris paribus* problem just mentioned also mars the logic of price discrimination theory even when as few as two separate prices are charged. Fortunately, even imperfect theory may be much better than none at all.

---

[1]A good discussion is that of James M. Buchanan, "Ceteris Paribus; Some Notes on Methodology," *Southern Economic Journal*, January 1958, pp. 259–70.

FIGURE 13–2   Price Discrimination—Fixed Supply

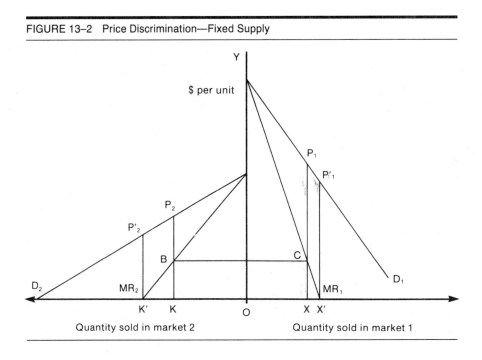

FIXED SUPPLY CASE

It was pointed out in Chapter 12 that a monopolistic seller may have on hand a commodity or service that is fixed in amount for the time period under consideration and that is not storable. Parking spaces, seats in a theater or stadium, and seating capacity of an airliner are examples of the fixed supply case. While the seats or spaces are themselves durable, their availability for a particular attraction or flight is limited, and their services are perishing so far as that particular demand is concerned. In Chapter 12 a single optimum price was assumed; in the present discussion it is assumed instead that the monopolist is able to separate the market into two segments for different treatment. Marginal cost is zero since the good in question is already on hand so that no additional production is involved.

Figure 13–2 shows the separate demand curves D_1 and D_2, the former being measured from the central axis OY to the right and the latter from OY to the left. Corresponding marginal revenue curves are similarly measured. To solve for the most profitable prices it is necessary to stretch a line BC which equals the fixed and perishing supply (in whatever units are specified on the horizontal axis) between the marginal revenue curves until it just touches each. Directly above B and C are the optimum prices P_2 and P_1. The lower price P_2 is charged in the market where demand (at any given price) is more elastic. Quantity sold is the entire fixed supply, BC, with OX sold in market 1 and OK in market 2. Marginal revenue is equated in each market. This is a rule for any price discrimination solution (except for perfect discrimination) since if MR were lower in one market it would pay the seller to divert sales from that market to the other.

A slightly different solution is involved if the fixed supply is larger than the quantity $K'X'$. In that case only $K'X'$ would be sold, marginal revenue would be zero in each market, and prices would be P_1' and P_2' in the two markets. (These prices would be at the points of unitary elasticity.)

Although the purpose of such price discrimination as youth or family fares on airlines is to increase the utilization of capacity, the airliner may still fly with some empty seats, corresponding to the theoretical case just examined. In recent years there has been much experimentation with different pricing schemes according to length of stay abroad, reserved or standby status, day of the week, and lead time of the reservation. Some of these devices do not follow the price discrimination model closely but are based on uncertainty of demand.[2] Most flights utilize a high first-class fare in order to secure more revenue from opulent passengers or those who travel on expense accounts that permit the extravagance.

CONTINUOUS PRODUCTION

The more common problem in price discrimination is how to treat markets differently in the sale of goods that are currently in production (rather than being on hand, as in the preceding section). Figure 13–3 shows the separate demand and marginal revenue curves based on some device for separating buyers for unlike treatment. Marginal cost is shown as rising when the rate of output is increased. The theoretical solution is that MC is equated to AMR—the aggregate marginal revenue curve secured by the *horizontal* addition of the two MR curves. This intersection determines total output. From the point of intersection, horizontal line BM is drawn to the left. This line serves the purpose of equating marginal revenue from sales in each market, such sales being determined by the intersections with MR_1 and MR_2, with prices located directly above on D_1 and D_2.[3]

Buyers in market 2 receive a substantially lower price (P_2) than buyers in market 1 (who pay P_1). Optimum sales in market 2 are OX_2. Optimum sales in market 1 are OX_1. Total sales OA are equal to OX_2 plus OX_1.

In Figure 13–3 demand at any price which is chosen for consideration is considerably more elastic in market 2 than in market 1. This is the reason for the profitability of charging less in market 2 than in the other

---

[2]Overbooking of reservations also occurs due to uncertainty as to whether passengers will show up for all reserved seats. Airlines are now being penalized when this causes passenger inconvenience.

[3]The theory of price discrimination was originated by Joan Robinson, *The Economics of Imperfect Competition* (London: Macmillan, 1938), chap. 15.

FIGURE 13–3   Price Discrimination When Output Can
Change

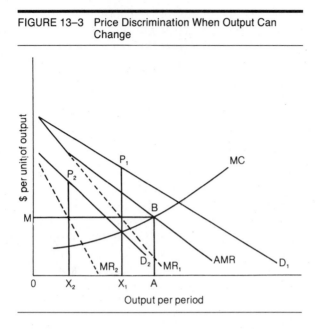

market. Customers who make up market 2 would desert the firm more extensively as measured by percentages than those in the other submarket if confronted by a high price.

INTERNATIONAL DUMPING

A variation of Figure 13–3 is useful in understanding the much maligned practice of international "dumping." A favorite claim of domestic firms and labor unions seeking government protection is that some foreign companies sell steel, TV sets, textiles, and other items more cheaply in the United States than at home. In theory this can occur if the seller has monopoly power at home, must meet competition abroad, and is protected against resale in the home market by tariffs, quotas, license requirements, or the high cost of reshipping.

In Figure 13–4 demand in the home country facing the firm is D_H and corresponding marginal revenue is MR_H. The firm faces perfect competition in the world market, however, making the demand curve D_W perfectly elastic at the prevailing world price. It will maximize profits by dumping abroad at price P_W but charging the higher price P_H at home because of its monopoly power. Total output will be OX, home sales OH, and exports HX. With close inspection, Figures 13–3 and 13–4 can be seen really to be similar since marginal revenue is equated in the two markets and total output is determined by the intersection of MC and AMR. This is because AMR in Figure13–4 follows MR_H down to the point B and then follows

FIGURE 13–4 Theory of Dumping

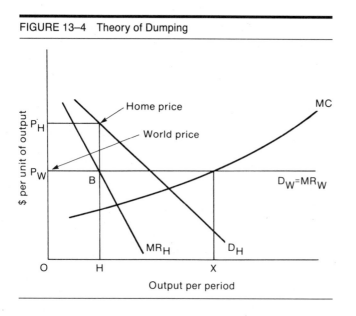

MR_W horizontally to the right. (AMR is the horizontal addition of marginal revenue curves and is dominated by MR_W to the right of point B.)

DISCRIMINATION AND DIFFERENTIALS WHEN PRODUCTS ARE DIFFERENTIATED

The theory of price discrimination, which has been described, is based on the assumption that a firm may find it possible to sell exactly the same commodity to two or more groups of buyers at different prices. Frequently, however, companies that are in a position to increase profits by means of price discrimination find it necessary or desirable to differentiate products from one another, so that similar—but not quite the same—goods are sold at two or more prices. The distinction in products may act as a barrier between the two markets. When air coach service was first introduced in the late 1940s at a price of 4 cents a mile instead of 6 cents per mile for first-class service, it represented an attempt to add revenue through getting new travelers who would not pay the higher fares. Late night departures and fewer amenities such as meals not only held down cost levels but served to prevent customers from being diverted from first class.

GEOGRAPHIC PRICE DISCRIMINATION

Frequently, markets that are subjected to unlike treatment by a firm are separated on a geographic basis—that is, transportation costs impose an economic barrier between markets. The case of dumping a commodity abroad at a low price while the domestic price is maintained has already been mentioned. Geographic price discrimination makes its appearance in numerous other forms also. For example, *blanket* freight rates are sometimes charged by the railroads that result in the same charge for transporting a unit of commodity over a wide geographic range, irrespective of the actual length of the haul. An outstanding example has been the movement of California oranges in carload lots from all points of origin in that state to any point between Denver and the North Atlantic seaboard at the same rate. This means, for example, that buyers in Chicago are discriminated against compared with those in New York, in that the former are charged the same price despite the lower marginal cost of transportation involved in placing California oranges in Chicago. More resources are used in delivering a box of California oranges to New York, but price does not reflect this fact.

BASING-POINT PRICING IN STEEL

A historically important, and still significant, form of geographic price discrimination is known as *basing-point pricing*. The most famous example of the practice was the "Pittsburgh-plus" system of pricing used by the steel industry prior to 1924. Under this system, mills all over the United States calculated prices not by reference to their own costs and shipping charges but by reference to the single set of basing-point prices at Pittsburgh, plus rail freight from Pittsburgh to the buyer's location. Thus, steel delivered to Washington, D.C., for example, was priced as if it came from Pittsburgh even if, in fact, it came by ship from nearby Baltimore. The steel industry changed to a multiple basing-point system in 1924 after the United States Steel Corporation was ordered by the Federal Trade Commission to "cease and desist" from the Pittsburgh-plus system. Under the amended system the delivered price at any city was calculated by adding to the mill price the freight from the *applicable* basing point. This was done by calculating the lowest combination of mill price and rail freight for any given buyer. The applicable basing point would always be the one from which rail freight was lowest if mill prices were the same, but might not be if mill prices were dissimilar. Any steel mill that wished to sell in a particular locality could offer its product at the delivered price thus computed. This required the absorption of part of the freight charge by more distant steel mills, however.

The portland cement industry was also a well-known practitioner of the multiple basing-point system of pricing; and historically, this system was second only to that of the steel industry in importance to the American economy. Cement prices charged by different companies were thus identical at any point of delivery. During the 1930s, about half of the cement mills were basing points and about half were not. Buyers located near the nonbasing-point mills were forced to pay some "phantom freight," while those near basing points were not at this disadvantage. In

1948, the Supreme Court upheld a Federal Trade Commission order that the portland cement industry "cease and desist" from selling cement at prices calculated in accordance with a multiple basing-point system or using other means to secure identical price quotations for the products of the various companies. Shortly after this decision, both the portlant cement and the steel industries abandoned the basing-point method of pricing and adopted systems of FOB mill pricing. They still are permitted to absorb freight to meet competitors' prices. What has been forbidden is the systematic and collusive aspects of multiple basing-point pricing.

MARKET PENETRATION

Advocates of basing-point pricing usually claim that the system is highly competitive because each seller can offer his or her product at the same price in any locality—that is, firms may compete freely for sales but may not compete in price. Any plant that has unused capacity, and whose owners are therefore anxious to increase sales, can offer its wares at the same price as others in any locality, although this may be possible only through *freight absorption*, which means a reduction in the *mill net* price realized. Although this may help utilize the excess capacity of the mill that penetrates the usual territory of another mill, it clearly tends to cause excess capacity in the plant whose market is being penetrated. If such freight absorption were not practiced and buyers were instead given prices equivalently lower, the resulting increase in total sales would help avoid excess capacity in both plants.

Market penetration, phantom freight, and freight absorption can perhaps be more easily understood from Figure 13–5. In this chart, A and B are mills producing the same commodity; but B is a basing point (the applicable one in the region considered), while A is not. Circles are drawn around B to reflect transportation costs from B; at each point on a circle the delivered price is the same. These delivered prices are shown by the numbers attached to each circle and are calculated by assuming the mill price at B to be $45 and the transportation cost from one circle to the next to be $1 per unit.[4]

If we assume that freight costs are the same in either direction and that equal distances represent equal freight costs, it is clear that mill A has a very favorable mill net price in selling near home. If mill A sells at point H, for example, the price will be $50, which includes a $5 freight charge from the basing point. Since actual freight from A to H is $1, the phantom freight collected by mill A is $4. On the other hand, if mill A sells at point F, the price will be $47, which includes $2 of freight. Since

---

[4]The use of circles assumes that transportation costs are uniform in all directions. Actually, they would be affected by the availability of railroads, highways, and waterways, and by mountains, and so forth; this would cause the isoprice lines to be irregular in shape.

FIGURE 13–5 Mill *A* Collects Phantom Freight to Left of *XY* but Absorbs Freight to Right of *XY*

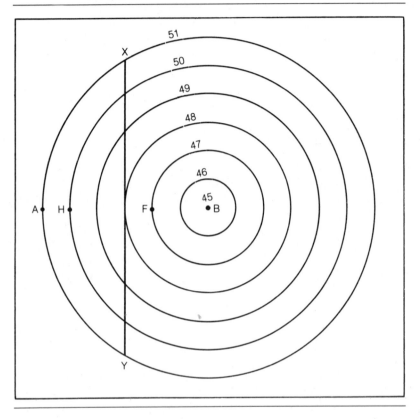

actual freight from *A* to *F* is $4, mill *A* must absorb $2 in freight costs in order to make the sale. On sales anywhere between *A* and the vertical line *XY*, mill *A* will realize phantom freight; while to penetrate beyond line *XY*, it will have to absorb freight. Line *XY* is drawn so as to be equidistant between the two mills.

It is also apparent from the chart that the basing-point mill *B* can penetrate the territory of mill *A* without penalty. If mill *B* sold at point *H*, for example, it would secure the same mill net as on a sale at point *F*, because the delivered price always includes full freight cost from point *B*. Mill *A* could make it more expensive for *B* to get such sales by giving nearby customers an FOB alternative. Its own mill net would be reduced; by how much would depend on the sale price it chose.

Under any system of pricing, a certain amount of *crosshauling* is bound to occur—that is, one mill shipping the same commodity into the natural territory of another mill at the same time the other mill is delivering in the territory of the first mill. This occurs even if the term cross-

hauling is defined strictly so as to require that a mill in city *A* be shipping a given commodity to a buyer in city *B* at the same time a mill at city *B* is shipping to a buyer at city *A*. The shipments are likely even to pass one another on freight trains headed in opposite directions. Under a basing-point pricing system, crosshauling is especially likely to occur, because the delivered price at any destination is the same regardless of origin of shipment. If shape, size, quality, and finish of the product are precisely the same, there is an obvious waste of transportation resources when this occurs.

PRICE DIFFERENTIALS AND DISCRIMINATION WHEN MARGINAL COSTS DIFFER

Conspicuous examples of large price differentials are found in such capital intensive industries as electric utilities and railroads. In order to assure fuller utilization of their plant over time, they may wish to offer substantial concessions in price to users whose demand is substantially concentrated in slack periods. For example, railroads may give special backhaul rates to avoid moving empty equipment. Electric utilities have large late night and winter troughs in demand. If more kilowatt-hours can be sold at these times, the only additional costs are likely to be those for fuel. Moreover, since their capital costs are dependent on the need to provide for peak demands, the long-run marginal costs of additional sales at non-peak hours remain low because such sales require little or no capital investment. Case 13–2, The Urban Electric Company, takes up a pricing decision of this type.

THE LEGALITY OF PRICE DISCRIMINATION[5]

Under the Robinson-Patman Amendment to the Clayton Act, price discrimination is made illegal only where the effect "may be to substantially lessen competition" or to "injure competition" with the "granter of the discrimination or his customers." Its basic provisions are enforceable only through civil suits, the result of which may be a cease and desist order. Even if injury is proved, the firm may, though experience shows it is difficult, prove that the price differentials made only due allowance for costs or were made in good faith to meet the price of a competitor.

Many forms of pure discrimination are legally acceptable. Identical prices to all customers are not legally considered discrimination even though the economist detects differences in *P/MC* ratios. Price discrimination in consumer markets is legally acceptable; usually the injury to competition is found in the secondary market when business executives

---

[5]Students who are interested in legal and policy issues concerning the law will find the Corwin Edwards' comprehensive study, "*The Price Discrimination Law* " (Washington, D.C.: Brookings Institution, 1959), illuminating.

in competition have paid different prices for the product. Many, if not most, firms have quantity discount schedules that have been unchallenged.

The greatest difficulties for management arise in trying to allocate costs to particular units of products. Most firms are multiproduct firms, and the attempt to relate overhead costs to particular products and orders is difficult and frequently involves somewhat arbitary judgments. The Federal Trade Commission has seemed to favor an average cost approach that requires such allocations rather than clearly identifiable marginal costs.

PRICE DISPERSION

A customer may feel she is discriminated against upon finding that she has just paid more for an article than the price charged by another store. This is not "price discrimination" in the economist's sense because the sales are not under a single control. Rather, it is "price dispersion" that can be traced in part to the impact of inadequate price information. The market may be characterized by lack of such information due, perhaps, to prohibitions against advertising (Case 12–3 and Case 13–5)—or there may be a lack of search for information on the part of the consumer.

Advertising has the important function of making search economical to the buyer. Price dispersion is consequently diminished by advertising, at least by advertising that gives important and accurate information. Price dispersion is promoted by advertising that implies differences when there are none, as in the case of aspirin and cornstarch.

CASE 13–1 _____
The Country Doctor*

Dr. Young served a rural area a substantial distance by ferry and automobile from other medical facilities. He estimated that to cover his family living expenditures and the fixed overhead connected with his small clinic, he required $15,000 gross income. On purely economic grounds, he could command more income elsewhere. Fifteen thousand dollars plus variable expenses represented a minimum gross necessary for him to continue to supply his services to the particular area, considering his sense of service and other noneconomic factors as well. In addition, he had certain variable expenses that would vary with the number

_____
*SOURCE: Dr. Young's case is set in the early 1960s before Medicaid and Medicare and the great escalation in medical costs.

of visits, and he estimated these at $1 a visit. (Obviously using a common unit, the visit, to describe the variety of medical services possible, is a great simplification.)

The population of the area consisted essentially of two groups, the new inhabitants and the older inhabitants. The first group was characterized by being mostly retired, generally well off, and primarily attracted by the resort aspects of the community. The second group were permanent residents who furnished services and participated in marginal agriculture and fishing.

Assume that the effective demand for Dr. Young's services among the two groups is described by smoothly drawn demand curves through the points in Exhibit 13–1A and that Dr. Young can provide 3,000 visits per year.

EXHIBIT 13–1A Hypothetical Demand Schedules
Confronting Dr. Young

Price	Visits, Group I	Visits, Group II	Total Visits
$18	0	0	0
15	475	25	500
12	900	100	1,000
9	1,100	400	1,500
6	1,300	700	2,000
3	1,450	1,050	2,500
0	1,500	1,500	3,000

Questions

1. a. Calculate the best single price (from Dr. Young's point of view) on the assumption that prices between those shown are all possible, that is, that the demand schedules are continuous.

   b. Calculate his net income above variable costs if perfect price discrimination could be carried out and demand schedules were continuous.

   c. What net income would Dr. Young receive from a five-price system ($15, $12, $9, $6, and $3)?

   d. What would be his net income from a two-price system—one price for group I and one price for group II?

2. Which of the above pricing systems (or modifications of these systems) would you recommend?

3. Suppose some patients had medical insurance covering office visits and others did not. What use could Dr. Young make of this situation?

4. Suppose Dr. Young had a financial interest in the only drugstore on the island. What would this suggest? (Hint: See Case 13–4.)

5. Is it socially desirable that all rural areas have a resident doctor?

CASE 13–2
The Urban Electric Company

In 1962, the Urban Electric Company, which served both metropolitan and rural areas in the Middle West, found itself in an unfavorable operating position because of the rapid growth of summer air conditioning, which had resulted in increased investment in utility plant and equipment without adequate increase in income. Obviously, a compensating type of load was needed to offset the unfavorable system effects of added air-conditioning load. Therefore the president of the company authorized the establishment of a "working" committee to bring in recommendations as to what measures should be taken:

1. To review the data previously prepared in the economic and rate research department to determine whether or not the company should encourage space heating.
2. To estimate the potential rate of growth in the residential space-heating market for the purpose of determining when a balance between summer and winter peaks could again be established.
3. To propose a price policy based on the necessary costs to the company to serve a residential space-heating load.

The committee had as chairman the manager of the rate department and staff representatives from the sales, operating, comptroller, and economic research departments.

During the course of the discussions, committee members developed the following attitudes:

The vice chairman, coming from the sales area, found himself on the horns of a dilemma. His evaluation of market growth, taking into consideration the intense competition to be encountered from gas and fuel oil interests, was that it was likely to be quite slow; hence, a special rate might not be justified at present. On the other hand, competition made it mandatory to be able to offer the lowest possible service rate to gain entrance into the space-heating market; hence, a special rate was required.

The representative of the comptroller's office was basically opposed to offering any special rates in the first place, but if a special rate were to be offered, he insisted that investment costs be included in determining company costs of service from the outset.

The representative from the operating department was all in favor of any promotional effort that would at least tend to equalize the rate of growth of summer and winter loads but was fearful that if domestic space heating once "caught on," it would have a runaway growth similar to that experienced in air conditioning in the postwar period. If this occurred, then the utility would be right back in the position it was in about 1930, with winter peaks far in excess of summer peaks. While this situation would be better than a permanent summer peak, it still was an undesirable situation because, on the basis of present knowledge, there would be no compensating summer load to be developed. If this happened, an unbalanced operating condition would become a permanent characteristic of utility operation.

The analyst from the economic and rate research department, who had been responsible for the basic technical and market research, was inclined to emphasize that the rate of growth of space-heating load seemed almost sure to be slow, while all the evidence tended to prove that the rate of growth of summer air-conditioning load for the next decade was sure to be large; hence, there would be an increasing gap between summer and winter peaks for most, if not all, of the period until 1975. He based his judgment that the rate of electric space-heating growth would be slow on what had actually happened, particularly in northern areas, during the 15 years elapsed since World War II. Electric space heating as the principal source of home comfort heating in the United States really had gotten its start in the Pacific Northwest, where a domestic conventional fuel shortage developed in 1942–43, and in wartime housing developments near military installations. These first systems were poorly engineered and poorly installed, so that electric space heating really had a setback in the first five years after World War II, both from the public and from the utility point of view. It was not until the very rapid rate of growth in summer air conditioning became apparent in the early 1950s that the utilities became concerned with the unbalanced seasonal load that was developing and started taking a genuine interest in electric comfort heating of homes.

The U.S. Census Bureau undertook in 1960 to conduct a housing census on a sample basis, and one item was the fuels being used in domestic comfort heating systems. A condensation of the result of the census survey is shown in Exhibit 13–2A.

If summer and winter growth trends were accurately forecast, space-heating load additions should not be charged with peak responsibility before the mid-1970s; hence, a low rate covering direct incremental expenses only would be justified until the winter "valley" was again filled. In his view a new point of equilibrium, assuming no change in general load conditions, would not occur before 20 to 25 years had elasped. The research analyst therefore favored a low incremental space-heating rate to meet gas competition, and reliance on future general load growth to balance future system peaks.

The Change in the Seasonal Peak

In the 1930s, the Urban Electric Company had a very distinct winter peak. This seasonal concentration of sales plus the late night lows in electric utilization mean the average load factor for the system (the percentage of actual current sold divided by what could have been sold if peak demand were sustained throughout the year) was only 50 percent. Increased industrial activity, the much greater use of electrical appliances

EXHIBIT 13–2A   Percentages of Households Using Various Space-Heating Fuels in 1960 (by regions of continental United States)

				Percent of Housing Units Heated by—		
	Gas*	*Petro-leum†*	*Coal*	*Electric*	*Liquid Petro-leum Gas*	*Other‡*
1. New England states (6 states)	12.8	77.8	6.0	0.1	1.5	1.8
2. Mid-Atlantic states (5 states and District of Columbia	28.1	53.8	15.6	0.2	1.0	1.3
3. South Atlantic states (6 states) . . .	22.7	39.1	13.3	3.3	8.5	13.1
4. North Central states (12 states). . .	45.5	30.2	17.1	0.3	4.5	2.4
5. South Central states (8 states) . . .	62.7	3.1	9.8	3.5	11.5	9.4
6. Rocky Mountain states (6 states). .	73.0	7.6	7.0	1.1	7.4	3.9
7. Pacific Coast states (5 states)	68.1	16.7	1.8	5.3	3.8	4.3
8. Total United States (including Alaska and Hawaii)	43.5	32.6	12.3	1.8	5.1	4.7

*Includes both natural and manufactured gas.
†Includes all grades of petroleum fuels used for heating (except "bottled" liquid petroleum gas).
‡Includes all types of electric heating where electrical heating is the principal, not the auxiliary, type of heating.
SOURCE: *1960 U.S. Census of Housing.*

EXHIBIT 13–2B   Quarterly Averages of Monthly Maximum Loads Expressed as Percentages of Previous Winter's Peak Load

	1932	1942	1954
December, January, February	95.5	100.0	99.0
March, April, May	79.8	90.4	91.2
June, July, August	66.9	88.8	94.9
September, October, November	86.4	95.5	94.2

in the home, and commercial air conditioning in the summer greatly transformed this pattern (see Exhibit 13–2B) and raised the average load factor to 60 percent.

By 1954, the Urban Electric Company had become concerned enough about the rising summer load to seek giving up certain long-standing rate schedules that gave unusually favorable off-peak rates to the users of air-conditioning equipment in the nonwinter months and to customers who established maximum demands outside of the traditional peak period. (See Exhibit 13–2G for such a rate schedule.) The switch to a summer peak was a disadvantage to utilities because the efficiency of utility plant and equipment goes down as ambient temperatures rise. The transmission and distribution efficiency problem is the same for all utilities regardless of whether or not hydro or steam power is used for generation, but the generating efficiency problem is much more acute for steam-generating systems than for the hydroelectric systems. The Urban Electric Company relied exclusively on steam generation and had testified before the state Commerce Commission that its overall plant and equipment efficiency is 14 percent less in hot weather than in cold weather.

Thus, in order to meet customer demands for service, 14 percent more plant and equipment had to be provided to meet summer demands than identically sized winter demands. Therefore, as soon as the differential becomes less than 14 percent, additional capacity would have to be provided on a summer basis rather than a winter basis. The last increment of capacity required to meet annual peak conditions also becomes unused capacity for more than half of the year; therefore, idle capacity was available in the spring, fall, and winter seasons.

Another aspect of the utility operating problem is that whereas prior to World War II, winter peaks were sufficiently above summer peaks so that generating and transmission equipment could easily be taken out of service for periods of several weeks up to two or three months for heavy maintenance and overhaul, the postwar load developments tended to level off monthly peak demands so that no comparatively long period of the year was really available for planned heavy overhaul maintenance. This problem was aggravated by the rapid increase in size of generating units in the large utilities from a 100,000- to 150,000-kilowatt capacity to 300,000-to 500,000-kilowatt capacity, with units being planned of from 800,000- to 1,000,000-kilowatt capacity. This increase in size of unit means fewer units and greater efficiency of generation, but it also means increasing total reserve requirements to meet emergency outages as well as normal maintenance and overhaul schedules. For lay-downs, a 12 percent inoperable reserve would be necessary plus a 5 to 10 percent operable reserve for emergencies.

The company was just achieving a comfortable reserve position after the strains of World War II when the shift from winter to summer peaks further embarrassed the operating men because reserve capacity had been planned on a winter, not summer, basis. Exhibit 13–2C shows in index terms what had actually happened to the load conditions being met by the company. The Ratio of Summer Peak to Winter Peak column is the important one in this tabulation. In absolute terms, summer peaks were below winter peaks until 1957, but only in 1950 was the differential as much as 14 percent. It was now predicted that this condition could become a permanent situation as summer temperature sensitive load had been averaging about 6.8 percent annual rate growth as compared to a 5.9 percent annual rate of growth for winter temperature sensitive load. (See Exhibit 13–2C). The spread was widening as air conditioning multiplied in residences in the late 1950s and early 1960s.

Electrical Space Heating

Electric heating had progressed to a point where quality equipment was commercially vendable at prices comparable to conventional heating

EXHIBIT 13–2C   Growth in Seasonal Peak Demand, 1947–60
(1947 = 100)

| Year | Relative Growth in Peak Demand | | Ratio of Summer Peak to Winter Peak |
	Winter	Summer	
1947	100.0	100.0	88.8
1948	104.5	104.4	88.7
1949	110.1	108.7	87.6
1950	120.5	110.6	85.3
1951	126.0	115.8	88.1
1952	134.2	119.2	89.3
1953	138.7	146.2	93.6
1954	144.9	154.7	94.8
1955	159.2	166.9	93.1
1956	169.5	180.2	94.4
1957	172.7	196.7	101.1
1958	184.3	200.5	96.6
1959	201.4	220.2	97.1
1960	209.9	240.2	102.5

equipment. Current equipment could be depended upon to operate satisfactorily if properly installed and if heated spaces were properly insulated. Insulation was extremely important with electric heating, as it does not require the same volume of outside air to supply needed oxygen as was required for flame types of fuel. The cost of operating an electric heating system could vary as much as 50 percent, depending on how well the building was insulated. Storm doors and windows would be a necessity for electrically heated homes, as well as wall, floor, and ceiling insulation.

Room or area control of resistance heating systems had been well developed, and resistance heating had been the fastest growing type of electric space heating in the past decade because it had the lowest installation costs.

Heat pumps for year-round air conditioning were little beyond the pioneering stage. While the component equipment parts were mostly standard items, each job had to be individually engineered and assembled. This made either ground-to-air or water-to-air installations expensive. The big equipment manufacturers came out, about 1955, with the air-to-air heat pump which, while it was the least efficient of the three types of heat pump, was the only one that could be factory assembled into a self-contained unit. Early air-to-air heat pumps had some operating "bugs" but could be produced for a cost low enough to compete with the price of a conventional furnace plus central air-conditioner equipment (about $2,000 for an average-sized installation). Satisfactory "electric" furnaces for hot-air or hot-water heating systems had been available on the market only for the past two or three years and were just beginning to be used.

EXHIBIT 13–2D   Comparison of Fuel Cost Ratios for Average Residential Customer under Existing Rates and at Varying Incremental Electricity Rates*

Fuel and Efficiency	Price and Unit	Relative Cost of Heating
Utility gas	8.00 cents/therm	1.00
Fuel oil (80% furnace efficiency)	14.30 cents/gal	1.00
Fuel oil (65% furnace efficiency)	14.30 cents/gal	1.20
Liquid petroleum gas (80% furnace efficiency)	14.00 cents/gal	1.60
Liquid petroleum gas (65% furnace efficiency)	14.00 cents/gal	1.80
Heat pump	2.45 cents/kwh	2.40
Heat pump	2.00 cents/kwh	1.95
Heat pump	1.75 cents/kwh	1.70
Heat pump	1.50 cents/kwh	1.46
Heat pump	1.00 cents/kwh	0.97
Resistance heating	2.45 cents/kwh	4.30
Resistance heating	2.00 cents/kwh	3.55
Resistance heating	1.75 cents/kwh	3.10
Resistance heating	1.50 cents/kwh	2.66
Resistance heating	1.00 cent/kwh	1.77

*While the relative cost of heating would hold approximately for a wide range of residences, calculations were based on a well-insulated 1,200-square-foot house. A season including 6,310 degree-days (65 degrees minus average temperature times days) would require an estimated 18,500 kilowatt-hours, and so electric resistance heating would cost approximately $450 as against a little over $100 for gas.

Tolerable Price Differential between Electric and Gas Systems

An analysis of relative operating costs of gas and electric space heating indicated that when the price per BTU[6] consumed for electricity was not more than two to two and a half times the comparable gas price, electric heating could be sold on a nonprice competitive basis because of its greater cleanliness, safety, and flexibility. As noted previously, resistance-heating installation costs, even allowing for extra insulation, were as low as or lower than conventional hot-air or hot-water heating systems, while air-to-air heat pumps could be installed at a cost approximately equal to that of a conventional hot-air furnace plus central air conditioning.

Exhibit 13–2D shows the relative operating cost of heating a 1,200-square-foot home[7] with an average heat loss of 50,000 BTU's per hour at approximately current electric and utility gas rates and costs per gallon of fuel oil and liquid petroleum gas.

It also shows how this ratio between electric space heating and utility gas space heating can be lowered if the effective electric heating rate is lowered to 2 cents, 1.75 cents, 1.5 cents, or 1 cent per kilowatt-hour.

---

[6]British thermal unit, the standard measure of heat.

[7]A 1,200-square-foot home is the approximate average size for a four-room, one-floor structure or a five-room apartment, and in the Midwest a 50,000 BTU heat loss per hour is considered average for well-insulated premises of this size.

Prospects for Reducing Electric-Gas Differential
through Rising Gas Prices[8]

Studies of the competitive cost of fossil fuels and electricity, and the probable future price trends of fossil fuels, tended to show that there would not be an acute shortage of natural gas and/or crude oil supply in the United States at least until the 1980s and probably not until after the year 2000. The indigenous U.S. supply was already being supplemented with Canadian gas, and there was talk of building a pipe line from the Mexican gas fields to the United States. Also, new ways were being tried out to liquefy natural gas and transport it in specially built tankers from overseas sources. New ways of producing synthetic or manufactured gas from coal at the mine mouth were being experimented with and might become commercially feasible before the natural gas supply runs out. Finally, chemical fuel cells of various types and midget atomic power plants have been under experimentation.

The conclusion reached from the fuel studies was that even assuming that natural gas rates rise more rapidly than electric rates (as they have in the past 15 years), to hope for equality of rates on a BTU basis between gas and electricity in less than 20 years was unrealistic. In fact, the more likely time for possible equalization of gas and electric rates was thought to be 40 years hence, rather than 20 years.

National Range of Space-Heating Rates

An analysis of the space-heating rates that were offered by private utilities in increasing numbers across the country indicated that the range of the space-heating charges by those companies that were beginning to do considerable space-heating business was seldom higher than 1.5 cents. Rates higher than 2 cents per kilowatt-hour were producing little business.

In analyzing the data of Exhibit 13–2E, the economic research department was particularly concerned with relating the annual penetration rate into the household heating market to the rates charged. The department recognized that the time the rate had been in effect and the climatic conditions were important factors in interpreting the data that were available.

The second critical relationship was the problem of interpreting the consequences of increased penetration in home heating for the winter peak. Home heating requirements could be expected to have a daily pat-

---

[8]The higher fossil fuel prices and environmental concerns of the 1970s were not fully anticipated in this forecast. Actually higher fuel prices, when electricity is generated from fossil fuel, work against electric heating, since generating and transmission make the heat/fuel ratio much less for resistance electric heating. In the longer run, environmental concerns are likely to favor electric heating as the clean fuels (natural gas and low sulfur oil) become scarce since pollutants can be better removed centrally.

EXHIBIT 13–2E   Saturation of Electric Space Heating in the United States (as of December 31, 1961)

Effective Date of Current Space-Heating Rate	Name of Electric Utility	Number of Residential Customers in Thousands	Principal State Served	Lowest Block Rate Applicable to Space and Water Heaters		Electric Space Heating Saturation as of Dec. 31, 1961	
				Space (Cents)	Water (Cents)	Heat Pumps —Per- cent Satura- tion	Resist- ance— Percent Satura- tion
1. NEW ENGLAND STATES							
1961	New England Electric System	756.5	Massachusetts	2.00[1]	1.30[2]	0.00	0.10
1958	Western Massachusetts Electric Company	125.1	Massachusetts	1.30[2]	1.30[2]	0.00	0.70
2. MIDDLE ATLANTIC STATES							
1958	New York State Electric and Gas Corporation	420.8	New York	1.20[2]	1.20[2]	0.00	1.00
1961	Public Service Electric and Gas	1,253.1	New Jersey	1.50	1.03[2]	0.00	0.02
1961	Philadelphia Electric Company[3]	926.2	Pennsylvania	2.00[4]	1.00[2]	0.00	0.01
1961	Baltimore Electric and Gas Company[5]	492.7	Maryland	1.60[4]	1.75[1]	. . .[6]	0.02
3. SOUTHEASTERN STATES (EXCLUDING TENNESSEE)							
1959[9]	Appalachian Electric Power Company	437.7	Virginia	1.50[1]	1.10[1]	0.20	1.50
1957	Georgia Power Company	642.1	Georgia	1.00[4]	1.00[1]	0.24	0.41
1962	Alabama Power Company[7]	577.0	Alabama	1.00[4]	1.20[1]	0.50	0.80
1962	Florida Power Corporation	257.9	Florida	1.60[4]	1.42[1]	3.00	5.40
83 (a). TENNESSEE (TVA)							
1939	Electric Power Board of Chattanooga	76.4	Tennessee	0.75[1]	0.40[1]	2.70	52.80
1938	Knoxville Utility Board	71.6	Tennessee	0.75[1]	0.40[1]	0.65	43.00
1959	Memphis Light, Gas and Water Division[8]	165.3	Tennessee	0.70[1]	0.70[1]	0.05	1.50
1939	Nashville Electric Service	117.1	Tennessee	0.75[1]	0.40[1]	0.00	40.00
4. GREAT LAKES AND UPPER MISSISSIPPI VALLEY STATES							
1961[9]	Ohio Power Company	418.4	Ohio	1.40[1]	1.00[1]	0.07	1.90
1949	Indiana and Michigan Electric Company	200.4	Indiana	1.50[1]	1.00	0.10	3.50
1959	Detroit Edison Company	1,177.0	Michigan	2.00[1]	. . .[10]	. . .[6]	0.02
1961	Central Illinois Public Service Company	203.4	Illinois	1.90[4]	1.40[1]	0.00	0.30
1961	Northern States Power Company[11]	654.0	Minnesota	2.00[1]	2.00[1]	0.00	0.07
1960	Union Electric Company[12]	550.8	Missouri	1.50[4]	. . .[12]	. . .[6]	0.40
5. SOUTHWESTERN STATES							
1961	Oklahoma Gas and Electric Company[13]	309.3	Oklahoma	1.20[4]	1.20[4]	0.23	0.12
1960	Central Power and Light Company	209.4	Texas	1.00[4]	1.90[2]	0.55	0.27
1952	Salt River Power District[15]	92.8	Arizona	1.00[4]	1.00[4]	4.22	1.01

EXHIBIT 13–2E *(concluded)*

Effective Date of Current Space-Heating Rate	Name of Electric Utility	Number of Residential Customers in Thousands	Principal State Served	Lowest Block Rate Applicable to Space and Water Heaters		Electric Space Heating Saturation as of Dec. 31, 1961	
				Space (Cents)	Water (Cents)	Heat Pumps —Percent Saturation	Resistance— Percent Saturation
		6. PACIFIC COAST STATES					
1961	Southern California Edison Company	1,470.7	California	1.40[1]	1.10[1]	0.50	1.40
1961[9]	Portland General Electric Company	233.4	Oregon	1.10[1]	0.70[1]	0.10	16.00
1960[9]	Tacoma City Light	57.0	Washington	1.20[1]	0.62[1]	0.00	9.60
1960[9]	Washington Water Power	129.0	Washington	1.20[1]	0.80[1]	0.03	10.00
1960	Idaho Power Company	114.6	Idaho	1.75[1]	0.90[1]	. . .[6]	0.86
Total for United States		36,193.8				0.02	1.10

Notes to Exhibit 13–2E

[1] Uncontrolled.

[2] Limited usage hours permitted.

[3] Philadelphia Electric Company seasonal space-heating rate is $2 per kilowatt based on 60 percent of connected resistance heating load, plus 2 cents per kilowatt-hour for all monthly usage above 500. Applicable from October through the following May.

[4] Seasonal data, applicable in heating season only.

[5] Baltimore Electric and Gas Company seasonal space-heating rate is applicable for billing months November through May, and provides a low rate of 1.6 cents per kilowatt-hour for all over 600 kilowatt-hours being billed.

[6] Less than 0.01 of 1 percent.

[7] Alabama Power Company's space-heating rate provides for a 0.2-cent reduction in kilowatt-hour charge for all kilowatt-hours consumed over 1,363 per month, November through April.

[8] The contract between the Memphis Light, Gas and Water Division and the TVA was renegotiated in 1959 after Congress refused to pass appropriations for TVA to build a special generating station for Memphis; hence the variation in rates.

[9] Promotional rate in effect before current rate.

[10] The Detroit Edison Company's water-heating rate is a flat monthly charge of from $4 to $7, depending on gallonage of tank. No metering is required, but a time switch is required to control heating hours to 20 per day.

[11] In Minneapolis, a 1.5 percent surcharge is applied to all bills. In St. Paul, the minimum rate is 2.1 cents per kilowatt-hour. In Winona only, the company has separate water-heating rates that are 1.5 cents per kilowatt-hour for uncontrolled water heating and 1.3 cents for controlled.

[12] The Union Electric Company has established a seasonal flat rate of 2 cents per kilowatt-hour for the four summer billing periods and 1.5 cents per kilowatt-hour during the eight winter billing periods for homes having both electric water heating and electric space heating; off-peak control for either is not required.

[13] Oklahoma Gas and Electric Company allows 0.9-cent discount for all kilowatt-hours consumed over 600 per month for the period from November through April for space-heating installations of 3-kilowatt capacity or over. This, in effect, extends the year-round water-heating rate to space heating during the winter months.

[14] Central Power and Light Company has an all-purpose seasonal residential rate with a bottom charge of 1.25 cents per kilowatt-hour. It also offers an alternate combination of rates; controlled water heating (year-round), 1 cent per kilowatt-hour, and a space-heating rate of 1 cent per kilowatt-hour from approximately November 1 through April. The customer's general usage (lighting, range, appliances, etc.) is charged for on the regular residential rate.

[15] Salt River water- and space-heating rate is applicable from November through April, when water heating and space heating are separately metered. Bottom step of general residential rate applicable to general usage is 1.7 cents.

SOURCES: "33rd Annual Appliance Survey," *Electric Light and Power,* May and August 1962. Rate data only: Federal Power Commission, *National Electric Rates.*

tern that would be reasonably constant in the current drawn from the system. The relatively minor daily peak could be expected in the morning hours and the demand at the usual winter peak times, 4:30–7:30 P.M., should be expected to be somewhat less than average because of the warming daytime effects and because of household activity in the early evening. On a cold January or February day, about 1 percent of annual heating requirements might be required.[9]

With these considerations in mind, the following calculations could be made:

Increase in kilowatt-hours generated per 1 percent increase in residential electric space heating saturation would be 1.6 percent (20,000 homes times 18,500 kilowatt-hours heating requirement divided by 23.3 billion kilowatt-hours, the total amount of current transmitted in 1961).

Probable increase in the winter peak load for each percentage increase in heating saturation would be the 1.6 percent times 3.65 percent or approximately 5.8 percent. The 3.65 factor recognizes that on a very cold day the heating demand of 1 percent of the year's requirements would be 365/100 of a load evenly spread throughout the year.

Cost Data

The committee considered three principal ways for determining cost to serve: (1) to charge full annual system peak responsibility to a particular type of load (as was becoming the practice for the air-conditioning load); (2) to average the chargeable responsibility for establishing the monthly maximum demands, and to charge the average monthly demand costs to the new load; and (3) to charge no peak or maximum demand responsibility to space-heating loads. The third method would produce a marginal cost-to-serve figure that includes incremental investment and maintenance charges (if any) directly chargeable to the new load and direct fuel and operating costs for the energy consumed, but does not prorate existing costs over the additional load expected.

The principal difference in these three methods was how peak or system maximum demand charges were assessed against the particular type of load being considered. The method of computing cost-to-serve off-peak night water-heating charges was one form of computation of incremental rates, since it was assumed that night water-heating loads did not add to system investment but rather increased the overall daily usage of utility facilities. In view of the finding that space-heating load was likely to have a slow rate of growth, an incremental method of computing cost to serve might be justified for the forseeable future.

---

[9]In the northern Illinois area covered by the Urban's system, annual degree days ranged from 6,100 to 6,500. (A degree day represents the daily difference between a 65° mean temperature and the actual average temperature.) The coldest day to be expected could show a minimum of −10 and a maximum of about 15° or an average of about 2.5. This would represent 62.5° days, about 1 percent of the total.

The average peak-load method of computation was a compromise between the full-peak and the no-peak charge methods. Its use was most suitable when the variation between monthly peaks was so reduced that there would be little chance for scheduling heavy overhaul in any one season of the year, thus requiring increased reserve capacity to provide overhaul periods.

If and when a substantial saturation of electric space heating could be achieved, such load would probably first become dominant during cold spells in January or February. Under already existing system conditions, an extra Christmas lighting was dropped, and early evening commercial lighting loads decreased with the increase of daylight, the time of the daily system peak of the electric system tended to shift in February from a 5:00–6:00 P.M. to a 10:00–11:00 A.M. peak produced by industrial load. Space-heating system loads that would be heaviest in prolonged cold spells could conceivably be the cause for changing the hour of the monthly January or February peak from 10:00–11:00 A.M. to 7:00–8:00 A.M. before other monthly peaks were affected. On the other hand, space-heating load would contribute nothing to July-August-September monthly peak loads, and would be unlikely to change the time of May, June, and October monthly maximum demands until a very high degree of saturation was attained. Therefore, by averaging the expected contributions of space heating for each of the 12 months of the year, a basis for computing investment charges on space-heating load could be established. Such an average charge is more than the incremental cost, but smaller than full-peak responsibility charges.

Exhibit 13–2F, based on an Urban Company space-heating cost-to-serve study, illustrates the comparatively wide spread in results obtained from computing costs on the basis of the three methods outlined. These figures do not include general administrative expenses and certain minor items that were not usually allocated by functions. In determining any rate required to meet the cost to serve, these unallocated expenses were added to the total of itemized costs on an overall percentage basis. They amount to about one eighth of the total.

The Rate Structure

There are various forms in which a winter space-heating rate can be offered. First, it can be a specific single-user or flat rate that applies only to electric space heating. Such a rate has to be made applicable in conjunction with the appropriate general service rate and also requires separate metering of heating load to administer.

Second, when the block form of rate rather than the demand form of rate is used, a new low block step can be added to an existing general service rate.[10] The problem in this type of procedure for the Rate Committee was to set the volume at which the heating step became effective great

---

[10]For an explanation of rate forms, see the section entitled "Note on Rates" below.

EXHIBIT 13–2F Comparison of Costs to Serve an Average Residential Electric Space-Heating Load during a Normal Winter Season

	Cents per Kilowatt-Hour		
	Full Peak Responsibility	Average Peak Responsibility	No Peak Responsibility
1. Capacity costs:*			
Generating†...............	0.435	0.375	—
Transmission‡	0.255	0.180	—
Distribution, including customer costs§	0.450	0.345	0.165
Total capacity costs	1.140	0.900	0.165
2. Operating and maintenance costs:#			
Generating	0.075	0.060	—
Transmission	0.008	0.003	—
Distribution, including meter reading and billing costs	0.045	0.015	0.015
Total operating and maintenance costs....	0.128	0.078	0.015
3. Fuel costs‖	0.450	0.450	0.450
4. Total costs to serve, excluding certain unallocated executive and financial costs.........	1.718	1.428	0.630
Percentage ratio of (1) to (2) and (3) to (2)	120.3	100.0	0.441
Percentage ratio of (3) and (2) to (1)..	100.0	83.0	0.334

*Capacity costs applied to plant—carrying charges of 12 percent based on a 30-year plant life were applied to plant costs. This percentage, computed by the level-premium method, assumes a 56.5 percent return on equity, a 52 percent debt ratio, a 3.85 percent cost of debt money, and a straight-line depreciation for tax purposes. State and local tax rates vary, depending upon location of plant within the urban area or the suburban areas served by the Urban Electric Company; therefore, a weighted average rate of 1.15 percent was applied for the combined state and local rates.

†Generating capacity costs include all costs to build a generating station, including land, structures, and equipment up to and including generating station transformer yards.

‡Transmission capacity costs include all costs to build and maintain the high-voltage transmission system (66,000 volts and higher) from generating station yard terminals to and including primary distribution centers, where the current is stepped down from high to medium voltage (12,000 to 66,000 volts).

§Distribution capacity costs include (1) land, structures, and equipment from the primary distribution center terminals through the secondary substations, where voltage is again stepped down from 12,00 volts or 4,000 volts or equivalent thereof; (2) from the distribution substation terminals through the alley transformers, where the current is stepped down from 4,000 volts to 110–20 to 220–40 volts (using voltages) or combinations, (3) company-owned low-voltage equipment on customer premises such as individual service drops and meter equipment.

#Operating and maintenance costs, except fuel, are all costs of labor and material used in operation and maintenance of the system, and appertain to the same segments of the electrical system as do the capacity costs. Meter reading, billing, and customer service costs are included under distribution costs.

‖Fuel charges are the cost of fuel on the kilowatt-hour basis used for generating electricity. They are normally converted to a coal-equivalent basis, although other fuels, such as natural gas and fuel oil, may be used seasonally or only during emergencies.

enough to ensure that the bulk of all other electric services furnished the customer would be charged for at the general-service rate levels during the nonheating season. On the other hand, the effective volume of the space-heating step should be set low enough so that all space heating would fall in the space-heating step, particularly during the heavy heating season (November through March in the geographic area served by the Urban Electric Company). Inasmuch as residential summer air conditioning, per se, tends to increase customer summer usage above winter general service usage levels, the balancing point for applicability of the space-heating step was not easy to determine. The chief advantage of the all-purpose rate was that it required no special metering or billing. The rate (at least theoretically) would be available for any customer using enough kilowatt-hours for any purpose to become eligible for the low steps of the rate.

A third form of space-heating rates was to establish, in effect, a "larger user" rate but restrict its applicabilty to customers whose principal means of space heating were all electric. It had all the advantages of the second form of rate but could adjust the blocks more readily for general usage and water-heating purposes, without making these adjustments available to all customers. Such a special rate could be offered only for a limited period of time and could then be dropped if found unsatisfactory for any but existing customers without further formal commission procedure.

Notes on Rates

There are three usual forms of general service rates: block, demand, and flat. Governmental rates normally follow the nonresidential form of rates, while so-called special rates, when used, can be in any form, but generally are in effect special contracts applying to only one large customer whose usage needs are peculiar to himself. Such special contracts are filed with the utility commission having jurisdiction, but they are normally not published as a part of the utility's rate schedule available to the public.

1. Residential rates are generally *block* rates, that is, the total consumption of the customer as recorded by a watt-hour meter is divided into steps or blocks, with the rate of charge per kilowatt-hour progressively declining for each block as the total consumption increases.

A hypothetical example of a block-type rate schedule is:

First	25 kwh at 5 cents per kwh
Next	75 kwh at 3 cents per kwh
All over	100 kwh at 2 cents per kwh
Minimum bill	$1

2. For nonresidential customers the *demand* form of rate is generally used, and it has been tried experimentally for large residential users. This form of rate differs from the block rate in that the two basic components of utility costs are separated and a separate charge is made for each component. The first component is frequently called the "readiness to serve"

EXHIBIT 13–2G   Rate 13—Industrial Electric Service (off-peak) (extract—includes selected paragraphs only)

AVAILABILITY

This rate is available only to customers receiving alternating current service hereunder at their present locations on November 22, 1954, for all commercial and industrial requirements, and who have not subsequently discontinued doing so. Upon the expiration of the customer's availability period under Rider 21, or upon the discontinuance of service under this rate by the Customer for any reason, whichever first occurs, he shall not again be served hereunder. . . .

EXPLANATION OF RATE

The charge for electric service under this rate is the sum of a charge for maximum demand created and a charge for the energy supplied. Three operating periods are specified corresponding to load conditions on the Company's system, namely, "peak," "daytime," and "nighttime," and a different demand charge is provided for demands created during each period. The peak billing demand is determined on an annual basis and the off-peak daytime and nighttime billing demands are determined on a monthly basis, as hereinafter provided.

CHARGES

Demand Charge

The number of kilowatts of peak, daytime, and nighttime billing demand shall be charged for in the order named, consecutively through the blocks of kilowatts in the following table, at the prices per kilowatt for the respective demand periods (for example—200 kilowatts of peak billing demand, 800 kilowatts of daytime billing demand, and 100 kilowatts of nighttime billing demand will be charged for at $2.15, $1.00, and $0.55, respectively):

Peak Billing Demand	Daytime Billing Demand	Nighttime Billing Demand		Kilowatts of Billing Demand for the Month
$2.15	$1.35	$0.75	per kilowatt for the first.	200
1.50	1.00	0.60	per kilowatt for the next	800
1.40	0.90	0.55	per kilowatt for the next	2,500
1.15	0.75	0.50	per kilowatt for all over	3,500

Energy Charge	*Kilowatt-Hours Supplied in the Month*
2.49¢ per kilowatt-hour for the first	6,000
1.14¢ per kilowatt-hour for the next	24,000
0.90¢ per kilowatt-hour for the next	70,000
0.68¢ per kilowatt-hour for the next	400,000
0.59¢ per kilowatt-hour for all over.	500,000

The energy charge for each kilowatt-hour supplied in the month is subject to adjustment in accordance with the provisions of the Company's Fuel Adjustment rider.

The gross energy charge shall be 10 percent more than the sum of the net energy charge and the "Fuel Adjustment," for the first 100,000 kilowatt-hours supplied in the month.

Minimum charge

The regular minimum monthly demand charge shall be $60 for the first month which includes any part of the peak period and for the succeeding four months. For all other months the regular minimum monthly demand charge shall be $40.

DEMAND PERIODS

The peak period is the period between the hours of 4:30 P.M. and 7:30 P.M. of each day from each October 15 to the next succeeding February 14, inclusive, except Saturdays, Sundays, Thanksgiving Day, Christmas Day, and New Year's Day.

The Company reserves the right, upon giving the Customer not less than three months' advance written notice, to change the peak period to not more than eight consecutive half-hours between the hours of 8:00 A.M. and 9:00 P.M. of each day in any period of not more than 124 consecutive days, Saturdays, Sundays, and legal holidays excepted.

EXHIBIT 13–2G *(concluded)*

The daytime period is the period between 8:00 A.M. and 9:00 P.M. of each day, except that it shall not include any period that is within the peak period.

The nighttime period is the period between 9:00 P.M. of each day and 8:00 A.M. of the following day.

Maximum demands

The peak maximum demand in any month shall be the greater of *(a)* the average of the three highest 30-minute demands established uring the peak period, if any, on different days of such month or *(b)* the number of kilowatts by which the daytime maximum demand exceeds 25,000 kilowatts.

The daytime maximum demand in any month shall be the average of the three highest 30-minute demands established during the daytime period on different days of such month.

The nighttime demand in any month shall be the average of the three highest 30-minute demands established during the nighttime period on different nights of such month.

---

cost. When a customer is connected to any public utility's lines, the utility by law is required to furnish the customer with any amount of service at any hour of the day or night he desires to use it (demand it), up to the capacity of all of his electricity-using equipment. This means that the utility must have generating and distribution capacity available at all times to meet the customers' demands. The utility calls these basic costs, which are incurred regardless of how much use the customers actually make of electric service, "readiness to serve" costs, or for billing purposes the "demand charge."

The second type of costs borne by a utility are the direct costs of producing and distributing electric energy. The charge made to cover these costs is called the energy charge.

Therefore, the bill of a customer who is on a demand rate contains two charges: *(a)* for the demand he created during the billing period, usually expressed in dollars or cents per kilowatt of demand; and *(b)* an energy charge computed in cents or decimals thereof per kilowatt-hour of energy actually consumed.

A hypothetical example of a demand form is shown in Exhibit 13–2G.

Questions

1. Assuming a flat rate were charged for space heating, what rate would you recommend? How could such a rate be administered?

2. Consider the advantages and disadvantages of a flat rate against a new step in block-rate structure. Would it help to restrict the step to October through April?

3. The committee's analysis led it to expect a slow rate of growth in demand. What does this suggest about the relevance for costs of full peak responsibility, average peak responsibility, or no peak responsibility?

4. Would you consider it price discrimination to be charging the kilowatt-hour rate for lighting of 2.45 cents and for space heating of 1.50 cents at the same

time of day? Why, or why not? What would the utility lose and gain by setting up a block-rate structure to avoid such separate rates?

5. The sharply higher fuel prices in the 1980s may affect both the social and private desirability of alternative rate structures for companies such as Urban Electric. Comment.

CASE 13–3
Frito-Lay, Inc.*

On January 6, 1976, the Federal Trade Commission issued a complaint against Frito-Lay, Inc., a wholly owned division of PepsiCo, Inc., alleging price discrimination in violation of subsection (a) of Section 2 of the Clayton Act, as amended, also known as the Robinson-Patman Act (1936).

Frito-Lay, the respondent, has approximately 49 plants in 25 states that produce a varied line of snack foods, including corn chips, potato chips, tortilla chips, pretzels, and several other lines.

The FTC complaint alleged that the company had been discriminating in price between different purchasers of its products of like grade and quality. An illustration of the practice was given by the FTC as follows:

> Respondent has for several years had in effect a quantity discount program in the Central Division of its Great Lakes Zone whereby any account purchasing $200 up to $499.99 within a calendar month is entitled to a 3 percent discount on total purchases of respondent's products delivered at regular store-door prices; any account purchasing $500 or more within a calendar month is entitled to a 5 percent discount on total purchases of such products. Discounts earned under this policy are paid by check on a calendar quarter basis. Under said pricing program multiunit accounts are permitted to accumulate purchases of each unit in order to realize the maximum discount. The discriminations resulting from this program favor the retail stores, among others, of the Kroger's Co.'s Indianapolis Division, in respondent's Great Lakes Zone. Many competitors of the Kroger Co. and other nonfavored customers, were discriminated against in that they did not receive the maximum discount, although their store units purchased in greater volume than did individual units of the favored customers. (p. 553)

The complaint was settled by a consent agreement under which Frito-Lay admitted all of the jurisdictional facts set forth in the complaint, but did not admit any violation of the law. Such an agreement is for settlement purposes only and avoids the necessity of going to court.

---

*SOURCE: Case is from *Federal Trade Commission Reports,* January 1, 1977–June 30, 1977, 89, p. 522.

The consent order required the company to cease and desist from selling to any retailer at a net price higher than the net price charged any competitive retailer. The following qualification was added:

> It is further ordered, that nothing herein contained shall prevent price differentials which make only due allowance for differences in the cost of manufacture, sale or delivery, resulting from the differing methods or quantities in which such products are sold or delivered to such purchasers or which are made in good faith to meet an equally low price of a competitor; nor shall anything herein contained prevent price changes from time to time where made in response to changing conditions affecting the market for or the marketability of the goods concerned, such as but not limited to actual or imminent deterioration of perishable goods, obsolescence of seasonal goods, distress sales under court process, or sales in good faith in discontinuance of business in the goods concerned; and it is further provided that all other defenses legally available to a charge of price discrimination under Section 2(a) of the amended Clayton Act are not waived by this order. (p. 555)

Questions

1. Why may snack foods be fairly suitable in physical nature to the practice of price discrimination? Name some goods or services that are by their nature even more suitable, and some that are less suitable, in this regard.
2. What is the significance of the claim by competitors of Kroger that their individual stores bought in lots as large as did individual Kroger stores?
3. If price differentials justified by cost differentials are not in violation of the Robinson-Patman Act, what sort of cost should be relevant—short-run average cost, short-run marginal cost, or long-run marginal cost? Why?
4. The Robinson-Patman Act is often called an antichain store law. Does it appear to be of this nature? Explain carefully.

CASE 13–4
Generic Drugs

Prescription drugs sold under brand names usually cost consumers much more than identical drugs sold in identical quantities under their generic names. These substantial price differentials are illustrated in the following advertisement by Medi Mart Drug Stores.[11]

---

[11] As shown in Staff Report to the Federal Trade Commission, *Prescription Drug Price Disclosures*, January 20, 1975, Appendix B.

YOU SAVE ON GENERIC DRUGS

All drugs are assigned two names—one the Generic name, which is the chemical name of the product, the second name is the trade name under which different companies market the same product.

Asking your doctor to prescribe a Generic drug is similar to buying a fine private label product. Your savings would be the dollars that a company would spend to sample, advertise, and otherwise promote their version (the trade name) of the product.

An example of this would be the use of a Generic penicillin vs. a trade name product.

	Generic Drug	Brand Name Drug
Generic name	Penicillin G	Penicillin G
Trade Name	NONE	Pentids
Strength	400,000 units	400,000 units
Retail for 100	$2.32	$11.00

The only difference is your savings of $8.68.

HERE'S MEDI MART'S LIST OF GENERIC DRUG PRICES

Chlorpromazine tabs 10mg	100	**2.92**
(compare to Thorazine)	100	4.72
Chlorpheniramine Maleate T.D. caps 12mg .	100	**2.44**
(compare to Teldrin-Chlor-Trimeton)	100	10.28
Conj. Estrogen tabs 1.25mg	100	**5.87**
(compare to Premarin)	100	6.69
Dioctyl Sod. Sulfosulfosuccinate 100mg . . .	100	**2.49**
(compare to Colace 100mg)	100	9.45
Meprobamate 400mg tabs	100	**3.29**
(compare to Equanil)	100	7.01
Penicillin G 400,000 units tabs	100	**2.32**
(compare to Pentids 400)	100	11.00
Papaverine HCL 150mg time release	100	**5.95**
(compare to Pavabid)	100	10.99
Prednisone tabs 5mg	100	**1.49**
(compare to Deltasone)	100	3.66
Propoxyphene HCL 65 mg	100	**4.95**
(compare to Darvon 65mg)	100	7.49
Propoxyphene HCL compound 65mg	100	**5.95**
(compare to Darvon compound 65mg)	100	7.59
Rauwolfia Serp. tabs 100mg	100	**1.19**
(compare to Raudixin 100mg)	100	8.49
Oxy-Tetracycline caps 250mg	100	**3.95**
(compare to Terramycin 250mg)	100	21.44
Reserpine 0.25 tabs	100	**1.19**
(compare to Serpasil 0.25)	100	4.73

Questions

1. Is the pharmaceutical industry practicing price discrimination by selling identical drugs at higher prices under brand names than under the generic names?

2. What do you think of the accuracy of the idea in the advertisement that the price difference is due to advertising and other promotional costs?

3. Name some circumstances that may account for the large differences between drugs in the price differential between brand name and generic name.

4. Doctors are noted for their careless handwriting. What is the relevance to the brand-name, generic name pricing situation from the consumer's point of view?

CASE 13–5
Price Dispersion in Optical Products in California*

A prime illustration of the effect of the absence of price information on the dispersion of prices is a survey of eyeglass prices in three California cities—Los Angeles, Oakland, and Sacramento—conducted in 1975. In each city the opticians and optometrists were asked for the price of their median-priced eyeglasses, with prices for the frames and lenses stated separately.

California law provided:

> No person, whether or not licensed under this division, shall advertise or cause or permit to be advertised, any representations in any form which in any manner, whether directly, or indirectly, refer to the cost, price, charge, or fee to be paid for any commodity or commodities furnished or any service or services performed by any other person, licensed as a physician and surgeon, optometrist, pharmacist, or registered dispensing optician, when these commodities or services are furnished in connection with the professional practice or business for which he is licensed.

The price dispersion found in the survey is shown in Exhibit 13–5A. Since rigid constraints were not provided on variations, it is possible that some of the recorded differentials are due to differences in types of materials.

Questions

1. Do the data illustrate price discrimination as defined by Joan Robinson?

2. What is the relation of the data to the California law regarding advertising?

3. How would you conduct a survey to determine whether price discrimination exists?

4. Comment on the similarity of the professional interest in this case and Case 12–3.

---

*SOURCE: Case is from Federal Trade Commission, Division of Special Reports, Bureau of Consumer Protection, "Advertising of Ophthalmic Goods and Services," January 15, 1976. Published as a matter of record, not as an order.

EXHIBIT 13–5A Price Dispersion—Los Angeles, Sacramento, Oakland

	Frames		Lenses				Contacts
			Single Vision		Bifocal		
	Plastic	Metal	Glass	Plastic	Glass	Plastic	
Los Angeles:							
High price ...	$40.00	$70.00	$37.50	$37.50	$58.35	$74.00	$250.00
Low price	12.00	15.00	18.00	18.00	23.00	17.50	115.00
Sacramento:							
High price ...	18.50	30.00	30.50	33.50	45.00	54.00	225.00
Low price	7.00	15.00	15.00	20.00	20.00	25.00	70.00
Oakland:							
High Price ...	25.00	33.00	40.00	n.a.	48.00	n.a.	250.00
Low price	10.00	27.50	21.50	n.a.	24.50	n.a.	145.00

n.a. = not available.

CASE 13–6
Price Discrimination at Harvard*

For 1982–83, Harvard University raised its undergraduate tuition about 15 percent to $8,195 a year ($5 above Yale and $5 below Brown). "Unlike some institutions, Harvard has affirmed that it will continue to meet the demonstrated financial need of any student admitted to the college." Despite this policy, "the pool of applicants from lower income families is shrinking at an alarming rate, only 15.8 percent of the applicants for the class of 1986 had parents who did not attend college compared with 26 percent for the class of 1983. It appears that less affluent students are selecting themselves out . . . before they learn of financial options at Harvard. If the present trend continues we will lose a vital part of the diversity of our student body."

In explaining the tuition rise that brought the level to more than triple that of 1971, the financial vice president stated that as long as endowment income does not keep up with inflation, student charges will go up faster than inflation. "Student fees now comprise 30 percent of the University's revenue and are viewed as the most elastic source of income."

President Derek Bok devoted his "President's Report to Board of Overseers" to the question of federal student aid and the curtailments proposed by the Reagan administration. While approving restrictions on the eligibility for subsidized loans to all families regardless of need, he was particularly concerned with cutbacks in the in-school loan subsidy, work-study programs, and supplemental grants as well as the proposed

---

*SOURCE: *Harvard Magazine,* May–June 1982.

elimination of the regular Guaranteed Student Loan Program for graduate students. He noted that in 30 years the enrollment of students in private colleges had shrunk from more than one half to less than one quarter of the total undergraduate population. With a dwindling potential student population, the government could permanently weaken the private side of a partnership (with public colleges) that has played an important role in lifting American higher education to a level unequaled in the world. (An odd result from an administration committed to a vigorous private sector.)

Questions

1. How does Harvard practice price discrimination? Consider how well its situation satisfied the requisites for price discrimination and what goals price discrimination serves for the nonprofit private colleges.
2. When the financial vice president speaks of student fees as being the "most elastic source of income" how is he using the word in a much different sense from that in the term "elasticity of demand"?
3. Why does the actual and prospective curtailment of federal loan and grant programs contain a particular threat to private institutions?

14

Price Strategies when Sellers Are Few

> People of the same trade seldom meet together, even for merriment and diversion, but the conversation ends in a conspiracy against the public, or in some contrivance to raise prices.
> —*Adam Smith*

A very common situation in manufacturing, wholesaling, retailing, financial services, and other fields is that of oligopoly, in which the number of sellers of a particular item is so small that each seller must consider rivals' reactions to his or her own actions. It has been pointed out that the oligopolist is not faced by a single demand curve but rather that the curve can assume a great variety of shapes (and even a positive slope), depending on the nature and extent of rivals' reactions to its pricing decisions. Both in monopoly and pure competition no such reactions of rivals alter demand: In monopoly, there are no rivals; in pure competition, the impact of one firm's action is negligible because of its small share of the market. Oligopoly thus differs sharply from both monopoly and pure competition, in both of which situations demand can be considered to "stay put" while the firm adjusts itself to the demand-cost situation.

Oligopoly is common in local markets throughout the country. Many towns and cities are large enough to support only a few drugstores, variety stores, department stores, theaters, building materials producers, and so forth. Especially where there is considerable geographic separation between cities, each such seller serves a substantial percentage of the local market and is usually highly sensitive to attempts of competitors to capture larger shares of the market by price cuts or other means.

The larger the market in which a product is sold, the more opportunity there is for a large number of firms (of efficient size) to participate. Nevertheless oligopoly is common also in industries that serve national and international markets. Here, the situation is usually not literally one of only a "few" sellers but frequently there are only a few large firms plus a number of small firms, with the dominant companies accounting for a large percentage of total sales. An oligopolistic situation then exists between the large firms, each being highly sensitive to the actions of the others. The small firms in the field may not be directly concerned with rivals' reactions, but the demand for their products and thus their own price-quantity decisions will be conditioned by the interaction of their major rivals.

REACTIONS TO PRICE CHANGES UNDER OLIGOPOLY

What are the assumptions that one of the few firms in an industry might make about the reaction of its rivals to a price change it makes? The two simplest ones are, first, that all other firms will promptly follow the same price change, and, second, that no firms will make any price changes. The demand curves resulting from these two reactions are shown in Figure 14–1. DD, the price leadership demand curve, is relatively less elastic than dd. Its elasticity can be considered essentially that of the total demand for the commodity insofar as the products of the different firms are homogeneous enough to constitute a commodity. In contrast, dd is more elastic since it reflects the gains or losses in sales by competitors who left their prices unaltered. With many firms, perfect information and standard products dd would be the demand curve facing the firm under perfect competition and DD would be irrelevant. (In that case dd would be horizontal.) The downward sloping dd curve in Figure 14–1 is appropriate with moderate product differentiation. With very substantial product differentiation so that rival firms furnish only distant substitutes, dd and DD coincide as the monopoly demand curve. The concept of price leadership would be irrelevant, since there would be no significant rival to follow.

In Figure 14–1 these four possible demand curves are shown: dxd, DxD, dxD, and Dxd. Let us consider them each in turn. First, dxd represents the limiting case of oligopoly. The consistent absence of any reaction to a firm's price changes would indicate that it produced a negligible proportion of a standard commodity or was the producer of a differentiated good with either so many close competitors that none was significantly affected by its actions (monopolistic competition) or with such great distinctiveness that no close competitors were present to retaliate (monopoly).

If each firm in this industry could assume that its price changes were always exactly duplicated as indicated by DxD, the monopoly model could be a rough approximation for the industry. The equilibrium price might be somewhat different from a single firm monopoly if there were economies or diseconomies of scale because of the difference in the relevant output range for the cost curves. The very condition (of several sellers rather than one) that distinguishes oligopoly from monopoly suggests that the barriers to entry are likely to be lower so that the prices will be set at levels low enough to limit entry and that oligopolies might have more limited prospects of monopoly gains even with strict adherence to the price leaders' choices.

Central to the issue of public policy toward oligopoly situations is the question under what market conditions will it be possible for oligopolists

FIGURE 14–1   Possible Reactions to Price Change under Oligopoly

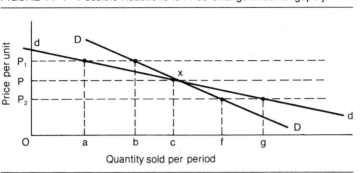

dd—No rivals' reactions.
DD—Price leadership.

to maintain prices based on the industry elasticity of demand that is reflected in *DxD*. Firmly established price leadership could be behavior consistent with the hypothesis advanced by Stigler and others that oligopolists wish to collude to maximize joint profits. But as Stigler points out, "such collusion is impossible for many firms and is much more effective in some circumstances than others."[1] Policing the operation of the tacit collusion involved in consistent price leadership is likely to be more difficult the greater the number of firms and the greater the difference in size of firms, in products, and in the purchase requirements of buyers.

The third possible demand curve from Figure 14–1 is *dxD*, the well-known *kinky or kinked demand curve*, initially advanced as an explanation of rigid oligopoly prices.[2] For a change in price upward from p, the *dx* portion indicates no rivals' reactions. Competitors are satisfied to enjoy the increased quantity of sales available to them since the price of the oligopolist making the price change was a significant determinant of their own demands. (Their respective *dd* curves were shifted to the right by the action of the firm making the price increase.) For a change in price downward, the *xD* portion indicates the price leadership situation of exact retaliation. Other firms would be compelled to respond to the shift of their relatively elastic *dd* curves to the left by meeting the price cut. To put the problems in terms of equalizing *MR* and *MC*, we can recognize a substantial discontinuity in the relevant *MR* curve at output *OC*. There is a substantial gap between the high *MR* associated with the elastic *dx* segment and the much lower and conceivably negative *MR* curve associated with the *xD* segment.

---

[1]George J. Stigler, *The Organization of Industry* (Homewood, Ill.: Richard D. Irwin, 1968), p. 39. Reprinted from *Journal of Political Economy*, February 1964.

[2]The kinked demand curve analysis is associated especially with Paul M. Sweezy, "Demand Conditions under Oligopoly," *Journal of Political Economy*, August 1939; and in a different form with R. L. Hall and C. J. Hitch, "Price Theory and Business Behavior," *Oxford Economic Papers*, no. 2 (May 1939).

The major prediction of the kinked demand curve analysis is that oligopolistic prices would be comparatively rigid in responding to cost changes (tremendous shifts in the MC curves could be accommodated in the discontinuity between the MR segments below x). The kinked demand analysis does not assist in explaining the level of the initial price P, but it was helpful in explaining price rigidities reported in many studies of the 1940s. In general economic analysis, the kinked demand curve has probably been downgraded in significance with widespread rise in prices including those of oligopolies which has been a feature of the postwar period.[3]

From the standpoint of the managerial economist, the kinked demand curve is a useful construct regardless of its general predictive power. In the postwar period, firms faced with rising costs have had to make provision for the possibility that the emerging of the kink would work against them in raising prices. A common pattern is for a firm to test for its existence by announcing a price rise effective as of a future date. If the other major firms follow it, the results are predicted by xD. If they do not follow, the firm will withdraw its prospective price increase to avoid the loss of market share indicated by the kink. Case 14–2 deals with the government's complaint about this practice in the aluminum industry.

It is also a construct that illustrates that the favorable results of an aggressive strategy such as a cut in price will hinge upon avoiding or at least postponing retaliation of other firms. Secret price cutting may thus be preferred to open cuts (see Case 12–2). Major increases in advertising expenditures that could be easily followed may be avoided, while attempts for uniqueness in advertising themes that could be less easily copied may be stressed.

The fourth possible demand curve shown in Figure 14–1, Dxd, has not received the extensive theoretical attention of the others, but it does have an interesting applicability in terms of levels of near capacity operation in an industry accompanied by upward pressures in costs. Why should rivals ignore a downward price change that threatened their sales and respond to an increase in prices? At high levels of operations, a firm initiating a price cut would have limited capacity to accommodate increased sales and thus would do little damage to the market position of competitors who may be already faced with the rising marginal costs of near capacity operations. At the same time, especially if there had been a general increase in costs reflecting a new labor contract or price rise in an important material, the expectations of all of the firms would be for higher prices by their competitors and there would be little fear of loss of market position through a price rise.

---

[3]As early as 1947, George Stigler published an influential article downgrading the importance of the kinked demand curve on empirical grounds that actual oligopoly prices were not significantly more rigid than others when actual prices charged, not posted prices, were taken into account. See G. J. Stigler, "The Kinked Oligopoly Demand Curve and Rigid Prices," *Journal of Political Economy*, October 1947.

The four demand curves shown explicitly in Figure 14–1 suggest the following possible quantities sold per time period in response to price changes from P to P_1 or P_2. For an increase in price, the firm is predicted to sell either oa or ob; for a reduction in price, either of or og. The only alternative reactions considered have been that all rivals react exactly and immediately or that none react at all. One range of possibilities ignored so far has been that an initial price cut might produce greater price cuts by the competitors so that even at the lower price less might be sold than the quantity oc associated with price P.[4] In effect, the initial price cut was the signal for a price war in which the motive of the firm's rivals was to discipline the initiator of the price cut and possibly to reduce capacity in the industry by eliminating weaker firms.

Another range of possibilities lies within the areas bounded by the dd and DD curves. Within these areas are points representing the effective demand curves if the reaction is delayed or takes the form of price changes smaller than those of the initiator. The reaction may not necessarily take the form of a price change but could be increased advertising or product improvements by the competitor to reduce losses and limit the initiator's advantage. Oligopolistic indeterminancy can be illustrated by drawing many possible demand curves through point x; the relevant demand curve depending upon the specific reactions of rivals.

CONCENTRATION OF AMERICAN INDUSTRY AND OLIGOPOLY

A popular statistical device for showing the existence of oligopolistic situations on a national basis is the *concentration ratio*. This measure is the percentage of total output, shipments, sales, or employment accounted for by the largest firms in a given industry. Such ratios are published from time to time by the Bureau of the Census and the Federal Trade Commission. The ratios are greatly affected by the broadness or narrowness of industry classification—for example, the "food and kindred products" industry covers such a wide range of activities that it can scarcely show up as concentrated.

Figure 14–2 shows selected industry concentration ratios based on the percentage of sales accounted for by the largest 4 and by the leading 20 firms in the industry. With a few exceptions, the listing is based on the five-digit Standard Industrial Classification for product classes, which usually more closely represent goods in actual market competition than do the four-digit industries.[5] A few ratios for four-digit industries are included when they more closely represent competitive realities and for

---

[4]This possibility is shown graphically in Figure 5–4 of Chapter 5 as curve D_3.

[5]For manufacturing, the SIC in 1972 included 20 two-digit manufacturing categories broken down into 143 three-digit broad industries. These in turn included 450 four-digit industries with 1,300 five-digit product classes. The finest seven-digit breakdown included 10,000 products.

FIGURE 14–2 Concentration Ratios for Selected Industries and Product Classes

SIC Code	Industry or Product Class	1972 4-Firm Ratio	1972 20-Firm Ratio	Earlier Date 4-Firm Ratio and Year	Value of Shipments 1972 ($ millions)
32111	Sheet (window) glass	100	100	95(58)	157
37111	Passenger cars	99+	100	98(54)	29,246
38615	Sensitized photo film and plates . . .	n.a.	99+	96(58)	1,085
3711	Motor vehicles and cars	93	99+	93(67)	41,054
20873	Flavoring sirups for soft-drink bottlers.	89	97	89(54)	6,371
21110	Cigarettes	84	100	90(47)	3,589
20670	Chewing gum and gum base	84	99+	84(54)	385
37112	Truck tractors, chassis and trucks . .	84	99+	77(54)	9,568
20430	Cereal breakfast foods	84	99	78(54)	935
28413	Household detergents.	84	97	n.a.	1,646
3211	Flat glass.	83	n.a.	90(58)	1,248
33347	Aluminum ingot produced in primary plants.	81	100	93(63)	1,510
30111	Tire casings for passenger cars	77	100	74(58)	2,860
22710	Woven carpets and rugs	62	95	50(58)	202
20821	Canned beer and ale	59	96	n.a.	2,206
33123	Hot rolled steel strip and sheet	54	98	56(58)	6,510
2082	Malt beverages.	52	91	27(54)	4,039
2841	Soap and other detergents	62	79	68(58)	2,862
3714	Motor vehicle parts and accessories	62	79	61(63)	19,399
3312	Blast furnaces and steel mills	45	84	55(54)	10,305
33417	Aluminum ingot from secondary smelters	50	89	44(63)	341
20860	Bottled and canned soft drinks	14	32	11(58)	4,801
20511	Bread, white, wheat, and rye	27	36	19(54)	2,444
2721	Periodicals.	22	50	31(58)	3,187
32410	Cement, hydraulic.	26	79	31(54)	1,758
20372	Frozen vegetables	35	82	52(54)	914
20111	Beef, not canned or used in sausage	30	58	36(54)	11,771
22112	Cotton sheeting and allied products.	28	77	24(54)	532
22720	Tufted carpets and rugs.	21	57	28(58)	2,626
24212	Sawmills and planing mills, softwood	20	40	n.a.	3,908
2421	Sawmills and planing mills.	17	32	10(63)	6,000
2835	Women's and misses' dresses	9	18	4(58)	3,535
28351	Ditto, sold at unit (not dozen) price. .	14	29	5(58)	1,826
3451	Screw-machine products.	5	15	12(54)	1,084
34512	Other screw-machine products	4	17	n.a.	639

n.a. = not available.

SOURCE: *Concentration Ratios in Manufacturing* (1972 Census of Manufactures, Bureau of the Census, U.S. Department of Commerce, 1975).

comparison. The 52 percent four-firm share for "malt beverages" (SIC #2082) probably better describes beer competition than the 59 percent four-firm share for "canned beer and ale" (SIC #20821), though the higher figure for the latter is suggestive of how the large national companies initially made their greatest inroads against locals and regionals in the cheaper-to-ship cans rather than bottles and kegs. The very great increase in malt beverages four-firm concentration ratio from 27 percent in 1954 to

52 percent in 1972, and very probably to about 70 percent at the time you are reading this text, is not representative of a general movement toward oligopoly. In Figure 14–2, the increases in concentration ratios are about balanced by the decreases.

The first group of product classes in Figure 14–2 with four-firm concentration ratios of over 80 percent, clearly appear to have earned the market status of oligopoly. Even George Stigler's study with data suggesting that "there is no relationship between profitability and concentration if the share of the four largest firms is less than about 80 percent" does not apply to them.[6] Questions can be raised, however, as to the significance of some of the ratios as a measure of collective market power. Only for sensitive film is the relevant market share probably over 90 percent, showing the influence of fineness of classification. Imports, which are over 20 percent of unit passenger car sales, reduce the significant number for the three motor vehicle categories. The 100 percent figure for the "sheet (window) glass" category scarcely describes the competition with plate glass as well as does the lower figure for the four-digit flat glass industry. Aluminum ingot from secondary smelters (SIC #33417) competes with primary ingot (SIC #33347).

The second group of industries and product classes almost certainly include oligopolistic relationships. In most cases, the four-firm ratios are 50 percent or more, and for each of the exceptions there is a strong case for assuming dominance by a few firms in relevant markets. Both for bread and cement, there is much greater concentration in regional markets, because of product perishability and high transportation costs respectively. Periodicals fall into highly differentiated classes such as national newsweeklies in which *Time, Newsweek,* and *U.S. News & World Report* dominate. While bottled and canned soft drinks are produced in many localities, most of their output is franchised by Coca-Cola, Pepsi-Cola, and a few others, in the highly concentrated flavoring syrup product class. For many of the industries, high 20-firm ratios suggest not only the lack of a significant competitive fringe of firms but also barriers to entry for new small firms.

The third group of product classes and industries have low enough ratios to suggest vigorous competition, in some cases with significant product differentiation. It is almost equally divided between industries in which four-firm concentration ratios have increased such as cotton sheeting, women's dresses, and sawmills, and in which they have decreased (frozen vegetables, beef, tufted carpets, and screw machine products). One would expect these contrasting trends to reflect a combination of industry growth (favorable to more firms and lower ratios) and increases in the minimum efficient scale of individual firms' operations (favorable to fewer firms and higher ratios).

---

[6]George J. Stigler, *The Organization of Industry* (Homewood, Ill.: Richard D. Irwin, 1968), p. 69.

Oligopolistic situations are certainly common in manufacturing, the industrial sector for which concentration ratios are calculated. A study suggests that as many as 75 percent of 7,000 manufactured products in the finest breakdown compiled by the Department of Commerce may have four-firm concentrations of 50 percent or more of sales.[7] Economists differ substantially in their estimates of what degree of industrial concentration is necessary for oligopoly elements to be significant. The list of concentration ratios in Figure 14–2 suggested a 50 percent share for four firms as appropriate, a figure that is in line with other studies of profitability and concentration. Carl Kaysen and Donald F. Turner using a broad grouping of industries set the minimum for oligopoly at an eight-firm concentration ratio of 33 percent and found that 62 percent of all manufacturing shipments in 1954 were then found in such industries.[8]

PURE AND DIFFERENTIATED OLIGOPOLY

Pure oligopoly may be said to exist when sellers of a homogeneous commodity are few in number. This situation is more common among producers of industrial materials than in the consumer goods fields. Most consumer goods are differentiated from one another by means of brand names, trademarks, and packaging, and usually by some differences in physical characteristics. Materials and components turned out by different companies for use as inputs into production processes are more frequently identical. Even if the name of the producer is stamped on the good, this is not apt to influence an experienced industrial buyer if the product is, in fact, identical with that of another firm. Consumers of finished products, on the other hand, are often influenced by brand names and advertising, even where no substantial difference in the commodity actually exists. (Aspirin is a famous example. Cornstarch also qualifies.) As a consequence, *pure oligopoly* may be said to be present in such fields as the manufacture of primary aluminum, primary copper, aluminum rolling and drawing, and certain gypsum products, whereas *differentiated* oligopoly exists for automobiles, cigarettes, hard-surface floor coverings, typewriters, sewing machines, and a great many other commodities.

When oligopolistic firms are few in number and have identical products, their demands are highly interdependent. As concentration of production diminishes, and as products are more differentiated, demands are less closely interdependent. If the number of firms selling in a market becomes large enough so that each can disregard the reactions of his rivals to his own price-output actions, the market situation is often designated by economists as *monopolistic competiton* or *pure competition*, depend-

---

[7]Dean A. Worcester, Jr., *Monopoly, Big Business and Welfare in the Postwar United States* (Seattle: University of Washington Press, 1967), chap. 4.

[8]In *Antitrust Policy: An Economic and Legal Analysis* (Cambridge, Mass.: Harvard University Press, 1959).

ing on whether differentiated or nondifferentiated products are sold. In each case a single demand curve confronts the firm: in the former case, this is a downsloping demand curve such as that designated as dd in Figure 14–1. In the latter case, it is a horizontal line. If there are no rivals selling the same commodity in the same market, the situation is designated as monopoly. The distinction between "monopoly" and "monopolistic competition" is not a clear one, however, since it encounters the same difficulty of classifying industries as is involved in compiling statistics on concentration. If *industry* is defined very narrowly and products are differentiated, there is only one firm in each industry (e.g., the "Campbell Soup industry"). If the industry is defined more broadly, the Campbell Soup Company becomes instead one firm of a number in the "canned soup industry." On a still broader basis, it is one of a very large number of firms in the "food and food products industry." Whether the company is "oligopolistic" or not depends on whether, in fact, its price adjustments will cause speedy reactions on the part of the other companies. If such reactions would occur, the company can be classified as a "differentiated oligopolist."

THE VARIETY OF OLIGOPOLISTIC SITUATIONS AS AN INFLUENCE ON BUSINESS DECISIONS

The analysis accompanying Figure 14–1 has been essentially designed to indicate the range of possible reactions that might have to be taken into account by a firm in its price decisions. It is not a simplified presentation of a generally accepted theory of oligopoly pricing. There are many oligopoly models, but there is no such generally accepted theory of oligopoly pricing. The absence of such a theory reflects the wide range of markets that may have some element of the oligopolistic interdependence that we have discussed.

   Concentration ratios and number of firms. Even when concentration ratios are well above the levels accepted by most economists as oligopolistic, the variations may be great. For example, in the domestic automobile industry, General Motors has usually accounted for just over 50 percent of the market and four producers for virtually 100 percent.[9] In the steel industry, U.S. Steel has had somewhat less than 25 percent, 8 producers have had three quarters of the market, but approximately 75 firms have produced some primary steel. In contrast, Traditional Depart-

---

[9]In the late 1970s, General Motors had pushed to 60 percent of the domestic production (Canada and the United States constitute a unified production area because of the tariff free arrangement on vehicles and parts). A fifth domestic producer, Volkswagen of America, had reduced the four-firm concentration ratio to less than 99 percent. Nonetheless, with imports running at 20 percent, General Motors frequently had less than 50 percent of unit sales.

ment Store (see Case 14–4) faced many competitors on most of its product types but was particularly conscious of the rivalry of two other downtown department stores.

International competition. In 1939, imports of goods and services were less than 4 percent of GNP; not until 1965 did they exceed 5 percent; in 1978 they passed 10 percent; and in 1984 were 12 percent. The general thrust of this increased international trade has been to reduce the significance of domestic concentration ratios and number of producers as measures of monopoly power in many oligopolistic industries such as automobiles, home electronic products such as TV, capital goods industries, and various industrial supplies. Despite common complaints about conspiracy among American oil companies, it was clear in 1979 that the price level of petroleum products was more clearly established by the production limitations of OPEC countries than by oligopolistic interdependencies among American producers and distributors. Recent troubles in OPEC have helped users of oil and gasoline.

Homogeneity of products. Compare automobiles that are differentiated in many features with steel ingot or with copper-beryllium alloys (see Case 14–1), both standard products. The close physical similarity of different classes of cigarettes has not stood in the way of strong brand preferences. Were everything else constant, less interdependence would be expected of the differentiated products.

Reliance on advertising. Cigarettes and beer are heavily advertised; steel very little. Automobiles receive substantial advertising, but as a percentage of the very large sales, the industry rates low.

Unlike other types of product differentiation, the image-building by substantial advertising may lead to greater pricing interdependence and identity rather than less. For example, accelerated advertising for beer, for which taste tests have indicated low brand recognition, has led to more rapid declines in the position of regional brands whose prices were significantly lower. This was conspicuously the case in the 1970s when Philip Morris took over the Miller Brewing Company and escalated advertising expenditures, along with introducing Lite and Löwenbräu beers. Its takeover of second place from Schlitz and challenge to Anheuser-Busch for first in the late 1970s was accompanied by industry-wide advertising increases. In the cigarette industry, ever since World War I a strong motive for following the price leader on price increases has been the provision of adequate margins for advertising.

Number of purchasers of the product. For example, the smaller the number of purchasers, the greater the advantages of secret price cutting for gaining sales. The automobile industry with thousands of purchasing dealers is in quite a different position than the beryllium industry with a few industrial purchasers.

Economies of scale in plant versus firm. If concentration rests on the economies of scale of single plants, barriers to entry may be larger than when large firms have been built up from many small plants. For example, the distilling industry had a four-firm concentration ratio of 64 percent in 1954 but the four firms operated 54 plants. Its profit record has not suggested that the oligopoly has been effective in maintaining high price-cost ratios.[10]

Rapidity of technological development. Unusually rapid technological developments may be productive of cost differences that encourage independent price cuts. For example, in the market for computer memories, competitors of IBM translated into lower prices the advances in the 1970s of the semiconductor industry in increasing the capacity of silicon chips from 1,000 to 16,000 bits. Thus, while in 1975 IBM charged 3.1¢ per bit, the lowest competitive price was 0.9¢. This discrepancy continued with prices being lowered until 1979 when IBM with its new 4300 line using a 64,000-bit chip met the competitive price of 0.15¢.[11]

Other differing characteristics such as the rate of growth of demand could be also cited. Underlying several of the market features above but worth stressing is the importance of barriers to entry in the determination of whether prices can be maintained significantly above the long-run cost levels. Which strategies will be chosen for reducing the uncertainties facing the oligopolistic firm that are discussed in the following sections will in part reflect this variety of market characteristics.

CARTELIZATION OR FORMAL AGREEMENTS

That the strictures of the Sherman Act against such restraints have not always been effective has been shown in the electrical price conspiracy case following Chapter 18. Even legal agreements to fix prices often break down since a firm that chooses not to abide by the agreement may have considerable incentive to cut prices if the rivals do not follow.

The experience of international cartels—such as those that have at times operated in such commodities as rubber and coffee—underlines the threat of the entry of new firms that can initially operate under the umbrella of the cartelized price and later, as they gain increased market shares, rupture the agreements. The sanction of government intervention frequently has been sought to make effective price and market-sharing agreements. The strong support by drug retailers for fair-trade pricing has been based on their desire that the minimum prices charged by their rivals will be predictable. Part of the past weakness of such price agreements had been that enforcement was left to private litigation. Proposals for strengthening price maintenance legislation by making the government

---

[10]Stigler, *Organization of Industry*, p. 54, calculated a rate of return on net worth of 7.55 percent from 1953 to 1957 in the industry, far below the 23.9 percent for sulfur and 20.3 percent for automobiles.

[11]Bro Uttal, "How the 4300 Fits IBM's New Strategy," *Fortune*, July 30, 1979, p. 62.

responsible for enforcement have failed. (See Chapter 18.) Other legalized cartel arrangements in the United States have been in the fluid milk industry—where prices in most parts of the country are controlled by federal or state commissions—and in sugar production—where import quotas and domestic quotas have been used to limit the supply and maintain a price that is usually far in excess of the world price.

Perhaps the particular price-fixing arrangements most familiar to men who still utilize their services is that of the master barbers associations in many cities. Local business is largely exempt from the federal antitrust laws, and few of the state laws are used. The most extensive government encouragement of price-fixing arrangements was found under the National Recovery Administration (NRA) codes of 1933 and 1934. Although the industry codes were not designed for this purpose, "560 of the first 677 codes contained some provisions relating to minimum prices or costs."[12]

PRICE LEADERSHIP AND OTHER CONVENTIONS

An effective method of avoiding price uncertainties and of limiting price competition may be found in the practice of price leadership. There have been antitrust questions raised about a firmly established price leadership convention, but in recent years suits against such parallel action have not been pushed. Under this system of tacitly collusive pricing, an important firm is usually the one to decide upon and initiate a price change, automatically followed by the other companies. It is, of course, difficult to generalize with respect to how much consultation takes place between industry officials prior to the initiation of a price change by the leader. If a great deal of interchange occurs, the system may not differ basically from that of overt agreement on price. If, however, the leader initiates the change after little or no advice from others in the industry, the form of collusion is quite different in nature. It is then primarily an "agreement to agree" on price rather than an agreement as to what the actual price should be. Frequently, the largest firm in the industry acts as price leader. If the product is sold in interstate commerce, there is danger in this practice, however, since the pattern may be too obvious to any interested antitrust investigator. For this reason, it may be safer to have other firms initiate the price change from time to time, with the "leader" a temporary follower. To carry out this sort of rotation of leadership, however, may require so much cooperation that the tacit collusion approaches overt price agreement.[13]

---

[12]Arthur R. Burns, *Decline of Competition* (New York: McGraw-Hill, 1936), pp. 471–72.

[13]"The essential combination or conspiracy in violation of the Sherman Act may be found in a course of dealings or other circumstances as well as in exchange of words. . . ," *American Tobacco Co. v. United States*, 328 U.S. 781 (1946).

Previously in this chapter an exploratory form of price leadership has been discussed. A firm may announce a price rise for a future date and find out whether its rivals go along without risking loss of sales. It can thereby reduce its uncertainty with relatively small costs compared with bearing the onus of proposing an immediate price rise.

Other conventions that aim at reducing the unpredictability of rivals' responses have been part of trade association activities. Systems of reporting prices at which immediately past sales have been made may well reduce the incentive for price cutting by increasing the likelihood of retaliation, and at the very least can reduce the uncertainties of association members as to prices of competitors.

EMPHASIS ON POLICIES THAT ARE DIFFICULT TO RETALIATE AGAINST

Market expanding activities of one of few sellers may well emphasize forms of nonprice competition. Both advertising and product differentiation are methods that may both serve to increase sales and by establishing greater distinctiveness for the product lead to less interdependence with the decisions of other sellers in the future.

More is involved in changing price than erasing just one figure. Whole price schedules including quantity discounts, charges for special services, and variations for quality differences frequently must be redrafted. Nonetheless, the changes can be accomplished rapidly and are essentially one-dimensional in comparison with the many alternatives involved in changing product quality or formulating advertising approaches. Prompt, exact retaliation is virtually impossible to product and advertising programs. Basic product innovations can establish a time gap of years. For example, while Ford introduced Maverick, a new small car, in the spring of 1969, General Motor's entry did not come until the summer of 1970.

In the late 1970s, General Motors' growing dominance of domestic automobile production rested on its lead of two years in downsizing cars, climaxed in the spring of 1979 with unusually roomy, frontwheel drive compacts such as the Chevrolet Citation.

That nonprice competition can be both a complement and alternative to price competition is discussed more fully in Chapter 15.

INDEPENDENT ACTION WITH LITTLE CONCERN FOR REACTIONS

One way of dealing with the complexity of possible reactions of competitors is to ignore them. Professor Baumol, on the basis of his work as a business consultant, has concluded that large firms may pay little attention to each others actions except where important long-range decisions must be made.[14] For example, in early 1955 when RCA cut its price on its classical long-playing records, it was primarily convinced "that the mass market was ready for a real assault," [15] and the response of its competitors was not a real issue.

Three characteristics of this episode are suggestive of circumstances under which reaction of competitors is immaterial; substantial differentiation of the product, the leading firm in the industry, and an aggressive move. The first two of these characteristics are fulfilled by General Motors, and in Case 14–3 it may be noted that its basic pricing formula with its emphasis on costs at a standard volume with a rate of return target is largely independent of competitors' reactions, although the pricing approach does allow for adjustments to meet market conditions.

Companies that are in the top four among the concentrated industries shown in Figure 14–2, and many others in manufacturing, transportation, mining, communications, electric power, banking, and other fields are often characterized as "big business." Officials of such firms inevitably emphasize the competitiveness of the activities in which they are engaged, and it is true that few are so well insulated from competition, actual and potential, that they can continue to prosper unless management is alert and ready to adapt to changing conditions. At the same time, large firms are in a better position to view profit making over the long run, partly because their financial strength nearly guarantees that they will be in business for a long time. A short-term opportunity to make unusual profits is more likely to be passed up by a very large company if it involves a possibility of damaging its "public image." The long waiting lists for some popular makes of cars following resumption of automobile production after World War II were an indication that sellers were not attempting to maximize immediate profits. (A queue of buyers can always be broken up by a sufficiently high price.)

It is sometimes said that many large firms set price to cover all costs and provide a target rate of return on capital. Such target rates can be consistent with profit maximization and may incorporate a longer run view of the effect of current prices on demand, entry of new rivals, union wage demands, and government action in such matters as antitrust, tariffs, and award of contracts. Examination of the pricing policy of large companies is especially difficult partly because many products are typically turned out by a single firm. Different degrees of control over supply, and consequently of price, are likely to prevail for various products. General principles regarding pricing policy of large firms, as far as they differ from the theory of price determination in general, cannot be stated with confidence. Perhaps the most revealing information is obtained by intensive study of particular firms. Two case studies (Case 14–2 and Case 14–3) of pricing by large companies follow.

---

[14]William Baumol, *Business Behavior, Value and Growth* (New York: Macmillan, 1959), chap. 4.

[15]*Business Week*, January 1, 1955.

CASE 14–1
The Riverside Metal Company*

On May 9, 1939, H. L. Randall, president of the Riverside Metal Company of Riverside, New Jersey, submitted the following statement of price policies to the Temporary National Economic Committee: "The price schedules issued by the Riverside Metal Company are contingent upon the prices published by the larger units of industry. From time to time these larger units publish their scale of prices, and our company has no alternative except to meet such published prices in order to compete."

Beryllium is an element that can be combined with copper, nickel, and certain other metals to produce alloys that possess great qualities of hardness, lightness, and strength. The principal industrial form in which this metal is used is in the alloy, beryllium copper, which consists of about 2 percent beryllium and 98 percent copper. The chief advantages of beryllium copper are the combination of extraordinary high-fatigue properties with good electrical conductivity. Beryllium alloys have many industrial uses, such as parts for electric motors, telephone instruments, diamond drills, and airplanes. Altimeters used in airplanes have beryllium copper diaphragms because these are more sensitive than other materials. Beryllium alloys are also used in bushings on machine parts.

Beryllium metal is derived from beryl oxide-bearing ores, which are refined by a relatively simple process. For technical reasons, refiners sell beryllium in the form of a master alloy, which contains 3.5–5 percent beryllium, with the remainder copper. Fabricators melt the master alloy and add copper to bring the final beryllium copper alloy to the desired weight, frequently 2 percent in beryllium content.

In 1939, beryllium master alloy was being produced from ore by two principal companies, the Beryllium Corporation of Reading, Pennsylvania, and the Brush Beryllium Company of Cleveland, Ohio. These companies also fabricated the master alloy into sheets, strips, castings, and other products. Both companies sold master alloy to fabricators of beryllium alloy products. The largest of these fabricators was the American Brass Company of Waterbury, Connecticut. The Riverside Metal Company was one of the smallest fabricating firms in the beryllium alloy industry.

The following testimony from the hearings of the Temporary National Economic Committee[16] describes some aspects of price policies used in the industry (see also Exhibit 14–1A).

---

*SOURCE: Material for this case was derived largely from *T.N.E.C. Hearings,* Part 5, 76th Cong., 1st sess. (Washington, D.C.: U.S. Government Printing Office, 1939).

Of the 51 cases in the original edition of *Business Economics,* this is the only one that appears in substantially the same form as it did in 1951. The original authors, Richard M. Alt and William C. Bradford, have been replaced, the number of chapters has increased from 8 to 18, and more words are printed on each page. Some business issues change but many remain the same.

[16]Ibid., pp. 2084 ff.

EXHIBIT 14–1A   Beryllium Copper Base Prices, 1935–1939

Date	Riverside Metal Co.			Date	American Brass Co.		
	Sheet	Wire	Rods		Sheet	Wire	Rods
February 25, 1935	0.97	1.25	0.97	February 6, 1935	0.97	1.25	0.97
June 28, 1935	0.96	1.24	0.96	June 27, 1935	0.96	1.25	0.97
August 22, 1935	0.96½	1.24½	0.96½	August 20, 1935	0.96½	1.24½	0.96½
September 19, 1935	0.97	1.25	0.97	September 27, 1935	0.97	1.25	0.97
October 27, 1936	0.98	1.26	0.98	October 27, 1936	0.98	1.26	0.98
November 7, 1936	0.98½	1.26½	0.98½	November 7, 1936	0.98½	1.26½	0.98½
December 15, 1936	0.99	1.27	0.99	December 15, 1936	0.99	1.27	0.99
December 31, 1936	1.00	1.28	1.00	December 31, 1936	1.00	1.28	1.00
January 14, 1937	1.01	1.29	1.00	January 14, 1937	1.01	1.29	1.01
February 16, 1937	1.02	1.30	1.02	February 16, 1937	1.02	1.30	1.02
February 22, 1937	1.03	1.31	1.03	February 22, 1937	1.03	1.31	1.03
March 8, 1937	1.05	1.33	1.05	March 8, 1937	1.05	1.33	1.05
March 31, 1937	1.06	1.34	1.06	March 31, 1937	1.06	1.34	1.06
April 6, 1937	1.05	1.33	1.05	April 6, 1937	1.05	1.33	1.05
April 20, 1937	1.04	1.32	1.04	April 20, 1937	1.04	1.32	1.04
October 26, 1937	1.03	1.31	1.03	October 26, 1937	1.03	1.31	1.03
November 23, 1937	1.02	1.30	1.02	November 23, 1937	1.02	1.30	1.02
January 20, 1938	1.12	1.30	1.12	January 20, 1938	1.12	1.30	1.12
January 28, 1938	1.11½	1.29½	1.11½	January 28, 1938	1.11½	1.29½	1.11½
May 20, 1938	1.10½	1.28½	1.10½	May 20, 1938	1.10½	1.28½	1.10½
July 5, 1938	1.11	1.29	1.11	July 5, 1938	1.11	1.29	1.11
July 25, 1938	1.11¼	1.29¼	1.11¼	July 25, 1938	1.11¼	1.29¼	1.11¼
September 19, 1938	1.11½	1.29½	1.11½	September 19, 1938	1.11½	1.29½	1.11½
October 10, 1938	1.11¾	1.29¾	1.11¾	October 10, 1938	1.11⅞	1.29⅞	1.11⅞
October 13, 1938	1.12	1.30	1.12	October 13, 1938	1.12	1.30	1.12
April 20, 1939	1.11	1.29	1.11	April 20, 1939	1.11	1.29	1.11

SOURCE: T.N.E.C. Hearings, Part 5, 76th Cong. 1st sess. (Washington, D.C.: U.S. Government Printing Office, 1939), pp. 2284, 2287–88.

Mr. Cox: You are the president of the Riverside Brass Co.?

Mr. Randall: Riverside Metal Co.

Mr. Cox: What is the business of that company?

Mr. Randall: The business of the Riverside Metal Co. is the fabrication of nonferrous alloys into rod, wire, sheet, and strip. We supply the manufacturer with a raw product.

Mr. Cox: You buy the master alloy and fabricate the material?

Mr. Randall: That is correct.

* * * * *

We make nickel silvers, phosphor bronzes, some brass; I think altogether we have an alloy list of over 80 different alloys.

Mr. Cox: Are all of the alloys which your company makes alloys which are also made and sold by the American Brass Co.?

Mr. Randall: I think that would be true.

Mr. Cox: How large a company is your company? Will you give us your capitalization?

Mr. Randall: Our capitalization is one and a half million dollars, and we are almost the smallest unit in the industry; there may be one or two smaller, but I think we are almost the smallest.

Mr. Cox: Can you give us any approximate figure to indicate what percentage of the industry your company controls?

Mr. Randall: Less than 1½ percent.

* * * * *

Mr. Cox: From whom do you buy the master alloys?

Mr. Randall: We buy the master alloys from the Beryllium Products Corporation.

Mr. Cox: That is Mr. Gahagan?

Mr. Randall: Mr. Gahagan.

Mr. Cox: Have you always bought all of your master alloy from that company?

Mr. Randall: Practically all; yes.

* * * * *

Mr. Cox: Mr. Randall, would it be correct to say that there is a well-crystallized practice of price leadership in the industry in which you are engaged?

Mr. Randall: I would say so.

Mr. Cox: And what company is the price leader?

Mr. Randall: I would say the American Brass Co. holds that position.

Mr. Cox: And your company follows the prices which are announced by American Brass?

Mr. Randall: That is correct.

Mr. Cox: So that when they reduce the price you have to reduce it too. Is that correct?

Mr. Randall: Well, we don't have to, but we do.

Mr. Cox: And when they raise the price you raise the price.

Mr. Randall: That is correct.

Mr. Cox: Do you remember that in February 1937, Mr. Gahagan's company reduced the price of the master alloy from $30 to $23 a pound?

Mr. Randall: I didn't know it at that time.

Mr. Cox: You did know there was a price decrease.

Mr. Randall: I do now.

Mr. Cox: Weren't you buying from Mr. Gahagan?

Mr. Randall: I think we were buying from them but it was quite some time after that I got the information that the price had gone down.

Mr. Cox: After the decrease in the price of the master alloy, it is a fact, isn't it, that there was no decrease in price of the fabricated product which you made?

Mr. Randall: I don't remember about that, I don't know, because I don't know when that decrease took place.

Mr. Cox: Looking at your sheet prices for the year 1937, you started at $1.01 a pound on January 14, 1937, and rose progressively until you reached $1.06 on March 31, and then on April 6, 1937, they dropped to $1.05. You remember those.

Mr. Randall: Yes; I remember those. That was copper.

*   *   *   *   *

Mr. Cox: But you do know there was about that time a decrease of $7 a pound in the price which you were paying to Mr. Gahagan.

Mr. Randall: Yes; I do know that.

Mr. Cox: I will put this question to you, Mr. Randall. Why didn't you reduce the price of the fabricated product following that decrease in the price of the master alloy?

Mr. Randall: Well, of course I would not make a reduction in the base price of beryllium copper unless the American Brass made a price reduction in beryllium copper.

Mr. Cox: And the American Brass Co. made no reduction at that time?

Mr. Randall: If they did, we did, as indicated on that sheet.

Mr. Cox: Assuming you didn't make a price change then, the reason you didn't was because the American Brass Co. didn't.

Mr. Randall: That is correct.

Mr. Arnold: You exercise no individual judgment as to the price you charged for your product, then, in a situation?

Mr. Randall: Well, I think that is about what it amounts to; yes, sir.

Mr. Arnold: When you say you have to follow, you don't mean anybody told you you had to follow?

Mr. Randall: No sir; I don't mean that at all.

Mr. Arnold: But you have a feeling something might happen if you didn't?

Mr. Randall: I don't know what would happen.

Mr. Cox: You don't want to find out, do you?

The Chairman: Well, as a matter of fact, Mr. Randall, if the American Brass Co. raised the price would the Brass Co. consult you about raising it?

Mr. Randall: No, sir; not at all.

The Chairman: You would, however, follow them without exercising any independent judgment as to whether or not it was desirable.

Mr. Randall: That is correct.

The Chairman: Suppose the American Brass Co. raises its price, but you are satisfied with your output and with the profit that you are making at the old price. Why is it necessary for you to increase your price to your customers, who are already paying you a price sufficient to give you a profit that is satisfactory to you?

Mr. Randall: I don't know that it is necessary; as a practical matter, if we didn't raise our prices the American Brass Co. or other companies, whoever they might be, would put their price back to where it was.

Mr. Chairman: That wouldn't bother you, because you were making a profit at the old price.

Mr. Randall: Not on beryllium copper.

The Chairman: Why do you do it?

Mr. Randall: It is the custom of the industry, at least of the smaller companies, to do that.

The Chairman: And other small companies do the same thing?

Mr. Randall: Yes, sir.

The Chairman: Is there any reason outside of custom for it?

Mr. Randall: No, sir.

The Chairman: Isn't it likely to reduce the amount of business that you obtain?

Mr. Randall: I don't think so.

The Chairman: Well, if a competitor raises the price for an identical product, isn't it likely to believe that the producer who does not raise the price would get more business?

Mr. Randall: I imagine it would, if the other price stayed where it had been raised to. I think that might work out over a period of time.

The Chairman: You see, I am trying to get some understanding of the exact reasons why this price policy is followed, and it is not an answer—understand me, I am not criticizing your answer—that carries conviction merely to say it is the custom of the industry. There is a reason for customs. What, in your opinion, is the reason for this custom to follow the leader?

Mr. Randall: Well, of course, that is a custom which has been prevalent, I think, in the industry for many, many years prior to my entry into it.

The Chairman: Oh, yes; we hear a lot about price leadership, but I am trying to get the picture of this practice as you see it, and why you follow it.

Mr. Randall: Well, I don't think I have ever given the matter very much consideration. We simply, when the new prices come out, print them just as they are. We don't give the matter any consideration. The prices are published and we print those prices.

The Chairman: Is there any sort of compulsion, moral or otherwise?

Mr. Randall: Absolutely none.

The Chairman: Do you think it is a good practice?

Mr. Randall: Well, I have never given the subject very much consideration.

The Chairman: Now, of course, it is one of the most important subjects in your business.

Mr. Randall: Yes; it is, of course.

The Chairman: The price that you get for your product.

Mr. Randall: I can't answer that question. I don't know whether it is a good practice or whether it isn't a good practice. I know that it has been the custom of the industry for years on end, and I know that it is what we do, that's all.

The Chairman: A moment ago, in response to either Mr. Cox's question or my question, you answered that if you did not follow the price up, then the American Brass Co. or some other company would come down again.

Mr. Randall: I don't think I said they would. I said they probably would or they might. I don't know what they would do.

The Chairman: Then I made the comment that that would not be a disturbing result, because it would mean merely the restoration of the old price. I could imagine, however, that you might start a price war, and that the other companies might go below you. Is there a possibility that that is what you have in mind?

Mr. Randall: I didn't have it in mind until this moment. That is a possibility; yes.

The Chairman: So you want the committee to understand that so far as you and your company are concerned, this price-leadership question is one to which you have never given any real consideration, and you have boosted your prices along with the American Brass Co. just as a matter of custom.

Mr. Randall: Yes.

* * * * *

Mr. Arnold: . . . but if this policy is continued, you will continue to follow the American Brass regardless of what your costs are, won't you, so that won't be an element in the picture?

Mr. Randall: Of course, to be perfectly frank, on that subject we don't know what our costs are on beryllium.

Mr. Arnold: It wouldn't make any difference if you did, so far as the present prices are concerned, would it?

Mr. Randall: No sir; I don't think it would.

Mr. Arnold: In other words, there is a situation here where there is a lot of competitors and no competition.

Mr. Randall: Well, we simply, as I said before, follow the prices that are published, and that is what we have been doing for a good many years.

* * * * *

At the conclusion of Mr. Randall's testimony, Mr. John A. Coe, Jr., general sales manager of the American Brass Company, was called to the stand. His testimony follows:

Mr. Cox: What is the nature of the business of the American Brass Co.?

Mr. Coe: The American Brass Co. is engaged in the production of copper, brass, bronze, and nickel silver in wrought forms, including sheet, wire, rods and tubes and other fabricated forms.

Mr. Cox: What is the capitalization of the company?

Mr. Coe: The American Brass Co. is a wholly owned fabricating subsidiary of the Anaconda Copper Mining Co.

Mr. Cox: Can you tell us what the capitalization of the company is?

Mr. Coe: I do not know what it is.

Mr. Cox: You heard Mr. Randall testify that his company did less than 1½ percent of the business in which he was engaged. Can you give us any approximate figure as to the percentage of the business which your company does?

Mr. Coe: Approximately 25 percent.

Mr. Cox: You heard Mr. Randall's testimony with respect to the system of price leadership which prevails.

Mr. Coe: Yes.

Mr. Cox: Would you agree with his description of that system insofar as it denoted your company as the price leader?

Mr. Coe: I wouldn't agree with that statement.

Mr. Cox: You wouldn't agree with the statement?

Mr. Coe: No.

Mr. Cox: In other words, it your position that your company is not the price leader in the industry?

Mr. Coe: We are not the price leader of the industry.

Mr. Cox: It is a fact, is it not, that your prices for beryllium copper have been substantially the same as those of Mr. Randall for a period between 1934 and the present time?

Mr. Coe: So far as I know, they have been practically the same.

Mr. Cox: Practically the same prices. Now, you say you are not the price leader. Is there any price leader in the industry?

Mr. Coe: There is none.

Mr. Cox: Then how do you explain the fact that the prices are the same?

Mr. Coe: We publish our prices; they are public information; anybody who wishes to, may follow those prices at his own discretion.

Mr. Arnold: They all wish to apparently, don't they?

Mr. Coe: They do not, sir.

Mr. Arnold: You mean they have not been following those prices?

Mr. Coe: On our product they have not, sir.

Mr. Arnold: I got the impression, I may be wrong, that the prices of competitors and your prices have been substantially identical.

Mr. Coe: To some extent they have been identical. There are always variations in many prices.

Mr. Arnold: You said that anyone who wishes to might follow. Some of them certainly wish to.

Mr. Coe: Some of them do wish to.

Mr. Arnold: And some of them did follow.

Mr. Coe: That is correct.

Mr. Arnold: And therefore to that extent you have been the leader.

Mr. Coe: To some extent we have been the leader in that we have put out our prices. However, others have put out prices and we have followed them at times.

Mr. Arnold: What other companies would you put in the position of price leadership aside from your own?

Mr. Coe: Practically any member of the industry.

Mr. Cox: Including Mr. Randall?

Mr. Coe: Including Mr. Randall.

* * * * *

Mr. Arnold: I take it that the prices are fixed generally by someone following someone else, and that sometimes they follow you and other times you follow others.

Mr. Coe: May I ask what you mean by "fixed"? We publish our prices; they become our prices; they are public information. In that way the prices of the American Brass Co. are fixed by us.

Mr. Arnold: Then you understand what we mean by "fixed" and I repeat my question: Is it true that prices are fixed in this industry either by someone following you or by your following others?

Mr. Coe: Not in all respects. Many times we do not follow others in all respects; many times they do not follow us in all respects.

Mr. Arnold: But there is a following on the part of the various companies in the industry?

Mr. Coe: A general following; yes, sir.

The Chairman: Not that you impose your ideas as to what the price should be upon anybody else, or that anybody else imposes it upon you, but when any company makes a change in price, the tendency is for all to follow that change?

Mr. Coe: That is the tendency.

The Chairman: And how long has that been the system?

Mr. Coe: As far back as I have been with the company that has been in vogue; water seeking its own level.

* * * * *

The Chairman: What factors go into the determination of the price?

Mr. Coe: The cost of our raw metals going into the alloys, plus our manufacturing differentials. The latter is determined by our price committee.

The Chairman: And if the price of the raw material should go down, then one would naturally expect the price of the finished product to go down, unless there was some countervailing change in some other factor?

Mr. Coe: There are other factors to be taken into consideration; yes, sir.

The Chairman: Well, now, would you say that the price fluctuates in the same degree that the price of these countervailing or these other factors fluctuate?

Mr. Coe: That is a difficult question to answer. I don't quite know what you mean by that.

The Chairman: Well, I tried to make it simple. The price of the finished product would naturally, one would suppose, depend upon the cost of the various factors which go into making the finished product?

Mr. Coe: That is correct.

The Chairman: Well, now, do you want the committee to understand that always the price of the finished product is determined by these other factors and by no other consideration?

Mr. Coe: The price is determined by the price of raw materials going into those products, plus our cost of manufacturing.

The Chairman: Yes; those are the other factors?

Mr. Coe: Those are the other factors.

The Chairman: And there is no other consideration that goes into the determination of the price?

Mr. Coe: That is correct.

The Chairman: And how about this leadership, why do you follow somebody else's lead sometimes?

Mr. Coe: We can get no more for our product than other people can get for theirs: will charge for theirs.

The Chairman: Here is another outfit which is supposedly competing with you, which is not as efficient as you are, and therefore which finds for example that there is a much heavier plant charge, let us say; therefore, it is not able to produce this finished product at as low a price as you, and because it doesn't produce it at as low a price as you, it has to raise the price, but according to your testimony when such a company raises the price, then you follow and raise your price, although your costs have not changed.

Mr. Coe: We have not necessarily raised our price.

The Chairman: Oh, now, let's drop the word "necessarily." You have just said that you have done that and that other companies follow you occasionally. Now, Mr. Coe, we are merely trying to get the facts here; we are not laying the basis for a case against the American Brass Co. I am trying to get through my mind this picture of price leadership in industry.

Now, you have told us as explicitly as it can be told that in some cases other companies in the same business as you follow the price that you fix, and you have told us how you determine that price, and then you say in other instances you followed the price of other companies, and when you do that necessarily you do it upon factors that are not reflected in your business, but on factors that are reflected in the business of the company which raises the price. Now why do you do it?

Mr. Coe: We can get as much for our product as any competitor can get for his product.

The Chairman: Now we are getting somewhere. If some other company raises the price and is getting that price, then you think you had better come up and equalize it?

Mr. Coe: I feel that our product is as good as any made by the industry.

The Chairman: It may be better.

Mr. Coe: I hope it is.

The Chairman: But the point in determining the price thing is that you base it not upon the actual costs of manufacture in your plants, but upon the highest charge that anybody in the industry makes by and large, isn't that the effect of this price leadership policy?

Mr. Coe: It is usually predicated on the lowest price that anybody makes.

The Chairman: Well, of course, there was an old familiar saying that the price the companies charge is what the traffic will bear. Now isn't that the motto which guides those who follow the practice of price leadership?

Mr. Coe: It depends on what you mean by "traffic." Of course we have to compete with many other things besides brass and copper.

The Chairman: Well, would you say the American Brass Co. puts its product out at the lowest possible price, bearing in mind all of these factors of cost?

Mr. Coe: It is necessary when we get our products to the ultimate consumer as low as we reasonably can, and still at a fair margin of profit, in order that we will not be—that our products will not be supplanted by substitutes.

The Chairman: But under this plan of price leadership, is it not inevitable that the tendency would be to raise the price so as to cover the cost of the less efficient member of the industry?

Mr. Coe: The tendency has been just the opposite. The tendency has been to lower the price.

Questions

1. Was the price policy of the Riverside Metal Company based on sound economic reasoning? What assumptions about retaliation had Mr. Randall made—to a price set above that posted by American Brass? To a price set below that of American Brass?
2. Can you suggest an alternative price policy that might prove more profitable for the Riverside Metal Company?
3. Some general principles of defense against probing questions can be gleaned from the case. Describe the more interesting ones.

CASE 14–2
Price Publicity in the Aluminum Industry

For many years in the aluminum industry the custom had been for widely publicized advance announcements of price changes, usually increases since World War II.

For example, the following sequences of announcements appeared in *The Wall Street Journal* in June 1977:

June 15, Kaiser plans to boost prices of aluminum products, including a 2-cent increase for ingots, as of July 5.

June 20, Alcoa will boost prices for ingots and fabricated products; increases parallel to those of Kaiser of slightly below 4 percent.

June 21, Reynolds, others, follow boost on unalloyed aluminum ingot to 53 cents a pound.

June 22, Three more primary aluminum producers announce 2-cent price increases.

June 23, Alcan Aluminum Corporation raising prices of ingot to 53 cents a pound, effective July 5.

In the summer of 1977 the Justice Department was pressing its probe on aluminum pricing. Among its complaints was the widespread advance publicity given to price announcements by the aluminum firms. On October 14, *The Wall Street Journal* noted that Aloca was quietly increasing some aluminum prices and that Kaiser followed with a 3-cent price increase; Alcan and Reynolds remained silent. *Iron Age* ran the story, "It's Not What Aluminum Did . . . It's How It Did It." It stated, "new lists sent to customers of Alcoa quietly began the latest round of increases of 3 cents a pound or about 4 percent. Kaiser followed. Other major producers did not . . . but it was considered only a matter of time before their prices caught up. . . . Without questioning Aluminum's right to a price hike, all that could be complained about was its manner in announcing the changes. Previous aluminum price increases this past spring and summer involving broader hikes on ingots and mill products were widely announced publicly."[17] The next announcement in *The Wall Street Journal* on November 7 noted that big aluminum firms delayed price boosts for distributor customers for the rest of 1977.

Questions

1. Consider the advantages of advance public announcements of price increases by aluminum firms such as Alcoa using the kinked demand curve as a starting point.

2. Why might antitrust authorities complain about the practice?

---

[17]*Iron Age*, October 24, 1977, p. 71. *The Wall Street Journal* citations are in *The Wall Street Journal Index, 1977* (Princeton, N.J.: Dow-Jones Books, 1978), pp. 594–95.

CASE 14–3 _____
Price-Level Determination by General Motors

For many years General Motors seems to have been following the same pricing procedures.[18]

1. The preliminary product planning so that a car such as Chevrolet may be sold within a general price range.
2. The establishing of standard prices on the basis of standard costs and a standard return at a standard volume
3. The setting of the prevailing or list price. (Actually, this price has been set at a retail level, with the price to the dealer allowing a margin of from 20 percent to 25 percent on a car with standard equipment.)

The following material is from the *Hearings before the Senate Subcommittee on Antitrust and Monopoly of December, 1955.*[19] Mr. Burns was counsel for the committee, and Mr. Bradley and Mr. Donner were vice presidents and directors of General Motors.

Mr. Burns: I would like to ask you some questions with respect to those principles, and the source of my information is the articles by Donaldson Brown, which I believe were published in 1924, entitled "Pricing Policy in Relation to Financial Return."

You are familiar with those articles?

Mr. Bradley: Yes.

Mr. Burns: And do they express in broad terms the pricing policies which have been used by the corporation since that time?

Mr. Bradley: That is correct.

Mr. Burns: Mr. Brown also made this statement with respect to attainable annual return and the pricing formula.

> The formulation of the pricing policy must be with regard to the particular circumstances pertaining to each individual business. When formulated, it is expressed simply in the conception of what have been defined as standard volume and the economic return available.

Now, would you explain for the benefit of our record what is meant by the term "standard volume"?

Mr. Bradley: Yes; I think I might illustrate the standard volume. We endeavor in planning for capacity to—we take the number of days there

---

[18]The most detailed exposition of the method is probably in Homer Vanderblue's article, "Pricing Policies in the Automobile Industry," *Harvard Business Review*, Summer, 1939, pp. 1–17. Other references are Kaplan, Dirlam, and Lanzillotti, *Pricing in Big Business* (Washington, D.C.: Brookings Institution, 1958), pp. 48–55, 131–35; and Joel Dean, *Managerial Economics* (Englewood Cliffs, N.J.: Prentice-Hall, 1951), pp. 448–49.

[19]Washington, D.C.: U.S. Government Printing Office, 1956.

are in the year, and then take out the Sundays and holidays, and then we take out the minimum number of days we produce this over a period of time to turn around—I mean, to bring out new models.

From that, we find there are 225, taking out all the Sundays, holidays, and Saturdays, and 15 full days, or 30 half days, for turning around, giving 225 days which we would like to run the plants, year in and year out.

But we don't use 225, we use 80 percent of that as a standard volume, because ours is a business that you might call cyclical, and while it has been on the upswing for a number of years, there have been times when we had downswings—in fact, for a number of years we averaged below standard volume.

So, to allow for that cyclical factor and other conditions beyond our control we take 80 percent of that 225 days, times the rated capacity per hour. So that gives us 180 days. And that, multiplied by our daily capacity, gives us a standard volume, which we work up by divisions, and which we hope to average.

Well, we have had years below it, and years above it.

Mr. Burns: How long a planning period do you use in your consideration of standard volume?

Mr. Bradley: Well, except for the number of days for the turnaround, we haven't changed our standard volume. The 80 percent of the rated daily capacity times 225 days, that has remained constant over the years.

Mr. Burns: When you are planning—

Mr. Bradley: Excuse me. We use that in planning capacity.

Mr. Burns: Now, when you are making your projections for either new models or plant expansion, do you use any particular length of time as a planning period?

Mr. Bradley: Well, of course, we make our economic studies for several years ahead, but they are not firm. They are subject to revision at any time. I mean, for example, we did not plan for as big a volume as we have had in the last 2 or 3 years. With the national income, which has grown faster—the gross national product—with the movement out to the suburbs, and so on, so the big market has been bigger than we anticipated, but we try to look ahead a number of years and plan accordingly. We have to plan at least 2 years ahead or we would not have the capacity.

Mr. Burns: Well, now, what profit margin or attainable return have you used in pricing policy in recent years?

Mr. Bradley: Well, actually in the back of our minds we have a standard, but one of the factors referred to there was competition. And the net profit may be below standard, or what he hope to have—the economic return attainable may be bigger in one business—one activity or one division than another. But we can always compare with what we expected.

We have not changed our general sights in a period of over 20 years.

Mr. Burns: What have been the general sights?

Mr. Bradley: Ours is a fairly rapid turnover business, and our operations will yield between 15 or 20 percent on the net capital employed over the years. . . .

*   *   *   *   *

Senator O'Mahoney: . . . What is this general overall percentage which is added to the cost of the car for overhead for the general staff?

Mr. Donner: The figure I haven't got in my mind. Maybe I can get in in a minute. It isn't a high percentage at all. I don't think it would be 1 percent.

Senator O'Mahoney: Let me ask you this way, then. What are the basic elements of cost that enter into fixing the price of the car that is sold to the average automobile purchaser in the United States?

Mr. Donner: Sixty percent of the cost is materials that we buy. Some thirty-odd percent is payroll.

Senator O'Mahoney: That includes all payrolls, the mechanics and the—

Mr. Donner: Right up to the president.

Senator O'Mahoney: Right up to the president?

Mr. Donner: There is a couple of percent depreciation—

Senator O'Mahoney: Yes, sir.

Mr. Donner (continuing):   And I think a couple of percent for taxes other than federal income taxes.

Now, that roughly adds up to a hundred percent of the cost.

*   *   *   *   *

[After putting in the record SEC figures for 1954 that showed profits after taxes as 9.9 percent of stockholder equity for all industry and 14.1 percent for motor vehicles and parts, Mr. Burns continued:]

Mr. Burns: I also would like to place in the record some figures from Moody's of the percentage of net income to net worth:

General Motors, 1948, 24.47; 1949, 31.37; 1950, 34.94; 1951, 20 percent; 1952, 20.59; 1953, 20.05; and their figure for 1954 is 24.43 percent. (1955 showed a 31 percent return.)

Competition in Price[20]

In a statement prepared for a Senate Subcommittee in October 1968, General Motors elaborated on some of the steps in the pricing policy as follows:

The MSP (Manufacturer's Suggested or list Price) represents a complex balancing of many and sometimes opposing factors. These include the

---

[20]The quotations in these sections are from *The Automobile Industry, A Case Study in Competition* (General Motors Corporations, October 1968), pp. 33, 37, 43.

EXHIBIT 14–3A   Operating Results for General Motors, 1961–1978

Year	Sales ($ millions)	Net Income ($ millions)	Share-holders' Investment* ($ millions)	Unit Sales, Cars and Trucks‡ (thousands)	Profit as Percent of Investment	Actual Unit Sales ÷ Standard†
1961.	$11,395	$ 893	$ 6,026	3,150	14.8	0.85
1962.	14,640	1,459	6,650	4,223	21.9	1.08
1963.	16,494	1,591	7,121	4,662	22.4	1.14
1964.	16,997	1,734	7,599	4,560	22.8	1.06
1965.	20,734	2,125	8,237	5,696	25.8	1.27
1966.	20,208	1,793	8,726	5,195	20.6	1.11
1967.	20,026	1,627	9,261	4,799	17.6	0.98
1968.	22,755	1,732	9,756	5,410	17.8	1.06
1969.	24,295	1,711	10,227	5,260	16.7	0.99
1970.	18,752	609	9,854	3,591	6.1	0.65
1971.	28,264	1,936	10,805	5,767	17.9	1.01
1972.	30,435	2,163	11,683	5,740	18.5	0.96
1973.	35,798	2,398	12,567	6,512	19.1	1.07
1974.	31,550	950	12,531	4,678	7.6	0.75
1975.	35,725	1,253	13,082	4,658	10.0	0.74
1976.	47,181	2,903	14,385	6,218	20.8	0.97
1977.	47,551	3,338	15,767	6,695	21.2	1.03
1978.	53,499	3,508	19,570	6,878	20.0	1.04

*Year-end.

†Based on long-run linear trend, standard has been computed as $S = 3,700 + 200t$; t is taken as 0 in 1961; units are thousands of cars. Thus, S for 1968 when $t = 7$ would be 5,100 thousands of cars. After 1975, the increment is reduced to 100,000 cars per year.

‡Unit sales are for the United States which in 1978 constituted 72.5 percent of total and accounted for 83 percent of net income.

SOURCE: GM *Information Handbook,* 1968, and subsequent annual reports.

competitive advantages the manufacturer believes his new product line offers in relation to his and other prior models, his estimate of the customer appeal of new competitive products, the prices of his competitors, his estimates of change in the cost of production and his appraisal of the market potential . . .

As an example, the report indicated how Chrysler had rolled back its average announced increase of $84 per car on 1969 models to $52 after General Motors announced increases of only $49 per car. Such modifications by Ford and Chrysler took place several times in the 1960s.

General Motors noted that the wholesale price index for cars declined about 2.5 percent between 1959 and 1968, although GM's hourly employment costs rose 63 percent, the costs of steel and copper rose 9 percent and 58 percent respectively, and the wholesale price index for all industrial commodities rose 8 percent. ". . . In these 10 years, General Motors countered its rising costs with imaginative efforts to increase efficiency and to develop and sell 'more car per car'—more optional equipment and a higher proportion of top-of-the-line models. For the first several years, our results were further favorably influenced by a rapidly expanding market as car sales doubled from 1958 to 1965. . . ."

The report went on to emphasize that GM's pricing methods are not of a mechanical cost-plus nature and indicated that the cost was frequently adjusted to the price range through product variations: ". . . The key test is whether a product of the type specified can be produced at a cost which will enable the manufacturer to sell at a profit in the defined areas of the price structure . . ."

A Target Rate of Return

General Motors' operating results from 1961 to 1978 have been quite consistent with these statements as to their pricing policy and their stated target rate of profits. Mr. Bradley's testimony above suggested that "their operations will yield about 15–20 percent on the net capital employed over the years." The mean profit for the 18 years as shown in Exhibit 14–3A is 17.7 percent.

Let us assume that General Motors' target from 1961 through 1973 was an 18 percent return on shareholder investment, and that this goal was expected to be achieved when the company achieved 100 percent of standard volume. In Exhibit 14–3A, the last column estimates the ratio of actual volume to standard volume, the latter being calculated by a long-run trend. The first five columns are from GM's statements, and we properly assume that these results were dominated by domestic car and truck operations, although recognizing they include appliance and international results.

The first step is to calculate as a percentage of sales the markup needed to achieve an 18 percent return on investment. That markup would depend on two factors: the proportion of sales at standard volume to stockholder investment, and the proportion of income before income taxes to the aftertax income. The following is the required formula:

$$\text{Markup} = \text{Target return} \times \frac{\text{Stockholders' investment}}{\text{Sales at standard volume}} \times \frac{\text{Pretax income}}{\text{Aftertax income}}$$

From 1961 to 1968, sales at standard volume were double or slightly more than double stockholder investment, so that the second term on the right had the value of one half or a little less. Income taxes were from 45 percent to 52.5 percent of GM's income, averaging about 49 percent, so that the third term on the right had a value averaging slightly over two. For the company during this period, the last two terms roughly cancel out and the required markup was between 15 percent and 18.5 percent of the sales price. In subsequent years the ratio of stockholder investment to sales dropped (partly because of inflation which would raise sales more than the value of such assets as plant and equipment) so the required markup on sales was approximately 13 percent from 1971 to 1978.

EXHIBIT 14–3B Prices, Costs, Margins at Various Outputs

	Ratio of Actual Volume to Standard Volume						
	0.65	0.80	0.90	1.00	1.10	1.20	1.30
Price.	1.180	1.180	1.180	1.180	1.180	1.180	1.180
ATC	1.081	1.038	1.017	1.000	0.986	0.975	0.965
AVC	0.850	0.850	0.850	0.850	0.850	0.850	0.850
AFC	0.231	0.188	0.167	0.150	0.136	0.125	0.115
Price—ATC	0.099	0.142	0.163	0.180	0.194	0.205	0.215
Predicted profits. . .	6.4%	11.4%	14.7%	18%	21.3%	24.6%	28.0%

It can be expected that profits would increase more than proportionally with volume because units costs would drop as fixed costs are spread over more units. In Mr. Donner's testimony cited earlier in the case, he estimated fixed costs at 15 percent of total costs at standard volume. Exhibit 14–3B shows the implications of this for average total costs and for margins. ATC is taken to equal unity at standard volume. Price is taken to be 1.18 which represents a markup of just over 15 percent of price which is about average for the period.

Since, coincidentally, the margin of 0.18 at the standard volume corresponds with the target rate of return on investment, the predicted profits as a percentage of investment given in the last row can be obtained by multiplying the ratio of actual to standard volume by the margin, that is, price minus ATC, which is given in the next to last row.

Questions

1. Are the actual profits as a percentage of investment of General Motors reasonably consistent with a target return of 18 percent at standard volume? (Compare the figures in Exhibit 14–3A with those in the last row of Exhibit 14–3B.)

2. Show diagramatically how increases in volume increase both dimensions of the rectangle of profits $[(P - ATC)\,Q]$. Use figures of Exhibit 14–3B.

3. What markup on sales would be called for to get a target return on 18 percent in 1962, in 1969? (The ratio of pretax income to aftertax income in each year was approximately 2.)

4. General Motors' approach has been termed "sophisticated cost-plus pricing." How does GM break the circle that prices determine volume and volume determines cost and cost determines price? How can GM bring demand considerations into its pricing approach?

5. Could the other automobile manufacturers successfully use a similar approach to pricing? What modifications might be necessary? With substantial imports of Japanese cars in the 1980s has GM been forced to modify its target return?

CASE 14–4
Traditional Department Stores, Inc.

Traditional Department Stores, Inc., was a medium-sized chain of department stores located in the Middle West, with stores in 10 cities.[21]

Mr. Marshall Jennings, the chief menswear buyer for the largest store in the chain, was explaining the manner in which his buyers operated in ordering and pricing men's clothing. Mr. Jennings was a college classmate of William Griffin, who was a professor of business and economics at a nearby university. Professor Griffin was interested in determining how price and "output" decisions were made by a retail organization. Professor Griffin knew that Mr. Jennings' store competed with two other large men's clothing stores in the trading area.

Mr. Jennings was quick to point out at the beginning of the conversation that while he could only talk in detail about his department, the general practice that he and his buyers followed was a more or less standard procedure used quite widely in all departments and in most department stores.

Professor Griffin suggested that Mr. Jennings first explain how the buyer determined what quantity of goods to order (and thus what quantity the store had to sell) and then discuss normal pricing and special pricing practices.

Ordering

Mr. Jennings began by explaining that there were two kinds of orders—advance orders and reorders. The size of the advance order depended largely on the estimated sales for the season for which the goods were being ordered, but also depended on the amount of "risk" involved in advance ordering. When items were highly seasonal in nature, so that selling an overstock after the season was difficult, advance orders as a percent of total orders were kept low, Mr. Jennings explained. Also, clothes of a very faddish or stylish nature presented a risky situation, since tastes could change easily and it was difficult to predict ahead of time what would sell well. Mr. Jennings estimated for Professor Griffin the percentage of estimated sales placed in advance orders for each of the four major buying seasons (see Exhibit 14–4A).

The basic estimates of sales volume for each period were based on sales for the last period and adjusted for shifts in timing of holidays, special sales, and so forth. Predictions were deliberately reduced somewhat from the last year's sales in order to decrease possible overforecasting, a mistake that was held against the buyer in judging his performance.

---

[21]This case is based in large part upon the research of Dean R. M. Cyert and Professor J. G. March of the Graduate School of Industrial Administration, Carnegie Institute of Technology, as reported in *The Behavioral Theory of the Firm,* © 1963. Adapted by permission of Prentice-Hall, Englewood Cliffs, N.J.

EXHIBIT 14–4A

Season	Percent	Order Dates
Easter	70	January 15–20
Summer.	50	March 10–15
Back to school	65	May 20–25
Holiday	75	September 20–25

Estimated sales forecasts did not have to be very accurate for ordering purposes, since the size of reorders could be varied to correct estimating errors.

By relying on reorders during the selling season, the buyers were able to utilize the most recent information on demand trends in terms of overall volume and specific items. Mr. Jennings warned, however, that the buyers had to balance this advantage against the disadvantages. Manufacturers required lead times for production, with the result that "out of stocks" might occur before the reorder was delivered. Moreover, since the manufacturer based both the type and the amount of recuttings on early reorders in order to decrease his risk of obsolete inventories, the buyer who waited till too late in the season to reorder might not be able to get the required amount or the exact styles and colors desired.

Mr. Jennings outlined the following method of determining reorder amounts. Shortly after the selling season began, the buyers checked each of their product style lines against the same line during the previous year, and then applied this ratio to the previous year's sales. For instance, if sales during the first two weeks of an item were 80 units, and sales during the same period of the previous year were 100, then the buyer calculated that sales for the remainder of the season would be 80 percent of last year's sales during the remainder of the season.

Once this new estimate of sales was determined, the inventory on hand was subtracted from this figure and any inventory desired at the end of the season added to it in order to calculate the reorder quantity. In some cases where sales had been much less than initially expected, the inventory on hand might be so large as to yield a negative reorder quantity by this calculation. In this case, past orders might be canceled or the price cut in order to move more merchandise. Once the selling season was under way and the reorder made, such a calculation was made every week to determine whether part of the reorder should be canceled, whether the price should be cut, or whether more should be ordered. This weekly check served as a control mechanism which prevented extraordinary overstocks on stock "outs" on each line.

Mr. Jennings stressed the importance of having a routinized method for handling the order problem. If each buyer had a free rein to buy as much as wanted whenever he or she wanted to do so, on hundreds of items, each coming in different styles and colors, the problem of controlling purchases, sales, and inventory levels would be tremendous.

EXHIBIT 14–4B   Sales and Competition Report (men's Bermuda shorts)

	Number of Pairs Sold	Traditional	Young's	Olds-Field's	Shopper's Discount
$4.95 summer line:					
1961:					
Easter	121	$4.95	$4.95	$4.95	—
Summer.	459	4.95	4.95	4.75	—
Back to school . .	315	4.25	4.25	4.50	—
1962:					
Easter	110	4.95	4.95	4.95	$3.95
Summer.	200	4.95	4.95	4.95	3.95
Back to school . .	300	3.95	3.95	3.75	3.75
$7.95 summer line:					
1961:					
Easter	60	7.95	7.95	7.49	—
Summer.	180	7.95	7.95	7.95	—
Back to school . .	120	7.95	7.95	7.95	—
1962:					
Easter	20	7.95	7.95	7.95	5.95
Summer.	100	7.95	7.95	7.49	5.95
Back to school . .	220	5.95	5.95	5.95	5.95

Mr. Jennings confessed that during the last year his staff had had more difficulty than usual in predicting sales volumes accurately, with the result that the department had had to cancel orders, sell goods at cut prices, and sell after the seasons were over. But occasionally, the store also found itself with too little stock. The trouble came from a new large discount store that had opened on the edge of the city, about four miles from the center of the business district. This store, according to Mr. Jennings, constantly engaged in special promotions and low markups. Mr. Jennings said he did not know how to take this store's behavior into account in forecasting sales for any one line. Prior to the opening of the discount store, he stated, he had not felt much need to take his competition into account in ordering, since the estimating method, which ignored these competitors, had in general worked satisfactorily. Professor Griffin then asked if he might see a record of an item with which Mr. Jennings had experienced trouble. Mr. Jennings had one of his assistants pull the records on men's Bermuda shorts (see Exhibit 14–4B).

Normal Price Determination

Mr. Jennings next described for Professor Griffin the concept of retail "price lining." The store carried only a limited number of different-quality items in the same product group. This simplified choice for consumers, resulted in stable product categories for manufacturers to produce in, and ultimately increased the retail stability of prices. Since the various price lines were reasonably well standardized, as were retail markups, the manufacturer knew the maximum his costs could be in order to sell his product at a particular price in the retail market. Likewise, each retail firm knew that the cost differences were not great for merchandise in any given

---

EXHIBIT 14–4C   Traditional Department Stores, Inc. (boyswear—
                normal markup)

Standard Costs	Standard Price*	Effective Markup
$ 3.00	$ 5.00	40.0%
3.75	5.95	37.0
4.75	7.95	40.2
5.50	8.95	38.5
6.75	10.95	38.3
7.75	12.95	40.1
8.75	14.95	41.5
10.75	17.95	40.0
11.75	19.95	41.0
13.75	22.95	40.0
14.75	25.00	41.0
18.75	29.95	37.4

*Calculated from the following rule: "Divide each cost by 60 percent (one markup), and move the result to nearest 95 cents."

price line, and thus that prices in that line among different stores would not vary significantly unless intended. Thus, price lining resulted in comparability for manufacturer, retailer, and shopper, according to Mr. Jennings.

Once price lines were selected, a large part of the pricing problem was solved. Merchandise was purchased to sell within a given price line and yield a "normal" markup. Normal markup for the menswear and boyswear department as a whole was 40 percent. This markup has been in existence in the industry as standard for 40 or 50 years, Mr. Jennings said. As a result of price-line standardization, the department was able to operate for the most part from a schedule of standard costs and standard prices. The schedule for the boy's section was as shown in Exhibit 14–4C.

The selection of price lines was an infrequent policy decision. Such a decision by high-level buying and administrative personnel was based on a wide range of factors—competitive lines in other stores, the economic characteristics of the community, the store's desired image, and so forth. For most decisions and to most buyers the price-line structure was a "given." The problem for the buyer, then, was to find goods that could be assigned prices that would enable the department to attain or improve the markup goal.

Although the average normal markup for the department was 40 percent, each product group had its own normal markup, which varied somewhat among product groups and which in general tended to be higher:

1. The greater the risk involved with the product.
2. The higher the costs (other than product cost).
3. The less the effect of competition.
4. The lower the price elasticity.

Risk was involved, for example, where the department dealt with foreign manufacturers. Products often varied in quality, and deliveries were not so dependable. As a result, the markup was increased 50 percent on these items, or to 60 percent of retail price.

Another exceptional markup occurred when the store handled a product on an exclusive arrangement. Since the consumer was not able to make comparisons, the price and margin were set higher according to the following company rule: "When merchandise is handled on an exclusive basis, calculate the standard price from the cost, then use the next highest price on the standard schedule."

Markups were also higher on large items that used up a great deal of floor space, and on items that required considerable personal sales attention. In both cases, costs were higher.

Price decreases were automatically made to match lower prices by the store's two major competitors, although when a competitor's plans to feature an item were known in advance, the store often did not stock and never displayed the identical item. The store also met the prices of lesser competitors such as drugstores if these stores actively promoted and displayed the product. (Information about competitors was gained through newspaper advertisements, manufacturers' salespersons, customers, and professional shoppers.) Mr. Jennings stated that last year he had felt it necessary to feature a month-long "back to school" sale on many summer clothes in order to clear out large inventories built up during the spring and summer months. He blamed these overstocks on the discount house. "To tell the truth," Mr. Jennings stated, "we were all a little surprised at the results of the sale. We were actually caught short of stock after two and a half weeks, and had to rush through a special order to continue the advertised sale."

Sales Price Determination

Mr. Jennings stated that a completely different set of rules governed sales pricing in order to achieve a price appeal. Special sales were limited in number. Usually, they occurred when a buyer was able to make arrangements for lines that were exclusive in the immediate market at lower than normal cost—in other words, at a special discount.

The management had promulgated certain policy directives for the buyers to follow:

1. Whenever the normal price falls at one of the following lines, the corresponding sale price will be used:

Normal Price	Sale Price
$1.00	$0.85
1.95	1.65
2.50	2.10
2.95	2.45
3.50	2.90
3.95	3.30
4.95	3.90
5.00	3.90

2. For all other merchandise, there must be a reduction of *at least* 15 percent on items retailing regularly for $3 or less and at least 16⅔ percent on higher priced items.
3. All sales prices must end with a zero or a five.
4. No sales prices are allowed to fall on price lines normal for the product group.
5. Whenever there is a choice between an ending of 85 cents and 90 cents, the latter ending will prevail.
6. Use the standard schedule of sales pricing for prices that are slightly higher (by 5 cents) than the listed values. Thus, if the price if $3 retail, assume it is the same as $2.95 in computing the sales price.
7. The smaller the retail price, the smaller must be the increments between sales price endings, in order to approximate as closely as possible the desired percentage reduction. Therefore, after determining the necessary percentage reduction from normal price, carry the result down to the nearest ending specified below:
   a. Retail price greater than $5, reduce to the nearer 90 cents or 45 cents.
   b. Retail price less than $5 but greater than $2, reduce to the nearest of 90 cents, 65 cents, 45 cents, or 30 cents.
   c. Retail price under $2, reduce to the nearer of zero or 5 cents.
   d. Reduce 5 cents more if the sale price is the same as another price line in the same product category.
8. When the special discount cost from the manufacturer is over 30 percent less than normal, pass some of the savings on to the customer by using the following formula:

$$\frac{\text{Special discount cost}}{1 - \text{Normal markup}}$$

if the resultant sales price using the normal rule is greater. [Mr. Jennings stated that "this usually happens when our relationship with the manufacturer has been one of long standing."]

When Professor Griffin asked if competitors' reactions were considered in setting sales prices, Mr. Jennings replied that they were not. He did say, however, that his store always met the sales prices of competitors on comparable items if their prices were lower, and competitors in turn would do likewise. The store had a firm policy, however, against raising prices to match competitors' prices where they were higher than those of Traditional.

Markdowns

Mr. Jennings next went into markdown pricing procedures. He explained: "We generally consider a markdown to be a decrease in price that the buyer feels will be permanent. However, there are exceptions in practice to this definition."

Mr. Jennings said that he like to look on markdowns as a kind of "emergency device" that the department used in its efforts to maintain sales and inventory control. Their use, he explained, could be roughly grouped into two categories—special cases and general routines.

Special Cases

Competition. When it was determined that a recognized competitor was selling an item at a lower price, the department would mark down the item to equal the competitor's price. However, explained Mr. Jennings, if the department had reason to believe that the price was the result of a mistake, a check would be made with the competitor first before reducing the price. "Frequently," according to Mr. Jennings, "it develops that the price discrepancy is unintentional, and the competitor's price is increased."

Customer adjustment. A returned defective item was marked down to zero and eliminated. Soiled or damaged merchandise was reduced in price. Merchandise that was returned by a customer after the line to which it belonged had been reduced in price was reduced accordingly.

Premature depletion. If the stock for a sale was prematurely depleted, regular stock would be transferred to the sale racks and be marked down to sale price.

Promotion item. At times during the year, as a stimulant to business, items that were in excess and also available in a large and balanced assortment were marked down by 4 percent.

Obsolescence differential. Some items were suitable only for one season because of a particular style, color, or material, and could not be sold in the succeeding season. To accelerate the sale of these items, they were marked down one or two dollars near the peak of the season. Said Mr. Jennings: "We view this reduction as small enough to avoid antagonizing recent purchasers of the items but large enough to stimulate sales."

Drop in wholesale price during season. When this happened, all items in stock, regardless of when they were purchased, were reduced to the appropriate level based on the new wholesale price.

Substandard merchandise. Items that did not meet the quality standards of the original samples were either sent back to the manufacturer or, if this was not convenient, reduced in price and reimbursement sought from the manufacturer.

General Routine

This category accounted for the largest amount of dollars of markdown, according to Mr. Jennings. The items were marked down when some signal (inventory figures, reports from salesclerks etc.) indicated that excess inventories existed. The exact nature of the price reaction depended on an analysis of the reasons for failure. Mr. Jennings outlined the pricing procedures followed for each of several common causes of excess inventories.

Normal remnants. These were the odd sizes, less popular colors, and less favored styles remaining from the total assortment of an item that sold satisfactorily during the season. These items were considered normal, since it was impossible to order precisely the right assortment. "In fact," commented Mr. Jennings, "the complete clearance of the stock of an item by the end of the season is taken as an indication that the buyer did not buy heavily enough and that he probably suffered lost sales."

Overstocked merchandise. These are items for which the buyer was overly optimistic—which had normal sales but still remained in a well-balanced assortment of styles and sizes at the end of the season with many acceptable items included.

Unaccepted merchandise. This was merchandise that had "unsatisfactory" sales. During the season the sales personnel tried to determine whether the lack of acceptance was due to overpricing or poor style, color, and so forth. "The distinction is usually made," remarked Mr. Jennings, "by determining whether the item was ignored or whether it got attention but low sales."

The markdown process. Usually, Mr. Jennings said, items were not marked down right away but were mentally "stored" in an "availability pool" until the store or department had a general clearance sale. However, Mr. Jennings pointed out, there were times during the year when the department could not wait till the next scheduled clearance due to lack of space or lack of funds. In this case, immediate markdowns were ordered, such as the "back to school" sale of overstocked Bermuda shorts mentioned previously.

Items were marked down 33⅓ percent in the first markdown, except in special conditions where space was extremely tight, when they were reduced 50 percent. Mr. Jennings remarked that the 33⅓ percent off was an easier rule to follow. All marked-down merchandise was advertised "at least one third off." The 33⅓ percent rule was developed into a standard "first markdown price" schedule with prices *reduced further* to the nearest 85 cents (to distinguish markdown from scale prices which ended in 90 cents). (See Exhibit 14–4D.)

There were two exceptions to the above rule, according to Mr. Jennings. Higher priced items were marked down by 40 percent or more. Experience had indicated that these items (over $15) did not have high rates of obsolescence so that when they were marked down, they were more soiled than were lower priced goods.

The second case involved manufacturers' closeouts of remnants of odd styles, sizes, colors, and so forth, that were purchased at low cost. In this case the department tried to sell these items for one season at the regular price and then cut the price by one half.

Second markdowns, for merchandise still not cleared by the initial markdown, followed no rule and were left to the buyer's discretion.

EXHIBIT 14–4D   Boyswear Section

Regular Retail Price		First Markdown Price
$ 5.00	. . . .	$3.85
5.95	. . . .	3.85
(6.95)*	. . . .	(4.85)
7.95	. . . .	4.85
8.95	. . . .	5.85
10.95	. . . .	6.85
12.95	. . . .	7.85
---

*Not considered a regular retail price.

Questions

1. How does the actual pricing practice of Mr. Jennings' department square with traditional price theory? In what ways do economic concepts apply? In what areas do they seem not to apply?

2. To what extent did these pricing practices seem to be influenced by the number of sellers?

3. What do you think is the reason for having such well-defined pricing practices? Do you think the buying and price decisions of this department could be made with a computer? Why, or why not?

4. Do you see any conflict between the "best"—that is, optimum—economic behavior of the firm and the practical needs of the organization? Explain.

15

Nonprice Competition

Selling costs are defined as costs incurred in order to alter the position or shape of the demand curve for a product.
—*Edward H. Chamberlin*

Frequently the term *nonprice competition* has been used to designate rivalry between firms in product specifications and in selling and advertising efforts. But this usage can be quite misleading. In one situation the competing firms may be charging identical prices and may take particular care that they always "meet competition" in price. As a matter of fact the major restraint against a firm's decision to cut prices is the probability of immediate retaliation by its rivals, as discussed in Chapter 14. The cigarette industry is one in which differences in wholesale prices sufficient to encourage a retail price differential are not tolerated. In a second situation a firm may charge a price that has little apparent relationship with that of other producers of similar products. The Rolls Royce at $70,000-plus is an illustration. Many other examples can be found in between these cases. For example, in many regions of the country less advertised brands of gasoline have typically sold for 2 cents per gallon below the standard brands. An attempt by an independent to increase the differential is likely to lead to retaliation. With favorable price differentials, private brands of bread, frozen orange juice, margarine, and canned vegetables have outsold nationally advertised brands both in corporate and voluntary food chain stores.[1]

The basic point is this: under most market structures that are intermediate between pure monopoly and pure competition, firms will be concerned simultaneously with the effects of price, product quality, and advertising on the quantity demanded. Nonprice rivalry does not take place without some attention to price. To paraphrase marketing experts,

---

[1] Jules Backman, *Advertising Competition* (New York: New York University Press, 1967), pp. 57–58.

firms aim at a satisfactory or optimal "mix" of product features, advertising, and price.[2]

Firms may agree, conspiratorially or tacitly, on price and at the same time leave the issue of quantity and relative market shares open to quality and advertising efforts. On the other hand, Rolls Royce may set a price figure that has so little relation to automobiles most nearly comparable with it that there is little point of making price changes when, say, Cadillac makes a price change. When price is taken as a given determinant of the quantity demanded, managements' concentration on product improvement and selling efforts to better meet or to shift consumer preferences represents nonprice aspects of market competition. They are methods of increasing sales that are alternatives to reductions in prices.

But it must be recognized that price changes, product improvements, and advertising may be complements in market rivalry. In a world of imperfect knowledge of market alternatives, advertising can make price and product decisions more effective. As examples: almost any retail grocery advertisement is essentially a price list; Polaroid may plug a new $34.95 (suggested retail price) camera; the cigarette companies launch advertising campaigns to present the virtues of new longer filter brands.

COMPETITION IN SERVICES AND OTHER TERMS OF TRADE

The close relationship between price and nonprice aspects of competition can be shown by examining the many terms of trade and collateral services that closely resemble price differences. Many concessions such as freight allowances, discounts, and trading stamps or coupons with definite cash value can of course be translated into price terms.

During the deep depression of the 1930s, the National Recovery Administration published a very comprehensive list of concessions designed to influence sales. This list is shown in Case 12–2 because one of the great difficulties that cartels face in trying to maintain prices at a monopoly level is the ease with which a "chiseler" can in effect reduce price without overtly making a price cut. The NRA list is also relevant to price discrimination since some customers can receive concessions not available to, or not utilized by, others. Still another value of the NRA list is in suggesting ways to get around rent or other price controls by offering extra inducements to the seller (in order not to be among those unable to rent or to buy goods when amount demanded exceeds amount supplied). For example, there may be favors to the landlord, entertaining of sellers, and employing of relatives of the seller.

In the context of the present chapter, interest centers on ways to increase sales in oligopolistic situations by means of devices that can be

---

[2]For simple mathematical models, see R. Dorfman and P. O. Steiner, "Optimal Advertising and Optimal Quality," *American Economic Review*, December 1954, pp. 822–36.

termed "nonprice" concessions. Inspection of the NRA list shows many of these including permitting deferred payment, giving guarantees and exchange privileges, making sales on approval, assuming liability for consequential damages, providing special containers, giving free engineering services, assuming reversed telephone charges, settlement of old accounts at less than full value, and signing "money-back" agreements. The basic idea is that "price" may not be a simple concept; there are a surprisingly large number of ways in which sellers and buyers can influence sales while price is nominally unchanged.

TYPES OF PRODUCT COMPETITION

In relatively few markets today are firms engaged in selling completely standardized products. This is especially true of final consumer goods, for which competition in quality, style, and design is a pervasive form of nonprice competition.

The concept of "quality" is by no means simple. It involves numerous variables, some of which can be measured; others defy measurement. Any one product can involve several quality variables. An automobile, for example, can be appraised as to horsepower, durability, gasoline consumption, probable frequency and cost of repairs, comfort, riding qualities, safety, and ease of handling.

Competition in some industries has served to give the consumer subtantial improvements over the years, with part of the gain reflected in lower prices and the rest in better quality. For example, since World War II, automobile tires have been both improved greatly in quality and lowered in price. Economy of operation is another aspect of quality competition that can be measured approximately. According to tests made by the Procurement Division of the United States Treasury in 1931, the average consumption of five makes of 6-cubic-foot refrigerators was 44 kilowatt-hours per month. A test based on 14 makes in 1938 showed average electricity consumption to have declined to 35 kilowatt-hours per month.[3] By 1954, this amount of current was sufficient to operate the average 8.3- to 9.6-cubic-foot refrigerators for a month, according to tests by Consumers Union.[4] After 1954, competition increasingly took the form of size, greater freezer space, automatic defrost, and other features, all of which increased energy consumption. For these later developments, see Case 15–1.

Although many quality changes are physically measurable in terms of performance, as a rule it is impossible to translate these changes into price equivalents. Where quality changes are of the intangible sort involving design, taste, and style, not even measures of physical performance are

---

[3]*Price Behavior and Business Policy*, TNEC Monograph No. 1, 76th Cong., 3d sess. (Washington, D. C.: U.S. Government Printing Office, 1940), p. 64.

[4]Calculated from data given in *Consumer Reports*, September 1954, p. 403.

available. Yet these intangible elements are often the chief determinants of consumer choice. In women's clothing, for example, the indefinable element of style is far more important than are thread count, tensile strength of the cloth, or quality of workmanship. The success of a new model of automobile frequently has been determined more by the design of the hood than by the efficiency of the motor, until the energy problems after 1972 made miles per gallon a most significant figure.

The degree to which quality competition emphasizes measurable elements of the product varies with commodities. Where industrial buyers constitute the chief market, there is a tendency to stress such features as operating economy, tensile strength, and durability. In consumer goods markets, sellers find it desirable to emphasize the intangible elements of quality, style, and design because these are less easily copied. Sellers of food products seldom mention their conformity with government standards of quality; sellers of dresses do not usually emphasize fiber content; and distributors of cosmetics do not ordinarily refer to the quality of ingredients of their products. Flavor, style, and attractive containers are more important selling features.

VARIETIES OF SALES PROMOTION

As an alternative or complement to varying the product, many business companies compete by incurring selling expenses that are directed primarily at creating demand. Collectively, these expenditures can be called *sales promotion*, including advertising, which involves outlays for newspaper and magazine publicity, direct mail, catalogs, television and radio programs, window displays, and billboards. The basic characteristic of these expenditures is that they are undertaken with a view to influencing the buyer, though some changes of the physical form of the product, as in packaging, may also be involved. Obviously, in some cases, it is difficult to distinguish changes in the product expressly designed for their effect on the consumer from those that have substantive utility. Who is to say whether a catsup bottle that is conveniently designed for table use may not also be the one whose contours catch the consumer's eye on the supermarket shelf?

Related to advertising is the use of trademarks and brand names. The purpose of these is to furnish an easy means of identifying a particular seller's product. It is conceivable that brands might be employed merely to enable the buyer to identify products embodying certain measurable quality differences. But usually, sellers combine the use of brands with advertising that attempts to persuade buyers that the product has certain desirable intangible characteristics that are unique or that it possesses in greater degree than competing goods. The brand is built into a limited monopoly, with a regular following created by advertising.

The effectiveness with which trademarks and brands can protect a product against price competition varies with different lines of goods. In fields in which comparisons are relatively simple, or in markets where buyers are well equipped technically (as many industrial goods markets), there is a strong tendency for buyers to switch to competing brands as soon as substantial price differences appear. On the other hand, where the consumer is unable to compare rival brands intelligently, the effective use of brands and trademarks frequently permits wide price differentials to be maintained between virtually identical products. A lack of correspondence between price and U. S. Department of Agriculture grade for particular food products often exists. In the case of grocery products the element of taste is so subjective that comparisons among brands are very difficult; as a result, sellers are presented with an opportunity to create demand through nonprice competition. Striking illustrations of the insulation from price competition afforded by brand names are in the drug and cosmetic field. The consumer is almost completely uninformed as to the merits of rival products; few are aware of the significance of specifications of the United States Pharmacopoeia. Advertising-sales ratios are higher for proprietary drugs and cosmetics than for any other industry.[5] In addition, elaborate sales promotion efforts are directed at physicians to encourage prescriptions by brand names.

Other devices of sales promotion include personal selling, free distribution of samples of the product, give-away contests, and other methods such as the use of coupons exchangeable for other products. With regard to personal selling, it should be noted that some use of salespersons' time is for "production," such as making estimates, giving instruction in the use of the product, handling complaints, and making collections. But it cannot be doubted that an important use of salespeople is for promotion of demand for the product. As such, personal selling is an alternative or a supplement to other means of sales promotion.

THE MAGNITUDE OF PRODUCT AND SELLING COMPETITION

What is the cost of these product and selling efforts? The total spending for industrial research and development was estimated for 1965 at $13,825 million, about half financed by government and half by industry.[6] Much of this was on process research (which frequently is connected with product changes); a great deal went into basic, military, or space research and development which scarcely fits the framework of this chapter; a fair approximation seems to be about 1 percent of the GNP, $6 to $7 billion in 1965, about $25 billion in the early 1980s.

---

[5] In 1977, 19 of the 100 leading advertisers were in drugs, toiletries, and cosmetics, spending from 1.9 to 24.2 percent of sales in advertising. Median expenditures for the group were 8.3 percent as compared with 5.7 percent for the next highest group—soaps, cleansers and allied products. *Advertising Age*, August 28, 1978.

[6] The source of this figures is the National Science Foundation. It was cited in Backman, *Advertising Competition*, p. 23.

Other production costs will also be affected. At a later point in the chapter an economic model will be presented indicating that for differentiated products, potential economies of scale may be unrealized. Costs of hundreds of millions have been incurred in the automobile industry alone for annual style changes.

A comprehensive series for advertising expenditures in the United States has been published by *Printer's Ink* magazine. In both the prewar and postwar periods, advertising amounted to about 2.25 percent of GNP and 1.5 percent of total corporate sales. It increased in proportion to consumption expenditures from about 3 percent to 3.5 percent. Advertising is only a fraction of total marketing costs, which include personal selling and the costs of physical distribution as well. For example, in a sample of 127 industrial companies, total marketing costs were found to be 15.1 percent of sales, of which advertising and sales promotion was 2.2 percent, or less than one seventh of total marketing costs.[7] On the other hand, for one of the most highly advertised consumer products, breakfast cereals, advertising and sales promotion expenditures were 17 percent of sales in 1964 while other components of marketing costs were 10 percent.[8] The median advertising-sales ratio for the 100 leading advertisers in 1977 was 3.1 percent with a high for Noxell Corporation of 24.2 percent and a low for Exxon of 0.6 percent.[9]

Many marketing costs, those related to the physical distribution of products, would be considered production costs rather than selling expenditures designed to increase the demand for the product. Personal selling costs may well involve such production functions as physical delivery of the product but also may be intended to influence demands for products. An example of how personal selling may be substituted for advertising is that of Avon products. While the cosmetic industry was estimated in 1963 to spend 15 percent of sales on advertising, Avon with its house-to-house representatives spent only 2.7 percent.[10] No attempt will be made here to assess the demand-influencing component of costs of nonprice competition. The results are also substantial in terms of the product choice offered the consumer and in the rate of product change over time.

AN ECONOMIC MODEL OF PRODUCT DIFFERENTIATION

Product differentiation is one result of product and sales competition. Products can be said to be differentiated if some buyers are willing to pay

---

[7]*Industrial Marketing—1963* (New York: McGraw-Hill, June 1964)

[8]*Studies of Organization and Competition in Grocery Manufacturing*, Technical Study 6, National Commission on Food Marketing (Washington, D. C., June 1966), p. 147.

[9]*Advertising Age*, August 28, 1978.

[10]*Printers Ink*, November 1, 1963, p. 30. Avon later tilted toward more advertising, 5.7 percent of sales in 1977. See footnote 9.

FIGURE 15–1 Initial and Equilibrium Position for Firm with Differentiated Product and Free Entry into Industry

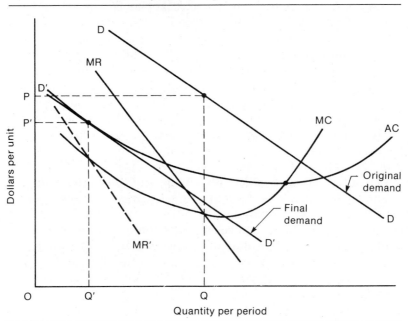

more for one firm's version of a commodity than for another firm's version.

Under the assumption that there are a large number of firms producing products that are tolerable, but at the same time distinguishable, substitutes for each other, the demand curve for the firm in Figure 15–1 can be drawn with the assumption that all other prices are held constant including those of competitors. Assume that initially the price is at P, the profit-maximizing position with output Q where $MC = MR$. If free entry exists, this is not an equilibrium position for the long run, since the high profits will attract new firms producing similar but not identical products. The effect of their entry is to shift the firm's demand curve to the left as its customers find the products of the new entrants more appealing. It is conceivable that this process could go on until the firm's demand was at $D'D'$. At this point its profit-maximizing price would have dropped to P' and the quantity produced to Q'.

This is not necessarily the only equilibrium position. A degree of product uniqueness and appeal could be postulated for the particular firm that could leave it with continuing profits despite the possibilities of entry into the industry. This latter case would approach that of monopoly. In fact, there is no clear line between monopoly and monopolistic competition. The issue hinges on the ease of substitution of competing products.

One generalization that has come out of the analysis of this type in Figure 15–1 is that where (a) product differentiation exists and (b) entry into the production of similar products is easy, then firms in the group or industry will be operating below the most efficient scale of production. This would necessarily be true when all profits were eliminated by the entry of new firms. A downward-sloping demand curve can be tangent only to a downward-sloping average cost curve.[11]

Examples most frequently cited are from the retailing field. The product differentiation in the service station industry is associated with location, the brand of gasoline, the cleanliness of washrooms, and the friendly smiles (of lack of them) of the station personnel. The gallonage of gasoline sold at many stations may be well below that possible at optimal capacity. More resources of land, labor, and capital have been devoted to the function of pumping gas than would be necessary with fewer stations. This extra use of resources may of course result in a locational convenience not otherwise available. In the 1970s the trend toward self-service and difficulties of getting assured supplies of gasoline significantly reduced the number of filling stations. Opponents of "fair trade" have pointed out that the druggists' hope for greater profitability under price-maintenance agreements is likely to be thwarted as long as entry is uncontrolled. The greater number of drugstores entering the business results in each encountering lower sales volume anad probably higher unit costs.

A MARGINAL APPROACH

How far should advertising or product quality be carried consistent with the maximization of profits? To examine advertising expenditures as a variable, the firm can select a particular price and quality of product. With the price given, a marginal revenue curve can be constructed at that price as in Figure 15–2. For a given quality of product, a marginal cost curve for production can be determined (technology and factor prices are assumed constant). If the price were determined in a purely competitive market, the intersection of the MR and MC_p curves in Figure 15–2 would indicate the profit-maximizing output. (Sales promotion expenditures would be neither necessary nor helpful with identical products that could not be differentiated by the consumer.)

The origin in Figure 15–2 represents a base quantity that could be either the quantity sold at price P with no advertising or that quantity sold with the minimum of advertising required to enter the market at all. With differentiated rather than identical products, the quantity demanded P may be increased by additional amounts of advertising (thus shifting a

---

[11]Even if profits are eliminated, opportunity costs are being met since these are included in average cost. The chart was devised by Edward H. Chamberlin. It has been criticized by members of the "Chicago School," especially George Stigler, partly because the various producers will have dissimilar cost curves, making the neat disappearance of profits questionable.

FIGURE 15–2 The Determination of Advertising Expenditures with Given Price and Product

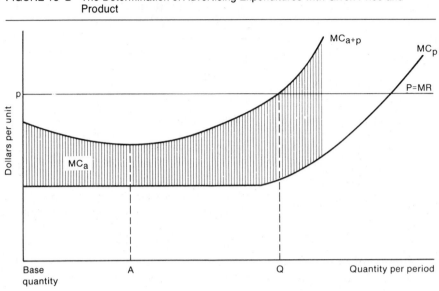

downward-sloping demand curve to the right). The shaded vertical distances indicating MC_a first show increasing returns in unit sales per dollar of advertising. This could reflect such factors as increased cumulative impact with greater frequency of advertising, cheaper advertising rates for greater quantity, or the use of more expensive and more effective media. To obtain sales beyond point A, decreasing returns are to be expected as additional or more expensive messages produce fewer added sales per dollar of expenditure. Finally at point Q, where the marginal costs of producing and of promoting an additional sale equal the added revenue per unit, further increases in advertising become unprofitable.

In addition to stressing its role in making consumers better informed, defenders of advertising have emphasized its role in promoting economic growth. The introduction of new or substantially modified products is frequently associated with marketing costs that are very large in proportion to sales for the first year or two.[12] Case 15–3 shows expenditures on advertising in 1983 and 1982 by leading advertisers, classified by the medium used. It is clear that this advertising was directed mainly at the final consumer rather than at industrial and commercial buyers.

It is difficult to draw useful charts when several variables such as

---

[12]For selected food products these were 57 percent for the first year and 37 percent for the second, in a study by Robert D. Buzzell and Robert E. Nourse, *Product Innovation, the Product Life Cycle and Competitive Behavior, Selected Food Processing Industries, 1947–1964* (Cambridge, Mass.: Arthur D. Little, 1966).

price, quality of product, and selling costs are all interdependent. If the hundreds of possible nonprice concessions are also kept in mind, the futility of a full graphic approach becomes evident. About all that can be said is that the astute businessperson should attempt to make all adjustments in product and conditions of sale where marginal revenue to be gained promises to exceed the marginal cost of the change.

Some variables may be of such a nature that they must be changed simultaneously and their combined effect on marginal revenue and marginal cost considered. At the very least these propositions show the complexity of many business decisions and suggest why most new enterprises are not successful. Oligopolistic interdependency adds to the complications that must be faced.

CONSUMERISM, PRODUCT, AND PROMOTION POLICIES

In Chapter 1, consumerism was cited as a challenge for business decision making. Essentially it calls for honesty and candor in product and promotional decisions. The rule of caveat emptor (let the buyer beware) may have tolerably served a marketplace where choices were few and products were simple. It is less appropriate for the changing and complex choices that consumers must make today. There is an asymmetry between the potential expertise of the producer and seller about the product offered and the consumer's knowledge about the many goods and services customers must buy that place a particular resonsibility upon sellers to fully disclose material facts about their wares.

Three approaches to consumer protection that represent constraints on business decision making constitute the main thrust of consumerism. One is litigation under the legal doctrines of implicit warranty or of fraud. The second is through legal regulation, either of product standards (as in building codes and motor vehicle safety requirements) or of the honesty or fullness of disclosure of promotion. The third is through private exposure such as the product information offered by Consumers Union in *Consumers Reports* or in the recording of abuses by a Nader task force. All three can be thought of as supplements to the provision of consumer alternatives in the marketplace.

It is not within the scope of this chapter to take up government restraints in general (some amplification is contained in Chapter 18). Rather it is to concentrate on the interplay between managerial decisions and consumerism in particular with reasonably representative situations— Case 15–1 with refrigerators and Case 15–2 with cigarettes.

The refrigerator case is of particular interest in the 1980s because its facts gave impetus to Senator Tunney's "truth in energy act" which was before Congress in 1974. Through the mid-1950s as indicated in this chapter, refrigerators had become larger, cheaper, and more economical in energy usage. They continued to become larger and cheaper in original price and offered new features such as no-frost operation and automatic icemakers. But by the 1970s the average refrigerator required four times as much energy to operate. The energy shortages of 1973–74 focused attention on the advantages for society of reducing energy demand, and more specifically on the fact that appliance purchasers were being offered little or no information on the energy cost of appliances, although these typically exceeded the purchase price. The prospect was that higher energy prices would make electricity or gas consumption information even more important for rational choice by consumers.

A latent consumerist issue had become a very active one. The approach of the "truth in energy act" was to require an estimate of annual operating costs in the labeling of refrigerators, freezers, ranges, air conditioners, clothes dryers, and water heaters. The supervision would be by the Federal Trade Commission and the National Bureau of Standards. The Association of Home Appliance Manufacturers opposed the operating cost provisions (presumably favoring energy usage), the administration had a voluntary alternative, others suggested the inclusion of other appliances. Refrigerator manufacturers faced not only the issue of what bill to support but what their own product and promotional policies should be concerning energy usage.

Another aspect of consumerism, the concern for product safety, is brought out in Case 15–2,"Upheaval in the Cigarette Industry." Such leaders in the antismoking campaign as the American Cancer Society may deplore the increase in the total number of cigarettes sold but can point to the decline in pounds of cigarette and tobacco products smoked, the sharp reduction in the percentage of men who smoke cigarettes, and the increased recognition of the rights of nonsmokers such as in various bans on smoking in public places. A triumph of sorts for women's liberation is suggested by the observation of Dr. Horn, director of the National Clearinghouse for Smoking and Health (an agency of HEW), who stated that "the girls have been keeping up with the boys" in cigarette smoking.[13] Significant contributions of the consumer advocates have been the publicizing of medical findings on smoking hazards, the exposure of the poor performance of cigarette filters in the 1950s, and the pressure on public agencies to act rather than to evade the health issue. A tangible gain has been the significant reduction of the tar content of cigarette smoke in the two decades after 1954. The requirement that tar and nicotine content, as determined by the FTC, be a part of all advertising is likely to mean further reductions. The specified warning that "The Surgeon General Has Determined that Cigarette Smoking Is Dangerous to Your Health" has added candor previously missing from national cigarette advertising.

---

[13] As quoted in *U.S. News & World Report*, December 17, 1973.

CASE 15-1
Refrigerators and Kilowatt-Hours

Even before the first energy "crisis" of the fall of 1973, the average price paid by consumers for a kilowatt-hour of electricity had started to rise. Its low had approached 2 cents per kilowatt-hour in 1969 and 1970. The extrapolation used in the MIT study[14] that is the source for much of the data in this case is for a doubling of the kilowatt-hour price by 1980. This prospect for higher prices, together with an increased public awareness of a social interest in energy saving, represented a challenge to the product and related policies of refrigerator manufacturers and distributors.

In many respects the consumer had been served well by vigorous and innovative competition in the industry. The average price for a refrigerator as expressed in constant dollars (1958) dropped from $320 in 1958 to $200 in 1972. The current dollar average price in 1972 was about $290, a demonstration that some prices do come down in a generally inflationary period. The cost index per cubic foot that adjusts for the fact that refrigerators were becoming larger showed an even more dramatic drop to 56 percent of its 1959 value. The service call index had dropped to less than half of its 1959 value. Performance characteristics such as "pulldown," the ability to cool food rapidly, had increased materially. Refrigerators took less overall room per unit of usable space; there were more "features" such as automatic icemakers and ice-water dispensers; and the proportion of low-temperature freezer space had been increased.

In one respect, however, the average new refrigerator of the model years of the early 1970s was distinctly more expensive than that of the 1950s; the average kilowatt-hour usage had increased from just over one to four per day. For the economy as a whole, home refrigeration has been estimated to use from 14.1 to 20 percent of total residential usage of current, which in turn is close to one third (32.7 percent) of total domestic usage of electric power. Thus, household refrigeration accounts for between 5 and 7 percent of total usage of electricity in the United States. Its estimated annual growth rate of 8.3 percent is slightly above that for the total U.S. load.

Life-Cycle Costs

Over the service life of a refrigerator, the household must incur three major types of costs: the initial purchase price, the costs of servicing, and the power costs. This concept was illustrated in a special study for the

---

[14]*The Productivity of Serving Consumer Durable Goods* (The Center for Policy Alternatives MIT—Report No. CPA-74-4, 1974).

EXHIBIT 15–1A   Discounted Life-Cycle Costs of No-Frost Refrigerator (15 cubic feet—1972)

	At $0.03 per Kilowatt-Hour			At $0.05 per Kilowatt-Hour		
	Annualized Life-Cycle Costs	PV* of Life-Cycle Costs	Per-cent	Annualized Life-Cycle Costs	PV* of Life-Cycle Costs	Per-cent
Purchase	$32.75	270	33	$32.75	270	22
Energy	55.20	455	54	92.00	758	69
Service maintenance	12.84	106	13	12.84	106	9
Total	$100.79	831	100	$135.59	1,134	100

* PV—present value.

MIT project[15] by estimating the costs for a 15-cubic-foot no-frost refrigerator of 1972 over its lifetime. The purchase price was taken to be $270, the power consumption was estimated as 1,840 kilowatt-hours a year, and the annual cost for outside servicing was assumed to be $9. The additional assumptions of the table below are: a life of 14 years, which has been the average scrappage age for many years; an increase of 50 percent in the servicing cost for years 11 to 14; a $3 imputed cost for the hour of annual time the household might spend on cleaning: two different prices per kilowatt-hour of electricity, 3 cents and 5 cents; and an interest rate of 8 percent. The life-cycle costs are given in Exhibit 15–1A.

The same study contrasted the cost of a no-frost refrigerator of the 1970s with a hypothetical "early" manual defrost machine. It assumed the same size and purchase price but the early machine would have just one door and a smaller freezer space, say 1.5 cubic feet against 4.5 cubic feet. The "early" refrigerator would use only 790 kilowatt-hours annually but would require five extra hours of user maintenance (four hours for defrosting and an extra hour for cleaning). The results are given in Exhibit 15–1B.

Clearly one way of reducing the life-cycle cost of refrigeration to the household would be the purchase of the early 15-cubic-foot machine and then the life-cycle cost advantage is almost doubled to $337 at the $0.05 per kilowatt-hour price that could prevail during the lifetime of a new refrigerator.

The MIT study thought this an unlikely solution: "So, in spite of the lower cost of manual-defrost machines with their inconvenient small freezer volumes, it would seem to be an exercise in futility to try to promote a return to the horse-and-buggy days of the refrigerator business."[16]

A course more likely to be successful in reducing energy usage in the study's judgment was to make engineering changes in the no-frost models.

---

[15]W. S. Chow and G. Newton, Jr., "Energy Utilization of Refrigerators and Television Receivers," Special study in *Productivity of Serving Consumer Goods*, pp. 175 f.

[16]Ibid., p. 183.

EXHIBIT 15–1B   Discounted Life-Cycle Costs of "Early" Manual Defrost Refrigerator (15 cubic feet)

	At $0.03 per Kilowatt-Hour			At $0.05 per Kilowatt-Hour		
	Annualized Life-Cycle Costs	PV of Life-Cycle Costs	Per-cent	Annualized Life-Cycle Costs	PV of Life-Cycle Costs	Per-cent
Purchase	$32.75	270	41	$32.75	270	34
Energy.	23.70	195	29	29.50	325	41
Service Maintenance*	24.50	202	30	24.50	202	25
Total	$80.95	667	100	$86.75	797	100

*Service is assumed to be only $6 a year instead of $9 for years 1–10 and 50 percent higher for years 11–14.

EXHIBIT 15–1C   Estimated Impact on Purchase Price and Energy Consumption of Engineering Changes for 15-Cubic-Foot No-Frost Refrigerator

Change	Increase in Purchase Price	Decrease in Annual Energy Use (Kilowatt-Hours)
(a) Substitution of polyurethane insulation for fiberglass	$14	438
(b) Increase efficiency of compressor motor from 65% to 75%	20	245
(a) and (b) together	34	625
(c) Tentative program including (a) and (b) and four other changes (increase in evaporator and condensor surfaces, etc.)	90	990

Two relatively simple changes were suggested as well as a tentative program that speculated on the cost effectiveness of several design changes made in combination. All the proposals had the effect of increasing the initial purchase price but of reducing energy requirements from the current estimated level of 1,840 kilowatt hours. The increase in purchase price is estimated at double manufacturer's cost, to reflect profit and distributor margins, in Exhibit 15–1C.

Competition in the Refrigerator Industry

During most of the postwar period, refrigerator production has had a four-firm concentration ratio of between 60 percent and 70 percent (Whirlpool—the usual supplier for Sears' Coldspot line, General Motors with Frigidaire, General Electric—Hotpoint, and plain Westinghouse.) The top 11 producers have accounted for 80–90 percent of production. In the late 1970s, White Industries acquired the refrigerator lines, first of Westinghouse and then of General Motors.

A number of factors have intensified competition. Substantial overcapacity was present from 1951 until the late 1960s. This stemmed directly from expansion to meet the postwar demand that led to a peak production of over six million in 1950, a total not again reached until 1972. Distributors with their own brands, conspicuously Sears, were in strong rivalry with the national manufacturers that sold through independent dealers as well as discount chains. Imports, particularly from Italy, became a competitive factor in the late 1960s, although the number, 874,000 in 1971, overstates their direct competitive importance. Most were of the smaller size serving mobile home, trailer, and similar markets. Imports represented only 4 percent of the dollar volume of U.S. production.

Alan F. Fusfeld has summarized various market surveys on refrigerator demand substantially as follows:[17]

1. Approximately 70–80 percent of all purchases are from new household formation or replacement due to unsatisfactory performance from age or reliability.
2. Price per cubic foot is the primary basis of brand choice for 45 percent of consumers.
3. Features provide the primary basis for approximately 35 percent of cases. . . . For those replacing units less than 10 years old in satisfactory condition (approximately 15 percent of demand) feature innovation has a stronger effect.
4. The elasticities are such that product-improvement efforts would be channeled towards improvement of costs per cubic foot and features.

It is not suprising that the peak period of product innovation, the mid-1950s to the mid-1960s, corresponds with the low household formation that reflected the low birth rates of the 1930s. In a saturated market, demand primarily rested on new household formation and replacement. *Electrical Merchandising Week* (January 1960) stated, "The problem of the industry is to continually create more design and performance innovations to dramatize the superiority of today's merchandise over antiquated boxes still throbbing away in millions of kitchens."

The general pricing policy of the industry has been to charge more for larger, feature-laden models than constant markup over cost would otherwise suggest, thus putting a profitability premium on product innovation.

Technological Change in the Product

While competitive pressures can keep prices in line with costs, cost-cutting changes in technology were required to reduce the constant dollar price of refrigerators. Scale economies are not a generally applicable explanation since the industry and firm volume has not materially increased since 1950. The major product change that reduced costs was in thin-

---

[17]*Application of the Technological Progress Function to Consumer Durable Products,* MIT Report, p. 225.

wall, straight-line construction that cut material usage per cubic foot of space drastically between 1956 and 1968. This change also yielded a feature attractive to consumers since the straight-line design cut down on exterior dimensions and saved space in the kitchen.

A feature that rapidly swept the market was no-frost, a totally frostless system requiring no maintenance by the consumer for either the fresh-food or the freezer section. It was available on 10 percent of the models in 1960 and on 90 percent by 1967.[18] It substantially replaced both the manual defrost and a cycle-defrost system that reached peak popularity in the 1950s. The combination of materials savings, larger inside volume, and the increased proportion of low-temperature freezer space, together with the no-frost feature, accounts for most of the increased energy consumption.[19]

Two other production features of significance were the popular automatic ice-makers and the magnetic door seal from which even a small child could force a way out. There were other marketing features that did not really represent technological changes, such as the side-by-side style for freezer and fresh foods, ice-water dispensers, humidifying drawers, and shelf changes.

Increasing Energy Efficiency

By 1977, most refrigerators had ratings on energy consumption certified by the Association of Home Appliance Manufacturers (AHAM) and attested to by a sticker on the appliance. *Consumer Reports* found that "there are refrigerator-freezers that do a good job on 25 percent to 30 percent less electricity than comparable models, but that may be one of the best-kept secrets of the advertising world."[20] It was not so much that "operating economy doesn't sell" but that promotion concentrated on "a minor feature—a switchable heater—that might save as little as 10 percent or so in electricity."

The AHAM ratings indicated that average energy usage would be lower than the 1972 figure of 1,840 kilowatt-hours used by the MIT study, about 1,450 kilowatt-hours for 15 cubic foot models.[21] *Consumer Reports* in rating 17–18 cubic foot refrigerators (more representative of the 1977 market) covered 16 models of 12 brands including 4 with high-efficiency design, presented data suggesting an average annual consumption of

---

[18]*Application of the Technical Progress Function*, p. 230. Fusfeld notes that the period 1956–64 was that of greatest innovative activity and that this corresponded with the period of greatest competitive pressure.

[19]Inside volume went from an average of 8 cubic feet in 1950 to 15 cubic feet in 1972; low-temperature freezer space went from less than 20 percent of total space in 1959 to almost 30 percent in 1965 and later models. By 1978, inside volume of 18 cubic feet was representative.

[20]*Consumer Reports*, January 1978, p. 23

[21]1977 Directory of Certified Refrigerators and Freezers, June 1977, *Association of Home Appliance Manufacturers*, 20 North Windsor Drive, Chicago, Illinois.

1,560 kilowatt-hours. The four high-efficiency models average 1,200 kil-owatt-hours as against 1,700 kilowatt-hours for the comparable regular refrigerators. The surveyed prices averaged $498 for the high-efficiency models and $465 for the regular models.[22] This comparison was between Whirlpool (including a Sears model) and General Electric (included Hot-point). Other companies offered partially automatic (freezer manual de-frost) refrigerators in the same energy range or lower with Fridgidaire the lowest at about 960 kilowatt-hours a year.

Questions

1. Evaluate the contribution of the engineering changes proposed in Exhibit 15–1C toward minimizing life-cycle cost. Assume 14 years' life, 8 percent interest, and $.05 price per kilowatt-hour.

2. Is there evidence that the industry had adopted some of these proposals by 1977? Why might a little promotional effort still be given to high-efficiency models? As a consumer, should you have purchased a high-efficiency box with electricity prices then ranging between 3 cents and 10 cents?

3. Evaluate the current role that energy economy is playing in the refrigerator industry by such methods as visiting appliance stores, studying advertise-ments, consulting *Consumer Reports,* and the current AHAM directory re-ferred to in footnote.

4. Why did competition into the 1970s stress original price and features rather than life-cycle costs?

CASE 15–2
Upheaval in the Cigarette Industry

In the 1980s, the cigarette industry has been a highly profitable oli-gopoly of six diversified firms making over $3 billion in cigarette profits on over $20 billion in sales. Annual sales of about 600 billion cigarettes were not growing, and consumption per capita (18 years and older) had declined from a 1963 peak of over 4,300 to 3,600. The industry manufac-tured over 200 product varieties of about 40 brands. In 1984, the leading brand, Marlboro, with eight varieties of length, tar content, flavor, and packaging, accounted for 21.6 percent of unit sales.

In 1912, the cigarette industry was dominated by three successor firms to the Tobacco "Trust" which had been dissolved by antitrust action. The three were American Tobacco, P. Lorillard, and Liggett & Myers. Their major products were in manufactured tobacco for pipe smoking and chewing. Total sales were only 14 billion cigarettes (about 230 per capita) but had doubled over those of 1907. Cigarettes were produced in many

---

[22]*Consumer Reports,* January 1978, p. 28

EXHIBIT 15–2A Per Capita* Tobacco Consumption Over
Time

	1912*	1950	1960	1981
Cigarettes—number	220	3,522	4,171	3,800
Cigarettes—pounds	0.5	9.54	9.64	9.61
Cigars—pounds	2.5	1.25	1.18	0.40
Tobacco—pounds	7.5	1.50	0.99	0.68
All products—pounds . . .	10.5	12.29	11.81	10.69

*Per capita base is population aged 18 and over, and 1912 figures are
estimated from production data.
SOURCE: *Historical Statistics of the U.S., Colonial Times to 1970;
Statistical Abstract of the U. S.*, various years.

varieties of types of tobacco, package size, and price. There were many
small firms in addition to the Big Three of the time (who in some corporate form are fourth, fifth, and sixth in industry sales in the 1980s).

By the 1920s and through 1931, cigarettes became standardized, and
three brands, Camels, Lucky Strikes, and Chesterfields, produced in one
variety and sold at identical prices, occupied over 90 percent of the market. Up to the "filter revolution" of the 1950s, the single-variety cigarette
firm dominated, and as late as 1947 the three brands had over 80 percent
of the market.

This case is concerned with the decisions involving product, price,
and promotional strategies that resulted, first, in product standardization
for the industry and later in the splintering of the cigarette market into
many segments. These decisions were influenced by economic events,
government policies, scientific studies, and social perceptions. It should
be noted at the outset since we are not going to analyze other tobacco
uses, that much of the period from 1912 to the mid-1980s was one of
gradual decline in the male consumption of tobacco products. The growth
of per capita cigarette consumption (with increasing feminine participation) was accompanied by a reduction in cigars and manufactured tobacco. The brief table in Exhibit 15–2A can be constructed from
government statistics.

***The introduction of Camels and the ascendancy of the Big
Three.*** R. J. Reynolds Company, a successor firm to the dissolution of
the original American Tobacco Company, had no cigarettes. Its winning
strategy in entering the market in 1913 was:

1. To produce a cigarette blending burley and some imported Turkish
    tobacco with bright tobacco in one package size (20 cigarettes).
2. To promote the brand heavily. (Joe, the Camel, proved an excellent
    symbol and has survived into the filter cigarette era.)
3. To price the brand aggressively; the retail price of 10 cents per pack
    was slightly below average for the time.

Reynold's share of the cigarette market rose from 0.2 percent in 1913
to 40 percent in 1917 and 45 percent in 1925. Noting the success of

Camels, the Liggett & Myers Company similarly concentrated advertising on its blend, Chesterfield, which had been launched in 1912. American Tobacco Company followed with the Lucky Strike brand in 1917. In 1926, the P. Lorillard Company challenged the Big Three with its Old Gold brand. It financed initial promotional requirements by the flotation of a $15 million bond issue. Since the Old Gold brand never achieved more than a 6.7 percent market share, even substantially higher advertising outlays per unit left its total annual advertising of $1,800,000 well below that of rivals that typically spent in the $5–$10 million range.

The price rise of 1931 and the new competitors. The wholesale price rise by the Big Three of 1931 from $6.40 to $6.85 per thousand cigarettes (which followed an earlier rise in 1929 from $6.00 to $6.40) was made in the face of a deepening depression and record low prices for tobacco.[23] By driving retail prices toward 15 cents a pack, it opened up a real opportunity for existing and new "10–cent brands" that seized 20 percent of the market. The motivation for the decision was apparently to try to maintain profits in face of a 5–10 percent decline in unit sales occasioned by the onset of the depression. The alternative of cutting advertising to below 25 cents per thousand cigarettes had had poor results for Reynolds, the price leader, in 1929 and 1930.

While the price cuts were rescinded in 1933, the low-priced brands remained significant until the prosperity, higher tobacco prices, and higher unit taxes of the 1940s reduced them to insignificance. The long-run consequences were the aid the episode gave to the establishment in the market of Philip Morris and Brown & Williamson (the American subsidiary of British American Tobacco). By the mid-1980s these firms have become first and third in unit sales, but in 1931 Philip Morris had 0.9 percent and Brown & Williamson 0.2 percent of the market. Brown & Williamson with Wings was the most successful of the low-price producers with over 10 percent of the market in 1939. Its line also included Raleighs, which has continued to use coupons, as a top 20 brand in the 1980s, and Kools, the mentholated cigarette in a nonfilter version. The Philip Morris brand benefited from the distributor ill will that the Big Three incurred as they attempted to cope with the "10-cent brands" by pressuring dealers to keep prices on their brands within 3 cents of the low-priced brands. Philip Morris sought to keep retailer margins up by encouraging maintenance of the 15-cent price and advertised heavily with such successful themes as Johnny, the bellboy, bellowing "Call for Philip Morris" over the radio sets of the country.

The postwar 1940s and the advent of Pall Mall. 1947 looked more like 1931 than 1939 with one conspicuous exception, the king-sized Pall

---

[23]This decision in 1931 that was made in a deepening depression when tobacco prices were at record lows was justified by Reynolds because "Courage was needed in the U.S.," by American "as an opportunity to make money," and by Liggett and Myers to get "more money for advertising." William H. Nicholls, *Price Policies in the Cigarette Industry* (Nashville: Vanderbilt University Press, 1951), p. 83

EXHIBIT 15–2B   Market Share of the Leading Cigarette Brands, 1931, 1939 and 1947.

	1931	1939	1947
R. J. Reynolds (Camels) 28.4		23.6	30.4
American Tobacco (Lucky Strike) 39.5		22.9	29.5
(Pall Mall) . . . . —		—	3.4
Liggett & Myers (Chesterfield) 22.7		21.6*	20.8
P. Lorillard (Old Gold) 6.5		5.8*	4.3
Philip Morris (Philip Morris) 10.9		7.1	6.9
Brown & Williamson (Three brands) . . 0.3		10.6†	3.0*
All others 1.7*		12.6†	1.7*

*Includes "10-cent brands."
†Predominantly 10-cent brands.
SOURCES: *American Tobacco Co.* v. *United States,* 328 U.S. 781 (1931 and 1939); and *Business Week* (1947).

Mall as shown in Exhibit 15–2B. The low-priced brands were comatose, but the market had more than tripled in size and was approaching 400 billion cigarettes.

The ability of American Tobacco to introduce a longer 85 mm cigarette with about 15 percent more tobacco reflected the fact that the Internal Revenue Code that imposed a federal excise of $3 per thousand on short cigarettes permitted a weight of up to 3 pounds per 1,000 cigarettes. Pall Mall possessed a unique combination of price and promotional appeal. Temporarily it sold at a premium, but quickly it was cut to regular prices and offered smokers an obvious price advantage. In addition, it had the promotional appeal of "traveling the smoke further" in an era where other brands were stridently claiming "better for the nose and throat."

The long-run signficance of Pall Mall was that its immediate success almost certainly retarded American Tobacco's entry into the filter market which was where the future was to lie. Pall Mall sales exploded to 12.4 percent of the market by 1953. It became the number one brand in 1959 with a 14.1 percent share. Its advertising theme, "Pall Mall's greater length travels the smoke further, filters its smoke and makes it mild," was correct for smokers who eschewed economy and threw away long stubs in that the extra (unsmoked) tobacco gave more protection than most early filters.

Adjusting to the Filter Revolution

Before discussing the series of management decisions that led to profound changes in the product structure of the industry, it is worth examining the medical findings whose wide public dissemination led to them and to government policies that conditioned them. The medical reports were widely circulated in the early 1950s and continued to be elaborated in Congressional Hearings, American Cancer Society reports, and magazines like *Readers Digest* and *Consumer Reports* throughout the decade and since. The clear-cut indication of their potential impact was indicated by a decline in per capita consumption of cigarettes from 3,509 in 1952 to 3,216 in 1954.

The medical findings and the industry response. The key external factor that was to influence strategies of the 1950s, 1960s and 1970s was discussed largely in scientific journals and medical meetings. But by 1953 and 1954, the basic findings of the strong statistical association of lung cancer, heart disease, and generally higher death rates with cigarette smoking were well established:

1. Correlation studies indicated that the rapid rise in lung cancer in the various countries of the world followed the establishment of widespread cigarette habits. The best of these studies made allowance for such other factors as urban rather than rural residence.
2. Retrospective studies of lung cancer victims indicated that the vast majority were regular cigarette smokers. These studies had become more persuasive as better control groups were set up that showed these victims differed from the rest of the population primarily in their smoking habits.
3. Human pathological findings found significant changes in the lungs of smokers that indicated precancerous conditions.
4. Experiments indicated that cancer could be induced in laboratory animals by components of the cigarette smoke.
5. Prospective studies, in which large samples of middle-aged men were classified as to smoking and other characteristics and were followed through several years to observe the time and cause of death, indicated death rates from lung cancer for heavy cigarette smokers of approximately 20 times that of nonsmokers. These prospective studies broadened the health issue from simply lung cancer to generally excessive mortality rates, particularly from coronary artery diseases, and confronted the public with such findings as the fact that heavy cigarette smokers in their late 40s and 50s die at rates of men who are seven or eight years older among nonsmokers.

Presumably influenced by the public health agitation and declining sales, 14 tobacco companies, including all of the majors, formed the Tobacco Industry Research Committee to study all phases of tobacco use, and from 1954 through 1962 contributed $6.25 million for about 400 grants to researchers. The public position taken by both it and the Tobacco Institute formed by the same companies in 1958 to advance public relations has been that the causative role of cigarettes in disease has not been proved and that more experimental research is needed. It was plausible to maintain this position through 1963 because the origins of cancer remained obscure, the causes seemed to be multiple, only long-continued cigarette smoking was the culprit pointed to by the studies, and the bulk of the evidence continued to be statistical.

The government role. The major government agency involved was the Federal Trade Commission which had jurisdiction over "false and misleading" advertising. It sought industry advertising policies that

misleading" advertising. It sought industry advertising policies that would make no health claims whatsoever, including claims about better filtration, and brought orders against the occasional effective filters that made such claims as "proved to give you the lowest tar and nicotine of all cigarettes" (made for the short-lived brand Life). This FTC position effectively ended, until 1964, industry efforts for low-tar filters since their possible advantages could not be advertised without a government challenge. Nonetheless, cigarette firms, stung by external criticism that filters were not filtering, modified the filters that had been mere mouthpieces to ones that did significantly reduce tar and nicotine levels.

The government role gradually changed after 1964 when the Surgeon General of the United States officially recognized cigarette smoking as a threat to the health of Americans. The FTC permitted firms such as American Tobacco and P. Lorillard to inform the public of the low-tar characteristics of Carlton and True. In 1965, the warning, "Caution, Cigarette Smoking May Be Hazardous to Your Health" was required on every cigarette package. The Federal Communication Commission prescribed free antismoking "commercials" for all broadcasters who carried cigarette commercials (one for every three was the working rule) in 1968. The antismoking ads apparently were so effective in reducing cigarette consumption (from 4,200 to 4,000 per capita while being run) that the industry was reasonably happy with the government decision to ban all cigarette TV advertising in 1970. (The prices of cigarette stocks rose with this decision. Wall Street saw the hundreds of millions spent on TV advertising as a drain on industry profits whatever the competitive necessity for the firm). The second action required all printed ads, as well as packs, to carry "Warning: The Surgeon General Has Determined that Cigarette Smoking Is Dangerous to Your Health." In addition, the tar and nicotine content, as determined by tests the FTC would set up, would be printed in all future ads.

The filter addition decisions, 1952–1962. This was the period in which a growing number of smokers wanted the assurance of a filter. With many potential switchers, it represented an opportunity for management to launch new filter products. Only R. J. Reynolds followed what in retrospect was the optimum strategy of establishing a strong position in both plain and mentholated filters, the latter to become increasingly important as filtration improved and the desire for a distinct flavor became more important. Reynolds rushed the Winston and Salem brands to the market rapidly, rather arbitrarily taking the names from its headquarters' city, Winston-Salem, North Carolina. The initial failure of the filters to be very effective was probably a commercial advantage since users of unfiltered cigarettes noticed little diminution in taste. The phrase "it's what up front that counts" added to the Winston jingle "Winstons taste good! Like a cigarette should!" was suitably modest about the effectiveness of the filter. Winston's market share of 12.1 percent and Salem's of 9.1 percent added to the regular Camel share of 13.2 percent gave Reynolds a commanding lead with 34.4 percent of the 1962 market.

American Tobacco, the leading firm in 1952, ignored the filter market except for the belated addition of a filter version to its second king-size brand Tareyton. Having Pall Mall as the leading brand in 1962 could not prevent American's future fall from second to fifth place in the industry. Unfiltered kings were shortly to join regular nonfilters in a precipitious decline. The third of the Big Three, Liggett & Myers, did little better and by 1962 had dropped to sixth place by a small margin. The filter brand it did establish, L&M, proved to be less promotable than those of competitors. The modest success of an 85 mm version of Chesterfield, which was a distant second to Pall Mall as an unfiltered king, was transitory.

The "little three" all improved their positions in this time of flux and attained shares of about 10 percent each in 1962. P. Lorillard, the filter pioneer with Kent and a later entry of Newport as a mentholated filter, was in the strongest position. It was helped by favorable articles about the effectiveness of its Kent filter but hurt by the inability to make advertising claims for the greater filtration. Philip Morris popularized an obscure brand, Marlboro, using the macho appeal of the now-famous Marlboro cowboy. Its advertising slogan "The better the makings, the better the smoke" carried out the theme that in 1962 was good for 5.1 percent market share. The willingness of Philip Morris to use an apparently male appeal for Marlboro despite the rapid increase in women smokers was probably related to the recessed filter that gave a feminine appeal to its second filter brand, Parliament. Brown and Williamson created filter versions of two established brands, the mentholated Kools and Raleighs, and added another plain filter, Viceroys.

After the Filter Revolution

The future structure of the industry was largely established in this period of the filter revolution. Ten of the filter brands newly established as leaders in the 1952–1962 period remained among the 20 leading brands in 1984, 4 of them at the top. The 11th, L&M, dropped out after 1978. A complete listing for 1967 through 1984 can be found later in Exhibit 15–2C. Market segmentation and brand proliferation was to go further. Exhibit 15–2D shows the situation as it was in 1973 and can serve as a benchmark for the changes in the late 1970s and 1980s. The 10 new filter brands with 1962 and 1984 rank are as follows: Winston (RY), 3, 2; Salem (RY), 4, 3; Kent (LO), 6, 11; Marlboro (PM), 7, 1; Viceroy (BW), 10, 19; Kool (BW), 11, 4; Tareyton (AM), 11, 18; Raleigh (BW), 12, 16; Parliament (PM), 13, 20; and Newport, (LO), 16, 12.

Steady as you go strategy. The greatest single success in the industry was to be Marlboro, the filter brand that moved cautiously but climbed from seventh in 1962 to a dominant first in 1984 with 21.2 percent. It stuck to its hard-bitten cowboy advertising theme. It followed the others with two additions in the 100 mm length (a soft pack and a box) and then three more varieties (a light filter-king, a light 100, and another box, all in tasteful Marlboro gold) when the low-tar appeal was at its peak in the late

EXHIBIT 15–2C   Market Shares and Ranks of the Leading Brands 1967, 1973, and 1978 (tar ranges of lines)

Brand (company)	1967		1973		1978		1984		Tar Range	
	Rank	Percent Share	Rank	Percent Share	Rank	Percent Share	Rank	Percent Share	1973	1978–79
Winston (RY)	1	15.6	1	15.2	2	14.2	2	11.9	20	13–20
Marlboro (PM)	5	6.5	2	13.6	1	16.8	1	21.2	14–18	12–17
Kool (BW)	7	5.4	3	9.8	3	10.1	4	7.1	17–22	7–17
Pall Mall (AM)	2	13.3	4	9.1	5	6.2	9	3.8	10–29	6–26
Salem (RY)	3	8.4	5	8.2	4	9.1	3	8.1	19–21	12–13
Kent (LO)	6	5.7	6	5.2	6	5.1	11	3.3	9–19	3–12
Camel (RY)	4	8.3	7	5.2	8	4.3	6	4.5	20–25	9–25
Benson & Hedges (PM)	14	2.3	8	4.0	7	4.5	5	4.9	10–18	10–18
Tareyton (AM)	9	4.0	9	3.3	11	2.2	18	1.1	19–20	8–20
Viceroy (BW)	11	3.7	10	3.2	13	2.0	19	1.1	17–18	9–1.
Raleigh (BW)	12	3.5	11	2.9	12	2.2	16	1.3	16–25	9–25
L&M (LG)	10	3.8	12	2.3	17	1.4	—	—	17–19	8–17
Lucky Strike (AM)	8	4.7	13	2.2	—		—		9–29	9–25
Parliament (PM)	16	1.6	14	1.7	20	1.3	20	1.0	15–19	10–12
Belair (BW)	15	1.7	15	1.7	18	1.4	—		16–18	13–15
True (LO)	20	1.4	16	1.5	14	1.9	17	1.2	12	5–12
Chesterfield (LG)	13	3.0	17	1.4	—		—		18–25	18–25
Vantage (RY)	—		18	1.3	9	3.1	10	3.5	11	6–12
Virginia Slims (PM)	—		19	1.3	15	1.6	13	2.7	17	17
Lark (LG)	17	1.6	20	1.1	—		—		17–18	8–18
Merit (PM)	—				10	2.9	7	4.2	—	8–10
Carlton (AM)	—				16	1.5	14	1.9	1–3	5–5
Newport (LO)	18	1.5			19	1.4	12	3.1	19–23	13–18
Philip Morris (PM)	19	1.4			—		—		23–29	—
Generics (LG)	—				—		8	4.2		
More (RY)	—				—		15	1.5		
Total sales (billion cigarettes)	529		575		603		600			

SOURCES: *Business Week*, December 15, 1967, and November 13, 1978; *Barrons*, October 29, 1973; FTC Report on Tar and Nicotine Content, April 1973; and 1978–1979 tar estimates from various advertisements.

EXHIBIT 15–2D   Unit Sales ($ billions); Total Market Segment Shares; and Number and Type of Brand Varieties, 1973

Company and Brand	Number and Type Brand Varieties	Total Company and Brand		85 mm Filters				100 mm Filters				Nonfilters			
				Plain		Menthol		Plain		Menthol		Regular		Kings (85 mm)	
		Sales	Share	Sales	Share	Sales	Share	Sales	Share	Sales	Share	Sales	Share	Sales	Share
All cigarettes sold	95	575.0	100	240.4	41.8†	102.6	17.8†	86.3	15.0†	43.8	7.6†	38.8	6.7†	49.7	8.6†
R. J. Reynolds	13	179.1	31.2	85.3	35.5	38.3	37.3	16.3	17.4	15.2	34.7	24.0	61.2	—	—
Winston	4, H, L*	87.7	15.2	69.5	28.9	—	—	16.3	17.4	1.9	4.3	—	—	—	—
Salem	2	48.5	8.4	—	—	35.2	34.3	—	—	13.3	30.4	—	—	—	—
Camel	2	29.8	5.2	5.8	2.4	—	—	—	—	—	—	24.0	61.2	—	—
Vantage	2 T	7.2	1.3	6.2	2.6	1.0	1.0	—	—	—	—	—	—	—	—
Doral	2	5.9	1.0	3.8	1.6	2.1	2.0	—	—	—	—	—	—	—	—
American Brands	19	92.9	16.0	16.8	6.9	1.4	1.4	21.1	24.4	3.8	8.7	11.5	29.6	39.4	79.2
Pall Mall	4	52.5	9.1	0.9	0.3	—	—	0.2	0.2	1.7	3.9	11.5	29.6	38.9	78.2
Lucky Strike	3 T	12.9	2.2	1.2	0.5	—	—	11.0	12.7	—	—	—	—	—	—
Tareyton	3 Ch	19.3	3.3	12.0	5.0	**	**	6.8	7.9	—	—	—	—	0.5	1.0
Carleton	3 T	2.5	0.4	2.5	1.0	—	—	—	—	*		—	—	—	—
Silva Thins	2	4.7	0.8	—	—	—	—	3.1	3.6	1.6	3.7	—	—	—	—
Iceberg 10's	1 T	1.0	0.2	—	—	1.0	1.0	—	—	—	—	—	—	—	—
Brown & Williamson	14	100.7	17.6	26.0	10.8	52.7	51.3	6.9	7.9	11.7	26.7	1.4	3.6	1.9	3.8
Kool	4 L, H*	56.2	9.8	—	—	45.9	44.7	—	—	8.9	20.3	—	—	—	—
Viceroy	2	18.4	3.2	14.9	6.2	—	—	3.5	4.0	—	—	1.4	3.6	—	—
Raleigh	4 C, L	16.4	2.9	11.1	4.6	—	—	3.4	3.9	—	—	—	—	1.9	3.8
Belair	2 C	9.6	1.7	—	—	6.8	6.6	—	—	2.8	6.4	—	—	—	—

EXHIBIT 15-2D   (Concluded)

Company and Brand	Number and Type Brand Varieties	Total Company and Brand		85 mm Filters				100 mm Filters				Nonfilters			
				Plain		Menthol		Plain		Menthol		Regular		Kings (85 mm)	
		Sales	Share	Sales	Share	Sales	Share	Sales	Share	Sales	Share	Sales	Share	Sales	Share
Philip Morris	22	121.9	21.2	78.7	32.7	2.8	2.7	28.0	32.4	10.3	23.5	0.4	1.0	1.8	3.6
Marlboro	6 2H	78.2	13.6	68.8	28.6	0.9	0.8	8.5	9.8	—	—	—	—	—	—
Benson & Hedges	5 T, Ch	23.0	4.0	2.4	1.0	0.2	0.2	13.2	15.3	7.2	16.4	—	—	—	—
Parliament	3 H, Ch	9.6	1.7	7.4	3.1	—	—	2.2	2.5	—	—	—	—	—	—
Philip Morris	2	2.2	0.4	—	—	—	—	—	—	—	—	0.4	1.0	1.8	3.6
Alpine	1 C	1.7	0.3	—	—	1.7	1.7	—	—	—	—	—	—	—	—
Virginia Slims	2	7.2	1.3	—	—	—	—	4.1	4.8	3.1	7.1	—	—	—	—
Lorillard (Loew's)	14	49.0	8.5	31.4	13.1	6.9	6.7	8.2	9.3	2.1	4.8	0.1	0.3	0.3	0.6
Kent	4 H	30.0	5.2	21.2	8.8	—	—	7.7	8.7	1.1	2.5	—	—	—	—
Newport	3 H	4.5	0.8	—	—	4.0	3.9	—	—	0.5	1.2	—	—	—	—
True	2 T	8.8	1.5	5.9	2.5	2.9	2.8	*	—	*	—	—	—	—	—
Old Gold	4 C	5.2	0.9	4.3	1.8	—	—	0.5	0.6	—	—	0.1	0.3	0.3	0.6
Liggett & Myers	13	29.6	5.1	15.3	7.3	0.0	0.0	5.6	6.5	1.3	3.0	1.4	3.6	6.0	12.1
L & M	4 H	13.2	2.3	10.2	4.2	0.0	0.0	2.3	2.7	0.7	1.6	—	—	—	—
Chesterfield	5 C	8.3	1.7	0.3	0.1	—	—	0.6	0.7	—	—	1.4	3.6	6.0	12.1
Lark	2 Ch	6.6	1.1	4.8	2.0	—	—	1.8	2.1	—	—	—	—	—	—
Eve	2	1.5	0.3	—	—	—	—	0.9	1.0	0.6	1.4	—	—	—	—

†Represents share of total market; obviously shares of each category would equal 100 percent.
Notes on other brand varieties: H = hard box; L = additional low-tar variety; C = couponed; Ch = charcoal; T = tar specified on package; * intro. in 1974;
** included under plain.

SOURCE: *Barron's,* October 29, 1973, pp. 11-15

1970s. In the mid-1980s, it was hard to conceive of its successor as number one since its leading rival, the fading Winston, had only an 11.9 percent market share, and industry reports estimated that over 40 percent of the young who were foolhardy enough to take up the noxious weed chose some version of Marlboro. Besides starting out with a successful image and the mangerial skills to make the necessary product and promotional fine tuning, Marlboro had one break from government policy. The banning of TV and radio ads robbed its rival Winston of its successful though ungrammatical jingles, for example "Winstons taste good, like a cigarette should."

That the "steady as you go" policy did not always work is illustrated by the L&M brands. It was eighth in 1962, barely behind Marlboro. It made the necessary additions of the 100 mm and light versions. It even added a box, but in 1984 its six varieties had a fraction of 1 percent of the market, and it was no longer promoted by Liggett & Myers.

The low-tar strategy. After 1964 when the Surgeon General's Report made the health danger of cigarettes official, American Tobacco, which had failed to establish a position in conventional filters, and P. Lorillard which had led the filter movement with Kent, dropped out of FTC-sponsored voluntary code for advertising to promote the low-tar brands they had developed, Carlton and True, respectively. After the publishing of tar and nicotine levels in all advertisements became mandatory in 1971, R. J. Reynolds promoted a new low-tar brand with wordy advertisements about the smoking problems and the advantages of choosing Vantage. In 1976, Philip Morris, whose reputation for successfully capitalizing on other firms' initiatives, followed with a similar promotion for Merit that stressed its additional flavor enhancers and passed Vantage after 1978.

As one can note in Exhibit 15–2C, these are the four low-tar brands that were the top 20 by 1984 with Merit leading at number 7 with a 4.2 percent brand share. The reason the shares are not higher was that all the filter brands found it competitively necessary to produce lower tar versions (15 mm of tar or less) with the public concern about health risks and numbers in all ads that required performance. See Exhibit 15–2C, the tar range columns for 1973 and 1978–79. (As for the two apparent exceptions, Virginia Slims introduced a light version since 1978, and Chesterfields were being produced without promotion or product modification to meet the demands of old customers.)

Costly business mistakes could be made in low-tar products. The redoubtable R. J. Reynolds, in hastily retaliating to the incursions of Merit, launched Real in 1977 with a $40 million promotional outlay to announce "the natural cigarette is here," a message surrounded by golden brown tobacco leaves. It turned out that lovers of the natural apparently did not smoke. The brand was withdrawn in 1980. Several companies overestimated the potential growth of ultra-low-tars (6 mg of tar or less) in which Carlton had established its reputation. The segment had rapidly grown in the late 1970s but peaked out at a little less than 10 percent of the market in the early 1980s. Part of the problem was that established brands, such as Winston, Kools, Vantage, and Merit, moved promptly into the higher-tar range (6 mg) of the segment with ultra-light varieties. Part was that people satisfied with the low-nicotine content of the very low brands were likely to become nonsmokers. The entry of Barclay (produced by Brown & Williamson, the British American Tobacco Company's subsidiary) produced a bit of a scandal as well as costing the company $150 million for promotion. It tested at 2 mg of tar on the FTC smoking machines. Its low score was apparently produced by air channels in the filter that diluted the smoke with air. When smoked by a person, the pressure of lips would shut off the air and result in much higher levels than those listed. The temporary answer was to forbid Barclay from listing the tar content until the FTC would devise new testing methods, a curious exception to the requirement that had not been finally resolved in mid-1985.

The extra-long strategy. The 100 mm length was first introduced for Pall Mall (AM) in 1966 which had lost its first place ranking to Winston (RY). Part of the appeal was extra value, and a price differential of about 2 cents per pack has continued for the longer cigarettes. For American Tobacco, a filter version of Pall Mall was necessary to preserve the brand since nonfilters were clearly on a continual decline. It succeeded only to a modest extent. Pall Mall was ninth in 1984, but its sales were down to a quarter of the 1962 peak.

For Philip Morris, the new length was an opportunity to strengthen its weak position in mentholated cigarettes. It took its minor filter brand, Benson & Hedges, and with a humorous advertising campaign featuring cigarettes being broken because of their extra length ("America's Favorite Cigarette Break"), it established Benson & Hedges as a leading brand. By 1984, it ranked fifth.

The popularity of the new length forced all the other leading filters to produce 100 mm versions. While companies recognized that most of the sales would be "cannibalized" from their own brands, the opportunity costs in losing customers to rivals were greater.

There was some evidence that the style of the longer cigarettes had a particular appeal to women. U. S. Health Service data clearly indicated that usage among men was declining more rapidly than among women. Forty-three percent of men and 30.9 percent of women were estimated as "present smokers" in 1970. In 1980, the percentages were 36.5 percent and 29.1 percent. Philip Morris was certainly aware of this when it launched Virginia Slims, thinner plain and mentholated versions of the 100 mm length, with the slogan "You've come a long way, baby." While earning the right to smoke seems a dubious blessing and having a segregated cigarette might seem to step back from equality, the brand succeeded in gaining 13th place by 1984 and was given the compliment of having established a feminine niche by other entries such as Eve (LG) and more recently Satin (LO).

EXHIBIT 15–2E   Concentration Ratios for 1973 in Subcategories of the Cigarette Market

Subcategory	Sales ($ millions)	Cumulative Percent of Sales by Brands				Leading Brands
		1	2	3	4	
85 mm plain filter . .	240.4	28.9	57.5	66.3	72.5	Winston, Marlboro
85 mm menthol filter.	102.6	44.7	79.0	85.6	89.5	Kool, Salem
100 mm plain filter .	86.3	17.4	32.7	43.4	55.8	Winston, Benson & Hedges, Pall Mall
100 mm menthol filter.	43.8	30.4	50.7	67.1	74.2	Salem, Kool, Benson & Hedges
Regular.	38.8	61.2	90.8	94.4	98.0	Camel, Lucky Strike
King	49.7	78.2	90.3	94.1	97.7	Pall Mall, Chesterfield
Hard-box.	44.8	82.1	89.2	95.5	97.4	Marlboro
Couponed.	41.7	39.3	62.3	82.1	95.8	Raleigh, Belair, Chesterfield Old Gold
Charcoal filter	29.9	63.0	85.0	92.5	99.4	Tareyton, Lark
Specified tar and nicotine	23.3	37.9	68.8	79.3	89.3	True, Vantage

Notes:

1. Last four categories cross boundaries of first six and cannot be added to total sales.

2. Firm concentration ratios are distinctly higher for first four categories (see Exhibit 15–2C) and for couponed cigarettes in which B&W has first two brands.

SOURCE: *Barrons*, October 29, 1973, pp. 11-15.

The only addition to the 20 leaders (other than the nonbrand generics) was the 140 mm long More (RY). Its appeals were value ("more puffs") and style (very long and thin and distinguished by a brown wrapper). It turned out to be particularly popular among women, and its later lower tar version, 120 mm in length, had a beige wrapper and a feminine advertising slant. Only Carlton (AM) among leading brands added a 140 mm version. More's success led to three new super-long brands by rivals that remained on the market without conspicuous success.

Other special categories.   Exhibit 15–2E sums up subcategories of the market as they were in 1973. The rivalry of the cigarette companies in finding new product features that will appeal to some segment of the market continues. Low-tar versions are now so general as to no longer be a special feature except for the lower half of the ultra-low group with almost no tar; some Carltons and the NOW (RY) brand are examples. Charcoal, as visual evidence of filtration, lost its special appeal when tar content was published. Lark (LG) and Tareyton (AM) suffered. Many brands have added boxed versions but have not emulated the success of Marlboro.

A trend in the 1980s is to seek a premium appeal with elegant packaging. The established Benson & Hedges (PM) is an example, as well as the new brands, for example Players (PM), Satin (LO), and Sterling (RY). By choosing a new length of 94 mm, Sterling avoided the necessity of carrying both 85 mm and 100 mm varieties.

In the mid-1980s products designed to appeal to Hispanics were being

EXHIBIT 15–2F   Advertising Expenditures in Cents per Carton for Selected Brands (1977, 1966, and 1961).

	1977	1966	1961	1977 Volumes (billions of units)
Five leading brands:				
Marlboro	6¢	11¢	7¢	97
Winston	8	9	5	88
Kool	8	11	6	60
Salem	9	9	7	54
Pall Mall	6	7	4	39
Low-tar brands:				
Vantage	19	—	—	17
Merit	26	—	—	14
True	19	34	—	11
Carlton	50	42	—	8
Now	67	—	—	3
Other brands:				
More	30	—	—	6
Benson & Hedges	15	25	—	26
Camels	6	6	3	24
Virginia Slims	18	—	—	10
Max	32	—	—	1
Unsuccessful introductions, 1977 estimates:				
Real	250¢			
Decade	180¢			

Notes: Students should recognize the real decline in advertising costs after TV ads were banned in 1970. They should also note the higher unit costs for promising and lower volume brands.

SOURCE: Calculated from *Advertising Age,* June 25, 1962, September 16, 1967, and August 28, 1978. Figures are estimated and include TV, magazines, newspapers, and billboards, but not point of sale, radio, and so on.

market tested. Philip Morris was testing its first all-mentholated brand, Rio, with this in mind, while Liggett was trying out Dorado.

The price dimension.   The most dramatic development of the 1980s was the development of significant price differentials between cigarettes. The generics produced by Liggett had become a leading "brand" in eighth place with a market share of 4.2 percent. Factors leading to this development included:

1. The recent wider use of temporary price cuts in the form of two-for-one deals and discount coupons that were particularly likely with new product introductions.
2. Enhanced price-cost margins reflecting price increases that at least incorporated inflation and relatively stable costs. Labor productivity was rising with new higher speed machines. Tobacco prices were relatively stable, and the dominance of filter cigarettes (including thinner products) had dropped tobacco content to well below two pounds per 1,000 cigarettes. The economist might point to the almost zero possibility of entry into an industry whose unit

sales had apparently peaked; whose variety proliferation left little real chance of an outsider achieving enough market share for effective production; whose consumers had persistent brand attachments so that large promotional efforts were needed to enter; whose product was considered the single greatest health threat in the United States; and whose companies were defending themselves against product liability suits.

3. The real key was having the right firm at the right time. Liggett had no attractive alternatives. Its market share had dwindled to 1.5 percent. Its existing brands seemed beyond promotional help. The opportunity costs of using the excess capacity of plant approached zero.

4. The time was right. Generics had become familiar to consumers through many grocery products. The combination of inflation followed by recession made consumers unusually conscious of lower prices, and cigarette prices were rising in contemplation of the increase in the federal tax to $8 per thousand.

The initial success of the generics was sufficient not only to induce Liggett to modestly advertise a nonbrand but encourage the interest of R. J. Reynolds and Brown & Williamson. Both felt the impact of lost sales with older, more price-conscious customers than those of Philip Morris. R. J. Reynolds had a particular interest in unit sales to restore its number one position in the industry. Reynolds chose two weapons, first a new brand Century with 25 cigarettes to a pack and nine packs to a carton. With the per carton price set at the regular rate, 12.5 percent more cigarettes would be available, 225 to 200. The second weapon was to sell a branded cigarette at generic prices; the obsolescent Doral name was available for this purpose. The two together achieved a market share of over 1 percent in 1984.

Brown & Williamson attacked the Liggett position directly with its own generics and also introduced a 25-pack Richland, a copy of Century. The effect of the generic entry was to put pressure on the wholesale price of generics. Liggett's move was to introduce Stride, a full-quality cigarette, with a price set to be $1 below the industry price. The economics of this decision are posed in an extended question at the end of this case.

Product diversification. Up until the late 1950s the cigarette companies were almost totally tobacco firms. The great incentive for diversification came from the generation of large profits in an industry in which the opportunities for reinvestment were limited and long-run decline seemed probable. Only Brown & Williamson, the American outpost of British American Tobacco, remains primarily in cigarettes. P. Lorillard and Liggett have been acquired by other firms. By the early 1970s, the cigarette business was less than 50 percent for American brands. The concerns of Philip Morris with beer and soft drinks were discussed in an earlier case. In 1985, Reynolds Industries became a leading "consumer products" company.

EXHIBIT 15–2G   Estimated Prices and Costs per Carton for (A) Standard Filter King, (B) a Cigarette Like Stride, and (C) Generic Brand.

	A	B	C
Retail price.	$9.00	$8.00	$7.00
Assumed state sales excise tax	1.50	1.50	1.50
Estimated distributor's margin	1.35	1.25	1.15
Manufacturers' wholesale price	6.15	5.25	4.35
Federal excise tax paid by manufacturer.	1.60	1.60	1.60
Revenue	4.55	3.65	2.75
Relevant AVC of production ($= MC$).	2.50	2.45	2.25
Net for promotion, corporate overhead, and profit	$2.05	$1.20	$0.50

Questions

1. Consider the price, product, and promotional aspects of the key decisions that led to the present-day dominance of Reynolds and Philip Morris.

2. What apparently was the great mistake that American made that led to its precipitous decline? What managerial decisions hurt Liggett? What aspects of Lorillard and B&W's strategy have led to an intermediate performance?

3. Develop an economic analysis that explains why cigarette profits remain high in an industry where growth has ceased.

4. Part of the problem the Liggett Group faced with Stride is outlined in Exhibit 15–2G. The state and federal taxes are based on units and cannot be lowered. Since the strategy calls for a cigarette just as good, manufacturing costs may be almost uncuttable. So the $1 price reduction comes almost entirely out of the amount available for promotion, corporate overhead, and contribution to profits. Heavy initial promotion investment is necessary for a brand like Stride.

    a. Assume this is $40,000,000, that 15 percent is the required return, and the life for this investment is infinite since annual advertising expenditures of $8,000,000 will maintain the product image. What will be the annual break-even volume, i.e., the cartons per year, that would justify this investment in initial promotion?

    b. If the volume were achieved entirely at the expense of Liggett's own generics, what volume would be necessary to be as well off as before the introduction of Stride?

    c. As an alternative to introducing Stride, why not simply cut the price of a carton of L&M (show sales in mid-80s were in the 10–15 million carton range) by $1? Little or nothing is being spent on it now for promotion.

5. What gives the cigarette industry particular interest for students of business economics is that the consequences of decisions to unit sales and market shares can be traced essentially through federal excise tax records. In a December issue of *Business Week,* the *New York Times* and other publications expert estimates are usually printed. As of 1985, questions of particular interest are:

    a. How big an inroad can lower price cigarettes make in the market? (They seemed to be topping out at about 6 percent in late 1984.)

b. Will the share of Marlboro continue to climb? Related to this are other aspects of the Reynolds-PM rivalry for the number one spot such as the success of Century's packs of 25 and Doral, the "branded generic."

c. Has brand and variety proliferation continued? Other research could involve advertising expenditures (see annual summary in *Advertising Age*), and investigation of current advertising appeals and tar ranges by reading magazine ads.

CASE 15–3
The Big Advertisers

The following table shows advertising expenditures by the seven companies that had the largest expenditures in each of six important media in 1983. For these companies, 1982 expenditures are also shown.

Company	1983 Expenditures ($ millions)	1982 Expenditures ($ millions)
NETWORK TELEVISION		
Procter & Gamble	$367	$390
General Motors	201	164
Ford Motor	172	129
General Foods	170	232
American Home Products	161	161
American Telephone & Telegraph	147	95
Sears, Roebuck	145	103
SPOT TELEVISION		
Procter & Gamble	$229	$179
PepsiCo	122	88
General Mills	113	108
McDonald's	105	94
General Foods	73	71
Coca Cola	71	59
Pillsbury	61	46
MAGAZINE		
R. J. Reynolds	$155	$111
Philip Morris	140	130
General Motors	89	86
Ford Motor	80	59
American Telephone & Telegraph	61	41
Jos. E. Seagram & Sons	45	62
Loews	45	29
OUTDOOR		
R. J. Reynolds	$ 89	$ 77
Philip Morris	55	51
Loews	37	24
Batus	22	43
Jos. E. Seagram & Sons	16	16
American Brands	13	12
Hiram Walker	8	9

Spot Radio

Anheuser-Busch	$ 41	$ 37
General Motors	29	31
American Telephone & Telegraph	28	19
Philip Morris	22	23
Adolph Coors	22	9
Chrysler	17	28
Delta Air Lines	15	12

Network Radio

Jeffrey Martin	$ 22	$ 33
Sears, Roebuck	11	11
Cotter & Co.	10	7
American Telephone & Telegraph	10	7
General Motors	9	8
Dow Jones	9	8
Warner-Lambert	8	7

SOURCE: *Advertising Age,* September 14, 1984.

Questions

1. Look up and list for each advertiser the principal products sold in these years. (Useful sources of information include *Standard & Poors, Advertising Age, Value Line Survey,* and this textbook.)

2. Try to explain:
   a. The reasons for the large advertising expenditures by some companies.
   b. The choice of media.
   c. Important changes from 1982 to 1983 in advertising expenditures.

3. Economists like to say "there is no such thing as a free lunch." Is this true when TV programs are broadcast without charge to viewers?

16

Product Line Policy

It has become cheaper to look for oil on the floor of the New York Stock Exchange than in the ground.
—*T. Boone Pickens*

Most of the discussion thus far has been concerned with demand, output, and cost for a single commodity produced by a firm or industry. This is obviously an unrealistic assumption for virtually all firms engaged in the wholesaling, retailing, or transporting of goods. Manufacturing establishments more frequently specialize in only one good (e.g., bricks, portland cement, a soft drink, airplanes, wheat, or tobacco) but, even so, usually produce the good in various sizes, models, packages, and qualities, so that it is not entirely clear whether they should be called single-product or multiple-product firms. In recent years, there seems to have been a particular emphasis on product diversification on the part of manufacturers—single-product firms becoming multiple-product producers and those already handling multiple products adding even more lines.[1]

The assumption of one product to a firm is a simplifying abstraction that is useful in developing numerous principles applicable to multiproduct companies as well. For the most part, profit-maximizing entrepreneurs handling many commodities should make short-run and long-run calculations in the same way as is suggested by economic theory for the single-commodity firm; they should equate marginal cost and marginal revenue in short-run operational decisions with respect to every product and should anticipate at least covering average costs (including normal returns to self-employed factors) when making new investment pertaining to any product.

The multiproduct firm is often a member of several industries when "industry" is classified according to the federal government's statistical procedure. It is equally appropriate, though usually less useful, to consider the firm to be a member of as many industries as the number of

---

[1]An early phase of this trend is interestingly described by Gilbert Burck in "The Rush to Diversify," *Fortune*, September 1955, p. 91.

distinct commodities it produces. Competitive conditions may differ greatly from good to good for any particular firm. Some commodities may be turned out under conditions approaching pure competition, where price is set by market forces outside the control of any individual company. Others may be turned out under monopolistic conditions, where the firm can choose its price, within limits, without regard to rivals' reactions. Other goods may be supplied to oligopolistic markets, where the power to set price exists, but where rivals' reactions are of prime importance (and where the conflict of interests may sometimes be usefully viewed as a "game" between firms).

GROWTH THROUGH DIVERSIFICATION

Alert management is usually in search of ways to promote the growth of the firm.[2] Very often, such growth is effected by adding new products; and frequently this is accomplished by the acquisition of entire companies. It is apparent that a systematic search for new investment opportunities will often indicate the best opportunities to be associated with commodities other than those already being produced, rather than with current products, simply because there are so many more items in the former category. This is especially true because new goods are constantly being developed through research. The scope for useful diversification is usually somewhat limited, however, by the desirability of having the new products of a firm related in some way to the old ones. The types of relationship making for compatibility are many; and often more than one type of relationship exists at the same time. Goods may be (1) cost related, (2) related in demand, (3) related in advertising and distribution, or (4) related in research. (Other relations conducive to multiple products might be named, but these appear to be the most important.)

A quantitative picture of the extent of product diversification by the 1,000 largest manufacturing firms was given in a voluminous compilation prepared by the Federal Trade Commission.[3] Figure 16–1 is partly derived from this report. The report indicated that diversification was very much related to the size of the firm. The largest 50 manufacturers most commonly made between 40 percent and 60 percent of their shipments in their principal industry; only 4 firms made 90 percent or more of their shipments in one industry. In contrast, about half of those firms ranked from 951 to 1,000 had 90 percent of their shipments in one industry; all but 4 of the 50 had over half their sales in one industry.

---

[2]Many corporations now employ a vice president who is primarily in charge of growth and development. While greater size often leads to larger and more dependable profits, part of the urge to grow is undoubtedly based on bigness as a goal in itself.

[3]*Federal Trade Commission, Report on Industrial Concentration and Product Diversification in the 1,000 Largest Manufacturing Companies* (Washington, D.C.: U.S. Government Printing Office, January 1957), p. 15.

FIGURE 16–1   Five-digit Products Produced by 1,000
Largest Manufacturers
(1950 and 1962)

Number of Products	Number of Firms, 1950	Number of Firms, 1962
1	778	49
2–5.	354	223
6–15.	432	477
16–50.	128	236
Over 50.	8	15

SOURCE: The 1950 data are from *Federal Trade Commission, Report on Industrial Concentration and Product Diversification in the 1,000 Largest Manufacturing Companies* (Washington, D.C.: U.S. Government Printing Office, January 1957), p. 15. The 1962 count is based on *Fortune's Plant and Product Directory.*

Figure 16–1 shows significant increases in the number of products handled by the 1,000 largest manufacturers between 1950 and 1962. The average of five-digit products produced by the 1,000 largest manufacturers rose from less than 10 to over 13. It should be noted that the standard industrial classification system specifies approximately 1,000 five-digit products. Examples are passenger cars and syrups used for soft drinks.

One can be quite certain that this process of product proliferation continued through the 1970s abetted by a large number of conglomerate mergers.

Case 16–1 traces the fortunes and misfortunes of LTV Corporation in such conglomeration. In the early 1970s, more attention was being paid to the shortcomings of rapid product expansion, and consolidation was forced by financial circumstances of LTV and other conglomerates. But from 1974 on, many firms made acquisitions in unrelated fields with the low stock prices of the acquired firm being a significant stimulus for such diversification. In the mid 1980s, corporate takeovers, often unfriendly, were epidemic. Case 16–3 is based on an unfriendly takeover in 1985.

JOINT COSTS

The most obvious cost relationship that brings about multiple products within the firm is that of joint costs. These exist when two or more products are turned out in fixed proportions by the same production process. Frequently proportions are variable in the long run but fixed in the short run. Fixed proportions are especially common in the chemical industry since nature may put substances together in a fixed way which man then breaks into components.

Joint costs are quite common in the processing of agricultural and fishing products. A famous example is the ginning of cotton where cottonseed and cotton linters are turned out in a weight ratio of about 2 pounds to 1. In the processing of oranges, juice, orange peel, and pulp (used as cattle feed), essential oils (used in flavoring extracts) and seeds (used in plastics and animal feed) appear in approximately fixed proportions.

If joint products are sold in perfectly competitive markets, their prices are determined by total demand and supply, and the individual firm has only the problem of deciding upon its own rate of output. The firm's short-run adjustment may be shown most simply if output units are defined in such a way as to keep the quantity of each product turned out always equal. If, for example, X and Y are joint products, and 3 pounds of X are secured simultaneously with 2 pounds of Y, we can usefully define 3 pounds of X as one unit of X and 2 pounds of Y as one unit of Y. Thus defined, the output of each, measured in the new units, would always be the same. If, for example, 300 pounds of X and 200 pounds of Y were produced during a given day, we could say that the output was 100 units of each good.

In Figure 16–2, units of output of two joint products are defined in this special way. One marginal cost curve and one average cost curve serve for both goods, but separate demand curves are drawn for each of the joint products since they are sold separately. Demand curves are horizontal lines, since the individual firm can sell all it wishes at the prevailing market prices. In addition, a line (D_{x+y}) that represents the sum of the two prices has been drawn.

The optimum output of the firm is OA units of each product per time period, since at this production rate the price OP received for the two goods regarded as one is equal to the marginal joint cost. Any higher rate of output would be unwise, because additional cost to the firm would exceed additional revenue from the sale of both goods; any smaller output would be nonoptimal because if less than OA were being produced, additional units could be turned out which would add more to the revenue than to cost. Since average cost (which is total cost divided by the quantity of either good) is below OP, the operation is yielding economic profit to the firm; that is, more than the usual returns are accruing to those receiving income on a noncontractual basis. If this situation is expected to persist, additional firms will enter the industry, gradually eliminating economic (but not accounting) profit.

From the point of view of an industry (rather than an individual firm), an increase in the demand for one of two joint products increases the price of that good but lowers the price of the other joint product, provided demand for the latter does not also rise. This is because the output of both goods will necessarily be stepped up in order to take advantage of a better demand for one good, and this will necessitate a lower price on the other in order to clear the market. Under perfect competition the price of any joint product can easily remain far below average cost of production, since as a long-run matter, average cost is covered by the sum of the prices of the joint products. As long as any positive price can be obtained for a

FIGURE 16–2   Joint Products under Competition—Firm Regards Two as One

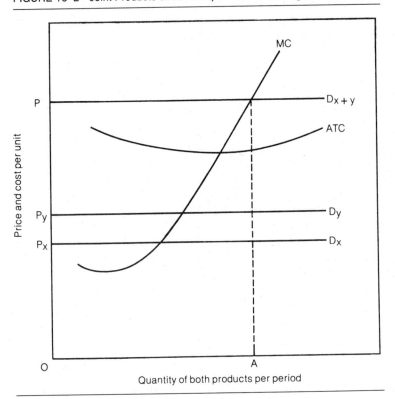

good, a competitive firm has no incentive to withhold any output from the market, inasmuch as its own sales will not depress price. If the price of a joint product falls to zero, it becomes a "waste product."[4] Students are urged to draw *industry* supply and demand curves.

JOINT COSTS AND MONOPOLY

When two or more joint products are produced for sale under monopolistic rather than competitive conditions, profit-maximizing behavior on the part of the firm is different. Assume again, for the sake of simplicity, that only two joint products are turned out by a firm and that units are so defined as to keep their rates of output equal. If the demand for both goods is sufficiently strong in relation to productive capacity, the determination of optimum output and prices is much like that of the single-product

---

[4] A waste product may also have a negative value in the sense that additional costs must be incurred in order to get rid of it. Orange peel, pulp, and seeds were formerly in this category but now constitute valuable by-products.

FIGURE 16–3   Monopolized Joint Products—Entire Output Sold

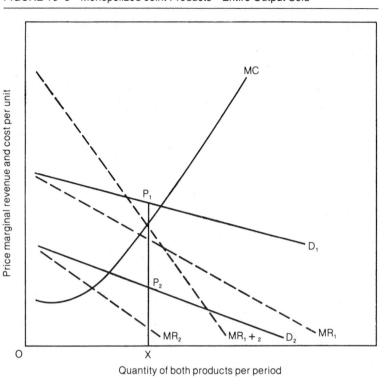

monopolist. In Figure 16–3, the separate demands are represented by D_1 and D_2, marginal (joint) cost is MC, and MR_1 and MR_2 are marginal revenue curves. Combined marginal revenue, MR_{1+2}, is derived by adding MR_1 and MR_2 vertically. (In the theory of price discrimination they are, instead, added horizontally.) The most profitable output (of both) joint products is OX, determined by the intersection of MC and MR_{1+2}. (This statement implicitly assumes that *average* cost curves, which are not shown, are not so high as to make it better to shut down the entire operation.) The separate prices P_1 and P_2 are found on demand curves D_1 and D_2 respectively and represent the prices at which the quantity OX can be sold. It is worthwhile for the firm to sell all of both joint products because marginal revenue from each is above zero at the optimum output. The "last" unit of each good makes a positive contribution to total revenue, and the sum of the contributions of the last unit of each good is just equal to the addition to cost which their production jointly entails.[5]

---

[5]Actually, any unit can be considered to be the "last" turned out, and this terminology has only the merit of convenience. The quantity axis measures rate of output per time period, and any unit can be considered to be marginal during that period.

A different theoretical solution is necessary if the demand for one product is substantially weaker than for the other (in relation to the joint production capacity). Figure 16–4 shows the solution for this case (which is also quite commonly encountered).

The optimum rate of output in Figure 16–4 is OC units (of each product) determined by the intersection of MC with MR_1. It is worthwhile to produce OC units of both goods in order to be able to sell that quantity of good 1. However, marginal revenue from the sale of OC units of good 2 would be negative. Consequently, profits can be maximized by selling only OB units of good 2 (where MR_2 is zero). The plethora BC of good 2 may be regularly destroyed by the monopolist, such as the continuous burning off of gas at a steel mill. Or it may be stored for future sale if demand and cost conditions are anticipated under which more of good 2 than will then be produced per period might profitably be sold, storage costs being considered.

If a monopolistic firm produces joint products which it then processes further (that is, treats the joint products as raw materials rather than goods for final sale), the analysis becomes quite complex and will not be presented here.[6] It is not difficult to see that there is a special incentive to process a quantity such as BC of good 2 which would otherwise bring in no revenue.

The term *by-product* has been frequently applied to less important joint products. The quantities in which such by-products are recovered will reflect the relevant added costs of recovery as well as the strength of elasticity of demand. An interesting example in 1969 of a potentially emerging by-product was sulfuric acid from high-sulfur coal. Between 5 and 10 percent of sulfur as a raw material has in the past come as a by-product from metal mining and natural gas production. As cities such as St. Louis set new standards for sulfur-dioxide emissions in the atmosphere, coal consumers faced requirements of reducing the sulfur either by purchase of more expensive, low-sulfur fuel or the elimination of the sulfur fumes. The additional relevant costs of sulfur recovery have been in effect reduced by legislation since sulfur must be eliminated in any case. It should be noted that although the sulfur market is dominated by two firms mining elemental sulfur, any by-product sulfur produced by coal would be offered under what amount to competitive conditions. The coal-burning firm would be a price taker offering a tiny fraction of the supply and thus facing a horizontal demand curve.

The analysis just presented can readily be extended to cover a situation where the firm has monopoly power in the sale of one joint product but must sell the other good in a perfectly competitive market. The student is urged to draw the chart for such a situation.

---

[6]The interested reader is referred to M. R. Colberg, "Monopoly Prices under Joint Costs: Fixed Proportions," *Journal of Political Economy*, February 1941, p. 109.

FIGURE 16–4 Monopolized Joint Products—Not All Sold

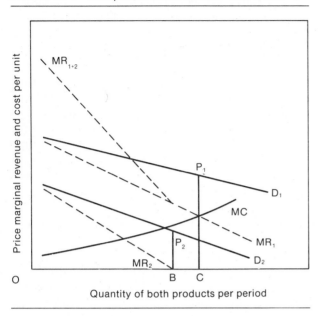

MULTIPLE PRODUCTS TO UTILIZE CAPACITY

Frequently, goods can be turned out more cheaply together than in separate facilities, even though they do not necessarily appear as the simultaneous product of the same process. For example, unless the available volume of one commodity is sufficient for a full trainload, it is obviously more economical to transport a number of goods at once than to have a separate train for each good. This advantage of transporting multiple products derives from the indivisibility of such resources as locomotives, engineers, and cars. If the capacity of any indivisible resource is not being fully utilized (because the train is too short, for example, or cars are not fully loaded), additional products can be hauled at a very low marginal cost. Additional revenue in prospect need not be great to induce the railroad company to carry extra items when excess capacity is present.

Similarly, a manufacturing plant that has excess capacity may have a strong incentive to add another product or products. Excess capacity may be due to a variety of causes. A decline in the demand for the product for which the plant was originally designed is clearly a possible cause. Or a plant may have been built purposely too large for present needs in anticipation of future requirements, and this may make at least the temporary installation of another product advantageous. Excess capacity may exist for a substantial period of time even under highly competitive conditions where inefficient firms tend to be driven out of the field. But excess capacity is more likely to be chronic when collusive pricing or a cartel arrangement among sellers (e.g., motel owners) both restricts total sales and attracts additional investment because of the temporary profitability of the high prices to those already in the field.

INDUSTRY DEVELOPMENT AND INTEGRATION

It has sometimes been observed by economists that firms in relatively new industries produce multiple products simply because the demand for any one of the products is insufficient to make possible its production in a volume sufficient to secure the advantages of scale. In this situation, some of these advantages can be secured by utilizing a large plant and producing several commodities.[7] However, if the demand for the principal commodity expands sufficiently, it may become more economical to cease producing the others and to specialize in this main good. This is because the indivisible factors are seldom equally adapted to all of the goods being produced, so that it pays to specialize output further if sufficient volume can be secured in one or a few goods.

Young industries are often forced to be vertically integrated (to produce at several stages) because the economic system is not geared to produce specialized raw materials and components that they require. As an industry grows, it is often both possible and profitable to turn over the production of these special raw materials and components to other firms. Similarly, as transactions on the New York Stock Exchange have grown in volume, brokers who do not wish to engage in extensive analysis of securities have been able to omit most of this work because of the growth of specialized market advisory services.

The tendency toward vertical distintegration as an industry grows depends, however, on the existence, or potential existence, of thoroughgoing competition at all stages of production. If it is necessary for a firm to pay monopolistic prices for materials or components, it may be better to undertake their manufacture itself, even if great efficiency cannot be secured in such production. Most raw material cartels have experienced trouble with customers who wish to integrate backward in order to avoid paying monopoly prices.[8]

During periods of war or postwar emergency, when the federal government allocates certain "scarce" materials in furtherance of its preferred programs (aircraft, atomic bombs, housing, etc.), a special advantage is inherent in integration in that the output of "captive" facilities producing in earlier stages is unlikely to be subject to allocation. Instead, such production will probably go automatically to the owning firms, just as the early items on a plant's assembly line do. Emergency conditions may have

---

[7] N. Kaldor, "Market Imperfections and Excess Capacity," *Economica*, N.S., vol. II, no. 5 (1935), p. 47.

[8] George J. Stigler, "The Division of Labor Is Limited by the Extent of the Market," *Journal of Political Economy*, June 1951, pp. 151–191. Stigler gives historical examples of cartels which have encountered this difficulty.

their impact mainly on the nonintegrated producers. Thus, vertical integration constitutes something of a hedge against emergency shortage of materials.

INTEGRATION IN FOOD DISTRIBUTION

Grocery chains in the United States are outstanding examples of integrated operations; and in this case, there does not appear to be a tendency toward disintegration as the industry grows. A&P, Kroger, and other food chains operate such facilities as warehouses, bakeries, milk-condensing plants, coffee-roasting plants, salmon and tuna-fish canneries, and plants for processing many special products such as mayonnaise, spices, jellies, and beverages. Reasons that have been cited for the growth of integration in this field are several. Probably the most important pertain to the savings of costs of transfer of ownership of goods from company to company. This saving can easily be exaggerated, however, since much intracompany bookkeeping with respect to such transfers is still required in an integrated operation. Certain advertising and other selling expenses can be eliminated by means of integration, since one stage does not have to "sell" the next. Freight and cartage costs may be lower when a number of products are shipped from the company warehouse to retail outlets. Faster handling due to uniformity of distribution channels under integrated operations may be especially important for fresh fruits and vegetables.

PITFALLS IN INTEGRATION

It has been noted that disintegration of operations has frequently been observed, especially as industries grow in size. In part, this is to permit management to devote its time to the production and sale of the principal end product, which is apt to be very different in nature from the raw materials and transportation that are required in the production-distribution process. That is to say, the multiple products turned out at different stages by a vertically integrated firm are especially likely to be incompatible from a managerial standpoint. Capital that can be obtained by selling facilities used in the earlier stages can often be better invested in the final stage, where the chief interest of the company is likely to lie.

A leading danger in integration is that demand at earlier or later levels provided by the firm's major operations may not be sufficient to justify production of the other commodities on a scale large enough to secure the full advantage of size. Fixed costs are especially high in transportation and in some types of mining. Consequently, a decline in demand for these items due to a decrease in output at the final-product stage will raise unit costs sharply for the firm. Unless quite a steady rate of output of the final good can be foreseen, it is usually better for a firm to purchase inputs from other firms in order to avoid this hazard. It may, of course, be possible to sell some of the output of the earlier stages to other firms; but this is not always feasible, since selling and advertising facilities are not likely to be well developed at these levels because, typically, only an intracompany transfer is required.

INTRACOMPANY TRANSFER PRICING

The dominance of large multiple-product, multiple-process companies in today's industrial world gives importance to the pricing of items transferred from one division to another. Morale of unit managers can be harmed if they feel they are treated unfairly because of being credited with prices that are too low. Salaries, bonuses, and promotions may be, or may be perceived to be, dependent on unit performance. Correct transfer prices are needed for attaining the managerial decentralization that is usually sought. Unfortunately, the best solution varies from one type of firm and product to another, and for some of the problems there are no theoretically correct solutions.

An economist is likely to say that products should be transferred to the next unit at marginal cost, and this is sometimes appropriate. But as shown earlier in this chapter, true joint costs cannot be allocated among two or more products produced in fixed proportions. If both or all of these products are transferred, the marginal joint cost could be the transfer price. But if the later stage within the same company needs only part of the output of the joint products, the situation resembles that of monopolists (Figure 16–4) who sell less than their entire output. The units of product necessarily produced but not needed in the next stage may be sold in the market to other firms if this is not detrimental to the company as a whole.

Sales divisions like to receive transfers at marginal cost because this maximizes their own apparent contribution to company profits since no fixed costs are in the prices they pay. The situation is similar to the dilemma in public utility regulation (Figure 12–6) where marginal cost pricing has social advantages but is impractical because fixed costs may not be covered by utility rates.

Two principal types of organizations within large firms can be termed *cooperative* and *competitive*.[9] Cooperative units must cooperate with one another and therefore bear a resemblance to different stages along a factory assembly line. Unit managers have relatively little autonomy since top management is involved in day-to-day operations, and control is exercised directly through subordinates. In its purest form, the cooperative unit does not have transfer prices. However, some organizations that approximate the cooperative type are in part "profit centers" that sell both within and outside the company.

Profit centers differ from cooperative or service centers in that much

---

[9]These and other arrangements are described by Robert G. Eccles, "Control with Fairness in Transfer Pricing," *Harvard Business Review*, November–December 1983.

autonomy is given to managers. This autonomy permits operational independence to a large degree, freedom to buy and sell in alternative markets both outside and within the firm, ability to separate its costs from those of other divisions, freedom to price its products, and in general to seek profits. "The modern integrated, multiple-product firm functions best if it is made into a sort of miniature of the competitive, free-enterprise-economic system," as stated by Joel Dean, a pioneer in managerial economics.[10]

The basic idea is that for many large, integrated companies it is best to permit a large degree of autonomy in order that there be an incentive to control costs, look for all sales opportunities both within and outside the firm, and earn profits. Top management must, of course, be careful to see that the overall situation of the company is aided rather than damaged by profit centers. For example, one reason for vertical integration is sometimes a desire to get away from monopoly in the earlier stages of production and distribution. A profit center should not seek monopoly profits from intracompany sales.

Resolution of conflicts within a large firm tends to be a difficult managerial problem. In fact, Joel Dean reported that a fist fight determined the intracompany transfer price policy in effect in a major oil company. The issue was the price at which gasoline would be transferred from the company's refinery to its marketing division.[11] This particular question also has considerable social significance since there is often a question whether independent service stations are treated as well as outlets of the oil companies, and legislation has been based on the question.

DEMAND-RELATED GOODS

Often, multiple products are turned out by a firm because they are related on the demand side instead of the cost side. (Or they may be related in both respects.) The motorist who buys gasoline is obviously a likely customer for oil, grease, tires, and soft drinks. The person who buys groceries is an excellent prospect for meat and fish, and the person who buys fire insurance on a home is a likely buyer of burglary or liability insurance. Usually, it pays the firm—once it has established contact with a customer—to be in position to sell the customer other products. The Mexican peddler, for example, is well aware of this possibility. Once he has secured a degree of attention from the tourist, he is usually prepared to present several types of jewelry or other goods rather than only one variety. Generally, he keeps his other wares hidden until he has sealed a sale on the principal item or has been definitely turned down on that item. The more difficult it is to secure contact with a customer, the greater the

---

[10]"Decentralization and Intracompany Pricing," *Harvard Business Review,* July–August 1955.

[11]Joel Dean, ibid., p. 65.

gain from handling a multiplicity of products is likely to be. Thus, traffic and parking congestion cause it to be difficult for the motorist to make several stops on a shopping trip. This factor leads a great many retailers to run something approaching a "general" store, where the customer can engage in satisfactory one-stop shopping. The "shopping center," however, permits stores to specialize to a greater degree by providing common parking with easy access on foot to a variety of shops.

Where parking is a municipal problem and the store is not located in a comprehensive shopping center, there is an especially strong incentive for a supermarket to carry nonfood items. This saves the customer the difficulty of going elsewhere for such items of frequent need as magazines, hair tonic, toothpaste, children's socks, and everyday glassware. It is important, however, that the nonfood items be easy to carry to the car, be difficult to steal, and have a rapid turnover, so that they do not tie up valuable space unduly. The high percentage markups on many nonfood items have been an important factor in the trend toward handling more of this merchandise in the chain grocery stores.

SEASONAL DEMAND

Frequently, multiple products are carried by the firm because they have opposite seasonal demand patterns. Coal and ice are famous examples of this demand situation. In the past, most firms that delivered coal in the winter used the same wagons or trucks for delivering ice in the summer. Commodities that are demand related in this way are at the same time cost related, since the purpose of handling multiple products is to utilize capacity that would otherwise be seasonally idle. Numerous other examples of such seasonal demand relationships can be found. An athletic stadium may be used for baseball in the spring and summer months, and for football in the fall. A clothing manufacturer changes the nature of her output from season to season in anticipation of temperature changes. The appliance dealer who stocks air conditioners in the summer may switch to heaters in the winter. In general, it is usually good business for the firm that has a seasonally fluctuating demand to install some item with an opposite seasonal demand to take up the slack. This may not be desirable, however, if the commodity is storable, since it can then be produced in the off season for sale later. The portland cement industry typically builds up inventories during the winter, to be drawn down during the spring and summer when construction is heavy. This policy is traceable to the ready storability of cement and to the desirability of limiting industry capacity, for the cement-manufacturing process uses a very high ratio of capital equipment to labor. Also, cement-producing equipment is highly specialized to that use instead of being adaptable also to other kinds of production. The industry finds the annual shutdown valuable for cleaning up the plants and making repairs.

A firm producing articles subject to sharp seasonal swings in demand sometimes finds it desirable to diversify by adding items that are stable in demand rather than opposite in seasonal demand pattern. This prevents the percentage decline in total business from being so sharp at any season. That is, a 30 percent seasonal decline in demand for one item can be converted into approximately, a 15 percent decline for the company as a whole by adding an item of equal sales importance but with no seasonal demand pattern. An example of this sort of diversification was the addition in 1949 and 1952 of utility company equipment such as transformers and circuit breakers by McGraw Electric Company. This helped offset the seasonal fluctuations in the Toastmaster and other home appliance lines. While such diversification may help only moderately in utilizing seasonally idle plant capacity, because of the specialization of machinery to certain products, it may provide fuller utilization of labor, management, sales facilities, and other more adaptable factors. This is especially true if the items of relatively stable demand are readily storable, since labor, for example, that is seasonally idle in one line can temporarily be added to the regular working force in the more stable lines. This may make it possible to carry a smaller regular labor force in the stable lines. Management as well as labor tends to gain if employment can be regularized in seasonal industries because labor turnover is reduced; consequently, the problem of training new workers is made less difficult.

BRAND-NAME CARRYOVER

An important force making for multiplicity of products in such fields as the manufacture of home appliances is sometimes referred to as "brand-name carryover." That is, a customer who is satisfied with a General Electric refrigerator, for example, is quite likely to buy such items as a washing machine, range, and television receiver from the same company. Opportunity is especially great in supplying "package kitchens" of particularly compatible appliances, all turned out by the same firm. In economic terminology the demands for such items are "complementary"; an increase in the rate of sale (and home inventories) of one appliance bearing a given brand name tends to increase the demands for other appliances with the same brand name.

Numerous examples of a rapid trend toward "full-line production" can be cited. Westinghouse introduced 27 new kinds of appliances between 1945 and 1955. General Electric (Hotpoint appliances), Philco, General Motors' Frigidaire division, Borg-Warner's Norge division, and American Motors' Kelvinator division have all steadily expanded their lines in past years. The full-line trend has brought on a wave of mergers of appliance makers. For example, a laundry equipment maker, a refrigerator producer, and the stove and air-conditioning division of the Radio Corporation of America merged under the name Whirlpool-Seeger (later changed to RCA-Whirlpool) and more recently the Whirlpool Corporation. Corporate affiliations changed with White-Industries acquiring the Westinghouse and Frigidaire lines and Kelvinator becoming the Kelvinator Appliance Company.

INTERNAL BRAND COMPETITION

Another force that frequently promotes multiple products within the firm is, in a sense, just the opposite of brand-name carryover. It consists in submerging the name of the company and using different brand names for two or more varieties of a product that are sold to the same group of customers. For example, two different qualities of canned corn may be turned out by a given firm under different labels. One brand may be so much poorer than the other that it is better not to emphasize that it is produced by the same company. To do so would be to run the same risk of unfavorable association as would a full-line producer of appliances who sold a decidedly inferior washing machine. When the quality of the product is not wholly under the control of the firm, as in the case of fruits and vegetables, there is likely to be especially good reason to avoid publicizing the company name. While the firm that cans tomatoes, for example, can choose to process only the best portion of its purchases, this may necessitate discarding large quantities that can instead be marketed under another brand name without greatly reducing sales of the top-quality product.

The phenomenon of internal brand competition is especially interesting when a given firm sells two or more varieties of a single product under different brand names to the same set of customers and when, further, the quality of the varieties is very much the same. The following appear to be among the leading reasons for this practice on the part of some of the larger firms:

1. Mergers or amalgamations of firms producing a given product may have occurred. Previous brand names are likely to be retained by the new company, at least in part, because of the customer following that might otherwise be lost.

2. Often, a sizable segment of the consuming public prefers one variety of a product, even though a larger segment prefers another variety. To concentrate on the latter alone would deprive the firm of large sales that could be secured by carrying both varieties. A case in point is the production of both standard and filter cigarettes by a given cigarette company.

3. The struggle between companies for display space in the supermarkets is a keen one. A given soap company, for example, is likely to be able to capture a larger portion of such space by producing more than one variety of soap for use in washing clothes or dishes. The various brands produced by a firm may be promoted as vigorously as if they were turned out by competing companies. It is generally felt that more sales are taken away from competitors than from other products of the company by such internal brand competition. Also, the various divisions of a firm are forced by both internal and external competition to be efficient in their operation. Procter & Gamble is an outstanding example of a firm that engages in vigorous internal brand competition.

4. By installing products very similar to those already being produced, a firm may be able to secure better distribution of its product than through exclusive dealerships. Regular dealers may receive only one variety of the product, while another variety is sold through discount houses or other channels. This practice is, of course, unpopular with the "exclusive" dealers. A manufacturer may in this way take advantage of high prices on advertised items and lower prices on much the same items in order to promote volume.

5. Under some circumstances, a firm's advertising may be more effective when it is distributed over two or more quite similar products than when it is concentrated on one brand. Two or more types of advertising appeal can be used simultaneously, and this may have greater total effect than an equal expenditure devoted to one product. Further, one product of the company might effectively be advertised on the package in which a rather similar product is sold. Armour-produced soap flakes, for example, have been advertised on the can in which an Armour liquid detergent was sold.

COMMODITIES RELATED IN ADVERTISING AND DISTRIBUTION

Frequently, firms find it advantageous to handle multiple products at least in part because they are related in advertising, even if the situation is not one of internal brand competition. The various items advertised individually by the roadside gift shop have a cumulative appeal that may cause the driver to pause in her headlong dash. A full-page advertisement may be optimal in attracting the attention of the newspaper reader; but once her attention has been gained, she is likely to be willing to read about a number of items carried by a firm rather than just one. (In fact, the housewife may be anxious to check many items at once in order to see whether a particular store is worth visiting on a particular weekend.) Also, a multiple-product firm is in a position to use coupons attached to one product to help sell another product. The coupons provide both a means of advertising and a direct financial incentive to the customer to buy the indicated commodity.

Multiple products are frequently carried by a firm largely because they are related in distribution. Salespersons who regularly call on drugstores, for example, can often quite easily supply these stores with other products of the same firm for which delivery facilities are suitable. The Gillette Company diversified its operations by entering the ballpoint pen field, buying the companies that made and distributed Paper Mate pens. The production and distribution facilities of Gillette were both considered by its management to be well suited to ballpoint pens. Similarly, Standard Brands, Inc., is able to use a common system of distribution for a variety of products bought by bakeries and grocers, including yeast, baking powder, desserts, coffee, and tea.

In moving its acquisition, the Miller Brewing Company, from second place in 1970 to a closing second place to Anheuser-Busch by the late 1970s, Philip Morris relied on general advertising and merchandising skills acquired in cigarettes. Its program included not only promotional revisions but the additional products, Löwenbräu, a premium brand, and Lite Beer, whose appeal of one-third less calories had analogies with the low-tar cigarettes.

COMMODITIES RELATED IN RESEARCH

A firm that has a strong research department is obviously apt to be frequently adding new products as these are developed. To the extent that new items can be patented, the legal system is likely to make possible substantial monopoly gains for a period of time. Even if other firms can readily add the same product or very similar items, the firm that first enters the field may reap substantial innovation profits before others are tooled up and otherwise adapted to turn out the good. Once qualified chemists, engineers, and others are hired and trained to work as a research department, a firm is likely to be making inadequate use of such a department unless it is ready to produce and distribute any promising new products that are developed. This is similar to the principle noted earlier that available unused capacity of any kind—in plant, management, or skilled labor—may lead to opportunities for product diversification on the part of the alert firm. Case 16–2 on General Electric's proposed introduction of a $10 energy-saving light bulb deals with the fruits of continuing research in a main area of company interest.

It has become very common in the annual reports of industries with changing product lines, such as chemical and processed foods, to find statements that a large percentage of sales are in products introduced in the last 10 years. For example: "In 1962, following a 10-year period in which 438 products were introduced by Monsanto's five chemical divisions, 293 of these products contributed 35 percent of those divisions' total sales and 37 percent of their gross profit. During the year, 78 new Monsanto products survived screening tests and were sold commercially."

The implication, however, of these product additions is not that the product lines inevitably become larger; product abandonments are also common under the pressure of new research and technology. Du Pont, which has shown great concern over the dwindling profit margins that can accompany a mature product line, announced in late 1962 the abandonment of silicon production because of overcapacity in the business and final termination of the rayon business which for over 40 years had constituted an important company activity.

THE FREE-FORM PRODUCT LINE

As shown earlier in the chapter, many firms have built up quite diversified product lines without merger, but usually at some point in the development of most new products there was a discernible demand, cost, or research connection of the new with the old.

In the 1950s and the 1960s, a numerous group of firms grew rapidly through mergers with almost totally unrelated firms. These "International Everythings" include such giants as Litton Industries which in 1969 produced inertial guidance systems, ships, office machines, and furniture among many other products; Gulf & Western which in 1960 sold $8.4 million of auto bumpers and raised its sales to $1.3 billion in 1968, largely through over 80 acquisitions including New Jersey Zinc Company, Paramount Pictures, South Puerto Rico Sugar, and Consolidated cigar; and Ling-Temco-Vought with 1958 sales of $6.9 billion and 1968 revenues of $2.8 billion which had as subsidiaries Wilson & Company (third in meat-packing), Jones & Laughlin Steel Corporation (sixth in basic steel), Braniff Airways Inc., LTV Aerospace Corporation, and five others (see Case 16–1).

Whatever economies of aggregation there may be for these conglomerates are to be found in two areas: management and finance. The fundamental proposition concerning management behind the free-form firms is "that talented general managers, applying modern management techniques, can effectively oversee business in which they have no specific experience.[12] Economists would weigh this as a significant argument only if such talents are scarce and would be underutilized if operating on a less broad canvas. Typically, these conglomerates have set up decentralized organizations. As an extreme example, Ling-Temco-Vought had a few more than 100 employees in its Dallas headquarters in 1969. The centralized management function largely concerns setting standards for operating managements, making managerial replacements where the performance has fallen short, and allocating capital among the subsidiaries and divisions. The experience at this time is too mixed to make generalizations as to whether or not such central managements are more successful in selecting, guiding, and developing operation managements than ordinary boards of directors would be.

The potential financial and capital advantages of the conglomerates can be divided into two categories. The first category consists of advantages of size which may make it possible to get stock exchange listing to sell securities to the public and to have access nationally to financial institutions such as banks, insurance companies, mutual and pension funds, and so forth. The larger free-form firms may have reached scales of

---

[12]William S. Rukeyser, "Litton Down to Earth," *Fortune*, April 1968, p. 186. Mr. Rukeyser was paraphrasing Litton's management.

operation that would make further economies of this type minor factors, but many mini-conglomerates could find greater size a significant financial advantage.

The second category of advantages concerns those related to ease of internal transfers of capital rather than external transfers. Industries in a dynamic economy grow at different rates as new technological possibilities are opened. In addition, some industries may be particularly susceptible to cyclical influences that reduce cash inflow at the very time long-run investments should be made. The management of a firm producing in several industries can channel funds generated by one product group into what are judged superior profit opportunities in quite different lines. Textron is an example of a large conglomerate that has completed the move out of the industry (textiles, particularly woolens) that was its original base into more rapidly growing product lines, including helicopters.

The cigarette firms, as discussed in Case 15–2, have been a salient example of channeling very substantial profits from an industry that with a high degree of certainty faces secular decline into industries with greater prospects of growth.

A significant reason for the relative attractiveness of internal transfers of acquired capital against reliance on external capital is to be found in the tax structure.[13] A key feature of the corporate income tax is that it applies equally to dividend payments and to reinvested earnings and at the same time dividend payments are subjected to progressive personal income taxes. Under the reasonable assumption the stockholders would wish to reinvest much of their gains, corporate managements are in a position to reinvest them undiminished by personal income taxes. The stockholder whose desire to reinvest is limited has the option to sell his securities at lower capital gains rates on the stock's appreciation.

Other provisions of the tax structure also encourage the corporate manager in this search for investment opportunities. Depreciation allowances particularly in such accelerated tax-approved forms as the sum-of-the-years'-digits and doubling-declining balance can result in substantial cash flows in advance of replacement needs. The provisions for carrying forward losses against future taxable income make it advantageous for firms with substantial losses to seek more profitable lines where the losses can be used to reduce taxable profits. Between 1956 and 1964, Textron made use of its substantial losses from its American Woolen subsidiary, and in the 1960s Studebaker Corporation found its past automobile losses helpful in its diversification program.

These tax considerations could encourage product additions either

---

[13]It is not maintained here that the tax structure caused corporations to rely heavily on reinvesting internal funds. The desire of entrepreneurs and managers to reinvest may well have influenced the kind of tax structure that the United States has adopted. This point is elaborated on in D. R. Forbush, "Product Additions: Business Rational and Economic Classification" (Ph.D. dissertation, Harvard University, 1953), pp. 133–51.

through "natural" growth or through mergers as means of selecting more profitable opportunities for the use of internally generated funds. But most of the "natural" product additions have been of the product extension type where the added product has been related to production, distribution, or research skills of the company. Even such a dramatic departure from past lines of business as the entry of Sears, Roebuck and Company into automobile and home insurance and then into life insurance, represented an extension of Sears' retail business that emphasized many products sold to automobile users and homeowners. The entry was made easier by available store facilities, an existing brand name (Allstate), and a strong consumer franchise. Before 1965, most conglomerate mergers were of this product extension type. From 1965 to 1968, there were 129 conglomerate acquisitions involving $9.5 billion of assets in which there was apparently no relationship between the products of the firms involved in any significant production or marketing sense.[14] For a free-form corporation, the merger may be helpful in an extension of product lines, and it becomes a virtual prerequisite for rapid entry into totally unrelated fields. The general managerial and entrepreneurial aptitudes on which the conglomerate firm is based usually need substantial infusions of more specialized talents and facilities to overcome significant barriers to entry of an unrelated industry.

Other factors that have contributed to the great move of conglomerate mergers were high levels of employment and profit and rising stock prices that accompanied them (negotiations leading to mergers seem to be eased by optimistic forecasts and bullish security markets help financing problems); the expectations of continued creeping or walking inflation (these place a particular premium on prospective profit growth by corporations that could more than offset the inflation in prices); the tax deductibility of bond interest (which encouraged firms to issue debentures in their acquisitions and thus reduce corporate income taxes); flexible accounting rules (that permitted firms considerable discretion in selecting a method of acquisition accounting that would emphasize rising earning trends); and the absence of restraining policies by government as discussed in Chapter 18. The full corporate tax deductibility of bond interest, the flexibility of accounting methods, and the lenient antitrust policy were all up for modification as the decade of the 1960s closed. Questions were also being raised by the securities market and by business analysts as to whether the merits of conglomeration had not been overrated. The merger fever of the 1960s was certainly contributed to by the early success of such free-form firms as Textron and Litton Industries and to its emulation by relatively young men, aggressively seeking power and wealth, who were ready to use somewhat novel financial techniques to build large

---

[14]Bureau of Economics, Federal Trade Commission, "Current Trends in Merger Activity" (Washington, D.C., 1969).

firms rapidly. Even if their entrepreneurial enthusiasm continues, the co-operation of business executives, financial houses, and the investing public which eased the path toward company-collecting seemed likely to be offered much more skeptically. Case 16–1 on Ling-Temco-Vought probes some of these issues more fully and emphasizes a turn in antitrust policy against conglomerate mergers by large companies.

TAKEOVERS AND MERGERS IN THE MID-1980s

With the onset of the great depression in 1929, merger activity among American firms declined sharply and remained at a low level until the end of World War II. It then revived, with marked acceleration in 1967 and 1968. In the 1980s, acquisitions and mergers have been an outstanding feature of the U.S. industrial economy, dramatized by takeovers even of very large corporations. Takeover specialists and stock arbitragers, including T. Boone Pickens, Carl Icahn, Irwin Jacobs, and Ivan Boesky, have done much to change financial—and sometimes physical—structures, especially in the oil industry.

Among the large mergers or acquisitions in 1983 (not necessarily involving the men just named) were:[15]

Santa Fe Industries and Southern Pacific Co.

Allied Corp. and Bendix Corp.

Xerox Corp. and Crum and Foster.

Diamond Shamrock Corp. and Natomas Co.

Phillips Petroleum Co. and General American Oil Co. of Texas.

CSX Corp. and Texas Gas Resources Corp.

Esmark, Inc. and Norton Simon, Inc.

Mesa Petroleum (Pickens) and Gulf Oil Corp. (13.2%).[16]

Kroger Co. and Dillon Cos.

International Business Machines Corp. and Intel. Corp. (16.3%).

Godfather's Pizza, Inc., and Chart House, Inc.

American Can Co. and Penn Corp. Financial, Inc.

Litton Industries and Itek Corp.

Corporate mergers and acquisitions may be either "friendly" or "hostile," the latter sometimes arousing extremely strong emotions among corporate officials who can lose very good jobs. An entire town, Bartlesville, Oklahoma, felt threatened when Mr. Pickens tried to acquire Phillips Petroleum in 1984.

---

[15]"100 Largest Transactions by Purchase Price, 1983," *Mergers and Acquisitions*, Almanac & Index, 1984.

[16]Gulf was later acquired by Chevron.

TYPICAL TAKEOVER SCENARIO

While details will differ from case to case, a typical set of events in an unfriendly merger might be as follows:

1. The "raider" engages in a great deal of research to find a corporation whose common stock appears to be undervalued substantially in the market. Oil and gas reserves, cash on hand, and cash flow may be special concerns.
2. The raider makes a tender offer for common stock at a price well in excess of the market price.
3. The offer is publicized in *The Wall Street Journal* and/or elsewhere.
4. The target corporation advises stockholders not to accept the "inadequate" offer for their shares.
5. The target company rejects the offer if it has the necessary power.
6. The target company issues all sorts of threats such as lawsuits, possible disposal of important properties, and issue of preferred stock as a dividend, carrying a right to demand cash if control is changed. The latter is called a "poison pill" defense. Selling off important properties is called a "scorched earth" defense.
7. The target company uses a "Pac-Man" defense in which it threatens or tries to swallow the pursuer.
8. The target company makes bylaw changes, for example, to require a larger stockholder vote on propositions.
9. The target company seeks a "white knight" who will instead provide a friendly merger.
10. The raider raises its bid price.
11. The target company agrees that the new bid is adequate and that the takeover may not be so bad after all (considering the large capital gains—taxed at a lower rate).
12. The acquired company hastens to provide "golden parachutes" for its executives, especially in the form of larger pension benefits.

Corporate takeover experts defend their efforts as being socially desirable because the targeted companies are not making sufficiently good use of their assets, such as oil reserves. They claim that the allocation of resources and management effort within the economy is improved by a merger. Very large capital gains are often made by stockholders, including officers of an acquired company and the raider firm. Arbitragers are extremely alert to opportunities to make quick capital gains, although losses are also possible, especially if a takeover attempt fails. Large fees are collected by attorneys and investment bankers. New York City mayor Edward Koch gave Mr. Pickens a crystal apple in honor of the $50 million that the Gulf fight had brought the city in legal fees and other payments.[17]

---

[17]"High Times for T. Boone Pickens," *Time*, March 4, 1985, p. 61.

Executives in diverse fields are worried about possible takeovers. Recently, ABC was sold to Capital Cities. At the time of this writing there is much interest in a possible unfriendly takeover of CBS. The public is likely to be especially aware of mergers in the field of television since the nature of news broadcasts can be sharply altered.

Case 16–3 relates to a 1985 hostile takeover of American Natural Resources Company.

CASE 16–1
The Redeployment of LTV

In the mid-1980s, the merger movement was substantially greater than that of the late 1960s. A *Business Week* article "Do Mergers Really Work?" cites 2,543 deals totaling $122 billion in 1984.[18] "Not very often" was the article's answer. When they did work, they involved companies in closely related deals, they were usually financed by stock deals or cash in hand, the price did not include lofty premiums, and the managements of the acquired companies usually stayed on to manage. *Business Week* listed seven deadly sins in acquisitions: paying too much, assuming a boom market won't crash, leaping before looking, straying too far afield, swallowing something too big, managing disparate corporate cultures, and counting on key managers staying. The experience of LTV is suggestive of the opportunities and pitfalls of growth by merger. It involves the paradox of a pure conglomerate settling down into one industry and thus embraces another feature of the 1980s, the striking increase in divestitures.

The Expansion of LTV and the concept of Redeployment

James J. Ling started the Ling Electric Company in 1947 with a $2,000 investment. It expanded rapidly in the conventional business of electrical contracting and wiring from a $70,000 to a $1 million gross by 1954. Its first experiment with what was later to be termed "Project Redeployment" came in the two years after Ling Electric, Inc., went public in 1955. A small acquired subsidiary making electronic equipment was renamed Ling Electronics. The parent company's name was changed to Ling Industries, and it traded its electrical contracting assets for the stock of a newly formed subsidiary using the old name of Ling Electric. The contracting business was later disposed of, and Ling Electronics became the vehicle for raising capital in an exciting growth industry.

---

[18]*Business Week*, June 3, 1985, pp. 88–100.

In 1959, Ling Electronics acquired Altec Companies, Inc., a major manufacturer of sound systems, through a stock exchange. This plus other acquisitions brought sales to $48 million and a change in name to Ling-Altec Electronics. The next two acquisitions, Temco and Chance Vought, both primarily in the aircraft industry and both with double Ling's previous sales, were difficult to digest. The newly named Ling-Temco-Vought Inc. ranked 158th among industrial firms in 1962 sales but slipped in *Fortune's* list to 204th in 1965. It was during this period of consolidation which included selling off such assets as Chance Vought's mobile home business that "Project Redeployment" was fully worked out.

LTV's assets were turned over to three newly created corporations in return for their stock. The parent company now offered one-half share of stock of each of the new corporations plus $9 for a share of LTV stock. The direct result was that 125,000 shares of each of the new corporations' stock were in the hands of the public with LTV retaining over a million shares in each of the three new companies. LTV reduced its own publicly held stock by about 10 percent. The indirect and gratifying result was a great increase of what Ling called the working assets of LTV since the now established market value of the new stocks was much greater than the book value of the assets that Ling-Temco-Vought had turned over to the subsidiaries. In mid-1966 the market values of LTV's share of subsidiary stock exceeded the book value of the assets turned over to subsidiaries, including the new acquisition of Okonite, as follows (the figures are given in millions):

	Book Value	Market Value
LTV Aerospace.	18.4	117.1
LTV Electrosystems, Inc..	8.6	47.1
LTV Ling Altec, Inc..	4.0	17.3
Okonite Company.	17.7	24.0
Total.	48.7	205.5

LTV was now in a position with sufficient market collateral to acquire a firm with three times its sales—Wilson & Company, the country's third largest meat-packer. It completed this deal in early 1967 using $81,504,653 of borrowed funds to gain a majority interest and $116 million of its own preferred stock to retire the rest. Wilson's assets were promptly redeployed into three companies: Wilson & Company, a meat-packer; Wilson Sporting Goods Company, the leader in a field with great stock market appeal; and Wilson Pharmaceutical & Chemical Company. These companies sold stock sufficient to pay over half of the debt incurred in buying them, and LTV's majority interest in them had a market value of approximately $250 million in the fall of 1967.

The success of these redeployments tempted LTV into the unfortunate

Greatamerica and Jones & Laughlin acquisitions. The subsequent financial problems obscured some virtues in the deployment idea. First, the redeployment made it possible to spin off acquisitions after LTV had completed financial and management reorganization of an acquired firm. If LTV had really made a contribution, this course could have been profitable and would have avoided the accumulation of parent company debt. Second, stockholders were given the kind of information about operations in particular fields in which the subsidiary companies operated—a great improvement over the lack of sales and operating information on particular groups of products that was given by many conglomerates. The apparent mistake of LTV was to use the financial collateral obtained by Project Redeployment for two overpriced acquisitions that offered little opportunity for effective reorganization. The company seemed to be dominated by the motive of growth for its own sake. Having taken on more than it could handle expeditiously, it had the misfortune of a bearish stock market that accompanied the 1969–70 recession and tight monetary policies designed to control continuing inflation. Almost insurmountable financial problems followed.

LTV did survive the crisis years of 1969 and 1970, but this was cold comfort for investors who bought anywhere near the 1967 peak of $169.50 per common share. The stock slid to $7.50 at the time of Ling's demotion in May 1970, and sold at just over $9 in August 1974. At that time the LTV management did feel confident enough of the availability of financial resources to recommend the acquisition of the 19 percent minority interest in Jones & Laughlin.

Significant elements for the student of business economics of the LTV experience are the following:

1. The conglomerate characteristics of LTV as representative of those of many firms with free-form product lines. Less common was the concept of "redeployment" of capital assets into specialized subsidiary firms which could serve as a basis not only for conglomeration but also as the basis for decentralization by corporate spinoffs.
2. Insights into particular financial transactions that sought particular corporate objectives by altering risk and time components in the corporate capital structure.
3. The significance of Section 7 of the Clayton Act as a limitation on product additions through mergers.

The Conglomerate Characteristics of LTV

A number of characteristics have been associated with the free-form product line concept and its attainment through the conglomerate acquisitions. Among them are the following:

1. A wide range of products with a considerable proportion of them in rapidly growing industries.

2. A strong emphasis on growth in earnings per share as the primary goal of the firm.
3. A heavy reliance on debt financing.
4. A complex financial structure stressing such instruments as convertible debentures, several classes of stock, warrants, and stock options. This itself makes results difficult to interpret and is sometimes accompanied by a flexibility of accounting treatment that may border on the deceptive.
5. Decentralization of the organization which leaves operating decisions to subsidiaries or divisions and leaves central management primarily with decisions about capital and top-management personnel.
6. One or a small group of aggressive entrepreneurs in whose shadow the aggregation has been built.

How did LTV measure up against these characteristics?

Product range. LTV's 1968 sales, including Braniff International, an unconsolidated subsidiary, broke down as follows:

Company	Major Product Area	Percent of Sales
Wilson & Co.	Meat and Food	29
Jones & Laughlin	Steel and ferrous metal products	29
LTV Aerospace	Aircraft, missiles, and space	15
Braniff	Air transportation	8
LTV Electrosystems	Government electronics	6
Okonite	Wire, cable, and floor covering	5
LTV Ling Altec	Consumer and commercial electronics	4
Wilson Sporting Goods	Recreation and athletics	3
Wilson Pharmaceuticals and Chemicals	Pharmaceuticals and chemicals	1

The range is certainly wide. The major discrepancy with the image of the conglomerate is the high proportion of sales in the relatively slow-growing meat and steel industries. The 58 percent in the figures above understates this since only seven months of Jones & Laughlin sales are included; those following the acquisition of 63 percent of the common stock in June 1968. Presumably the LTV management felt this emphasis in slowly growing industries was consistent with the company's "Project Redeployment" and their expressed hope that by the Jones & Laughlin acquisition the cash flow from steel operations could be used to finance growth elsewhere.

Growth in earnings per share. LTV's performance had been extraordinary through 1968 in this characteristic. *Fortune* rated them third out of the 500 largest industrials with an average annual growth in earnings per share from 1958 to 1968 of over 51 percent (from 14 cents to $8.90).[19] These figures have several upward biases, not uncharacteristic of conglomerates. Extraordinary gains amounting to over 25 percent of net income were realized in 1968. *Fortune* used a figure for number of shares that did not recognize fully the potential dilution in terms of common stock and from the exercise of warrants and the conversion of securities (see later). A third bias is one that can arise from merging with a company whose price-earnings ratio is lower than that of the acquiring company. About $2.25 per share of LTV's earnings growth has been estimated to come out of such "free earnings" even though in its period of greatest absolute growth its price-earnings ratio ranged from only 13 to 17.5.[20]

Leverage. The transactions of 1968 through which LTV tripled the asset and liability totals of its consolidated balance sheet were accompanied by a large increase in the debt-equity ratio of the company as shown in Exhibit 16–1A.

The substantial swing away from current toward physical assets on the asset side and the great increase in the debt-equity ratio of the liability side of the balance sheet is explained by the payment in excess of $400 million cash for Jones & Laughlin stock that gave LTV a heavy interest in its physical plant, and by the issuance of $474,316,000 in 5 percent subordinated convertible debentures for the stock of Greatamerica Corpora-

---

[19]*Fortune,* May 15, 1969, p. 169.

[20]Arthur M. Lewis, "Ten Conglomerates and How They Grew," *Fortune,* May 15, 1969, pp. 151 ff.

A widely quoted example of such "free earnings" is one that appeared in *The Wall Street Journal* in July 1969. Before "International Everything" acquired "One Product" the situation was this:

	International Everything	One Product
Number of shares	1,000,000	1,000,000
Price per share	$30	$10
Net income	$1,000,000	$1,000,000
Earnings per share.	$1	$1
Price-earnings ratio (2 ÷ 4)	30	10

After International Everything gave one-half share (worth $15) for each share of One Product:

	International Everything
Number of shares	1,500,000
Price	$40
Net income	$2,000,000
Earnings per share.	$1.33
Price-earnings ratio (2 ÷ 4)	30

This growth of $0.33 in earnings per share is what is referred to as free earnings. No increase in total earnings has occurred. The $40 price assumes that the market will value the stock at the same price-earnings ratio.

EXHIBIT 16–1A Summary of Balance Sheets for LTV Consolidated for 1967 and 1968
Unconsolidated for 1968 ($ millions)

	1967	Percent	1968	Percent
Current assets	$636	72	$1,171	44
Investments and other assets	61	7	489	18
Plant and equipment (less depreciation)	184	21	988	38
Total assets.	$881	100	$2,648	100
Current liabilities (including deferrals).	$379	43	$ 880	33
Long-term debt	205	23	1,237	47
Minority interest in subsidiaries	51	6	355	13
Shareholders equity	245	28	175	7
Total liabilities	$880	100	$2,647	100

Unconsolidated—1968

Current assets	99	8%	Current liabilities.	249	22%
Investments, etc	1,048	90	Long-term debt	748	63
Property, plant, and equipment.	25	2	Shareholders equity . . .	175	15
	1,172	100%		1,172	100%

SOURCE: *LTV Annual Report, 1968.*

tion whose main asset was its stock in Braniff.[21] After these acquisitions, LTV embarked on a further transaction that was quite revealing as to the emphasis it placed on growth in earnings per share and its willingness to increase further what many firms would consider an excessive debt-equity ratio. LTV acquired almost 2 million shares or 35 percent of its own common stock (thus revising the denominator for calculating earnings per share) by offering its stockholders stock in subsidiaries with good price-earnings ratios that were based on good future prospects but with small current earnings. As the company put it, "Equity dilution is a consistent special concern of LTV's management."[22]

Interestingly enough, *Fortune* reported that LTV had the seventh highest sales per dollar of stockholders' capital, $15.79,[23] a figure exceeded only by firms almost totally in meat packing where sales-capital ratios are expected to be high.

Financial structure. LTV had made use of both convertible debentures and convertible preferred stock, but in 1968 it made substantial reductions of amounts of these outstanding and emphasized the use of warrants, that is, rights to purchase shares of a common stock at a specified price before a given date. Both convertible securities and combinations of debentures and stock warrants represent methods of offering

---

[21]LTV sold other Greatamerica holdings in insurance, banking, and its National Car Rental subsidiary.

[22]*LTV Annual Report, 1968*, p. 4.

[23]*Fortune*, May 15, 1969, p. 187.

security holders a dual-purpose package, a reasonably certain fixed income immediately and the prospect of exercising the conversion feature or the warrant when real or inflationary growth has increased per share earnings.

At the end of 1968, when LTV had only 2,072,000 common shares outstanding, it had reserved over 7 million shares; over 1.25 million shares for the possible conversion of preferred stock or guaranteed debentures and almost 6 million shares for the exercise of warrants. In its 1968 annual report, LTV explained how these warrants could be useful in reducing its large debt-equity ratio:

> There are presently outstanding common stock purchase warrants with an aggregate exercise price of $604,000,000. We expect that most of these warrants will be exercised by cash payment or by surrender of those of our debentures which are usable at face value in the exercise of warrants. Assuming exercise of all warrants. . . . $604 million of our long-term debt could be eliminated.[24]

The extent to which LTV considered its function to be the financial one of "redeploying capital" for long-run growth is indicated by its issuance in 1968 of a Special Class AA stock in exchange for preferred and common shares. No cash dividends were to be paid (an advantage for tax-conscious investors), but automatic growth relative to common shares was insured by the following provisions:

> These shares are convertible through December 30, 1969 into .85 of a share of common stock, which ratio increases incrementally on December 31 each year through 1980 to a maximum of 1.50 shares of common stock for each share of Special Stock. The shares of Special Stock, Class AA, are entitled to cumulative stock dividends of 3% in each year through 1992. Such dividend shares will also be convertible into common stock on the basis described above.[25]

Decentralization of operations. What distinguished LTV's decentralization from that of most other conglomerates was that it chose in 1965 to place its operations under subsidiary companies each with sufficient minority ownership to obtain separate listing on the stock exchanges. At the end of 1968, the LTV equity ranged from 63 percent and 66 percent in the newly acquired companies, Braniff Airways and Jones & Laughlin, to 86 percent in the Okonite company. In the three companies created to run LTV's varied operations in aerospace and electronics with most sales aimed at governmental military and space agencies (LTV Aerospace, LTV Electrosystems, and LTV Ling Altec), the parents' equity stood at from 69 percent to 74 percent. The successors to Wilson & Company (the third largest meatpacker), whose acquisition in 1965 approximately doubled LTV's sales, included Wilson & Company (81 percent owned), Wilson

---

[24]*LTV Annual Report, 1968,* p. 3. The consequences of this exercise would also be to reduce the share of existing stockholders in profits.

[25]*LTV Annual Report, 1968,* p. 43.

Sporting Goods Company (75 percent owned), and Wilson Pharmaceutical & Chemical Corporation (77 percent owned).

LTV stressed the managerial advantages of this organization in these terms: Instead of being "highly competent general managers" executives now "are highly motivated presidents of very visible companies with public ownership and public accountability . . . Each had an equity stake in the company . . . for whose fortunes he was responsible . . . each had stock options tied into operating performance." . . . In every subsequent acquisition, "the operating managements did not oppose the acquisition and chose to remain with the company."[26]

The financial advantages include the ready marketability of listed securities that would allow LTV to sell stock in subsidiaries as money for expansion was needed (or to increase its equity ownership if this seemed profitable). The public quotations for subsidiaries' stock could show market valuations that would help the parent company in borrowing.

The aggressive entrepreneur. The development of many of the conglomerates has been associated with one man: Textron with Royal Little; Gulf & Western Industries with Charles Bludhorn; Northwest Industries with Ben Heineman; and Ling-Temco-Vought with James Ling, former bookkeeper, draftsman, and master electrician. The combination of drive for wealth and power, sales ability, financial intuition, and leadership may be uncommon but not rare. The circumstances of prosperity with inflation, the tax structure, the development of takeover techniques and suitable financial instruments and markets, and techniques of centralized and decentralized management abetted by computer and communications technology provide the occasion for the man.

The Section 7 Charges

In the late 1960s, the government was interested in testing the amended antimerger Section 7 of the Clayton Act as a legal weapon to slow up the trend toward macroconcentration. Subsequently, as discussed in Chapter 18, this attempt has been abandoned since the language of the law calls for showing that "competition may be substantially lessened" in "a line of commerce." It is difficult to find such "a line" with firms as unrelated in product lines as the then Ling-Temco-Vought and Jones & Laughlin Steel.

The government charges of 1969 were settled in 1970 by a consent decree that allowed LTV (probably unwisely) to maintain its interest in Jones & Laughlin if it disposed of Okonite (a "potential competitor" in wire and cable) and Braniff which operated in the regulated air transport industry. "The only principle that seemed to issue from the consent decree (and a similar one permitting ITT to keep Hartford Fire Insurance)

---

[26]*LTV Annual Report, 1968,* pp. 8–9.

was that if you are going to take over some venerable American Corporation, the Justice Department is going to make you suffer in some way to
be agreed upon in court.[27]

The government made clear its essential concern in paragraphs 16–18
of its complaint.[28] It was with the increase in concentration abetted by
mergers as measured by the ownership of productive assets. Paragraph 16
stated, "The proportion of total assets of the nation's manufacturing corporations held by the 200 largest firms increased from 48.1 percent in
1948 to 54.2 percent in 1960 and 58.7 percent in 1967." Paragraph 18
pointed out that "912 manufacturing and mining concerns (each with over
$10 million assets), with combined assets of $31 billion, were absorbed
from 1948 to 1966." Paragraph 19 stressed the rapid increase in such
activity in that $24.9 billion of these assets were absorbed from 1966 to
1968, with 192 firms and $12.6 billion assets absorbed in 1968. The 200
largest firms accounted for 70 percent of the assets absorbed. Twelve firms
each with over $250 million in assets were absorbed in 1968. (Jones &
Laughlin Steel with $1,092,800,000 in assets was the largest; in dollar
terms it was the largest acquisition in history.)

Since the concern of the Clayton Act is with the probability of a
substantial lessening of competition in a line of commerce, the government specified the various lines of commerce into which LTV and its
subsidiaries had been considering entry and those that Jones & Laughlin
had considered. Eleven industrial areas including primary aluminum,
various building materials, and industrial automation processes were
found on both lists. In addition, LTV was noted as a potential competitor
in several of J&L's lines of steel, and J&L Steel as a potential competitor
in copper and aluminum wire and cable. The government therefore alleged a lessening of potential competition in several industries, a number
of which were already highly concentrated.

The Antitrust Division also predicted the probability of lessening of
competition in the use of "reciprocity," defined as "a seller's practice of
utilizing the volume or potential volume of its purchases to induce others
to buy its products or services," which could be expected to grow with an
increase in purchasing requirements and product diversity.

The government seemed more concerned with LTV's (then Ling-
Temco-Vought) takeover of Jones & Laughlin Steel in 1968 than with the
acquisition of Lykes Corporation (owner of Youngstown Steel and Tube)
in 1978. The combined share of the two firms in the steel industry after
the 1978 merger was 8.5 percent for third place after U.S. Steel and Bethlehem Steel with a combined 37 percent. Normally 8.5 percent in a rather

---

[27]Stanley H. Brown, *Ling* (New York: Atheneum, 1972).

[28]The complaint Civil Action No. 69–438 was actually filed April 15, 1969, before the
U.S. District Court of Western Pennsylvania in Pittsburgh and included the preliminary
injunction agreed to by consent mentioned before. The companies filed their answers
May 5, 1969.

concentrated industry would be occasion for prosecution under Section 7 of the Clayton Act, and Bethlehem Steel had lost such a case when it sought to merge with Youngstown in 1954. Attorney General Griffin Bell apparently was persuaded by "the Failing Firm doctrine" since the plight of both firms, particularly Lykes, was serious, and one survivor might be the most that could be expected.

In February 1984, the Justice Department was prepared to challenge LTV's proposed acquisition of Republic Steel, number 3 taking number 4 to become the second largest steel firm. After an internal struggle in the Administration, the guidelines for horizontal mergers were modified. Imports, despite being limited by quotas, were counted in determining market shares, and potential increases in productive efficiency were given greater weight. The merger was quickly approved with the provision that two Republic plants that contributed to undue regional concentration be disposed of.

LTV Approaching 1990

While James Ling, the firm's creator and chief executive officer until 1970, and LTV itself may have suffered, it was not from the government's action. Assets had to be disposed of to meet the debt obligations incurred by the acquisition. Ironically the LTV Corporation (whose official name until 1972 was Ling-Temco-Vought, Inc.) sold the Okonite stock to Ling in his new role as head of Omega-Alpha, a new conglomerate that ran into serious difficulties in 1973. Much of the Braniff stock was exchanged for $200 million of the nearly half billion in 5 percent debentures issued in 1968 to acquire Greatamerica, a holding company whose major asset had been the Braniff stock.

Paul Thayer, the new chief executive officer, was credited with a minor miracle in preventing the collapse of LTV in the early 1970s. The combined LTV-Lykes' sales of $7.25 billion in 1978 would have placed the merger in 25th place on the *Fortune* list of the 500 largest industrial corporations. But the company was absolutely last in average return to investors from 1968 to 1978 with −22.7 percent annual percentage returns (reflecting virtually no dividend and a collapse of its stock price from the $150–$170 range to a $5–$11 annual range). Whether the company could be turned from a sickly, cyclical giant with over half its sales in steel, almost one third in meatpacking, and the rest split between aerospace, ocean shipping, and oil rig equipment (the latter two acquired from Lykes along with Youngstown Steel) was the problem.

In discussing future prospects, the 1978 annual report of LTV stated "1978 marked the start of a new era. . . . It was a year in which LTV merged with Lykes Corporation and became in essence a new LTV—more firmly based on steel than ever before and at the same time more widely diversified."

The annual report was right in that LTV's future was to be firmly based

EXHIBIT 16–IB   Continuation of Note to Question 3

	1968–1978			1974–1984		
	RK-78	TR	GR E/S	RK-84	TR	GR E/S
The conglomerates:						
ITT.............	11	− 3.12	3.50	21	14.88	− 1.99
LTV............	42	− 22.74	− 9.60	48	2.47	Loss in 84
Gulf & Western . . .	58	1.22	11.97	77	18.85	7.56
Litton Ind........	72	− 9.98	Loss in 78	75	39.82	Loss in 84
Textron.........	89	− 1.08	7.85	122	17.19	0.85
Northwest Ind.....	122	6.49	7.44	242	24.40	− 8.66
The *Fortune* 55 ave. .	—	2.85	10.00	—	18.65	5.90
Diversified cigarette companies:						
Philip Morris	46	18.15	20.00	32	16.38	16.48
Reynolds Ind.	47	7.29	9.23	23	16.92	11.38
American Brands..	83	9.50	8.90	84	14.70	10.81

on steel after its acquisition of Republic Steel in June 1984. It was wrong in that it would remain widely diversified. The marginal Wilson meat-packing operations were spunoff to the stockholders before the merger. The new Wilson Foods was number 192 in the Fortune 500 list in 1984 (it had been number 81 before its acquisition in 1967). Lykes ocean shipping business had been sold off for badly needed cash. Ironically, for a "free form" firm, LTV in the second half of the 1980s had become essentially a steel company at a time when the industry was struggling with import competition. It had a debt-equity ratio of 4–1, and its long-term bonds were selling to yield 17 percent, about 5 percent more than the corporate average. Its stock price of $7 was close to historic lows and less than one twentieth of the highs of the 1960s. While LTV was second to U.S. Steel in market share, it could be said to be the largest steel firm, since U.S. Steel, after acquiring Marathon Oil, could be classified as a petroleum company based on greater sales in that industry.

Questions

1. Can you see any joint product advantages in combining steel and meat-packing with lesser participation in aerospace, shipping, oil field equipment, and other products?

2. Which, if any, of the seven deadly sins of acquisitions listed by *Business Week* (see first paragraph) did LTV commit? What, if anything, did LTV do right?

3. The following note compares the performance of six conglomerates with the averages for the *Fortune* 500 and with three diversified cigarette companies. The time is the two overlapping decades 1968–78 and 1974–84. Why might these conglomerates have done relatively poorly in the first decade and so relatively well in the second? Why might LTV have had the poorest performance in both decades?

Note: In Exhibit 16–IB, RK refers to the standing of the firm among the *Fortune* 500 in sales; TR designates the average annual rate of return for the decade to investors in the stock including price appreciation on the stock plus dividends that are assumed to be reinvested in the stock; and GR E/S designates the annual rate of increase in earnings per share that would make first year earnings equal to 10th year earnings. During both of the decades, the rate of inflation averaged about 7 percent. The period 1968–78 was clearly bearish with real returns on the average stock being negative.

CASE 16–2
General Electric and the $10 Light Bulb

In June 1979, General Electric announced a new household light bulb with a projected price of $10 and a planned introduction date of early 1981. The most closely comparable incandescent bulb in its line was a three-way 50/100/150-watt bulb. The new bulb was announced to have two settings equivalent to those of a 75-watt bulb (with lumen ranging from 1,075 to 1,170 in various incandescent models) and a 150-watt bulb (with present lumen output from 2,200 to 2,790 lumens). Since it was estimated to be three times as efficient, the actual current requirements would approximate 25 watts and 50 watts.

The second selling feature was an estimated average bulb life of 5,000 hours that was approximately four times the bulb life of the present 50/100/150-watt bulb. At a 100-watt setting the latter was anticipated to last 1,200 hours. This life was characteristic of the "soft light plus" and "long life" bulbs GE was selling in 1979. General Electric was also still distributing, at somewhat lower prices, "the soft light" line with average lives of 750 hours and moderately higher lumen/watt ratios.

The following could be considered representative prices at 1979 levels for three alternatives for providing an average of 1,640 lumens:

	Price	Average Wattage Used	Average Life (hours)
New bulb ("Electronic Halarc")	$10.00	33	5,000
50/100/150-watt soft light plus	1.60	100	1,200
100-watt "soft light" (without multiple feature but somewhat more lumens) .	0.60	100	750

An additional drawback of the new light was that it was larger than present bulbs and had somewhat the appearance of two lights jammed together with the lower bulb a plastic base containing electronic components. It used the incandescent principle only for start-up for 30 seconds. It in fact was a miniature version of a metalhalide lamp used in outdoor lighting.

There was a potential of 1.65 billion sockets to fill, over 95 percent in homes since commercial and industrial lighting largely relied on fluorescent tubes with a similar energy efficiency margin over the incandescent bulb (a 40-watt tube could produce as much light as a 150-watt lamp). While patents had been taken out on socket-fitting fluorescent tubes, none were being commercially produced.

General Electric estimated that it had spent $20 million in research and development and would spend $20 million more in production facilities by the time of the commercial introduction of the bulb.

Questions

1. Work out the price per kilowatt-hour for current that would yield the $20 saving estimated by GE over the 5,000 hours of the "Electronic Halarc" (as compared with the three-way lamp).

2. Would the "Electronic Halarc" be a good replacement for guest room lamps used 100 hours a year (average use is 1,000 hours) already containing a half-used 100-watt "soft light" if the price per kilowatt-hour was $0.03 and the interest rate was 10 percent? How many hours of annual use would make it worthwhile to discard an existing bulb at a $0.03 price; at a $0.10 price per kilowatt-hour?

3. Why is the "Electronic Halarc" likely to be an addition to the product line for an indefinite period in the future rather than a product improvement replacing the ordinary incandescent bulb? Compare this case with that of the "soft light plus" versus "soft light."

4. What annual market penetration would GE need for a 20 percent pretax return on estimated investment in the new bulb assuming $1 per bulb margin over AVC? Assume 10 years of production.

CASE 16–3 _____
American Natural Resources Takeover in 1985*

American Natural Resources Company (originally American Natural Gas) had an 80-year history of successful operations and increased dividend payments. Although it had diversified into such fields as trucking, coal, synthetic fuels, and energy technology the interstate transportation,

---

*SOURCES: 1983 and 1984 Annual Reports of American Natural Resources Company; *Value Line Survey,* January 11, 1985; Drexel Burnham Lambert; and various issues of *The Wall Street Journal.*

storage, and sale of natural gas remained its primary source of revenue. Sales in Michigan and Wisconsin accounted for 95 percent of total gas sales. ANR also explored for crude oil and gas in the United States and Canada. At the end of 1984, interests in 1,528 oil and gas wells were owned, and a net acreage position was held in 183,000 developed and 825,000 undeveloped acres.

The least satisfactory division was trucking where 1984 losses were $31.3 million despite record high operating revenues and a 4.3 percent gain in tonnage hauled. A new chief executive officer and other senior managers were appointed for the ANR freight system.

As a surprise to most persons, the Coastal Corporation on March 4, 1985, made an offer "to purchase any and all outstanding shares of common stock of American Natural Resources Company at $60 per share." Shortly before the offer, ANR was trading around $45 and had been as low as 27¾ within the previous 52-week period. After the Coastal Corp. offer, the stock of ANR sold at or a little above $60. Management of American Natural urged stockholders not to accept the "inadequate" $60 offer, and they turned out to be right as Coastal Corporation soon "sweetened" the bid to $65. (At a price of $38, American Natural Resources was considered by *Value Line Survey*, January 11, 1985, to have "no particular investment merit at this time.") Book value per common share was $31.35 at the time. ANR's dividend policy was conservative. The 39,276 stockholders owned 37.8 million common shares and secured 1984 dividends of $2.22 per share. Net income in 1984 was $196.1 million.

Coastal Corporation was also the owner of a natural gas pipeline that it felt would nicely complement that of American Natural Resources. It owned four oil refineries that lost about $2.5 million in the third quarter of 1983. It explores for gas and oil, with proven reserves of 20.6 million barrels of oil and 1.02 trillion cubic feet of gas. Coastal's dividend payout in 1984 was only 23 percent of net profit. Corporate executives owned about 8 percent of the common stock while ANR's executives owned less than 1 percent of their outstanding shares.

Starting in the summer of 1984, Coastal acquired more than 1.6 million shares of ANR. Under federal law, Coastal would have been required to disclose its purchases if they exceeded 5 percent of all outstanding shares. In order to acquire American Natural, about $2.2 billion was borrowed by Coastal, in part by the sale of bonds that paid high interest rates.

Before accepting the Coastal offer of $65 per share, the president of ANR tried unsuccessfully to find a "white knight." He also considered asking his employees and others to attempt a "leveraged buyout" in which debt is incurred to be paid off with future cash flow. A "poison pill" tactic was mentioned as well as a "scorched earth" action. ANR also charged Coastal in court of tipping some insiders prematurely of an intended takeover action. Eventually, however, the two companies agreed to a (more or less) friendly merger. Buying American Natural has made Coastal a major gas transmission company.

Questions

1. Why would it have been poor strategy for Coastal to have acquired 2.6 million shares of ANR, starting in the summer of 1984, rather than the 1.6 million actually bought?

2. An "executive incentive plan" in effect at American Natural Resources at the end of 1984 provided that 343,320 shares of common stock could be acquired at prices ranging from $18.16 to $33.31 per share. If the average price was $25, about how much was the takeover worth to ANR executives?

3. The "rational anticipations" approach espoused by some economists suggests that market prices for stocks at any moment are "about right," reflecting what is known about companies. (Some economists have even said that throwing a dart at a stock market page will provide a suitable way to pick stocks to purchase.) What do you think of that theory?

4. Arbitragers may have research staffs and extensive contacts in order to try to anticipate takeovers. Can you suggest some "cheap" ways of anticipating takeovers? (A good answer may make you rich, especially if you do not disclose it in full.)

17

Production and Social Costs

I remember that a wise friend of mine did usually say, "That which is
everybody's business is nobody's business."
—*Izaak Walton*

Concern over environmental deterioration has brought the subject of social costs into great prominence. Virtually all types of production impose
some costs on other persons. Firms, in some fields, such as paper, plastics,
and nylon production, may impose very large costs on others. Such effects
are called *externalities*. While some externalities are beneficial—for example, pleasure from a neighbor's flower garden—the ones that cause
concern are unfavorable.[1]

As was emphasized in earlier chapters, private costs are taken fully
into account by a firm in deciding upon production processes, output
rates, plant expansion, contraction, and product abandonment. Costs
placed upon others may be partially considered by conscientious executives but are very unlikely to be taken fully into account unless financial
rewards or penalties induce such action. As a definitional matter, it is
general practice to let the term *social costs* include the sum of internal
and external costs rather than pertaining to the latter alone. The broad
problem facing all economies (socialist as well as capitalist) is how to
ensure that social costs of production will be taken into account by economic units.[2]

---

[1]This is not to say that favorable externalities always require no action. Steven N. S.
Cheung, "The Fable of the Bees: An Economic Investigation," *Journal of Law and Economics*, vol. 16, no. 1 (April 1973), points out that the services of bees and flowers, which
often provide uncompensated external benefit, have been marketed since World War I.
Bee hives are moved from farm to farm in the western fruit growing areas. In some cases,
fruit farmers pay for pollination services; in other cases, beekeepers pay for nectar extrac-
tion. Case 17–3 shows a similar market in Florida.

[2]The USSR is said to have as serious environmental disruption as ours. Marshall I.
Goldman, "The Convergence of Environmental Disruption," *Economics of the Environment*; R. Dorfman and N. S. Dorfman, eds. (New York: W. W. Norton, 1972), p. 294.

PRIVATE BARGAINING

Under favorable conditions the price system itself can cause firms to consider all costs—not just private costs. Suppose a retail store erects a sign bearing its name on its own property in such a way as largely to obscure the sign of an adjacent theater from passing motorists. The damage is two-way. The store's sign reduces the value of the theater's sign, and the latter's sign reduces the value of the store's sign. Although the second firm to erect a sign may have been somewhat unethical or careless in its decision, subsequent economic behavior is not based on which sign appeared first. A private bargain between the firms under which one firm pays all or part of the cost of moving the other firm's sign is a possibility. The theater owner is likely to be under more pressure from the conflict of signs, since he changes the advertised feature frequently. In the absence of any legal liability the theater owner may bribe the store owner to move his sign to another location.

The store owner should consider the proferred payment as an opportunity cost of leaving the sign in its present location. (Sacrificed income is equivalent to a cost.) An appropriate offer and locational adjustment may remove the external cost imposed by each sign. If the store owner finds it to be cheaper, the theater owner can, of course, move his own sign. If ill will arises between individuals, a private bargain becomes less likely. For example, the store owner may feel it worthwhile to sacrifice some income in order to punish the theater owner whom he does not like.[3] Malevolence can be a powerful economic force.

Not all adverse "neighborhood effects" should be removed. The costs of removing a given amount of noise, traffic congestion, air and water pollution, and litter may exceed the benefits, just as the cost of moving one of the conflicting signs may exceed the benefits.

There is frequently an indirect payoff to the individual who undergoes pollution. For example, an individual may be able to buy or rent a home more cheaply if it is known beforehand that there will be noise from a nearby highway or airport. She may prefer to save on housing cost rather than pay for a quiet environment (especially if she is a bit deaf). This is another example in which the price system may operate in what appears to be an equitable manner.

POLLUTION AND COMMON PROPERTY

The more difficult externality problems facing society and business arise from air and water pollution where many firms and individuals both contribute to, and are adversely affected by, the externality. In large measure the pollution problem is due to the common property status of most air and water. Any single firm or individual has little incentive to take

---

[3]A famous article dealing with the entire problem is Ronald Coase, "The Problem of Social Cost," *Journal of Law and Economics*, vol. 3 (1960).

care of a resource when he cannot appreciably appropriate the benefits of his own conservation. This explains why the same person who carves his initials in a park bench will not do the same with his dining room table. It also helps explain why there is overfishing of popular species such as lobsters that belong to anyone until they enter a trap.

When no charge is made for use of the common environment, firms, municipalities, and individuals can reduce their own costs by using the air, water, beaches, and so forth, as a receptacle for wastes. From a social point of view there is too large an output of commodities that are produced without meeting all costs. In part this may explain why Americans are so well supplied with paper, plastics, cans, and plumbing. From the point of view of the firm, the desirability of having minimal and uniformly applicable restrictions is clear. A firm in a particular industry that is subject to more costly restrictions than its competitors may find itself seriously disadvantaged. The recycling of bottles and aluminum cans may be useful to large companies for its public relations value, even if the process is not inherently very efficient.

SOLUTION BY MERGER

Under favorable circumstances it is possible to "internalize an externality" through merger of the firm that is harmed and the firm that is polluting. The situation is then improved in that the entire cost will be taken into account by one company. A problem is that the firm that has been able to get rid of some of its costs is not likely to want to absorb them through merger. A more likely solution for merger is found in the "common oil pool case" where pollution is not involved but where firms affect one another's costs. If several different oil companies are pumping from a common oil pool, each has an incentive to pump at an uneconomically high rate in order to maximize its net revenue from the pool. (Each wants to get the oil before it is taken by the others.) A merger of such firms can change the rate of pumping to an optimal one since there will be a single decision maker in a more predictable situation.

The oil pool is an example of an exhaustible resource. In theory the owner of such a resource seeks to maximize its present value, rather than its current production of income. The owner always has the option of selling the property and consequently has an incentive to mine at a rate that keeps the total value at a maximum. It might be thought that this could be done by not working the mine at all but that is not likely to be the case since the owner sacrifices interest income on the valuable resource as long as it remains in the ground.

REGULATION BY AUTHORITIES

Of far greater importance than outright prohibition of pollution is its regulation by authorities who are established by legislative bodies. In addition to state and local authorities, the Federal Environmental Protection Administration, established in December 1970, exercises regulatory powers of great significance to business. National air and water quality standards have been set, and EPA is engaged in the difficult and costly mission of securing reductions of emissions by industry, municipalities, and other government units and individuals. Subsidies play an important role. In 1979, over $4 billion was awarded for sewage disposal plants.[4] Other devices and weapons used are enforcement conferences, 180-day notices, and civil or criminal suits. Voluntary compliance is sought before suits are filed. Often the firms that are cited will agree before the trial to install the necessary pollution abatement equipment.

EPA is often challenged on technical grounds because a great deal of information about the effects of different levels of pollution is required in addition to knowing what technology is available. There is also a difficult socioeconomic problem, especially because jobs are involved. Some 200–300 mainly small and less efficient factories were expected to shut down by 1976 because of air and water quality standards.[5]

In addition, there is now a much greater problem of locating new refineries, pipelines, and utility plants, and this contributes to higher prices and shortages. Delay in construction of the Alaska pipeline because of environmental objections and abandonment of the partially built Cross-Florida Barge Canal on environmental grounds are outstanding examples of the new problem that firms and government agencies face in addition to the more usual profitablility or cost-benefit criteria. The problem viewed broadly is one of balancing all costs against all gains, considering alternative locations and processes. Emotions and guesses may have more weight than careful calculations, especially because valid calculations are so hard to make.

The nature of the problem is illustrated by required emissions standards for cars. Many areas of the country have no serious air pollution, but since automobiles are by nature highly mobile, there is no assurance that a car not equipped with emission control devices will not end up in daily use in a city where smog is prevalent. The awkward administrative solution is to require expensive additional equipment on all new cars, knowing that many will not really need the devices. Also, gasoline consumption is increased.

TAXES ON POLLUTANTS

In the literature of economics the classic form of government intervention where there are important unfavorable externalities consists of a special tax on the polluting firm. If there is a fixed relation between the rate of

---

[4]Michael Thoryn, "Resource Recovery Means Waste Not, Want Not," *Nation's Business*, vol. 67, no. 5 (May 1979), p. 96.

[5]Y. Cameron, "The Trials of Mr. Clean," *Fortune*, April, 1972, p. 103.

FIGURE 17–1   Tax on All Output

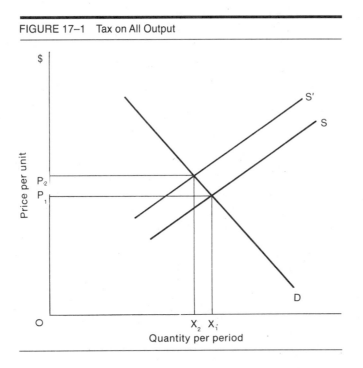

output of a good and the output of a "bad," it is possible to reduce the problem by taxing the product.

Figure 17–1 illustrates the imposition of a specific tax per unit of product on a competitive industry. The supply curve is S prior to the tax. Because each unit of output will have its marginal cost raised by the amount of the tax, the new supply curve will be S' lying above S by the tax per unit of output. Industry output will be reduced by the amount X_2X_1. This approach is actually used for cigarettes and liquor, to the extent the taxing authorities are trying to reduce adverse social effects rather than simply raising revenue. The effectiveness of the tax in reducing pollution will be greater the larger the tax, the less the negative slope of the demand curve, and the less the positive slope of the supply curve. Since the slope of the supply curve decreases as more time is allowed for adjustment, the long-run effect of the tax in reducing pollution should be greater than its immediate impact.

A more common situation is that the effluent discharge from a plant can be altered by the use of appropriate equipment. Output of the useful product itself is not necessarily affected greatly, although its greater cost will reduce the amount demanded, other things remaining the same. In Figure 17–2 a curve of marginal damages to the community constitutes a sort of demand for pollution reduction. Damages are highest if 100 percent of the effluent is discharged, as indicated by the intersection with the vertical axis. Marginal damages are shown to fall to zero with less

FIGURE 17–2   Effluent Charge to Reduce Pollution

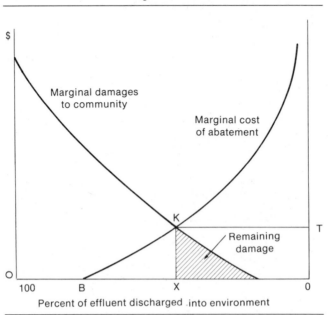

Percent of effluent discharged into environment

than a complete elimination of pollution by the firm in question since the natural cleansing power of water and air will often take care adequately of some effluent discharge. The upsloping curve shows the marginal costs of abatement if carried out optimally by the firm. Complete elimination may be impossible so the curve is stopped short of the right-hand vertical axis. On the other hand, some reduction may be virtually costless so the marginal cost of abatement is shown to appear only after a small reduction has been effected[6] (point B).

A tax on the effluent will be needed to cause the firm to act. This tax should be set at the level OT if the authorities are perfectly informed regarding marginal environmental damages and the firm's marginal abatement costs. (A big order!) With a flat charge of OT imposed on the discharge, the firm will find it least costly to reduce effluent discharge to point X since it can abate this amount for less outlay than if the tax were paid. The shaded area represents the dollar tab placed on community damages that would still be suffered (but should be endured in the sense that more resources would have to be spent on further cleanup than the cleanup would be worth socially). The tax paid is OXKT.

---

[6]The chart is a modification of the one used by Allen V. Kneese and Blair T. Bower, "Causing Offsite Costs to Be Reflected in Waste Disposal Decisions," reprinted in R. Dorfman and N. S. Dorfman, eds., *Economics of the Environment* (New York: W. W. Norton, 1972), p. 137.

It is not difficult to see that a cost-reducing improvement in abatement processes would make possible a greater reduction of pollution and a lower tax. On the other hand, a revaluation upward of estimated marginal damages to the community would call for a higher tax and fuller abatement.[7]

Effluent taxes are not in wide use and have been dubbed "a license to pollute" since they are unlikely to stop effluent discharge completely. However, an administrative agency that utilizes direct orders will ordinarily also have to permit less than 100 percent abatement in order not to have devastating effects on firms and on municipalities that own sewage disposal facilities. To that extent the authorities will also indirectly issue "licenses to pollute."

SUMMARY OF SOME IMPORTANT PRINCIPLES

There are a few problems that society and many business firms must face that are more difficult than that of reducing environmental damage. The student should train himself or herself to see both sides of the picture— both the value of the product or service that causes pollution and the harmful effects imposed. The social problem is one of maximizing welfare by means of appropriate actions that will usually be strongly supported by some groups and opposed by others, since income distribution is affected.

In some situations, private bargaining between involved parties can solve the problem. This solution does not always require that one party be liable for damages. Contrary to the theme of many western movies, it is not always easy to know who is the good guy and who is the bad guy. The upstream rancher who denies water to the new and poorer rancher below may have a large herd that could not otherwise survive. The small rancher below may have purchased his land very cheaply because of the probability of the very water problem that he now encounters. Like some other externalities, this one may be happily settled by merger (marriage of the rich rancher's daughter and the poor rancher's son). (The poor rancher must have sons to help him blow up the dam.)

There are some possibilities of useful private bargaining even when a considerable number of persons are involved. An association of upstream manufacturers may be able to bargain with an association of downstream fishermen in such a way that both sides will feel they have gained. Often the "free rider" problem will be encountered, however. Some members of either or both groups will try to obtain the benefits without paying dues, bribes, or other costs.

Government agencies themselves cause much of the pollution prob-

---

[7]In reading the chart, think of pollution becoming greater as one moves to the left and abatement being fuller as one moves to the right. Also remember that the area under any marginal curve is the corresponding total. For example, area BKX is total direct expenditure on abatement. Area BKTO is total abatement and tax cost to the firm.

lem (municipal waste discharges, dumping by the Navy, sonic booms by the Air Force, runoff from interstate highway construction), but government must often be brought in to alleviate the problem. A great many possibilities for government action exist. These include direct prohibition, liability decisions by the courts, regulation by administrators, education of the public, subsidies, and taxation. In some cases no action should be taken at all. Optimal pollution, rather than zero pollution, is a rational social goal.

A MORE POLITICAL VIEW

The need to control serious pollution usually means that government must become a chief actor, although as pointed out earlier, some unfavorable externalities can be removed by private bargaining. As also stated by Ronald Coase, "Nothing could be more 'antisocial' than to oppose any action which causes any harm to anyone."[8] Much good judgment is required to do more good than harm.

Control of pollution to improve the environment can be considered to be a "public good." A public good is one that must be consumed jointly by all (affected) persons. National defense is the clearest example because the pertinent population is large and well defined. It is clear that many individuals would be "free riders" if voluntary contributions, rather than taxes, were relied upon to finance national defense. There are, of course, great differences among individuals in the amount of national defense they deem desirable, as bitter congressional debates show, but individuals can do little to alter the amount they must buy.

While a public good is often defined as one that is available to all if it is provided to anyone, some of the difficult questions of public policy arise from the question who "all" covers. A radio or television signal is available to all within its range but not those more distant.[9] An interstate highway system is available to most persons but not directly to those without an automobile or other vehicle. Some goods are "quasi-public goods" in that the recipients can be quite a restricted group. Fire protection may qualify.

Pollution controls imposed on a national level are likely to have quite different effects in various areas of the nation. An economist has shown that the 1970 Clean Air Amendments provided substantial net gains to persons living in New York City and vicinity and other densely populated places but provided benefits worth less than their costs in such states as Wyoming and Alaska.[10]

---

[8]Coase, "The Problem of Social Cost," p. 35.

[9]Radio and TV signals are examples of public goods that can be provided privately. To a lesser extent in the United States they are also provided publicly.

[10]Henry Peskin, "Environmental Policy and the Distribution of Benefits and Costs," *U.S. Environmental Policy,* ed. Paul R. Portney (Baltimore: Resources for the Future, Johns Hopkins University Press, 1978).

Complex technical questions greatly complicate the whole field of pollution control. (Case 17–4 illustrates this as applied to atomic waste.) It is strongly felt by most observers that acid rain is a leading cause of lake, stream, and forest deterioration in the United States, Eastern Canada, and Northern Europe, but how much reduction of emissions from which factories is necessary to solve the problem optimally is the subject of heated debate. Politicians sometimes find this sort of field an ideal one in which to secure political contributions because some wealthy interests feel strongly about public policy while the general public is poorly informed and often not very interested.

The relatively new discipline of "public choice,"[11] which considers politicians and bureaucrats to be motivated mainly by considerations of personal utility rather than by the "public interest" is especially applicable to environmental questions. The theory has been discouragingly illustrated at times by federal officials having strong affiliations with firms responsible for poor practices regarding toxic wastes. "Government failure" is now widely discussed along with "market failure" (due to monopoly, poor information, misleading advertising, etc.)."

CASE 17–1
Pollution Problems in the Dairy Industry*

There is a pronounced trend toward fewer and larger dairy plants in this country. Fluid milk plants decreased about 75 percent in number between 1948 and 1958. A marked decline in the number of cheese and butter plants occurred prior to 1948. Ice cream plants have also declined in number.

As dairy food plants become larger, they have a greater need to be located at places having good access to major highways. This increasingly places them near interstate highways and often in the suburban areas of small to medium-sized cities.

The trend is for dairy plants to service larger areas, trucking in raw milk from considerable distances and hauling out packaged products in semitrailers for distances as great as 500 miles.

---

[11]The leading economist in developing this approach is James M. Buchanan. A recent book that provides an introduction to modern theories of public choice is James Buchanan and Robert Tollison, eds., *Theory of Public Choice—II* (Ann Arbor: University of Michigan Press, 1984).

*SOURCE: Information is mainly from U.S. Environmental Protection Agency, *Dairy Food Plant Wastes and Waste Treatment Practices*, Water Pollution Control Research Series 12060 EGU, March 1971.

FIGURE 17–1A   Dairy Food Plants and Effluent Charges

Proprietary Companies in Region	Number of Plants	Plants with Surcharge on Waste Composition
A	32	0
B	35	2
C	9	2
D	19	2
E	75	2
F	10	0
G	15	1
H	12	1
I	5	0
J	11	0
K	8	0
L	27	1
M	20	0
N	7	Unknown
O	15	2
P	5	2
Q	15	1
Cooperatives		
R	9	0
S	9	0
T	1	0
U	27	5
V	21	0
W	7	0
X	23	3

SOURCE: U.S. Environmental Protection Agency, *Dairy Food Plant Wastes and Waste Treatment Practices,* Water Pollution Control Research Series 12060 EGU, March, 1971, p. 20.

Where dairy plants utilize the municipal waste treatment facilities, they can be major contributors to the load of the municipal systems. The average milk plant of 1980 (250,000 pounds of milk per day) can be predicted to have waste loads equivalent to a population of 55,000 persons unless special efforts are made to pretreat or otherwise markedly reduce these wastes.

The most visible pollutant of the dairy industry is whey. The significance of this is great, since about 20 percent of the total milk produced in this country is converted into whey. Cottage cheese whey represents a more serious problem than sweet whey because of its acid nature which limits its utility as a food or feed.

Surveys have indicated that a great many managers of dairy plants are not aware of the pollution potential of the industry (or just wish the problem would go away).

Figure 17–1A shows that surcharges on waste discharge (effluent taxes) have not yet been heavily utilized in the dairy industry. There have been some instances in which dairy food plants have been closed down after the imposition of surcharges by municipalities.

Questions

1. Assuming that a municipality imposes an effluent tax on a dairy food plant that uses its waste disposal facilities, how would you describe the optimal levy in theoretical terms?

2. Dairy product plants have traditionally been located near large markets, with cheese being produced farther from the market than fresh milk. Explain why. (Reference to Chapter 10 may be helpful.)

3. What developments have tended to change locational determinants for dairy food plants?

4. Milk prices are usually kept artificially high by federal or state marketing orders. Can you think of a plan to redesign this sort of government intervention so as to reduce the pollution threat?

5. When it is possible to convert a "waste product" into salable dairy products, theoretically how far should additional direct processing costs be incurred by a profit-maximizing firm?

6. Suppose the dairy plant is otherwise subject to an effluent tax on the waste product. How does this change the theoretical maximizing position with respect to converting the waste product into a salable product?

CASE 17–2 _____
Noise in Moscow*

Many people believe that environmental problems stem mainly from the tendency of private industry to avoid some production costs by discharging "bads" into public water and air. This belief leads quite naturally to the idea that a centrally planned economy with social ownership of firms would much more easily protect the environment. There is evidence that such is not the case.

> Life in Moscow goes on in an often noisy environment. A common sight on the streets is a vendor promoting lottery tickets, excursions or books with a megaphone or a portable public address system. Even the police use loudspeakers to provide lectures and public ridicule to disorderly persons, jaywalkers, etc. The usual level of sound in a Moscow movie house is so high that a moviegoer may leave after a show with a headache and a feeling of fatigue. The big sports stadiums make life difficult for people in nearby housing, especially when spectators in open bleachers express their enthusiasm at soccer matches.
>
> One aspect of the noise problem in any location is the effect noise has on sleep. A Moscow sleep survey involving a 65-question canvas of 5,650 people showed that almost half of them suffered from poor sleep and that

---

*SOURCE: Information from U.S. Environmental Protection Agency, _An Assessment of Noise Concern in Other Nations_, vol. I (December 31, 1971), pp. 38–51.

the majority of these blamed this on external disturbances, primarily noises. Loss of sleep, of course, can have economic as well as social implications in the lowering of labor productivity, a higher incidence of breakage on the job, and other costly malfunctions. The investigators' observation that a fourth of West Germans and a third of Americans suffer from poor sleep implies that they consider sleep disturbance in the USSR to be equal to or possibly greater than such difficulty elsewhere.

The law concerning disturbing the peace (hooliganism statute) was adopted by the RSFSR (Russian Federation) in 1966, but the Moscow City Council passed its own stricter version in 1960. A typical public-nuisance ordinance, it applied to all public places, including communal apartments and dormitories, on their balconies, in the streets, etc. It specified that there was to be no loud singing, playing of musical instruments, radios, etc., if it might disturb other citizens, from 11 PM to 8 AM. Fines were up to 100 rubles if the case went as far as the "Neighborhood Commission" of the city council or up to 25 rubles if paid on the spot to the arresting policemen. A similar ordinance prohibiting loud playing of radios, etc., was passed by the Moscow City Council on 11 November 1969.

Perhaps after the 1969 city ordinance was passed, some enforcement was again temporarily achieved. But despite the 1969 resolution of the city council, applicable noise nuisance ordinances have not been vigorously enforced in the streets; the various sources of street noise such as street vendors and militiamens' megaphones still go unregulated.

The new official emphasis on noise control also seems to be deficient in practice in the area of industrial noise emissions to the community, as a 1971 report from Moscow illustrates. According to this report, a certain electric transformer substation (No. 179) was the constant source of complaints about noise for years in the Moscow "Semenovskaya" neighborhood. The loyal SES (Sanitary-Epidemiological Station) sent a list of offending substations, including No. 179, to the Moscow Power Authority (Mosenegro), and to the national Ministry of Energetics and Electrification with the demand that the transformer noise be abated. The SES also secured a directive from the Moscow City Council (December 1968) that the transformer substation nuisances be abated and that several unenclosed substations, including No. 179, be enclosed in soundproof buildings in the course of the 1969–71 period. However, these measures achieved nothing except the promise of the director of the Moscow Power Authority that action would be taken. No action was taken.

Questions

1. Explain how the universal tendency of individuals to maximize personal utility contributes to the noise problem in any society.

2. Soviet plant managers often receive bonuses for meeting or exceeding planned output. Explain how this can contribute to noise and other pollution in the USSR.

3. How is social ownership of firms likely to affect prospects for bargaining between affected parties as a means of removing noise or other disturbing circumstances?

4. In some ways it may be easier and in some ways harder for an environmental protection agency to put pressure on another agency of government than on privately owned firms. Consider this question and apply to the relative problems of the United States and USSR in protecting the environment.

A Note to Case 17–2*

A decibel is the unit that is used to measure sound. One decibel is the quietest sound a human can hear. "Each decibel step upwards from zero represents a 26 percent increase change in sound intensity."[12] Here is a list of several items and their respective decibel readings:[13]

Vacuum cleaner	70
Alarm clock	80
Power mower	105
Jet engine	140
Live rock music	90–130

"The Occupational Health and Safety Administration says we can tolerate 8 consecutive hours at 90 decibels but only 15 minutes at a level of 115 decibels."[14] Listening to loud sounds can do unrepairable damage to the human ear; yet noise pollution continues to grow due to industrialization, increases in the standard of living, and the need to meet the demands of a quick moving society. Loud, prolonged noise can cause tension, anxiety, lack of sleep, and other undesirable circumstances. Accidents at work are many times related to these situations with noise being a direct link to the situations that lead up to the accidents.

CASE 17–3
The Bees and the Flowers in Florida†

As noted in the text, a market for the services of bees, and the reciprocal services of flowers, exists on the West Coast of the United States. A very important market of a similar sort exists in Florida. Colonies of bees are used not only to help in pollination of orange blossoms but are used

---

*SOURCE: The authors are indebted to Dr. John H. Lauck of Ball State University for material in this note.

†SOURCE: Material for this case was furnished by Clark Reeder, a student at Florida State University.

[12]"What Is Noise," *Science Digest*, May 1974, p. 62.

[13]Dava Sobel, "Noises that Really Do Hurt Your Ears," *Good Housekeeping*, November 1978, p. 305.

[14]Ibid.

also in watermelon and vegetable production. Over 70 percent of the acres planted in vegetables are pollinated by the use of bees.

Vegetable growers pay rental fees of $15 to $25 per hive per season to beekeepers. The latter face considerable costs and risks in providing the services of the bees. The hives are moved at night. Bees can be lost to insecticides used on the vegetable crops and whole colonies may be stolen by another beekeeper. While most beekeepers remain within the state, some may migrate as far north as Maine and as far west as California.

In the use of bees in Florida orange groves, the beekeepers may pay instead of being paid because of the desirable citrus honey which results. Often the trade of pollination services and citrus honey is considered to be an even one. Statistics are largely unavailable, as most deals are worked out on a private basis.

While much "natural" pollination occurs in Florida due to the wind and the insects, better control of pollination occurs when bee colonies are used. With the use of bees the grower may be able to set the blooms before the first frost, before substantial insect damage occurs, harvest earlier, and secure higher prices.

One factor often overlooked is the value of pollination to succeeding generations of crops. Insect-pollinated legumes have the ability to collect nitrogen from the air, store it in the roots, and ultimately leave it to enrich the soil.

In 1975, approximately 360,000 colonies of bees were in use in Florida. It is probable that an increase in their number and use as pollinators would be socially desirable.

Questions

1. As fully as you can, cite the factors that should, in theory, determine whether beekeepers are paid or have to pay in the market for pollination and nectar-gathering and how large payments will be. Include high gasoline prices as a factor.

2. If you were a beekeeper looking for a small piece of land on which to locate hives, what would be some important considerations: (*a*) if you plan to rent out bee colonies and (*b*) if you plan only to sell honey. Bee imaginative in your answer.

CASE 17–4 _____
Atomic Waste Management*

The subject of this session is no less than one of the great dilemmas of our time; that is, how can the public constructively participate in major

*SOURCE: Excerpts from U.S. Environmental Protection Agency, Bill Perkins, Atomic Industrial Forum, Inc., "Radioactive Waste and Public Acceptance," *Proceedings: A Workshop on Policy and Technical Issues Pertinent to the Development of Environmental Protection Criteria for Radioactive Wastes,* Albuquerque, N. M., April 12–14, 1977.

governmental and social complexities to their own satisfaction? The very vagueness of the question demonstrates the difficulty of answering it. Who, actually, is the "public"? What "constructive" participation can the public be expected to bring? Can participation at any level be satisfactory if the decision itself is not?

The most difficult part of our question is a simple one: who is the public? Or for that matter, who represents the public? For most of my talk I have assumed that the public is just that—the tens of millions of men and women, of all ages, interests, education levels, and lifestyles that make up our country. Obviously, no rational technical program could ever pretend to accommodate all their views—especially since the vast majority has no interest in the subject. In the Issues and Objectives paper that the Environmental Protection Agency (EPA) provided for this session, the term was re-defined as the "concerned and affected public." This is a more realistic description of the participants in most decisions involving the public. But it should be recognized, then, that the participants outside the normal decision-making process do not generally represent the disinterested public, but a range of *other* special interests—scientists interested in the technology, labor officials interested in jobs, landowners interested in property values, nuclear critics interested in any issue that may provide yet another stumbling block to nuclear power. All of these viewpoints have their place, but it would be naive to believe that any truly represent the public. Or, for that matter, that even a consolidation and compromise of these allows them to understand the issue without a thorough background in radiation effects, chemistry, geology, and nuclear physics. That would require the pre-digestion of this information by a credible source who could, in lay terms, describe the issue in the proper perspective.

That, I contend, is exactly what is missing from the current debate over radioactive waste: the credible source and the perspective. Like most of the nuclear controversy, this issue is presented in the terms of two extremes—absolutely dangerous or absolutely safe—because all parties have become so completely polarized. Even independent scientists and professors find it nearly impossible to avoid being labeled 100 percent for nuclear power, or 100 percent against it. A moderating voice must be found to sort out the overstatements on both sides—and especially in the area of waste management, the government must come up with a firm decision based on the best information available and be willing to advocate it as the agreed-upon national policy. Hoping that the country will come to understand the subject through osmosis or continuing to speak with various points of view will only perpetuate the current confusion and controversy. Somehow, despite the various interests of the agencies, the government needs to demonstrate its own confidence in waste management programs and present them to the public more consistently and effectively.

The most appropriate way to consider and present the issue of waste management, I believe, is in the style of this session rather than typical technical approaches. That is, not by presenting detailed technical facts in a vacuum, but in the full context of the benefits and risks of nuclear power and its alternatives. This context is usually absent from discussions of radioactive waste, just as it is here today, but it is a perspective that needs to be emphasized. A radioactive waste repository, alone, has no societal benefit, and it would seem that any risk is too great. The public needs to be reminded that the repository is directly tied to the benefits of nuclear power plants. Moreover, waste management programs of almost the same size would be required even if there were no nuclear power plants, because of military activities that create considerably more radioactive waste; the benefits are made possible by a small incremental risk. Similarly, a discussion of the risks of waste management can be complete only with a consideration of alternatives—the risks of other sources of power, or of the alternative of no nuclear power. Any context but the broad one of relative risks and benefits is an incomplete one and overemphasizes what has been called the unique risks associated with radioactive wastes. In fact, the uniqueness is the public's perception. Important as that is, it should not deter regulators and public officials from their basic responsibility—to develop policies based on real risks, real benefits, and real facts. The perception of the public, as opposed to technical facts, must not be underestimated as an important contribution to such decisions. A number of surveys has shown that the basic assumptions and values of technologists often vary markedly from that of the general public, and even more so from those of people who consider themselves environmentalists. It is this different set of assumptions and values that the public can contribute to decisions such as this one, and these values can lead to a questioning of basic premises that has often been missing from such procedures in the past. Still, it must also be kept in mind that the participants from the public are usually not disinterested, but members of their own special interest groups; that their sources of information may or may not be valid; and that their perspective might be a constricted one. Public officials must weigh all of these contributions, while making their decisions based on the best available information and in the context of alternative options. After the decision is made, it should be pursued and advocated diligently, minimizing the opportunity for continued obstructions and giving the public at large a reason for confidence in the decision and in the program.

Questions

1. How does "rational ignorance" enter into the problem of atomic waste management?
2. Would the field of atomic waste management be a suitable field for holding a public referendum when disposal policy is under review? Contrast such a referendum with one pertaining to the desirability of a state-operated lottery.

3. What are the main difficulties in defining "the public" and the "public interest"?
4. Is atomic waste disposal a "public good" (or at least a "quasi-public good"?)
5. How does a broad concept of "marginal cost" enter into civilian atomic waste disposal?

18

Antitrust Limitations on Business Decisions

The sole consistency that I can find in litigation under Section 7 (antimerger) is that the government always wins.
—*Supreme Court Justice Stewart, 1966*

Mergers are healthy for the economy.
—*William Baxter, Head of Antitrust Division of the Department of Justice, 1982.*

The Sherman Act and other antitrust laws have been termed a "brooding omnipresence" over the American economy. The strictness of judicial interpretation and scope of administrative application may vary over time. The quotations above indicate that mergers that would have been disallowed in the 1960s would escape scrutiny in the 1980s. But the antitrust laws have endured and almost certainly will continue to endure as an expression of preference for competitive free enterprise. The interest of business economics in the antitrust laws is in the framework they establish and the constraints they set upon firms' decisions.

The basic laws that may act as restraints on such decisions are the following: the Sherman Act (1890); the Clayton Act (1914); the Federal Trade Commission Act (1914); the Robinson-Patman Amendment to the Clayton Act (1936); the Wheeler-Lea Amendment to the Federal Trade Commission Act (1938); and the Anti-Merger Amendment to the Clayton Act (1950). The basic provisions of these laws are presented as an appendix to this chapter.

THE PROHIBITION OF PRICE FIXING AND RELATED AGREEMENTS

The particular antitrust provision that probably has had the greatest effect on business decision making is Section 1 of the Sherman Act that states, "Every contract, combination in the form of trust or otherwise, or conspiracy, in restraint of trade or commerce among the several states or with foreign nations is hereby declared to be illegal." This provision was the first to be effectively applied in decisions against the Trans-Missouri Freight Association and the Addystone Pipe & Steel Co. in 1899. The first case held illegal a railroad price-fixing agreement and the second rendered invalid a pooling agreement by cast-iron pipe manufacturers who sought to reduce competition by sharing markets.

In later litigation, the reasonableness of particular restraints has frequently been an issue, but agreements to fix prices, to restrict production, and to divide markets have generally been illegal per se, or in themselves. The classic statement on the illegality of price fixing was delivered in the Trenton Potteries Case in 1927. Producers of vitreous pottery fixtures for use in bathrooms and lavatories were members of a trade organization which had been found guilty of fixing prices. They appealed on the grounds that the prices were reasonable. Justice Harlan Stone of the Supreme Court in finding against the firms stated, "The aim and result of every price-fixing agreement, if effective, is the elimination of one form of competition. The power to fix prices, whether reasonably exercised or not, involves the power to control the market and to fix arbitrary and unreasonable prices. The reasonable price fixed today may through economic and business changes become the unreasonable price of tomorrow."[1]

What this has meant for the business firm is that to act legally in important market and production decisions, it is called upon to act independently. For the broad range of American firms, cartelization is effectively prohibited. This has not meant that firms never, in fact, fix prices collusively, but rather that the ability to do so openly and with legal sanctions to back the agreement is impossible. In Chapter 14, we recognized that when sellers are few, tacit agreements based on such conventions as consistent price leadership may well be common. Trade association activities that may approach price fixing will be discussed below. Nonetheless, the United States has encompassed into law prohibitions to meet the observation of Adam Smith that "people of the same trade seldom meet together, even for merriment and diversion, but the conversation ends in a conspiracy against the public or in some contrivance to raise prices."[2]

Case 18–1 which touches upon what has been called the "Great Electrical Price-Fixing Conspiracy" indicates that sanctions may be severe. Several business executives who agreed in clandestine meetings to fix prices on bids for electrical equipment were sent to prison in 1961 and their companies paid many millions of dollars in damage suits to public and private utilities.

Recently, both the FTC and the Antitrust Division have been active in antitrust litigation against horizontal conspiracies, and 15–20 cases might be under litigation at a time. A landmark successful prosecution was that

---

[1] *U.S. v. Trenton Potteries Co.*, 273 U.S. 392 (1927).
[2] Adam Smith, *Wealth of Nations*, Book I, chap. 5.

against 23 manufacturers of paperboard boxes (including Container Corporation, American Can Company, International Paper Corporation, and Weyerhaeuser Company). A criminal suit brought *nolo contendere* pleas from most firms and officers and criminal trial convictions of the rest. The Antitrust Division failed to get the new tougher guidelines or penalties it desired. Instead of 18 months, the roughly one third of the officers sentenced to jail averaged 10 days. Personal fines averaged $5,000 instead of the sought-after $50,000, and corporate penalties were far less than the proposed 10 percent of sales (about $1 billion in this case). Private, treble damage suits, provided for by Section 4 of the Clayton Act, have become more important as antitrust sanctions. More than a thousand such suits a year were filed in the 1971–83 period.[3]

A Federal Trade Commission Order in 1983 against du Pont and Ethyl Corporation was designed to limit "price signaling" similar to that among aluminum companies in Case 14–2. One of the firms would announce price changes in antiknock compounds in advance of when they would be effective. This would allow the determination of the others' reaction when there was still time to adjust the price and could thereby strengthen price leadership. The order was overruled by a federal appeals court in 1984 on grounds of constitutional right to free speech. Unless a reversal occurs in the Supreme Court, the prohibition against price signaling is likely to remain effective only when there is evidence of conspiracy.

EXCEPTIONS FROM THE PROHIBITION ON PRICE FIXING

While the thrust of antitrust policy is to promote independent market decisions, there have been a number of significant exceptions. Perhaps the most debated has been retail price maintenance legislation, euphemistically called fair-trade laws. Enforcement of the Sherman Act covered not only agreements between competitors but price-fixing agreements between manufacturers and dealers. In the 1930s when downward price pressures resulting from excess capacity were great, many states (finally all but three) passed legislation permitting manufacturers to require their dealers to maintain particular prices on products with trademarks. A legal justification for such a requirement was found in the idea that the manufacturer owned the trademark and that widespread price cutting on such an identified product could diminish the reputation of the product and thus the property value of the trademark.[4] Such legislation stood in conflict with the Sherman Act prohibitions on agreements when applied to interstate commerce. It was necessary that Congress pass legislation to exempt such agreements from the Sherman Act prohibitions, and the McGuire-Keogh Act in 1951 reinforced this legislation by making it clear

---

[3]Robert D. Blair and David L. Kasserman, *Antitrust Economics* (Homewood, Ill.: Richard D. Irwin, 1985), table 4–1, p. 71.

that nonsignatories to the price-fixing contracts could also be bound. In state after state, these nonsigner's clauses were nullified for violating state constitutions so that by 1975, when Congress repealed the retail price maintenance legislation, only 21 states had effective laws. Manufacturers had switched to "suggested retail prices" and had to accept legal risks for blatant attempts to enforce them as mandatory floors. For example, Levi Straus & Co. had to modify its attempts to maintain retail prices on jeans by cutting off dealers suspected of price cutting after an FTC suit in 1976.

There is no exception under current legal rulings for the fixing of maximum resale prices for a distributor by a producer. From the consumer's viewpoint, it would seem laudable that prices be kept down. However, the Supreme Court ruled against two liquor distillers who agreed not to sell to wholesalers who refused to respect the maximum resale prices. The Court stated that such prices "cripple the freedom of traders and thereby restrain their ability to sell in accordance with their own judgment."[5]

A second exemption to antitrust prohibitions against price agreements occurred in the enactment of NRA legislation in 1933. General price deflation was associated with the depression and the National Recovery Act encouraged industry codes which permitted firms to get together to draw up specifications as to fair market behavior and frequently included price-fixing agreements. The Blue Eagle symbolizing the NRA had a short life. The major permanent effect of the legislation was in the encouragement of trade associations whose discussion of mutual industry problems such as production rate and prices have sometimes led to antitrust violations. Whether such activities constitute illegal agreements to fix prices has depended upon whether the price information collected refers to present and future rather than past prices, whether its dissemination is limited to members of the trade association and whether any recommended list prices agreed to were in fact effective.[6] Most associations are discreet enough in discussions they may have on price so that the government is not provided with written evidence as to price collusion. The courts have found that one or two letters between company presidents as to agreed-upon prices are legally far more convincing than hundreds of pages of economic testimony indicating that the similarity in price changes was not purely coincidental.

Legislation has also been passed exempting particular groups from the antitrust strictures on price-fixing and market-sharing agreements. The Webb-Pomerene Act of 1919 was designed to exempt price-fixing agreements that involved only the export activities of American firms.

---

[4]*Old Dearborn Distributing Co. v. Seagram Distillers Corp.* 299 U.S. 183 (1936).

[5]*Kiefer-Stewart Co. v. Joseph E. Seagram & Sons,* 340 U.S. 211 (1951). Blair and Kasserman, *Antitrust Economics,* cite a series of newspaper and gasoline dealer cases from 1968 to 1980 that confirm this rule, pp. 348–49.

[6]These are among the distinctions between illegal and legal activities in the case, *Tag Manufacturers Institute v. F.T.C.,* 774F.2d452 (1st Cir., 1949).

The justification for this exemption was that American firms were frequently placed in competition with foreign cartels and could need to form a united front. Agricultural and labor organizations were exempted by the Clayton Act. One approach toward the agricultural problem was to encourage increased market power among farmers. That this approach was not very successful is indicated by a succession of later government interventions into agricultural markets. A final example of an exemption is that of the Reed-Bulwinkle Act of 1948 that exempted the rate-making activities of railroad traffic bureaus.

Serious efforts were being made in the late 1970s to reduce government regulatory practices that could reinforce price-fixing, such as the Interstate Commerce Commission use of these traffic bureau rates as mandated minimums. The CAB, under Alfred Kahn, did eliminate most rate minima for air passenger traffic in 1978, and all regulations by the CAB of prices and entry ceased when the agency was abolished by the end of 1984. The administration in 1980 was partly successful in sharply curtailing the ICC's power to mandate minimum trucking rates. Both carriers and unions lobbied heavily in Congress for continued minimum price controls.

It is worth noting that permission to make price agreements is not necessarily effective in raising prices. Many ingenious forms of price cutting were found to bypass the NRA codes; only in a few agricultural industries where producers are relatively few have farmers been effective in setting prices by agreements. Fair trade prevented price cutting in only a few lines of commerce where the support of the idea was virtually unanimous, such as drug retailing.

MONOPOLIZATION

Not only did the Sherman Act prohibit price agreements but it also prohibited monopolization in Section 2, which stated that "every person who shall monopolize, or attempt to monopolize, or combine or conspire with any other person or persons, to monopolize any part of the trade or commerce among the several States, or with foreign nations, shall be deemed guilty of a misdemeanor. . . ." This particular section was of little legal force until the 1946 decision concerning Alcoa.[7] Earlier cases against firms with monopoly power largely rested on records of predatory practices and specific restraints of trade they were using to build monopoly power. As a concomitant to discouraging cartelization by its firm line on agreements, Sherman Act enforcement encouraged the building of dominant firms by merger that eliminated the necessity for continuing agreements between separate firms.

The building up of monopoly power is not the result of a particular

---

[7]*U.S. v. Aluminum Company of America et al.*, Court of Appeals, Second Circuit, 148F.2d, 416 (1945).

business decision, except in the relatively rare case where all significant firms in an industry simultaneously agree to merge. It usually is the result of a series of decisions including some mergers and some successful innovations which may have initially been protected by patents. Strong monopoly positions outside of the regulated utilities are comparatively rare. In determining monopoly power, court decisions have concentrated on the power to fix prices and to exclude competitors. Monopolizing embraces something more than monopoly alone. To be guilty of monopolizing, the firm must know what it is doing and act in a way that tends to preserve or enhance its monopoly power.

What has this meant for decision making by firms? If a firm approached a two-thirds share of a significant market, decisions that might result in further enhancement of its market position could well bring about an antitrust prosecution. In the du Pont Cellophane case a market share of about 75 percent together with actions that showed du Pont was active in setting and keeping this position was held to constitute monopolizing of the cellophane market. Du Pont's acquittal depended upon satisfying a majority of the Supreme Court that cellophane was merely one of a number of flexible wrapping materials and thus did not constitute the relevant market upon which to judge the workability of competition.[8]

In looking back at the Cellophane case, it seems highly probable that the court's decision was influenced by the prospect that the cellophane monopoly would soon be swamped by the technological development of cheaper transparent films made of polyethylene and polyvinyl.

The outcomes of the two great monopolization cases of the 1970s and early 1980s were similarly influenced. The dismissal of the IBM case in part refelected the innovative competitive leapfrogging in electronic data processing. The willingness of AT&T to divest its operating subsidiaries was motivated by the changes in communications technology that had diminished its monopolistic position and the desire for freedom to use its scientific expertise to enter other fields, including electronic data processing.

In a third case, Xerox chose to accept a consent order in 1975 in a near record time of just three years after the Federal Trade Commission brought monopolization charges. (The FTC used its broad discretion under Section 5 of the Federal Trade Commission Act directed at unfair competitive practices.) The student may judge from Case 18–3 whether government intervention was necessary in view of the influx of technologically competent competitors.

The aborted antitrust attack on IBM. The Justice Department filed its complaint in January 1969; amended its complaint after Telex received a favorable decision in its private suit against IBM in 1973; brought the case to a six-year trial in 1975; started a review of the case under a new assistant attorney general in charge of the Antitrust Division, William F.

---

[8]*U.S. v. E. I. du Pont de Nemours and Company*, 351 U.S. 377 (1956).

Baxter, in 1981; and dropped the case in January 1982, with the stipulation that "the case is without merit." A discussion on *Telex* v. *IBM* is included as Case 18–2 as an example of an antitrust case against a dominant firm. It gives the flavor of the government case. While IBM lost none of the 19 private triple damage suits brought against it during the period of antitrust prosecution (the decision for Telex was reversed on an appeal), it incurred substantial costs in legal expenses and out of court settlements.

In building its case, the government cited evidence of a large market share, "69% to 80% of the total revenues from the sale or lease of general purpose computers"; large reported profits; substantial barriers to entry; and IBM's anticompetitive behavior in various marketing and pricing practices and policies designed "to restrain competitors from entering, remaining, or expanding in the market for general purpose electronic digital computer systems, or in the submarkets for said peripherals (disk drives, etc.)."[9]

"Folded, Spindled, and Multilated,"[10] is the title of a 1983 monograph that took the position that these adjectives were appropriate for what the government case did to correct economic analysis in the *U.S.* v. *IBM* case. A better market definition that would have included revenues from all electric data processing (EDP) would have shown a decline from 93 percent to 43 percent for IBM between 1952 and 1972.[11] The large profits represented competitive innovation that improved the performance/price ratio dramaticaly over time, not long-run equilibrium monopoly profits. The record of entry, 68 companies in 1961 and 617 in 1972, that reported EDP revenues was neglected. The so-called anticompetitive behavior, such as that reported in the Telex case, was typical of the competitor "leapfrogging" that took place constantly in the industry. Specifically, the Fixed Term plan (FTP) cited in Telex was not a "predatory" money-losing scheme to eliminate competitors but a profitable move to enhance IBM's competitive position.

THE DEMISE OF MOTHER BELL

In June 1983, a consent decree between AT&T and the Justice Department was approved in final form to settle the Section 2 complaint filed by the Antitrust Division against "Mother Bell."[12]

The actual divestiture in 1984 under the decree transformed the 22

---

[9]From amended complaint (Civil Action, No. 69CIV200) cited on p. 360 of reference in following footnote.

[10]Franklin M. Fisher, John J. McGown, and Joen E. Greenwood, *Folded, Spindled, and Mutilated* (Cambridge, Mass.: MIT Press, 1983). Fisher, a professor of economics at MIT, was chief economic consultant to IBM.

[11]Ibid., p. 117.

[12]*U.S.* v. *AT&T,* U.S. District Court for the District of Columbia, Civil Action No. 74–1698 (1974).

operating companies under AT&T control into seven independent regional holding companies: NYNEX, Bell Atlantic, Bell South, Ameritech, Southwestern Bell, U.S. West, and Pacific Telesis. For each share of AT&T stock, stockholders received 0.1 share in each of the new regional companies. The largest firm became eight successor firms ranked in the first 50 in the United States in terms of assets.

The government obtained the separation of AT&T's manufacturing subsidiary, Western Electric, and the Long Lines Department from the Bell operating companies. It had argued without success in previous antitrust litigation that the vertical integration between Western Electric and the operating companies resulted in a virtual telephone equipment monopoly since the operating companies purchased almost exclusively from Western Electric. This intracorporate connection also was held to frustrate the regulation of local telephone monopolies because the prices of equipment included in their rate bases were not determined in arm's-length transactions. With the advent of the microwave and satellite technology, the Federal Communication Commission had permitted limited long-distance competition by such firms as MCI. One provision of the decree was that equal access to local systems be provided to all long-distance carriers by 1987.

AT&T was able to retain the Bell name only for Bell Laboratories, its research and development division. (Local companies had the exclusive use of the Bell name and logo though only three of them did.) It did keep Western Electric in an unregulated subsidiary, AT&T Technologies. It no longer can sell telecommunications equipment in a quasi-captive market but has gained freedom to sell computers and other products. A third division, AT&T Communications, now operates the Long Lines Department, which is designed to be just another long-distance carrier by 1987.

Immediate results did not clearly indicate that the increased reliance on competition as the regulator in telecommunications would benefit all. The end-to-end responsibility of Mother Bell has been done away with and consumers with faulty service face difficulties in tracking it down. Local service rates have gone up as the cross-subsidization from long-distance revenues has been eliminated. The supposedly monopolistic local companies are threatened by technological change that permits the bypassing of their use by large users. Regional holding companies thus have sought other revenues such as those from telephone equipment and computer retailing.

The handful of other dominant firms have also been subjects of attacks under the antitrust laws. Berkey Photo, Inc., won an award of 81 million dollars in 1978 (subject to appeal) in a private suit against Eastman Kodak. The allegedly anticompetitive business policy stressed was the sudden, simultaneous introduction of a new film with a new camera with the intention to use it to the detriment of other camera manufacturers. This was seen by the judge as "honest industrial" conduct for a firm without monopoly power but illegal for Eastman Kodak which was extending its monopoly power in film to cameras. Kodak agreed to modify its product introduction procedures. In 1976, the H. J. Heinz Company sued Campbell Soup (70 percent share in soup market) for such allegedly anticompetitive practices as selective price cutting. Campbell made the common response to a private antitrust suit of countersuing.

Even though there are several important markets where a few firms control over 70 percent of the market, and while recommendations have been made that the antitrust laws should be strengthened so that the dominant position of a few firms could be reduced, they seldom have come under legal prohibitions of Section 2. In a few cases, of which the most prominent example was the suit against the major tobacco companies that was settled in 1946,[13] monopoly convictions have been obtained where the actions of a group of dominant firms was held to be sufficient to exclude competitors or to fix prices. At the turn of the decade into the 1980s, a continuing case was that of the FTC against the "shared monopoly" of the three leading breakfast cereal manufacturers. It is the subject of Case 18–4. Past experience suggested that the probability of court acceptance of the key remedies of partial divestiture and trademark licensing was low. The FTC dropped the case in 1982.

Merger guidelines in the 1980s. The language of the amended Clayton Act, Section 7, prohibits mergers, "where in any line of commerce in any section of the country, the effect of such acquisition . . . may be substantially to lessen competition, or to tend to create a monopoly." The Justice Department guidelines of 1982 and 1984 make it clear that only a very small percentage of mergers would be challenged.[14] As the quote at the beginning of the chapter indicated, the head of the antitrust division felt that "mergers are healthy for the economy." For guidance to firms contemplating mergers, it used a single number as a measure of market concentration, the Herfindahl (or Herfindahl-Hirschman) index. The guidelines made it clear that this was not a "mechanical" approach and that other considerations, such as ease of entry and effects on efficiency, would enter the final decision to challenge the merger. The Antitrust Division was also careful in indicating how the relevant market "line of commerce" would be defined—broadly enough to include all products that would significantly limit a "hypothetical monopolist's" power to set monopoly prices but narrowly enough to exclude products that were substitutes only when monopoly prices were being charged.

The Herfindahl index is simply the sum of the squares of shares in the relevant market and as used by the Justice Department, no decimal points were used. A completely monopolized market would have an index of 10,000 (100 squared). A market consisting of 100 firms, each with a 1 percent share, would have index of 100 (100 times 1 squared). Using

---

[13]*American Tobacco Co.* v. *U.S.*, 328 U.S. 781 (1946).

[14]Published in *Justice Department Merger Guidelines,* June 14, 1984, in Special Supplement, *Antitrust and Trade Regulation,* Report, S.1–S.16 (June 14, 1984).

the proper decimal expressions of percent market shares, as is frequently done, would set the maximum Herfindahl at 1.

The standards for usage of the index are particularly applicable to horizontal mergers. No challenge to a merger would be made if the index was below 1,000, except under extraordinary circumstances. Such a market would have to have at least 10 firms (10 times 10 squared equals 1,000). In such an unconcentrated industry no substantially lessening of competition would be presumed.

With a moderate concentration, with the values of the index between 1,000 and 1,800, mergers would be carefully scrutinized but those that did not increase the Herfindahl index by more than 100 would be permitted. To illustrate, if 1 of 10 equal-sized firms purchased another, the Herfindahl would increase by 200 (20 squared minus 2 times 10 squared) and such a merger could be challenged if it made the index greater than 1,000.

With an aftermerger Herfindahl index greater than 1,800, most mergers would certainly be challenged. Case 18–4 deals with ready-to-eat cereals, a market with an Herfindahl of well above 2,000. In such a market a merger that added less than 50 to the Herfindahl could be exempted. The limits for such a merger would be a firm with 6 percent of the market taking over a firm with 4 percent. (This would result in an increase of 48 in the Herfindahl: 52 premerger to 100 postmerger for the two firms involved.)

The guidelines essentially say that horizontal mergers between firms with significant shares of the market are proscribed. They have permitted acquisitions of previously unprecedented size in industries in which concentrations are moderate or low. Thus, in 1984 alone, Texaco, the sixth largest industrial corporation, was able to take over Getty, number 24, and become number 5; Chevron, the ninth largest acquired Gulf, number 11; Mobil, number 3, took over Superior Oil, number 196; and LTV Corporation moved up from 78 to 48 by merging with Republic Steel, number 145 (concentration in steel was moderate only when imports were included).

For vertical mergers, the guidelines focus on the structure of the acquired firm's industry. The risk of legal challenge is essentially limited to concentrated markets with Herfindahl values of over 1,800. The 1984 guidelines do not discuss conglomerate mergers separately. These are discussed under the heading of "Horizontal Effects of Nonhorizontal Mergers." The emphasis is on the probable effects of the merger on competition in a well-defined market, a specific "line of commerce" referred to in the law. The practical significance would be that the acquirer must be one of a very few potential competitors likely to enter a concentrated industry as defined by a Herfindahl index of over 1,800. An additional guideline suggests that if the acquired firm has less than 5 percent of its market, no challenge would be made, but that if it exceeds 20 percent, it is likely to be challenged. This guideline would seem to continue to ban a merger such as that proposed of Clorox by Procter & Gamble that is noted later.

They also make it clear that the possibility of using the Clayton Act to prevent increased macroconcentration, such as the growth of the largest 200 corporations by merger, is not within the law. This is in contrast to the position taken by McClaren and Mitchell in 1969. As discussed below, this position was taken at the end of a period when as the chapter-leading quotation by Justice Stewart complained, the government always won Supreme Court decisions on mergers.

PRICE DISCRIMINATION

The antitrust law that has probably been the most criticized is the Robinson-Patman Act, an amendment to Section 2 of the Clayton Act, which prohibits discrimination "in price between different purchasers of commodities of like grade or quality . . . where the effect of such discrimination may be substantially to lessen competition or tend to create a monopoly in any line of commerce, or to injure, destroy or prevent competition with any person who either grants or unknowingly receives the benefit of such discrimination or with customers or with either of them."

As a restriction of business decisions it should be noted that all price discrimination is not prohibited, and in Chapter 13 we have been concerned with the situations in which it is economically and legally justified.

The price discrimination involved in such delivered price systems as the basing point system has been successfully attacked where the government in addition has been able to demonstrate collusive agreements to enforce the system. The economics of such pricing arrangements were also discussed in Chapter 13.

Objections to the Robinson-Patman Act have centered on its test of injury to competitors rather than to competition and on such *per se* provisions as 2c, that makes it unlawful for a firm to receive a discount because it chose to deal directly with the manufacturer rather than through a broker. This brokerage provision was aimed directly at the chain stores that sought to introduce economies of vertical distribution in retailing and that were prepared to bypass traditional distribution channels.

EXCLUSION OF COMPETITORS

In a competitive economy, the very success and growth of some firms is likely to eliminate competitors from the market. A number of the provisions of the antitrust laws are aimed at particular practices that suggest that the exclusion is unfair.

The most specific prohibition on business tactics is Section 3 of the Clayton Act which made unlawful tying agreements and exclusive dealing contracts which "may substantially lessen competition or tend to create a monopoly in any line of commerce." Such tying arrangements require that a purchaser or lessor must purchase one commodity as a condition for the purchase or lease of another. For example, a firm that required the use of its material along with the purchase of a patented machine could be risking an antitrust prosecution. An exclusive dealing arrangement requires the dealers to purchase only from a specified manufacturer. Conspicuous examples in our economy have been in contracts that require a service station to purchase all its gasoline from a particular refiner, or an automobile agency to purchase all of its automobiles and spare parts from a particular manufacturer.

The restrictions have not been so tight as to make it impossible for many firms to bind their customers quite closely to them. For example, in the automobile industry, the threat of losing a dealer franchise together with considerable advantages in concentrating on a particular automobile line has produced a retail system in which most dealers in fact handle only Chevrolets or only Fords. Many other franchising arrangements that amount to exclusive dealing are made in competitive markets such as the roadside restaurant business where the probability of lessening competition is remote. Serious antitrust questions, however, have been raised concerning tying arrangements such as those between IBM cards and the business machines that they were designed to be used with. As a matter of fact, IBM was called upon as part of the settlement of a Sherman Act case against it to recreate competitive conditions in the card business, in which its name had become generic, and to reduce its market share in "IBM" cards to less than 50 percent.

THE DECISION TO MERGE

The first real merger movement in this country came immediately after the passing of the Sherman Act. The climax of this merger movement was the formation of U.S. Steel—a combination of several previous combinations of steel producers and fabricators. Three hundred other combinations occurred between 1890 and 1904 creating dominant firms in many industries. The Sherman Act proved ineffective in dissolving many of these combinations, although the dominant positions created in many industries were eroded away by the entry of new competitors. The Clayton Act in 1914 sought to remedy the situation by prohibiting stock acquisitions that may substantially lessen competition between the two firms or tend to create a monopoly, but its effectiveness was limited by the fact that it was not applicable to merger through the purchase of assets and because its application to vertical mergers was unclear. A second merger movement of considerable size took place in the prosperity of the 1920s and ended with the depression. In 1950, at what seemed the peak of a new postwar merger movement, the Clayton Act was amended to make it clear that all types of mergers regardless of the method of accomplishment could be prohibited.

The strict decisions of the 1960s. The enforcement agencies were relatively slow in using their new powers, and the first major case to be decided was the rejection of the Bethlehem-Youngstown proposed merger in 1954. Subsequent decisions have made it clear that there is a real antitrust risk wherever a horizontal or vertical merger involves a modest percentage of a particular line of commerce. The most definitive decision has been the Brown Shoe Case[15] in which the Brown Shoe Company's acquisition of G. R. Kinney Company was ruled void. Brown Shoe had produced about 4 percent of the total shoe output and Kinney produced 0.5 percent, although it retailed more, about 1.2 percent. The court noted that in a large number of cities the combined share of the two companies exceeded 5 percent. This figure may guide future decisions, although the Supreme Court made it clear that other circumstances such as a trend toward vertical integration by several companies that tended to foreclose retail outlets from competitors was a factor. In commenting on the significance of the case, David Dale Martin stated, "In essence the new policy is simple: both vertical and horizontal mergers are likely to be held illegal unless companies can demonstrate that mergers are likely to increase competition and thus promote the public interest."[16]

The government has also been successful in dissolving such product extension mergers as the acquisition of Clorox, the leading bleach producer, by Procter & Gamble on the grounds that Procter & Gamble's significant power in related products could result in a lessening of competition in the bleach market.[17]

Merger activity accelerated through 1968 despite these legal victories. The number of manufacturing and mining firms acquired in 1968—2,442—was more than double that of any previous year except 1967 (with 1,496 such mergers). Similar increases also took place in trade and service mergers to bring the total number in 1968 up to 4,003. This proved to be a peak as both the number of assets of mergers fell off, influenced by the bearish stock market of 1969 to 1974 and the financial difficulties of hastily expanded conglomerates typified by LTV.

A low in merger activity was reached in 1972 with less than $3 billion of assets in acquired firms as compared with about $10 billion in 1968 and 1969. By the late 1970s, assets acquired by merger had risen above those of the late 1960s in dollar levels (admittedly depreciated dollars). Low stock prices (price-earnings ratios under 10, often much under) made acquisition by merger cheaper than other forms of expansion for cash-rich companies. Both the acquiring corporations and their partners were frequently large. For example, in 1976, General Electric acquired Utah International with over $2 billion of assets, the largest to date. In both 1978 and 1979, six of the *Fortune 500 Largest Industrials* disappeared as merger partners of other list members. Several others were deleted because their

---

[15]*Brown Shoe Co., Inc. v. U.S. 370 U.S. 294 (1964).*

[16]David Dale Martin, "The Brown Shoe Case and the New Antimerger Policy," *The American Economic Review,* June 1963, pp. 340–58.

[17]*F.T.C. v. Procter & Gamble,* 386 U.S. 568 (1967).

results were no longer separately available, either because they had acquired or had been acquired by nonindustrial firms. No less than 13 of 1978's *Second Five Hundred Industrials* were noted as being acquired by a company in the first 500 in the 1979 listing.[18]

Why so much merger activity in the face of the amended Clayton Act? The significant mergers of 1968 were essentially conglomerate mergers in which there is no important vertical relationship of supplier and customer or horizontal relationship of offering similar products in the same market. In 1968, 84 percent of the number and 89 percent of the assets involved for the acquisitions of firms with over $10 million of assets were of this type; a great increase in recent years.

Donald F. Turner, the head of the Antitrust Division under President Johnson, felt that these mergers were essentially unreachable under the existing law which specified as unlawful "mergers which may substantially lessen competition in any line of commerce." The problem was to find a line of commerce shared by companies in different industries. In 1969, the Nixon administration with John Mitchell as Attorney General and Richard W. McClaren as head of the Antitrust Division, challenged the conglomerate merger movement with several suits including the challenge to the stock acquisition by Ling-Temco-Vought, Inc., of Jones & Laughlin Steel Corporation on three basic grounds.[19]

1. The increase in manufacturing concentration so that the 200 largest corporations controlled 58 percent of total manufacturing assets in 1968 as against 48 percent in 1948, which was abetted by mergers. The trend "leaves us with the unacceptable probability that the nation's assets will continue to be concentrated in the hands of fewer and fewer people."
2. The decrease of potential competition since Ling-Temco-Vought was a potential competitor in "cold rolled sheet stainless steel wire" and Jones & Laughlin was a potential competitor in "copper and aluminum wire and cable." Both firms were potential competitors in a number of concentrated industries such as primary aluminum and gypsum.
3. The increase in the probability of reciprocity, that is, for Jones & Laughlin and Ling-Temco-Vought to make purchases from each other, or to use their combined purchasing power to increase their sales to the detriment of competition.

Attorney General Mitchell laid down this guideline for firms contemplating mergers:[20]

---

[18]*Fortune*, June 18, 1979, p. 182.

[19]Case is included in Chapter 16 elaboration on this point. Complaint was filed before the U.S. District Court, Western District of Pennsylvania (1969). Direct quotations are from that complaint and from Attorney General Mitchell's speech which is cited below.

[20]Attorney General Mitchell's speech of June 6, 1969, before the Georgia Bar Association as quoted in *The Wall Street Journal*, June 9, 1969, p. 4.

1. The Nixon administration "may very well" file suit to prevent mergers among any of the largest 200 manufacturing firms or firms of comparable size in retailing and other industries.
2. "Will probably" file suit if any of the 200 seek to merge with any "leading producer in any concentrated industry."
3. And "of course will continue to challenge mergers" that regardless of the size of the companies involved may substantially lessen "potential" competition or develop a situation of substantial potential of reciprocity.

The transition to 1980s' guidelines. In the mid-1970s there was evidence that antitrust strictures against mergers might be loosening. McClaren had resigned as head of the Antitrust Division to take a federal judgeship after Nixon had opposed his prosecution of IT&T in its acquisition of the Hartford Fire Insurance Company, a case settled by consent decree.[21] A more conservative Supreme Court with four Nixon appointees found against the Antitrust Divisions in several bank merger cases involving the issue of substantially lessening potential competition. The acquisition of the United Electric Coals Companies by General Dynamics was allowed to stand despite, "government figures showing the substantial percentages of the coal mining business in various markets controlled by the merged companies."[22]

As the 1980s commenced, Senator Edward M. Kennedy was leading a movement to sharply limit mergers between large companies. Mergers between firms with over $2 billion in assets or $2.5 billion in sales (approximately the largest 200 firms of the date) would be prohibited. Companies with $350 million in sales ($200 million in assets) would have to prove their mergers would add to competition or would yield increased efficiency. If combined assets were more than $1 billion, the proof requirement would hold if each partner had more than $100 million in assets. Such legislation would almost certainly reduce greatly the number of larger mergers as the required proofs would be difficult and uncertain and would thereby contribute to less centralization of business decision making.[23] The legislation failed to pass.

In the middle years of the 1980s it seemed clear that amended Section 7 was an obstacle only to substantial mergers in industries where concen-

---

[21]Nixon told Kleindienst, "I don't want McClaren to run around prosecuting people, raising hell about conglomerates. . . . Now you keep him the hell out of that . . . Don't file the brief." Kleindienst denied this pressure in his confirmation proceedings for Attorney General and in 1974 was convicted of a misdemeanor for this denial. From White House tapes as reported in the *Boston Globe,* July 7, 1974.

[22]"Tipping the Scales, High Court Favors Business More Often in Antitrust Cases," *The Wall Street Journal,* May 21, 1974.

[23]For arguments against such legislation, see A. F. Ehrbar, "Business Becomes the Target of Trustbusters," *Fortune,* March 29, 1979, pp. 34–40. One stressed was the replacement of inadequate management, which would be more persuasive if some provision for spinning off the revamped acquisition were usual.

tration was already high. It seemed unlikely that the administrative zeal and favorable judicial rulings of the 1960s would be repeated to stretch the language of the law to cover small mergers or to deal with the subtle threat of increased macroconcentration. Concerns about takeovers of large firms (16 firms in the *Fortune* 500 were taken over in conglomerate mergers in 1984 in addition to four large horizontal mergers cited) were essentially not about the antitrust issue of monopoly power and were widely expressed within the business community. The criticisms included: (1) the substantial managerial resources devoted to devising takeover plans and defenses instead of being devoted to more tangible contributions to the economy, such as technological development; (2) the tremendous increase in debt incurred in the process of highly leveraged acquisitions at a time when it seemed appropriate that scarce savings might be better applied to investments in productive capital; and (3) the ethical issues raised were the difficulty in preventing insider gains in the takeover process, the "greenmail" extracted by corporate raiders from corporation assets to prevent takeovers, and the apparent pressure on managements to emphasize short-run financial, over long-run institutional, objectives. The new era of corporate takeovers was described in more detail in Chapter 16 and exemplified in Case 16–3.

SETTING A PLANE FOR COMPETITION

The price, product, advertising, and production policy of business is increasingly affected by legislation demanding higher and fairer standards of honesty and awareness of the noncommercial consequences of business actions. In simpler, primarily agricultural economies, the rule of caveat emptor, that is, let the buyer beware, was reasonably appropriate. The consumer choice between commodities was limited to those that were fairly familiar. Most transactions were with acquaintances rather than with strangers. On the few occasions that the buyer made unfamiliar transactions, he could act with an attitude of distrust. With the growing complexity of consumer choice and with a rapidly changing technology that continually results in new options, the consumers must be able to act with reasonable trust and confidence. Perfect knowledge of all alternative product characteristics and of relative prices has become impossible.

The basic antitrust law in this area is Section 5 of the Clayton Act that forbids "unfair" competitive practices with the Wheeler-Lea Amendment with forbids "deceptive" practices (1938). In a number of ways, legislation has proved inadequate; and in the 1960s there was continuing pressure for greater consumer protection which led to such legislation as the Cigarette Labeling Act in 1965, the Fair Packaging and Labeling Act of 1966, and the Truth in Lending Act of 1968. Other legislation that does not really fall under the heading of antitrust also has been concerned with the problems of honesty in labeling and advertising or with more complete knowledge for the consumer. For example, the Food and Drug Administration has been concerned with adulteration, misbranding, and the safety of food and drug products under a succession of legislative acts starting with the Food and Drug Acts of 1906. In 1962, drug amendments were passed that, among other things, made it necessary that a manufacturer in applying for approval of a drug must prove not only that it is safe but also that it is effective and that drug labels and advertisements must contain information of injurious side effects. The impetus for this legislation came from the thalidomide disaster that resulted in the birth of more than 7,000 European babies without normal arms or legs. The United States had been saved a similar experience by the resoluteness of Dr. Frances Kelsey, an FDA examiner. To keep the pill off the market, she resisted heavy pressure from the drug industry.

The amended FTC legislation leaves manufacturers considerable leeway for puffing in advertising that can be quite misleading. The FTC may obtain a stipulation with the company's agreement that it will discontinue what the FTC considers misleading advertising, but the company is not penalized further nor are the past effects of the advertising removed.[24] If such an agreement cannot be made, the FTC can issue a cease and desist order against the advertising themes. This order can be challenged in the courts, and a period of several years may elapse before a legal injunction against the advertisement is obtained. By this time it is quite likely that the company will want a fresh approach and would give up the advertising in any case. The cigarette industry case in Chapter 15 illustrates this process.

The legal constraints under which business firms must operate have set a minimal but rising plane for competition. Many business firms may well wish to select higher standards of candor. It is important that they lead the way since the long-run acceptability of any economic arrangements is likely to rest on their fundamental honesty in meeting society's needs.

Different types of standards quite outside the scope of the antitrust laws are also being developed. Their economic justification is sufficiently similar to make them worth mentioning here. These standards seek to make competitive firms consider the social costs in the form of environmental pollution of their choice of products and production methods. Examples are specifications for exhaust emission of automobiles, for the amount and chemical composition of smoke placed into the atmosphere, and for discharges of pollutants into rivers and lakes. Most of these regulations require increased costs by producers and, unless required by the federal government and thus applicable to all firms in an industry, are likely to be infeasible for firms operating in competitive sectors of the economy where additional costs for an individual firm would jeopardize

---

[24]Occasionally, the FTC has succeeded in getting remedial advertising, as when Warner Lambert was required to include the sentence, "Listerine will not help prevent colds or sore throats," in $10 million of advertising.

its survival. Constructive leadership in meeting these problems and in developing acceptable standards that eventually will be mandated by the government is a challenge to managerial policy making for the infra-marginal firm. (Case 17–1 deals with taxation of effluent discharge as one approach to the problem.)

In the 1980s, considerable controversy has arisen regarding the rapid extension of regulatory policies designed to protect consumer and worker interests. In the period 1962–74, Congress had passed 22 regulatory laws, of which 11 were concerned with product safety, 2 with safety of employees, 2 with environmental controls, 2 with honesty in the provision of products and services, 4 with discrimination in employment, and 1 with the financial security of employees.[25] Some criticized the inadequacy of enforcement; others were concerned with a "mindless" pursuit of safety that imposed large costs on business and ultimately the consumer by inadequate benefit-cost analysis. One critic expressed this sentiment, "What is made safe for the village idiot will cost the person of common sense more."[26]

APPENDIX
The Antitrust Laws

The Sherman Antitrust Act (1890)
An Act to protect trade and commerce against unlawful restraints and monopolies.

Be it enacted by the Senate and House of Representatives of the United Staes of America in Congress assembled.

Sec. 1. Every contract, combination in the form of trust or otherwise, or conspiracy, in restraint of trade or commerce among the several States, or with foreign nations, is hereby declared to be illegal. Every person who shall make any such contract or engage in any such combination or conspiracy, shall be deemed guilty of a misdemeanor, and, on conviction thereof, shall be punished by fine not exceeding five thousand dollars, or by imprisonment not exceeding one year, or by both said punishments, in the discretion of the court.

Sec. 2. Every person who shall monopolize, or attempt to monopolize, or combine or conspire with any other person or persons, to monopolize any part of the trade or commerce among the several States, or with foreign nations, shall be deemed guilty of a misdemeanor, and, on conviction thereof, shall

---

[25]Tabulated from table 1–1 of Murray L. Weidenbaum's *Business, Government, and the Public Interest* (Englewood Cliffs, N.J.: Prentice-Hall, 1977).

[26]Walter Gezzardi, Jr., "The Mindless Pursuit of Safety," *Fortune*, April 9, 1979, p. 64. "Person" has been substituted for "man" in the quotation to avoid promoting sexism.

be punished by fine not exceeding five thousand dollars, or by imprisonment not exceeding one year, or by both said punishments, in the discretion of the court. . . .

[The fine limit was raised to $50,000 in 1955 and to $500,000 for individuals and $1 million for firms in 1974.]

Sec. 4. The several circuit courts of the United States are hereby invested with jurisdiction to prevent and restrain violations of this act; and it shall be the duty of the several district attorneys of the United States, in their respective districts, under the direction of the Attorney General, to institute proceedings in equity to prevent and restrain such violations. Such proceedings may be by way of petition setting forth the case and praying that such violation shall be enjoined or otherwise prohibited. When the parties complained of shall have been duly notified of such petition the court shall proceed, as soon as may be, to the hearing and determination of the case; and pending such petition and before final decree, the court may at any time make such temporary restraining order of prohibition as shall be deemed just in the premises. . . .

Sec. 7. Any person who shall be injured in his business or property by any other person or corporation by reason of anything forbidden or declared to be unlawful by this act, may sue therefore in any circuit court of the United States in the district in which the defendant resides or is found, without respect to the amount in controversy, and shall recover threefold the damages by him sustained, and the cost of suit, including a reasonable attorney's fee.

Note: Section 3 makes the act applicable to territories and the District of Columbia. Section 5 deals with subpoena power of court; Section 6 gives right to seize property of violators in transit; and Section 8 defines "persons" to include associations and corporations.

The Federal Trade Commission Act (1914)

An Act to create a Federal Trade Commission, to define its power and duties, and for other purposes.

Be it enacted by the Senate and House of Representatives of the United States of America in Congress assembled, That a commission is hereby created and established, to be known as the Federal Trade Commission (hereinafter referred to as the commission), which shall be composed of five commissioners, who shall be appointed by the President, by and with the advice and consent of the Senate. Not more than three of the commissioners shall be members of the same political party. The first commissioners appointed shall continue in office for terms of three, four, five, six, and seven years, respectively, from the date of the taking effect of this Act, the term of each to be designated by the President, but their successors shall be appointed for terms of seven years, except that any person chosen to fill a vacancy shall be appointed only for the unexpired term of the commissioner whom he shall succeed. The commission shall choose a chairman from its membership. . . .

Sec. 5. That unfair methods of competition in commerce are hereby declared unlawful.

The commission is hereby empowered and directed to prevent persons, partnerships, or corporations except banks, and common carriers subject to the Act to regulate commerce, from using unfair methods of competition in commerce.

Whenever the commission shall have reason to believe that any such person, partnership, or corporation has been or is using any unfair methods of competition in commerce, and if it shall appear to the commission that a proceeding by it in respect thereof would be to the interest of the public, it shall issue and serve upon such person, partnership, or corporation a complaint stating its charges in that respect, and containing a notice of a hearing upon a day and at a place therein fixed at least thirty days after the service of said complaint. The person, partnership, or corporation so complained of shall have the right to appear at the place and time so fixed and show cause why an order should not be entered by the commission requiring such person, partnership, or corporation to cease and desist from the violation of the law so charged in said complaint. . . . If upon such hearing the commission shall be of the opinion that the method of competition in question is prohibited by this Act, it shall make a report in writing in which it shall state its findings as to the facts, and shall issue and cause to be served on such person, partnership, or corporation an order requiring such person, partnership or corporation to cease and desist from using such method of competition. . . .

If such person, partnership, or corporation fails or neglects to obey such order of the commission while the same is in effect, the commission may apply to the circuit court of appeals of the United States, within any circuit where the method of competition in question was used or where such person, partnership, or corporation resides or carries on business, for the enforcement of its order. . . .

The findings of the commission as to the facts, if supported by testimony, shall be conclusive. . . .

Sec. 6. That the commission shall also have the power—

(a) To gather and compile information concerning, and to investigate from time to time the organization, business, conduct, practices, and management of any corporation engaged in commerce, excepting banks and common carriers subject to the Act to regulate commerce. . . .

(b) To require, by general or special orders, corporations engaged in commerce to file with the commission in such form as the commission may prescribe annual or special reports or answers in writing to specific questions, furnishing to the commission such information as it may require. . . .

(c) Whenever a final decree has been entered against any defendant corporation in any suit brought by the United States to prevent and restrain any violation of the antitrust Acts, to make investigations, upon its own initiative, of the manner in which the decree has been or is being carried out, and upon the application of the Attorney General it shall be its duty to make such investigation.

(d) Upon the direction of the President or either House of Congress to investigate and report the facts relating to any alleged violations of the antitrust Acts by any corporation.

(e) Upon the application of the Attorney General, to investigate and make recommendations for the readjustment of the business of any corporation alleged to be violating the antitrust Acts, in order that the corporation may thereafter maintain its organization, management, and conduct of business in accordance with law.

(f) To make public from time to time such portions of the information obtained by it hereunder, except trade secrets and names of customers, as it shall deem expedient in the public interest; and to make annual and special reports to the Congress and to submit therewith recommendations for additional legislation; and to provide for the publication of its reports and decisions in such form and manner as may be best adapted for public information and use.

(g) From time to time to classify corporations and to make rules and regulations for the purpose of carrying out the provisions of this Act.

(h) To investigate, from time to time, trade conditions in and with foreign countries where associations, combinations, or practices of manufacturers, merchants, or traders, or other conditions, may affect the foreign trade of the United States, and to report to Congress thereon, with such recommendations as it deems advisable. . . .

Sec. 10. That any person who shall neglect or refuse to attend and testify, or to answer any lawful inquiry, or to produce documentary evidence, if in his power to do so, in obedience to the subpoena or lawful requirement of the commission, shall be guilty of an offense and upon conviction thereof by a court of competent jurisdiction shall be punished by a fine of not less than $1,000 nor more than $5,000, or by imprisonment for not more than one year, or by both such fine and imprisonment. [While the fine for violation of an FTC order remains at $5,000, it can be applied for each day of violation.]

The Clayton Act (1915)

An Act to supplement existing laws against unlawful restraints and monopolies, and for other purposes.

Sec. 2. That it shall be unlawful for any person engaged in commerce, in the course of such commerce, either directly or indirectly, to discriminate in price between different purchasers of commodities, which commodities are sold for use, consumption, or resale within the United States or any Territory thereof or the District of Columbia or any insular possession or other place under the jurisdiction of the United States, where the effect of such discrimination *may be to substantially lessen competition or tend to create a monopoly in any line of commerce:* Provided, That nothing herein contained shall prevent discrimination in price between purchasers of commodities on account of differences in the grade, quality, or quantity of the commodity sold, or that makes only due allowance for differences in the cost of selling or transportation, or discrimination in price in the same or different communities made in good faith to meet competition: And provided further, That nothing herein contained shall prevent persons engaged in selling goods, wares, or merchandise in commerce from selecting their own customers in bona fide transactions and not in restraint of trade.

Sec. 3. That it shall be unlawful for any person engaged in commerce, in the course of such commerce, to lease or make a sale or contract for sale of goods, wares, merchandise, machinery, supplies, or other commodities, whether patented or unpatented, for use, consumption, or resale within the United States or any Territory thereof or the District of Columbia or any insular possession or other place under the jurisdiction of the United States, or fix a price charged therefor, or discount from, or rebate upon, such price, on the condition, agreement, or understanding that the lessee or purchaser thereof shall not use or deal in the goods, wares, merchandise, machinery, supplies, or other commodity of a competitor or competitors of the lessor or seller, where the effect of such lease, sale, or contract for sale or such condition, agreement, or understanding may be to substantially lessen competition or tend to create a monopoly in any line of commerce.

Note: Sections 4 and 5 provide, respectively, for triple damage suits by private injured parties and fo final judgments in a suit brought by the government as being prima-facie evidence in private suits in the matters involved.

Sec. 6. That the labor of a human being is not a commodity or an article of commerce. Nothing contained in the antitrust laws shall be construed to forbid the existence and operation of labor, agricultural, or horticultural organizations, instituted for the purposes of mutual help, and not having capital stock or conducted for profits, or to forbid or restrain individual members of such organizations from lawfully carrying out the legitimate objects thereof; nor shall such organizations, or the members thereof, be held or construed to be illegal combinations or conspiracies in restraint of trade under the antitrust laws.

Sec. 7. That no corporation engaged in commerce shall acquire, directly or indirectly, the whole or any part of the stock or other share capital of another corporation engaged also in commerce where the effect of such acquisition may be to substantially lessen competition between the corporation whose stock is so acquired and the corporation making the acquisition or to restrain such commerce in any section or community or tend to create a monopoly of any line of commerce. . . .

Sec. 8. . . . That from and after two years from the date of the approval of this Act no person at the same time shall be a director in any two or more corporations, any one of which has capital, surplus, and undivided profits aggregating more than $1,000,000, engaged in whole or in part in commerce, other than banks, banking associations, trust companies, and common carriers subject to the Act to regulate commerce, approved February fourth, eighteen hundred and eighty-seven, if such corporations are or shall have been theretofore, by virtue of their business and location of operation, competitors, so that the elimination of competition by agreement between them would constitute a violation of any of the provisions of any of the antitrust laws. . . .

Sec. 11. That authority to enforce compliance with sections two, three, seven, and eight of this Act by the persons respectively subject thereto is hereby vested: in the Interstate Commerce Commission where applicable to common carriers, in the Federal Reserve Board where applicable to banks, banking associations, and trust companies, and in the Federal Trade Commission where applicable to all other character of commerce. . . .

Sec. 14. That whenever a corporation shall violate any of the penal provisions of the antitrust laws, such violation shall be deemed to be also that of the individual directors, officers, or agents of such corporation who shall have authorized, ordered, or done any of the acts constituting in whole or in part such violation, and such violation shall be deemed a misdemeanor, and upon conviction therefor of any such director, officer, or agent he shall be punished by a fine of not exceeding $5,000 or by imprisonment for not exceeding one year, or by both, in the discretion of the court.

Sec. 15. That the several district courts of the United States are hereby invested with jurisdiction to prevent and restrain violations of this Act, and it shall be the duty of the several district attorneys of the United States, in their respective districts, under the direction of the Attorney General, to institute proceedings in equity to prevent and restrain such violations. . . .

Robinson-Patman Amendment to the Clayton Act (1936)

An Act to amend section 2 of the Act entitled "An Act to supplement existing laws against unlawful restraints and monopolies, and for other purposes," approved October 15, 1914, as amended (U.S.C., title 15, sec. 13), and for other purposes.

Be it enacted by the Senate and House of Representatives of the United States of America in Congress assembled, That section 2 of the Act entitled 'An Act to supplement existing laws against unlawful restraints and monopolies, and for other purposes' approved October 15, 1914, as amended (U.S.C., title 15, sec. 13), is amended to read as follows:

'Sec. 2. (a) That it shall be unlawful for any person engaged in commerce, in the course of such commerce, either directly or indirectly, to discriminate in price between different purchasers of commodities of like grade and quality, where either of any of the purchases involved in such discrimination are in commerce, where such commodities are sold for use, consumption, or resale within the United States, or any Territory thereof or the District of Columbia or any insular possession or other place under the jurisdiction of the United States, and where the effect of such discrimination may be substantially to lessen competition or tend to create a monopoly in any line of commerce, or to injure, destroy, or prevent competition with any person who either grants or knowingly receives the benefit of such discrimination, or with customers of either of them: Provided, That nothing herein contained shall prevent differentials which make only due allowance for differences in the cost of manufacture, sale, or delivery resulting from the differing methods or quantities in which such commodities are to such purchasers sold or delivered: Provided, however, That the Federal Trade Commission may, after due investigation and hearing to all interested parties, fix and establish quantity limits, and revise the same as it finds necessary, as to particular commodities or classes of commodities, where it finds that available purchasers in greater quantities are so few to render differentials on account thereof unjustly discriminatory or promotive of monopoly in any line of commerce; and the foregoing shall then not be construed to permit differentials based on differences in quantities greater than those so fixed and established: And provided further, That nothing herein contained shall prevent persons engaged in selling goods, wares, or merchandise in commerce from selecting their own customers in bona fide transactions and not in restraint of trade: And provided further, That nothing herein contained shall prevent price changes from time to time where in response to changing conditions affecting the market for or the marketability of the goods concerned, such as but not limited to actual or imminent deterioration of perishable goods, obsolescence of seasonal goods, distress sales under the court process, or sales in good faith in discontinuance of business in the goods concerned.

'(b) Upon proof being made, at any hearing on a complaint under this section, that there has been discrimination in price or services or facilities furnished, the burden of rebutting the prima-facie case thus made by showing justification shall be upon the person charged with a violation of this section, and unless justification shall be affirmatively shown, the Commission is authorized to issue an order terminating the discrimination: Provided, however, That nothing herein contained shall prevent a seller rebutting the prima-facie case thus made by showing that his lower price or the furnishing of services or facilities to any purchaser or purchasers was made in good faith to meet an equally low price of a competitor, or the services or facilities furnished by a competitor.

'(c) That it shall be unlawful for any person engaged in commerce, in the course of such commerce, to pay or grant, or to receive or accept, anything of value as a commission, brokerage, or other compensation, or any allowance or discount in lieu therof, except for services rendered in connection with the sale or purchase of goods, wares, or merchandise, either to the other party to such transaction or to an agent, representative, or other intermediary therein where such intermediary is acting in fact for or in behalf, or is subject to the direct or indirect control, of any party to such transaction other than the person by whom such compensation is so granted or paid.

'(d) That it shall be unlawful for any person engaged in commerce to pay or contract for the payment of anything of value to or for the benefit of a customer of such person in the course of such commerce as compensation or in consideration for any services or the processing, handling, sale, or offering for sale of any products or commodities manufactured, sold, or offered for sale by such person, unless such payment or consideration is available on proportionally equal terms to all other customers competing in the distribution of such products or commodities.

'(e) That it shall be unlawful for any person to discriminate in favor of one purchaser against another purchaser or purchasers of a commodity bought for resale, with or without processing, by contracting to furnish or furnishing, or by contributing to the furnishing of, any services or facilities connected with the processing, handling, sale, or offering for sale of such commodity so purchased upon terms not accorded to all purchasers on proportionally equal terms.

'(f) That it shall be unlawful for any person engaged in commerce, in the course of such commerce, knowingly to induce or receive a discrimination in price which is prohibited by this section.'

Note: Section 3 of the act, which has not been used, prohibits regional price discrimination for the purpose of "destroying competiton or eliminating a competitor."

Wheeler-Lea Amendment to the Federal Trade Commission Act (1938)

To amend the Act creating the Federal Trade Commission, to define its powers and duties, and for other purposes.

Sec. 3. Section 5 of such Act, as amended (U.S.C., 1934 ed., title 15, sec. 45), is hereby amended to read as follows:

'Sec. 5. (a) Unfair methods of competition in commerce, and unfair or deceptive acts or practices in commerce, are hereby declared unlawful.'

Sec. 4. Such Act is further amended by adding at the end thereof new sections to read as follows:

'Sec. 12. (a) It shall be unlawful for any person, partnership, or corporation to disseminate, or cause to be disseminated, any false advertisement—

'(1) By United States mails, or in commerce by any other means, for the purpose of inducing, or which is likely to induce, directly or indirectly, the purchase in commerce of food, drugs, devices, or cosmetics, or (2) By any means, for the purpose of inducing, or which is likely to induce, directly or indirectly, the purchase in commerce of food, drugs, devices, or cosmetics.

'(b) The dissemination or the causing to be disseminated of any false advertisement within the provisions of subsection (a) of this section shall be an unfair or deceptive act or practice in commerce within the meaning of section 5.'

Antimerger Amendment of 1950

To amend an Act entitled 'An Act to supplement existing laws against unlawful restraints and monopolies, and for other purposes,' approved October 15, 1914 (38 Stat. 730), as amended.

Be it enacted by the Senate and House of Representatives of the United States of America in Congress assembled. That sections 7 and 11 of an Act entitled 'An Act to supplement existing laws against unlawful restraints and monopolies, and for other purposes,' approved October 15, 1914, as amended (U.S.C., title 15, secs. 18 and 21), are hereby amended to read as follows:

'No corporation shall acquire, directly or indirectly, the whole or any part of the stock or other share capital and no corporation subject to the jurisdiction of the Federal Trade Commission shall acquire the whole or any part of the assets of one or more corporations engaged in commerce, where in any line of commerce in any section of the country, the effect of such acquisition, of such stocks or assets, or of the use of such stock by the voting or granting of proxies or otherwise, may be substantially to lessen competition, or to tend to create a monopoly. . . .'

CASE 18–1 _____
The Electrical Price Conspiracy Cases and
General Electric Directive 20.5*

On February 6 and 7, 1961, Judge J. Cullen Ganey, in the U.S. District Court in Philadelphia, fined 29 corporations engaged in the manufacture of electrical equipment a total of $1,787,000 (General Electric paying $437,500; Westinghouse, $372,500). In addition, he fined 44 executives of these firms $137,500 and sentenced 30 of these men to 30 days in jail. All but seven were given suspended sentences "reluctantly," Judge Ganey said, because of the defendant's age, health, or family situation. The seven ordered to jail the following week included three men from GE, two from Westinghouse, and one each from Cutler-Hammer, Inc., and Clark Controller Company. (Eight of the suspended jail sentences went to GE men.)

The sentencing by Judge Ganey brought to a close the first phase of the antitrust suits brought a year earlier in Judge Ganey's courtroom by

_____
*SOURCE: The authors acknowledge the assistance of Clarkson students John Thorne and David Banker in securing material for this case which has been prepared from various news and other sources of the time and from General Electric's Policy Directive 20.5.

Attorney General William Rogers and his Antitrust Division head, Robert Bicks. The sentences ended the criminal cases brought by the federal government, but still remaining were civil suits concerned with the same offenses. Companies involved in criminal cases may be fined up to $50,000 for each offense; individuals may be fined up to $10,000 and sentenced to a year in prison, or both. Most of Judge Ganey's sentences were less than those recommended by the government prosecutors. No testimony about the alleged offenses had been heard by Judge Ganey, since all defendants had pleaded either guilty (in the seven suits regarded as "major" by the Department of Justice), or *nolo contendere* (no contest, admitting no guilt but not fighting the charges) in the remaining 13 suits. Yet to be filed were numerous suits by purchasers of equipment against the manufacturers as a consequence of the sentences. Such suits would allege overpayments by these purchasers coupled with a demand for reimbursement and perhaps for treble damages as well.

The case had begun with the empaneling in 1959 of a grand jury in Philadelphia to hear evidence presented by the Antitrust Division, subpoena documents (since it was to consider the return of criminal indictments), and subpoena individuals. A second grand jury was empaneled in mid-November 1959. More and more evidence was presented to the two grand juries; and on February 16 and 17, 1960, they handed down the first 7 indictments, charging 40 companies and 18 individuals with fixing prices or dividing the market. Thirteen more indictments followed during 1960. The Justice Department filed a deposition opposing the acceptance of *nolo* pleas, and Judge Ganey so ruled at the arraignment on the first seven indictments in April 1960. At that time, Allis-Chalmers and its employees pleaded "guilty"; most others pleaded "not guilty." As more evidence came to the attention of the companies involved, however, an effort at rapid settlement was made. On October 31, 1960, attorneys for the companies and for the Justice Department worked out a package of guilty pleas in the seven major cases and nolo pleas in the others. These pleas were heard and accepted by Judge Ganey in December 1960, and the stage was set for the sentencing in February 1961.

In announcing the sentences, Judge Ganey stated:

> This is a shocking indictment of a vast section of our economy, for what is really at stake here is the survival of the kind of economy under which America has grown to greatness, the free enterprise system.
>
> The conduct of the corporate and individual defendants alike, in the words of the distinguished assistant attorney general [Bicks] who headed the Antitrust Division of the Department of Justice, have flagrantly mocked the image of that economic system of free enterprise which we profess to the country and destroyed the model which we offer today as a free world alternative to state control and eventual dictatorship. Some extent of the vastness of the schemes for price fixing, bid rigging and job allocations can be gleaned from the fact that the annual corporate sales covered by these bills of indictment represent a billion and three-quarter dollars. . . .
>
> It is not to be taken as disparaging of the long and arduous effort the

Government has made, and even more the highly efficient and competent manner of its doing, that only in these instances where ultimate responsibility for corporate conduct amongst those indicted, vested, are prison sentences to be imposed. Rather am I convinced that in the great number of these defendants' cases, they were torn between conscience and an approved corporate policy, with the rewarding objectives of promotion, comfortable security and large salaries—in short, the organization or the company man, the conformist, who goes along with his superiors and finds balm for his conscience in additional comforts and the security of his place in the corporate set-up.[27]

Some Facts Concerning the Price Conspiracies

The electrical conspiracy involved numerous independent agreements to fix prices on particular types of electrical equipment. At the time of the initial jury investigation, some of the conspiracies had been in operation for as long as eight years. Twenty-nine manufacturers of electrical equipment were involved including such firms as General Electric, Westinghouse, and Allis-Chalmers. Prices were fixed on electrical equipment ranging in size and value from $2 insulators to multimillion dollar turbines. As indicated by Judge Ganey's summary, annual sales of the products involved at one time or another in the charges was $1,750,000,000.[28]

Economic reasons for the price fixing included these: During the 1950s the entire industry was plagued with overcapacity. The major manufacturers were faced with increased competition from smaller manufacturers who began broadening their product lines. The industry's position was further weakened by the wide usage of the competitive sealed bid. Competitive bidding in some cases had resulted in price quotations on heavy equipment that gave discounts as high as 50 percent off list. General Electric, the major company involved and the one without which the conspiracy could not have taken place, faced organizational problems.

The company had been reorganized into a decentralized structure in 1950 when Ralph Cordiner took over as president. General Electric was divided into 110 nearly autonomous companies. The head of each company was given responsibility for operating results as well as the price level on goods his branch produced. Under Cordiner, the company heads were faced with strong pressure to increase profits as a percentage of sales and at the same time to increase sales volume. Given the intense competition and overcapacity, these goals were incompatible. One approach accepted by several General Electric managers was to meet with officials from other companies and and to predetermine price levels. An important

---

[27]These introductory paragraphs were prepared by Dr. John A. Larson from contemporary news reports as an introduction to case MR216R1 of the Northwestern University School of Business.

[28]"The Incredible Electrical Conspiracy," *Fortune*, April 1961, p. 132 summarizes many of these.

example involved price fixing on switch gear equipment. Between 1951 and 1958 the conspiracy affected some $650 million worth of sales. Sales were broken down into two categories—sealed and open bids. The sealed bid business was divided among four companies (the only producers in the United States at that time) on a fixed percentage basis. General Electric was allotted 45 percent; Westinghouse, 35 percent; Allis-Chalmers, 10 percent; and Federal Pacific, 10 percent. Meetings were held periodically to determine who would get what bids and what the price should be for the prechosen successful bidder.

The open bid market was controlled by upper level executives (general managers and vice presidents) who met to set book prices. (Attendance lists at these meetings were called Christmas card lists and meetings were called, oddly enough, "choir practices." Each company was given a code number; GE–1, Westinghouse–2, Allis-Chalmers–3, Federal Pacific–7, to be used for telephone communication. The companies were tempted to and often did break the rules by secretly setting lower prices on bids. Occasionally one of the companies would become dissatisfied with its market share and would go it alone on the open market for a period of time. In late 1953, General Electric dropped out of the conspiracy. In 1954–55, the famous "white sale" occurred in which prices on all types of electrical equipment were discounted by as much as 45 percent off book. Hard hit by the sale, the General Electric switch gear division decided to reactivate the old cartel arrangements that were reasonably successful in 1956 and early 1957. These arrangements broke down in 1957 when a discount violating the agreement by Westinghouse instituted a chain reaction that resulted in a price war similar to that of 1954–55.

In 1958, the cartel was reborn with revised shares for sealed bids. General Electric was reduced from 45 percent to 40.3 percent, Westinghouse from 35 percent to 31.3 percent, and Allis-Chalmers from 10 percent to 8.8 percent. Federal Pacific was increased to 15.6 percent, and I-T-E received a 4 percent allotment. This last stage relied upon a formula based on the phases of the moon to determine successful bidders and prices.

The year 1959 was the beginning of the end for the electrical conspiracies. The TVA had become extremely suspicious concerning the almost identical bids and rapid price hikes on turbine generators and had informed the federal government of its suspicions. The Antitrust Division was able to build up evidence by using relevant documents that had been obtained under subpoena to get testimony from individuals with lesser involvement. The ultimate object was to determine whether the major manufacturers and top executives were active participants in the conspiracy. As William Maher, chief of the Antitrust's Division at Philadelphia, put it, the idea was to "go after the biggest fish in the smallest companies, then hope to get enough information to land the biggest fish in the biggest companies."[29]

---

[29]*Fortune*, May 1961, p. 163.

General Electric Directive 20.5

General Electric had a specific, written "Directive Policy," which could not be rescinded or changed by any member of management, for compliance with the antitrust laws. It had originally been issued in 1946, and in an amended version at the time of the antitrust trials it was a one-page document. It briefly stated the need for a Directive Policy because of the decentralization of the company and of the substantial injuries to the company that could result from "expensive litigation, treble damage liability, and injunctions or orders affecting its property and business."

The Directive Policy itself was a few short paragraphs stating:

> It is the Policy of the Company to comply strictly in all respects with the anti-trust laws. There shall be no exception to this Policy nor shall it be compromised or qualified by anyone acting for or on behalf of the Company.
>
> No employee shall enter into any understanding, agreement, plan or scheme, expressed or implied, formal or informal, with any competitor, in regard to prices, terms or conditions of sale, production, distribution, territories or customers; nor exchange or discuss with a competitor prices, terms or conditions of sale or any other competitive information; nor engage in any other conduct which in the opinion of the Company's counsel violates any of the anti-trust laws.
>
> Each employee responsible for the Company's conduct or practices which may involve the application of the anti-trust laws should consult and be guided by the advice of counsel assigned to his component.
>
> Where an employee who has acted in good faith upon the advice of counsel for the Company nevertheless becomes involved in an anti-trust proceeding, the Company will be prepared to assist and defend the employee through attorneys representing the Company in the case. However, if an employee is convicted of violating the law, the Company cannot as a matter of law save the employee from whatever punishment the court may impose upon him as a consequence of such conviction.
>
> It is the obligation of each employee of the Company in his area of responsibility to adhere to the above stated Policy.

The fact that the policy had not been a complete success was indicated by 36 successful antitrust suits against General Electric since 1941.

Dealing with the Convicted Executives

One of the troublesome issues that Ralph Cordiner, then chairman of the board of General Electric, had to face was that of company sanctions against the executives involved. In January 1960, he stated that after careful consideration,

> I came to the only possible conclusion: that the Company could not ignore such flagrant disregard of the Company Directive Policy 20.5. . . .
>
> A man who is General Manager has tremendous ethical responsibilities. He must also be held accountable for his own performance and the performance of his Component. Thus I concluded that the persons responsible for these violations of Company policy must be disciplined by such penal-

ties as resignations from their officership, removal from their present assignments, demotion in rank, decrease in pay, and assignment to positions where the offenders can have no authority or responsibility for pricing. These penalties are being imposed as rapidly as the cases of violation can be fairly reviewed and as the restaffing can be carried out consistent with maintaining service to customers and protecting the jobs of innocent employees.[30]

Within two months of the time of the sentencing, all 16 executives of General Electric had resigned from the company, and later interviews indicated that at least some of the resignations were forced. Other corporate defendants were much more lenient than General Electric, and in most cases their convicted executives continued their roles with the company. They justified this leniency on the grounds that the executives had been punished sufficiently and had essentially been acting in their companies' interests as they saw them.

Top Management's Responsibility

One of the most embarrassing aspects of the case to the top management of General Electric was the question raised as to how it could have been unaware of price conspiracies that were so widespread. Senator Estes Kefauver addressed Mr. Cordiner after a congressional hearing in which Cordiner had testified as follows: "It is hard to understand how you in sales and executive positions did not find out and know about or were not put on your suspicion about these meetings with competitors until so late in the game."[31]

John Brooks wrote a satirical article, "The Curious Wink," for the New Yorker whose theme was the apparent difficulty of communication in General Electric and raised the question of whether the administration of Directive Policy 20.5 was sometimes conducted with a wink.[32]

At the 1961 stockholders' meeting, resolutions offered by James B. Carey, president of the International Union of Electrical, Radio and Machine Workers were decisively beaten. One proposed:

> Resolved that the Directors of General Electric Company appoint an impartial committee of recognized integrity, none of the members of which is an officer, director or employee of the Company, to investigate and determine (1) whether the Chairman of the Board, any other directors, or any officers of the Company reasonably should have known of the existence of the conspiracy to violate the Federal anti-trust laws prior to the 1960 indictments; and (2) whether the Incentive Compensation Plan or any other

---

[30]Speech of Ralph G. Cordiner at General Electric Management Conference, Hot Springs, Va., Janury 5, 1960.

[31]Hearing of the Subcommittee on Antitrust and Monopoly of the Senate Judiciary Committee, June 5, 1961.

[32]John Brooks, "The Curious Wink," New Yorker, May 26, 1967.

incentive policies of the Company serve to encourage its officers and employees to engage in such conduct. . . .[33]

The Civil Suits and Consent Decrees

In addition to the criminal suits, the electrical companies were subject to 18 civil suits covering the conspiracies. The government's purpose was to get court injunctions against the practices involved that would permit quicker and more rigorous action since future violations could be adjudged as being in contempt of court. Rather than going to trial, the companies chose to negotiate consent decrees. After tough bargaining with the Justice Department, all 18 suits were settled by consent decrees on September 25, 1962; General Electric agreed to such provisions as the issuance of new price lists, independently arrived at, for each of the 18 product lines (involving about $500 million in annual sales), the submitting of affidavits swearing each sealed bid to the government was made independently, and the selling of component parts to less integrated manufacturers.

The Private Treble Damage Suits

Altogether 2,000 suits were filed, mostly by utility companies. Proving damages was not simple particularly since there was no trial record because all of the criminal cases had been settled by "guilty" or "nolo contendere" pleas. The basic principle was to try to establish the difference between what prices would have been without the conspiracy and with it. The first settlement by General Electric was for $7,470,000 on government purchases mostly by the TVA. This represented a little over 10 percent of purchases of $69.6 million of GE products covered by the suits. General Electric did not concede that customers had been damaged but pushed a policy that it was worth money to compromise to get cases settled. By 1965, most of the major suits were settled. General Electric had paid out $225 million and estimated that this would be 99 percent of the total. (About $110 million had been paid by Westinghouse and $45 million by Allis Chalmers.)[34]

Company Policy 20.5, as of June 8, 1964

This postconspiracy version of the directive was expanded to four pages with two additional pages outlining the procedures for compliance. It included an acknowledgement sheet for the employee to sign. This indicated the employee's understanding and compliance. A second signature was required by a manager who thus indicated that the policy had been reviewed with the individual. Along with the directive were 19 pages summarizing the provisions and giving guides for compliance with Sections 1 and 2 of the Sherman Act; Sections 2 (as amended by the

---

[33]*General Electric Notice of Annual Meeting and Proxy Statement*, March 17, 1961, pp. 23–34. This notice included a lengthy review of the antitrust cases.

[34]"The High Cost of Price-Fixing," *Time*, September 10, 1965.

Robinson-Patman Act), 3, and 7 (as amended in 1950) of the Clayton Act; and Section 5 of the Federal Trade Commission Act.

Added provisions to the Directive Policy itself that seem to reflect the convictions of 1961 include:[35]

As to Need:

The character of our free society and the unmatched success of the economy of the United States is based solidly on the concept of a free and competitive market. The future of the General Electric Company depends upon the continued existence of such a free, competitive market. Our growth and success will reflect the extent to which we are able to innovate, to provide superior products and services to our customers and to show competitive initiative in all areas of the Company's business. In General Electric, the only effective and enduring business philosophy is one of fair, vigorous competition. As a matter of good business judgment, there is no excuse for collusive activities in violation of the antitrust laws. As a matter of economic, ethical and legal principle, it is the unequivocal policy of the Company to avoid actions which in any way restrain or restrict competition in violation of the antitrust laws.

As to Application:

The provisions of this Directive Policy prescribe mandatory courses of action upon all Company officers and managers. No employee has any authority to act in any manner inconsistent with the provisions of this Directive Policy, to qualify or compromise it, nor to authorize, direct, or condone violations of its terms by another.

As to Relationship with Competitors:

. . . no employee shall give to or accept from a competitor, nor discuss with a competitor, any information concerning prices, terms or conditions of sale, or other competitive information.

As to Company Discipline:

Any employee who violates, or who orders or knowingly permits a subordinate to violate, this Policy, shall be subject to severe disciplinary or other appropriate action, including discharge.

Similarly the Procedure for Compliance provisions seemed influenced by the case in the following provisions:

As to Auditors:

At the request of the General Counsel and in consultation with him, the Comptroller has devised and put into effect a continuing program whereby the Traveling Auditors on his staff expand the scope of their regular audits to examine in depth any records which may indicate the failure of employees to abide by the Company's Directive Policy 20.5.

As to Supervision:

Furthermore, it is the basic responsibility of each Manager to ask each employee, directly, any specific questions concerning the subject matter of, and compliance with, Directive Policy 20.5 which may seem appropriate in the light of the duties of the particular employee. . . . It is one objective

---

[35]"Directive Policy on the Compliance by the Company and Its Employees with the Antitrust Laws," June 8, 1964, General Electric Co., pp. 1–3, 7, 15.

of this procedure to develop at an early state information on any areas of operations which are generating doubts among our own people before such doubts arise outside the Company. . . .

Careful examination and inquiry will continuously be made by each General Manager into any circumstances which might evidence lack of vigorous competition in the business of any Department.

Guides to Compliance:

For Section 1 of the Sherman Act the following guides to relationship with competitors were given:

Compete vigorously and independently at *all* times and in *every* ethical way.

Maintain your own freedom to compete by avoiding any kind of agreements or "gentlemen's understandings" with representatives of competitors . . .

Act at all times so your customers, the public and the trade press will know that you are competing vigorously . . .

Secure from the market place—and not from competitors—as much "competitive intelligence" about your competition as you ethically can.

Vigorous competition frequently produces or compels similarity or identity of competitor's prices, programs or policies. Your business records should be such as to demonstrate that decisions concerning your prices, policies and programs are the result of your *independent* judgment, and not agreements or understandings with others.

Questions

1. What three legal weapons were available to the government and injured parties under Section 1? What decisions did General Electric have to make upon how to confront each?

2. The production of electrical equipment involves heavy capital and other fixed costs. Discuss the apparent demand and cost situation in the 1950s that made conspiracy particularly tempting.

3. How might the revisions in policy statement 20.5 make it more effective?

CASE 18–2
Telex versus IBM: The Problem of
Plug Compatible Peripherals*

Introductory Note

As indicated in the chapter, Telex lost the battle but won the initial skirmish. This case, written from the perspective of 1975, illustrates the

---

*source: In the technical jargon of the day, plug compatible peripherals are ancillary equipment such as memory units that can be used with, that is, plugged into, the main computer unit. The body of the case was written by Daniel H. Forbush, and the authors express their appreciation for his permission to edit and use it.

continuing managerial problems for a dominant firm of competing strongly yet fairly. From 1974 to 1978, IBM's share of worldwide shipments of computer systems were estimated to have dropped from 70 to 58 percent. In 1979, however, new threats for competitors were raised by the introduction of the 4300 line with greatly improved price-performance ratios.

"In the constellation of multinational corporations," wrote William Rodgers, "International Business Machines illuminates the economic firmament more than any other."[36] In early 1974, IBM's 575,000 stockholders owned 146,061,750 shares with a sale value of $36.5 billion. IBM was marketing its products in four out of every five nations on earth. It ranked sixth among U.S. corporations in total revenue. Predicted by some to become the world's largest corporation by the end of the century, IBM's net income for the second quarter of 1974 was up 35 percent from the year before, the highest such increase in the company's history.

This was hardly the description of a firm in trouble. Yet in recent years, IBM has undeniably fallen in uncomfortable straits. Its more serious problems have been of a legal nature and, ironically, stem to a large degree from its own incredible success. By a combination of marketing genius, technological wizardry, and both proved and alleged anticompetitive business practice, IBM has captured and maintained between 70 percent to 80 percent control of the domestic computer business and half the world market. IBM has become a potential antitrust defendant.

The Antitrust Assault

The assault came on two main fronts. The first attack came from the Justice Department on the last business day of the Johnson administration. For monopolizing the electronic data processing industry and particularly the mainframe market, the government sought a radical restructuring of IBM into "several, discrete, competitive entities."

It was not the first time that IBM and the Justice Department have confronted each other. In 1935, IBM was found guilty by a federal court of illegally requiring lessees of its tabulating machines to buy punch cards exclusively from IBM. In 1952, the Justice Department charged IBM with monopolizing the tabulating-machine business itself but a trial was averted when IBM accepted a consent decree from governmental lawyers four years later.

A less drastic but costly threat to IBM is the second source of legal attacks the giant must defend itself against—its bloodied competition, Control Data Corporation, which pioneered the development of huge computers, filed against IBM in late 1968, a month before the Justice Department. It charged IBM with, among other things, attempting to ruin Control Data's market by announcing large computers it had no intention of producing (as Control Data put it, "paper machines and phantom computers"). The case was later settled out of court with IBM paying Control

---

[36]William Rodgers, "IBM on Trial," *Harpers*, May 1974, p. 79.

Data roughly \$110 million and Control Data turning over to IBM the \$3 million index of internal IBM documents it had made in preparation for the case. Since then, other firms have followed Control Data's lead. In the spring of 1974, a total of 12 punitive and triple-damage suits were pending against IBM, seeking a collective \$4.3 billion.[37]

Large as that sum may seem, it could go higher. IBM lost a monopolization suit to the Telex Corporation in 1973 and was assessed \$259 million in damages. It faces a rash of additional suits from other manufacturers of computer accessories if the verdict withstands IBM's appeal. As many as 40 firms, according to a 1974 estimate, were in position to file. With a catalogue of IBM's anticompetitive practices already on the record as a result of the Telex action (it obtained 40,000 internal IBM documents to make its case), all a potential litigant needs, "is a Xerox machine and a month of discovery to bring the record up to date."[38]

The Telex case involved a far narrower issue than the Justice Department suit. While the government accused IBM of a broad range of monopolistic practices in a number of computer markets, the Telex decision dealt only with IBM's dominance and marketing practices in accessories for IBM's own computers. These accessories are such peripheral "plug compatible" products as magnetic tape and disk storage devices (upon which information is stored and fed into the "mainframe" or "central processing unit"), main memories, printers, and communication controllers.

In further contrast to the government's suit, which considers IBM's behavior over an extended period, the time frame of the Telex suit is just four years—1969 through the recession in 1970 and 1971 to recovery in 1972. This was a critical time for the industry, bringing the first serious sales downturn it had ever suffered. Revenue rose 6 percent or less in 1970 and 1971 compared to regular annual increases of 10 percent before 1969. Total shipments of new equipment actually dropped slightly in 1970. IBM was additionally pressed by the infant independent peripheral manufacturers who, offering products equivalent to IBM's at lower prices, found ready acceptance by budget-conscious computer users. For its attempt to "destroy" this new competition by predatory pricing practices and market strategy "bearing no relationship to technological skill, industry, appropriate foresight, or customer benefit," Judge A. Sherman Christensen found IBM in violation of Section 2 of the Sherman Act.

The Plug Compatible Problem

The origin of IBM's plug compatible competition was uncomplicated. Du Pont, discontented in 1966 with an IBM refusal to lower its price on a

---

[37]Ibid., p. 81.

[38]The estimator and source of the quotation is Jack Biddle, executive director of the Computer Industry Association, as quoted in *Business Week*, September 22, 1973, pp. 18–20.

tape drive, asked Telex, a relatively small communications outfit based in Tulsa, Oklahoma, to copy the device. Others spotted their opportunity in the field and moved in. Output grew rapidly in the latter part of the 1960s, and the independents moved into production of the newer, faster disk drives in addition to the tape units. By the turn of the decade, plug compatible equipment was recognized as an important market in itself.[39]

"Their business strategy was magnificently simple," says *Fortune* magazine of the peripherals. "Copy and, where possible, improve upon an IBM design, and undersell IBM to its own customers."[40] Through "reverse engineering," which meant simply purchasing a device from IBM, disassembling it, and erecting an assembly line to produce a similar machine, the independents offered savings of about 20 percent on IBM equivalents. Frequently they offered a better product as well. While IBM, making its pitch as a "total systems vendor," hung on to the large majority of the market share, sophisticated users turned increasingly to the independents.

For the independents, 1970 was a heady year. In that year they shipped half of all disk and tape drives they had ever installed. The purchase value of the plug compatible manufacturers doubled in the period, from $150 million at the end of 1969 to more than $300 million by the end of 1970. Of the tape drives attached to IBM mainframes in 1976, 13 percent had been installed by independents, while 6 percent of the disk drives had been installed by independents. This was in a market that only a few years before had been 100 percent IBM's.

How did the independents penetrate the once exclusive province of IBM so quickly? For one thing, IBM's pricing policies, which yielded profits as high as 50 percent on some items, created an umbrella wide enough for the peripheral manufacturers to slip beneath. In addition, IBM failed to devote the same development effort to its peripherals that it did to the development of its mainframes. As a result, most of IBM's peripheral products were regarded as inferior, even by IBM management. In a frank evaluation of 26 pieces of equipment in its own product line, IBM judged 16 as deficient, 4 superior, and 6 as equal to the competition.[41]

The incursion by the independents might seem to testify against IBM's possession of undue market power. But it was not until 1970 that IBM took steps to counter the problem. When the U.S. Budget Bureau advised government agencies to switch to non-IBM peripherals in early 1970, IBM executives became alarmed. In February, the peripheral problem was designated a "key corporate strategic issue," and a month later a "peripherals task force" was appointed to, among other things, recommend product strategies to impede the growth of the competition.

---

[39]Except when other citations are given, text material is based on the opinion of Judge A. Sherman Christensen handed down in the United States District Court, Tulsa, Okla. (September 17, 1973).

[40]Louis Beman, "IBM's Travails in Lilliput," *Fortune*, November 1973, pp. 148–50.

[41]Rodgers, "IBM on Trial," pp. 82–83.

The task force urged counteraction in the form of faster development of its peripheral products including improvements midway through a product's life cycle. Called "mid-life enhancements," the improvements were intended to make competitors' inventories obsolete. The task force further recommended consideration of price changes. This advice was put into effect in September, 1970, when IBM announced a new bargain-priced disk drive publicly called the 2319A. Internally, however, it was known as "the Mallard" and actually was nothing more than a reworked disk drive first delivered over three years earlier. But this time the device was priced about 25 percent lower and was available only to customers buying or leasing new systems. It fit only one new IBM computer. The object of Mallard was to reach those customers who were looking for lower prices—and who were thus most susceptible to buying from IBM's competition—without cutting prices for all users. That route would have reduced IBM's revenue by an estimated $120 million a year.[42]

By the fall of 1970, a second peripherals task force had concluded that Memorex and Telex were IBM's strongest competitors in disk drives. It was demonstrated that should IBM cut prices on its other disk drives to a point below the price of the plug compatible equivalents, Memorex and Telex too would have to cut prices with a "very serious impact" on the profits and revenues of both.

In December, IBM broadened its price reductions to all its disk devices. As expected, the independents dropped their prices and, as expected, they were hurt. But from February 12 to April 9, 1971, they increased their installation of disk drives more than 50 percent and threatened to erode IBM's control over printers and memories. Telex still appeared to IBM as a "viable" competitor that could "manage impressive earnings." Clearly, a stronger remedy was required.

It came in late May in the announcement of the "Fixed Term Plan," which called for extended leases of IBM peripherals at sharply reduced rates. To offset the losses in revenue, IBM called for a 3 percent to 8 percent increase in the price of its central processing units. Under FTP, for customers willing to lease IBM peripherals for one or two years, the saving was 8 or 16 percent respectively. For some users, the saving went as high as 30 percent because extra-use charges on IBM computers were also eliminated. "It's a shocker," said a New York securities analyst at the time. "IBM is just wrecking the profitability of the whole area."[43]

FTP was indeed strong medicine. As it turned out, it was also the cure. IBM's Commercial Analysis Section, described as "a kind of corporate CIA," reported happily at the end of the year that the monthly sales of the plug compatibles were off 48 percent in disks and 62 percent in tapes. Badly battered, Telex filed suit against IBM on January 21, 1972.

---

[42]Beman, "IBM's Travails in Lilliput."

[43]*Business Week*, September 22, 1973, p. 19.

Provision of the Judge's Decision

The day Judge Christensen announced his decision in Tulsa's District Court—September 17, 1973—the level of IBM stock plunged 26 points. The firm was in shock. From its point of view, the plug compatibles were parasites who would not even have had a market if not for IBM's mainframes. Cutting prices and temporarily lowering profits—swallowing "whatever financial pills are required . . . irrespective of financial considerations of one or two years," as Chairman Thomas Watson, Jr. urged in a particularly damaging memo—seemed natural to IBM if that would make its competitors reluctant to challenge its dominance again. According to *Fortune* magazine, IBM's lawyers were so certain of their legal grounds they made no serious effort to settle out of court with Telex.[44] The Greyhound Corporation, after all, had filed charges against IBM in 1970 and the judge not only dismissed the complaint but complimented IBM for its diligence and competence. Christensen rejected IBM's contention that the relevant market in the case was the entire electronic data processing industry. Instead, he limited it to peripheral devices plug compatible with IBM central processing units.

"If the percentage of a relevant market controlled by an alleged monopolist is high, an inference of market power may be drawn," he ruled. "Market power," he said, "was simply the economic ability to charge unreasonable high prices and to exclude competition." According to its own documents, IBM in 1970 sold or leased 80 percent of the tape drives, 94 percent of the disk drives, and 99 percent of the impact printers that were plugged into its central units. These shares of the relevant submarkets combined with testimony concerning the effects of IBM's predatory practices on its plug compatible competition led Christensen to the guilty verdict.[45]

To ". . . obviate the found monopoly, and to restore a healthy competitive climate within a reasonable time," Christensen ordered IBM to do the following:

—Pay Telex $352 million (this was later revised to $259 million).
—Price all the functionally different devices that go into a computer system separately and to apply "substantially uniform" markups over actual costs of development, manufacture, and marketing of each unit.
—Establish separate prices for existing central processors and memories, which previously had been priced together.
—Eliminate all penalty payments on customers for premature termination

---

[44]Beman, "IBM's Travails in Lilliput."

[45]Actually, both parties were found guilty, IBM of the anticompetitive practices already enumerated and Telex of violating copyrights and misappropriating trade secrets. For its transgressions, Telex was ordered by Judge Christensen to pay IBM damages of $21.9 million. In January 1975 the U.S. Court of Appeals reversed the decision, ruling that IBM had only followed ordinary marketing methods. Telex planned an appeal to the Supreme Court.

of long-term lease agreements, providing customers give 90 days' notice of termination. This provision shall be limited to a three-year period and is intended to open the market for competitive substitution.
—Refrain from all predatory pricing, leasing, or other practices or strategies intended to obtain or maintain a monopoly of the market for equipment compatible with its computers, or any relevant submarket.

Questions

1. As the chapter indicates, this case was reversed and the government suit was dropped. How can IBM actions be interpreted as being vigorously competitive?

2. IBM continues to dominate in the production of complete computer systems although its share of electronic data processing sales has dropped. Does this case suggest practices that might be modified for a firm in this position while remaining vigorously competitive?

3. Is the survival of Telex, and of other medium-sized firms like it, important for the economy? (It had survived through 1985. There were over 20 firms other than IBM among the *Fortune* 500 who had important stakes in some segment of computer production.)

CASE 18–3
Xerox Before and After the 1975 Consent Order

Case 2–2, Haloid to Xerox, encompassed the time period to early 1973 and ended with the FTC complaint against Xerox alleging monopolization of the copier industry. The initial charges of illegally monopolizing the office-copier-machine industry were made on December 12, 1972, and formally issued in February 1973. The charges estimated that Xerox had a 60 percent share of 1971 industry revenues of $1.7 billion from the sale and lease of copiers and the sale of supplies[46] and a 95 percent share of the "plain-paper" copier market. Minnesota Mining & Manufacturing Co. and IBM, a new entrant in 1970, were among two dozen competitors which also included Eastman Kodak, the leading domestic competitor by the 1980s.

The 1973 Complaint

The complaint charged that Xerox maintained its monopoly position through a series of unfair acts and practices; its insistence on leasing and discouragement of sales of its copiers; price discrimination among customers including illegal package-leasing plans and quantity discount

[46]Of the $1.1 billiion for the sales and lease of office copiers the Xerox share was estimated at 86 percent.

rentals; its monopolization of patents, their use to gain technology used by competitors and limitation of their licensing to coated-paper copiers; maintenance of market power through agreements with Rank Xerox to divide world markets. (Rank Xerox agreed not to operate in the United States and Canada.)

The remedies proposed included: the divestiture by Xerox of its 51 percent stock interest in Rank Xerox and the freedom of the latter to sell in the United States; the granting of royalty-free and unrestricted licensing of all existing office copier patents and the granting of such licenses in new patents for 20 years after the conclusion of litigation; prohibitions on refusal to sell copiers and exclusive maintenance contracts; a ban on acquisitions of, and joint ventures with, manufacturers of office copiers or supplies.

Xerox's initial reply was that only 2 of 17 major copier-duplicator products were limited to leasing and that this was an initial market arrangement to assess manufacturing costs and revenues. It perceived an intensely competitive situation with 50 domestic competitors and foreign companies that could be expected to enter the U.S. markets. Mr. McColough, the chief executive officer, stated "It is clear that the Commission feels we have been too successful in securing these constitutionally statute-protected patent rights—and that we must simply give them away prior to their nature expiration. . . . We will fight every aspect of the complaint and we will win."

The Consent Order of 1975

One person who thought Xerox won when a consent order was formally adopted by the Federal Trade Commission in mid-1975 was Richard Sexton, vice president of general counsel of SCM Corporation, who stated, "The consent order was a failure of federal antitrust enforcement and a knuckling under to Xerox" and its behavior "will have to be dealt with in private suits rather than before the FTC." This company commenced an action in 1973 charging Xerox with monopolization of the plain paper office copier market and xerographic technology and acquisition of patents and technology. SCM asked treble damages of $1,522 million and injunctive relief. In 1978, a jury awarded $37 million in damages, to be trebled, but the trial judge set aside the money damages and the case was appealed. The Xerox 1978 Annual Report noted that five other private suits were outstanding in 1978. Patent litigation with IBM was ended in 1978 with a $25 million payment by IBM and an exchange of licenses.

James T. Halverson, director of the FTC's Bureau of Competition, felt that the order could lead to significant gains for the public by opening the copier market to new competition. He stated that the agreement attacks the fundamental problem faced by competitors, "a lack of technological know-how and a fear of the massive patent advantage possessed by Xerox."

C. Peter McColough, chairman of Xerox, expressed pleasure rather than triumph, "we are pleased that the matter has been concluded. Taking everything into consideration, this consent arrangement is in the best interests of the company."

Major provisions of the order were on patents. Xerox was required to license 1,700 copier patents and some future patents with sharply limited rights to get patents in return. A competitor could receive three patent licenses without paying royalties. The next three per product could require royalties of up to 0.5 percent of product revenues each, with additional patents royalty free. A competitor could be required to cross-license its patents on a one-for-one basis only after receiving three patents. It could receive reasonable royalties from Xerox (up to 6 percent of product sales) and Xerox could not use such patents until four years after the commercial availability of the competitor's product.

No divestiture was required of Rank Xerox Ltd. but the firm was required to grant worldwide licenses on past and future patents (for six years). Xerox agreed to forgive all past infringement liabilities by any company taking out a patent license under the order.

Another provision banned outright for five years Xerox's pricing plan for large users in which it gave package rates for a range of machines, presumably to the disadvantage of firms with narrower lines. Xerox was also required to announce a selling price at the same time it gave leasing terms on new copiers.

Since the Consent Order

At the time the consent order was concluded, Xerox was estimated to have 85 percent of the plain copier market, a drop from the 95 percent reported in the original complaint of 1971. By 1978, as shown in Exhibit 18–3A, its operating revenues had grown to $5.9 billion, about double the 1973 level. Xerox broke down these revenues into $3.4 billion in domestic operations (about 55 percent of the total) and $4.6 billion (almost 80 percent) in copiers and duplicators. Its domestic copier revenues thus can be estimated at over $2.5 billion or 50 percent more than the broad all-copiers-plus-supplies domestic market of which Xerox estimated to have 60 percent in 1971 (amounting to about $1 billion or a little over half of Xerox's 1971 revenues). Virtually all of these increases can be considered as real, that is, not due to price increases. The first modest increases in copier prices for several years were in 1978. The copier field clearly had continued its growth, albeit at a far lower pace than in the hectic 1960s, and Xerox has remained dominant. As shown in column 5 of Exhibit 18–3A Xerox's rate of return on equity dropped rapidly through the 1960s and had settled down in the 17–18 percent range after 1975 in which large losses were incurred as the company disposed of its unprofitable computer business which had been acquired with Scientific Data Systems in 1969. The ratio of income before taxes to total operating data is shown in note 3 of the exhibit. In the five years before the consent decree it ranged from 22.5 to 29.0 percent. In the three subsequent years it ranged from 17.4–18.2 percent.

EXHIBIT 18–3A

	(1) Operating Revenue	(2) Net Income	(3) Equity	(4) R&D	(5) Income ÷ Average Equity	(6) Income per Share	(7) Dividends per Share
1963	176	23	85	15	34.4%	$0.39	$0.08
1968	1,224	129	601	60	24.0	1.88	0.50
1972	2,338	256	1,249	117	22.4	3.24	0.84
1973	2,915	283	1,475	154	20.8	3.57	0.90
1974	3,505	329	1,733	179	20.5	4.14	1.00
1975	4,054	244	1,898	198	13.4	3.07	1.00
1976	4,418	360	2,173	226	17.7	4.49	1.10
1977	5,082	404	2,460	269	17.4	5.03	1.50
1978	5,902	477	2,786	311	18.2	5.92	2.00
1979	6,852	515	3,259	367	17.0	6.12	2.40
1980	8,037	565	3,630	430	16.4	6.69	2.80
1981	8,510	598	3,728	526	16.3	7.08	3.00
1982	8,455	424	3,724	565	11.4	5.00	3.00
1983	8,464	466	4,222	555	11.7	4.42	3.00
1984	8,792	376	4,543	n.a.	8.6	2.53	3.00

Notes: 1. 1963 and 1968 data are taken from Exhibit 2–2B, 1972–78 figures are from the Xerox annual report for 1978, and the slight discrepancies in 1972 data from that of Exhibit 2–2B reflect company revisions.
2. The 1975 drop in earnings reflected large losses incident to discontinued operations, essentially the computer operation acquired with Scientific Data Systems in 1969.
3. The ratios of income before taxes to total operating revenues were for 1970–74: 29.0 percent, 27.2 percent, 26.6 percent, 23.7 percent, 22.5 percent; and for 1975–78: 18.7 percent, 18.2 percent, 17.4 percent, 18.2 percent.
4. Columns 1, 2, 3 and 4 are expressed in $ millions.
n.a. = not available.

In 1985, Xerox was estimated still to hold about 50 percent of the world copier market as against 80 percent in the late 1960s. Its earnings had peaked in 1981 at $7.08 a share. Despite a drop of earnings to $2.53 a share caused largely by its write-off of Shugart Associates, the disk-drive manufacturer it had acquired in 1977, and losses from an insurance acquisition, it maintained its dividend at its peak of $3 a share. This gesture could be thought of as an indicator of its resolve to be a leader in office automation.

The new machines Xerox had ready were slanted toward the "output" aspect of automation, documentation preparation, and storage and printing. Xerox had developed a system called Ethernet of cable and computer programs to tie its automation system with data processing equipment of other manufacturers. The Xerox stress on "output" reflected its continued strength in copiers. Outside analysts questioned whether its consolidated sales force, used to dealing with office managers for copiers, would be successful in wooing management information officers on office automation systems, against IBM, Wang, and Digital Equipment, who were strong in microprocessors. Xerox had had great success in individual items such as high speed laser printers and electronic typewriters, and its research department had produced many individual automation products.

Questions

1. How might the practices complained about by the FTC help Xerox maintain its dominant position in the copier market? How could the remedies proposed by the FTC help erode that position?

2. The data on rate of return for equity and operating margins are consistent with reduced monopoly power. Does this indicate that government intervention was effective?

3. Why, apparently, was the Xerox management willing to accept the consent order in view of their prediction that "we will win"?

4. Assume that Xerox is "successful" in its venture into "office automation systems." Would it be possible for it ever to achieve the rewards for stockholders achieved by those who held stock before 1961?

5. Check its performance since 1984. Would you term it successful? Should Xerox continue to maintain R&D expenditures at levels that approximate its net income?

CASE 18–4
Kellogg Company versus the FTC

Four companies were charged with "shared monopoly" of the ready-to-eat (RTE) cereal business in 1972 by the FTC. Charges were dropped in 1978 against Quaker Oats (9 percent of the market in 1970). Two of the remaining defendants, General Mills (21 percent share in 1970 and 19 percent in 1978) and General Foods (16 percent share in both years) were widely diversified food manufacturers with no more than 10 percent of their total sales in cereals. The Kellogg Company, the leader in the field with a 42 percent market share in 1978 (slightly below its 45 percent share in 1970 cited in the FTC case), was the firm with most at stake with over 70 percent of its 1978 sales of $1.7 billion, and 80 percent of its 1978 profits of $145 million in cereals. Its net return on capital of 21.5 percent was the highest for a large firm in the food industry.

Kellogg's Strategy for the 1980s

Growth-oriented strategists suggested that because of gloomy demographic trends, 1980 was "the time for Kellogg to use its mature but rich cereal operation to finance a breakneck diversification time into faster growing businesses."[47] Their argument was based not so much on the "shared monopoly" case, which proposed as one of the remedies the split

---

[47]*Business Week*, November 26, 1979, p. 81.

of Kellogg's cereal operations into several competing companies (see below), but on a recent slowdown in growth of physical volume in the industry (less than 2 percent annually from 1976–79 as against 7 percent from 1970 to 1976) and its anticipated continuation in the 1980s as the number of people under 25 decline (the per capita consumption of those under 25 of 11 lbs. had been more than double that of the 25–50 age group). Additional difficulties were the decline in presweetened cereal sales in 1978 of 5 percent, the first since the development of the category in the 1950s. It represented one third of Kellogg's cereal sales and was under heavy attack by consumer groups as being "equivalent to candy" with many brands having a 60 percent sugar content. An FTC staff report in 1978 recommended the prohibition of television advertisements directed to children under six and limiting ads for sugared products aimed at any pre-teen audience.[48]

Kellogg's response to these actual and potential unfavorable developments included first, a strong legal, political, and publicity attack. A new law firm sought to force rehearing of the FTC case. It launched an advertising campaign stressing the nutritional value of presweetened cereals as part of a "balanced breakfast." It joined other businesses that sought to curb the regulatory power of the FTC by subjecting its actions to congressional reversal. Kellogg's president, William S. LaMothe, allocated 40 percent of his time to lobbying and public relations work stressing the theme "to try to punish success in a free enterprise system is a terrible direction for our country to be taking."[49]

Second, Kellogg was very active in new cereal additions with five in 1979 including Most, a high-fiber cereal with 100 percent of the daily recommended requirements of 10 vitamins and iron, which had gained a 0.8 percent market share in a few months (0.7 percent was Kellogg's goal for a new product). It launched a new effort toward promoting cereals for older audiences and was developing a fortified breakfast bar. It hoped that the nation's per capita cereal demand might be boosted from 8.6 pounds to 12 pounds by 1985.[49]

A third policy was to increase cereal penetration in South America and even in the Middle East and Asia, areas where corn meal and crushed wheat have been traditional.

Kellogg's diversification efforts were much more cautious than those of other food firms. Its major acquisitions from 1969 through the 1970s were Salada Tea, Mrs. Smith's (pies), Fearn International and Pure Pack Foods. It refused to pay "outrageous" prices for acquisitions (Tropicana Products received twice as much from Beatrice Foods as Kellogg's bid). Its growth was largely internal, such as with lower calorie and yogurt pies for Mrs. Smith's.

---

[48]Ibid., p. 89.
[49]Ibid., p. 86.

Kellogg at Mid-Decade

Kellogg could look back with satisfaction to the dismissal of the FTC suit in 1982. With this legal challenge behind it, "Kellogg's no longer is pulling its punches" in increasing market share. It reversed a trend that had briefly taken its share in RTE cereals to 35 percent in 1982, and stood at 39.4 percent in 1984 and 41 percent in early 1985. It was fourth among the *Fortune* 500 in 1984 returns on equity with 51.4 percent. Modest progress was made in increasing overall per capita consumption of RTE cereals to an annual 9 pounds per capita.

The basic strategy of sticking to, and attempting to find, growth in RTE cereals continued. Its advertising budget increased 20 percent a year since 1982; 10 cereals were introduced including Nutri-Grains, which made whole grains into flakes, and Raisin Squares, that wrapped cereal around a fruit, which were technological innovations. Kellogg's international efforts stressed the European market.

The Shared Monopoly

While the government has had occasional legal success in getting convictions against tight oligopolies on the basis of identity of behavior rather than overt conspiracy, it never won a remedy that significantly altered the market structure. The FTC's complaint in 1972 charging "unfair competition" under Section 5 of the Federal Trade Commission Act with the possible remedies of divestiture and royalty-free licensing of trademarks was potentially ground-breaking.

The FTC's allegations included "proliferation of brands," "artificial differentiation of product" through advertising to children, control of supermarket shelf-space "particularly by Kellogg," and exercise of monopoly power by failure to cut prices and by following price increases. Kellogg denied any monopolistic practices, said less than 20 percent of breakfast main dishes were cereals, and attributed its success to "bringing the housewife what she wants"; General Mills was not only "distressed" but "puzzled"; General Foods was confident that the Post cereal business was good for the consuming public; Quaker Oats found it impossible to see how its 9 percent share (up from 3 percent) was a basis for a monopoly charge.

The economic analysis of a consultant to the FTC in the case was that "the privately optimal entry-deterrence strategy involves high prices, brand proliferation and some degree of overspending on advertising."[50] Brand proliferation was the key since it split the cereals' "product space" into such small segments as to make it unlikely that a new entrant could achieve the 3 percent share needed for efficient production. Only 2 of the 80 brands introduced in the 1950–72 period ever achieved this level, but,

[50]Richard Schmalensee, "Entry Deterrence in the Ready-to-eat Breakfast Cereal Industry," *The Bell Journal of Economics*, Autumn 1978, p. 313.

as indicated before, Kellogg felt a 0.7 percent share was the test of success for a leading firm.[51]

Heavy advertising would reinforce product differentiation and reduce incentive by sellers for price competition. Increased advertising as a kind of fixed cost would discourage potential entrants. Low limit prices were not necessary as a deterrent to entry in addition to brand proliferation and advertising. They probably would not have been effective since, with the small group of firms involved, mutually beneficial post-entry price rises might be expected by a potential entrant.

The one opportunity for entry came in the early 1970s when the established companies did not anticipate the growth of natural cereals to 10 percent of the market by mid-1974. Colgate, International Multifoods, Pillsbury, and Pet all entered, but only Pet hung on after the entry of the major cereal producers and a decline of this market segment in the late 1970s.

The Proposed Relief and its Impact

There were four components to the relief proposed by the FTC, the first two of primary importance and novelty.

1. The creation of five new firms by divestiture of certain established brands and trademarks of the three defendants; three from Kellogg, one from General Foods, and one from General Mills. To avoid delays existing shareholders would simply receive shares in the new companies.
2. The licensing of existing trademarks (and provision of needed formulae) to all nonrespondent firms willing to meet quality control standards. Similar licenses would be required after five years on new products. All would revert to originating firms after 20 years.

The other provisions were a ban on acquisitions to make divestiture effective, and a prohibition on the supermarket shelf-space plans allegedly used by defendants.

Economist Richard Schmalensee felt that the "fall in concentration should directly increase price competition," particularly by weakening the tacit agreement that made major producers reluctant to engage in private label production. But "divestiture may not by itself constitute an adequate remedy."[52] Under licensing, copies of the largest RTE cereals are likely with price competition eroding margins and forcing reductions in prices of other brands. The proposed divestiture would create a set of firms well situated to take out licenses, and the ability to take out licenses

---

[51]Kellogg had one of these, Sugar Frosted Flakes, with 6 percent share (3d in industry). Its other leaders, Corn Flakes (7.5 percent, 1st), Raisin Bran (4.7 percent, 4th), and Rice Krispies (4.5 percent, 5th) were long established.

[52]Schmalensee, "Entry Deterrence," p. 322.

should enhance the viability of the new firms plus other outsiders who could gain a toehold by producing copies of leading brands.

Government success in this case would have represented an unprecedented restructuring of an oligopoly to influence conduct and performance. There seemed to be no middle ground (except possibly restrictions on advertising to children) between these significant structural changes and the willingness to accept the status quo.

Questions

1. Assess Kellogg's policy of continuing emphasis on RTE cereals. Measures of its recent profitability (the number in the parentheses represents its rank in *Fortune* 500) follow. Figures are for 1984 and are in millions (except for percentages): sales, 2,602 (143); assets, 1,667 (182); net income, 250.1 (71); stockholders' equity, 487 (255); employees, 0.017 (211); net income as a percent of sales, 9.6 (43); and of equity 51.4 (4); growth rate in earnings per share 1974–84, 13.08 (115); total return to investors, 28.8 percent (39); 1974–84 average total return, 15.9 percent (272). Note the median for the 42 food companies in the 500 was 17 percent for 1984 return and 18.4 percent for the 1974–84 average total return.

2. Why should one expect a high return on equity for a company that successfully spends about three times as much on advertising as compared to the average consumer product (think—what is its major asset likely to be?)? The extraordinary 51.4 percent return in 1984 (rather than previous returns in the 20's percent) reflected the purchase of 15 million shares from the Kellogg charitable trust for $570 million, which reduced shares outstanding by almost 20 percent and cut the equity shown on the balance sheet to less than half. The debt-equity ratio was raised to about 0.70. Is this financial decision consistent with the emphasis on RTE cereals?

3. Assess the FTC's case and the proposed remedies in the light of the fact that it was dismissed in 1982.[53]

4. Show that the amended Section 7 of the Clayton Act very much applies to the cereal industry by computing an Herfindahl index for 1984 given these figures for market shares: Kellogg's 39.4 percent; General Mills 20.6 percent; General Foods 14.9 percent; Quaker 8.1 percent; Ralson 5.9 percent; and Nabisco 5.0 percent. Specifically consider whether a merger of Quaker with Ralston would be challenged according to the guidelines.

5. Check a local supermarket to see whether distributor brands and generics provide lower-price alternatives for RTE cereals.

---

[53]According to Alfred F. Dougherty, Director of Competition of the FTC, the cost to consumers of the competitive restraints in RTE cereals were over $100 million annually. These included "excessive profits" (200 percent of average for all manufacturing) and "excessive advertising" (300 percent of its proportion to sales for all consumer products). This figure was about 5 percent of industry sales (thus 3–4 percent of consumer expenditures on RTE cereals). It can serve as a starting point for your assessment (*New York Times*, November 27, 1979, p. A22).

Index of Cases

Accounting, Leeway in, 9
Advertisers, The Big, 424
Air Conditioning and Related Industries, Productivity in, 188
Aluminum Industry, Price Publicity in the, 376
American Natural Resources Takeover in 1985, 460
Arbitrage in Stocks, 44
Atomic Waste Management, 476
Badger and Siegel, 145
Bees and the Flowers in Florida, The, 475
Broadway, On, 39
California and Arizona Lemons, Demand for, 97
California and Florida Avocados, Demand for, 99
Capital Budgeting, Problems in, 206
Capital Investment, Problems in, 184
Chicago-Vancouver Route Controversy, 121
Cigarette Industry, Upheaval in the, 408
Coincident to Lagging Indicators, Ratio of, 63
Collective Bargaining in the Basic Steel Industry, 234
Country Doctor, The, 328
Cow Pastures or Condominiums, 32
Cows Are Laughing, Even the, 283
Component Manufacturing Company, The, 209
DeBeers and the CSO, 308
Demand Analysis for the Firm, Problems in, 124
Demand Analysis for Industry, Problems in, 96
Discrimination and Employment, 232
Dow Chemical in Europe, 263
Electrical Price Conspiracy Cases, The, and General Electric Directive 20.5, 504
First House: Inflation, Interest, and Taxes, 212
Forecasters, Bad Times for the, 59
Forecasting, Problems in, 60
Frito-Lay, Inc., 345
Frozen Orange Concentrate, Demand for, 83

General Electric and the $10 Light Bulb, 459
General Motors, Price-Level Determination by, 377
Generic Drugs, 346
Haloid to Xerox, 35
Harvard, Price Discrimination at, 349
Hul Gul—An Application of Game Theory, 123
Insulation, How Much, 208
Interest Rate Formulas, The Use of by Managers and Engineers, 182
Kellogg Company versus the FTC, 522
Leading Indicators and Cyclical Turning Points, 61
Learning Curve and Military Aircraft, 191
Linear Programming Methods—A Graphic Example, 154
LTV, The Redeployment of, 448
Mason, (L. E.) Company and Optimal Inventory Policy, 148
Medical Advertising, 307
Minimum Wage, How High a, 239
Monopoly Pricing, Selected Problems in, 311
Moscow's Taxi Business, 282
Nissan in Tennessee, 256
Noise in Moscow, 473
Nordon Manufacturing Company, 146
Optical Products in California, Price Dispersion in, 348
Options on Stock Indexes, 43
Paragon Parking Lot, 207
Pepsi-Cola for Vodka, 264
Philately, Prices in, 277
Pollution Problems in the Dairy Industry, 471
Price Controls, Nixon, 298
Puts, Calls, and Straddles, 40
Reed, Waite, and Gentzler, 257
Refrigerators, The Demand for, 89
Refrigerators and Kilowatt-Hours, 403
Riverside Metal Company, The, 365
Robbins Manufacturing Company, 187
Smaller Plants, Trend Toward, 189
Soft Drinks, Market Share in, 118
Sunland Tailoring Company, 143
Telex versus IBM: The Problem of Plug Compatible Peripherals, 512
Traditional Department Stores, Inc., 383
Unemployment, How the Government Measures, 236
Union and Nonunion Rubber Plants (March, 1979), 229
Urban Electric Company, The, 330
Ways to Chisel on Price, Hundreds of, 301
Women in Business, 120
Worker Alienation, Combating, 230
Xerox Before and After the Consent Order, 518

Index

ABC Network, 448
Abrams, Bill, 118
Accounting
  cost, 128
  leeway, 9
  profit, 13
Acid rain, 471
Act to Regulate Commerce, 295
Adaptability, 140
Addystone Pipe & Steel Co., 481
Adolph Coors, 425
Advertising
  beer, 360
  cigarettes, 360
Agglomeration, 254
Aid to families with dependent children, 239
Air Canada, 122
Air conditioning industry, 188
Airline Deregulation Act, 121, 296
Alaska, 466, 470
Alcoa pricing, 376, 484
Alienation, worker, 226, 230
Allied Corp., 446
Alcan Aluminum Corp., 376
Alchian, Armen, 163, 168
Alchian cost curves, 169
Allis-Chalmers, 505–6
All-or-none decision, 139
Alt, Richard M., 365
Aluminum industry, 376
American Brands, 424, 458
American Brass Co., 371
American Can Co., 446, 482

American Home Products, 424
American Motors, 439
American Natural Resources Co., 448, 450
American Telephone & Telegraph, 255, 424–25, 485
American Tobacco Co., 408, 488
American Woolen, 444
Anheuser-Busch, 360, 442
ANR freight system, 461
Anthony, Robert N., 15, 425
Arbitrage
  nature, 23
  stocks, 44
  in takeovers, 447
Arizona lemons, 97
Armour, 441
Aronson, Jonathan D., 256
Assets, net, 16
Atlantic Richfield, 255
Atomic waste, 476
AT&T Communications, 487
AT&T Technologies, 487
Autocorrelation, 85
Avon products, 397

Backman, Jules, 392, 396
Balance sheet, economist's, 15
Bank of America, 255
Banker, David, 504
Bargaining power
  companies, 222
  labor unions, 221

Bartlesville, Oklahoma, 446
Battelle Memorial Institute, 36
Batus, 424
Baumol, William J., 19, 109, 154, 158–59, 363–64
Baxter, William F., 480, 486
Bayes, 19
Beatrice Foods, 523
Becker, Gary S., 225
Bell, Frederick W., 71
Bell Laboratories, 487
Beman, Louis, 515–17
Bendix Corp., 446
Benishay, Haskel, 75
Berkey Photo, Inc., 487
Beryllium copper prices, 366
Bethlehem Steel, 456–57, 492
Bicks, Robert, 505
Biddle, Jack, 514
Bird, Larry, 205
Bittlingmayer, George, 224
Blair, Robert D., 482–83
Bludhorn, Charles, 455
Boesky, Ivan, 446
Bonini, Charles P., 47
Borg-Warner, 439
Bower, Blair T., 468
Box, G. E. P., 49
Bradford, William C., 365
Brand, Horst, 188
Brand name carryover, 439
Braniff Airways, 443, 451, 453–54
Break-even charts, 142
Brimmer, Andrew, 240
British Petroleum, 255
Broadway plays, 39
Brooks, John, 509
Brown, R. G., 48
Brown Shoe case, 492
Brown, Stanley H., 456
Brown and Williamson, 410
Brozen, Yale, 224
Buchanan, James M., 319, 471
Building permits, 51
Bunting, Robert L., 219
Burck, Gilbert, 426
Burns, Arthur R., 362
Burton, John C., 10
Business
  formation, 51
  slumps, 62
Butler, Eamonn F., 274, 277
Buzzell, Robert D., 400
By-product, 432

California
  avocados, 99
  lemons, 97
  marketing quotas, 103
  oranges, 324
Camel cigarettes, 409
Cameron, Y., 466
Campbell Soup, 488
Capital budgeting
  chart, 204
  problems, 206
Capital Cities, 448
Capitalization
  concept, 170
  finite income, 171
  perpetual income, 170
Carlson, Chester F., 36
Carnegie, Andrew, 58
Carnegie-Mellon University, 60
Cartels
  chiseling in, 293
  coffee, 361
  defined, 292
  milk, 362
  OPEC, 293
  rubber, 361
  sugar, 362
Carter, Jimmy, President, 122, 223
Cash flow, 174
Cason, Roger, 10
CBS Network, 448
Cellophane case, 485
Cereal consumption, 523
Certainty, 18
Ceteris paribus, 127
Chamberlin, Edward H., 102, 288, 392, 399
Chaplin, Charlie, 230
Chart House, Inc., 446
Chance-Vought, 449
Chase Manhattan Bank, 255
Chesterfield cigarettes, 409
Cheung, Steven N. S., 463
Chevron, 489
Chicago
  merchandise mart, 254
  route controversy, 121
Chicago Board Options Exchange, 43
Chisolm, Roger, 47
Chow, W. S., 404
Christensen, A. Sherman, 514–15, 517
Christensen, L. R., 167
Chrysler, 380, 425
Cigarettes
  after filter revolution, 414

Cigarettes—Cont.
  filter revolution, 413
  generic, 422
  labeling, 495
  market shares, 415
  medical findings, 412
  unit sales, 416
Cigarette companies, diversification, 422
Cigarette excise tax, 411
Civil Aeronautics Board, 121, 296, 484
Clayton Act
  antimerger amendment, 480
  exemptions, 484
  provisions in full, 500
  Robinson-Patman amendment, 490,
    502
  section 3, 490
  section 4, 482
  section 5, 495
  section 7, 450, 455, 488
  stock acquisitions, 491
  Wheeler-Lea amendment, 495
Clark, J. J., 199, 202
Clark, Lindley H., 59
Clark, M. T., 199
Clean Air Act, 5, 470
Clorox, 489, 492
Closed shop, 222
Coase, Ronald, 102, 464, 470
Coastal Corporation, 461
Coca-Cola
  advertising, 424
  in China, 265
Colberg, Marshall R., 32, 224, 250, 432
Colgate, 525
Collective bargaining
  industrywide, 248
  steel industry, 234
Common oil pool, 465
Common property, 464
Competitive model, implications, 276
Complements, 74
Concentration ratios, 356, 359
Conference Board, 55
Conglomerates, 443
Consolidated Cigar, 443
Cook, James, 256
Consumer good orders, 51
Consumerism, 4, 401
Container Corp., 482
Continental Illinois National Bank, 9
Control Data Corporation, 513
Coolidge, Calvin, President, 1
Coors (Adolf), 425
Cordiner, Ralph, 506, 509

Cost
  accounting, 14
  direct, 140
  equity, 14
  explicit, 14
  fixed, 132
  historical, 16
  implicit, 14
  joint, 430
  long run, 163
  marginal, 15
  opportunity, 14
  original, 14
  overhead, 140
  short run, 163
  social, 463
  standard, 140
Cost of capital
  dividend based, 200
  equity, 200
  internally generated, 201
  with growth, 200
Cost Accounting Standards Board, 15
Cottler & Co.; 425
Cournot, Augustin, 66, 110–11
Cowhey, Peter F., 256
Crateology, 58
Cross-Florida barge canal, 466
Crum and Foster, 446
CSX Corp., 446
Cyert, R. M., 383

Dairy food plants, 472
Davenport, Herbert J., 268
Davenport, John, 263
Davis-Bacon Act, 224–25
Dean, Joel, 192, 377, 437
DeBeers diamond cartel, 309
Debt, cost of, 198
Decibels of sound, 475
Delivery costs, 243–44
Delta Air Lines, 425
Demand
  advertising and, 75
  curve, 67
  elasticity, 69
  empirical, 76
  income and, 72
  law of, 69
  related goods, 437
  seasonal, 438
Dempsey, Paul S., 222
Depreciation, economic, 132
Diamond Shamrock Corp., 446

Digital Equipment, 521
Dillon Cos., 446
Dirlam, Joel B., 377
Discounting, 192
Disintegration of industry, 434
Disposable personal income, 85–86
Distilling industry, 361
Diversification, 427
Divisibility, 140
Dorfman, N. S., 463, 468
Dorfman, Robert, 154, 159, 393, 463, 468
Dougherty, Alfred F., 526
Douty, H. M., 224
Dow Jones, 425
Drew, Daniel, 12, 29
Dumping
    international, 323
    theory of, 323
Duopoly
    Cournot solution, 111
    defined, 110
    interstate bus, 296
DuPont, 2, 255, 442, 482, 485
Duesenberry, J. S., 53, 203
Dynamic analysis, 105

Eastman Kodak, 255, 487–88, 518
Eccles, Robert G., 436
Economies of scale
    firm, 361
    plant, 360
Edwards, Corwin, 327
Efficient markets theory, 52
Effluent charge, 468–69, 472
Ehrbar, A. F., 494
Elasticity
    arc, 71
    constant, 69
    cross, 74
    demand, 68
    geometric calculation, 69
    income, 73
    market share, 109
Elder, Peyton, 223
Electronic Halarc, 460
Elgers, P. T., 199
Emission standards, 466
Employment, composition of, 233
Entry barriers, 361
Environmental
    movement, 5
    Protection Agency, 5, 465
Epstein, Edward J., 309
Equipment, value of, 169, 171

Esmark, Inc., 446
Espionage, industrial, 58
Ethyl Corp., 482
Evans, Michael K., 53, 59
executive
    incentives, 227
    turnover, 226
Externalities, 463
Exxon, 255

Fair, Ray C., 46
Fair Labor Standards Act, 223
Fair Packaging and Labeling Act, 495
Fair trade laws, 294, 361, 482
Farm problem, 248
Feasible region, 157
Federal Communication Commission, 487
Federal Pacific, 507
Federal Trade Commission, 328
Federal Trade Commission Act
    antimerger amendment, 504
    passage, 480
    provisions, 498
    Wheeler-Lea amendment, 480, 503
Financial Accounting Standards Board, 15
Firestone Tire & Rubber Company, 229
Firm size, 167
Fisher, Franklin M., 486
Florida
    avocados, 99
    frozen orange concentrate, 84
Food and Drug Acts, 496
Food and Drug Administration, 495
Forbush, Daniel H., 512
Forbush, Dascomb R., 308, 444
Ford, Henry, 230
Ford Motor Co., 255, 363, 380, 424
Forecasters, bad times for, 59
Forecasting
    Box-Jenkins, 48
    complex naive, 48
    consumer attitudes, 54–55
    econometric, 53
    generalized adaptive filtering, 48
    loaded dice, 57
    naive, 45
    projection, 45
    requirements, 55
    survey methods, 54
Franklin, Charles B., 32
Free form product line, 443, 450
Free rider, 469–70

Freight
  absorption, 325
  crosshauling, 326
  phantom, 325
Friedland, Claire, 295
Friedman, Milton, 7, 52, 67, 266
Friend, Irwin, 200
Fromm, G., 53
Fusfeld, Alan F., 406–7
Futures
  contracts, 22
  defined, 22
  foreign exchange, 27
  inflation, 32
  interest rate, 26
  options on, 30

Gaines pet food plant, 231
Games
  loss leader, 115
  motel, 114
  saddlepoint, 113
  theory of, 112
  zero sum, 112
General Accounting Office, 225
General American Oil Co., 446
General Dynamics, 494
General Electric, 255, 405, 439, 442, 459,
    492, 506, 508
General Foods, 424, 522
General Mills, 424, 522, 524
General Motors
  concentration, 359
  downsizing of cars, 363
  operating results, 380
  output schedules, 55
  pricing, 364, 377
  rate of return, 379
  size, 255
  standard volume, 382
  target returns, 381
Getty Oil, 489
Gezzardi, Walter, Jr., 497
Gillette Company, 441
Godfather's Pizza, Inc., 446
Golden parachute, 447
Goldman, Marshall I., 463
Goldwyn, Samuel, 45
Goodrich, B. F. Co., 229
Goods
  complements, 73
  inferior, 73
  normal (superior), 73
  substitutes, 73

Goodyear Tire and Rubber Co., 229
Gordon, Myron J., 199
Gore, Albert, 190
Gould, John P., 224
Government failure, 471
Greatamerica Corp., 450, 452
Greene, W. H., 167
Greenhut, Melvin L., 242–43, 250
Greenmail, 495
Greenwich, Connecticut, 6
Greenwood, Joen E., 486
Gulf Oil, 255, 446–47, 489
Gulf & Western, 443, 455–56, 458

Hadley, George, 154
Hailey, Arthur, 4
Hall, R. L., 353
Haloid, 35, 518
Halverson, James T., 519
Hammer, William, 36
Hampton, John J., 199, 201
Harlow, C. V., 22
Hartford Fire Insurance, 455, 494
Healy, Paul, 9
Heineman, Ben, 455
Heinz (H. J.) Co., 488
Herfindahl index, 488–89, 526
Hewlett-Packard, 255
Hedging
  agricultural, 24
  defined, 21
  financial, 26
  long, 25
Hertz, David B., 201
Hiram Walker, 424
Hirshleifer, Jack, 103
Hitch, C. J., 353
Hoagland, Edward, 32
Houthakker, H. S., 76
Huffstutler, Clyde, 188
Hul Gul and game theory, 123
Human capital, 225

Icahn, Carl, 446
Idaho, right to work, 222
Indicators
  coincident, 50, 52
  coincident over lagging, 63
  index of leading, 50
  lagging, 50, 52
  leading, 50–51, 61
Industrial parks, 254
Integration, vertical, 167, 434–35

Intel Corp., 446
Interest as cost, 132
Internal brand competition, 440
Internal rate of return, 195
International Business Machines Corp.,
    36, 255, 446, 485–86
International competition, 360
International Multifoods, 525
International Paper Corp., 482
International Telephone & Telegraph,
    255, 455, 458, 494
Interstate commerce
  commission, 295, 484
  defined, 223
Inventories
  just in time, 256
  net change in, 51
  optimum, 152
Isocosts, 131
Isoquants, 130
Itek Corp., 446

Jacobs, Irwin, 446
Jaeger, Carol M., 91
Japanese work ethic, 256
Jeffrey Martin, 425
Jenkins, G. M., 49
Johnson, H. G., 23
Johnson & Johnson, 255
Johnson, J., 143
Johnson, Lyndon B., President, 493
Joint costs
  agriculture, 428
  competition, 429
  cotton gins, 429
  fishing products, 428
  further processing, 432
  monopoly, 431, 433
Jones & Laughlin, 443, 450–51, 454, 456,
    493

Kahn, Alfred, 296, 484
Kaiser Aluminum, 376
Kaldor, N., 434
Kasputys, Joseph, 60
Kasserman, David L., 482–83
Kaysen, Carl, 358
Kefauver, Estes, 509
Kellogg Company, 522
Kelsey, Frances, 4, 496
Kelvinator Appliance Company, 439
Kendall, Donald, 264
Kennedy, Edward M., 494

Keynes, John Maynard, 23
Kiefer-Stewart Co., 483
Kinney, G. R. Co., 492
Klein, L. R., 53
Kneese, Allen V., 468
Knight, Frank H., 266
Koch, Edward, 447
Koten, John, 118
Kreps, Juanita, 120
Kroger Co., 446
Kuh, E., 53

Labor mobility, 248
Labor surplus areas, 248
LaMothe, William S., 523
Land rent, 249
Lanzillotti, Robert F., 377
LaPlace, 19
Larson, John A., 506
Lauck, John H., 475
Least squares, 80
Learning curve, 169, 191
Leftwich, Richard H., 270
Lerner, Abba P., 286
Leveraged buyout, 461
Levi Straus & Co., 483
Lewellen, Wilbur G., 201
Lewis, Arthur M., 452
Limited production run, 168
License fees, 133, 287
Liggett & Myers, 408
Linear programming, 143, 154
Ling, James J., 448, 455
Ling-Temco-Vought, 428, 443, 446, 448,
    458, 489, 492–93
Lintner, John, 200
Lite beer, 360, 442
Little, Royal, 455
Litton Industries, 443, 445–46, 456, 458
Location
    competition, 252
    and demand, 250
    interdependence, 250
    two-plant monopoly, 251
Locklin, D. Phillip, 246
Loews, 424
Long position
  in construction, 22
  defined, 21
Long run
  costs, 179
  defined, 126
Lorillard, P., 408
Löwenbräu beer, 360, 442

LTV Aerospace, 451
Lucky Strike cigarettes, 409
Lutz, Friedrich A., 175–76
Lutz, Vera C., 175–76
Lykes Corp., 456

McClaren, Richard W., 493–94
McColough, C. Peter, 519
McDonald's, 424
Macesich, George, 227
McGown, John J., 486
McGraw Electric Company, 439
McGuire-Keogh Act, 482
McKinsey, J. C. C., 118
McLaughlin, Robert L., 50
Maher, William, 507
Malabre, Alfred L., 59
Malkiel, Burton G., 198
Marathon Oil, 458
March, J. G., 383
Marginal efficiency of capital, 195
Marginal factor cost, 220
Marginal productivity
    competitive seller, 216
    concept, 214
    fixed proportions, 219
    monopolists, 218
Marginal revenue product, 218
Markdown, price, 388
Market failure, 471
Market orientation, 245
Market penetration, 325
Market separation
    age of buyer, 316
    buyer income, 315
    location of buyers, 316
    market function, 317
    newness, 316
    quality, 317
    quantity, 316
    time of purchase, 315
    use, 316
Market share, 109, 485
Markups, price, 386
Marlboro cigarettes, 418
Marshall, Alfred, 68, 126, 171, 228, 267, 276
Martin, David Dale, 492
Martin, S., 19
Material gathering cost, 243–44
Maximax, 20
Maximin, 19
Mazda, 255
Meltzer, Allan H., 60

Memorex, 516
Mergers
    early, 491
    friendly, 446
    hostile, 446
    solution, 465
Mesa Petroleum, 446
Michelin plants, 222, 230
Michigan, University of, 54
Milk prices, 294
Miller, D. W., 19
Miller, Merton H., 200, 202–3
Miller Brewing Co., 360, 442
Milling-in-transit, 246
Minimum wage rates
    effects, 223
    schedule, 223
    youth, 240
Minnesota Mining & Mfg., 255, 518
Mintz, Morton, 4
Mitchell, John, 493
Mobil Oil, 255, 489
Modigliani, Franco, 200, 202–3
Monetarism, 52
Money supply, 52
Monopolistic competition, 288
Monopolistic pricing, 286
    existing supply, 290
    short run, 291
Monopoly
    bilateral, 221
    degree of, 286
    natural, 295
    sources of, 287
Monopsony
    defined, 219
    input, 221
    rural, 220
    and training, 225
    wage rate, 221
Montreal Exchange, 32
Monsanto products, 442
Moore, Geoffrey H., 49
Morgenstern, Oskar, 112
Mother Bell
    demise of, 486
    local holding companies, 487
Motor Carrier Act, 1980, 295
Motor Vehicle Safety Act, 4
Multicollinearity, 85
Multinational companies
    early, 254
    Forbes, 255
    Fortune, 255
    present day, 255

Multiple products
  advertising, 441
  distribution, 441
Multiproduct firm, 426, 433
Myers, Steward C., 200

Nabisco, 526
Nader, Ralph, 401
National Bureau of Economic Research,
    49, 52
National Car Rental, 453
National Labor Relations Act, 222
National Recovery Administration, 294,
    362, 393, 483
Natomas Co., 446
Nature, states of, 17–19
Nepotism, 241
New Jersey Zinc Company, 443
New York City, 447, 470
Nicholls, William H., 410
Nissan
  size, 255
  in Tennessee, 256
Nixon, Richard M., President, 33, 494
Nonrecourse crop loans, 275
North Carolina, unions, 222
Northwest Industries, 455, 458
Norton Simon, Inc., 446
Nourse, Hugh O., 243
Nourse, Robert E., 400
Nonpecuniary gratifications, 242

Objective function, 155
Occidental Petroleum, 255
Oi, Walter Y., 166, 226
Okonite Co., 449, 451, 454
Okun, Arthur M., 50
Old Dearborn Distributing Co., 483
Olden, Julia, 128
Oligopoly
  demand, 108
  differentiated, 358
  kinky demand, 108
  monopoly as limits, 109
  pure, 358
  reactions, 352
Omega Alpha, 457
OPEC, 96, 313
Options
  calls, 27–28, 40
  commodity futures, 30
  puts, 27–28, 40
  sellers, 28

Options—*Cont.*
  stock index, 29, 43
  straddles, 40
Opportunity cost
  defined, 127
  home owner's, 127
  transformation chart, 129
Orange concentrate, demand, 83
Oregon, marketing quotas, 103
Output, competitive, 138

Pac-Man defense, 447
Pall Mall cigarettes, 410
Parity in agriculture, 275
Patton, Arch, 228
Payoff matrix, 17, 112
Paramount Pictures, 443
Pennock, Jean L., 91
Pepsico, 424
Perry, L. Glenn, 10
Perry, William "The Refrigerator," 205
Peskin, Henry, 470
Pet, 525
Peterson, J. M., 224
Philadelphia, production in, 259
Philco, 439
Philip Morris, 255, 360, 410, 425, 442,
    458
Philips, 255
Phillips Petroleum, 255, 446
Pickens, T. Boone, 205, 426, 446–47
Pillsbury, 424, 525
Pinkston, Elizabeth, 296
Pittsburgh-plus pricing, 324
Planning curves, 163, 179
Plant location
  demand and cost, 242–43
  flour mills, 246
  highway facilities, 253
  oil refining, 246
  steel, 247
Plant and equipment orders, 51
Plants
  replication, 166
  smaller, 189
Poison pill defense, 447, 461
Pollution, 464
Population and demand, 75
Portland cement
  basing points, 324
  inventory policy, 438
Price control
  gasoline, 274
  general, 274
  Nixon, 274, 298

Price differentials, 313
Price discrimination
  basing point, 324
  continuous production, 321
  fixed supply, 320
  geographic, 323
  multiple basing point, 324
  perfect, 317
Price dispersion, 328, 348
Price leadership, 362
Prices
  common stocks, 51
  sensitive materials, 51
Private bargaining, 464
Processing costs and location, 243–44,
  246
Procter & Gamble, 255, 424, 440, 489,
  492
Product differentiation, 397
Production function, 12, 126, 128, 130,
  180
Profit
  accounting, 13
  economic, 13
  expected, 18
Profit centers, 436
Public good, 470
Puckett, Marshall, 200
Pure Pack Foods, 523

Quaker Oats, 522, 524
Quasi rent, 171

Rank-Xerox, 36, 519, 520
Rational expectations, 52, 462
RCA, 364
Reagan, Ronald, President, 224
Reaganomics, 224
Reed-Bulwinkle Act, 484
Reeder, Clark, 475
Refrigerators
  competition, 405
  demand for, 89
  Frigidaire, 405
  Italian, 406
  kilowatt hours, 403
  life cycle costs, 404
  new owners, 90
  replacement, 90
Rent control
  Britain, 273
  New York, 274
  Paris, 274

Replacement, machine, 177
Republic Steel, 457, 489
Revenue
  average, 70
  marginal, 103–4
  total, 70
Reverse engineering, 515
Reynolds, R. J., 424, 458
Reynolds aluminum, 376
Richman, Sheldon, 296
Right-to-work laws, 222
Risk, 18
Riverside Metal Co., 365
Robichek, Alexander A., 200
Robinson, Joan, 313, 321
Robinson-Patman Act, 316, 327, 480
Rodgers, William, 513
Rogers, William, 505
Rolls Royce, 392
Roosevelt, Franklin D., President, 56
Roth, Cecil, 57
Rothschild, N. M., 57
Royal Dutch/Shell, 255
Rubber plants, union and nonunion, 229
Rukeyser, William S., 443
Ruston, Richard E., 43

Saab plant, 227
Saddlepoint, 113–15
Sales promotion, 395
Santa Fe Industries, 446
Scale
  diseconomies, 164
  economies, 164
Samuelson, Paul, 154
Scheidell, John M., 105
Schlitz, 360
Schmalensee, Richard, 524–25
Schuettinger, Robert L., 274, 277
Schultz, T. W., 225
Schwartz, Anna, 52
Schwartz, Eli, 203
Scientific Data Systems, 37, 521
SCM Corp., 519
Scorched earth defense, 447, 461
Sears, Roebuck, 227, 255, 406, 424–25,
  445
Sebastian, Pamela, 43
Sexton, Richard, 519
Scrap value, 174
Seagram, Jos. E. & Sons, 424, 483
Section 14-B, Taft-Hartley Act, 222
Securities and Exchange Commission, 9
Service sector, size, 256

Sharpe, William F., 201
Shearer, Lloyd, 222
Shell Oil, 255
Sherman Act
  passage, 480
  provisions, 497
  section 1, 480
  section 2, 484
Sherman, Steve, 128
Shiskin, Julius, 49
Short position, 21
Short run
  cost, 163
  defined, 126
Shubik, Martin, 112, 117
Shugart Associates, 521
Siemens, 255
Slope, 68
Smith, Adam
  on conspiracy, 481
  pin factory, 226
  on specialization, 230
Smithies, Arthur, 251
Sobel, Dava, 475
Social costs, 463
Soft drinks, market shares, 118
Solow, Robert, 154
Sommers, Albert T., 55
South Carolina, unions, 222
South Puerto Rico Sugar, 443
Southern Pacific Co., 446
Soviet Russia, planning, 228
Speculator
  arbitrager, 23
  bear, 23, 28
  bull, 23, 28
Spot prices, 22
Spurr, William A., 47
Standard Brands, Inc., 441
Standard Oil
  California, 255
  Indiana, 255
  Ohio, 255
Standard & Poors Stock Index, 30
Starr, K., 19
Static analysis, 104
Steel companies, major, 234
Steiner, P. O., 393
Stewart, Supreme Court Justice, 480
Stigler, George J., 140, 166, 214, 288,
  295, 353–54, 357, 361, 399, 434
Stone, Justice Harlan, 481
Straszheim, Donald H., 59
Stone, H. L., 22
Studebaker Corp., 444

Style goods, location, 245
Subsidies, industrial, 249
Substitutes, 74
Substitution, marginal rate, 133
Suits, D. B., 53
Sulfur, 432
Sun Company, 255
Superior Oil, 489
Sweezy, Paul M., 353

Tag Manufacturers Institute, 483
Takeovers, 446
Taussig, Helen, 4
Tax
  corporate income, 14
  pollutant, 466
  shield, 193
Taylor, Lester D., 76
Telex, 485–86
Temco, 449
Tenneco, 255
Teweles, R. J., 22
Texaco, 255, 489
Texas Gas Resources Corp., 446
Textron, 444–45, 458
Thalidomide, 496
Thayer, Paul, 457
Thorne, John, 504
Thoryn, Michael, 466
Tollison, Robert, 471
Trade associations, 363
Trademarks, 395
Traditional Department Stores, 383
Training of workers, 225
Transfer pricing, intracompany, 436
Transformation, marginal rate, 128
Trans-Missouri Freight Association, 481
Trenton Potteries Case, 481
Tropicana Products, 523
Truth in Energy, 401–2
Truth in Lending and Fair Packaging
    Act, 495
Toyota, 255
Treble damage suits, 510
Tunney, John, 401, 493
Turner, Donald F., 358
Tying agreements, 491

Ubiquitous materials, 245
Uncertainty
  defined, 16
  nontransformable, 20
  transformable, 20

Unemployment benefits, 51
Unilever, 255
Union shop, 222
United Electric Coals Cos., 494
Uniroyal, Inc., 229
United Mine Workers, 229
United Rubber Workers, 229
U.S. Steel, 10, 255, 359, 491
U.S. Treasury Securities
  defined, 26
  futures, 26, 61
United Technologies, 255
Utah International, 492
Utility pricing goals, 296
Uttal, Bro, 361

Vanderblue, Homer, 377
Vancouver, B.C. route controversy, 121
Van Horne, James C., 201
Vendor performance, 51
Vermont, 33
Veterans Administration, 58
Viner cost curves, 169
Volkswagen, 255
Volvo, 231
Von Neumann, John, 112
Von Thünen, Johann Heinrich, 249

Walter, James E., 200
Walton, Izaak, 463
Walton, Richard E., 227, 230
Wang, 521
Warner-Lambert, 425
Waste product, 430
Watson, Thomas, 517
Webb-Pomerene Act, 483
Weidenbaum, Murray L., 497

Weight losing, 245–46
Weirton Steel, 227
Wendt, Paul F., 200
Western Electric, 487
Westinghouse, 405, 506
Weston, J. Fred, 199
Weyerhaeuser Co., 482
Wharton Econometric Forecasting Associates, 59
Whirlpool Corporation, 89, 405
Whitaker, Gilbert R., 47, 75
White, Bouck, 29
White Industries, 405
White knight, 447
Whitin, Thomas M., 153
Wicksteed, Philip H., 268
Wiebull distribution, 91
Wilcox, William, 59
Williams, David, 60
Wilson & Company, 443, 449, 451, 454
Wilson Pharmaceutical & Chemical Co., 449, 451, 455
Wilson Sporting Goods Co., 449, 451, 455
Winston cigarettes, 418
Winter, Ralph E., 229
Wood, Richardson, 247
Worcester, Dean A., 358
Working, E. J., 77
Workweek, average, 51
Worthy, Ford S., 9
Wyoming, 470

Xerox Corp., 35, 446, 485, 518

Youngstown Steel and Tube, 456, 492
Yugoslavia, 227

This book has been set Linotron 202 in 10 and 9 point Melior leaded 2 points. Chapter numbers are 22 point Melior and chapter titles are 18 point Melior. The size of the type page is 28 by 48 picas.